istory of Psychoanalysis Series

Brett Kahr and Professor Peter L. Rudnytsky (Series Editors)

ed and distributed by Karnac Books

itles in the Series

KARL ABRAHAM

The H

Professo
Publishe

Other t

Her Hou
edited

Rescuin
by Pe

Ferencz
edite

Freud i
by E

Ferenc
edite

The C
by

Sando
edi

The
by

Feren
Psyc
by

Look
by

Psy
b

The
b

The

Fre

Th
O

KARL ABRAHAM
Life and Work, a Biography

Anna Bentinck van Schoonheten

Translated from the Dutch by
Liz Waters

KARNAC

First published in Dutch as *Karl Abraham: Freuds rots in de branding*
© Garant, Antwerp, 2013

First published in English in 2016 by
Karnac Books Ltd
118 Finchley Road, London NW3 5HT

Translated by Liz Waters

British Library Cataloguing in Publication Data

A C.I.P. for this book is available from the British Library

  ISBN: 978 1 78220 184 7

Edited, designed and produced by The Studio Publishing Services Ltd
www.publishingservicesuk.co.uk
e-mail: studio@publishingservicesuk.co.uk

Printed in Great Britain by TJ International Ltd, Padstow, Cornwall

www.karnacbooks.com

CONTENTS

ACKNOWLEDGEMENTS

The writing of this book would not have been possible without the help of friends, colleagues, and the staffs of archives in many countries, since the archives of psychoanalysts have become dispersed around the world.

First of all I would like to thank the late Professor Dr Gerhard Fichtner, who received me with great hospitality in Tübingen, familiarised me with the history of psychoanalysis, and was always ready to advise and assist. Unfortunately, he did not live to see the book completed.

Dr Bettina Decke invited me to stay in her house and showed me around Bremen, Karl Abraham's native city. Her research into his childhood years was of great importance for this book.

It was Dr Marion de Ras who suggested that I should gain a doctorate. I had many discussions about Abraham with her and she provided a critical commentary on my texts on the subject.

Thanks also to Karl Abraham's relatives, Lottie Levy-Abraham (who died in 2012), Anja Amsel, and Steven Burgner. We had long conversations in London and Edinburgh about the fortunes of the Abrahams and the Burgners (the family of Abraham's wife). I would also like to thank Jeremy Lewison, son of Hilda Abraham's good friend Dinora Pines, for the information he gave me.

I am grateful to Dr Arnold Enklaar, who suggested writing a book about Karl Abraham, Henry Strick van Linschoten in London, who provided critical remarks, Ursula Heyl-Keese for her transcriptions from Sütterlin script, and Anne Folkertsma for a meticulous final edit of the Dutch edition.

I would also like to thank the following for their advice and contributions: Deirdre Bair (New Haven), Pieter van den Berg, Anne Birkenhauer (Jerusalem), Dr Gabriela Bosch of the Military History Research Office (Potsdam), Dr Gertie Bögels, Emile Brugman, Dr Leonardo Bruno of the LoC (Washington), Wolfgang zu Castell-Castell (Castell), Joyce and Richard

Darilek (Washington), Professor Dr Trudy Dehue, Sylvia van Deursen, Nel Floor, Ab Gieteling, Ludger Hermanns of the Archives of the Karl-Abraham-Institut (Berlin), Dr Sanford Gifford (Boston), Professor Dr Albrecht Hirschmüller (Tübingen), Sarah Hutcheon of the Schlesinger Library (Cambridge, MA), Mrs Joos-Bleuler (Zurich), Ann Kelland, the Melanie Klein Trust (London), the Kristine Mann Library (New York), Dr Willem Melching, Michael Molnar of the Freud Museum (London), Herr Mösli (Zurich), Gerbrand Muller, Thomas Müller (Ulm), Professor Dr Herman Philipse, Professor Dr Brita Rang (Frankfurt), Professor Dr Hans Renders, Ken Robinson, Allie Dillon and Joanne Halford of the Archives of the British Psychoanalytical Society (London), Michal Saft of the Israeli State Archives (Jerusalem), Anne-Marie Sandler (London), Ellen Schalker, Professor Dr Heinz Scott (Bonn), Leonard Shengold (New York), Professor Dr Speck of the University Archives in Freiburg, Dr Marcus Sporn of the University Archives in Würzburg, Dr Barbara Stadler of the State Archives in Zurich, Dr Nellie Thompson (New York), Professor Dr Frans Verhage, the Wellcome Institute (London), Professor Dr Daniel Widlöcher (Paris), and Professor Dr Itta Shedletzky (Tel Aviv).

Anna Bentinck van Schoonheten, PhD, is a psychoanalyst in private practice in Amsterdam. She is a member of the Dutch Psychoanalytic Group, the Dutch Psychoanalytic Society and the IPA, and President of the Board of the Dutch *Journal of Psychoanalysis*. She specialises in the early history of psychoanalysis, with a particular focus on Freud and the secret committee. She has conducted extensive research on Karl Abraham and the role of the secret committee in the development of psychoanalytic theory.

ABBREVIATIONS

Ψα; ΨA; Ψα: psychoanalysis.

Allg. Zsch. Psychaitr.: *Allgemeine Zeitschrift für Psychiatrie und psychisch-gerichtliche Medizin*Burghölzliarchiv: Staatsarchiv des Kantons Zürich, Burghölzliarchiv.

CP: Abraham, K., *Clinical Papers and Essays on Psycho-Analysis*, H. Abraham (Trans.). London: Karnac 1979 (reprint of 1955 edition).

Eitingon archive: Jerusalem State Archive, Eitingon archive.

F/A: The Complete Correspondence of Sigmund Freud and Karl Abraham 1907–1925, Completed Edition, edited by Ernst Falzeder. London: Karnac 2002.

F/Bleuler: Schröter, M. (Ed.) (2012). *Sigmund Freud—Eugen Bleuler. Ich bin zuversichtlich, wir erobern bald die Psychiatrie. Briefwechsel 1904-1937.* Basel: Schwabe.

F/Eit: Schröter, M. (Ed.) (2004). *Sigmund Freud und Max Eitingon, Briefwechsel 1906–1936*, edited by Tübingen: Edition Diskord.

F/Fer: Falzeder, E., & Brabant, E. (Eds.) (1993, 1996, 2000). *The Correspondence of Sigmund Freud and Sándor Ferenczi, 1–3, 1908–1933.* Cambridge, MA: Belknap Press of Harvard University Press.

F/J: McGuire, W. (Ed.) (1974). *The Freud/Jung Letters.* London: Hogarth Press and Routledge & Kegan Paul.

F/Jones: Paskauskas, R. A. (Ed.) (1993). *The Complete Correspondence of Sigmund Freud and Ernest Jones.* Cambridge, MA: Belknap Press of Harvard University Press.

F/Rank: Lieberman, E. J., & Kramer, R. (Eds.) (2012). *The Letters of Sigmund Freud and Otto Rank,* Baltimore, MD: Johns Hopkins University Press.

HA: Abraham, H. C. (1974). Karl Abraham. An Unfinished Biography. *International Review of Psycho-Analysis*.

IZP: *Zentralblatt für Psychoanalyse* (1910–1913), *Internationale Zeitschrift für Ärzliche Psychoanalyse* (1913–1920), *Internationale Zeitschrift für Psychoanalyse* (from 1920).

Jahrbuch: *Jahrbuch für psychoanalytische und psychopathologische Forschungen. Jahrbuch der Psychoanalyse* (from 1960).

Korrespondenzblatt: *Das Korrespondenzblatt der Internationalen Psychoanalytischen Vereinigung 1910-1941*. Available on CD-ROM. Giefer (2007). Citations from the *Korrespondenzblatt* are given the same year and page number as used on the CD-ROM.

LoC: Library of Congress, Washington.

PS: Abraham, K. *Psychoanalytische Studien. Gesammelte Werken in zwei Bänden*, J. Cremerius (Ed.). Giessen: Psychosozial, 1999.

S. E.: *Standard Edition of the Complete Psychological Works of Sigmund Freud*.

SP: Abraham, K. (1927[1988]). *Selected Papers of Karl Abraham*, D. Bryan & A. Strachey (Trans.). London: Karnac.

Shortly after the tragic and untimely death of Karl Abraham at the age of forty-eight years, on Christmas Day, 1925, his long-standing psychoanalytical colleagues began to pay plentiful tribute to the man who had devoted his life to psychological science.

Sigmund Freud (1925a, p. 41) described Abraham as his "rocher de bronce" ["*rocher de bronze*"] (Freud, 1925b, p. 591) and, also, borrowing a phrase from the odes of the Roman poet Horace, immortalised his German colleague as "Integer vitae scelerisque purus" ["He whose life is blameless and free of guilt"] (Freud, 1925a, p. 41; cf. Freud, 1925b, 1926). Ernest Jones (1926, p. 181)—Freud's British amanuensis—venerated Abraham in almost similarly poetic terms, explaining that, "Amid the turmoils of personal emotions and the clash of discordant tendencies Abraham stood always firm, a central steadiness in the shifting eddies around". Indeed, Jones (1926, p. 155) lamented, "There can be no doubt that of all the blows the science of psycho-analysis has yet suffered the death of Karl Abraham is much the most cruel and severe". Jones (1926, p. 181) concluded his obituary by memorialising Abraham as "*un preux chevalier of Science, sans peur et sans reproche*".

These encomia might well have helped the grief-stricken pioneers of psychoanalysis to manage the pain of their bereavement, but, by having branded Abraham as the fearless and blameless "*chevalier*" who could do no wrong, they succeeded in sanctifying him in a potentially unhelpful and idealised fashion.

Indeed, one wonders whether these early funerary tributes ultimately served to inhibit a more balanced, more honest, and more nuanced understanding of the founder of the psychoanalytical movement in Germany. Certainly, the publication in 1965 of the highly expurgated edition of Abraham's correspondence with Freud (Freud & Abraham, 1965a,b), which eliminated much of the shadowy side of Abraham's relationship with the founder of psychoanalysis, solidified the notion of Abraham as the spotless and unwaveringly loyal man of science. Only in 2002, with the appearance of Ernst Falzeder's complete, scholarly edition of these letters, would students of psychoanalytical history come to appreciate the complexity of Abraham's character and, also, his relationship to Freud, more fully (Freud & Abraham, 2002; Freud & Abraham, 2009a,b).

Abraham's early death, combined with a lack of availability of his extensive correspondence, not to mention the lingering presence of his daughter Hilda Abraham—herself a practising psychoanalyst—might have prevented historians from delving more enthusiastically into a study of Abraham's life and work. Consequently, apart from his daughter's brief biographical essay (Abraham, 1974; cf. Abraham, 1976), few scholars have dared to explore Abraham's life and legacy in a more comprehensive fashion (cf. Decke, 1997; De Masi, 2002; Sanfeliu Santa Olalla, 2002; Lemaigre, 2003; May, 2012; Zienert-Eilts, 2013; Sanfeliu, 2014), and certainly none has done so in a truly magisterial fashion.

During my own training, senior teachers regarded Karl Abraham predominantly as either a footnote to Sigmund Freud or as a precursor to Melanie Klein, rather than as a profound and original contributor in his own right. Over time, Abraham has become increasingly marginalised, at least in English-speaking countries.

The dearth of "Abrahamiana" might be explained, in part, by his early death, and, in part, by the paucity of readily accessible primary source materials, many of which—such as family letters—have not survived. But, additionally, most scholars have avoided engaging with Abraham owing to the *lack* of salacious gossip surrounding this steadfast man. Unlike Alfred Adler, Wilhelm Stekel, Carl Gustav Jung, Sándor Ferenczi, and Otto Rank, each of whom fell out spectacularly with Freud, and unlike Ernest Jones, who became embroiled in many a sexual scandal, historians have come to view Abraham as, perhaps, a bit staid, even somewhat *boring*, compared to the more colourful, dramatic personalities who peppered the early psychoanalytical movement. Indeed, even Ernest Jones (1957), who had no difficulty in speaking ill of his psychoanalytical "siblings", described Karl Abraham as "divinely normal" (quoted in Roazen, 2000, p. 83).

Abraham has, however, presented potential biographers with an even greater challenge, namely, *the sheer magnitude of his work*. A brilliantly cultured man, Abraham could lecture freely not only in German, but also in English and even in Latin (Jones, 1926). He steeped himself in research projects almost as compulsively as Freud did, and he, too, mastered many bodies of literature, whether psychiatric, historical, or linguistic. Therefore, in order to pay true homage to Karl Abraham, a chronicler must not only navigate the biographical and historical contextual data, but must, in addition, grasp the totality of Abraham's formidable contributions to both clinical and applied psychoanalysis.

After all, Abraham's publications ranged from studies of such psychopathological topics as dementia praecox (e.g., Abraham, 1907, 1908), the war neuroses (Abraham, 1919a), and narcissism (Abraham, 1920), to historical and literary explorations of such diverse figures as Amenhotep IV (Abraham, 1912) and Giovanni Segantini (Abraham, 1911), to the construction of an intricate theory of psychosexual developmental psychology (Abraham, 1923, 1924), to the investigation of neurotic resistance in clinical practice (Abraham, 1919b), to the elucidation of characterology (e.g., Abraham, 1925), and so much more besides (e.g., Abraham, 1921). Thus, in order to grapple with the totality of Abraham as clinician, theorist, and writer, one must be a practitioner–scholar of great depth, scope, and sophistication.

Happily, Dr Anna Bentinck van Schoonheten—both psychoanalyst and historian—has risen to the challenge of engaging with the enormous fullness of Karl Abraham and has, after many years of hard labour, produced a magnificent biography which engages not only with Abraham's life history in an intricate and frank manner, but also provides a detailed study of every one of Abraham's major professional and scientific achievements.

Endowed with considerable archival and historiographical skill, Bentinck van Schoonheten has travelled the world, scouring documentary repositories and unearthing new primary source materials. Over the course of many years, the author visited a multitude of research institutions on several continents, ranging from the Library of Congress in Washington, DC, to the Israel State Archive in Jerusalem (where she consulted the papers of Abraham's colleague, Max Eitingon), with, *inter alia*, stops along the way in London, Amsterdam, Berlin, Freiburg im Breisgau, Potsdam, Tübingen, and Würzburg. A consummate detective, Dr Bentinck van Schoonheten not only uncovered large quantities of buried treasure, but she then incorporated this "forgotten" data into a compelling narrative that allows us to enjoy a more complete and more human portrait of Karl Abraham.

Owing to the formidable heft of detail of Abraham's daily life contained in his correspondence with Freud, any biographer requires great stamina to study, analyse, and incorporate the highlights of this material into a tightly woven narrative. Fortunately, Bentinck van Schoonheten has done just that, and she has succeeded admirably in weaving Abraham's letters, his published works, and the unpublished archival source materials into one truly integrated text.

A consummate stylist, Bentinck van Schoonheten has written her book, *Karl Abraham: Life and Work, a Biography*, in clear, concise—indeed delicious—prose. Her sentences flow so beautifully that one soon forgets that the author has written a profound work of history, replete with nearly two thousand endnotes. By contrast, one imagines oneself reading a great novel on the beach during an August analytical holiday. However, unlike a summertime work of fiction, Bentinck van Schoonheten has checked each fact carefully, and has sculpted a portrayal of Abraham rich in scope and in intricacy and, I would argue, reliability as well.

This new biography—likely to be the definitive work for quite some time to come—provides us not only with a newer and fuller depiction of Abraham, but also of the father of psychoanalysis, Sigmund Freud. While many scholars have, in recent years, written extensively about Freud's incapacity to tolerate diversity and criticism, often with much justification, Bentinck van Schoonheten's book reveals not only an Abraham able to engage in creative dispute, but also a Freud who could do likewise.

Certain young students and, indeed, elderly practitioners as well, often balk at the prospect of reading a weighty, substantial biography. Many of these less academically vigilant individuals prefer to learn simply the basics of theory, without bothering to study the historical and biographical context. Such an attitude strikes me as deeply unfortunate, especially when offered a book such as this one by Anna Bentinck van Schoonheten. Her formidable biography of Karl Abraham offers students and teachers alike an opportunity to ground their understanding of Abrahamian theory in its biographical milieu so that the two strands inform one another and also reinforce one another. By taking the time to engage fully with this book, one feels stimulated, enhanced, educated, and treated to a real "master class" in history, theory, and technique.

Nowadays, psychoanalysis has become deeply preoccupied with such "modern" topics as its relation to neuroscience, its links with attachment theory, its reconfiguration of the politics of gender, not to mention its flirtation with such technological developments as Skype. In view of this, many students might wonder whether Abraham, who died more than ninety years ago, truly merits an examination. Has he not become "old hat"? Fortunately, Dr Bentinck van Schoonheten's book provides us with rich evidence of the very contemporaneity of Abraham, reminding us of his unique clinical contributions to such diverse areas of concentration as the psychoses, depression, and, above all, the emphasis on the pre-oedipal, arguing that Abraham, perhaps more than Freud himself, underlined the developmental significance of the mother rather than that of the father during the earliest years of human growth. In this respect, Abraham laid much of the groundwork not only for the substantial work of Melanie Klein, but also, one might argue, for the contributions of Michael Balint, John Bowlby, Erik Erikson, Margaret Mahler, Donald Winnicott, and many others.

I hope that this new biography of Karl Abraham will serve not only as an important contribution to the growing literature on the history of psychoanalysis, but also that it will help to ignite interest in Abraham's "forgotten" clinical essays, which still have great relevance today. As a little example of the ongoing usefulness of Abraham as a clinical teacher, it might be of interest to know that I recently presented a paper to a conference on the treatment of psychosexual difficulties, and drew heavily upon Abraham's (1917) almost completely neglected paper "Über Ejaculatio praecox", in which he hypothesised a crucial interconnection between premature ejaculation and the unconscious wish to soil the woman's body. Many of the conference participants—mostly devotees of modern methods of psychosexual therapy who prescribe practical genital exercises for couples struggling with premature ejaculation—listened in open-minded fashion as I described my work with several patients whom I treated in a classical Abrahamian fashion, and whose *ejaculatio praecox* vanished after we had thoroughly explored the split-off hostilities. After the conference, many participants asked me for the reference to Abraham's paper, explaining that they had never come across this essay, or, indeed, upon Abraham himself!

We owe so much to Karl Abraham, not only in terms of his huge institutional achievements (e.g., Decker, 1977; Fuechtner, 2011) but, above all, due to his wide-ranging work as one of the principal architects of pre-oedipal psychology (e.g., Abraham, 1918), and for his elucidation of many of the more severe forms of psychopathology, in consequence of which Abraham helped "to free psychiatry from the nightmare of therapeutic nihilism" (Jones, 1926, p. 167) which characterised so much of the early twentieth century.

I congratulate Dr Anna Bentinck van Schoonheten for having shared her copious researches with us in such a generous and engaging manner, and I recommend *Karl Abraham: Life and Work, a Biography* most warmly for providing us all with a marvellous opportunity to embrace the legacy of one of the most creative contributors to the entire field of human psychology.

Professor Brett Kahr,
London

References

Abraham, Hilda (1976). *Karl Abraham: Sein Leben für die Psychoanalyse. Eine Biographie*, Tom Burgner, Marion Burgner, & Dinora Pines (Eds.), Hans-Horst Henschen (Trans.). Munich: Kindler.

Abraham, Hilda C. (1974). Karl Abraham: An Unfinished Biography, Tom Burgner, Marion Burgner, & Dinora Pines (Eds.). *International Review of Psycho-Analysis*, 1: 17–72.

Abraham, Karl (1907). Ueber die Bedeutung sexueller Jugendtraumen für die Symptomatologie der Dementia praecox. *Centralblatt für Nervenheilkunde und Psychiatrie, 30*: 409–415.

Abraham, Karl (1908). Die psychosexuelle Differenzen der Hysterie und der Dementia praecox. *Zentralblatt für Nervenheilkunde und Psychiatrie, 31*: 521–533.

Abraham, Karl (1911). *Giovanni Segantini: Ein psychoanalytischer Versuch*. Vienna: Franz Deuticke.

Abraham, Karl (1912). Amenhotep IV. (Echnaton): Psychoanalytische Beiträge zum Verständnis seiner Persönlichkeit und des monotheistischen Aton-Kultes. *Imago*, 1: 334–360.

Abraham, Karl (1917). Über Ejaculatio praecox. *Internationale Zeitschrift für ärztliche Psychoanalyse*, 4: 171–186.

Abraham, Karl (1918). Untersuchungen über die früheste prägenitale Entwicklungsstufe der Libido. *Internationale Zeitschrift für ärztliche Psychoanalyse*, 4: 71–97.

Abraham, Karl (1919a). Erstes Korreferat. In: Sigmund Freud, Sándor Ferenczi, Karl Abraham, Ernst Simmel, & Ernest Jones, *Zur Psychoanalyse der Kriegsneurosen*, pp. 31–41. Vienna: Internationaler Psychoanalytischer Verlag.

Abraham, Karl (1919b). Über eine besondere Form des neurotischen Widerstandes gegen die psycho-analytische Methodik. *Internationale Zeitschrift für ärztliche Psychoanalyse*, 5: 173–180.

Abraham, Karl (1920). Zur narzißtischen Bewertung der Exkretionsvorgänge in Traum und Neurose. *Internationale Zeitschrift für Psychoanalyse*, 6: 64–67.

Abraham, Karl (1921). *Klinische Beiträge zur Psychoanalyse aus den Jahren 1907–1920*. Vienna: Internationaler Psychoanalytischer Verlag.

Abraham, Karl (1923). Ergänzugen zur Lehre vom Analcharakter. *Internationale Zeitschrift für Psychoanalyse*, 9: 27–47.

Abraham, Karl (1924). *Versuch einer Entwicklungsgeschichte der Libido auf Grund der Psychoanalyse seel-ischer Störungen*. Vienna: Internationaler Psychoanalytischer Verlag.

Abraham, Karl (1925). *Psychoanalytische Studien zur Charakterbildung*. Vienna: Internationaler Psychoanalytischer Verlag.

Decke, Bettina (1997). Karl Abraham: Familie, Kindheit und Jugend in Bremen. *Luzifer-Amor, 10*(20): 7–60.

Decker, Hannah S. (1977). *Freud in Germany: Revolution and Reaction in Science, 1893–1907*. New York: International Universities Press.

De Masi, Franco (2002). *Karl Abraham: (1877–1925). La vita e le opere. Alle radici della teoria analitica*. Rome: Armando Editore/Armando Armando.

Freud, Sigmund (1925a). Letter to Ernest Jones. 30th December. In: Sigmund Freud & Ernest Jones (1993), *Briefwechsel: Sigmund Freud. Ernest Jones. 1908–1939. Originalwortlaut der in Deutsch verfaßten Briefe Freuds* (pp. 41–42), Ingeborg Meyer-Palmedo (Ed.). Frankfurt: S. Fischer.

Freud, Sigmund (1925b). Letter to Ernest Jones. 30th December. In: Sigmund Freud and Ernest Jones (1993), *The Complete Correspondence of Sigmund Freud and Ernest Jones: 1908–1939* (p. 591), R. Andrew Paskauskas (Ed.), Frauke Voss (Trans.), Cambridge, MA: Belknap Press of Harvard University Press.

Freud, Sigmund (1926). Karl Abraham. *Internationale Zeitschrift für Psychoanalyse*, 12: 1–2.

Freud, Sigmund, & Abraham, Karl (1965a). *Briefe: 1907–1926*, Hilda C. Abraham & Ernst L. Freud (Eds.). Frankfurt: S. Fischer.

Freud, Sigmund, & Abraham, Karl (1965b). *A Psycho-Analytic Dialogue: The Letters of Sigmund Freud and Karl Abraham. 1907–1926*, Hilda C. Abraham & Ernst L. Freud (Eds.), Bernard Marsh & Hilda C. Abraham (Trans.). London: Hogarth Press.

Freud, Sigmund, & Abraham, Karl (2002). *The Complete Correspondence of Sigmund Freud and Karl Abraham: 1907–1925*, Ernst Falzeder (Ed.), Caroline Schwarzacher, Christine Trollope, & Klara Majthényi King (Trans.). London: Karnac.

Freud, Sigmund, & Abraham, Karl (2009a). *Briefwechsel 1907–1925: Vollständige Ausgabe. Band 1: 1907–1914*, Ernst Falzeder & Ludger M. Hermanns (Eds.). Vienna: Turia und Kant.

Freud, Sigmund, & Abraham, Karl (2009b). *Briefwechsel 1907–1925: Vollständige Ausgabe. Band 2: 1915–1925*, Ernst Falzeder and Ludger M. Hermanns (Eds.). Vienna: Turia und Kant.

Fuechtner, Veronika (2011). *Berlin Psychoanalytic: Psychoanalysis and Culture in Weimar Republic Germany and Beyond*. Berkeley, CA: University of California Press.

Jones, Ernest (1926). Karl Abraham: 1877–1925. *International Journal of Psycho-Analysis, 7*: 155–181.

Lemaigre, Bernard (2003). *Karl Abraham*. Paris: Presses Universitaires de France.

May, Ulrike (2012). Karl Abraham's Revolution of 1916: From Sensual Sucking to the Oral-Aggressive Wish of Destruction, Daniela Haller (Trans.). *Psychoanalytic Quarterly, 81*: 83–109.

Roazen, Paul (2000). *Oedipus in Britain: Edward Glover and the Struggle Over Klein*. New York: Other Press.

Sanfeliu, Isabel (2014). *Karl Abraham: The Birth of Object Relations Theory*, Kate Walters (Trans.). London: Karnac.

Sanfeliu Santa Olalla, Isabel (2003). *Karl Abraham o el descubrimiento de la melancholía*. Madrid: Biblioteca Nueva/Editorial de la Biblioteca Nueva.

Zienert-Eilts, Karin (2013). *Karl Abraham: Eine Biografie im Kontext der psychoanalytischen Bewegung*. Gießen: Psychosozial-Verlag.

Introduction

In 1997, I was given a small, beautifully bound book with a red cover containing the correspondence between Sigmund Freud and Karl Abraham (or part of it; the complete collection of letters was published several years later). The book was edited by Karl Abraham's daughter Hilda and by Ernst Freud, son of Sigmund Freud.

At that stage I knew little about Karl Abraham. During my training as a psychoanalyst, I had read an article by him and I was aware of him as an analyst from the earliest phase of psychoanalysis, but I had no idea that he had been a member of a secret committee close to Freud.

I was astonished by what I read. Freud's wonderful writing style was familiar to me, but Abraham turned out to have an attractive, crystal-clear way with words as well, and a real sense of humour. The biggest surprise, though, was the way he dealt with Freud. He was clearly very fond of him and admired him greatly, but, in writing to Freud, he remained entirely himself. There was none of the obsequiousness or sycophancy that so often surrounded the founder of psychoanalysis. Their exchange of letters involved many intricacies and significant differences of opinion. Sometimes, Abraham allowed himself to be persuaded by Freud. At other times, although always friendly and polite, he clarified his views further without yielding any ground. Freud could be a good deal less than friendly and polite, but he was clearly fond of Abraham.

The Foreword to the book was written by Edward Glover, well known in British psychoanalytic circles, who had been in analysis with Abraham in 1920.

The correspondence made me curious to know who Karl Abraham was and what kind of place he had created for himself in the world of psychoanalysis. I went in search of articles and books and found precious little: his collected works had been published, his daughter had written a partial biography, there were a few articles, he was quoted here and there, and a handful of published responses to his work were available, but he was mentioned mainly in connection with a number of major conflicts that had taken place in the history of psychoanalysis.

I decided to study Karl Abraham in more depth and to write a book about him, which eventually became a biography examining both his life and his work. Over the years I spent on my research, interest in Karl Abraham increased markedly, especially in Germany. Articles about him appeared quite regularly, and those welcome additions enabled me to gain a clearer impression of him for my biography. To this day, however, his work remains largely undiscussed.

Karl Abraham was buried in a wooded area of the Lichterfelde cemetery in Berlin, in a grave now surrounded by tall trees and rhododendrons. His gravestone gives no indication at all of his orthodox Jewish background. Two smaller stones have been placed nearby. To the right and a little further forward is a slab bearing the Berlin coat of arms, above which are the words "EHRENGRAB LAND BERLIN". Almost up against the large gravestone, angled backwards slightly, is a stone that reads:

Dr. Karl Abraham
1877–1925
Begründer der Psychoanalyse
In Berlin

It is a family grave. The space beneath Abraham's name on the main gravestone, reserved for his wife, remains empty. Hedwig Abraham was forced to flee Nazi persecution in 1933, along with her children, Hilda and Gerd. Karl Abraham, who felt wholly German and abandoned his orthodox Jewish faith to embrace secularism, was spared the trauma of exile since he had died eight years earlier, at the age of forty-eight, of an inflammation in his throat caused by swallowing a fishbone. These were the days before the discovery of antibiotics.

Freud's renown has eclipsed the close colleagues who helped to make psychoanalysis what it later became. In a sense, they disappeared from the picture, leaving only Freud. Yet, it was not until fairly late in life, when he was over fifty, that Freud (1856–1939) made a name for himself, and even then it was not for some years that he became truly famous. One of the colleagues who made powerful contributions to Freud's growing fame was a contemporary, Eugen Bleuler (1857–1939), director of the Burghölzli Clinic in Zurich and one of the most eminent and well-known psychiatrists of his day. Bleuler became interested in psychoanalysis and asked a young doctor's assistant who worked with him, Carl Gustav Jung, to read and comment on Freud's *Journal of the American Psychoanalytic Association*. Jung (1875–1961) was less than impressed at first, but gradually he grew fascinated by the work and became an enthusiastic champion of both psychoanalysis and Freud.

A number of young doctors came into contact with psychoanalysis through Bleuler, Jung, and the Burghölzli Clinic, and, working in co-operation with Freud, they gave it a huge boost. They were Karl Abraham in Berlin, Sándor Ferenczi in Budapest, and Ernest Jones in London. From 1912 onwards, together with Hanns Sachs and Otto Rank in Vienna, they formed the "secret committee" that shaped, along with Freud, the development of the psychoanalytic movement over the next fourteen years.

It was an astonishingly creative and productive group, continually in contact with Freud. The young doctors produced a stream of scientific articles and books. Karl Abraham and Sándor Ferenczi were the most important members, and, aside from his intellectual contribution, Abraham was of great significance in an organisational sense. Under his leadership, Berlin became the centre of psychoanalysis.

By the end of his life, Abraham had the most important leadership role in the world of psychoanalysis after Freud. Jones writes that it was not in Abraham's nature to aspire to such a position, and, indeed, Abraham took quite some time to adjust to it. Jones thought his ability to perform in such a role rested on a natural authority. Among Abraham's defining characteristics were a refreshing youthfulness and an optimistic outlook. These are not qualities that would immediately qualify a person to become a leader, but his youthful optimism was accompanied by a sceptical caution, calm and sober powers of judgement, and an intelligent sense of humour.

His personality made Abraham extremely attractive to women, and men were captivated above all by the energy he exuded at all times. He came across as controlled, cheerful, polite, and friendly, but behind all that lay great determination and restraint. Jones called it a reserve whose depth not even his friends, or perhaps Abraham himself, could fathom.[1]

According to Jones, Freud rightly believed that Abraham was the most intelligent of the group, and, for that reason, Abraham's endorsement was the most important to him—not that it always came as readily as it did from some of the others. Abraham told Jones that he always needed time to absorb and think through each new theory launched by Freud and was satisfied only when able to link it to the crucial Oedipus complex.[2]

Abraham had exceptional powers of empathy, which made him admirably suited to the work of a psychoanalyst.[3] But occasionally he might suddenly fail to empathise at all, without even realising it. He could be utterly blind to fear in other people.

When they fled to England, Abraham's wife and children were able to take only a few of their belongings with them. They decided to make a priority of all Abraham's correspondence on the subject of psychoanalysis. As far as we know, everything he wrote in his youth, including all his love letters and personal correspondence, has been lost almost in its entirety, so at first I had doubts as to whether it would be possible to write a biography. As it turned out, a great deal of personal information was to be found in the psychoanalytic correspondence and in the articles he wrote. Hilda Abraham's biographical sketch of her father, which includes all kinds of everyday details, was of inestimable value.

It remains true to say, however, that the sources are rather one-sided. We know that Abraham had broad cultural interests, especially when it came to the classical world, its art, literature and languages. It is an aspect that would no doubt emerge more fully were the sources more diverse. According to Hanns Sachs, for example, in his free time Abraham read his favourite author, Aristophanes, in Greek.[4] At the same time, it seems typical of Abraham that no personal letters have survived, since, for all his cordiality and courtesy, he kept much of his inner life private, just as it is typical of him that he never chose to be analysed himself.

The process of writing this book was just as enlightening and fascinating as my initial reading of Abraham's correspondence. He turns out to have been far more important to the early years of psychoanalysis than I had previously realised, and far more original than contemporary writers led me to suspect.

CHAPTER ONE

Childhood in Bremen

K arl Abraham was born on 3 May 1877, in extremely unsettled times. The political structure of his fatherland, Germany, changed so much in the second half of the nineteenth
century that relationships between the most powerful nations in Europe were radically
altered. After the revolutions of 1848–1849, a federal system had been introduced so that independent German states continued to exist but a central government took charge of important
matters like the postal service, defence, foreign affairs, and the currency.[5] Another twenty years
passed before the German Empire was established, in 1871.

In 1862 Otto von Bismarck became prime minister of Prussia. Nine years and three wars
later, the German federation was defunct, Austria was excluded from German affairs and a
German empire had been founded with a highly reluctant William I as emperor and Bismarck
as chancellor.[6] The change wrought by Bismarck was immense. The part of Central Europe
occupied by people who regarded themselves as Germans had always been a region of loosely
connected states, most small or medium in size, two of them large, from which neighbouring
countries had little to fear. Now, suddenly, there was a vast, contiguous, extremely powerful
and organised state in their midst, structured along military lines.

From 1850 onwards, German economic growth was spectacular. A solid bourgeoisie developed and its capital and self-confidence steadily increased.[7] Karl Abraham's family was part of
that middle class.

In the first two years of the German empire's existence, from 1871 to 1873, the economy
overheated and share prices rose inexorably. Everyone bought shares, young and old, rich
and poor. The consequences of the crash of 1873 were devastating and it would be another
twenty years before the economy recovered. As a result of the crash, anti-Semitism flared up
after a comparative lull. The Jews were blamed for the crisis. There was talk of a Jewish
conspiracy.[8]

The German empire was destined to last only until 1918, forty-seven years after it came into being, although the German republic remained in existence until 1945. For more than nine centuries, until 1862, the year Bismarck came to power, the German lands had only rarely been at war with each other and they had not attacked other countries. They had, though, beaten back invasions and engaged in three major internal conflicts—the Schmalkaldic War, the Thirty Years War and the Seven Years War—none of which involved aggression against neighbouring countries. In the twentieth century, the German Empire launched attacks abroad on two occasions. Two World Wars resulted, and its own downfall.[9]

Karl Abraham's family background

In 1908, the year in which Karl Abraham began his psychoanalytic practice in Berlin at the age of thirty-one, he gave a lecture entitled "The significance of intermarriage between close relatives in the psychology of the neuroses".[10] His daughter Hilda writes in her biography that he was probably speaking about his own family, of which several generations had married close relatives.[11] In his lecture, Abraham disputed the widely accepted idea that a marriage between members of the same family will have damaging consequences for their offspring. Children born as the result of inbreeding certainly had all kinds of disorders, but Abraham believed this was not a result of the close biological relationship between the parents. In fact, he was convinced it was the other way round; people with neurotic character traits tended to marry within their own family. He was referring not to families who lived in isolation and, therefore, had little choice, but, rather, to those whose members married out of mutual sympathy. This meant, Abraham said, that they lacked the capacity to transmit feelings of love to strangers, while at the same time their feelings of love for their own families were more intense than normal. Their sexuality was disturbed to the extent that it was reduced—finding a partner from within the family circle requires less initiative—and remained focused on love-objects from early childhood, the mother or father. They might seek a partner who resembled a parent, never marry, or marry very late.[12]

Karl Abraham's grandfather, Moses, married a close relative and had six children, of whom five lived to adulthood. Three remained single, and of the other two one married outside the family while the other married a cousin. Those first cousins were Karl Abraham's parents.[13] They fitted the description he gave in his lecture. Moses Abraham (1799–1870) lived in Nienburg as a butcher, religious teacher, and preacher to the Jewish community there.[14] Towns that could not permit themselves a rabbi often engaged the services of a preacher. Rabbis had usually graduated from a university or other institution of higher education, whereas the training received by preachers was more diverse. Elders mostly came out of the traditional Talmud schools of Central Europe, or were rabbis who had not yet found suitable posts. Young men were schooled at the Jewish teachers' seminary. A preacher's salary was very low, so he would usually combine the task with a trade of some kind.[15]

Moses must have been a progressive thinker, since he sent his daughter Johanna (1836–1916) to Hannover and Aachen to be trained as a seamstress and as a buying agent in the fashion business, a remarkable decision in the mid-nineteenth century when women rarely received any vocational training. In 1863, Johanna applied to become a citizen of Bremen, where her brother Nathan was living by then. She wanted to start her own company there and her father provided the financial guarantee demanded by the municipal authorities in such situations.[16] Moses sent his youngest son, Nathan (1842–1915), Karl Abraham's father, to a private school in Hannover that was founded in 1848, where he was trained as a teacher. In that sense, Nathan was following his father's course in life.[17]

In 1861, at the age of nineteen, Nathan was appointed by the Jewish community in Bremen as preacher and religious teacher.[18] In 1872, he was granted citizenship.[19]

Bremen

Today's Bremen is but a shadow of what it once was, one of the most powerful and wealthy cities of what is now northern Germany. Founded in 787 by Charles the Great as a bishopric, by the tenth century it had become a major port city, one of the oldest in Germany. In the mid-thirteenth century, it joined the Hanseatic League and became one of the most important of the German members. Throughout the Middle Ages it was a city state and from 1815 onwards it enjoyed an independent status as a free Hansa city.[20] When Karl Abraham was born there in 1877, Bremen had officially been part of the German Empire for six years. In Bremerhaven, Bremen had one of the most important ports in Germany, second only to Hamburg and a key transfer point for tobacco and cotton. The Bremen shipping company Norddeutscher Lloyd, founded in 1857, quickly became one of the most important shipping concerns of its day, taking emigrants and other passengers to New York and returning with freight.[21]

Ever since the Middle Ages, Bremen had operated a policy aimed at strictly limiting the number of Jews who settled there. It was far tougher in that regard than, for instance, Hamburg, and for a long time Jews were not given the right of residence or citizenship. As a result, the number of Jewish inhabitants was smaller than in other comparable German cities.[22] The majority of the population was either Lutheran or Reformed. The city was run by rich merchants and lawyers, and when Nathan settled there in 1861 its Jewish community consisted of just twenty families, some 150 people in total. Not until 1871 could Jews settle freely in Bremen. From then on their numbers steadily increased.[23]

Family

Nathan worked as a teacher of religion for eleven years.[24] He would gladly have continued in that profession, but his future parents-in-law, who were farmers and cattle traders, did not want their daughter to be married to a poverty-stricken teacher. Nathan complied with their wishes and became a tobacco merchant. In 1873, he married his cousin Ida Oppenheimer (1847–1929).[25] He started working for his brother-in-law, husband to Ida's younger sister, and in 1880 he set up his own wholesale tobacco business.[26]

Hilda describes her grandfather Nathan as a handsome man, small in stature with a patriarchal appearance, scholarly, well dressed and fearless. He looked a little like Sigmund Freud or Wilhelm Fließ. Nathan Abraham was an Orthodox believer with a strong faith and at the same time tolerant, but he was always serious. He was treated with respect at home, as befitted the head of the family.[27] Until his death, he was the leader of the Jewish community in Bremen as well as of B'nai Brith.[28] So, Karl Abraham grew up in an orthodox German–Jewish environment.

In nineteenth-century Germany, the Jews gained equal rights to a large extent but, at the same time, anti-Semitism was very much in evidence. Three thousand Jewish students attended university in Berlin in the early years of the century, but they could not become lecturers or professors. Most studied law or medicine and went on to pursue careers within the Jewish community.

They had Napoleon to thank for their rights. In 1806, he defeated the Prussians and occupied Berlin, uniting the thirty-eight states of the Rhine under the same legislature, which guaranteed equality under law for the Jews. In France, the Jews had been declared free and equal in 1791, in the new Republic.[29] The Edict of 1812 granted the following to Germany's Jews:

- the right to full citizenship;
- the right to settle wherever they chose;
- the right to buy land as long as they adopted German names;
- the right to join the army;
- the right to marry whomsoever they liked, Jewish or non-Jewish.

All discriminatory taxes were abolished, yet, under pressure from King Frederick William IV of Prussia, and partly in response to the demands of the aristocracy, Jews were banned from holding public office, with the exception of local government. Since universities were supported by the state, this excluded them from academic careers.[30] In the period after 1812, the rights granted by the Edict were gradually curtailed and this tendency was not reversed until 1871.

In 1815, at the Congress of Vienna after the fall of Napoleon, the map of Europe was redrawn and Posen was given to Prussia. The 80,000 Jews in Posen were excluded from the Edict, which meant that, in Prussia, a third of Jews lived under the old restrictions until well into the nineteenth century. The other thirty-seven states were given the right to reverse the Edict, so the situation for the Jews after 1815 was extremely unclear.[31]

In her article about Abraham's childhood, Bettina Decke describes how, in the mid-nineteenth century, Jews were officially forbidden to settle in Bremen. There was no Edict giving them the right to live wherever they liked. She suspects that Nathan Abraham was allowed to move there because, in 1859, the Senate of Bremen had adopted a rule that allowed for an exception to be made in the case of "foreign" religious leaders, but immediately after his appointment in 1861 he was confronted with considerable anti-Semitism. An appeal to the Senate for permission to build a synagogue at a suitable place in the city was refused.[32] The mayor, Karl Mohr, explained the decision as follows:

> Everything the constitution allows, they enjoy (the Jews in Bremen, B.D.). They are not a generally recognised religious community, and they are certainly not equal to the three Christian

denominations. They cannot even make a claim to equality. Pure good-naturedness does not apply here either, since in principle people want nothing to do with the Jews.[33]

Times were changing, however. Two years later, at the urging of liberal forces within the Senate of Bremen, the Jewish religious community was recognised. The turning point came in 1871, under Bismarck, at the same time as the German Empire was established. Jews were given the rights of the Edict of 1812, although with certain limitations: they could not become high-ranking army officers, they were hardly ever admitted to teaching professions, and they could take public office only in the more lowly positions. They were allowed to become judges but not to hold the more highly respected post of public prosecutor.[34]

Mother's family

Ida's father, Samson Oppenheimer, Karl Abraham's maternal grandfather, married three times because his first two wives died. With his third wife, Julie, he had four children, of whom Ida was the eldest and her favourite brother, Albert, the youngest. The generations of Oppenheimers overlapped, as illustrated by the fact that Ida was present as a two-year-old at the wedding of her oldest half-sister, while her mother had a baby at the breast.[35]

Karl Abraham's mother, Ida, was pretty, dominant, possessive, loving, and generous. Her warmth, domesticity, and sense of humour pervaded the house. She liked to feed her family on plenty of rich food. She was intelligent and, by the standards of the time, well educated. She was able to speak and write English, which she had learnt when Albert moved to Britain and married there.[36]

Ida and Nathan wed in 1873 and settled in Bremen.[37] Ida's parents moved in with them, as did Nathan's older sister Johanna, who had a business of her own in fashion items and made it financially possible for them all to move into the house at number 32 Bismarckstraße. Nathan's sister Jeanette joined them there, too. She was mentally disturbed and for a while extremely difficult to handle.[38] Adolph, Nathan's unmarried brother, had a home of his own but came to eat at the Bismarckstraße every day and spent weekends with the family.[39]

In September 1874, their eldest son Max was born.[40] Hilda writes that he was a difficult and sickly child, who became an extremely neurotic adult. He was severely asthmatic and his mother was possessive and overprotective in caring for him. He did justice to his brother's article about marriage between relatives to the extent that he lived with his mother until the age of forty-seven. At that point he married and his mother went to live with him.[41]

Karl Abraham

Karl Abraham was born two and a half years after Max, on 3 May 1877. Although only mildly asthmatic, he was subjected to the same strict regime as his brother. He is said to have enjoyed a harmonious first year of life. His daughter, Hilda, believed his liveliness and sense of humour were attributable in part to these early months. The idyll was interrupted after that first year of life by a series of deaths that hit the family hard. March 1878 saw the death of Karl's grand-father, who lived with them. In 1879, his mother's sister Rosa followed, at the age of only twenty-eight, and a year later Rosa's husband died. In that same period, Karl's mother fell down the stairs in the dark and suffered a miscarriage. She mourned deeply for her stillborn daughter and would return to that loss for the rest of her life. It had a lasting effect on her younger son. In 1883, Karl wrote to his father: "Dearest Papa! God be thanked my night was a little better, but Mama had a bad night because of my coughing and did not sleep very much. The night before was better. Grandmama and Aunt Jeanette are fine. Today just a lot of kisses, from your loving Karl".[42]

Karl was more concerned about his mother than about himself. He was only six and a half when he wrote that letter, an age at which you would expect a child to care more about his own cough than about his mother's lack of sleep. That Karl put her feelings first suggests he was anxious about her, which, in turn, indicates parentification.[43] His anxiety no doubt had its origins in the grief and depression to which she fell prey after the loss of her unborn daughter. When Abraham visited his parents in the summer of 1911, with a four-year-old daughter of his own, his anxiety about his mother revived. The little girl had slept poorly in the oppressive heat under thick covers, but what made the greatest impression on her was that her father asked her to say nothing about her uncomfortable night, to avoid upsetting grandma. It was one of many occasions on which Abraham asked the young Hilda to take account of the feelings of others.

Hilda Abraham writes that her father and his brother had an upbringing in which a great deal of emphasis was placed on order and regularity. There was also prudishness about sexual matters. Anal jokes were told with great enjoyment, but there were never any erotic jokes.

Because of their asthma, their anxious, possessive mother forbade the boys from taking part in sport or doing anything that was physically demanding, so, to work off their energy, they sought an outlet in the house and garden and found it in their aunts, on whom they regularly played tricks. Max would later describe to his small daughter, Lottie (1923–2012), every evening before she went to sleep, the practical jokes he and Karl got up to at their aunts' expense.[44]

In those days, effervescent tablets were sold for making fizzy lemonade. The boys put them into their aunts' chamber pots, which caused great commotion in the middle of the night. The aunts wore skirts with starched petticoats held up by a button at the back. The boys would hide behind the hedge and tie a thread around the button when the aunts came past. They jerked the thread so that the button came off and the petticoats fell to the ground. Hilda writes that she believes her father had just one real anal-erotic character trait. On rare occasions, he had sudden outbursts of rage—his mother called him a little keg of gunpowder—that would vanish as quickly as they came and leave him full of remorse. Max's daughter Lottie also spoke of those unpredictable rages.[45]

Karl's parents were delighted by their vital, energetic younger son, but he found their strict rules a torment and disliked being treated in almost the same way at his rather sickly older brother. Both boys were protected from draughts, a close watch was kept on their health, and they were not allowed to play with other boys. Another factor in all this was that Karl occasionally fainted and had very poor sight in one eye. It later transpired that he had a congenital eye disorder and he eventually became blind in his right eye. When feeling tense, he would lose his appetite.[46]

At the age of six, Karl was sent to a small private school with such meagre resources that he once came home blue with cold. He said the teacher had been so kind as to allow the children to sit on their hands to keep them warm. At seven years old, he was top of his class.[47] When he was almost eight, in March 1885, he was sent to the best and most expensive school in the city, where Max was already a pupil. It consisted of an elementary school, a trade school, and a humanist grammar school. In the autumn of 1886, Karl was admitted to the grammar school, at the then standard age of nine.[48]

Karl Abraham's relationship with his mother

Hardly any letters or other documents have survived that give us any insight into Karl Abraham's relationship with his mother, but, from his work, we can deduce that it must have been extremely problematic. He was always preoccupied with the subject of mother–son relationships, especially in his early years as a psychoanalyst and as a married man. He wrote time and again about mothers and sons, including love and hatred towards the mother.[49]

Karl's mother was warm, cheerful, funny, and dominant. Her prominent presence must have given the young Karl a sense of warmth and security, but she was also extremely possessive and anxious. Because his brother was not allowed to play with other children, Karl could not either, which must have made him lonely. He was active and full of energy but was allowed only to walk a little, so he must have felt cooped up. It took him a great deal of effort to separate himself from his mother, but the reverse must have been true as well.

When her sons were adults, Ida Abraham found it hard to have to compete with her daughters-in-law. Karl's wife, Hedwig, seems to have disliked her and with Max's wife, Else, things became so bad that the marriage was threatened. In the 1920s, when Ida moved in with Max and Else, she tyrannised the household to such a degree that Else packed her bags and left. It took Max a considerable effort to persuade her to come back.[50]

A recurring theme in Abraham's work is traumatic early abandonment by the mother, of the kind he experienced when he was two. His mother was still physically present, but unreachable because of her depression. Abraham writes that such a trauma stays with a person for a lifetime and can suddenly raise its head as an overwhelming sense of abandonment.[51]

There was a second recurring theme, anxiety, and, in particular, the absence of anxiety. Karl Abraham, described by his wife and by his analysand Theodor Reik as a person with an exceptional gift for empathy, could not feel anxiety in others.[52] He felt none in himself, either. It was as if, as a very young boy, he had been so anxious that he repressed that feeling for ever. This had far-reaching consequences, both for himself—he took great risks climbing mountains, for example—and for others. He might fail to notice that his children were feeling fearful, and sometimes he had the same blindness with regard to his patients. Abraham's own fear no doubt had to do with the fact that he felt his mother had disappeared, in an emotional sense, after her miscarriage. On top of that, he grew up in the same house as his severely disturbed aunt Jeanette, who sometimes smashed everything in her room. That must have been particularly frightening for a child of two who could not seek comfort from his mother and whose father kept his distance.

At grammar school

The Abraham brothers were among a tiny number of Jewish boys who attended the grammar school in Bremen. In Karl's class, there was just one other. (When Freud went to grammar school in Vienna, the proportion of Jewish pupils was high: forty-four per cent in 1865 and seventy-three per cent in 1873.) The two boys were extremely good pupils, but they were different; on Saturdays, they were not allowed to write or to play, and during Jewish celbrations they were kept home from school. They were never allowed to eat another child's sandwich or go for a meal at a friend's house. Karl was forbidden to take part in sports.[53] Schooldays cannot have been easy for either of them. They spent a lot of time together until just before puberty, when Max began to observe Jewish rituals meticulously. Karl was not only a good pupil, he turned out to have a talent for languages and he devoted more and more of his free time to learning them, developing a phenomenal ability later in life.[54]

During his time at grammar school, when he was fifteen years old, Karl Abraham wrote a small book that has never been published.[55] It was written in Bremen between August and October 1892 and he kept it with him throughout his life. After his death, when his family moved to London, the book went with them. He gave it the title *Grammatik der abiponischen Sprache. Abhandlungen und Notizen aus Ethnologie und Etymologie* (Grammar of the Abiponish Language. Treatment and notes from ethnology and etymology). There are seven chapters, of which three deal with Native American tongues: Abiponish, the language of the indigenous people of what is now Paraguay, Nahuatl, the language of the Aztecs in Mexico, and Delaware, a North American language. He also decided to compare the word "father" in 320 languages and to collect all the words he could find for numerals.

The thoroughness of Karl Abraham's study of languages is surprising in a fifteen-year-old boy, but Decke points to an even more remarkable aspect of the book.[56] He writes about the languages of countries far from Bremen, which was such an oppressive place to him. It was written in the very hot summer of 1892, when the cholera epidemic in Hamburg was at its height. The disease had broken out in August. People still drank untreated water from the Elbe in those days and this was the last great cholera epidemic in Germany, killing more than 8,000 people. There were fears that Bremen would be infected—a dual blow to the Jews, since they not only ran the risk of contracting the disease but were blamed for having caused it. Karl seems to have buried himself in his studies; he was probably kept indoors most of the time.

In early 1896, he took his final exams, in which he came second out of a class of eleven. The essay he wrote for that exam has been preserved in the municipal archives in Bremen.[57] The most striking thing about it is that the eighteen-year-old Karl includes a description that could easily apply to his later relationship with Freud.[58]

The title of the essay is "Instruenda est vita exemplis illustribus. Der Mensch soll sich durch erlauchte Beispiele leiten lassen"—a quotation from Seneca ("We must instruct ourselves using illustrious examples"). The essay begins as follows: "Everyone has once had—at least in childhood—some kind of ideal. He has admired some exceptional man whose work he has read or heard or even seen with his own eyes".[59] And, a little later,

> Above all we have to admit that every person, before he can give free play to his own individuality, has to study the example of others whose insights and ways of acting have proven

themselves. He then has to follow their example and if he wants to be truly worthy of his pre-decessor, which is his duty, then he must always act according to the word of Seneca. The duty of piety obliges him always to walk in the footsteps of great men who have striven for the same goals before him.[60]

Karl Abraham then left Bremen for good.

CHAPTER TWO

Student years

K arl Abraham would have liked to make a profession of his hobby, comparative linguistics. In 1896, he took his leaving exams at the grammar school. Nathan Abraham had
decided at an early stage that his elder son, Max, must take over the business from him
one day and Max's obvious unsuitability to do so was apparently not something Nathan took
into consideration. Max would have preferred to become a rabbi and to spend his days studying.[61] He never did make a success of commerce.[62]

The fact that his brother followed Nathan into the family business meant it was Karl who
had the opportunity to study. His uncle Adolf paid his university fees, but the family rejected
the idea of comparative linguistics. Karl did not want to be a schoolteacher and, in 1896, it was
practically impossible for a Jew to make a career at a university.[63] A degree in comparative
linguistics would, therefore, not lead to paid employment, so the family proposed dentistry
and Karl reluctantly complied. Hilda Abraham writes in her biography that he began a
dentistry course in Würzburg but came home after the first semester and said he would prefer
to study medicine.

> He demurred, but agreed to study dental medicine, and his father's brother Adolf offered to
> finance his studies. So he became a dental student at the University of Würzburg in South
> Germany in 1895, but after the first term he returned home and announced that he would rather
> study medicine than dentistry.[64]

The striking thing about this is that Karl Abraham did not begin a degree course in dentistry
or any other subject in 1895: in fact, he was still at the grammar school. That Hilda mistook the
year is not particularly surprising, since it all happened long before her time. Karl took his final
school exams in early 1896 and began studying in Würzburg immediately, in the summer

semester.[65] The 1896 *Inscriptionsliste* or student register for Würzburg makes clear that he studied medicine right from the start.[66] Decke wrote in 1997 that Karl let it be known before leaving school that he intended to study medicine—and put it in writing on his application forms for the school leaving exams—before going on to study dentistry instead.[67] It is impossible from this distance in time to discover the precise course of events, but quite possibly he wavered between his own second choice after comparative linguistics, medicine, and the preference expressed by the uncle who would be paying his fees. Dentistry was a less costly course of study. University fees were high in those years, at 1,200 to 1,500 marks a year.[68] To give a comparison, at the start of the twentieth century a mineworker would earn three marks a day and an employee of the mint works twenty-three marks per week, while six nights in a good hotel cost twenty marks.[69]

In Würzburg, Abraham took part in all the sports previously forbidden to him. He went swimming, played tennis, and, in due course, took up mountaineering, the sport that would become his great passion. His daughter, Hilda, believed that climbing mountains satisfied his need for new discoveries and she quotes in her biography what Abraham later wrote about oral and anal character development.

> People who have been gratified in the earliest oral stage are bright and sociable; those who are fixated at the oral–sadistic stage are hostile and malicious. While moroseness, inaccessibility and reticence go together with the anal character. Furthermore, persons with an oral character are accessible to new ideas, in a favourable as well as an unfavourable sense, while the anal character involves a conservative behaviour opposed to all innovations—an attitude which certainly prevents the hasty abandonment of what has been proved good.[70]

Hilda had a feeling that her father is describing here the behaviour he had observed in himself and his brother.

In his first university semester, Karl contracted scarlet fever. His friend, Iwan Bloch, informed Karl's parents and Ida Abraham rushed to Würzburg to care for her son. Iwan was several years older than Karl. In 1896 he was working on his dissertation.[71]

In Würzburg, Abraham took the usual subjects for the first semester of a degree course in medicine, which included experimental physics taught by Professor Wilhelm Röntgen.[72] The discovery of electromagnetic radiation had been made on 8 November 1895, and Röntgen was working on his first publications about it. Abraham also opted for two non-compulsory subjects, Professor Oswald Külpe's history of modern philosophy and Schopenhauer, taught by Dr Karl Marbe.

Külpe was an ordinary professor of philosophy at the University of Würzburg and founder of the Würzburger Schule der Denkpsychologie. Marbe was also attached to the Würzburger Schule, as a *Privatdozent*. In Germany, anyone who had gained a doctorate in one of the faculties of a university could apply for a *Habilitation*, which involved writing a professorial thesis. Compared to such theses, dissertations tended to be short. A work of thirty pages was often sufficient to gain a doctorate, whereas a *Habilitation* was a far more comprehensive test of ability that involved demonstrating command of the subject, including giving two lectures. The faculty concerned had to approve the applicant's proposal for a professorial thesis beforehand and, on its completion, check that the resulting work was of a sufficiently high standard. The scholar was then qualified to teach independently at university level, as a *Privatdozent*, who was not paid by the university but instead received fees for lectures, paid at the start of each semester by the students, subject by subject. The sum he received therefore depended on the number of students who subscribed. He could teach whatever he liked and, in theory, the student was free to choose subjects to study, although in the case of medicine many were compulsory.[73] For an academic career it was important to become a *Privatdozent*, since if a paid post at the university fell vacant it would often be filled from among their ranks. Freud was a *Privatdozent* at the University of Vienna and Abraham attempted to become one in Berlin, without success.[74]

After his summer term in Würzburg, Abraham moved to Freiburg. The medical faculty there was well known and it was common in those days to study at three different universities. The semesters were short, the vacations long, adding up to some twenty-two weeks per year.[75]

Freiburg

Today's visitor to Freiburg im Breisgau sees almost nothing of the city that Abraham knew, in those days one of the most beautiful in Germany.[76] After German unification in 1871, when the states came together as an empire led by Prussia, with Wilhelm I as emperor, the number of students in Freiburg rose, slowly at first but then increasingly quickly.[77] The expansion of medicine there, and physics in its wake, was facilitated by an energetic building policy from 1860 onwards, driven by physiologist and anatomist Alexander Ecker, who worked tirelessly to improve working conditions in his field of expertise through renovation and construction. He managed to convince the relevant governmental bodies of the need for a new building to house anatomy, and when Karlsruhe declined to provide the necessary financial support, the city and the university took the costs of the construction project on the Albertstraße upon themselves.[78] Its inauguration in 1867 marked the first major step towards the creation of a medical faculty that rapidly filled an entire urban district. The hospital, built in the 1870s, had become too small, so it was extended with several new buildings, then a botanical institute with a garden was added, as well as a chemistry institute, a zoological institute with its own collection, and so it went on. When Abraham arrived in Freiburg in the second semester of 1896, he was able to work in a brand new medical faculty. "The Medical Faculty, for its good facilities alone, also enjoyed an excellent reputation as a modern and progressive place of training."[79]

Freiburg was the first university to admit female students, starting in 1899–1900. Karen Horney, who later became Abraham's analysand, studied there in 1906–1908.[80]

Abraham registered as a student in Freiburg on 4 November 1896.[81] He was nineteen years old, one of the youngest of the 339 students who registered that term, of whom ninety-eight were there to study medicine. At registration, each student's faith was noted. The majority were Catholic, just seventeen Jewish, ten of them studying medicine, six law, and one chemistry. Abraham registered for a remarkably large number of subjects, eleven in his first semester at Freiburg, ten in the next. In subsequent years, he studied eight, dropping to seven for one term. Few students registered for so many subjects.

As he had in Würzburg, Abraham took several non-medical subjects in his first semester at Freiburg, and in that semester only, including Italian and "Geographical Issues of the Day". The professors whose lectures he attended included a number who were famous names at the time. Robert Wiedersheim (1848–1923), professor of anatomy at Freiburg from 1883 to 1917, was intensely involved with the new science of origins, brought into being by the ideas of Charles Darwin, and he wrote a bestselling book of popular science on the subject called *Der Bau des Menschen als Zeugnis für seine Vergangenheit* (The Bodily Structure of Humans as Evidence of their Past). He was both a productive writer and an excellent teacher.[82] Abraham took two of his courses in the first semester: "Systematic Anatomy of Humans" and "Dissection". He also chose "Comparative Anatomy of Vertebrates", taught by Ernst Gaupp (1865–1916), who had qualified as a *Privatdozent* in 1895. Gaupp belonged to the group associated with Wiedersheim and he devoted himself, among other things, to comparing the skulls of different vertebrates. He was a gifted teacher, and popular with students as a result.[83] Anatomy was always strongly represented among Abraham's study options.

Franz Keibel (1861–1921), with whom Abraham later worked for two years and carried out his doctoral research, had been first assistant to Wiedersheim since 1889. In the summer term of 1897, Abraham took two of Keibel's courses: histology and embryology. Keibel's career at the university did not run smoothly. Despite many publications and international renown, he remained an assistant for twenty-five years. He did become an honorary professor in due course, which meant he carried out the work of a professor but without a salary. Wiedersheim remained at the university until the advanced age of sixty-nine and at last, aged fifty-three, Keibel became a full professor in Strasbourg.

Max Schottelius (1849–1919) was another professor of Abraham's who was well known in his day. Originally a pathologist, he became prominent in the new field of hygiene and in bacteriology. The study of hygiene was of great importance in view of the outbreaks of typhus and cholera that were still occurring at regular intervals. In Freiburg in 1884, Max Schottelius gave the first ever lecture on bacteriology and in 1885 he introduced practical courses on bacteria and hygiene. In 1889 hygiene became an independent subject, distinct from pathology, and Schottelius was appointed professor of hygiene. In 1895–1896 a special institute for hygiene was built and the building met all the requirements of hygiene in its lighting, heating and ventilation, so students were able to learn directly from the building itself. In his final term, the summer semester of 1900, Abraham took both theoretical and practical courses in hygiene. It was an exciting time to be involved in medicine, with important discoveries being made continually.

Abraham had not yet begun to study psychiatry; that came later, in Berlin. He was at Freiburg from the winter of 1896–1897 to the summer of 1898, for four successive semesters. He spent the winter semester of 1898–1899 studying in Berlin and in the summer semester of 1899 he was at Freiburg again. He then spent the winter semester of 1899–1900 in Berlin and the summer semester of 1900 at Freiburg.

In Berlin, as well as the clinical subjects that were a regular part of his medical studies in the later semesters, Abraham studied psychiatry. In 1898–1899 he took "Diseases of the Nervous System" and in 1899–1900 "Diseases of the Nervous System and Psychiatry", both taught by Professor Emanuel Mendel. In the 1899–1900 semester, he also studied "Investigations of Mental Illnesses" under Professor Max Köppen, who would present a psychiatric patient in the lecture theatre and examine him or her there.[84]

On 31 January 1901, Abraham took his final exams, and on 5 February he officially qualified as a doctor. On 14 June that year, he completed his doctorate.[85] The subject he chose for his
doctoral thesis was the developmental history of the budgerigar.[86] On 27 February 1901 he paid
300 marks as a fee for his doctorate, a considerable sum in those days.[87]

Abraham's dissertation was an embryological study, a comparative description of the development of organs in the budgerigar and in other bird species. The dissertation states that it was
published under the auspices of the anatomy institute of the University of Freiburg im
Breisgau, which was headed by Wiedersheim. Abraham dedicated it to Professor F. Keibel, with
his sincere gratitude.

In the foreword, he explains his intentions, writing that he is grateful above all to his teacher
Professor Keibel, who had suggested the subject to him and entrusted him with the research
material, which consisted of thirty embryos. Those would have been extremely hard to obtain
and therefore represented an impressive gift. Abraham also thanks Keibel for his friendly
engagement with the study and the bountiful advice that was of use to him in carrying out the
work.

It was usual practice for a student achieving a doctorate to give fulsome thanks to a teacher,
but Keibel seems to have offered Abraham a truly rare opportunity by giving him the embryos.
It suggests they got along particularly well. Hilda writes that Abraham met a young lecturer in
Freiburg, meaning Keibel, who succeeded in interesting him in histology and embryology, and
that Abraham would remain interested in those subjects for the rest of his life. Keibel was not
particularly young, at sixteen years older than Abraham.

Wiedersheim's assessment of the thesis, which has survived, was highly complimen-
tary.[88]

How did Abraham experience his time in Freiburg? As far as we know, not a single piece
of personal correspondence from that period has been preserved. He faithfully wrote to his
parents every week, but all those letters have been lost.[89]

Abraham stayed in Freiburg for a considerable time and seems to have felt at home there.
His co-operation with Keibel was important in that respect and the number of subjects he chose
to study suggests that he worked extremely hard. He will undoubtedly have devoted some
time to mountaineering; in fact, it was in Freiburg that his great love of the mountains developed.[90] Other than Bloch, we know nothing of his friends during his student years. Hedwig,
his future wife, mentioned that he had a brief friendship with a girl in Freiburg, but no details
have been discovered.[91]

Abraham did not join the Jewish student association Ghibellenia, established in 1897. His
name is not on the list of members. Most student fraternities not only refused to admit Jews,
but discriminated severely against them. Abraham must have been confronted with anti-
Semitism, but it is astonishing how little sign of it there is in the material about him or in his
own writing. Medical faculties were notorious for their anti-Semitism and many doctors later
became Nazis.[92] There was a great deal of anti-Semitism among the residents of Freiburg, too,
most of whom were Catholics. In his autobiography *Mein Weg Als Deutscher und Jude* (My Life
as German and Jew), writer Jakob Wassermann, four years older than Abraham, wrote a
passage set in Freiburg in the period shortly before Abraham arrived there. Wasserman was
looking for work and had put an advert in the newspaper:

An insurance agent from Freiburg in Baden replied and asked me for a photograph and personal details. After receiving them he took me on. I was the only clerk in his office and I had ten hours of writing work to do every day. The man into whose service I had entered was tough, mean, devious and hard to please. In his behaviour he was emphatically correct. He had all the charm of a lieutenant in the reserve.

One Sunday morning, when I went to the office to finish some urgent work, he arrived as well, praised my diligence but then said that I could leave the work and go to church instead. I was amazed that he had not been informed on this point and I answered what there was to answer. His face darkened frighteningly. After an angry silence he reproached me for intentionally leaving him in ignorance; it had been my duty to make specific reference to my religion in my letter of application. He had never thought of such a thing, since he had been misled by my photograph and then by my appearance and regarded this as deception. He said nothing further, but because he did not dare simply to throw me onto the street, he prepared the most hatefully difficult tasks for me, grumbled at every stroke of the pen, at every greeting, and, out of low expectations, laid a trap for me.[93]

Wasserman was dismissed shortly afterwards. His book concerns the fact that he saw himself first of all as a German. He felt a close bond with the language, the culture, the country, but he noticed that others suddenly turned out to see him not as German, but as Jewish, expressing an astonishing degree of hatred towards him.

There was a great deal of anti-Semitism in the German population as a whole, but it was particularly strong among students. Among German Jews, a significant social change had taken place in the nineteenth century in the sense that many had climbed up from a marginal economic position and achieved a solid middle-class standing.[94] In this respect, Abraham's father was one among many.

By about 1880, an anti-Semitic movement had emerged with the aim of stripping the Jews of the entitlement to equal rights that they had gained (up to a point) in 1871.[95] In 1881 Chancellor Bismarck was handed a petition with 265,000 signatures and the following demands:

1. Prevention or at least restriction of immigration by foreign Jews.
2. Exclusion of Jews from all official functions and restriction of their activities in the judicial field, and especially as judges.
3. Maintenance of the Christian character of elementary schools by appointing only Christian teachers. The admission of Jewish teachers in other types of school only as thoroughly justified exceptions.
4. Reopening of the official statistics regarding Jews.[96]

Only 0.6% of the German population actually signed the petition. Shockingly, however, a full 19% of students did so. In its wake, student associations were established that regarded anti-Semitism as one of their main tasks. They were known as *Vereine Deutscher Studenten*, and, in December 1880, one such association was founded in Berlin. In February 1881, Halle-Wittenberg, Leipzig, and Freiburg followed, in March 1881, Göttingen, and then others.[97] Despite considerable opposition, they succeeded in gaining official recognition and came together under the umbrella of the Kyffhäuserverband der Vereine Deutscher Studenten, thereby amounting to an organised national student movement. Still a relatively marginal matter in the German empire as a whole, the "Judenfrage" became a central issue in the student world.[98]. The following guidance gained considerable influence:

> In the election and official activities of student representatives we have always, on occasions with lively agitation and with complete success, acted in such a way that those who had such a position filled it in the traditional spirit. For that reason we always regarded it as necessary to prevent Jewish fellow students from holding positions in the representation of our academic young people.[99]

The anti-Semitic student association in Berlin, for example, managed to pose the "Jewish question" repeatedly in the period 1880–1914 and to make it a central subject during student meetings, many of which had been called to discuss other matters entirely. Practically all its opponents allowed themselves to become caught up in this unproductive subject.[100] The same happened in other university cities, with far-reaching consequences. There were many different student societies, ranging from social clubs to musical, sporting, and scientific associations. After a while, despite much internal resistance, almost all of them began refusing to accept Jews as members. A third of Berlin's student acrobatics society were Jews, yet eventually all Jewish students were expelled from it.[101]

By the time Abraham began attending university, it was practically impossible for a Jewish student to join any mainstream student society. In response, Jewish fraternities were established from 1886 onwards. They emphasised their conviction that Germany was their fatherland and vowed to combat anti-Semitism, but their mission was also to reinforce Jewish identity and self-consciousness.

In 1894–1895, social sciences student associations (*Sozialwissenschaftliche Studentenvereinigungen*) suddenly sprang up. In a university climate in which it had become almost impossible to set up a new student society without excluding Jews, these were societies established and run jointly by Jewish and Christian students.[102] Later, when he worked in Dalldorf in Berlin and was no longer a student, Abraham joined one such society and made his most important friends there.

CHAPTER THREE

Doctor's assistant in Dalldorf

A braham was not required to do military service. The asthma of his childhood had caused slight emphysema, so he failed the medical test. On 17 May 1901, before he had finished his doctorate, he started working as a doctor's assistant in the Dalldorf psychiatric clinic in Berlin.[103] Dalldorf was his second choice. In Freiburg, he had become interested in the ideas of Eugen Bleuler, director of the Burghölzli psychiatric clinic in Zurich, and had tried to get a place as an assistant there.[104] He succeeded only much later.

Before Abraham got down to work at Dalldorf, he wrote to his father that in his new job he would not be in a position to respect the Jewish dietary laws, or to keep the Sabbath. His father answered that this decision, which would affect his entire future, was one he alone could make. Hilda had the feeling that the great tolerance contained in her grandfather's answer was typical of him. Her father was no less tolerant of his own environment, she wrote.[105] But it can surely not have been as simple as that. Hilda was writing in 1970 when she was well into her sixties and her mother approaching ninety. The two women shared the London house where Hilda carried on her psychoanalytic practice.[106] Hedwig, Karl Abraham's wife, was emphatic in her judgements and opinions and she provided Hilda with information for use in the biography of Karl. Hilda was nineteen when her father died, so much of the information must have come from her mother. Karl's father, Nathan, was strictly orthodox and his life revolved around his religion, so his son's decision must have been very difficult for him. It cannot have been easy for Karl, either. He was extremely attached to his parents. Did he feel he was betraying them? We know what Hedwig thought about the Jewish rituals. She writes, "Knowing my mother's enormous resistance to religious beliefs in general and Jewish ritual in particular, we can be sure that it carried the day over her conscious solicitude".[107]

Dalldorf had once been outside Berlin, some distance from its outer suburbs. In 1869, the municipality of Berlin bought the Dalldorf estate to establish a psychiatric institution there and,

19

in 1880, a clinic was built for 500 patients and made ready for use.[108] The estate covered sixty-six hectares, which meant there was room for an eighteen-hectare farm next to the institute. The clinic was built in the shape of a large square, with a building for the management and administrative staff, and ten pavilions. The word "pavilion" was slightly misleading, since the buildings in which the patients were accommodated were tall and solid, and their mostly barred windows, connecting walls, and iron railings made them look more than anything like a prison.

Dalldorf had a psychiatric department and a department for sick psychiatric patients and epileptics. Both had a medical director, and the director of the psychiatric department was also the general director. That department also had a senior doctor, four doctors' assistants, two volunteer doctors, and 140 care staff, both male and female.[109] In the early decades, most of the staff lived in the grounds of the clinic with their families, and Abraham probably lived there, too.

The salaries paid to the care staff were low. A senior care worker earned 1,000 marks per year, plus bed and board, his female equivalent 750 marks. The ordinary care staff earned 450 marks, 350 in the case of the women, and their working conditions were tough. They often had to sleep on the wards along with the patients and they were required to ask permission before leaving the premises. There was a high turnover of staff.

In those days, the patients' disorders were assumed to be organic in nature and treatment consisted above all of isolation from the outside world and from the city. Little force was used, except that solitary confinement was frequently imposed. The hope was that the patients' unease could be channelled by means of therapeutic orderliness and consistency, manual labour, and other occupations. The men worked in the fields or in one of the workshops, making furniture, shoes, or clothes. The women were kept busy sewing, knitting, and darning, with a small number cooking or doing other domestic work. The male patients were given ten pfennigs and the women five pfennigs for a working day that lasted a minimum of six hours. The payment was intended as an incentive to work. In 1900, a new treatment was introduced in the form of bed rest. All patients had to spend their first eight days in bed, where they were given medication to make them sleep and to calm their nerves. Restless patients were treated with warm baths (32–37°C) in which they had to stay for between six and fourteen hours. Special baths were used for this purpose, in which the patient was enclosed up to the neck.

In Berlin, there were a number of competing institutions: private clinics, the university clinic known as the Charité, and various others. As a result, Dalldorf was mainly a place where people from the lower ranks of society were treated. The Charité would regularly send on to Dalldorf patients whom it was unable to help any further.[110]

Abraham went to Dalldorf on the recommendation of his teacher, Keibel, because Hugo Karl Liepmann was working there as a brain pathologist. Abraham was interested in cell research and did not take up the post in order to become involved in psychiatry.[111] Professor Liepmann (1863–1925), from an old Jewish family in Berlin, was a doctor at Dalldorf from 1899 to 1914. Even while still at school, Liepmann was greatly interested in ancient languages and philosophy.[112] His career followed an unusual course. He studied philosophy and sciences with an emphasis on chemistry and, in 1885, obtained his doctorate with a thesis on the mechanism of the *"Leucipp-Democritschen Atome"*, which later won considerable praise and was much used in research. He wrote a book about Schopenhauer, but by the time it was published, in 1891, he had switched to studying medicine. Liepmann eventually opted for the real world and moved away from philosophy with its purely mental constructs. He started work at Dalldorf as a neurologist and psychiatrist in 1899 and carried out a great deal of brain research. His specialist field was apraxia, a term he introduced in 1900 to refer to the inability to carry out intentional acts or certain combined actions despite the absence of any muscular paralysis or sensory disorder. The cause lies in damage to specific parts of the brain. Liepmann gained his *Habilitation* in 1901 and became an honorary professor. He never obtained a university post as a full professor and his Jewish origins no doubt played a part in that. Abraham got along well with him and remained in touch after he left Dalldorf. He found the work he was able to do with Liepmann interesting and published several articles about it, but, aside from that, Dalldorf did not suit him.[113]

A tight circle of friends

Abraham had one close friend in Berlin with whom he spent a good deal of time. Salomon Altmann was a student of economics who later taught at Heidelberg University and then became an economics professor at Mannheim. He came from a strict religious background. Altmann was a member of the Berlin Sozialwissenschaftliche Studentenvereinigung (Berlin social sciences student association), one of those associations mentioned at the end of the previous chapter that rejected the norms of the traditional student societies. Despite the name, it took pains not to be thought of as revolutionary in any sense, since it would then run the risk of being banned by the university authorities.

The association also voiced opposition to the recently established Jewish student societies, which placed a strong emphasis on courage, manliness, and drinking (although members did not engage in duels), distancing themselves from everything that could point to the negative image of the bookworm and the lack of decisive vigour associated with it. In that sense, they were very much like the existing German student fraternities. Duelling was not something they had freely decided against, far from it, but Jews were not permitted to challenge anyone to a duel.[114]

The social sciences student associations believed that the new Jewish student societies were responding to anti-Semitism in a way that made them hopelessly old-fashioned. Instead of imitating conservative societies that were themselves dated, they ought instead to find an answer suitable to modern times. The first social sciences student association was set up in Berlin in 1891 and the second in Freiburg in 1895.[115] Within the Berlin association, Abraham developed a tight circle of friends, who also met up at seminars given by Ignaz Jastrow. The society admitted both men and women, which was highly unusual in those days.

In Berlin, there was fierce opposition to the admission of women to the university. Whereas Freiburg had female students as early as 1900, there was none in Berlin until 1908, but from the winter semester of 1895–1896, after much pressure had been applied, women were allowed to attend lectures and participate in seminars as *Gasthörer* or "guest listeners". They could not graduate, and the lecturer or professor had to give his permission for them to be admitted. Ignaz Jastrow (1856–1937) allowed women to attend. He was an economist and historian who, from 1895 onwards, taught at Berlin University, where he became a professor in 1905. In 1928, Adele Schreiber wrote the following about him and the group of friends who attended his lectures:

> There was once a professor who was part of this most progressive minority. In his summer house in Charlottenburg he gave a seminar, with tea and cakes. The real students and several guest listeners who were not yet real students visited both the university and the seminar in the summer house, and they were in those days real friends.[116]

It was quite an extraordinary group. They came together in the summer house in Jastrow's garden and after his lecture they would go to a café near what is now Berlin's Gedächtniskirche to drink coffee and engage in endless discussions.[117] Several of them later became famous. Adele Schreiber (1872–1957), journalist, feminist, and politician, would serve as a member of the Reichstag in the 1920s. Alice Salomon (1872–1948) became an important campaigner for women's rights and one of the first women in Germany to gain a doctorate, in 1906, with a thesis about unequal pay for men and women. She was the founder and director of the Soziale Frauenschule in Berlin.[118] Walter Kaesbach, art historian and famous collector of modern art, became director of the art academy in Düsseldorf in 1924 and appointed Paul Klee, among others, as a lecturer there.[119] Elisabeth Gottheiner (1874–1930) gained her doctorate in Zurich in 1904, and in 1924 she was appointed professor of economics in Mannheim, making her Germany's first female professor. From 1912 onwards, she was editor of the *Jahrbuch der Frauenbewegung*. She married Abraham's friend Salomon Altmann (1878–1933).

Another member of the seminar group was Hans Bürgner (1882–1974), who became one of Abraham's best friends. He and Abraham would walk back and forth between each other's houses all night long, debating and philosophising. They both had a thorough grounding in the classics and they based their approach on Aristotle's peripatetic school, so called because Aristotle always walked around while engaging in debate. The two friends enjoyed each other's company enormously. Hans Bürgner became a lawyer and notary and his clients included many analysts. He was later involved with the founding of Berlin's psychoanalytic polyclinic. He and Abraham shared a love of nature and art. One of Bürgner's clients was Marc Chagall, who gave him paintings as payment. In 1929, he married the artist and illustrator Dodo Wolff.[120]

In 1902, a very short article by Abraham was published in the Viennese weekly *Die Zeit*.[121] In it, Abraham expressed his indignation that the rector, Professor Kékulé von Stradonitz, had decided to ban the Berlin social sciences student association. There had been problems before, when talks it organised were forbidden by the university, but this was a much more far-reaching measure. It was prompted by the fact that for the winter season 1901–1902, two talks were planned that would be given by women.[122] This was unprecedented, the rector felt. He ordered that instead two men must give talks about the issue of the place of women. The association agreed, but in its announcement it asked women to take part in the discussion so that their views would be heard, not just those of men. At that point the rector banned the society. Abraham's engagement here is remarkable, as is the fact that he became part of a group that was greatly concerned about the emancipation of women. In his later work, the position, influence and psychological development of women was an important theme.

Engaged

Through Hans Bürgner, Abraham got to know his future wife, Hedwig, Hans' older sister.[123] Hedwig attended lectures about German language and literature as a *Gasthörer* and did secretarial work for the social sciences student association. Hans had two sisters, Hedwig being the oldest of the three children.[124] Their father, Philipp Bürgner, was born in southern Hungary in 1844, the fourth of six children in a family that lived comfortably as small landowners. They were practising Jews but not strictly orthodox.

Philipp left home at the age of seventeen and pursued a business career in Vienna. When he arrived in Berlin, he was in his early twenties.

Hans and Hedwig's mother, Clara Cohn, born in 1851, had grown up in Berlin.[125] Her father was from a Jewish family in Berlin and her mother from the Harz region. Clara had an older brother, Hermann, and another brother seven years younger called Richard. They spent their childhood in the centre of the city, playing on the square outside the Alte Museum, with games of hide-and-seek among the sarcophagi. The family had settled into the life of Berlin and they were not practising Jews.

Clara and Philipp met through Clara's older brother, Hermann, and were married in 1877. According to Hilda, it was a happy marriage. Philipp was lively and quick-tempered, and Clara, an attractive woman, rather mild. Hedwig was the eldest, next came Else, born in 1879, and Hans, 1881. When the children were small, the family went on an outing during which Hans fell into a stream while playing. His sisters knew that if their parents found out, the trip would be over, so they stood some way apart and told Hans to run back and forth between them until he was dry. Hilda thought this was a nice anecdote, but it does make clear that the sisters were given responsibility for their little brother from an early age.

Hedwig had a great deal to cope with in her childhood. When she was seven, her grandmother, Clara's mother, came to live with the family after her husband died. The children resented never having their mother to themselves any longer and the situation worsened when their grandmother developed dementia. Else, Hedwig's younger sister, had a spinal deformity as a result of rickets and in her teens she developed a hump. When Hedwig was twelve, Clara was discovered to have a heart valve defect. At the age of fourteen, Hedwig accompanied her mother when she went to take healing baths and would stay awake at night for fear she might miss a heart attack and be unable to help. Clara died when Hedwig was seventeen. Philipp was grief-stricken and for support he turned to Hedwig, who closely resembled her mother and who took the household upon herself.

For Hedwig, this must have meant that she missed out on a great deal of her childhood. From the age of twelve, she increasingly acted as the caring parent and, at seventeen, she found herself looking after her father, her younger sister, who was starting to show signs of psychosis, a twelve-year-old brother, and a demanding grandmother. She left school, although she would have liked to attend university.

Instead, Hedwig took private lessons with Helene Lange (1848–1930), a standard bearer of the women's movement and early feminism in Germany.[126] That she chose Lange as a teacher surely indicates that women's emancipation was important to her. Hedwig wanted to train to be a teacher of English and French, but that was incompatible with her household tasks.

Moreover, her father made clear to her that it would ruin her chances of marriage. In the end, she contented herself with attending lectures on German language and literature, and, along with her brother, she went to lectures on sociology by Georg Simmel.[127] Hedwig was clearly hugely ambitious and maintained close relations with campaigners for the emancipation of women.

Hedwig and Karl became friends in the winter of 1901–1902 when they were both attending Simmel's lectures and their relationship developed quickly from there.[128] In the summer of 1902, four members of the group, Elisabeth Gottheiner, Salomon Altman, Abraham, and Hedwig went on a walking holiday together in Switzerland. Since Hedwig's father might have objected to such an undertaking, they took Hedwig's brother, Hans, with them as a chaperone. They laughed about that a good deal, but it must indeed have been reassuring for Philipp Bürgner. Abraham wrote a very long epic poem for the occasion that began in the style of Nietzsche's *Zarathustra* and included passages from the Bible as well as lines of poetry specially selected for each member of the quintet. Hedwig was addressed in Nibelungen-style, while for Hans Bürgner, Abraham adapted some lines by Wilhelm Busch.[129]

Karl Abraham and Hedwig Bürgner became engaged in 1904, shortly before Abraham left for Zurich to take up his next job.[130] His parents travelled to Berlin to meet Hedwig, and his mother sent her a leather folder with five photographs and some poems, so she would still have Abraham with her after he left for Switzerland.[131] Max, Abraham's brother, also came to meet Hedwig. She made a great effort to cook kosher food for him, but then put everything on the table without separating the meat from the dairy products. Max barely ate anything and Hedwig was deeply hurt.[132]

Abraham's choice of partner

With the help of an article by Abraham about neurotic exogamy, along with the article about intermarriage mentioned earlier, Hilda discussed in her biography the relationship between her parents and her father's sexual development.[133] When Abraham wrote about inbred families he clearly included his own:

> In the paper mentioned above I have shown that in order to appreciate correctly the psychological significance of the tendency towards inbreeding, this phenomenon must be ranged with certain other manifestations. At one end of the scale we find true incest. This is far less rare in psychopathic families than has been hitherto supposed. At the other extreme is complete and permanent avoidance of all heterosexual relationships.

> Closely akin to the first extreme is the inclination towards cousins and other cognate members of the family. Closely akin to the other extreme is the manifestation which I should like to call "neurotic exogamy". This occurs where a man experiences an insuperable aversion to any close relationship with a woman of his own people or nation. Or, to put it more correctly, of his mother's people This is an indication of special measures taken to avoid the possibility of incest. The neurotic takes flight from women who typify his mother and turns to women who in appearance and character are as different as possible from his mother or sister. This flight is a result of his exaggerated phobia of incest.[134]

Hilda wrote, probably echoing her mother's opinion, that she did not think it would be going too far to say that much of this was of relevance when it came to her father's own choice of partner. Hilda described her mother as a modern-looking woman, an intellectual who wanted nothing to do with religious practices of any kind, a progressive woman who loved the theatre, concerts, and a busy social life, the opposite of Abraham's mother in every way. She believed Karl Abraham would have chosen a partner who was as different as possible from his mother.

In fact, Abraham had chosen a woman who resembled his mother in many ways. Hedwig had the same nationality. She, too, was from the well-to-do German–Jewish middle class and was highly demanding. Hilda's description says a great deal about Hedwig's attitude to Abraham's orthodox Jewish family, which was not from the pulsating metropolis of Berlin, but from provincial Bremen. Clearly, Hedwig did not much like the Abrahams. After Karl's death she barely saw them again.[135] The way she treated her niece, Max's daughter, in later years suggests that she looked down on her husband's family.[136]

CHAPTER FOUR

Burghölzli

A braham's attempts to secure a position as doctor's assistant in Zurich were finally successful. On 8 December 1904, he started work as second assistant in the Burghölzli Clinic.[137] It came as a revelation after the soul-destroying Dalldorf. A few years later he wrote to Freud:

> The Berlin colleagues I know well. I was a physician at the Berlin mental hospital Dalldorf for more than three years, until I could bear it no longer. I know how difficult it is in medical Berlin to stand up against an established doctrine. In Zurich I could breathe freely again. No clinic in Germany could have offered me even a fraction of what I have found here.[138]

The uninspiring environment was not the only reason why Abraham moved on. He wanted to marry, but, in Dalldorf, there was no prospect of a salary large enough to support a family. He left with glowing references, stating that he had begun as a volunteer, unpaid but with bed and board, and later worked as an assistant.[139] There was praise for his conduct towards patients, management, and colleagues.

When Abraham made application for a residence permit at the Ministry of Health, his new director, Bleuler, wrote that he came highly recommended by his previous director and with many years of experience in independent psychiatric work at Dalldorf. He also wrote that Abraham wanted to come and work in Zurich because his race stood in the way of promotion in Berlin, adding that his North-German speech was a shortcoming that should not weigh too heavily. Every institution, especially a clinic, benefits from a fresh breath of air from elsewhere. An excellent foreigner was preferable to a less competent fellow Swiss.[140] Abraham's way of speaking was problematic because, in Zurich, everyone spoke Swiss German and the patients found it hard to understand the accent and idioms of northern Germany. Hilda Abraham made no mention of the impossibility of promotion at Dalldorf because of her father's Jewish background, concentrating instead on his plans to marry. Bleuler, however, is entirely frank about the problem.

Eugen Bleuler

There is no telling how psychoanalysis might have developed without Eugen Bleuler and Zurich's university psychiatric clinic, the Burghölzli.

Practically all the important psychoanalysts in those early years spent time at the Burghölzli, where they came into contact with Freud's work and received their training. To name just a few: Carl Gustav Jung (1875–1961) and Ludwig Binswanger (1881–1966), both of whom were Swiss; Johan van Ophuijsen (1882–1950) from the Netherlands; Sabina Spielrein (1885–1942) from Russia; Otto Gross (1877–1920) from Austria; Max Eitingon (1881–1943), who was born in Russia before moving to Leipzig at the age of twelve, and Abraham A. Brill (1874–1948) from the USA. Ernest Jones (1879–1958) came from England to visit Jung at the Burghölzli Clinic, having met him at the first psychiatric congress in Amsterdam.[141] Jones then attended the first psychoanalytic congress in Salzburg, where he met Freud. Sándor Ferenczi (1873–1933), from Hungary, was taken to Jung at the Burghölzli by his colleague Dr Stein, and he then visited Freud in Vienna on 2 February 1908. A close friendship quickly developed between Ferenczi and Freud.[142]

In his article "The creation of a scientific community: The Burghölzli, 1902–1914", Peter Loewenberg compares it with other "clusters of gifted people", such as the Bauhaus (1920–1933) in Weimar and Dessau, and the Enrico–Fermi group of nuclear physicists in Rome (1925–1938), both of which likewise brought together a huge amount of creativity and were the focus of mutual inspiration.[143]

At the start of the twentieth century, Zurich was an extraordinary city. The little town quickly grew and it was not just a centre for textiles, machinery, and steel, but the breeding ground of extremely diverse cultural and political developments. The right to political asylum was laid down in the Swiss federal constitution of 1848. In the nineteenth century, Russian revolutionaries such as Alexander Herzen and Michael Bakunin fled to Switzerland and, as the twentieth century approached, German socialists such as Wilhelm Liebknecht and August Babel moved to Switzerland to escape Bismarck's antisocialist laws.

Before the First World War, James Joyce lived in Zurich, as did Albert Einstein and Lenin. In those days it was the only German-speaking city in which anarchists could express their views without fear of arrest. It also had the only German-language university where women could study medicine. The first female student was admitted in 1870. Rosa Luxemburg, born in Poland, went there to study in 1889, gained her doctorate, and remained in residence until 1898.[144]

The Burghölzli Clinic became famous under Auguste Forel (1848–1931), who was its director from 1879 and at the same time professor of psychiatry at Zurich University. It became world famous under Forel's successor Eugen Bleuler, who became director and professor of psychiatry in 1898. He was from a farming family in Zollikon on the eastern shores of Lake

Zurich.[145] Bleuler was the first in his family to be educated beyond elementary school. His father left the farm to start a small shop in the village and to work as bookkeeper for the local school. Eugen's father and grandfather were both involved in the political scuffles that would eventually lead to the reforms put in place by the Zurich liberals in 1830, which allowed the peasants to engage in trade, to work in the professions, and to be admitted to higher education at Zurich University, which was founded in 1833. Bleuler's family simply accepted that Eugen would pluck the fruits of his father and grandfather's political activities and study medicine, specialising in psychiatry because his sister suffered from severe psychosis.[146]

Bleuler studied first in Zurich and later in Paris under Charcot.[147] He became Forel's assistant at the Burghölzli and, in 1886, at the age of twenty-nine, he was appointed director of the psychiatric clinic at Rheinau. Twelve years later came his appointment as director of the Burghölzli Clinic.[148]

Many people in Bleuler's home village of Zollikon earned extra money by working at the Burghölzli, so from a young age he heard stories about directors who paid no attention to the patients, concerned themselves only with their own research, and could not even understand what the patients said because they themselves spoke High German and were unfamiliar with the Swiss dialects. Bleuler decided to take a different approach as director. He wanted to concentrate first of all on the patients and speak to them in their own dialect.[149]

In the late nineteenth century, psychiatry had reached a dead end and Bleuler was looking for new ways of explaining his patients' problems. He was enthusiastic about Freud's ideas and defended them against fierce criticism from established German psychiatry.

Like Charcot, Bleuler was one of the pioneers who brought order to the wildly inaccurate diagnoses of mental illnesses prevalent in those days. He introduced the concept of "schizophrenia" to replace "dementia praecox" and added the terms "ambivalence" and "autism". His books, *Dementia praecox oder die Gruppe der Schizophrenien* (Dementia Praecox, or the Group of Schizophrenias) of 1911 and *Lehrbuch der Psychiatrie* (Textbook of Psychiatry) of 1916, were groundbreaking.

In *Dementia praecox* Bleuler classified the symptoms of schizophrenia under four headings that later became known as the four "A"s:

1. Associative disturbance. The most important symptom of schizophrenia is a looseness of associations comparable to what happens in dreams or daydreams.
2. Affective incongruity. In other words, indifference and inappropriate behaviour.
3. Autistic thinking. The term autism was used to mean that contact with the environment was largely absent and all the patient's attention was concentrated upon his or her own world.
4. Ambivalence. This term was invented by Bleuler and later taken up by Freud to indicate conflicting emotions.

Bleuler's therapeutic principle was that a strong personal bond must exist between the patient and the person treating them. He and his family lived among the patients, and the family dining room gave directly on to the clinic's women's department. It was not unusual for patients to eat their meals along with the doctors or to assist with research. Bleuler regarded psychotic symptoms as treatable. There was always hope of improvement. He stressed that attention must be paid to both the patient's personality and that of the doctor. In the case of the latter, this included taking account of countertransference, or the totality of conscious and unconscious feelings the doctor or therapist had for the patient.[150]

Bleuler and Freud corresponded by letter from 1904 to 1937 and they had great respect for each other. Their correspondence began when Bleuler sent Freud an account of some of his dreams, asking Freud to help interpret them.

Bleuler was convinced of the existence of a dynamic unconscious and of early childhood sexuality. He believed repressed sexuality was converted into anxiety. He wrote to Freud that the interpretation of dreams in the Burghölzli had become a group activity. He also described his own dreams to his wife and the assistants. On one occasion, Bleuler described a dream to the group and was then called away. By the time he came back the others had interpreted his dream, but in such a way that he no longer recognised himself in it. The complexes of his wife, who had taken over leadership of the interpreting session, came through in it loud and clear. Bleuler wrote to Freud that such beginner's errors no longer occurred. Experience at the Burghölzli had shown that an interpretation was correct only if the dreamer had the feeling: yes, that's it.[151]

Freud was very conscious of the importance of Bleuler and the Burghölzli for the development and dissemination of psychoanalysis. He wrote in 1914, in "The history of the psychoanalytic movement", that the Burghölzli Clinic in Zurich was the only place where such a tight group of adherents existed, where it was possible to carry out psychoanalytic research in a general clinic, and where teachers incorporated psychoanalytic theories as an integral part of their courses. Only in Zurich did the opportunity exist to learn the new method and work with it in practice. Freud also wrote that most of his followers and staff in that period came from Zurich.[152]

In his biography of *Freud: The Man and the Cause*, Ronald Clark writes that Switzerland did more than simply ensure Freud's ideas were widely distributed. They could be applied to a far larger and completely different range of people in that country than could ever have been treated by small group of Viennese doctors with their own private practices.[153]

Bleuler's interest in the introduction, development, and dissemination of psychoanalysis has been seriously underestimated. It is possible to point to a number of reasons for this. First of all, Freud became and remained so famous that people are incapable of imagining a time when he was not. Yet, in 1907, when Freud was fifty-one, he was known to only a few colleagues and his ideas were controversial. Only a small number of copies of *The Interpretation of Dreams* had been sold. Bleuler, roughly the same age as Freud, was one of the most famous psychiatrists of his time, with an excellent reputation. The fact that Bleuler concerned himself intensively with Freud's work for years on end and inspired others to do the same gave Freud his breakthrough.

Second, Jung acquired such a prominent place in the early years of the psychoanalytic movement that he was wrongly assumed to have introduced psychoanalysis at the Burghölzli.[154] In fact he came into contact with psychoanalysis through Bleuler. When Jung had only just begun working at the Burghölzli Clinic as a doctor's assistant, Bleuler asked him to talk about *The Interpretation of Dreams* at a staff meeting. Jung read and discussed the book, but he was not impressed. It was only on a second reading, in 1903, that he became enthusiastic.[155]

Third, Freud and Bleuler grew apart over time because Bleuler had a different attitude to psychoanalysis. For each patient, he sought the method of treatment he felt would suit them best, which might be psychoanalysis or something else. Freud concentrated solely on psychoanalysis. Because of this gradual parting of ways, psychoanalytic historiography has wrongly placed Bleuler in Jung's enemy camp, overlooking the fact that contact between Bleuler and Jung was itself extremely problematic.

Fourth, Jones' history of psychoanalysis in his three-volume biography of Freud was extremely influential.[156] Written by a psychoanalyst who watched the specialism develop at first hand, it is of great importance. At the same time, it contains quite a few errors. Jones writes in Volume 2, for instance, that interest in psychoanalysis at the Burghölzli was shown primarily by Jung, while Bleuler studied it in depth. In fact, it was Bleuler who showed an interest first, a long time before he awakened Jung's enthusiasm.[157] Jones also credits Jung with inventing association tests, whereas Jung actually carried them out on Bleuler's orders. It was Bleuler who came up with the first series of words for which patients were asked for associations. Jones attributes the problems between Jung and Bleuler to the fact that Jung had started drinking alcohol again in 1909.[158] In reality, Bleuler was extremely put out by the fact that Jung had begun a relationship with a patient. Jones' description of Bleuler is unambiguously negative. He barely knew him and probably relied upon information from Jung. Jones stresses Bleuler's ambivalence and thereby creates the impression that he was sometimes in favour of psychoanalysis and sometimes against.[159] But Bleuler was, in fact, a critical enthusiast; he found some parts of psychoanalytic theory of great value and other parts unscientific.

Carl Gustav Jung

In December 1900, immediately after graduating, Jung joined Bleuler's staff at the Burghölzli as a doctor's assistant. In her lengthy biography of Jung, Deirdre Bair describes Bleuler waiting for Jung at the door and startling him by taking his modest luggage from him and carrying it all the way to the top floor.[160]

Jung had studied medicine in Basel, where he publicly quarrelled with his professor, Wille, about the treatment of psychiatric patients and was told he would not be recommended as a doctor's assistant but would have to look for a post elsewhere. That was why Jung sought a job in Zurich, although he anxiously kept the reason a secret.[161]

Jung was the son of a far from wealthy pastor in Keswill, Switzerland, and he lived in Switzerland all his life. He was the fourth child of the family but the first to survive, followed much later by a sister. His father was a tyrant at home and could sometimes burst into a towering rage, but in the company of others he seemed accommodating. Paul Jung (1842–1896) had wanted to live a studious life rather than become a pastor. Jung's mother, Emilie Preiswerk (1848–1923), unhappy and unstable, had grown up in a family where having visions was regarded as the most normal thing in the world.[162] Emilie reacted to the arrival of stillborn children in 1870, 1872, and 1873 by withdrawing from reality, preferring the company of her ghosts over the life of the parsonage. She became extremely fat and remained so for the rest of her life. Jung's parents frequently moved house and eventually went to live near Basel.[163]

Jung reacted to his parents' difficulties and arguments by withdrawing. He became self-absorbed and from an early age he was troubled by confusing dreams. He nourished his imagination by reading anything he could lay his hands on, but he also had friends and got up to mischief. All his life, Jung made a contradictory impression on people.[164] He was friendly but difficult, sometimes entertaining and at other times withdrawn, apparently full of self-confidence but extremely sensitive to criticism. He seemed strong, with his robust presence, Germanic features, and articulacy. Ernest Jones, who met him for the first time in 1907, describes his quick mind, energy, and cheerfulness, but also his irritability.[165] In 1907, at the psychiatric congress in Amsterdam, Jung gave a talk about psychoanalysis and overran the time allocated to him. When this was pointed out, he reacted fiercely, as if under personal attack, which made a poor impression on the audience. The subject of his talk was Jung's first psychoanalytic treatment of the patient Sabina Spielrein.[166]

Several times in his life Jung went through a serious crisis and, like his mother, he retained a powerful attachment to the occult.

Daily life in the Burghölzli

The clinic had a small staff relative to its considerable tally of patients, so everyone was under pressure and had to work extremely hard. In 1870, there were 121 patients, but, by 1907, the number had risen to 410.[167] Alongside Bleuler as medical director, there was a second doctor and three doctors' assistants, sometimes supported by volunteers. Daily life at the clinic was organised by eighty male and female carers.

Everyone was obliged to board, which meant the staff remained at the clinic day and night. The director and the second doctor lived there with their families. The doctors' assistants and the volunteers had rooms of their own, while the carers slept on camp beds in the wards or corridors. Married carers were allowed home for one day a week.

Bleuler was the personification of work and duty and he expected the same commitment from his staff, with unlimited devotion to the patients.[168]

The in-house doctors made their rounds early in the morning, before the daily staff meetings at 8.30, when they reported on the patients. Two or three times a week there was a meeting at which, under Bleuler's leadership, the case histories of new patients were discussed.[169]

The evening rounds took place between five and seven. There was no clerical staff, so the doctors and doctors' assistants had to type out their own case histories, which often took them until ten or eleven at night. The doors to the clinic were shut at ten. Junior assistants did not have keys, so if they wanted to come back after ten, they had to borrow a key from an older staff member.

Bleuler was astonishingly dedicated. Five or six times a day he made brief rounds of the wards.[170] Alphonse Maeder, who worked in the clinic in that period, mentioned later that everything revolved around the patients. As a student, you learnt to talk to the patients. The Burghölzli was a kind of factory where you worked extremely hard for little pay. Everyone, from the professor to the youngest staff member, was completely absorbed by their work. Teetotalism was compulsory. Bleuler was friendly to everyone and never bossed others around.[171]

It is remarkable that Jung, who worked at the clinic for nine years, from 1900 to 1909, does not mention Bleuler's name once in his autobiography and writes of the Burghölzli that the psychiatrists there were interested only in describing symptoms and labelling patients. He claimed that the psychology of the psychiatric patient was seen as irrelevant, a statement contradicted by every other person who worked with Bleuler.[172]

As director of the psychiatric clinic in Rheinau, Bleuler had spent twelve years developing his own method of working. His starting point was a desire to understand a category of patients no one had succeeded in comprehending: the schizophrenics.[173] All those years he lived among his patients, talking to them in their own dialect and attempting to fathom their supposedly meaningless statements and delusions by every means possible. He continued his research at the Burghölzli and it was in this connection that in 1901 he gave Jung the task of carrying out association experiments. That research became famous, and with it Jung.[174]

The association study initially had nothing to do with psychoanalysis. In those days the method of treatment for hysterical patients at the Burghölzli—if they were treated at all—was hypnosis, which had been introduced by Forel.[175] In carrying out the association study, Jung co-operated mostly with Franz Riklin.[176]

After a while, Jung started to discover similarities between his observations regarding hysterical patients and Freud's theory, especially when attention was paid less to the regularities than to the irregularities. Patients might sometimes suddenly respond to a word after a long pause, or make slips of the tongue. It often turned out that behind those silences or slips lay a repressed, extremely emotional charge. Jung discovered that many of the strange symptoms and behaviours of his patients were not meaningless at all if seen in the context of the course their lives had taken, and their wishes and desires.[177]

Jung became increasingly enthusiastic about psychoanalysis, all the more so when he carried out his first analysis, of Sabina Spielrein, who, within six months, was transformed from a deeply psychotic patient terrorising the entire department into a reasonably well-functioning young woman who resumed her medical studies and helped with experiments in the clinic. It was astonishing. She remained an inpatient at the clinic for another six months, from late 1904 to 1 June 1905, and then spent four years being treated by Jung as an outpatient.

In 1908, a romantic relationship between Spielrein and Jung began that led to her treatment being broken off in 1909.[178]

Abraham's post at the Burghölzli Clinic

Karl Abraham entered a completely new stage of life in late 1904, with inspiring work, engagement to be married, and the move to Switzerland. He was fairly soon promoted from second to first assistant, in May 1905, with a salary of 2,200 francs a year. His new position had come free because Jung became the second doctor and moved to the first floor of the Burghölzli with his family. Jung and Abraham got along well initially. When Hedwig Bürgner came to visit in 1905, Jung even threw a party in her honour.[179]

Abraham and Hedwig kept in touch by sending many letters (which, sadly, have not survived) and presents, and visiting each other whenever possible. In May 1905, they celebrated Karl's birthday together on the Wannsee in Berlin, an event that he described twenty years later in verse, on what would be his last birthday. Along with the presents, he sent Hedwig countless love notes. Hilda still had them in her possession in the 1960s, but they have since been lost. Hilda writes that those little notes showed how warm and tender her father was and that they struck a sympathetic chord with her mother, who was herself more reserved by nature. Abraham never gave up the habit of writing notes and poems for Hedwig and for his two children. Hilda admitted that they did not always appreciate this at the time. As they started to grow up they considered it childish of him.[180]

Switzerland was extremely bureaucratic and, for permission to take holidays, Abraham could not simply turn to the director of the clinic but had to submit a request in writing to the Direktion des Gesundheitswesens des Kantons. The day after his holiday finished, he had to send word that he had resumed his work. Bleuler was required to report, in writing, everything that went on at the clinic. This generated a huge amount of paperwork, which makes it all the more surprising that he was able to devote so much time to his patients.[181]

Abraham's future father-in-law, Philipp Bürgner, spent the summer vacation of 1905 in Elem in the Swiss canton of Glarus, along with his son, Hans, and daughter, Hedwig. Abraham joined them whenever possible. Hans later remembered a climb of the Churfirsten along with Abraham, who believed there was a quicker and easier way to the top. After two hours of fruitless searching, they had to take the same route back down. It was a pattern that kept recurring: Abraham would look for a new and better route and often fail to find it. On another trip, Hedwig accompanied her brother and her fiancé. Their guide had not slept because his wife had given birth that night. He was so tired that they got lost and had to spend the night outdoors.

Abraham was a good mountain climber. *Alpina*, the magazine of the Swiss alpine club, reported that, with his guide, G. Fiorelli, he was the first to climb the Punta Scione and from there a second and unnamed summit, to which he gave the name Punta Daelli after a climber who had recently been injured climbing it.[182]

Abraham and Hedwig wanted to marry as soon as possible, but there was a problem. The Burghölzli Clinic had no provision for such an outcome. There was room for two families, those of the director and the second doctor, but not for a married assistant. Abraham asked those in charge to allow him to live outside the clinic. Bleuler supported the request with a letter of his own, in which he stated that for the current treatment of the patients it was important to have another experienced doctor alongside the first and second doctors. That would be possible, however, only if the doctor's assistants were able to marry. Bleuler added that Abraham was thoroughly trustworthy and would carry out his duties whether or not he lived outside the clinic.[183]

Abraham was given permission to marry, uniquely in the history of the Burghölzli Clinic, and, once he was living elsewhere, he was allocated a thousand francs extra a year for bed and board, and a telephone so that he could be reached quickly.

The couple rented an apartment in a beautiful new Jugendstil building not far from the clinic. It can still be seen today, although many more buildings have gone up around it. Jung had rented an apartment in the same block for his mother and sister.[184]

The relationship

The wedding, on 23 January 1906 in Berlin, required a good deal of organisation to satisfy everyone. Abraham's parents would have been deeply hurt if it had been merely a civil wedding, while Hedwig's family, although Jewish, no longer had any attachment to religious customs and rituals. The ceremony finally took place in a hall and was conducted by a rabbi. According to Hilda, her mother had trouble keeping a straight face because Karl and Hans kept making jokes about the rabbi, whom they had met only once before.

Is that really how it went? The information comes from Hedwig, who was always eager to stress that she was completely unreligious. Perhaps Abraham made a joke to Hans during the ritual, but it is hard to imagine that he would have made the entire ceremony seem ridiculous when he was so fond of his parents.

At the wedding dinner, all the guests who ate kosher had specially marked chairs and the wedding day passed off harmoniously.

After a brief honeymoon, the young couple moved into the apartment on the Forschstraße. Hedwig found it hard. She missed her family and friends and she missed Berlin. She was alone much of the time because Abraham worked such long hours. At first, Jung's mother and sister were extremely warm-hearted, but from one day to the next, in the winter of 1906–1907, they suddenly stopped talking to Hedwig. Hilda suspects the change came about when problems arose between Abraham and Jung.

When he first came to work at the Burghölzli, Bleuler had begun a discussion group with his friend and colleague Constantin von Monakow, a neurologist of Russian descent. Monakow was an associate professor in Zurich and had a small private clinic. In 1906, the group consisted of the doctors at the Burghölzli, Jung, Abraham, and Emma Fürst. Later that year, Ludwig Binswanger and Max Eitingon joined them, as well as staff and guests of Monakow. Finally, there was Hedwig Waser, Bleuler's wife, who had a doctorate in German, Jung's wife, Emma, and Abraham's wife, Hedwig.[185] It was extraordinary that doctors' wives took part in discussions and described their dreams. As the group's knowledge of unconscious desires and impulses increased, however, the doctors forbade their wives from relating their dreams. Hedwig later said that the Bleulers, the Jungs, she and Karl, and Dr Meijer told each other their dreams in order to practise interpreting them. Abraham tried out psychoanalytic theory on his patients.[186]

Hedwig tried to make her husband's field of interest her own by reading and going to talks about psychiatry. She was fascinated by psychoanalysis and always read Abraham's articles, which they discussed between them. They both also loved literature, especially work by Heinrich Heine and Gottfried Keller.

Hilda describes how her parents treated each other with great affection and how, in particular, her father gave her mother many little tokens of affection. Hedwig was more reserved, but nevertheless she wrote a poem every year for his birthday.[187] They were often visited by friends and family, and whenever possible they took long hiking trips. Hilda's description of the sexual relationship between her parents is extremely veiled. She writes as follows:

> Clearly the years 1906–7 brought to my father the two most important and lasting relationships of his adult life. His marriage became what he describes under the heading of the genital phase

and under that of a genital object-relationship. He speaks of the overcoming of oedipal strivings and rivalry. Thus we shall see that the attainment of the highest level of the organisation of the libido goes hand in hand with the final step in the evolution of object love. In an earlier part of the same paper he speaks of the attainment of genital maturity as a state of post-ambivalence in which the love-object is seen as a whole object and where the most favourable traits of each developmental stage are present.[188]

She goes on to quote Abraham himself at the end of his life when he wrote about the subject:

> The final stage of character formation shows traces everywhere of its association with the preceding stages. It borrows from them whatever conduces to a favourable relation between the individual and his objects. From the early oral stage it takes over enterprise and energy; from the anal stage, endurance, perseverance and various other characteristics; from sadistic sources, the necessary power to carry on the struggle for existence.[189]

Hilda continues in her own words: "This passage, written near the end of his life, was a summary of what he felt worthwhile to achieve for himself and what he looked for in his wife and those close to him. He must also have seen Sigmund Freud as possessing these qualities".[190]

The striking thing here is that Hilda is actually writing about ideals to live up to and expressing the view that both Abraham and Freud did so. She does not divulge any intimate personal details and she avoids talking about the sexual relationship between her parents.

In her account, the image emerges of a man who set very high standards for himself and believed his wife and children should live up to them as well. A little later in her biography, Hilda notes an anecdote about her parents that says a great deal more than all the psychoanalytic jargon and shows that Abraham did, in fact, carry childhood traumas with him.

Hilda describes how Abraham proposed to his heavily pregnant wife (who was expecting her first child, Hilda) that they should climb the Rigi by moonlight. He had forgotten, however, that there would be no moonlight during the descent. It was an extremely uncomfortable trek down. Hedwig was terrified of falling, so she moved on hands and feet as soon as they lost the path. Hilda adds that this undertaking was typical of her father, who always set off to do daring things impulsively and never believed anything could go wrong.[191] This incident will be examined further in Chapter Eight. Abraham did something very dangerous and, in that sense, extremely aggressive towards the unborn baby and its mother, inviting a repeat of his own mother's accident. They had Hedwig's presence of mind to thank for the fact that all was well in the end.

Aggression and jealousy directed at the dead sister of Karl's early childhood, along with anger at his mother, who was unreachable for him after the accident because of her depression, must have been a factor here. Hilda wrote that her father wanted a daughter, whereas her mother cared little whether the baby was a boy or a girl.[192] She said he must have wanted to replace the little sister he had lost, and may possibly have had unconscious feelings of guilt about that.

Hilda did not make a connection with the mountain walk, although she did say that her father possibly wanted to give his mother a granddaughter to compensate for the loss she had suffered twenty-seven years earlier. At the point when Hilda wrote her father's biography, eighty-seven years had passed since that tragedy, which means that the stillborn sister must have been a permanent presence in Abraham's parental family, for his mother and, subsequently, for him and his own family.

Hedwig would have liked the baby to be born on her dear brother Hans' birthday on 17 November. The contractions started that day, but labour was protracted because of Hedwig's narrow pelvis and Hilda was born on 18 November.

The time immediately following Hilda's birth was very difficult. Hedwig could not produce enough breast milk. Hilda was healthy to begin with but very soon had to be fed with a bottle and she turned out to be intolerant of cow's milk. It gave her intestinal cramps.[193] Hedwig's father came to their aid by sending his trusted housekeeper. First, they fetched milk from a nursing mother and in the end, when the baby began to show signs of rickets and contracted a middle ear infection, they found a wet nurse.

Hedwig longed for Berlin and her family and friends, and she did not find it easy to make contacts among the Swiss. Abraham was extremely busy, so she barely saw him. He wrote many notes saying how much he would like to be with his love and his little love and how jealous he was of their closeness. He also wrote notes on behalf of Hilda to both parents.[194]

Abraham married in January 1906 and by November that same year he had a daughter. In between came the scene on the mountain in the dark. In the first few months after the birth, amid problems with Hilda, Hedwig felt unhappy. In the spring of 1907, Abraham tried to find another job as a doctor in Switzerland but did not succeed and, immediately after the summer of 1907, he decided to leave Zurich. All these major events followed each other extremely quickly.

Abraham wrote to Freud: ". . . I do not find it easy to leave. But I have to think of the future, especially since I am married".[195]

Between the lines, it becomes clear that the early years of Abraham's marriage were far from easy. He had been so happy with Zurich after the suffocating city of Berlin—literally as well as figuratively, because the mountain air was good for his lungs. Now he would have to go back to Berlin. The reasons for their hasty departure seem to have lain mainly with Hedwig, who could not stand Zurich and was deeply unhappy there. In the years that followed, Abraham would continually write on the subject of a man who is so attached to his mother that it is hard for him to let go. When he does so, he turns to a woman with whom his relationship is just as intense, not so much because that is what he wants as because he cannot behave in any other way.[196]

CHAPTER FIVE

The first meetings between Freud and staff from the Burghölzli Clinic

Nowadays, it is almost impossible to believe that in 1907, at the age of fifty-two, Freud was virtually unknown, with hardly any followers in the German-speaking countries, let alone in the USA. The interest shown in him by staff at the Burghölzli Clinic was a godsend.

Freud's work was read at the Burghölzli for years before contact was made, first on paper and later in person.[197] The correspondence with Bleuler began in 1904[198] and in 1906 Jung sent Freud his *Diagnostic Association Studies*, in which he cites Freud and at one point compares his own association experiments with psychoanalysis.[199] Freud's first letter to Jung, dated 11 April 1906, was a response to that book, which he warmly welcomed,[200] and six months later he sent Jung part one of his *Collection of Shorter Writings on the Theory of the Neuroses*. In late 1906, Jung sent Freud his *Dementia praecox*, published in December that year. We do not know Freud's reaction, but Jung's hurt response leaves no room for doubt that it was critical, in part at least:

Dear Professor Freud,

I am sincerely sorry that I of all people must be such a nuisance to you. I understand perfectly that you cannot be anything but dissatisfied with my book since it treats your researches too ruthlessly. I am perfectly well aware of this. The principle uppermost in my mind while writing it was: consideration for the academic German public. If we don't take the trouble to present this seven-headed monster with everything tastefully served up on a silver salver, it won't bite, as we have seen on countless occasions before. It is therefore entirely in the interest of our cause to give heed to all those factors which are likely to whet its appetite. For the time being, unfortunately, these include a certain reserve and the hint of an independent judgment regarding your researches.[201]

Jung did not dare to declare himself explicitly in favour of psychoanalysis. Freud softened his criticism immediately in his next letter; Jung was, after all, of great importance to him. He stressed his enthusiasm, saying it was precisely the reason for his critical response.[202]

Freud's lack of genuine enthusiasm is perfectly understandable. In his introduction to *Dementia praecox*, Jung had praised Bleuler, Riklin, and Freud, only to add that he did not attribute such importance to childhood sexual trauma as Freud did. He added that Freud's therapy was, at best, one of many treatment strategies and did not always live up to theoretical expectations. In the remainder of the book, Freud is mentioned only in passing, despite the fact that Jung includes one of his case studies. In general, *Dementia praecox* was less than favourably received.[203]

Neither is Jung's reticent attitude to psychoanalysis particularly surprising. Since the publication of Forel's articles, the Burghölzli had become one of Europe's most famous clinics. Bleuler had an excellent reputation, while the association experiments had made Jung's name. Both men would be hazarding their reputations should they enter into too close an association with Freud. Jung was cautious.[204]

A visit to Freud

In January 1907, Freud received his first visitor from the Burghölzli. Max Eitingon (1881–1943), the son of a wealthy Russian fur trader, had grown up in Germany. Because of a severe stammer, he was unable to finish secondary school, which meant he could not go on to take medical exams. By a circuitous route through various other university courses, he eventually managed to qualify as a doctor in 1909, in Zurich, where he had settled in the winter semester of 1904–1905.[205]

During his student days, Eitingon worked with Bleuler and Jung at the Burghölzli Clinic for two short periods, as a volunteer: from 12 April to 30 April 1906 and from 2 March to 24 April 1908.[206] There, he struck up a friendship with Abraham. He made a deep and extensive study of psychoanalysis and, in late 1906, he approached Freud to enquire whether he was in a position to accept a twenty-seven-year-old patient of his for analysis. In January 1907, Eitingon accompanied the patient to Vienna, and for him the most important aspect of the trip seems to have been his meeting with Freud. This was an extremely important moment for Freud; Eitingon's visit was a turning point, since it heralded the end of Freud's isolation. Eitingon stayed for two weeks, attended meetings of the Wednesday Society (*Mittwochgesellschaft*) and was analysed by Freud during several long evening walks.[207]

In his "History of the psychoanalytic movement" of 1914, which he described as his "bomb", Freud lays great stress on his isolation in those years and the change that Eitingon's visit brought about.[208] He does not even mention his visitors of two months later (on Sunday 3 March 1907), Carl Gustav Jung, his wife Emma, and Ludwig Binswanger, who at the time were regarded as far more important than Eitingon. By 1914, when Freud wrote his historical account of the psychoanalytic movement, he had broken off contact with Jung. The account was written with the express purpose of making clear that several of his followers had gone astray, specifically Adler, Stekel, and Jung.[209]

The visit by Jung and twenty-six-year-old Binswanger in 1907 was, however, of enormous significance for Freud. Both had excellent reputations in the psychiatric world of the time and Jung was not a Jew. Freud was afraid that psychoanalysis would remain a Jewish affair. Ludwig Binswanger (1881–1966) came from a famous and highly respected family of psychiatrists; in 1857, his grandfather had established a private clinic in Kreuzlingen called the Bellevue Sanatorium, and his father and later Binswanger himself became medical director there. Ludwig's uncle, Otto Binswanger, was professor of psychiatry at Jena.[210]

In his *Erinnerungen an Sigmund Freud* (Memories of Sigmund Freud) Binswanger gives a fascinating account of this first visit.[211] I quote it at length here because it paints a picture of the staff at the Burghölzli and shows how Freud's behaviour overwhelmed his young visitors.

> In the spring of 1906 I had completed my medical qualifications and in June that same year I started working at the Burghölzli in Zurich as a volunteer doctor. Eugen Bleuler had already aroused my admiration for his personality during the clinical semesters and developed to the utmost my inherited love of psychiatry. Even then he was busy preparing to write his book *Dementia Praecox; or the Group of Schizophrenias*, which radically changed the theory of dementia praecox.[212] I can still see him in front of me, at every opportunity writing notes on a small piece of paper that he pulled out of his waistcoat pocket. Karl Abraham, my predecessor in the male wing, was more reticent in character, but because of his high intelligence and his fine, often somewhat ironic nature he too had an effect on younger colleagues. One of my assistants was H. W. Maier, with whom I had been friends at school. C. G. Jung, the clinic's senior doctor at the time, with whom I wanted to work on my doctorate, proved himself a true fire spirit, his temperament and the richness of his ideas continually taking his pupil's breath away.
>
> If I feel compelled to describe that year at the Burghölzli as by far the most exhilarating of my years of training in psychiatry, then that is mainly because the Burghölzli in 1906 was already at the centre of, indeed was carried along by, the intellectual movement emanating from Vienna that bore the name psychoanalysis and traced itself back to a single name, the name of Sigmund Freud. Which is why it does not take a great deal of imagination to understand how willingly and gratefully I said yes to the question with which Jung surprised me one day: whether I would like to accompany him and his wife on his first visit to Freud in Vienna. The journey took place in late February 1907. If I remember rightly, Professor and Mrs. Jung spent almost a week in Vienna; to my great joy I was able to stay about a week longer.
>
> On the day after our arrival Freud asked Jung and me about our dreams. I no longer remember Jung's dream, but I do remember the interpretation Freud gave him. It was to the effect that Jung wanted to dethrone him and step into his place. I dreamed of the entrance to the house at Bergstraße number 19 and the old chandelier that had needed to be moved for renovations to take place. Freud's interpretation, which I did not find completely convincing – and which he still remembered thirty years later when we visited him on the occasion of his eightieth birthday – was that the dream contained a wish to marry his oldest daughter, but at the same time reluctance, since he said – I remember the precise words of the interpretation – "I'm not going to get married in a house that has such a shabby chandelier."
>
> From these interpretations you can easily tell how informal and friendly the atmosphere was from the first day of our visit. Freud's dislike of any formality and etiquette, his personal charm, his simplicity, natural openness and kindness and not least his humour allowed no awkwardness to

arise. And yet not for a moment could the impression of the greatness and dignity of his person- ality escape one's attention. For me it was a joy, if mixed with some degree of scepticism, to see the enthusiasm and trust with which Freud treated my teacher Jung and immediately saw in him his scientific "son and heir".[213]

In his biography of Freud, Jones writes that Jung gave him a hugely enthusiastic account of that first meeting and expressed a great sense of admiration,[214] yet the correspondence between Freud and Jung makes clear that Jung was initially far more ambivalent. This is understand- able in view of the fact that the day after he arrived as a house guest, Jung was told by his host that his dream of the previous night meant he wanted to dethrone Freud and take his place—despite the fact that, as yet, there was no throne in prospect. Freud named him as his heir and successor at that first meeting, which must at the very least have taken him by surprise.

Jung waited several weeks before writing a letter of thanks, in which he stated that he no longer doubted the validity of Freud's theory but did have reservations about early childhood sexuality.[215] There followed an intense exchange of letters, with frequent references to demen- tia praecox, the condition nowadays known as schizophrenia. Jung had spent several years working with schizophrenic patients and "dementia praecox" was the diagnosis applied to most patients at the Burghölzli, only two per cent of whom had been diagnosed as hysterical. Freud had almost no experience at all with schizophrenia but he nevertheless tried to develop a psychoanalytic theory to cover it, using Jung as a sparring partner to test his ideas. Freud believed that patients diagnosed with dementia praecox had regressed to an early childhood phase of autoeroticism, which had destroyed their potential for object-love and with it the possibility of sublimation. Freud must have discussed the matter during the visit by Jung and Binswanger, since, in his letter of 31 March, Jung writes, "Autoerotism as the essence of Demen- tia praecox strikes me more and more as a momentous deepening of our knowledge – where indeed will it end?"[216] Jung also repeatedly quotes Bleuler. This suggests that Freud's ideas were a perpetual subject of debate at the Burghölzli, although Jung often takes the opportunity to place Bleuler's position in a negative light. On 17 April 1907, for example, he writes, "Bleuler is leaning more and more towards autoerotism but in theory only".[217] It is a mischievous remark that does little justice to Bleuler's admittedly critical but profoundly sincere interest in psychoanalysis.

Abraham's first articles on psychoanalysis

On 17 April 1907, Abraham gave a talk to the German Psychiatric Society in Frankfurt. He sent the written version to Freud, who was favourably impressed.[218] Abraham had come into contact with Freud's ideas immediately on his arrival at the Burghölzli in 1904 and subse- quently read Freud's work with enthusiasm. He had been present at many debates about it and joined in the discussion, but he had not yet undertaken psychoanalysis in practice. In the clinic, the assistants were not allowed to treat non-resident patients,[219] who were reserved for the director and the next most senior doctor, meaning Bleuler and, from 1905, also Jung. There were hardly any hysterical patients among the residents who could have benefited and Abraham had not undergone psychoanalysis himself. In his articles "On the significance of sexual trauma in childhood for the symptomatology of dementia praecox" and "The experiencing of sexual traumas as a form of sexual activity", which appeared a few months apart, he attempted to apply psychoanalytic theory to the schizophrenic patients with whom he was working.[220] In the first of the two articles, he wrote,

New research—I am referring, among other things, to the publications by Bleuler (1906) and Jung (1907)—has shown that Freud's theories are also extraordinarily fruitful for the understanding of dementia praecox, that in the symptoms of dementia praecox we are dealing with the same material as in hysteria, that, here as there, sexuality plays a dominant role, and that here as there the same psychic mechanisms are at work.[221]

Abraham illustrated this with a number of vignettes featuring patients who had been sexually traumatised in childhood by incest or rape and had later become psychotic. He did not believe that dementia praecox was caused by trauma, but, rather, that traumas could determine the symptoms. It is clear from the article that Abraham was taking his very first steps in the field of psychoanalysis. He was aiming to show that dementia praecox, like hysteria, had its origins in early childhood sexuality. In his opinion, it could be caused either by a predisposition or by a trauma in that particular phase of life.

Freud reacted to the article Abraham had sent him by writing a short and friendly letter, including the following in the final paragraph: "I eagerly await your communications. If I can offer you something of use through my remarks on your new findings, I shall gladly do so. I particularly like that you have tackled the sexual side of the problem, the side that hardly anybody is willing to approach".[222]

So began the correspondence between Freud and Abraham. Freud had found someone who, unlike Bleuler and Jung, accepted early childhood sexuality unreservedly as a basic assumption, and would continue to do so.

Abraham must have sent Freud his second treatise, "The experiencing of sexual trauma as a form of sexual activity", shortly after this, since, on 7 July 1907, Freud wrote a response several pages long.[223] An earlier letter to which Freud was also responding has been lost. Freud's letter can be seen as a combination of approval for the path Abraham was taking and an explanation of psychoanalysis, a field Abraham was only just beginning to explore.

This second psychoanalytic article by Abraham dealt with the fact that some children show far greater resistance than others to sexual seduction, while a few even seem to seek it out or unconsciously invite it. Like the earlier article, it included concise case histories, Abraham's trademark from the start. In his letter, Freud discusses at length the fact that Abraham regards all the events described by patients as having actually happened and is not yet aware of the possibility that some might be phantasies.

Much later, in 1920, Abraham apologised for his article, writing,

The above essay, written in the year 1907, contains many errors in its representation of Freudian ideas. Its author was then just beginning to work his way into the world of ideas that is psychoanalysis. A general indication of this now seems to him more appropriate than a belated correction of specific points, especially since the results of the research were not influenced by these errors.[224]

The *Jahrbuch der Psychoanalyse* issue number 52 (2006) was entirely devoted to this second article by Abraham, a rather remarkable editorial decision, given how few articles have ever been written about Abraham's work. In this special issue, Ulrike May looks at what exactly it was that Abraham later regarded as erroneous and describes with great clarity how complex Freud's theory of seduction was even at this relatively early stage. Freud was continuing to insist on the importance of sexual experiences that had taken place in reality, but he had added two contrasting dimensions: hereditary disposition and phantasy. The hysterical patient phantasises his need for object-love back into childhood, superimposing his current phantasies of love and seduction on an autoerotic childhood. Some of the traumatic childhood experiences patients talk about arise as a result.[225]

It is understandable that Abraham had yet to develop a comprehensive view of the matter, since he was in the early stages of familiarising himself with psychoanalytic theory. He thought it was simply a question of hereditary disposition and of sexual experiences that had actually taken place.

The second "error" concerned normality and abnormality. Whereas Abraham distinguished between a normal sexual constitution and one featuring inherited abnormalities, Freud believed that aberrations, perversions, anal-eroticism and suchlike existed in everyone; at most there were differences of degree. This is an important and lasting theoretical difference between the two men.[226]

The start of the Freud, Jung, Abraham triangle

Of the original group of psychoanalysts described above, all of whom came into contact with Freud through the Burghölzli Clinic, two would go down in history as mutual enemies: Carl Gustav Jung and Karl Abraham. In 1907, they were thirty-two and twenty-nine years old, respectively. In accounts of their life and work, one particular excerpt from a letter written by Jung to Freud is invariably quoted. It expresses a damning verdict on Abraham. Since it is usually the only reference to the relationship between Jung and Abraham, it has come to function almost as a screen memory, making it impossible to see what actually happened. As a result, this particular letter has had a huge influence on the way Abraham is regarded today.

The excerpt usually quoted, which comes from a letter dated 19 August 1907, written by Jung in response to a letter from Freud of 10 July 1907, is as follows:

> In one of your earlier letters you asked for my views about Dr. Abraham. I admit at once that I am "jealous" of him because he corresponds with you. (Forgive me this candour, however tasteless it may seem!) There are no objections to A. Only, he isn't quite my type. For instance, I once suggested that he collaborate on my writings, but he declined. Now he pricks up his ears whenever Bleuler and I talk about what we are investigating, etc. He then comes up with a publication. Of all our assistants he is the one who always holds a little aloof from the main work and then suddenly steps into the limelight with a publication, as a loner. Not only I but the other assistants too have found this rather unpleasant. He is intelligent but not original, highly adaptable, but totally lacking in psychological empathy, for which reason he is usually very unpopular with the patients. I would ask you to subtract a personal touch of venom from this judgment. Apart from these cavilings A. is

an agreeable associate, very industrious and much concerned with all the bureaucratic affairs of the Clinic, which nobody can say of me. A little drop of venom may derive from that source too, for in this respect my chief has long since reached the pinnacle of perfection.[227]

To judge by this, Abraham could do nothing right in the eyes of his colleague Jung, but Jung is at pains to qualify his impression three times in the same letter. He says he is jealous because Abraham is corresponding with Freud; he asks Freud to discount the venom in what he says; he writes that Abraham is pleasant company. It was unusual for Jung to temper what he wrote in this way. In many of his letters to Freud, he takes a swipe at a third party without the slightest restraint. A few examples from the autumn of 1909 will suffice: Bleuler had told Jung that he intended to explain the degree to which he had moved in the direction of psychoanalysis and how far he would or could pursue it. Jung wrote to Freud, "Naturally I am dying to know what sort of obliquities will come out".[228] Then there is Eitingon, who was in Vienna at the time and was analysed by Freud during evening walks. Jung writes, "Eitingon's company cannot be counted among the highest joys. His vapid intellectualism has something exasperating about it".[229] And as for Binswanger, "Besides, there is a colossal and apparently still unresolved father complex rumbling in his depths".[230]

It is striking that in each case Jung is referring to a colleague who, at the time of writing, was directly involved with Freud. When that was not the case, as with Johann Jakob Honegger, Jung was capable of a far more approving tone: "I spend much of my time with young Honegger – he is so intelligent and subtle-minded. Hardly a day goes by without an exchange of ideas".[231] It seems Jung had quickly developed such a powerful transference relationship with Freud that he could not tolerate anyone else being close to him and felt compelled to undermine potential rivals without delay. The most extreme example concerns Freud's visit to Jung in Zurich, from 18 to 21 September 1908.[232] Freud was on his way home after a visit to England and then to Berlin. Jung was living in the Burghölzli Clinic, on the first floor, above Bleuler's apartment on the ground floor. Jung managed to persuade Freud not to visit Bleuler.[233] This was a serious affront, given Bleuler's stature and his importance to psychoanalysis. Even today, such an omission would be extremely hurtful, but in the early twentieth century it was an unimaginable insult to pass over the professor and director of the clinic and visit only the senior doctor.

Jung's attitude shows that he wanted Freud entirely to himself. The fact that Freud complied is almost beyond belief. He must have been so enthralled by Jung, probably verging on falling in love, that he lost sight of his own best interests and those of psychoanalysis, quite apart from the importance of maintaining contact with Bleuler. In the correspondence between Bleuler and Freud, the results of Freud's "faux pas" are clearly visible. The intimate tone of Bleuler's letters vanishes overnight to be replaced by reticence and mild distrust.[234]

Freud later regretted his decision. On 25 November 1910, he wrote to Jung about difficulties with Bleuler: ". . . his whole performance looks to me like revenge for the situation when I was staying *with* you, *above* him, and neglected to call on him. That was really a mistake. I shouldn't have given in to you. Now it serves me right".[235]

All this throws fresh light on Jung's criticisms of Abraham. He was attempting to wipe every rival off the map and in Abraham's case there was a particular reason for wishing to do so, which will be examined later in this book.

First, back to that extract from Jung's letter about Abraham in which Jung writes, "he isn't quite my type". That may well have been how Jung felt when he wrote the letter, but there are several indications that his antipathy was new. Hilda writes that Abraham and Jung initially worked harmoniously together.[236] When Hedwig came to visit, she found Jung extremely attentive towards her. As we have seen, he even threw a party in her honour. When Karl and Hedwig married, they moved into an apartment in the building where Jung's mother and sister lived and initially the contact between them was affectionate, until it was suddenly broken off by the mother and sister. Unfortunately, Hilda does not say exactly when this happened, but even in early 1908, after Abraham had left the Burghölzli, Jung wrote him a warm letter.[237] What should we make of the sentence "I once suggested that he collaborate on my writings, but he declined."?[238] Jung called upon everyone, even patients, to assist with his association experiments.[239] It seems Abraham was averse to the idea. In those days there was a strict hierarchy that meant Abraham was not really in a position to refuse such a request from a superior, but he did so, none the less.[240]

"Now he pricks up his ears whenever Bleuler and I talk about what we are investigating, etc. He then comes up with a publication." This is a remarkable claim, since, before he arrived to work at the Burghölzli, Abraham had written a number of articles that were published before and during his time there.[241] In his first few years at the clinic, he published nothing; a version of the lecture he gave in April 1907 was his first publication about the work he was doing in Zurich. His next article appeared in the autumn of 1907, several months after Jung's letter.

The sentence that comes next seems even more remarkable in this context: "Of all our assistants he is the one who always holds a little aloof from the main work and then suddenly steps into the limelight with a publication, as a loner". What can Jung have meant by "the main work" (*die großen Werke*)? Ninety-five per cent of what went on at the Burghölzli consisted of hard toil by a small staff looking after 400 seriously disturbed patients. Abraham could not possibly have shirked his duties in that sense. Several letters from Bleuler, one dated 29 August 1908, for instance, describe just how dedicated, hardworking, and meticulous Abraham was.[242] Virtually the only possible conclusion is that by "the main work" Jung meant his own experiments.

What exactly was going on here, aside from the jealousy that Jung mentions himself? A letter from Jung to Freud dated 5 October 1906 makes things a little clearer.[243] Jung thanks Freud for the present he has sent, namely his *Collection of Shorter Writings on the Theory of the Neuroses* (1906), and then goes on to write that, in general, he has a slightly different view both of Freud's theory on sexuality and on the origins of hysteria, which was that sexuality is of great significance but not all-determining. This might seem a minor difference, but, in fact, it was fundamental. The core of Freud's theory concerned the overwhelming importance of sexuality.

Freud replied in his letter of 7 October 1906 that, after reading Jung's work, he had expected him to think this way but had not wanted to relinquish the hope that in due course Jung would move far closer to his own theory.[244] This expectation proved unfounded. The point of friction that Jung identified in his very first letter always remained, ultimately leading to a rift between Freud and Jung.

So, after his visit to Freud in 1907, Jung found himself in a complicated situation. He was fascinated by Freud and wanted to have him all to himself. It was a transference relationship in which Freud's approval had become extremely important. Jung showed great dedication to psychoanalysis, but there was a fundamental theoretical difference between the two men. It is important to bear in mind that Jung had an excellent reputation, which he would be risking by straightforwardly endorsing Freud's ideas.

Then along came Abraham, with no reputation to lose. He embraced Freud's theory unreservedly and Freud was suitably pleased. Jung's letter to Freud of 19 August, in which he describes Abraham, was written out of frustration. Freud, however, took what Jung said on trust and responded as follows:

> I was predisposed in Abraham's favour by the fact that he attacks the sexual problem head on; consequently I was glad to provide him with what material I had. Your picture of his character seems so apt that I am inclined to accept it without further examination. Nothing objectionable, yet something that precludes intimacy . . . which is bound to clash with your open, winning nature. . . . By the way, is he a descendant of his eponym?[245]

This last point was of great importance to Freud, who feared that psychoanalysis would be disadvantaged if it were seen as a purely Jewish affair. As already mentioned, it was one of the reasons why Freud wanted to do all he could to keep Jung, a Christian, on board.

The fact that Freud immediately went along with Jung's verdict, even though he had never met Abraham, is disconcerting, as is the fact that intimacy was a criterion. Freud revised his opinion of Abraham drastically after getting to know him in December 1907, when he visited Freud for the first time one month after leaving the Burghölzli to settle in Berlin as an independent psychoanalyst. Abraham returned from that visit filled with enthusiasm.

Leaving the Burghölzli

A letter from Hedwig to Jones dated 24 February 1926 shows how Abraham felt about leaving the Burghölzli:

> Karl was hoping to be able to stay in Switzerland. But this hope was not fulfilled, since every time he applied to the various institutes for a more senior position, Swiss citizens were given preference. When eventually relations became really too unproductive as a result of the Bleuler–Jung conflict, Karl discussed with Hermann Oppenheim (whose wife was close to him) his plan to settle in Berlin. O. promised to refer patients to him, but wanted to be sure they would be treated only according to the method he recommended. He categorically rejected Freudian theories.[246]

The conflict between Bleuler and Jung that made Abraham decide to leave is described by Deidre Bair in her biography of Jung.[247] He had proposed to Bleuler that he, Jung, should set up his own psychological laboratory, an independent institute under the wing of the Burghölzli of which he would be the director. He had also proposed that the professorship of psychiatry at Zurich University should be given to a researcher instead of to the director of the Burghölzli, meaning to him rather than to Bleuler. Jung seems to have been unaware of the astonishing arrogance, if not delusions of grandeur, these proposals revealed. They amounted to nothing less than an attempt to dethrone Bleuler, who occupied Switzerland's most prestigious university post in psychiatry.

Abraham was now thirty. Since the age of twenty-four, he had worked as a doctor's assistant and it seemed there was no prospect of a job as a doctor, no matter how well he performed. In August 1907, he had even been left in charge of the Burghölzli while Bleuler and Jung were both away. The medical authorities reprimanded Bleuler as a result, since this was not officially permitted.[248]

Abraham's lack of prospects was not unusual. Ever since 1880 there had been an excess of doctors as a result of an exponential increase in the number of medical students, and from 1890 onwards there were explicit warnings that many doctors had too few patients and were unable to make a decent living. Fifty-nine per cent had insufficient income.[249]

On 6 October 1907, Abraham wrote to Freud that he was giving up his post at the psychiatric clinic. As a Jew in Germany and a foreigner in Switzerland, he had not succeeded in advancing beyond "a junior position".[250] This was not the full story. Abraham had only recently begun applying for jobs and he made no mention of his personal reasons for leaving. He asked Freud for support should he settle in Berlin and Freud responded immediately with encouragement:

Dear Colleague,

I soon suppressed the first impulse of regret I felt on reading your letter. No harm can come to a youthful man like you from being forced into open life "*au grand air*", and that as a Jew you will encounter more difficulties will have the effect, as it has with all of us, of bringing out all your productive capabilities. That my sympathy and best wishes are with you on your new path goes without saying; and more than that, whenever possible. If my intimate friendship with Dr W. Fließ from Berlin still existed, the way would be levelled for you; but now unfortunately that road is completely blocked.[251]

Freud added that he had repeatedly been forced to say to patients over recent years that he had no confidant in Germany to whom he could send them, but in future he would recommend Abraham. Should his own reputation grow, that would undoubtedly work to Abraham's advantage. He added, "and if I may forthrightly refer to you as my pupil and follower – you do not seem to me to be a man to be ashamed of that . . ."[252]

It was remarkable, of course, for Freud to speak in this way about someone he had never met and who had recently been deeply disparaged by Jung. It seems to fit in with a strategy Freud first developed when he discovered that his theory had found supporters in Zurich. From that moment on, Freud turned his attention to psychiatrists abroad who might be able to disseminate his work, and he clearly thought of Abraham as one of them. In Isidor Sadger's book, *Sigmund Freud, persönliche Erinnerungen* the obverse of this strategic approach comes to the fore. The Wednesday Society had been meeting in Freud's house since 1902. It was a small circle of Viennese followers who had supported Freud in the years when hardly anyone had heard of him. This group felt passed over when Freud started to focus intensively on foreigners, first Bleuler and Jung, then Abraham, soon to be joined by Ferenczi and Jones.[253]

Abraham was extremely pleased by Freud's response and called it the best encouragement he could have received. Being called a pupil by Freud was to him a form of recognition.[254]

CHAPTER SIX

A private practice and the first psychoanalytic conflict

Berlin

In early November 1907, Karl, Hedwig, and the infant Hilda moved into number 22 Schöneberger Ufer, Berlin.[255] Today, the street running along the Landwehr Canal is still called the Schöneberger Ufer, but the row of houses that included number 22 has gone. There were trees on both sides of the canal and flowers and vegetables were sold from barges on the water.[256] Hilda remembered little of the house, since she was not yet four at the time, but she did recall that they looked out over gardens. There was a large balcony with red-and-white tiles, and a coloured awning.

In Zurich, Abraham had felt very much at home, whereas Hedwig had struggled to adjust to an environment in which she could not find her niche. Now the tables had turned. Hedwig was back in the city where she grew up, with family and friends around her. Abraham had previously lived in Berlin for several years, but now he needed to build a new life with a practice of his own.[257] This was a risky undertaking, and he was far from the Burghölzli and the mountains where he felt he belonged. Hedwig's homesickness for Berlin will undoubtedly have been one of the reasons for the move.

Berlin had an astonishing power of attraction in those days. The city was growing at a speed almost impossible to fathom. In 1861, it had 528,900 inhabitants and when it became the capital of the new German Empire ten years later, the figure had grown to more than 800,000. By 1880, the number of residents had passed the million mark, at 1,122,330. In 1910, there were more than two million, and in 1920, almost four million Berliners. So, in late 1907, Abraham and his family settled down in a hectic, modern city with new buildings going up everywhere. At the same time, it was home to Wilhelm II's extremely conservative royal household and a great deal of attention was paid to the army and to parades.[258]

First visit to Freud

On Sunday 15 December 1907, Abraham visited Freud for the first time, staying until Thursday 19 December. It would be a turning point in his life.

On the 18th, he attended a meeting of the Wednesday Society, which that evening discussed sexual trauma and sex education for children.[259] Abraham expressed a remarkable view on the subject of sexual trauma. Whereas the others mainly discussed the pros and cons of informing children about sex, he argued that a mother's tenderness was of great importance—a perspective hardly ever mentioned in those days. Freud called Abraham's article on sexual trauma a step forward.[260]

One report of Abraham's visit to Freud has survived. In Zurich, Hedwig and Karl Abraham had become good friends of Max Eitingon, and they both wrote letters to him in the new year. In his letter, Abraham describes his recent trip.

Dear Mr. Eitingon,

We have kept you waiting for a proper letter for a long time. As you can see, however, there is every intention to do better in 1908. Naturally you wish to hear about Vienna. I shall therefore begin by telling you that Freud spoke of you in a friendly way, especially of your meeting in Rome.[261] He only regrets that you did not creatively collaborate. I met with a most pleasant welcome in his home. He himself, his wife, sister-in-law and daughter took me all over Vienna, to art galleries, the theatre, cafés, to Heller's bookshop, to an antique dealer, etc. They were delightful days. They were also fruitful in other ways. I profited greatly from the daily discussions, often continued until late at night. Most of all I have been enriched by the personal acquaintance with a man of his stature. We talked about his various interests. I have come to know every object in his collection of antiquities, to which he added several precious pieces during my visit. In Rome he had a serious mishap in an antiquities shop with a Roman glass worth about 800 lire. He swept it from the table with his sleeve; it broke clean into two pieces. Great upset about the damage and the apparent wrecking of his theory. Do try to imagine why he broke this glass. The unconscious motivation is very interesting.

Freud has come to divide his followers into three grades: those in the lowest have understood no more than *The Psychopathology of Everyday Life*; those in the second the theories on dreams and neuroses; and those in the third follow him into the theory of sexuality and accept his extension of the libido concept. (I cannot literally repeat his wording.) He includes me in the third grade, which is very gratifying for me. The work on the borderlines between dementia praecox and hysteria and on the concept of dementia has taken more tangible shape in Vienna. Freud very much wants me to deal with this subject very soon. I also outlined another project to him for the Gradiva Collection: the dreams in Hebbel's diaries.[262] They are a goldmine of material for us. I would like to ask you not to talk of these projects.

There is no need for me to describe Freud's personality to you. I now admire him even more than before. Unfortunately, he seems to be worried by his old age complex. He is very pleased with any collaboration; the formerly suppressed wish for recognition is now clearly apparent. I am all the more pleased that we shall probably soon have a journal (you may have heard of Jung's preparatory work) and even a congress of our own in Salzburg at Easter.[263] If the practice makes it financially possible I shall go there and my wife would accompany me. Would you come too?

I am not too enthusiastic about the Viennese followers. I attended the Wednesday Meeting. He is too far in advance of the others. Sadger is like a Talmudic scholar; he interprets and observes every rule of the master with orthodox Jewish strictness.[264] The best impression among the medical members was made by Dr Federn. Stekel is superficial, Adler one-sided, Wittels too verbose, the other insignificant. Young Rank seems very intelligent as also Dr Graf, editor of the *Freie Presse*.[265]

Everything else we can discuss when we meet sometime soon. I must just tell you one pleasant incident. I had shown great interest in the Egyptian antiquities. During our farewell Freud secretly slipped a box with some small bronze statues into my briefcase! I am still filled with all those pleasant impressions. I also like his wife very much; she and his eldest daughter will visit us soon on their way through Berlin. Now it only remains for me to thank you for advising me so pressingly to make this journey.

The news from the Burghölzli has amazed me. Miss Fuerst told us about it post haste as you can imagine. Do let us have all your news soon. We are well. My wife will tell you in more detail.

With cordial greetings,

Yours, Karl Abraham[266]

Many years later, Hedwig wrote to Jones that Freud had made an enormous impression on Abraham, both during fascinating conversations in Freud's study that lasted for hours and on their long walks through the streets of Vienna. He also very much enjoyed being accepted into Freud's family circle. He got to know Freud's wife and his sister-in-law Minna Bernays, both of whom visited him in Berlin in the years that followed.[267] Abraham became especially fond of Freud's wife.[268]

In December 1907, Abraham set up his own practice. Initially, patients were referred to him by Oppenheim as promised, and he worked for a while as a volunteer at Oppenheim's polyclinic, but as he began increasingly to devote himself to psychoanalysis, Oppenheim referred fewer patients, and they were mostly difficult or hopeless cases whom an analyst could not help any more than anyone else could.[269]

On 2 January 1908, the day after Abraham's letter to Eitingon about his visit to Freud, Hedwig wrote to him about their new life in Berlin:

My husband has made no mention to you of his practice, yet he has good reason to be satisfied with it. It is true that he has not yet had an analytic case and we are both sorry about this, but the fact that there were patients from the outset has exceeded our expectations. Eventually there will be Freudian cases too, I hope. It seems a pity that the Congress is not to take place in the summer – there would surely be more participants if one could combine it with a summer holiday. Dr. Jung, whose idea the Congress is and who has convened it, has once again handled it very well. Are you, Mr Eitingon, a resident on the Burghölzli staff now and a real M.D.?[270] I hope the question is not an indiscreet one between good friends. I sincerely hope that you have finished working for your examinations and I can well imagine how much you are looking forward to your future work and better health. What is the medical administration of the Burghölzli like at present? You see, I still think a lot about Zurich but quite frankly without any longing. I feel too happy and warm in this turbulent metropolis and in the old, well-known circle, even though it shares few of our interests. But it gives us the personal interest we missed for so long for ourselves and our little one who has suddenly become the centre of attention. I shall write another time about Berlin's cultural pleasures. The move followed by the Christmas activities has not given us time to think of such things. Write soon and tell us a lot about yourself – for it will be a long time before you come here. You must know that a place of a friend who shares our interests is kept for you.[271]

Many heartfelt greetings and – if you'll accept them – best wishes too for the new year that has begun from

Your Hedwig Abraham.[272]

Clearly, Hedwig was relieved and happy to be back in Berlin, but for Abraham it was a difficult time in which he seems to have felt extremely unsure of himself. Freud, who had a keen eye for the state of mind of those around him, recognised as much during Abraham's visit. On 14 January, he wrote to Jung that Abraham was rather inhibited in his conversations with him, far more so than in his letters.[273] Freud assumed this was because of Abraham's worries about his Jewishness and his future, which he could perfectly well understand. He also wrote that fortunately Oppenheim had taken an interest in Abraham. Although Oppenheim was not a friend, he was a decent person.[274] Abraham's uncertainty is obvious from the two lengthy letters he sent to Freud on 8 and 15 January 1908, as is his need to make a favourable impression on Oppenheim, who had referred two obsessive-neurotic patients to him. Oppenheim had even asked him to try psychoanalysis on one of them, all of whose previous treatments had failed.[275] After two sessions, Abraham did not know how to continue and he asked Freud for advice.[276] Freud responded immediately and very supportively, explaining how to proceed. On 9 January he wrote,

The chief rules are: 1. Take your time, in the words of the Salzburg motto. Mental changes are never quick, except in revolutions (psychoses). Dissatisfied after only two sessions. At not knowing everything! 2. A problem like: How do I go on? must not exist. The patient shows the way, in that by strictly following the basic rule (saying everything that comes into his mind) he displays his prevailing Ψ surface.[277]

Then, on 19 January, he added,

If, as an experienced senior, I may give you some advice, conduct the psychoanalysis of the O.[ppenheim] patient without a great deal of "sexual displacement" [*Sexualverlegung*] and without any ambition to impress O. by rapid success. For in the first place it will go better like that, and in the second the case is not suitable for being developed into a show-piece. Such a long-standing obsession in a man nearing the 50s is technically very difficult and therapeutically rather unfavourable. Obsession must be treated early, in persons who are still young, and then the treatment is a triumph and a pleasure. But do not allow [yourself] to be discouraged, and keep the man as long as possible; such patients generally become easily attached and are often satisfied when the physician is not. So far as details are concerned, I shall always tell you what I can divine from a distance, and thus try to compensate for the lack occasioned by the technique not yet having been published in detail.[278]

Abraham felt lonely during this first period in Berlin, since there was no one around who shared his enthusiasm for psychoanalysis. He was regularly to be found at Oppenheim's clinic, but could detect no interest in psychological mechanisms there at all. He missed the exchanges about Freud's ideas that were a feature of the Burghölzli.

That first year in Berlin, while setting up his practice, Abraham still had some free time. Later, he would have almost none. He led an active social life along with Hedwig, who wrote to Eitingon that they went to receptions, which she found rather tedious, whereas she greatly enjoyed the talks, plays, and operas she attended, either alone or with her husband.[279] They continued seeing their friends from the days of the social sciences student association. The couple with whom they had gone to Switzerland in 1902, Salomon Altmann and Elisabeth Gottheiner, had kept their attachment a secret for years from their Jewish and Protestant families and now they were finally to marry. It was actually Elisabeth's father, who had Jewish roots, who insisted they should have a church wedding, while Salomon's family refused to accept that the ceremony would not take place in a synagogue. In the end, a compromise was found. The marriage was solemnised in the synagogue in the morning and in the church that same afternoon.[280]

On 8 March 1908, Abraham wrote to Freud about the wedding.[281] He was reading *The Interpretation of Dreams*, the part about the "either-or principle".[282] He wrote that a friend had come to stay with them (from Hilda's biography we know this to be Elisabeth Gottheiner), who wanted to marry a Jewish man and was of Jewish extraction herself on her father's side.[283] Both families were firmly opposed to the marriage and, at the time of Elisabeth's visit, the differences of opinion had come to a head. On the first night of her stay, Elisabeth had a dream that Abraham was immediately able to interpret, with the result that she became extremely interested and the next morning told him about five dreams. Abraham wrote to Freud that he had the feeling these dreams were illustrations of the either-or principle, about which he had just been reading. In his *Interpretation of Dreams*, Freud writes that a dream cannot express a choice between one thing and another, just as it cannot express a "no". Instead, it transforms the two alternatives into a single whole. In the dreams that Abraham cites, something quite different happened: all the possibilities were dreamed one after the other.

Abraham wrote that Elisabeth Gottheiner had clearly dreamed the dreams in the hope that he would interpret them. They represented the following possibilities:

1. The lovers could live together without marrying.
2. They could marry in a register office without either of them having to state their religion.
3. He could be baptised and then marry in a register office only.
4. She could convert to Judaism and then marry in a register office only.
5. She could change her faith and they could marry according to the Jewish rites.

He adds that, in each of the five cases, the couple was represented by relatives or friends who were suitable for the purpose and that he found this a wonderful example of "either-or". He wanted to hear what Freud thought.

On 13 March, Freud replied that Abraham's interpretation was undoubtedly correct and would make a good supplement to the passage in the *Interpretation of Dreams*.[284] By 1908, dream interpretation had become a party game at the breakfast table in the Abraham household. The dreams do seem rather too good to be true.

Preparations for the psychoanalytic meeting in Salzburg

The idea of holding a psychoanalytic meeting originated with Stein and Ferenczi from Budapest.[285] Only in retrospect would it come to be known as the first psychoanalytic congress.

On 2 January, Jung wrote a letter to Freud in which he said his depiction of his colleague Abraham "was, after all, too black".[286] Now that Freud had met Abraham, Jung was clearly uneasy about the impression his description had made. As we have seen, on 3 January Jung sent Abraham an affectionate letter, apologising for his delayed response. He had heard about the good start in Berlin and hoped it would continue. He wrote about various things, including a hysteria analysis he was undertaking, and told Abraham about the planned psychoanalytic meeting. The decision had been made to hold it in Salzburg. He would send Abraham the proposed date and duration.[287]

On 22 January 1908, Jung wrote to Freud that he wanted to do his best to prepare a talk for Salzburg about dementia praecox, perhaps in co-operation with Riklin.[288] On 25 January, he followed up by writing that Dr Abraham had announced he would give a lecture in Salzburg on "the psychosexual differences between Dem. praecox and hysteria", a subject very close to Jung's own.[289] He made no further comment and Freud did not respond on the subject.

Then, on 30 January, Jung wrote to Abraham that he was pleased to hear that he intended to give a lecture at the Salzburg meeting and requested him to limit it to twenty minutes, since a good deal of time would have to be reserved for Professor Freud.[290] It seems likely that Jung received the announcement about Abraham's lecture between 22 and 25 January. Neither he nor Freud made any mention of the thematic overlap in their letters to Abraham. That both men had chosen the same subject was not surprising, since at the Burghölzli it was the diagnosis they both dealt with most frequently and each of them had debated at length with Freud about dementia praecox and autoeroticism. Jung had published a book on dementia praecox and Abraham believed that during his visit to Freud he had received an explicit request to develop further Freud's ideas on dementia praecox and hysteria, as his letter to Eitingon of 1 January 1908 makes clear. He responded at once to the request.

On 3 March 1908, Jung sent Freud a letter that included the draft programme for Salzburg,[291] and, on 5 March, Freud wrote back that he had noticed that Riklin (Jung had planned his talk along with Riklin) and Abraham were missing from it.[292] Jung had "forgotten" to allocate Abraham a slot in the Salzburg programme and he responded to Freud on 11 March as follows:

> Of course the devil had to put a spoke in my wheel with that lecture of colleague Abraham's; I can hear you chuckling. The lecture displeases me because it puts forward what I have fantasied out loud under your stimulation and what I wanted to work up later myself, once it had matured.[293]

It is the first occasion on which Jung expresses displeasure at the fact that Abraham and he had chosen the same subject. Abraham had still heard nothing of this.

Salzburg congress

The Salzburg congress has gone down in history as a successful gathering with one unfortunate episode: a difference of opinion between Jung and Abraham, attributable mainly to the latter.[294]

That was Freud's interpretation of the whole affair, and it has become common currency simply because several of his biographers adopted the same standpoint (see for example Gay,[295] Clark,[296] and Jones). Jones wrote of the congress (where he met Freud for the first time) that it took place on Sunday 26 April 1908 and was different from all the congresses that followed it in the sense that it had no chairman or secretary and there was no formal discussion of organisational matters.[297] Freud felt deeply honoured by Bleuler's presence and would have liked him to chair the meeting, but Bleuler refused. Forty-two people attended and eight lectures were held. Freud began at eight in the morning with a talk about an obsessive patient who would later become famous as "the rat man". Freud talked non-stop until eleven and everyone listened attentively. He wanted to end there, but his audience persuaded him to continue and he went on speaking until about one o'clock.[298]

Other talks followed in the afternoon. Jones describes the discord between Jung and Abraham as follows:

> It was one of those stupid little disputes over priority that have so often marred scientific progress, from Newton and Leibniz onward. It arose from Abraham omitting to mention or give any credit to Bleuler and Jung in his Congress paper for their psychological investigations into dementia praecox, which Jung took very much amiss at the time.[299]

Only a few writers (Brome,[300] Cremerius,[301] and Kuhn[302]) have described the possibility of a different version of events, in which Abraham became caught up in the extraordinarily complicated and hypersensitive relationship between Freud and Jung. Freud could not bear the fact that there were difficulties between them, and he increasingly managed to convince himself (and others—see the biographies) that the dispute did not concern him and Jung but was a matter of a fairly trivial rivalry between Jung and Abraham.

What exactly had happened? On 23 July 1908, Freud wrote to Abraham: "At the time I gave the same suggestion to each of you and had no intention other than that each should take it up and work on it independently".[303] Freud had discussed with both Jung and Abraham his hypothesis that in dementia praecox there was a regression to an early childhood phase of autoerotism in which the potential for object-love was destroyed and with it the ability to sublimate. This subject crops up time and again in the correspondence between Freud and Jung. Between the time of Jung's visit to Freud in early March 1907, during which it seems they spoke at length about dementia praecox and autoerotism, and the summer of 1907, there was hardly a single letter in which the subject was not at least touched upon. Jung's doubts were not dispelled. The letters between them also make clear, as do Bleuler's letters to Freud, that Bleuler and Jung discussed the subject as well.[304] Having published a book about dementia praecox and having engaged in many debates with Freud, it is hardly surprising that he regarded the subject as his (and perhaps Bleuler's), but Jung had never published anything about dementia praecox from a psychoanalytic perspective. In a more general sense, Jung had not written anything of any depth about psychoanalysis, or about Freud's libido theory. He had not gone much further than to make a case for the mental causes of psychiatric disorders in his lecture at Zurich town hall in January 1908, entitled "Der Inhalt der Psychose" (The content of the psychoses).[305]

Jung's letter of 22 January 1908 makes clear that he wanted to give a lecture about dementia praecox at the congress, but he does not write that he intends to address the subject from the perspective of psychoanalysis.[306] Nevertheless, we can assume that Jung was planning to give a lecture about psychoanalysis, or, at least, to include psychoanalytic elements; this was, after all, the first psychoanalytic congress, he had organised it himself, and his letter of 11 March 1908 indicates that his plans were along the same lines as Abraham's.

On 29 January 1908, Abraham wrote to Freud,

> I have received an invitation to Salzburg from Jung. As I hope to be able to take part in the meeting, I have announced a talk on "Psycho-Sexual Differences between Hysteria and Dementia Praecox". Some new points of view on this subject have occurred to me, which fit in well with the theory of auto-eroticism. I hope you like the subject. Since you have previously acknowledged that in the early work I had tackled the problem from the most important angle, that of sexuality, I thought it important to stress at this, our first congress, that sexuality forms the nucleus of the problem.[307]

Clearly, Abraham was unaware of any difficulty and he continued to think and write about what he had discussed with Freud during his visit to Vienna. Did Freud foresee what would happen if he encouraged both Jung and Abraham to work on the same ideas? It seems unlikely. Freud was a good judge of people, but his perceptiveness deserted him as soon as he formed a strong attachment to someone, as was clearly the case with Jung. Did he perhaps think that a bit of competition would ensure the subject was debated more thoroughly? If so, he was seriously mistaken, since Jung's reaction was simply destructive and damaging to his relationship with Freud.

Kuhn goes even further by suggesting that Freud acted "as an agent provocateur surreptitiously goading Jung—by way of coded warnings—that he had a serious rival in Abraham and if he still wanted Freud's attentions he had better look to his ideas".[308] Still, it seems rather implausible that Freud went about things in such a calculated manner. It is safer to assume that Freud, in his idealising of Jung, underestimated the latter's devastating jealousy. Furthermore, Freud did not take Jung's doubts about the libido theory seriously. He expected Jung to be convinced by it over time. Although Jung had not published any truly psychoanalytic articles and continued to disagree with Freud on essential points, he made huge efforts on behalf of psychoanalysis, both at an organisational level—the Salzburg congress being one example, preparations for a periodical another—and by the way in which he managed to stimulate and galvanise a succession of young doctors who would later become important figures in the field. Freud had Jung's infectious enthusiasm to thank for his rapidly growing fame.

That Jung looked up to Freud is indisputable, as is the fact that, for Jung, being admired and in the position of an adored favourite son was of enormous importance. In that situation, competition was hard to tolerate.

On 27 April 1908, Abraham delivered his lecture in Salzburg: "The psycho-sexual differences between hysteria and dementia praecox". Later published as an article under the same title,[309] it is written in Abraham's characteristically lucid style. He claims that the psychoanalytic method has revealed important similarities between hysteria and dementia praecox, both of which have their origins in sexual complexes. He does, however, want to look at the differences. Towards the end, he says that his main concern is to differentiate between dementia praecox, hysteria, and the obsessive neuroses, and that in this article he is merely making a start in that respect. He looks mainly at dementia praecox and only briefly at hysteria. Based on Freud's *Three Essays on the Theory of Sexuality* (1905d), he writes that the earliest expressions of the libido in children are autoerotic in character. At that stage, the child recognises no sexual objects outside itself. Only in the next stage of development do we see object-love. In hysteria, Abraham says, love for one person is intensified to a pathological degree at this point, while simultaneously another person is fiercely rejected.

In dementia praecox, by contrast, we see either indifference or a persecution mania that spills over into explicit hostility. It leads to the obliteration of both object-love and sublimation. Abraham thought this was a result of an abnormal disposition and a developmental disorder, such that the stage of autoerotism was not passed through as it should be and feelings became blocked. He regarded hysteria, too, as hereditary.

It is an interesting article. Abraham is attempting to give an initial boost to the development of psychoanalytic theory on dementia praecox, which he is keen to distinguish from hysteria.

Based on this talk, in a letter to Freud dated 7 May 1908, Jung accused Abraham of plagiarism, saying he had stolen ideas from him and from Freud. He wrote that he would not be prepared to include Abraham's article in the *Jahrbuch* as it now stood, "for a journal edited by me has to be thoroughly clean and decent and should not publish any plagiarism of your intellectual work or mine".[310]

Kuhn writes that on rereading Freud's letters on the subject, he came to the conclusion that the approaching rift between Jung and Abraham was caused by Jung's accusation of plagiarism, which arose from Abraham's failure to mention the work of Bleuler and Jung in his Salzburg lecture.[311] It is regrettable that Kuhn does not mention which letters led him to draw this conclusion. Jones does not use the word plagiarism, writing that although Jung resented the fact that Abraham had not mentioned him or Bleuler in his talk, that is a quite different issue. Abraham's later behaviour points in the same direction. He credited Bleuler and Jung in retrospect, and, in a letter to Freud dated 11 May, he explains why he did not name them in Salzburg. The only use of the word plagiarism is in the letter written by Jung to Freud of 7 May 1908, quoted above.

Was it a question of plagiarism? The day in Salzburg went as follows. Freud spoke all morning. In the afternoon there were eight talks, the third by Abraham and the sixth by Jung.[312] So, Abraham spoke before Jung. If Jung believed Abraham was guilty of plagiarism, why did he not bring up the matter immediately when his turn came to speak? In his lecture, Abraham tried to distinguish, within psychoanalytic theory, between two concepts: dementia praecox and hysteria. Bleuler and Jung had published nothing on the psychoanalytic approach to dementia praecox, so what did Jung mean when he said Abraham was guilty of plagiarism? Plagiarism means including texts or theories in your own work without naming the original authors. Both Bleuler and Jung had published on dementia praecox, but not in the context of the theory of psychoanalysis, and a failure to identify your teachers is a very different thing from plagiarism. Abraham had named Bleuler and Jung explicitly in his first article on dementia praecox.[313]

Jung was the sixth speaker that afternoon. At this first congress for the followers of Freud, which he had organised himself, he gave a talk in which psychoanalysis was not mentioned. Freud must have regarded this as a huge insult, one that no one commented upon. Jung claimed that dementia praecox was caused by an abnormality in the brain that had something to do with psycho-toxic substances.[314] The exchange of letters between Jung and Freud shows that Jung still had his doubts about Freud's sexual theory, which he found extremely valuable while at the same time believing that it applied only to some patients and that physical factors were also relevant. Jung's sudden decision to make no mention at all of Freud's theory when he spoke in Salzburg suggests real agitation, the result not just of jealousy towards Abraham, but of anger that Freud was not taking his doubts seriously. This points to a degree of arrogance on Freud's part. After all, Jung had a great deal of experience with dementia praecox patients whereas Freud had none at all.

So, at the Salzburg congress, a major intellectual conflict was going on between Freud and Jung that had nothing to do with Abraham, yet it has gone down in history as a conflict between Jung and Abraham. How could this happen? The correspondence between the three is our main source of information on subsequent developments, while Hilda's biography shows how unhappy Abraham was that Freud had unfairly identified him as the cause of problems with Jung, claiming they arose from rivalry and jealousy. Given his enthusiasm for Freud, Abraham must have felt profoundly disillusioned.

On 30 April 1908, directly after the congress, Jung wrote to Freud, "I beg you to have patience with me, and confidence in what I have done up till now. I always have a little more to do than be just a faithful follower".[315] This comment on the conflict fell somewhere between a sneer and an attempt at reconciliation. Freud responded three days later, on 3 May, completely passing over the insult contained in Jung's lecture: "So you too are pleased with our meeting in Salzburg? It refreshed me a good deal and left me with a pleasant aftertaste. I was glad to find you so flourishing and every suspicion of resentment melted away when I saw you again and understood you".[316]

Later in the same letter, he shifts the blame for the conflict on to Abraham:

> I have a great favour to ask of you. It has not escaped me that a rift is in the making between you and Abraham. There are so few of us that we must stick together, and a rift for personal motives is less becoming in us psychoanalysts than in anyone else. I regard him as a man of great worth and I should not like to be obliged to give him up, though there can be no question of his replacing you in my eyes. Accordingly, I have this request to make of you: be helpful if he consults you about the publication of his dementia paper, and accept the fact that this time he took the more direct path, whereas you hesitated.[317]

That same day, Freud wrote to Abraham,

> I recollect that your paper led to a slight conflict between you and Jung, or so at least I concluded from a few words you said to me afterwards. Now, I consider a rivalry between the two of you to be inevitable, and also quite harmless within certain limits; in dealing with the matter at issue

I did not hesitate to say that you were in the right and to attribute Jung's sensitiveness to his vacillation. But I would not like any serious bad feeling to come between you. We are still so few that disharmony, especially because of any personal "complexes", should be out of the question among us. It must also be of importance for us that Jung should find his way back to the views he has just forsaken, which you have stood by so consistently. I believe there are prospects for this; Jung also writes to me that Bleuler shows signs of being very much influenced and almost inclined to abandon again the concept of the organic nature of dementia praecox.

So you would virtually do me a personal favour if you informed him in advance of your publication and asked him to discuss his former objections with you so that you would be able to take them into account. Such an act of courtesy will certainly nip the nascent disagreement in the bud, would greatly please me, and would show me that all of us are capable of also drawing practical benefit for our own mental activities from the practice of psychoanalysis. Do not take the little victory over yourself too hard.

Be tolerant, and do not forget that really it is easier for you to follow my thoughts than it is for Jung, since to begin with you are completely independent, and then you are closer to my intellectual constitution through racial kinship, while he as a Christian and a pastor's son finds his way to me only against great inner resistances. His association with us is therefore all the more valuable. I was almost going to say that it was only by his emergence on the scene that psychoanalysis was removed from the danger of becoming a Jewish national affair.

I hope you will give your attention to my request and send you the most cordial greetings.

Yours,

Freud[318]

Abraham had done nothing, yet he was being asked to lay the conflict with Jung aside for the sake of the cause, a conflict in which Freud completely disregarded his own role. Six days later, Freud wrote an even more insistent letter.[319] He had not yet received an answer from Abraham and was writing again to add further emphasis to his request.

On 11 May 1908, Abraham sent Freud a calm and carefully considered response.[320] Of the three, he seems to have acted the most wisely by far in the circumstances. He writes that he set Freud's request aside for a few days in order to think it over. He was not entirely in agreement, but he had in the meantime drawn the conclusion that it outlined the right approach and had written a draft letter to Jung. He had left that in turn to one side for a while so that he could look at it again, just in case his overtures still contained anything hostile, before writing the definitive letter to Jung. He hoped that in doing so he was serving the cause of psychoanalysis. He went on,

Actually I became involved in the conflict quite innocently. In December I asked you whether there was any risk of my colliding with Jung on this subject, as you had communicated your ideas to him as well. You dispelled my doubts at the time. My manuscript for Salzburg contained a remark that would certainly have satisfied Bleuler and Jung; following a sudden impulse, I omitted to read it out. I deceived myself for the moment by a cover-motive—saving time—while the true reason lay in my animosity against Bl.[euler] and J[ung]. This came from their latest all too conciliatory publications, from Bleuler's address in Berlin, which made no reference to you *at all*, and from various trivialities. That I did not mention Bl. and J. obviously means: "Since they turn aside from the theory of sexuality, I really will not cite them in connection with it."—It naturally did not come into conscious thought at that moment that this omission might have serious consequences.

Even before delivering his lecture in Salzburg, Abraham had heard from Eitingon that Jung's talk would contain not a word about psychoanalysis or any reference to Freud. Annoyed that the same had been true of Bleuler's lecture in Berlin a short time before, he had not mentioned either of them in his own talk. There was, in fact, no need to do so, but it would have been courteous to name them.

In an article about the scandal in Salzburg, in which he mainly looks at the origins of Freud's version of events, Kuhn writes that, despite all the evidence to the contrary, Freud emphasised repeatedly that the conflict came down to a dispute about who had primacy, about "who had the right to lay the first authentic paranoid claim for having planted the Freudian libido flag in the field of dementia praecox".[321] Kuhn claims that in this way Freud papered over the fact that the dispute was about plagiarism. Yet, there are many indications that although the dispute was about plagiarism, the issue of primacy was also important, not so much in the case of Abraham, who saw himself as a beginner in the field of psychoanalysis and had asked Freud whether there was a risk he would be getting under Jung's feet, but more so for Jung, who accused Abraham of a very strange kind of plagiarism. It was an offence that would not stand up in a court of law, but, for Jung, it seems to have been hugely important: plagiarism of a phantasy. In the letter from Jung to Freud quoted earlier in this chapter, he writes of Abraham's talk: "The lecture displeases me because it puts forward what I have fantasied out loud under your stimulation and what I wanted to work up later myself, once it had matured".[322] Freud had discussed his ideas about a psychoanalytic approach to dementia praecox with both Jung and Abraham. With Jung, he had exchanged thoughts on the matter earlier and for longer. Abraham had prepared a lecture and an article, believing that Freud had explicitly asked him to do so. He was doing it for Freud. Jung, too, had been planning to give a lecture and write an article; he could see the content in front of him in a phantasied form. He did not develop his ideas further, perhaps because he was angry that Abraham was ahead of him, but even had that not been the case, it is possible that no article by Jung would have been published on the subject, for two reasons. First, Jung was still wrestling with the libido theory, which he could not fully accept. He could have included his doubts in an article, but, second, Jung did not have the gift for extremely lucid thinking and writing that Abraham had, and we may wonder whether he ever truly understood Freud's libido theory. As for Jung himself, in a letter to Freud of 30 April 1908, he put it down mainly to lack of time: "Maybe I have done too little analytical work on Dem. praec. these last nine months, with the result that the impressive material has become too much of an imposition on me. The chief obstacle is my pupils; training them and overseeing their papers consumes my time".[323]

In writing to Freud, Jung's rage against Abraham becomes increasingly fierce. In the letter in which he makes his accusation of plagiarism, dated 7 May 1908, he writes,

For that very reason I have an undisguised contempt for some of colleague A.'s idiosyncrasies. In spite of his estimable qualities and sundry virtues he is simply not a gentleman. In my eyes just about the worst thing that can happen to anyone. I am always ready to subordinate my judgment to someone who knows better, but in this case I find myself in agreement with a large number of people whose opinions I respect.[324] In Salzburg I was able to prevent a scandal only by imploring a certain gentleman, who wanted to shed light on the sources of A.'s lecture, to abandon his plan. This gentleman wasn't a Swiss, nor was he one of my pupils, who (like me) can only gaze in quiet wonderment at such productions but can't help taking note of the facts. Up till now nothing has ever been done from my side that might have led to the rift; on the contrary it is A. who is pulling in that direction. The latest piece of effrontery (which, be it said, I could not imagine him capable of before) is the news that he will send me his lecture unaltered for publication. Naturally I wouldn't put up with that, for a journal edited by me has to be thoroughly clean and decent and should not publish any plagiarism of your intellectual work or mine.[325]

In his lecture in Salzburg, Jung made no mention of plagiarism by Abraham, but now, in this letter, he writes that he has prevented a scandal by dissuading someone else from talking about it. Of all the participants in Salzburg, Jones is the only one to whom this could refer, but in his account, written decades later, Jones does not use the word plagiarism.[326]

The way in which Jung deals with Abraham in this letter to Freud comes close to slander. Abraham cannot be accused of behaving like anything less than a gentleman. Jung was at fault in failing to mention Freud's ideas in his lecture, but he used all his verbal firepower to put the blame on Abraham. Although at first this had little effect, it worked in the long run.

Freud's response to Jung's allegations was quite tactful.[327] He understood what Jung meant up to a point, but felt he was being too hard on Abraham, who had heard about dementia praecox from both Jung and Freud and had then written about it. To Freud, this was acceptable. Abraham had since credited Bleuler and Jung in his published article.

In the period that followed, all this gradually became very unpleasant for Abraham, so much so that it stayed with him for the rest of his life and seventeen years later on 27 October 1925, from his sickbed, two months before his death, he wrote about it again.[328] There were two reasons why it was so disturbing for him, one being that Jung did not respond to the paragraph in Freud's letter in which he defends Abraham, just as he did not respond to the letter Abraham wrote to him at Freud's request. The second reason was that Freud seemed increasingly to idealise Jung.

In May and June 1908, the correspondence between Freud and Jung was mostly about the new periodical, but they also discussed Jung's analysis of Otto Gross.[329] Jung makes a great many excuses for being slow to respond. In June, Freud's tone becomes almost rapturous.[330] He writes that he has noticed Jung's ideas have now come close to his own. He had been worried about that for a while, but when he saw Jung in Salzburg—there had been no opportunity to speak to him—he knew they would converge. Freud seems to have entered into a kind of dream world as far as Jung was concerned, since it was in Salzburg that Jung's performance had been so insulting to Freud. Moreover, Jung's ideas had not in any sense moved closer to his own.

Abraham shook Freud out of his dream with a single sentence in his letter of 9 July 1908: "I do not want to write anything about Zurich today. You will draw the right conclusions about it for yourself in any case".[331]

Freud responded fiercely in a letter of 11 July 1908, saying he had received no news either from Zurich or from Jung, regretted the quarrel deeply, and had the impression that both sides lacked a desire to set things right.[332] This latter conclusion was extremely unfair to Abraham who, having done nothing wrong, had written a long letter to Jung in an attempt to put the matter to rest. Jung had not answered him, and in his letter of 9 July, Abraham was referring not to the conflict between himself and Jung but to colleagues in Zurich who were turning their backs on Freud.

In Freud's case, the issue of guilt took a remarkable turn. An outsider would think it was Freud who had instigated the conflict. This does not appear to have occurred to Freud. Initially, he regarded Jung as the cause, writing to Abraham on 3 May 1908, "In dealing with the matter at issue I did not hesitate to say that you were in the right and to attribute Jung's sensitiveness to his vacillation".[333] Then, on 10 May 1908, Freud wrote to Jung that he had gone too far in his accusations of plagiarism by Abraham. From that moment on, Jung never mentioned plagiarism again. When Abraham shook Freud out of his dreams about Jung on 9 July 1908 with his hint at bad news about Zurich, Freud shifted the blame on to both men, and soon he was placing it solely on Abraham, where it would remain. On 16 July 1908, Abraham wrote to Freud,

> I really ought to leave you in peace just now at the beginning of your holiday, but I do have to reply to some points in your letter. My brief reference to Zurich in my last letter was *not* meant to refer to my personal disagreement with Jung, but to the whole present attitude adopted in Zurich. To deal with the former first: I have not the slightest wish for an estrangement from Zurich. My letter to Jung was as accommodating as possible (I could send you a copy). Not to reply is really rather rude. But should harmony be re-established, now or later, either through your mediation or in some other way, I for my part will certainly not be the sulky one! On the contrary, I should like to keep in touch with the Burghölzli. Even though a number of unpleasant things happened before I left, I brought so many agreeable memories away with me that I certainly do not wish to disturb the peace.
>
> Actually the matter goes deeper. Jung's behaviour to me is, after all, only a symptom. I believe all the gentlemen in Vienna had the impression in Salzburg that not much more could be expected from Zurich. I have news from a reliable source about the latest developments, and it was under the impact of this that I wrote to you last time. I do not wish to pester you with details. But the sudden death of the Freudian evenings, so well attended until April, is striking. Jung seems to be reverting to his former spiritualistic inclinations. But please let us keep this between ourselves! However, if Jung gives up for this reason and for the sake of his career, then it is simply over at the Burghölzli. Bleuler, however efficient he may otherwise be, will do nothing on his own.[334]

Later, it would turn out that Abraham had been right in what he said about Zurich, but for now Freud was incensed at the disturbance of the idyll he saw when he thought about Jung and Zurich.

On 23 July, Freud wrote an extremely odd letter to Abraham that began with a great compliment for Abraham's article on dementia praecox and hysteria.[335] Freud said he had such admiration for the resolute tone and clarity of the article that Abraham should not think he had failed to notice its beauty. But Abraham ought never to have written it. Freud had given the idea to both Abraham and Jung, and by taking it up Abraham had driven Jung into a corner. Instead, he should have been considerate enough to let it lie. Freud seems to have forgotten that Abraham had asked him whether it could do Jung any harm if he wrote the article and

Freud had answered in the negative. After all these peregrinations, the blame was firmly laid at Abraham's door, where it would remain.

The conflict can be approached from many different points of view: that of the rivalry between Jung and Abraham, the existence of which is beyond dispute; that of Jung's realisation that he was intellectually inferior to Abraham; that of Jung's frustration at Freud's desire to force him into a particular pigeon hole; that of Abraham's annoyance at finding both his former colleagues (Jung and Bleuler), whom he had once so admired, suddenly abandoning psycho-analysis, and so on. Yet, at the centre lies the issue first broached by Cremerius,[336] which was that Freud had a number of favoured disciples on whom he lavished all his attention, and those who disturbed his idyll by pointing out reality brought Freud's fury down upon themselves. They were made to bear all the blame for his disillusionment.

CHAPTER SEVEN

Psychoanalysis in Berlin

Opposition

Abraham had thought carefully beforehand about how to introduce psychoanalysis in Berlin. He knew he could count on having few supporters and many opponents. He had decided not to give a talk too soon and when he did to make certain that the subject he chose would not provoke too much resistance. Ellenberger wrote in his standard work about the history of psychoanalysis that Abraham portrayed the opposition he encountered as worse than in fact it was, but Ellenberger was confusing Abraham's first and second talks.[337] The first, in the autumn of 1908, was quite favourably received. At his second talk, a year later, he was panned.

Abraham was also intending to set up a Berlin Psychoanalytic Society and he succeeded remarkably quickly. On 21 August 1908, he wrote enthusiastically to Freud that it was already up and running. The Berlin Psychoanalytic Society was due to meet for the first time on 27 August, with Magnus Hirschfeld, Iwan Bloch, Otto Juliusburger, and Heinrich Koerber as members.[338] At first, it was more a sexological than a psychoanalytic group. Iwan Bloch (1872–1922) was a friend of Abraham's from his student days in Würzburg, and the only one to have his forename included in the letter to Freud. In 1896, Bloch had been working on his doctorate while Abraham, five years his junior, was still a first-year student. The son of a cattle dealer from Delmenhorst near Oldenburg, Bloch was a dermatologist and sexologist. He discovered the manuscript of *The 120 Days of Sodom, or the School of Libertinism* by the Marquis de Sade, which everyone though had been lost, and, in 1904, he published it under the pseudonym Eugène Dühren. In 1908, he was already famous in Berlin. In a single year, 40,000 copies of his *Das Sexualleben in unserer Zeit in seinen Beziehungen zur modernen Kultur* (1907) were sold.[339] The book, published in English the following year as *The Sexual Life of our Time in its*

Relations to Modern Civilization, was regarded as marking the start of sexology as a science in its own right. Bloch was a member of the Berlin Psychoanalytic Society for only a short time, but the connection between Bloch and psychoanalysis went back quite a long way. Freud named works by both Bloch and Hirschfeld as sources for the first essay in the 1905 edition of his *Three Essays on the Theory of Sexuality*. As for Bloch, his attitude to psychoanalysis was one of benevolent neutrality.[340] To him, it was among the possible methods to be used in sexology, but he found purely psychological explanations for neurosis, such as were usual in psychoanalysis, insufficient. The physiological–anatomical side was, in his view, no less important.

We do not know how they met, but it is clear that Abraham visited Magnus Hirschfeld (1868–1935) on 11 May 1908.[341] A few days later, Hirschfeld referred a homosexual man to him and after that frequently sent him patients. Hirschfeld was nine years older than Abraham and had settled in Berlin as a doctor in 1895. In 1897, he set up the Wissenschaftlich-humanitäre Komitee, whose aim was to advance the emancipation of homosexuals. Among other things, the committee campaigned for the reform of paragraph 175 of the German Criminal Code, which forbade sexual contact between men. Like Iwan Bloch, he lived from his private practice and from his books. Hirschfeld wrote a great deal. In 1899, he founded the journal *Jahrbuch für sexuelle Zwischenstufen*, which published scientific articles written by a variety of scientists from many different countries.

It was this journal that published a questionnaire Abraham and others would later assist with, consisting of eighty-five questions to be answered in writing. They concerned a person's mental and physical health, life history and, in particular, sex life. Hirschfeld probably collected several thousand of them. Initially, he focused mainly on information about homosexuals, but after 1915, when the list became known as the Psychobiological Questionnaire, he included heterosexuals as well. He was interested above all in finding out about people who had not consulted doctors with a problem of any kind, a group that had never previously been investigated by sexologists.[342] This empirical work made Hirschfeld an important pioneer who collected data about the sexual life of his day. Years later, Alfred Kinsey was able to build on the foundation he laid.[343]

In 1913, Hirschfeld set up the Ärztliche Gesellschaft für Sexualwissenschaft und Eugenik, with Bloch as vice-chairman. He remained a member of the Berlin Psychoanalytic Society for some years, although he did not work as a psychoanalyst himself. He left the society after he was grossly insulted in public by Jung at the congress in Weimar. Jung expressed hostile views about homosexuals on a number of occasions.[344] Abraham found Hirschfeld's decision highly regrettable and tried in vain to persuade him to stay.

Hirschfeld and Freud were opponents in a theoretical sense when it came to male homosexuality. Hirschfeld believed it was congenital, whereas in his *Leonardo da Vinci and a Memory of his Childhood*, Freud wrote that homosexual men had in their backgrounds a powerful erotic bond with a female individual in early childhood, usually their mothers. That bond was reinforced by extremely loving treatment by the mother and withdrawal by the father during childhood. Because the father made himself unreachable, the boy was subject to female influence alone.[345]

With two heavyweight sexologists like Bloch and Hirschfeld, it is no wonder that discussions at the Berlin Psychoanalytic Society were mainly about sexology.[346] In his letter of 24 August

1908, Freud congratulated Abraham on setting up the new society on the difficult but important territory of Berlin and said that he expected only Juliusburger to turn out to be a real asset to psychoanalysis.[347]

Otto Juliusburger (1867–1952), the son of a Jewish merchant from Breslau, was head doctor at the Kurhaus Lankwitz, which opened in 1907 as a private psychiatric clinic with twenty-five beds for the wealthy bourgeoisie. Lankwitz was part of the Private Heil- und Pflegeanstalt Berolinum in the south of Berlin, with more than 500 beds.[348] In Lankwitz, Juliusburger applied psychoanalytic insights to mentally ill people and alcoholics. He was the first doctor to give a talk about psychoanalysis to the Berlin Psychiatric Society.[349] Like Forel, Bleuler's predecessor in Zurich, Juliusburger was a leading figure in the temperance movement. He later became a good friend of Albert Einstein, whose nephew he treated in 1917.[350]

Heinrich Koerber (1861–1927) started out as a family doctor, but from 1905 onwards he worked as a psychotherapist in Berlin. His house was a meeting place for avant-garde artists, writers, and psychoanalysts. He mainly wrote articles about sexuality, and he gave a series of talks about psychoanalysis. He was chair of the Berlin branch of the Deutsche Monistenbund, established by Ernst Haeckel, and the only one of the four founding members of the Berlin Psychoanalytic Society who remained a member for many years.[351]

Moshe Wulff (1878–1971), who was born in Odessa and raised in Berlin, joined the group a little later. He started to read Freud's work in 1907 and soon became enthusiastic. After reading a report about a case of kleptomania in the bulletin of the Berlin Neuropsychiatric Association, which presented the phenomenon from a psychoanalytic perspective, he got in touch with the report's author, Juliusburger.[352] In 1908 he became Juliusburger's assistant and it seems he was trained in psychoanalysis by Abraham, although without being analysed by him. Wulff returned to live in Russia in 1911, and there he was an active supporter of psychoanalysis, but, in 1927, after the political climate became too dangerous, he returned to Berlin. In 1933, he fled to Palestine, as had Eitingon. He, Anna Smelianski, Ilja Schalit, and Walter Kluge, founded the Palestine Psychoanalytic Society in 1934.[353]

Abraham had gathered a group of medical men around him who, with the exception of Wulff, all occupied prominent places in their specific fields. None but Koerber and Wulff ever worked as psychoanalysts, but they all continued to look very favourably on psychoanalysis.

Abraham's practice slowly got off the ground in 1908 and he used his free time to write articles. On 8 March, he wrote to his friend Eitingon,

Dear Mr Eitingon,

Tonight I will drop the laudable plan to work in favour of the even more laudable one of at last replying to your letter. I am in the middle of working out the theme about which I wrote to you. Some fifty pages have been written but the most difficult part remains to be done. Freud agrees with the subject of *Dreams and Myths* and is glad to accept it for his series. Riklin will soon appear in print, then Jung, *The Content of Psychoses*, then Rank, *The Birth of Heroes*, i.e. the myths of the births of Moses, Cyrus, etc. My *opus* will therefore be volume 5. I hope to finish it in some weeks. Then I must prepare for Salzburg. Are you coming? I hope you are now more ready for your examination, so that you can soon play an active part in the Freud corps.[354] Nothing is doing here as far as Freud is concerned and I greatly miss the exchange of ideas.[355]

Abraham was working on a substantial treatise called *Dreams and Myths: A Study in Folk-Psychology*, which was published in book form in 1909.[356] The idea had come from Freud. Sadger, one of the earliest members of Freud's Wednesday Group, describes in his book *Sigmund Freud, persönliche Erinnerungen* how Freud was overwhelmed by ideas, which he passed on to his followers, extremely selectively, for them to develop further. [357] *Dreams and Myths* is a clear example of an idea of Freud's that was further developed by Abraham. It was the last time Abraham worked on one of Freud's ideas in this way. After *Dreams and Myths*, he developed ideas of his own, although there was often a close connection with Freud's.

Dreams and Myths had as its central theme the premise that all products of the human mind can be examined under a single heading, since they all spring from the human phantasy. They may sometimes be pathological disorders such as hysteria or obsessions, but they may equally well be poems, jokes or myths. The work connects with Freud's "Creative writers and day-dreaming".[358] According to Freud, a child organises the world in its game into an order that suits it, so that its wishes are fulfilled. Adults have ceased this overt game but they have not abandoned it. They phantasy instead. Adults build castles in the air and create day-dreams. Phantasying by adults is far harder to observe than the games played by children. Adults are ashamed of their phantasies and hide them from others, cherishing them like their most intimate possessions; in fact, they are more willing to admit to "misdeeds" than to share their phantasies. A person who is happy does not phantasy; phantasies are a correction to a dissatisfying reality. Unsatisfied wishes are the motive force behind them.

In *Dreams and Myths*, Abraham wrote that collective phantasies also exist, whether generated by large groups of people or by whole nations. Such wish-fulfilment dreams are expressed as fairytales and myths. Abraham worked out these ideas based on the story of Prometheus, who stole fire from the gods to give it to man. An interesting theme, but Abraham's treatment was academic and, therefore, a challenging read.

Freud praised the book in his letter of 7 June 1908, with the double-edged comment that he wanted to thank Abraham and to express his full appreciation because he was not certain whether he would get it from others.[359] He expressed very different thoughts about it to Jung, saying it was support for the theory that, however, lacked any creative spark.[360]

Abraham wrote a brief supplement to the book in 1911, in which he described how the body of the mother and sometimes also the desire to flee back into the mother's body in fearful situations is represented both in dreams and neuroses and in popular culture.[361] It often prompted thoughts of a lonely house in a garden where one felt one had been before, or of a hidden space with a narrow entrance. He made reference to the little-known local Russian religious sect of the mother cult, known as the opening-worshippers. They performed their religious rituals facing a hole in the wall of their house and the prayer went: "My house, my opening, deliver me!"

Meanwhile, Abraham was as productive as ever. On 21 August, he reported to Freud that he had written the reviews for the *Jahrbuch*. Immediately after the Salzburg Congress finished, a small group of attendees had come together to set up the *Jahrbuch für psychoanalytische und psychopathologische Forschungen*, edited by Freud and Bleuler and published by Jung. Freud and Jung had been writing to each other for months about the possibility of setting up a new journal. Present at its founding were Freud, Bleuler, Jung, Abraham, Brill, Ferenczi, and Jones.[362]

Freud had neither consulted the members of his Vienna Psychoanalytic Society nor invited them to the meeting, and they were deeply offended.[363] Abraham was asked to write reviews about the psychoanalytic works thus far published and he set about the task with great dedication. In the second issue of the *Jahrbuch* of 1909, two articles by him were published: "Freuds Schriften aus den Jahren 1893–1909" (Freud's writings of the years 1893–1909) and "Bericht über die österreichische und deutsche psychoanalytische Literatur bis zum Jahre 1909" (Report on Austrian and German psychoanalytic literature up to the year 1909).[364]

Abraham had by this point also written an article about the relationship between sexuality and alcoholism for Hirschfeld's *Zeitschrift für Sexualwissenschaft*.[365] In it, he described how urges in early childhood that are in due course repressed and sublimated suddenly reappear during drunkenness, when resistance falls away. The first example he gave was homosexuality. Drunken men throw their arms around each other in a bar, whereas when sober they keep their distance. His second example was sadism, which can easily emerge during drinking sprees, and his third was exhibitionism. He described how the small child knows no shame and does not yet repress his or her exhibitionist and voyeuristic tendencies. (He claims that in cases where the child does not learn to repress them, a perversion arises.) If an adult drinks alcohol, resistance disappears, as can be seen, above all, in the obscene jokes that are made. Freud studied this obscene wit in his *Jokes and their Relation to the Unconscious* and came to the conclusion that its purpose was "exposure".[366]

Bleuler reacted enthusiastically to Abraham's article in a letter dated 29 August 1908.[367] Bleuler was extremely interested in alcoholism—in the Burghölzli Clinic alcohol was taboo— but he wrote that, like Freud, Abraham generalised too much. Abraham had written that when sublimation is absent or falls away, sadism or masochism arise in place of their sublimated forms: pity and repugnance. Bleuler was not convinced that all sympathy was necessarily sublimated sexuality. At the time, he was unreservedly enthusiastic about Freud's *Interpretation of Dreams* but rather less impressed by *Three Essays on the Theory of Sexuality*.[368] He felt it was too much of a generalisation to trace all psychiatric problems back to early childhood sexuality.

Bleuler, a missed opportunity

The letter from Bleuler to Abraham, and its favourable yet critical tone, is remarkable in another sense as well. On 29 September 1908, exactly four weeks after it was written, Freud wrote to Abraham: "It will come to nothing with Bl., his breaking away is imminent, the relations between Bl. and J. are strained to breaking-point. Jung is giving up his position as assistant but remains head of the laboratory and will work completely independently of Bl".[369]

Freud wrote this after spending several days with Jung in Zurich without visiting Bleuler. The information that Bleuler was on the point of breaking away probably came entirely from Jung. Based on Bleuler's letter to Abraham, it seems quite likely that Jung had transformed his own serious problems with Bleuler into Bleuler's problems with psychoanalysis. Bleuler did not break away, but he was very critical. A letter from Abraham to Freud dated 18 October 1910, two years later, suggests Bleuler was far less dismissive of psychoanalysis than Jung had led Freud to believe:

Now I must tell you about Bleuler, who spent hours with me in order to abreact. You are familiar enough with his complexes. Naturally, he justifies his staying away from the Society with various scruples, for which he does not find the real motives, even with a great deal of help. All the
same, I have a number of things to say in his favour and should like to ask you, dear Professor,
whether it would not be appropriate now to meet him half-way, in order to make good certain
mistakes and to serve our cause. I have talked much psychoanalysis with B., and I must say that
he is taking a keen interest in the cause. During the congresses he had many discussions with
Kraepelin, Aschaffenburg, and others, and they all considered him, as I personally heard, a really
convinced partisan.[370] I believe his service to our cause in this respect more than outweighs the
occasional harm he may have done to it by being too reserved. And, finally, the main point: both
before and at the time of the founding of the Zurich group, Bl. was very obviously grossly
insulted. You know that I am quite critical of Bl., but if one makes it a principle in Ψα not to insult
the complexes, why should one behave differently towards Bl., of all people? Bl. *wants a rapproche-
ment*. He is at odds with himself and suffers from it. Should not there be a way to come to an
understanding?[371]

Bleuler had no wish to become a member of the IPA, but he was extremely interested in
psychoanalysis. He thought it an important movement, although he did not see it as a theory
that explained everything and made all other theories obsolete. He was too much of a scientist
for that. Psychoanalysts tended to explain this as resistance on the part of Bleuler, arising from
his complexes. Abraham thought the same way; at the start of the letter quoted above he was
rather disparaging about Bleuler, but he also spoke up for him and tried to persuade Freud to
be reconciled with him. He was convinced of Bleuler's great importance and regarded the
differences of opinion as a secondary matter. Bleuler believed that in setting up a scientific association it was crucial not to make scientific debate impossible, but instead to welcome it. He felt
that was missing at the IPA. In a letter to Freud of 13 October 1910 Bleuler put it like this:

I understand perfectly well that the Association was founded . . . But it is the sound that makes
the music. The statutes are of an exclusivity that does not correspond with my character. That I
am not mistaken was confirmed to me verbally by Jung; yes, with his explanations he has gone
far further than I expected. One wants to remain secluded . . . But if one wants a scientific association that goes further than merely exchanging experiences between members and discusses those
opinions, if one wants therefore to have a scientific discussion, and if one wants to present oneself
to the public as a scientific association, one cannot make dissent impossible beforehand; on the
contrary, one should welcome it.[372]

Here, Bleuler touches the Achilles' heel of psychoanalysis. If an academic field is to be truly
scientific, it must enter into discussion not just with those of like mind but with critical out-
siders. Why psychoanalysts are, as often as not, fearful of doing so is an important question.
Abraham, incidentally, was a psychoanalyst who did venture into debate. That others dismissed Bleuler's opinion as opposition, of course, reflects very poorly on them.

In this period, Jung caused a great deal of harm. He insulted Bleuler profoundly on a
number of occasions and in the end Bleuler permanently withdrew from the Zurich Psychoanalytic Society as a result. On 27 November 1911, Bleuler explained to Freud exactly what
brought him to that point. He had invited his assistant, Dr Hans-Wolfgang Maier, to a meeting

of the Zurich Psychoanalytic Society, but Jung forbade the guest to attend because he was not a member. He gave Maier a choice: become a member or stay away.[373] This shows that any debate with those who thought differently was avoided, as Bleuler had earlier pointed out. By this refusal, Jung was also insulting his former boss. Bleuler was particularly put out that Jung had made a decision that ought to have been put to the group as a whole, and furthermore had communicated it directly to Maier. Bleuler regarded that as a violation of the rules of the Society and felt that the fact he had not been consulted was outrageous. Hans-Wolfgang Maier succeeded Bleuler as director of the Burghölzli Clinic in 1927 and remained in that position until 1941.

Bleuler's departure from the Zurich group and his refusal to become a member of the IPA was a huge loss. He was respected and valued by his European colleagues and highly regarded in the academic world. Prominent colleagues such as Emil Kraepelin and Gustav Aschaffenburg regarded him as a supporter of psychoanalysis. In losing Bleuler, psychoanalysis lost its connection with the university.

Psychoanalysis within the family, and its supporters and opponents

In a lecture she gave in 1970 on the occasion of the fiftieth anniversary of the founding of the Psychoanalytic Institute in Berlin, Hilda Abraham said that in the early years in Berlin, psychoanalysis was almost a family affair.[374] At meetings of the early Berlin Psychoanalytic Society, which met every three weeks at Karl Abraham's house, Hedwig was always present. One evening, at the home of Hugo Karl Liepmann, Abraham's former boss in the Dalldorf clinic, a lively debate about Freud arose in which Abraham defended the theory of wish fulfilment in dementia praecox in one room, while Hedwig did the same for the theory of repression in a neighbouring room. As material on which to practise, Abraham sent accounts of both his own dreams and Hedwig's to Freud.

On 9 November 1908, Abraham took the step of giving a lecture on psychoanalysis to the Berlin Society for Psychiatry and Neurology with the title "The significance of intermarriage between close relatives in the psychology of the neuroses".[375] In a letter to Freud of 10 November 1908, Abraham described it as a successful evening.[376] Admittedly, Abraham was vehemently attacked, especially by Ziehen, but a lively discussion arose during which Oppenheim was extremely sympathetic, Liepmann spoke up for Abraham, while several other colleagues expressed intense interest after it was over.[377] Given the general hostility towards psychoanalysis, this was better than had been expected. The exchange of letters between Freud and Abraham was frequent in this period and extremely cordial, except when they were writing about Jung.[378]

Meanwhile, psychoanalysis was starting to come into vogue in Berlin. In Charlottenburg, in those days an independent town to the west of Berlin, a group of Freudians had emerged in the autumn of 1908. One of Abraham's first patients, a philologist who taught at a school in Charlottenburg, was extremely grateful to Abraham for the treatment he had received and he developed a good understanding of psychoanalysis. Prompted by an incident involving a number of pupils, he gave his headmaster Freud's writings. The headmaster read them thoroughly and then demanded that the school doctor familiarise himself immediately with Freud's theory about sex, even examining him on the subject. The headmaster expected the same of the teachers. Abraham described all this in a letter to Freud of 18 December 1908, and added that any of the teachers who did not know Freud's work were now regarded as old-fashioned, and naturally that was an impression none of them wanted to give.[379]

In that same letter, Abraham complains to Freud that Jung informed him only after the first *Jahrbuch* had gone to press that the reviews to which Abraham had devoted so much time, and that had been ready by the summer, were to be held over for the following issue. Abraham believed that Jung had inserted an article of his own at the last moment in place of the reviews. There was indeed an article by Jung in the first *Jahrbuch*, about the significance of fathers. It was made up of four case histories and there was no psychoanalysis in it at all, apart from the fact that the term was mentioned a couple of times.

Freud reacted like a viper stung, accusing Abraham of having a "persecution complex".[380] Jung had taken an editorial decision; Freud had deliberately refrained from influencing the contents of the *Jahrbuch* and he felt Abraham should do the same. Freud was, of course, correct in saying that Jung was ultimately responsible and had the right to do this, but it was nevertheless a remarkable move on Jung's part. Abraham had been specifically asked to review all the psychoanalytic literature written in the German language up to that point and had done so in two lengthy articles, which were not so much reviews as concise recapitulations. His overview seemed particularly suitable for a first issue of the journal.[381] Abraham did not respond for some time to the angry letter from Freud—so long, in fact, that, on 10 January 1909, Freud wrote,

> Dear Colleague,
>
> I told you not long ago that I owed you some amends.[382] I remember this as I write to you today, though your long silence points to your feeling seriously offended by the criticism in my last letter. You know that that criticism is consistent with the friendliest feelings towards you or, rather, derives from those feelings, because it was from my liking for you that I assumed the right to draw your attention to a wrong emotional turning along which I saw you making your way. Permit me to hope that you are not capable of taking frankness amiss for long, and show this soon.[383]

Abraham replied immediately that he had not been offended in any way.[384] He had visited his parents over Christmas, contracted influenza afterwards and then, for the first time, found himself with a great many patients to see.

Was it true that he did not feel offended? Jones writes that Abraham sometimes failed to notice when another person was extremely angry.[385] But perhaps Abraham was simply being sensible. He had based his entire existence, including his income, on Freud. His practice was just starting to get off the ground. He could not afford any trouble.

Abraham was satisfied with his first year. The point at which he could actually live from his practice seemed closer than he had anticipated. In early 1909, his expenses still exceeded the amount coming in, but the number of patients was growing. He was, however, still carrying out very little psychoanalysis. Hirschfeld helped him enormously by referring patients to him for expert testimony for the courts and for other bodies, which brought Abraham much-needed income. A number of such documents are held at the Karl Abraham Institute in Berlin. They make interesting reading because of Abraham's cautious and respectful assessments. In the middle of one of the handwritten reports are a number of blue pages with scribbles, as if five-year-old Hilda was trying to trace out letters while her father was writing.

Throughout 1909, Abraham's practice continued to grow. In May, he reported to Freud that his day was filled with ongoing treatments.[386] He had nine patients in his diary for the following morning alone, six of whom would be coming for psychoanalysis. From that moment on, Abraham's practice would always be oversubscribed, with the exception of the war years.

Meanwhile, Freud had accepted an invitation to give a series of lectures at Clark University in Worcester, Massachusetts, in September.[387] The trip was discussed several times in their correspondence. Freud would leave at the end of August and visit Abraham on his way back from America. Yet, Freud did not once mention that Jung would be going with him. Only on 11 July, almost in passing, did he say that he would be travelling with Ferenczi to meet the boat and did not yet know where they would be meeting up with Jung who, as Abraham knew, had also been invited.[388] Abraham answered that he had had no idea Jung had been invited as well.[389] Clearly, Jung was still an extremely touchy subject that Freud preferred to avoid.

Freud did indeed visit Abraham on his way home in September 1909. He stayed for dinner and Abraham travelled with him for some hours in the train bound for Vienna so that they could continue talking.[390]

On 7 April 1909, Abraham wrote the following remarkable passage in a letter to Freud,

> I have tracked down a symptomatic action in myself. While I am analysing and am waiting for the patient's reply, I often cast a quick glance at the picture of my parents. I know now that I always do this when I am following up the infantile transference in the patient. The glance is always accompanied by a particular guilt feeling: what will they think of me? This has of course to do with my separation from them, which was not too easy. Since explaining this symptomatic action to myself, I have not caught myself at it any more.[391]

Abraham's understanding of transference at that point was as follows:

> Transference: The patient transfers his repressed desires – whether love or hate – onto the doctor, in whom he confides. For the doctor it is an important task to explain to the patient the essence of what is happening, to trace the transference back to its source just like any other symptom of illness.[392]

It is, of course, remarkable that Abraham regarded transference as a symptom of which patients needed to be helped to rid themselves. But here he is writing about his own countertransference. With his patients, he went in search of the sources of transference, which lay in sexual desires in early childhood in relation to the child's parents. We do not know, incidentally, how Abraham went about psychoanalysing his patients. He had never undergone analysis himself, and neither had he trained as a psychoanalyst. Did he enter into a search along with his patients, or did he explain to them the significance of what they told him? His assertive way of writing suggests that the latter is more than possible.

The question is: what were Abraham's guilt feelings with regard to his parents about? He was no thankless son. He visited his parents regularly and wrote to them every week. He had a close bond with his mother and a tendency to worry about her. That will not have made moving away from her any easier, but the relationship with his father might have been of great importance as well.

In a lecture in 1970 titled "Die Anfänge von Karl Abraham's wissenschaftlicher Arbeit in Berlin" (The start of Karl Abraham's scientific work in Berlin), Hilda Abraham spoke about "Amenhotep IV", a long treatise by Abraham that is examined further in Chapter Ten.[393] Amenhotep IV (ca 1351–1334 BC), an Egyptian pharaoh of the eighteenth dynasty, made a radical break with his father's faith and established his own monotheistic religion.[394] Hilda thought it was Abraham's special interest in the father–son relationship that had led him to write about Akhenaten, as Amenhotep chose to call himself. Oddly, she does not mention the similarities between Abraham and Akhenaten, as a son who broke with his father's religion and put another religion in its place. When Abraham analysed his patients, he looked at the portrait of his mother and father and felt guilty. He had dispensed with the faith of his deeply religious father and put another (psychoanalysis) in its place, with Freud as a substitute father.

The Berlin Psychoanalytic Society met only occasionally in the first half of 1909. Hirschfeld was away travelling a great deal. Juliusburger was troubled by panic attacks and entered into analysis with Abraham for that reason. He, too, was then away travelling for a period.[395] He was sorely missed when Abraham gave his second talk to the Berlin Neurological Association on 8 November 1909, speaking to a room full of contemptuous faces before being angrily attacked by Ziehen, who called the talk a "hotchpotch" and, as chair, prevented any debate from taking place.[396] Abraham attributed the hostile reception to resistance among the audience, which was, after all, made up of extremely sceptical doctors. But Ziehen was not entirely wrong: Abraham's talk was indeed a hotchpotch.

His lecture, "Hysterical dream states", was about dream states that patients found themselves in during the day, when they were awake.[397] Abraham based his talk and his later article on the same subject on an article by Leopold Löwenfeld in the *Centralblatt für Nervenheilkunde und Psychiatrie*, which included the following passage about how patients experienced such states: "The outside world no longer makes an ordinary impression. That which is known and seen daily seems changed, as if unknown, new, peculiar. Or the entire environment gives the impression of being a product of phantasy, a sham, a vision".[398]

The condition described here by Löwenfeld is nowadays called depersonalisation, or dissociation, a state in which patients have lost all sense of contact with their surroundings and everything, no matter how regularly encountered in the past, seems strange and, therefore, extremely frightening. Abraham tried to find a psychoanalytic explanation for this phenomenon and to trace it back to a repressed desire to masturbate.[399]

The problem with the article lies in its confused perspective on the state of such patients' mental health. Abraham always worked from case histories and stuck to them as closely as possible. He writes about what he experienced with his patients. To his article about dream states, he added six case histories and, in doing so, he lumped together depersonalised patients who had lost all sense of contact with their surroundings and experienced everything as strange with patients who continually fantasised and daydreamed, a quite different problem.

Eitingon comes to Berlin

In November 1909, Eitingon settled in Berlin. This greatly pleased Abraham, who had been feeling very isolated and longed for a kindred spirit who was as powerfully engaged as he was.[400] He wrote to Freud that he felt far less lonely now that he was regularly meeting up with the "Peripatetics" Karpas, Eitingon, and others. The old habit of walking together to debate matters was still extant.[401]

Eitingon had been planning to stay for one year, but he ended up living in Berlin for twenty-four years. After gaining his doctorate in Zurich, he first spent six weeks in Vienna, where he was psychoanalysed by Freud during evening walks. He attended several meetings of the Wednesday Society and read a paper at Freud's seminar at the university. In Berlin, Eitingon wanted to specialise in neurology at Oppenheim's clinic.[402] In the early years of his stay in Berlin, Eitingon and Abraham kept in close touch. Eitingon was a welcome and regularly guest at the Abraham family home.[403]

Hilda writes that, to her parents' great regret, this began to change in 1912. Eitingon was married that year, to a Russian actress who was not the least bit interested in his professional activities and avoided contact with his colleagues, making an exception only in the case of the Freud family, a number of Russian colleagues, and Lou Andreas-Salomé, who was also of Russian extraction. Eitingon was extremely wealthy and had a large and luxurious house in Berlin where members of the Freud family regularly came to stay.

1910, the Berlin Psychoanalytic Society

Meanwhile, Abraham was steadily working at promoting psychoanalysis in Berlin. In January and February 1910, he gave a course in psychoanalysis for doctors. In response to demand, he immediately gave a second course in March. The participants were enthusiastic and Abraham derived a great deal of pleasure from teaching them.[404]

Freud exchanged regular letters with many acquaintances, including Ferenczi, Jung, Abraham, Binswanger, and Bleuler. Since most of this correspondence has been published, it is possible to make comparisons. The differences are striking. In the correspondence, Jung's quickness to take offence was an important theme. He required flattery at regular intervals and had to be won over to the cause. Freud's correspondence with Abraham was usually cheerful, friendly, and between relative equals, that between Freud and Ferenczi far more personal in nature than with the others; in fact, it might be described as psychoanalysis on paper. On 1 January 1910, for example, Freud wrote to Ferenczi that Binswanger wanted to visit in January or February and he asked Ferenczi whether he would like to come at the same time or on a separate occasion.[405] In his reply, Ferenczi kept getting Binswanger mixed up with Abraham. He became aware of this himself and wrote,

> all of a sudden I notice that up to now I have always been reading Abraham instead of Binswanger—or maybe I read Binswanger, but certainly I have been thinking Abraham! That tiresome brother complex is still playing tricks on me. I was evidently afraid that Abraham would be the guest; he is the more significant one (perhaps the most significant after Jung); it is evidently

my secret wish to be able to measure myself against him; not to be capable of it—the motive of anxiety and antipathy![406]

Ferenczi felt embarrassed by his mistake and wrote to Freud that there was a lot of work left for him to do (including a lot of self-analysis).

Abraham and Freud both travelled a little ahead of time to the psychoanalytic congress in Nuremberg (30–31 March 1910) so they could meet up before it started. Abraham gave a talk on fetishism. Bleuler was unable to come because he was suffering from appendicitis. He used his time in bed to reread Freud's *Three Essays on the Theory of Sexuality*, which he praised fulsomely in a letter to Freud.[407]

This second psychoanalytic congress was a good deal less harmonious than the first, in Salzburg, had been.[408] Ferenczi gave a talk that included a proposal to set up an International Psychoanalytic Association (IPA). It was established there and then, and the IPA became the umbrella organisation for all the local psychoanalytic societies. Ferenczi proposed appointing Jung as the IPA's president for life with Riklin, who came from Zurich and was a blood relative of Jung, as its secretary. This meant the centre of psychoanalysis would move from Vienna to Zurich, and in that sense Ferenczi had taken yet another swipe at the Viennese.[409] He also proposed that all articles should be shown to Jung before publication. The IPA was Ferenczi's idea, while the move to Zurich was Freud's. The Viennese felt greatly deprived and resisted strongly. It took Freud a huge amount of effort to calm the waters. At the congress, Jung's term as chairman was reduced to two years and peace was restored in Vienna with the appointment of Adler as president of the Vienna Psychoanalytic Society and Adler and Stekel as editors of a new journal, the *Zentralblatt für Psychoanalyse*.[410]

Abraham was not involved in any of this. He was full of enthusiasm about the congress. On the way home in the train, he, Koerber, and Eitingon spoke about nothing else.[411]

The Berlin Psychoanalytic Society became the first subsidiary of the new IPA, with Abraham in the chair and nine members: Eitingon, Hirschfeld, Juliusburger, Koerber, Marcinovski, Simon, Stegmann, Stohmayer, and Warda.[412] Bloch was no longer among them and, in late 1909, Wulff had returned to Odessa after encountering difficulties at work because of his interest in psychoanalysis.[413]

In a letter to Freud dated 28 April 1910, Abraham mentions the arrival of three new analysands. They were very probably Karen Horney, who also sent her friend Ida Behrmann to Abraham, and a friend of Horney's husband, Oscar, called Carl Müller-Braunschweig.[414] Karen Horney was the first in a long line of Abraham's patients who later became famous in the field.

Karen Horney

Karen Horney (1885–1952), née Danielsen, was the youngest daughter of the second marriage of an authoritarian, devout ship's captain to the daughter of a famous Bremen architect. She had an older brother, Berndt, whom she admired greatly, and four half-brothers and half-sisters from her father's earlier marriage. Her parents divorced in 1904. Horney went to Freiburg in 1906 to study medicine, in a period when women had only recently been admitted for the first time.[415] After Freiburg, she continued her studies in Göttingen and Berlin, graduating in 1913 and gaining her doctorate in 1915 with Karl Bonhoeffer as her supervisor. In that year, she also became secretary to the Berlin Psychoanalytic Society.[416] In 1909, she married Oscar Horney. Their eldest daughter was born in 1911, the second in 1913, and the third in 1916. Horney entered into psychoanalysis with Karl Abraham in 1910 and it seems clear from the way his practice developed that she must have been one of the earliest to do so.[417]

It is not clear how Horney came to Abraham. She had worked as an assistant to Oppenheim for a year and it may have been while she was there that she became aware of Abraham. Or her *avant-garde* friends may have pointed her in the direction of psychoanalysis, which was increasingly in vogue in such circles.[418] Her problems were serious and they had crippled her especially since her marriage. She was deeply depressed, which made her tired and listless. She had difficulty concentrating and from time to time considered suicide. She had become almost unable to work.

From the moment Horney began psychoanalysis with Abraham, it shaped her entire life. She was still training to be a doctor and she was careful not to reveal her positive attitude towards psychoanalysis at the university because of the great hostility towards psychoanalysis at the medical faculty. Horney's dissertation—*Ein kasuistischer Beitrag zur Frage der traumatischen Psychosen* [A Casuistic Contribution to the Question of Traumatic Psychoses]—contains no reference at all to psychoanalysis, even in the bibliography.[419]

Horney kept a diary for a while, including the period when she was in analysis with Karl Abraham. It gives an impression of how she experienced analysis and of how Abraham operated.[420] She came to him six times a week, as was usual in those days, beginning in April 1910 and continuing until the summer. It is not clear exactly when her psychoanalysis ended, but it might have been when Abraham went away on his summer holiday. Until that time, Abraham had done little psychoanalysis, but that was soon to change. He was inexperienced, and the profession itself was still in its infancy. He had to draw all his knowledge from the limited number of books and journals that had been published on the subject. Hardly anything had been written as yet about the actual technique.[421]

Horney's analysis was remarkably short, especially in view of the fact that her problems gave grounds for a long treatment. It is not clear from her diaries on whose initiative her sessions stopped. Abraham seemed to assume at this stage that psychoanalysis ought not to take more than a few months: first find out what is wrong and then deal with the resistance.

On 18 April 1910, Horney wrote that Dr A, as she referred to him in her diary, had offered many possible explanations for her fatigue.[422] She seems to have talked non-stop in the first few weeks and Abraham responded with many different interpretations. Then a point was reached when Horney was unable to come up with very much more and Abraham said they must now wait, because there was too much resistance. Horney wondered in her diary what might happen next; she was unable to imagine what else Abraham could have to say. So Abraham's role was very much that of a doctor who explains what is wrong.

Abraham attributed Horney's apathy and fatigue to masturbation, which he believed caused lassitude after the initial arousal. Horney, however, wrote in her diary that masturbation was not a particularly important part of her life. She had done it a lot as a child, and still did occasionally, but its place had been taken by telling stories to herself, by fantasising and the accompanying excitement. Now she tried to stop fantasising, which suggests Abraham advised her to do so. On 19 April, she wrote something remarkable. She had asked Abraham what he thought was yet to be discovered, and Abraham told her that was precisely the question people asked when there was resistance. The resistance might yet increase, he said, before it could finally be broken.

It was another four years before Freud published "Remembering, repeating and working-through".[423] That "working through" was lacking in Horney's treatment. Her analysis actually seemed to start out very well. Much was discussed, including her prostitution fantasies and her desire for a forceful man. Her difficult relationship with her mother and the sexual problems she was experiencing with her husband were talked of as well, and Horney wrote that coitus was a poor substitute for masturbation, which allowed her to fantasise about all the things she desired.[424] There was a powerful transference, as Horney recognised. She even wrote some-where that Abraham had taken the place of her husband, Oscar. She also recognised the nega-tive transference, which was her aversion to Abraham. At the same time, she had a strong desire to be his most extraordinary patient. She fantasised that he wrote about her as a special case. Horney's condition improved rapidly during analysis and it seems that discussing her repressed negative feelings towards her mother, Oscar, and her baby (by this point she was pregnant) made a significant contribution to this. Horney's mother had effaced herself, the victim of a brutal husband, and she had a demanding and coercive character. After she married, Horney arranged for her mother to move to Berlin, where she lived close by. In discussing all this, Horney became able to see her mother rather more as she actually was, and she also started to notice the similarities between the two of them. They both needed to be at the centre of attention at all times. Her sexual relationship with Oscar improved and she became slightly more positive about the baby. She wrote in her diary that she was less tired and had more self-confidence. Oddly, Abraham's interpretations do not seem to have had much to do with all this. He believed her depression and sense fatigue were the results of early masturbation, which created feelings of emptiness and exhaustion when it was over. It was a view that did not con-vince Horney in the slightest.[425]

When Horney felt a little better and sexual relations with Oscar had been restored—their first baby was born nine months later, truly an analysis baby—the psychoanalysis ended. But in early 1911, Horney's symptoms returned with a vengeance. Her mother died suddenly in February that year. Abraham seems not to have regarded life events of this kind as influential. Horney's father had died in 1910 and she became deeply depressed. Then, when her mother died in 1911, she had a serious relapse. She was continually fatigued. She slept for ten hours a night and another three in the afternoons. Abraham was still central to her thoughts and she continually wondered whether to go back to him but did not. When her daughter was born, Abraham announced he would come to visit and every time someone arrived she thought it might be him.

Central to that "working through" that had yet to be introduced is the notion that new insights never fall into place immediately but have to be discussed, examined, and worked on again and again. Resistance recurs repeatedly and has to be tackled afresh each time. It is a long process that demands a great deal of patience and determination from both analyst and ana-lysand. In 1910, Abraham obviously assumed that an insight and the tackling of the resistance that went along with it were sufficient. The term "crack" that Horney uses indicates that the whole process was seen both as a single event and as something quite heavy-handed. We should note, however, that it is not clear where the term "crack" came from. It may have originated purely with Horney, and her desire for rough men.[426]

Horney was unfaithful to Oscar quite early on in their marriage, as he was to her. They had agreed to leave each other free, which was not unusual in the *avant-garde* circles of Berlin in which they moved. Horney's hunger for men took quite extreme forms until she was of advanced years, however, and she conquered one man after another before dropping them no less abruptly.[427] She even quite regularly chose trainee psychoanalysts for the purpose. Susan Quinn, her biographer, mentions a suspicion that she emigrated to America in 1932 partly because her reputation had been damaged by her promiscuous behaviour.

Abraham interpreted her need to conquer men as originating in early childhood and with her love for her brutal father. She was always in search of brutal men to whom she could then submit. That may have been part of the explanation, but Quinn mentions something more important.[428] Horney's loved and feared father was a ship's captain and away a great deal. Therefore, he left her time and again. All her life Horney was affectionate towards men only to leave them shortly afterwards. If you are the one to leave, then they cannot leave you.

Intriguingly, Horney did the same with Abraham. Her diaries and her later life show that his analysis helped her a great deal. She went on to be extremely active and productive, yet she treated Abraham the way she treated her lovers. While he was her psychoanalyst, he was the focal point of her life. After their sessions ended, she said she had gained nothing from them. The success of the treatment seems to have had more to do with Abraham's alertness to the aggression and willingness to discuss it than with his interpretations concerning early childhood sexuality. The crucial theme of separation anxiety was not addressed.[429] Despite this, Abraham seems to have suspected it to some extent when he explained a relapse as Horney's need to hold his attention. Horney was in analysis for too short a time to allow for the working through of her separation anxiety. On several occasions she considered going back, but in the end she believed she ought to analyse herself. Her narcissism led her to take that route rather than putting herself in the hands of someone else.

CHAPTER EIGHT

Segantini and depression

The birth of Gerd

In August 1910, Hedwig gave birth to a son, Gerd, and everything went far more easily than it had the first time. Labour was quick and problem-free, Hedwig found she was able to breastfeed, she was in Berlin among her family and friends, and Abraham's practice was going well. Their future seemed assured and she was delighted by the fact that she now had a son.

Anja Amsel, the daughter of Hedwig's brother Hans, described what the atmosphere was like in England, where Hedwig lived with Hilda in later years, whenever Gerd (there known as Grant) came to visit.[430] It was as if he descended from Mount Olympus; from the moment he walked in, everything revolved around him. Hilda mentions that Abraham must have looked with pleasure and some nostalgia at how the bond between mother and son developed, but she says nothing about her own reaction.[431] She does describe how caring Abraham was towards her. Hilda saw little of her father. He worked until eight in the evening and often went to meetings when he had finished, but after Gerd was born he introduced a new ritual. After lunch he would pick up four-year-old Hilda and take her with him to his study, where she was otherwise not allowed. There he would put her down on the carpet, in the middle of the room, to play with his chess or draughts pieces. Abraham would then sleep for a short while. Hilda kept very quiet until he woke up and came to sit on the floor and play with her.[432]

They had, meanwhile, moved to a larger house at number 24 Rankestraße. Abraham had arranged the move while Hedwig was in hospital recovering after childbirth. She was disappointed not to have been actively involved. It seems that Abraham set about organising the move without taking very much account of her wishes. The new apartment was spacious. Abraham's consulting room, waiting room, and sitting room were at the front, well separated from the rooms at the back, so the children could move around freely without disturbing their father's work.[433]

Abraham's practice was going well, but the small group of psychoanalysts in Berlin still faced an unfavourable climate. They were isolated. At the neurological congress in late 1910, there was an official call for a boycott of psychoanalysis and the naming of doctors who engaged in it. Abraham spoke of "la Mafia Neurologica" in Berlin who saved him the trip to Sicily.[434] In this period, he focused firmly on writing.

Segantini

It was now that Abraham wrote *Segantini*, a treatise with two main themes.[435] They were the early relationship between mother and child with all the ambivalences that accompany it and, in the same connection, depression. The choice of themes made it unique for its time. Until then, the relationship with the father had been to the fore in psychoanalysis, and although Freud had on several occasions attempted to develop a psychoanalytic theory about depression, nothing had yet come of it.[436] Writing *Segantini* cost Abraham a good deal of effort and he took an unusually long time by his standards. He first wrote to Freud about it on 14 February 1909 and he sent it to be assessed by him a full two years later, on 11 February 1911.[437] Freud was full of praise: "Your Segantini is fine and beautiful, it goes deep without causing offence, and is probably also discreet".[438] It made him think of Leonardo da Vinci.[439] Segantini was published in 1911 as a monograph in the series *Schriften zur angewandten Seelenkunde*. In 1924, Abraham added a new final paragraph.

The painter Giovanni Segantini (1858–1899) was born in Arco near Lake Garda, which was then part of the Austro-Hungarian Empire. He was famous in the late nineteenth century but rather faded from view in the twentieth.[440] Abraham wrote that Segantini's older brother died when Segantini was six months old, followed by his mother when he was five.[441] His mother had never properly recovered from Segantini's birth, eventually becoming bedridden. After his mother's death, he was sent to live with a stepsister who treated him so badly that he ran away. Abraham writes that the father had left for the USA, but in reality he was a poor tradesman who came and went.[442] Abraham based his account on the 1907 biography by Franz Servaes and on Segantini's autobiography, which later turned out to have been partly invented.[443] Segantini found himself in a reformatory. He eventually became a painter but would suffer from periods of severe depression all his life. He died at the age of forty-one after climbing a mountain in the snow despite being ill. Remarkably, he died of the same illness, peritonitis, that killed Abraham, also well before his time.[444]

Abraham's aim was to apply psychoanalysis to Segantini in an effort to understand him. He was careful to point out the difference between this and psychoanalytic treatment, in which the doctor commits to working with the patient. As the treatment goes on, the doctor gains more insight into the unconscious and waits until the gaps in the material are filled by whatever comes into the patient's head. With a painter who is already dead, that is not possible. There would, therefore, be more gaps in the analysis.

What Abraham then went on to describe was remarkable for its time. He wondered whether Segantini, as a result of having been deprived of a mother at such an early age, had become the painter of motherly love, but he came to the conclusion that it was more complicated than that. Segantini painted many loving mothers with their babies, but he also painted horrifying mothers with babies. This was not a matter of Abraham recognising the far-reaching impact of the early loss of a mother. He thought that Segantini was an exception and that most children who had to deal with such a loss—not uncommon in the early years of the twentieth century—soon got over it. He believed that neurosis was created by overly strong passions and desires, and in this case by powerfully incestuous desires on Segantini's part towards his mother. On 14 February 1909, he wrote to Freud about Segantini: "It is astounding how great a role is played here by the sublimation of component instincts, the repression of incestuous phantasies, the transference onto non-human objects, etc".[445] Abraham claimed that in his autobiography Segantini wrote about his mother not as a loving carer, but as if she were a lost lover who, in his imagination, as an ideal image, occupied an increasingly important place as the years went by. In the words of the adult, echoes could be heard of the eroticism of the child. This was a child focused on the unlimited possession of the love-object. Its feelings of love were combined, however, with an aggressive, even cruel side. Abraham went on to say that the extreme, colliding feelings of love and hate, which gave rise to fierce emotional conflicts, are characteristic of people who later suffer from obsessional neurosis. The libido cannot develop in a normal way because the conflicting emotions keep obstructing each other. Abraham referred to Freud's rat man and developed ideas about feelings of hatred that were completely new.[446] In *Segantini*, he sees them as a counterpart to oedipal love, but after a while he began to locate them much earlier. In the year the book was published he wrote:

> The thought of having caused the death of a beloved person is encountered very frequently in neurotics. As already mentioned, the childhood libido of a neurotic is characterised by strong feelings of hatred. These express themselves in phantasies of the death of the loved person or, if the latter really dies, in feelings of satisfaction, even of cruel pleasure. Later, when repression gains in power, guilt-feelings arise against which the neurotic is powerless to defend himself, although in his conscious mind he finds no grounds for such self-reproaches. He accuses himself of responsibility for the death of his father or mother, although in fact his childhood crime consisted in no more than forbidden phantasies and feelings. These self-reproaches are followed by attempts at making reparation for such crimes, which take an exaggerated form in obsessional neurotics. The memory of the loved person is cherished with excessive fervour and becomes sanctified. Alternatively an attempt may be made to repress the fact of the death into the unconscious, and in phantasy to resurrect the dead one.[447]

One striking aspect of Segantini's paintings is the contrast between the loving mothers, cradling their babies in their laps, and the bad mothers, who float through the air over a dead landscape, sinister as ghosts, trailing their half-starved babies. Abraham felt that in both cases feelings of hatred were being expressed. The mother who is at first loved disillusions her child by turning away. The holy loving mother is a transformation of feelings of hatred, while in the bad mother, feelings of hatred break through.

All these paintings depict mothers with babies. Not one of them shows a mother with a five-year-old son. The perspective is therefore not oedipal but pre-oedipal. The intensity of the hatred felt is also archaic and more pre-oedipal than oedipal.

In the additional chapter that Abraham wrote in 1925, he looked in greater depth at how depression arises. He believed that a bout of depression was connected to an event with which a person in their mental state at the time was not able to cope. That event was a loss that caused a profound inner shock and was experienced as unbearable. It was always the loss of someone who was at the centre of the person's life. Loss did not necessarily mean death, but an intense relationship with another person was suddenly destroyed, for example by a disappointment that could never be set right. The feeling of total abandonment that resulted would then trigger depression. A disappointment of such magnitude could only happen in early childhood with regard to the mother and it would cause a desire for revenge that was hard to control. Hidden deep beneath that vengefulness was a nostalgia for the original mother, for the earliest sense of satisfaction at the mother's breast.[448]

Abraham's treatise on Segantini is sixty pages long. The writing is extremely compact, containing a great wealth of facts and ideas. It is not an easy read; it demands study on the part of the reader. No wonder, then, that it took a long time to write and the level of difficulty might help to explain why articles that were published about *Segantini* concentrated on autobiographical elements. One exception is a 1997 article by Ulrike May-Tolzmann, which has a succinctness and a wealth of information that almost match Abraham's own. She gives *Segantini* a place in the development of the understanding of depression and sets out Abraham's unique contribution to it.

She writes the following:

> Whereas Freud's early ideas about hysteria, compulsive neurosis, anxiety neurosis, neurasthenia, and borderline psychotic and psychotic images, like ideas about paranoia and hallucinatory confusion, were published in the decade before the turn of the century, it was not until 1911 that the first innovative contributions on the subject of depression appeared. They were not Freud's, rather they originated with Abraham. Freud's first work about depression, "Mourning and Melancholia", came into being only several years after that.[449]

And, a little later:

> His *Segantini* has always been thought of as a contribution to applied psychoanalysis . . . As the following will show, however, it also belongs in the category of works on the theory of depression and furthermore represents Abraham's first contribution to forming a picture of this illness.[450]

She describes a number of specific characteristics of Abraham's treatment of the subject:

– The mother is in the foreground. Previously, psychoanalysis was primarily about the father.

– The son does not only focus libidinous desires on the mother. There are also death wishes and wishes for revenge. The stress on the hatred between mother and son was distinctly unusual at the time and it touched upon the most fundamental issues in Freud's theory.[451]

– Abraham believes that the son's hatred derives from a constitutionally strong sadism on the one hand and on the other the feeling that his mother does not love him enough (which arises partly from rivalry with the father, whom she loves more).

Several months after *Segantini* was published, Abraham gave a talk at the congress in Weimar (21 and 22 September 1911) in which he further developed his argument based on a clinical example.[452] He laid out in that talk the mechanism of depression. His starting point was the conflict between love and hate. He postulated a powerful sadistic component that was inborn: the libido's preponderant disposition towards hatred, which was first applied to close family but then became more general. He also presumed powerful feelings of inadequacy. They were initially formulated as: I cannot love people; I have to hate them. This discomforting inner realisation is repressed and projected outwards, so that patients have a sense that people close to them do not love them but hate them. That hatred is then detached from the original disposition and linked to other mental or physical deficiencies. The second formula then becomes: People don't like me; they hate me because I have congenital deficiencies. That's why I'm unhappy and depressed.

Those congenital deficiencies could be all kinds of things. Abraham's case history concerned a patient of middling intelligence who had an older brother who was extremely intelligent, but it might equally well be something a patient regarded as a physical deficiency. He believed that the second formula was not the end of the story, however, since the sadistic inclinations had a tendency to return to the consciousness and they might appear in various forms, perhaps simply in dreams or in parapraxes, in other words, symbolic acts, or they might produce a tendency to hurt those who were close, or give rise to fiercely vengeful desires or criminal impulses. The latter do not become visible, because they are not converted into acts, but they do emerge when the patient is questioned.

Patients are more likely to locate the origin of these impulses in an agonising feeling of physical and mental inadequacy than in their own sadism. A side-effect is the sense of guilt. The fiercer the unconscious urge for revenge, the greater the delusions of guilt. Those delusions could be quite extreme. Patients might think that all the evil in the world originated with them. Such thoughts point to inexhaustible sadism, yet are, at the same time, so unbearable that they amount to a serious depressive psychosis. The patient, nevertheless, also nurtures a desire to be the greatest sinner on earth.

On 1 May 1912, Paul Federn spoke about Abraham's talk and related article at a meeting of the Vienna Psychoanalytic Society (Abraham was not present since he was in Berlin) and he was critical on many different grounds.[453] The central point of Abraham's highly original article concerned the relationship between sadism and depression: sadistic traits and aggression were extremely influential in depression, just as they were in obsessive neurosis. Federn's opinion was that Abraham's case history contained nothing that showed that sadistic traits had caused the pathology. He stated that it was wrong to conclude that depression arose from a conflict between love and hate, since there were some depressive patients who had no sadistic tendencies. Nor was it the correct formula, he said. In fact, Federn claimed Abraham's argumentation was incorrect in all sorts of ways. At the same time, he did not discuss the content.[454] The impression all this gives is that Federn rejected Abraham's theory about depression first because it was unknown, and second because Abraham was describing something extremely disturbing: powerful feelings of hatred. Freud endorsed Federn's view. Oddly, Freud spoke of a *Patientin* (female patient), despite the fact that Abraham's detailed case history clearly concerned a man. The only thing Freud found useful was Abraham's idea that mania was a product of failed repression.[455] The next day he wrote to Abraham:

At the Society yesterday we had talks on the last two issues of the *Zentralblatt*, and we are to make our Ψα literature the subject of regular discussions. Your paper on melancholia was very sensibly criticised by Federn, and then all sorts of things dawned on me which may lead further. We are still only at the beginnings in that respect.[456]

Freud chose to leave his own criticism to one side. He did not enter into debate with Abraham.

Autobiographical elements?

On 14 December 1910 Abraham wrote to Freud that his work on Segantini was delayed because his subject so strongly resisted analysis, adding later in the letter that the theme presented unprecedented difficulties, but that he now had the feeling he had solved all that could be solved.[457] On 11 February 1911 he wrote to Freud: "The Segantini manuscript goes off to you together with these lines. I send it to you with a request for your criticism that seems particularly necessary to me this time, as it is a piece of work with some personal complexes behind it".[458]

Little is known about what went on in Abraham's mind, so it is not surprising that this sentence has prompted much speculation. What did he mean by personal complexes? Remarkably enough, it was his daughter Hilda who started the speculation. Having cited the above passage, she wrote, "Unfortunately, we cannot tell what he felt these complexes were and we have to attempt, instead, to draw conclusions from Abraham's personal history up to the time he wrote this paper".[459]

By "we", she meant Hedwig and herself, Abraham's wife and daughter. Hilda did not write that they did not know but rather *"können wir nicht sagen"*, "we cannot tell", and she took the reader along with her in her attempts to find out what those complexes were. It is uncomfortable to be led off on a search by someone who knows but refuses to say.

Hedwig, Abraham's wife, was an intelligent, intellectual woman, who knew a great deal about psychoanalysis and had read a lot about it. She had attended psychoanalytic meetings in the Burghölzli Clinic and in the early years in Berlin she ran a psychoanalytic family business together with her husband and was present at meetings of the Berlin Psychoanalytic Society. Abraham asked her to read all his articles. Moreover, discussing dreams had become almost a game in the Abraham household. Given that Abraham worked on *Segantini* for two years and must have struggled with it towards the end, Hedwig surely knew exactly which complexes he meant. If Hedwig knew, then Hilda did, too. Why could it not be told?

This is an example of how problematic it can be for a daughter to write a biography of her father with her mother as her most important source of information. Were mother and daughter concerned to portray Abraham in as good a light as possible, or did they intend to create an image of him that matched how they wanted the world to see him? Can close family members do anything other than the latter? After all, their own identity is involved.

This might be connected with the fact that in her biography Hilda does not quite manage to evoke a man of flesh and blood. Was there an aspect of her father that she did not want to describe? Or was it simply a matter of loyalty? There were certain things Abraham did not speak about except with Freud, who clearly knew which complexes were involved. Would Hilda have regarded it as disloyal to write about them?

Remarkable in this connection is something Hedwig said in 1953.[460] When Eissler asked Hedwig whether her husband had undergone analysis, Hedwig's answer was: never. She said he had had no opportunity to do so. He was the only psychoanalyst in Germany and he could not have gone away for months once he was a married man with children. On the face of it, Hedwig's view of the matter seems very clear: it was an impossibility. But for her or for Abraham? He could, after all, have undergone analysis for a few weeks as Ferenczi did in 1916.[461]

Hedwig told Eissler that Abraham had a rare capacity for empathy, a marvellous thing that others perhaps failed to notice. She went on to say that analysis would, of course, have been useful in many ways, but she believed his patients were unaware that it had not taken place. She mentioned again that he was the only psychoanalyst in Germany at the time and that all later analysts were his pupils. Finally, Eissler asked Hedwig whether there was any personal matter that made her think he ought to have undergone psychoanalysis. At first her answer was rather evasive; then she said her husband had certain slight inhibitions and such things that possibly . . . She did not finish her sentence but added, "I mean, doesn't everyone have such . . ."; Eissler helpfully agreed. Hedwig went on to say that psychoanalysis would all the same probably have been useful in all kinds of ways. At that point, sadly, Eissler started to fill in the gaps. He asked whether Abraham perhaps had difficulty speaking in public. This was a very clumsy suggestion, since if there was any problem Abraham did not have then it was public speaking. He was a gifted speaker. Hedwig merely contradicted Eissler and said nothing more, although a moment before she had seemed about to say why Abraham might have benefited from psychoanalysis. The difficulty was, of course, that Eissler had said something that showed he knew very little about Abraham. It caused a breakdown of trust. Eissler was rather too impatient because he was mainly after information about Freud.

Lack of personal information

Why do we have so little personal information about Abraham, as Mächtlinger remarked?[462] She suggested that Abraham was extremely tight-lipped. There was another reason, however. Although occasionally personal matters are mentioned in his correspondence with colleagues, none of Abraham's personal letters has survived, despite the fact that he wrote very many of them. How can it be that they have all disappeared?

Abraham wrote a letter to his parents every week, from the time he left home almost until his death, from 1896 to 1925.[463] After his father died, he continued to write weekly letters to his mother, so there must have been some 1,500 altogether. A good number, if not all of them, must surely have been kept. Abraham's mother lived with Max, her eldest son, and after her death in 1929 he will surely have held on to some of them.

Max was very fond of his brother. He was hoping for a son and would have named him Karl.[464] But Max and his wife were killed by the Nazis in 1941, in Minsk. All their belongings, which included everything left by Max and Karl's parents, were lost. Their daughter, Lotte, was able to flee to England in 1939, but without taking anything with her. Max and his wife tried several times to flee and they sent some of their personal property to Antwerp, but those belongings disappeared, too, and all Abraham's letters to his family were lost with them.[465] All the same, if Abraham wrote 1,500 letters to his parents, they must have written a considerable number to him. Moreover, Hedwig and Karl wrote to each other frequently while they were engaged, and then there were those many notes that Abraham wrote to members of his family and others.

Hedwig, Hilda, and Gerd fled to England in 1933. At that point it was still possible to take some personal possessions, but there will have been a limit to how much they could carry. Gerd, later Grant, who outlived his sister and mother by some twenty years, deposited letters in the Library of Congress, including Abraham's correspondence with Freud, circular letters, and various letters to and from colleagues. Not a single personal letter survives, although Hilda clearly still had some when she was writing her biography.

From today's perspective, it is difficult to understand why Abraham's family thought him important enough for a biography to be written yet did not keep his letters. Neither Grant nor Hilda had children, but there were heirs in the form of the children and grandchildren of Hedwig's brother, Hans. Their legacy did not include any letters by or to Abraham.[466] Lotte Levy inherited a little money but nothing else. It seems as if Hedwig, Hilda, and Grant wanted to preserve only those things that were directly connected with psychoanalysis.

Caution is advisable with regard to both Hilda's biography and any conclusions drawn about Abraham as a person based on his work. The reader of her biography needs to take into account the inevitable bias caused by the fact that the author was Abraham's daughter. In coming to any conclusions about Abraham, it is important to bear in mind that much has been deduced over the years because of the lack of personal information and, in reading secondary literature, we are, therefore, dealing with hypotheses, as Mächtlinger clearly stated in her 1997 article.[467] Nevertheless, Daniel Widlöcher remarked in 1977 that Abraham was so selective in noting the themes of Segantini's life story that his choices bring out his own personal complexes, his countertransference.[468]

Widlöcher shows in his article that, in describing Segantini, Abraham concentrated on the artist's bond with his mother, on ambivalences and love–hate emotions, and on how those urges can be sublimated to make possible a stable relationship with the world. Abraham left the bond with the father out of account, and, indeed, Segantini's later dependence on the art dealer Vittore Grubicy, who made him famous.[469]

Abraham's personal complexes

Abraham wrote of Segantini that he was reserved and shy in relation to the female sex. Unlike most young men, he was unable to form relationships and then break them off. Not until he was twenty-two did he experience true love for the first time and his choice of woman at that point was decisive. Abraham describes Segantini as extremely monogamous and he linked this with the fixation of Segantini's libido on his mother and the resulting unusual limiting of his object-choice. In an earlier passage in her biography, about his relationship with Hedwig, it was precisely this character trait that Hilda attributed to her father. For Segantini, the description did not actually fit; in reality he had a child with a model he took into his home. Abraham was probably strongly fixated on Hedwig in his younger years but later he undoubtedly paid attention to other women. Lotte Levy describes, for example, how fond her mother was of her brother-in-law, the handsome Karl Abraham, with whom you could laugh and talk about any subject, and she says Hedwig was jealous.[470]

Hilda also wondered why her father chose that particular subject in 1910. She decided that Hedwig's pregnancy and the birth of Gerd made him think about his own happy early childhood years. But, in fact, Abraham was working on *Segantini* as early as February 1909, as is clear from a letter to Freud.[471] Simple arithmetic is sufficient to show that Gerd (born in August 1910) had not been conceived at that time.

Monogamy and the birth of Gerd, breastfeeding, the mother–child relationship, and Abraham's own happy infancy were the subjects Hilda raised in connection with *Segantini*. She made no mention at all of depression, death wishes, and feelings of hatred for the mother. Did Abraham suffer from depression? Or, to be more specific, did he have periods of depression? There are a number of reasons to think that he did.

Abraham wrote to Freud that *Segantini* touched upon some of his personal complexes and that writing it had cost him much effort. The book was full of love–hate towards the mother, with death wishes and feelings of guilt. These are central themes and they must have been connected with the personal complexes he mentioned.

At the age of about two, Abraham experienced one of those central events that an individual's emotional state at the time is not able to deal with: the loss of the person who was the focal point of his life. This event is described in Chapter One. Abraham's mother became depressed as the result of a series of bereavements, so little Karl suddenly lost the centre of his world. On top of that, his father's psychotic sister was living in the same house. She sometimes had attacks in which she would smash furniture and smear faeces on things, which must have been very frightening for a little boy who was unable to seek comfort from his mother.

Abraham described paintings by Segantini that are dominated by total desolation. They had titles such as "The Bad Mothers". Segantini painted mothers who had abandoned their children and were punished as a result. According to Abraham, Segantini's resistance to depression and with it his resistance to his aggressive impulses became increasingly fragile. He described how an abandoned child like that becomes overwhelmed by fear, jealousy of rivals, and feelings of hostility towards the mother.

In her 1997 article, Mächtlinger convincingly located the powerful sadistic component and the temporary emergence of hatred in the event in which Hedwig was pregnant with Hilda and Abraham took her on a mountain walk by moonlight, forgetting that there would be no moonlight on the way back and thereby risking a fatal fall in the dark.[472] It was a remarkable initiative that almost led to a repeat of his mother's accident. Mächtlinger suggested that the writing of *Segantini* worked as a form of self-analysis that made it possible for Abraham to sublimate his sadistic impulses.

Abraham hated cold winter weather. He loved sun and warmth and found winter bearable only in skiing resorts high in the mountains.[473] It is possible that he suffered from seasonal depression. He describes how Segantini moved higher and higher into the mountains in an increasingly desperate attempt to throw off the depression that threatened. Each time, just before he moved house, Segantini's paintings grow darker. Immediately afterwards, once the painter has settled at a higher altitude, they are bathed in light.

Abraham was a passionate mountaineer. He reached some of the major summits. He believed mountain climbers were cursed with certain complexes, especially lovers of the Engadin.[474] Mountaineering was, and remains, one of the most dangerous of sports, with a higher percentage of fatal accidents than any other. We should not forget that Abraham had very poor sight in one eye and, therefore, lacked a sense of depth.[475] It meant he was taking serious risks.

Abraham's articles differ on one particular point. He could write about people with great empathy and warm interest, evoking them in his writing in such a way that the emotional link between author and subject is obvious. This was clearly the case with Segantini and with "the imposter".[476] There are, however, also articles in which Abraham writes about his patients as if they are things with which he has no emotional contact. This total lack of empathy had an effect almost as if he affixed them firmly to their problems, for which he blamed them. This kind of writing can be found, for example, in "The experiencing of sexual traumas as a form of sexual activity" and in his article about war neuroses, which he read out at the congress in Budapest in 1918.[477]

It is as if Abraham had periods of extreme depersonalisation, in which he lost all emotional contact with himself and those around him. He had written about such a state in his article "Hysterical dream-states". It must have been one aspect of his depression.[478] The times at which these depersonalised articles were written are of relevance. "The experiencing of sexual traumas" was written in 1907, in the period when his future was extremely uncertain. He wanted to stay in the Swiss mountains, probably regarding it as an essential means of keeping control of his depressive moods, and he wanted a job as a fully qualified doctor, for which he had been ready for some time. He had been a doctor's assistant for far too long. He could not find such a job in any of the Swiss clinics and the repeated rejection of his applications must have made him despair. We should not underestimate Hedwig's role in all this. She wanted to return to Berlin because she was unhappy in Switzerland. She must have put pressure on Abraham that he could not ignore. She became another woman for whose ups and downs he had to make sacrifices, as he had for his loving mother, whom he experienced as suffocating. That conflict must have aroused aggression.

The article "Psycho-analysis and the war neuroses" (1921a) was written at a time when Abraham had years of war behind him and was feeling ill and depressed. The war years must have been terrible for him. He worked as a doctor in a military hospital. Furthermore, Abraham was not good at putting up with being unwell, a point examined later in this book.

Descriptions of Abraham by others vary so much that it is hard to build up a picture of him as a single individual. The inconsistency probably flows partly from the fact that a depersonalised Abraham seemed different from an Abraham who was emotionally present. Given the striking number of people who sooner or later became angry with him, even after his death, we can assume that in a depersonalised state he made a rigid, rather aggressive impression.

Hilda wrote, "It has been stressed that my father's own mood was mainly happy and hopeful, as can be gathered from his correspondence. Whether he had to fight off depression I do not know. He showed no signs of it that I can remember".[479] But Abraham wrote of Segantini,

"The struggle against repressed instinctual forces is, however, a silent one, of which a man as sensitive as Segantini shows as little as possible to the outside world".[480]

Abraham's *Segantini* is a treatise about a pre-oedipal mother–son relationship. By writing it, Abraham gave a whole new direction to psychoanalysis. The relationship could not at that stage be called pre-oedipal, since the "pre-oedipal organisation" was introduced by Freud only in 1913. Like Freud himself, Freud's other pupils began to pay attention to the pre-oedipal phases in 1911–1913.[481] Abraham was their forerunner.

There is a striking similarity between Abraham's theory about early trauma, with the sense of total abandonment and the depression that goes with it, and André Green's theory about the "dead mother". The similarity is examined in the afterword to this book.

CHAPTER NINE

A meeting with Fließ, family life, and the failed *Habilitation*

A braham's articles were serious. They were solid and well considered and his sense of humour was not much in evidence. That was given more space in his letters. He managed to amuse Freud greatly with the following anecdote. In the clinic run by Ziehen, the psychiatrist who had attacked Abraham so fiercely when he gave a talk, a patient with obsessive neurosis was shown to an audience. The patient had the obsessional thought that he must put his hand up the skirts of women on the street. Ziehen told his audience that it was necessary to find out whether there was any sexual content to the obsession and he asked the patient whether he felt the same urge when he saw older women. The patient answered, "Alas, Professor, even with my own mother and sister." At which Ziehen declared, "You see, gentlemen, that there can be nothing sexual at all at work here." He went on, "Patient suffers from a non-sexual but senseless obsessional idea!"[482]

In that same letter of 11 February 1911, Abraham wrote to Freud about Fließ:

At the moment I find myself in a dilemma. The other day I mentioned to a colleague that I had found, in a very striking way, masculine and feminine periods in a mild case of circular psychosis. She spoke of this to Fließ, with whom she is friendly, and a few days later told me of Fließ's request that I should visit him. On the one hand, I would not like to be discourteous; on the other, I find it unpleasant to have to force myself to adopt as much reserve as is necessary in this case.

Abraham was well aware of Freud's friendship of many years and his eventual break with Fließ. He wanted to visit Fließ, but not without Freud's approval. Just how sensitive this matter remained for Freud became clear when he answered Abraham immediately:

Dear Friend,

I am replying by return of post because of what you say about Fließ, and I am taking the liberty of giving you my advice unasked, that is, telling you my attitude in the matter. I cannot see why you should not call on him. In the first place, you will meet a highly remarkable, indeed fascinating man, and on the other hand you will perhaps have an opportunity of coming scientifically closer to the grain of truth that is surely contained in the theory of periodicity, a possibility that is denied to me for personal reasons. Now, he will certainly try to sidetrack you from $\Psi\alpha$ (and, as he thinks, from me) and to guide you into his own channel. But I am sure you will not betray both of us to him.[483]

Wilhelm Fließ (1858–1928) came from a family of Sephardic Jews and was born in Arnswalde in the German state of Brandenburg. His parents were orthodox Jews and his mother adhered strictly to the religious rituals. When Fließ grew up, he distanced himself from the Jewish religion and led a secular life, something he had in common with Abraham. Fließ's childhood was pervaded by grave and traumatic events. His father killed himself when Fließ was nineteen and his younger sister died when he was twenty. He had no brothers, except for one who was stillborn, so after his sister's death he found himself alone with his mother. He settled in Berlin, became an ear, nose, and throat doctor and built up a good reputation. His theory of vital periodicity, according to which men and women are subject to biorhythmic cycles of twenty-three and twenty-eight days respectively, based on which all kinds of diseases and defects could be diagnosed, is regarded today as a peculiar superstition but it gained many adherents at the time.[484]

Freud first encountered Fließ when, at the advice of Josef Breuer, he attended several lectures by him in 1887.[485] In November of that same year, Freud wrote a letter to Fließ saying that he would like to get to know him better, since he had made a great impression on him.[486] It was the start of a close friendship, which was played out mainly in letters but also in meetings they called conferences. In this early phase of the development of Freud's psychoanalytic theory, Fließ was his confidant and discussion partner. Their split, after Fließ accused Freud of collaborating on the plagiarising of his work by Swoboda and Weinigner, always remained a source of pain for Freud.[487]

Abraham was received with great warmth by Fließ and he reported to Freud on 26 February that although he had not found the man fascinating, he did think Fließ was "a penetrating and original thinker", if lacking true greatness.[488] What struck Abraham about Fließ's scientific work was that it was based on valuable ideas but then went no further than a concern to prove them correct. All the same, he had heard much that was interesting and regarded it as one of the most valuable meetings he had yet had with a Berlin doctor. Fließ, meanwhile, had visited Abraham in turn. Freud replied on 3 March with a number of warnings about Fließ, but he also wrote that Abraham's description of Fließ's research methods seemed to him "remarkably true". With something like nostalgia, he added, "I once loved him very much and therefore overlooked a great deal".[489]

On 9 April 1911, Abraham wrote that he had again visited Fließ, who had referred a female patient to him, recommending both Abraham and psychoanalysis. Fließ continued to refer patients to Abraham, many of whom were suitable for psychoanalysis, and the two men became friends. Abraham came to trust Fließ. He found the theory of vital periodicity interesting and attended lectures by Fließ. Among other places, they would meet at the Ärztliche Gesellschaft für Sexualwissenschaft. Abraham attended ten times between 1913 and 1920, twice as a sponsor and four times as a panel member. Fließ was present thirteen times in the same period and gave talks.[490] Over the years, Abraham seems to have taken him more and more into his confidence, and he turned to Fließ when he or Hedwig had physical problems of various kinds.

Family life

Because of the birth of Gerd, Karl and Hedwig were unable to go on holiday in 1910. For some time now, Abraham's practice had been extremely busy. He was tired and decided to take an extra holiday in April 1911.[491] They went to Bad Schandau, a beautiful place near Dresden, but close enough to Berlin to allow the meeting of the Berlin group to take place in Dresden for a change. Abraham's sense of duty was quite extreme. The whole family spent the summer in the village of Skagen at the northern tip of Jutland in Denmark. The children caught chicken pox, so the journey there in the train was miserable. Hilda remembered little of their stay except that her father taught her a couple of Danish words so that she could fetch milk for the baby from the hotel kitchen, and she remembers spending days on the beach. The weather was beautiful and the unlimited quantity of strawberries and cream made a deep impression. On the way back, Abraham took Hilda to Bremen to visit her grandparents. It was one of many visits to the old-fashioned home, where the atmosphere was warm and affectionate.[492] Grandmother Ida was extremely fond of her grandchildren and loved playing with them. She told endless family anecdotes and read to them, as she had to her own children. Her favourite activity was writing little verses for all possible occasions, which was where both her sons, Max and Karl, acquired the habit.

The Abrahams' house on the Rankestraße in Berlin was not far from the Tiergarten zoo with its large playground. The children often went there with their nanny. From time to time their mother joined them, sometimes accompanied by their grandfather, Philipp Bürgner, and they would be taken along to a café for something to drink. Their house had a back garden, where the children had a sandpit and where friendly neighbours lowered pieces of cake down to them on a string. The greatest attraction, however, was the fire station across the street. Abraham's consulting room was at the front of the house, so the children could look at the fire station only when there were no patients. They could never get enough of watching the fire engines drive out, bells ringing. Abraham had invented a fictional fireman called Piefke. He was deployed from time to time to keep the children in order. Hilda recalled a powerful thunderstorm during which their father sat them on the window seat and shouted "hoorah" at every thunderclap to prevent them from being afraid.[493]

Hilda

Freud believed that symptoms found in adult patients had their origins in childhood and especially between the ages of three and five. He encouraged his followers to collect material about that period.

In one of the first letters that Freud wrote to Abraham, on 5 July 1907, he says, "My impression is that the age of from three to five is that to which the determination of symptoms dates back. Later traumas are mostly genuine, earlier ones or those falling within this period are *prima facie* doubtful. So here is a gap to be filled in by observation".[494] In his introduction to "Little Hans", he added, "With this end in view I have for many years been urging my pupils and my friends to collect observations of the sexual life of children – the existence of which has as a rule been cleverly overlooked or deliberately denied".[495]

Abraham took this encouragement to heart and made notes as he watched his own children. In 1917, he published a short article based on observations of his daughter Hilda in 1910.[496] Born on 18 November 1906, Hilda was four years old at the time. That the notes really were about Hilda is confirmed by Hilda herself in her biography of Abraham and by Pines, a good friend of Hilda's.[497] They include the following[498]:

> Helen, aged four, once gave vent to her feelings whilst having dinner with her father in her mother's absence in these words: "Isn't it nice that mummy is not at home today?" When her father asked her why she was so pleased about it, the little girl replied: "Because she cannot butt in when we talk."

For a whole month, little Hilda regularly asked her mother how long she thought she might live. She never put such a question to her father. She once asked her father, over lunch, whether she could see him naked. After Hilda had for some time uninhibitedly expressed death wishes regarding her mother, several weeks followed in which she was neither particularly hostile nor particularly affectionate. Then Hilda started telling her mother to look into all kinds of shop windows when they were out walking, asking her which things her mother liked best: which dress, which hat, and so on, the way parents tend to ask children. When Hedwig pointed to something, Hilda would invariably say, "When I'm big I'm going to give you that." Abraham concluded that Hilda had overcome her desire for her mother's death and found a remarkable sort of compromise. Instead of death, a reversal of roles would suffice: when I'm big I'll have money because I'll be father's wife; you'll be our child and I'll have to buy things for you. Hilda's hostility in the same period towards her baby brother—she asked the nurse to drown him—is described in another article, called "Little Hilda".

In 1913, Hilda was seven and Gerd three. Hilda's teacher complained that Hilda was dreamy and failed to pay attention in lessons. Hilda wrote about her mother's reaction to her dreaminess:

> One of my memories of this time is of doing some homework with my mother sitting beside me, and being recalled from wherever my thoughts may have been by her fist banging the table and making me and my books jump. She was of course less trained to understand, and easily lost patience in such a situation.[499]

Abraham reacted differently. He decided to try to analyse his daughter's problem. He wrote about his efforts in his "Little Hilda" article, which was never published.[500] Several years before Hilda wrote her father's biography, she was given the manuscript of the article by her mother and she put it into the hands of her own psychoanalyst, Hilde Maas.[501]

Today, it is clear to everyone that psychoanalysts should not analyse their own family members, but in the early days no one really gave the issue much thought.[502] Several analysed their own children, starting with Jung, who began analysing his daughter Agathli in 1910, followed by Abraham with Hilda.[503] Paul Roazen revealed in 1969 that Anna Freud was in analysis with Freud for years, from October 1918 to the spring of 1922 and from May 1924 until the summer of 1925.[504] The letters between Freud and Lou Andreas-Salomé about Anna Freud's analysis were not included in their published correspondence.[505] Ernst Kris analysed his two children, Anna and Tony, and Melanie Klein her youngest son. Anna Freud's first patients were her young nephews, Heinerle and Ernst Halberstadt.

In the case of Karl Abraham and Hilda, however, no actual analysis took place. According to his notes, Abraham went for a walk with Hilda on three occasions, on 3 and 5 November and on 21 December 1913, and talked to her about what was wrong. Between times he had shorter conversations with her, but those, as he wrote, did not produce any new material. The conversations helped. Hilda's dreamy inattentiveness was reduced. The extra focus on her probably played its part.[506] Abraham wrote of his daughter that she was extremely absent and dreamy. She might change her shoes or clothes, for example, and halfway through remain sitting motionless, impossible to stir despite exhortations. She was finding it hard to get to sleep at night. Abraham wrote that she had allowed herself to masturbate, a choice of words that reveals his disapproval. He told her not to do it, as an old-fashioned father: she must not masturbate or she would lie awake at night and be tired the next morning rather than "fresh and lively" like the other children.[507] Hilda reacted to that by immediately changing the subject.

On 3 November 1913, Abraham went for a walk with Hilda and told her that as a doctor he wanted to understand her dreaminess and difficulty getting to sleep. He persuaded her to talk about her daydreams. Hilda told him she tried to think about pleasant things but often found herself thinking about things that were nasty and frightening. She often thought about apes, as if there was a trap door in her bedroom with apes under it, and she often imagined a flame that might suddenly come out of the floor of her room. She thought about giants and bad men. In the next conversation she spoke about burglars that might take her away. After talking about burglars she was very affectionate and kissed her father's arm. She asked him whether he dealt with other patients the same way and whether they then came more often. Abraham noted that she clearly wished he would pay attention to her more frequently. He regarded the dangerous animals, burglars, and bad men as expressions of Hilda's inner anger, possibly directed at her brother and mother. Hilda's own comment later was that she failed to understand why he did not interpret her daydreams as arising from castration anxiety.[508]

The final conversational walk took place on 21 December 1913. On 16 December, Hilda had had her tonsils removed.[509] She had been taken to the ear, nose, and throat doctor a number of times for recurring sore throats and ear infections. In order not to make her unnecessarily fearful, she was told merely that she was going to be examined again. Both parents went with her, although her mother stayed in the waiting room. The doctor looked at Hilda's throat, nodded to Abraham and rang a bell. Two nurses came in, one carrying two large enamel buckets. The other sat Hilda on her lap and held her tight while an ether mask was put on her. Hilda screamed and gasped for breath. She could hear her mother rattling the door handle. When she woke, she was lying on a couch. She was relieved to see that only the bottom of one of the buckets was covered in blood. They went home by taxi and Hilda's clearest memory of that morning was that the bedcovers were pulled back ready for her and her nanny was standing next to the bed. Hilda's conclusion was that the nanny must also have known what was going to happen. In his report of their last walk, Abraham wrote that Hilda had undergone a fairly severe tonsil operation on 16 December and was oversensitive afterwards. She cried a lot in her sleep and was hard to wake. It would be a few minutes before she could speak and in the morning she no longer remembered anything about it. Abraham's total lack of sympathy for the fact that his small daughter had been given the shock of her life is striking. It is as if he was blind to fear in others. Chapter One deals with the fact that Abraham was often insensitive to fear in himself. As a result, he sometimes seemed to be completely unaware of fear in other people. His children fell victim to this on a number of occasions. Even Hilda, who has not a bad word to say about her father anywhere in her biography, comments on his reaction to her period of recovery from surgery and points to the stark contrast between Abraham's caring and cautious approach to her problems during their walks and the way he dealt with her tonsillectomy.

During that last walk, Hilda talked non-stop about her fear of bad men who might come and take her away, yet not for a moment did Abraham make any connection with the operation of five days before, or with the fear that might have been induced by the surprise attack on her while he was sitting there knowing what was about to take place. His explanation concerned feelings of guilt about masturbation. He wrote that she was afraid of bad men because she perhaps thought she had done something bad herself by masturbating. Abraham was so preoccupied by his daughter's masturbation that he failed to notice her fear.

Life in the Abraham household might not have been particularly easy for Hilda. Abraham was a caring father, but his caring attitude might sometimes drop away completely. Moreover, Hilda saw very little of him. He treated patients eleven hours a day, worked on articles and on his *Habilitation*, chaired the Berlin Psychoanalytic Society and was generally extremely busy. Hilda's remark about patients who got more of his time than she did was not without foundation. Her mother, Hedwig, was at least as ambitious as her father and rather less caring. From what has been written about her, Hedwig emerges as a person who set great store by the intellectual aspects of life, who was lively company, and had broad interests, a person with whom you could have a good laugh, who could sometimes be extremely condemnatory and preferred to let other people look after her.[510] As we have seen, because of the illness and death of her mother, Hedwig had to care for an entire household at far too young an age. She was unable to finish high school and although she would have liked to go to university, that was impossible. It is as if she had had enough of caring for other people. The circle of friends of which she and Abraham were part in the time they got to know each other included many who would later become prominent figures in the movement for women's emancipation, which was surely no coincidence.

For Hilda it cannot have been easy, either, to deal with the fact that her mother had a strong preference for her brother, who was four years younger.[511] The nanny was very important to Hilda, so it was a blow to discover that she was involved in the betrayal surrounding her tonsillectomy.

There was fun and affection in the Abraham household, too. Because he was busy until late in the evenings, Abraham made sure he had breakfast and lunch with the children.[512] Breakfast was a hurried affair, lunch rather less so, although Abraham had an ability to eat hot soup very fast. Hilda was accused of dawdling. The nicest part of the day during the week was coffee time:

> We would join our parents after their short rest and a special game with an almost ritual charac-
> ter followed. My father would put a lump of sugar on his tea-spoon and then close his eyes,
> announcing how much he looked forward to having it when he had had a nap. We would in turn
> creep up and steal it amid much giggling and when my father "awoke" he would call for the help
> of the police or of the famous fireman from across the road to find the thief. In my memory this
> game went on for years, which is obviously unlikely, but lumps of sugar dipped into coffee
> remained a delicacy of grown-up life.[513]

On Sundays, everyone had a lie-in. Hedwig's brother and sister, Hans and Else, would always arrive in time for lunch and the children were served non-alcoholic white wine, which made them feel proud. The afternoon was for the children and they could choose which games to play. Visitors were always welcome as long as they were willing to join in, and Hilda writes, "I think this was an excellent way of making us feel wanted".[514] This shows that Hilda was concerned about whether she was wanted or not. If you truly feel wanted, you take it for granted and will not give any more thought to the matter.

Developments within the Berlin Psychoanalytic Society

In late 1911, Abraham felt sombre about his Berlin Psychoanalytic Society.[515] He badly needed someone who would not simply take part receptively; everything still always had to come from him. Two members (Warda and Strohmayer) had left when the subscription was raised. That was hardly any loss scientifically speaking, but it was a reduction in numbers. Juliusburger had been sulkily keeping his distance since the congress in Weimar, leaving just five people: Eitingon, Koerber, Stegmann, Abraham himself, and, as Abraham wrote, "Dr. Horney".[516] Abraham wrote to Freud that two years ago Horney had undergone analysis with him success-fully. He described her as extremely diligent. She would start working as a psychoanalyst as soon as she was sufficiently trained.

But why did Abraham describe Horney in his letter to Freud as more qualified than she was at that point? In late 1911 Horney had not yet graduated, she was still a medical student. She graduated in 1913 and gained her doctorate in 1915. On 27 April, a woman had become a member of the Vienna Psychoanalytic Society for the first time, Dr Margarethe Hilferding.[517] It seems Abraham did not dare to tell Freud that the first woman to join the Berlin Psychiatric Society was a student, just as in the early years he chose not to write that his own wife was attending meetings of the new Berlin Psychoanalytic Society.

Freud reacted warmly and supportively on 2 January 1912: "I know how difficult a position you have in Berlin and always admire you for your unruffled spirits and tenacious confidence. The chronicle of our undertaking is perhaps not always pleasant, but that may be true of most chronicles; it will yet make a fine chapter of history".[518]

In his letters, Abraham meticulously kept Freud informed. In late 1911 he had rather fewer patients for a time, but in February 1912 he was pleased to be able to tell Freud that he was up to his neck in patients. He never worked less than ten hours a day now, and he was no longer dependent on Oppenheim's support.[519] Freud, who could be very caring, urged Abraham to increase his fee. Abraham needed colleagues to whom he could refer patients. Recently, he had referred a patient to Eitingon, but Eitingon generally worked fairly short hours. He was independently wealthy. In the small Berlin Psychoanalytic Society it was business as usual. Horney had given a talk called "Sexualpedagogik im frühen Kinderalter" (sexual instruction in early childhood) and Abraham was very pleased by the fact that she was so firmly in command of her material. That was not always the case with such talks.[520]

Abraham was so busy he hardly found time to write articles. "I always wonder how you manage to write so much in addition to your practice", he wrote to Freud.[521]

Lou Andreas-Salomé

At the psychoanalytic congress in Weimar that took place on 21 and 22 September 1911, Abraham met Lou Andreas-Salomé and was deeply impressed by her.[522] She had first come into contact with psychoanalysis through Rainer Maria Rilke. German doctor and psychoanalyst Viktor Emil von Gebsattel had advised Rilke to undergo psychoanalysis, which led Lou Andreas-Salomé to focus her attention on all works on the subject. In 1911, during a summer stay in Stockholm, she got to know psychotherapist Poul Bjerre and together they went to the third psychoanalytic congress in Weimar, where she met Abraham. She then spent some time in Berlin—according to Winship, so that she could study psychoanalysis under Abraham.[523] On 28 April 1912 Abraham wrote the following to Freud:

> One of the visitors to the Weimar Congress, Frau Lou Andreas-Salomé, has just spent some time in Berlin. I have come to know her very closely and must say that I have never before met with such an understanding of Ψα, right down to the last details and subtleties. She will visit Vienna in the winter and would like to attend the meetings there.[524]

Her visit to Vienna in late 1912 lasted several months and was a success. She attended meetings of the Wednesday Society and was in analysis with Freud for some time. Freud came to value her greatly and after the First World War their contact blossomed into a firm friendship and regular correspondence, although Freud avoided discussing her theoretical works.[525] She also became good friends with Anna Freud, who even spent a brief period in analysis with her.[526] Jones believed that Lou Andreas-Salomé had a special place among the intellectual women with whom Freud became friendly; he admired her refined personality and her ethical ideals, which surpassed his own.[527]

Lou Andreas-Salomé lived in Göttingen, 350 kilometres from Berlin. She often visited Berlin and stayed in touch with Abraham. She was a regular guest at his home.[528]

Family and faith

Abraham and his family spent the summer holiday of 1912 in Switzerland, in a hotel above Brunnen on the edge of Lake Lucerne.[529] It rained virtually the whole time and Abraham contracted bronchitis. He was regularly ill and seems to have overstrained himself with his sometimes extremely demanding weekly schedule. The children could do little but play noisily on the covered balcony, and in brief dry spells Hilda went out to pick bilberries. One of Abraham's colleagues from Hamburg came for treatment, as he had done the previous year.[530] It was not unusual in those days for patients to come to a psychoanalyst's holiday home. It brought in some money at a time when there was no other income. Hilda wrote in her biography that the year before, this particular colleague had paid some attention to her but that this year, to her dismay, he focused entirely on her brother. Hilda was jealous. Her remark also gives us an insight into how they all interacted. The visiting patient had contact with the entire family.

Abraham took the opportunity to visit his colleagues in Zurich, whom he had not seen for five years. He had some hope that the difficulties with the Swiss psychoanalysts could be resolved. Freud was pessimistic because of the change in Jung's behaviour. Whereas, four years earlier, Jung had been disloyal mainly behind Freud's back and allowed himself to be corrected, he had now entered into open confrontation with Freud.[531]

Much sickness arrived in 1912, culminating with a death in the family. Abraham's father-in-law died in late September after a stroke that left him in a coma for nine days. It was the first time Hilda had seen Hedwig grieving and her father said she must comfort her mother. What Hilda does not mention is that her grandfather had become extremely devout in the period before his death and suffered a stroke while he was fasting for Yom Kippur. The family felt that fasting had been too much for his fragile health.[532] What must the attitude of the Abrahams have been to this return to the faith? Atheism had become almost a norm among them, so much so that six-year-old Hilda, who had just started school, said in a bible lesson that her mother had told her God did not exist. She said mother, not father. Hedwig was open about being an atheist, but Abraham's orthodox upbringing must have made that far more complicated. After Hilda's remark in class they decided to be more careful about what they said in front of her.

Abraham's Habilitation

Abraham had felt for some time that he wanted to try to become a *Privatdozent* at the university, which would give him the opportunity to deliver lectures there. It meant writing a *Habilitation*.[533] One condition was that a faculty of the Humboldt university, in this case the medical faculty, had to be willing to accept first the plan for a *Habilitation* and then the *Habilitation* itself. Abraham had pinned his hopes on Karl Bonhoeffer, who had recently succeeded Ziehen as professor and whom Abraham personally found far more likeable.[534] Liepmann, with whom Abraham had kept in touch since Dalldorf, had written a glowing letter of recommendation to Bonhoeffer on his behalf. Abraham had earlier heard from Freud that Friedrich Kraus was increasingly sympathetic towards psychoanalysis and he asked Freud whether he would be willing to send a letter of recommendation to Kraus.[535] Abraham thought that if Bonhoeffer and Kraus spoke up for him he would have a reasonable chance. He added that the faculty's anti-Semitism would remain an obstacle. Freud answered by return post that he would certainly write to Kraus but he was afraid nothing would come of it. Ten days later, Freud wrote that the letter to Kraus had reached its destination long since, "but whether also its purpose?"[536]

At the end of December 1912, Abraham went to Vienna for a few days to visit Freud and was received with great warmth.[537] Freud had written to Abraham in advance of the visit that he must tell his dear wife they would not allow Abraham to get indigestion anywhere else than with them and that he was looking forward to seeing him again. As on his first visit in late 1908, he had received presents from Freud, and when he checked out of the hotel he discovered that Freud had secretly been there and paid his bill.[538] Freud had invited Ferenczi as well, but Ferenczi was ill and unable to come. Clearly troubled by all the attention paid to Abraham instead, Ferenczi wrote Freud a ten-page letter the day after Abraham left, with an extensive self-analysis and dreams, then a follow-up letter three days later.[539] Freud dealt with this in his usual tactful manner, replying that he had read Ferenczi's auto-analysis but had not yet studied it. He never returned to the subject.[540]

The first reports concerning Abraham's *Habilitation* were good. Freud received a letter from Kraus saying that he was prepared to support Abraham's application, counted on approval from Bonhoeffer and believed Abraham had a good reputation even among his opponents.[541]

Kraus was himself reasonably positive about psychoanalysis. He had devoted two enthusiastic lectures to it in early 1912, and, in early 1913, he did so again.[542] Shortly before New Year, he asked Abraham to come to see him and revealed that he had obtained information about him, which turned out to be favourable. He advised Abraham in any case to submit a *Habilitations-Schrift*. Kraus promised to do what he could to support the project and asked for a list of early articles by Abraham on subjects other than psychoanalysis.

After that conversation, Abraham decided to choose an uncontroversial subject for his *Habilitation*, one that was not connected with psychoanalysis.[543] On 29 January 1912, he wrote to Freud that he was about to start on a thesis and, on 3 March, that he was working on association experiments with healthy elderly people and patients with mild senile dementia, adding with levity that it would be "a good old Prussian piece of work, forcing open doors".[544] He had heard from Liepmann that Bonhoeffer's response was negative, but when he asked for more details on the matter it turned out that Bonhoeffer had said that if Abraham wrote a good paper he would not be opposed on principle. Liepmann had regarded this as a negative reaction, possibly because he himself had been rejected four or five times in applying for a full professorship.[545]

Jewish academics were able to qualify for the post of *Privatdozent* in those years and to become honorary professors, but the post of full professor was almost always denied them. Abraham regarded Bonhoeffer's reaction as positive.[546] In the period that followed, he regularly reported to Freud that he was working on his *Habilitation*, saying how busy it made him in combination with ten hours a day treating patients and all his other commitments.[547]

Then there was a hitch.

Abraham never finished his *Habilitation*. There is no trace of it in the archives of Humboldt University in Berlin, not even among the rejected applications. The hitch was probably the psychiatry congress in Breslau on 13 and 14 May 1913, an annual meeting of the German Psychiatric Association with 200 participants.[548] One of the items on the programme was a debate about psychoanalysis. Abraham sent Freud the programme in his letter of 3 March 1913 and added that there would probably be little point in going, but that he would take part if Freud wanted him to.[549] Freud answered that no, it would not be worthwhile attending, except that then they could then report on it in their *Zeitschrift*.[550] Falzeder and Burnham have described how, in advance of the congress, a well-organised group of German psychiatrists conspired to undermine psychoanalysis. It was by no means the first time that neurologists and psychiatrists had mounted an attack on psychoanalysis, but a conspiracy ahead of a congress was new. There were two central characters. The first was Alfred Hoche, professor of psychiatry at Freiburg im Breisgau from 1902 to 1933.[551] He was active in German psychiatry but not particularly authoritative, since he had published little of any scientific importance. He is known mainly for his lifelong attacks on the followers of Freud and psychoanalysis, which he called a morbid doctrine, a form of evangelism for decadent people and for all kinds of weaklings, of whom there would always be more than enough.[552] Hoche had sent all participants in the congress a letter in which he asked his colleagues to report to him cases of patients who had been damaged by psychoanalytic treatment, so that he could speak about them at the congress.[553] The second central character was Bleuler, who, in contrast to Hoche, was a man of great renown. He had actively supported Freud for many years. In the first *Jahrbuch für psychoanalytische und psychopathologische Forschungen*, of which Bleuler was editor-in-chief along with Freud, he defended psychoanalysis in a 110-page article and criticised Hoche, among others, several times.[554] Bleuler's support for psychoanalysis was regarded with alarm by his colleagues. He was conferring prestige on a movement that they felt was undermining the psychiatric profession. On top of that, more and more patients were hearing about psychoanalysis and competition was starting to emerge. Psychoanalysis had grown rapidly since the memorable year 1907 to become an active, internationally organised movement of which Bleuler was not actually a member but which he did support. In psychiatric circles, Bleuler was held responsible for its increasing influence.[555]

The congress was attended by the *crème de la crème* of psychiatry, including Emil Kraepelin and Karl Bonhoeffer. Representing psychoanalysis were only Max Eitingon and Arnold Stegmann from Dresden. Bleuler opened with a speech in which he systematically worked through the various fields of psychoanalysis point by point. He had some serious criticisms, especially concerning the structure as a whole, but there was much that he regarded as an important addition to psychiatric knowledge.[556] Falzeder and Burnham described Bleuler's speech as follows:

> In essence, while Bleuler dismissed much of the general metapsychological superstructure, he actually approved of most of the cornerstones of psychoanalytic theory and therapy. His paper can be seen as a masterful example of legendary Swiss neutrality, or one of ambivalence and indecisiveness. In fact, however, he undoubtedly made an honest and fair-minded attempt to evaluate psychoanalytic theory and therapy on the basis of the contemporary state of scientific and therapeutic knowledge—a rare exception in the heated atmosphere of those times.[557]

Bleuler tried to investigate and express with great precision and thoroughness which aspects of psychoanalytic theory he approved of and where his criticism lay. He devoted a great deal of time to it. He had published extensively on the subject in 1910 and at the Breslau congress he continued his line of argument.

Generations of psychoanalysts were of the opinion that it was because of Bleuler's ambivalence, in other words, his personal complexes, that he did not embrace everything about psychoanalysis but had criticisms.[558] It has gradually become one of the black pages in the history of psychoanalysis. In their article, Falzeder and Burnham, despite their nuanced approach, also tended to describe Bleuler as ambivalent, as can be seen from their own summary of the article in which they write of Bleuler's half-hearted support for psychoanalysis. But what was half-hearted about a person who had been intensively involved with psychoanalysis for fifteen years and had admiration for it as well as criticism?

After Bleuler, Hoche addressed the congress. Bleuler summed up Hoche's performance in his letter to Freud of 24 July 1913:

> With Breslau I was dissatisfied to the extent that a clear description of the antitheses was not possible. Hoche was intelligent enough to summon up mainly a lot of errors made by psychoanalysts, and his own error was in essence that he acted as if the whole of psychoanalysis consisted of such errors.[559]

What Bleuler did not say was that Hoche did this to such an extent that the entire audience roared with laughter throughout. Hoche summed up all the abuses about which information had been sent to him. Falzeder and Burnham were of the opinion that the debate demonstrated the extent to which the attack on psychoanalysis was stage-managed. One speaker after another undermined psychoanalysis and only Stegmann stood up against them. Bleuler maintained his own standpoint in his final response and explained that Hoche had based his judgement purely on answers he had received to his circular letter. Hoche had asked only for examples of abuses and had not been the slightest bit interested in positive experiences. Using Hoche's method it would be easy to show, for example, that all surgeons kill their patients, Bleuler said.[560] Hoche concluded at the end of the debate that psychoanalysis had been rejected unanimously by those present with the exception of Dr Stegmann and he offered Bleuler his ironic condolences.

Later, a letter from William Powers to Smith Ely Jelliffe revealed that what happened at the congress was prearranged in order to give Bleuler, who was regarded as extremely influential, a chance to distance himself publicly from Freud's school. The hope was that without Bleuler's support, Freud's theory would be doomed.[561] Moreover, there was a desire to put German psychiatrists down on record officially as opponents of Freud's teachings. Powers wrote in his letter that this had emerged from a conversation he had with Kraepelin after the congress was over. Powers had said that he was not particularly impressed by the arguments used against psychoanalysis and Kraepelin replied that they had never been intending to have a proper debate. Instead, this was an organised move against psychoanalysis. Liepmann had protested during the congress at the way the matter was handled.[562]

The congress took place in the period when Abraham was writing his *Habilitation* and it destroyed his chances. The ranks, which included Bonhoeffer, had closed.

Was Freud's tactic of avoiding confrontation, an approach also adopted by his followers, really sensible? As far as this congress is concerned, it seems not. The fairly cheap attempt to undermine psychoanalysis would have been harder if more of those present had counterattacked, and Bleuler would have been supported in his courageous performance. Now the congress had alienated him from his colleagues in psychoanalysis. Abraham had discovered on several occasions that when psychoanalysis was strongly attacked, he did at least garner support by his performance. At this point he was very much in need of support for his *Habilitation*.

In the world of psychoanalysis, it seems that Bleuler has, none the less, received most of the blame for the debacle of the congress. Emil Oberholzer, a member of the Zurich Psychoanalytic Society, wrote a letter to Eitingon on 3 June 1913 in which he mentioned criticism by Bleuler, saying that two years earlier Bleuler had still been sympathetic but this was now the work of a negative and adversely influenced person.[563] Oberholzer found it incomprehensible that Abraham was still sending people to the Burghölzli to train as psychoanalysts.

A second attempt to gain access to the university

After the First World War, the climate for psychoanalysis improved.[564] At the psychoanalytic congress in Budapest in 1918, participants even included a number of dignitaries. Abraham, therefore, tried once more to gain access to the university. As a result of his political activities, Ernst Simmel had contacts in the Ministry of Education and the Arts.[565] Influential people at the ministry had told him that people were reasonably positive about the idea of setting up a chair of psychoanalysis at the university.[566] Simmel had discussed the matter with Eitingon and he felt there were three people eligible for such a post: Abraham, Eitingon, and himself. Eitingon declined to be a candidate and said that he believed no one was qualified except Abraham. Simmel was persuaded and spoke with the relevant head of department at the ministry.[567] The civil servant then asked Abraham to visit him at the ministry. Abraham was requested to write a comprehensive, scientifically sound memorandum about the introduction of psychoanalytic education by the Berlin Society. He did so. In the end he succeeded in getting the green light from the ministry despite a change of guard as a result of the Kapp Putsch.[568] But the medical faculty had to give permission as well and there things came to a standstill. It was still a bulwark of anti-Semitism. Abraham would be allowed to become a *Privatdozent* only if he had himself baptised, which he refused to do.[569]

Eitingon's father, Chaim Eitingon, who lived in Leipzig, later also made an attempt to establish a chair in psychoanalysis. In his will, dated 2 May 1927, he left the University of Leipzig 50,000 marks for that purpose. In 1931, he withdrew the bequest because of rapidly increasing anti-Semitism at the medical faculties of German universities, especially in Leipzig.[570]

CHAPTER TEN

Akhenaten

Until 2011, a veritable battle went on between Egypt and various major museums in the USA and Europe over the art treasures taken from excavations in Egypt that have ended up in collections all over the world. Egypt wanted its art treasures back. Germany was asked several times to return the world-famous bust of Nefertiti, wife of Akhenaten, the pharaoh to whom Abraham devoted a long essay. The bust is one of the prime exhibits at the Neues Museum in Berlin. The most recent request came shortly before revolution broke out in Egypt in January 2011. After the revolution and the destruction at the Egyptian Museum in Cairo that coincided with it, the issue was put on hold. Germany has always refused to give the bust back, arguing that it was acquired legally and is too fragile to move. It was discovered in 1912 by a team led by Ludwig Borchardt, during excavation of the house of the sculptor Thutmose, and brought to Berlin in 1913.[571]

Around the turn of the twentieth century, a series of excavations was underway in Amarna, a city on the Nile that was founded by Akhenaten (1374–1335 BC). Initially called Achetaten, it was for a short time the capital of Egypt. In Germany, there was huge interest in the excavations and Abraham was not the only person to be inspired by them. The Egyptian collection at Berlin's Neues Museum was already one of the most important of its kind in Europe and it included many objects from the Amarna period.[572] Else Lasker-Schüler (1869–1945), a famous poet and painter from Berlin and a contemporary of Abraham's, was inspired by the astonishing portraits of Akhenaten in creating one of her main characters, Jussuf.[573] Akhenaten is often shown with his head held high, his neck stretched forward, and his forehead sloping back. Else Lasker-Schüler gave Jussuf a similar look.[574] She did not adopt in her Jussuf pictures the remarkable round, feminine belly that is often a feature of statues of Akhenaten.

Applied psychoanalysis

In his early years in Berlin, Abraham published a number of major works on the subject of applied psychoanalysis. In *Dreams and Myths* of 1909, psychoanalysis was applied to folklore. In *Segantini* of 1911, he applied it to art, and in "Amenhotep IV", about Akhenaten, to ancient Egypt, specifically to a pharaoh of the eighteenth dynasty who lived in the fourteenth century BC.[575]

Was *Segantini* about the mother and "Amenhotep" about the father, as Abraham's daughter Hilda wrote?[576] Amenhotep was certainly about a son who dispenses with his father's faith and puts a new religion in its place.

On 11 January 1912, Abraham wrote to Freud as follows:

> Only a few lines today to thank you very much indeed for your kind wishes and encouraging words![577] The latter have helped; I have just completed the preparatory work on my paper for the new journal. I know that its theme will interest you: it is about Amenhotep IV and the Aten cult. The subject has a particular attraction for me—to analyse all the manifestations of repression and substitutive formation in a person who lived 3,300 years ago. The Oedipus complex, sublimation, reaction formations—all exactly as in a neurotic today. I did the preparatory work partly in the Egyptian department of the Berlin Museum and was reminded more than once of the first instruction of Egyptology that I enjoyed in Vienna in December 1907.[578]

Freud wrote back, "Well, well! Amenhotep IV in the light of $\Psi\alpha$".[579] It is as if he was surprised, but not really pleasantly surprised. Was Freud particularly interested in Amenhotep IV at the time, in the way that he was later interested in Moses? Might Freud have told Abraham about Amenhotep IV during the visit to Vienna that Abraham writes about in his letter of 11 January? Had Abraham beaten him to it in dealing with the subject?

Abraham stressed the ambivalence of the pharaoh in the opening lines of "Amenhotep IV". He was a ruler who neglected his empire, yet he was ahead of his time in the fields of religion, art, culture, and ethics:

> He was neither a conqueror nor a statesman, as some of his ancestors had been. On the contrary, during his short reign the young king looked on passively while the world empire which they had built up fell into ruin. His greatness lay in another realm: the spiritual realm. . . . At the age of ten Amenhotep IV ascended the throne; at the age of twenty-eight he died. In the few intervening years he brought about great revolutionary changes in religion, ethics, philosophy, and art. All we know of this spiritual revolution leads us to the conclusion that the king was far in advance of his time.[580]

He then outlined the image he had formed of Amenhotep IV and his ancestors, who had conquered vast territories. Thutmose III (1501–1447 BC) extended the Egyptian empire as far as the Euphrates. Amenhotep's father, Amenhotep III, who reigned from 1390 to 1353 BC, was not particularly warlike by nature and concentrated mainly on the hunt, but the immense empire was defended successfully under his rule. He married the daughter of a priest from Asia who was a confidant of the court. She was called Tiye and at first she bore him no sons, so Amenhotep took a second wife. Later, however, Tiye had a son, Amenhotep IV.

To judge by the facts garnered by Abraham, Amenhotep III left the government of his country increasingly to his wife. Foreign policy remained unchanged but Tiye tried to impose religious changes by giving the cult of the god Aten a more prominent role than that of Amen. Thebes, which lies within present-day Luxor, was Amen's city. The priests of Amen had great influence both at court and among the people.

When Amenhotep III died, ten-year-old Amenhotep VI succeeded him. During his eighteen-year reign he abolished the Amen cult and switched to a monotheist religion devoted to Aten. He neglected the defence of his vast empire, which began to fall apart as a result, and focused all his attention on art and philosophy.

According to Abraham, Amenhotep's mother was more powerful than his father and their son had an extremely strong bond with her. Abraham describes the relationship between mother and son as follows:

> Such a strong and lasting attachment of the libido to the mother leads in later life to certain effects upon the eroticism of the maturing or adult son. It makes it more difficult for him, as I have demonstrated in an earlier paper, to detach his libido at the time of puberty from his mother and to transfer it to new love-objects. Not infrequently such detachment fails entirely.[581] In most cases it succeeds but partially, and a tendency becomes apparent to form a monogamous attachment to one person, who becomes a substitute for the mother. The transference of the libido, once established, is usually final and irrevocable. This monogamous trait is to be found in the young king to a marked degree.[582]

Oddly, Abraham wrote that he had addressed this subject in 1908, but not that he had published work on it again in 1911. He attributed exactly the same characteristics to Akhenaten as to Segantini.[583] "Amenhotep" was again about a man who was so attached to his mother that, Abraham felt, he had great difficulty turning his attention to a new love-object and once he had done so never departed from that choice.

"Amenhotep" looked primarily at the king's relationship with his mother and only secondarily at that with his father. Abraham described the relationship with the father in such vague terms that the reader gains no clear impression of it at all. When Amenhotep was fifteen, he took the government upon himself and initially followed his mother's line but, Abraham writes, he then began to react more and more strongly against his long-dead father. Abraham added that unfortunately we do not know what Amenhotep's attitude to his father was like when he was a young boy, but he assumed there was an unconscious inner fixation on the father. Amenhotep IV took up arms against the inner image of his father, whose dominion had to be shaken off. Paternal authority, including in a religious and political sense, was rejected and immediately exchanged for something else. According to Abraham, this shows that Amenhotep had an undiminished need for authority in his life.

As soon as Amenhotep IV came to the throne, he completely broke with his father's religious tradition, the tradition of Amen, and turned to a single god, Aten, whose name means the disc of the sun. He no longer called himself the son of his father but instead the son of Aten. He founded a new residence, 450 kilometres north of Thebes, called Achetaten, and changed his name to Akhenaten, which means "horizon of the Aten". Fierce conflict erupted with the Amen priests of Thebes, but Akhenaten persisted, drove the priests from their lands and made

Aten the country's only god. He had the name Amen and the name of his father chiselled off inscriptions everywhere. Abraham writes that this was the old, long repressed or sublimated hostility of the son breaking through. Instead of burying his mother next to his father, he laid her to rest at a place where he could eventually be buried next to her. So the rivalry with the father for possession of the mother was fought out even beyond the grave.

Abraham found Akhenaten's life history intriguing. His vassals from border areas sent messengers time and again to plead for help, saying they were in danger of being overrun by enemy hordes. Year after year, Akhenaten failed to respond to their appeals. He was busy laying out beautiful gardens, making music, writing poems, and preaching love. Instead of impressive kingly robes he wore simple clothes (after all, the truly great have no need of imposing costumes). Meanwhile, his empire declined.

In creating Aten, Akhenaten put in place a single universal god who was equally close to all creatures, a monotheist religion. Abraham believed that Akhenaten's doctrine contained not just all the essential constituents of Old Testament Jewish monotheism, but those of Christendom, too, which was 1,300 years younger. In the traditional prayers and hymns, Aten came to the fore as a loving and wholly benevolent being, transcending space and time. Such goodness and mildness were completely foreign to the earlier Egyptian gods, and, indeed, to the believers. Aten knew no hatred, jealousy, or vengeance, unlike the later god of the Old Testament. He was the king of peace, not of war, and free of all passions. Akhenaten did not imagine him as physical, like the old gods, but as spiritual and impersonal. He forbade images, with the exception of the image of Aten as the sun with rays, each of which ends in a hand.

Abraham stressed Akhenaten's ethics, which involved a far-reaching sublimation of all sadistic urges. Akhenaten rejected all expressions of hatred and violence, just as Jesus Christ later did, and wanted to rule only though love. He also advocated a different, more influential position for women.

For all his opposition to his father, Abraham believed, Akhenaten could nevertheless not do without an authority of a similar kind. So he created one to meet his own needs and dressed him in the omnipotence that every child initially ascribes to its father. Akhenaten gave this god the characteristics he possessed himself and created him in his own image as humans have done so often. Behind this, as Abraham saw it, lay the desire to have conceived oneself, to be one's own father.[584] Whereas throughout his treatise he continually makes mention of sublimation, at the end it is suddenly all about repression:

> An exaggerated sexual repression disturbs a person's emotional relationship to other people and robs him of the sense of reality. This leads to the auto-erotic restriction so often met with in neurotics, and especially in the most gifted ones; their own wishful-phantasies become the exclusive centre of their interest. Thus the neurotic no longer lives in the world of real events, but in another world created by his phantasy. He becomes indifferent to real happenings, as if they did not exist for him at all. Ikhnaton's behaviour is in perfect conformity with this.[585] Living entirely in his own world of dreams and ideals, in which there is only love and beauty, he is blind to the hatred and enmity, the injustice and misery, to which men are subject in reality. . . . Thus he turned a deaf ear to the cries for help from his Asiatic subjects; so, too, he was blind to the atrocities which took place in his provinces. His eyes saw only beauty and harmony whilst his empire fell in ruins.[586]

On what did Abraham base his version of the Akhenaten story? Present-day historians describe this period in Egyptian history differently. Bryan (2000), for example, tells of the long reign of Amenhotep III, Akhenaten's father, as a highpoint of the eighteenth dynasty. He was in power for thirty-eight years, a period characterised by peace and plenty. Wilson (2008) mentions Amenhotep III's love of hunting, but he does not say that the pharaoh neglected his kingly duties as a consequence of it. His wife, Tiye, was a highly important figure at the court and extremely influential towards the latter part of her husband's reign. Bryan does not claim, however, that she reigned in his stead.[587] It was Amenhotep III who actually introduced the Aten cult and there was no regency between his reign and that of his son. Nowhere is it written that along with the erasure of the names of the gods on inscriptions the name of Amenhotep III was removed as well, although the sources do say that Nefertiti, the beautiful queen, wife of Amenhotep IV, had an important position at court. It was a period in which women at the court had an extraordinary amount of influence.

Abraham was writing about Akhenaten a hundred years ago. The differences between Abraham's version of his life and those of modern historians might flow from new facts that have come to light over the past century from discoveries in the grave of Tutankhamen, Akhenaten's successor, for example.[588]

In the early twentieth century, there were others who wrote similarly on the subject. Abraham was able to choose between various interpretations. He listed all his sources in a note on the first page of his article.[589] In the period when Abraham was writing "Amenhotep", the standard work about Egypt was James Henry Breasted's *History of Egypt* (1905).[590] It remains so to this day. Abraham names it as a source, but his ideas about Akhenaton's monogamy, so unusual in those ancient times, come from Weigall.[591]

An assessment of Abraham's "Amenhotep IV"

Three themes can be found in "Amenhotep" that deeply preoccupied Abraham. The first was the relationship between son and mother. Abraham chose one version of the Akhenaten story, in which the position of the mother is very strong. She even ruled for a long time in her son's stead. Of the various interpretations of Akhenaton's life, Abraham chose the version in which a son has a loving but suffocating relationship with a dominant mother, as he did with his own mother. Moreover, he attributed to Akhenaten the same problems as to Segantini. He wrote about a strong and fixated attachment of the libido to the person of the mother, such that it has a powerful influence on the sexuality of the son, who has great difficulty detaching himself from his mother and choosing a new object. Once he has chosen a new love-object, he tends to make an irrevocable choice for monogamy. Abraham had a loving, very dominant mother. He must have had difficulty detaching himself from her, and he felt very restricted by her and concerned about her wellbeing. Given that he was preoccupied by that theme, it must have arisen to some extent in his marriage. The sense of being trapped and having to adjust to another person must have been present there, too. As mentioned earlier, he would have preferred to stay in the Swiss mountains or perhaps close to the mountains of southern Germany, but Hedwig wanted to return to Berlin. Dinora Pines, who knew Hedwig well in later life in England, described her as follows:

Until the end of her long life, for Hedwig Allan-Abraham lived until she was 91, and so I knew her well, she was a highly sophisticated, charming and elegant woman. She took great pride in her own appearance and also in the elegance with which her home was run. But she could also be cold and self-centred. She was extremely interested in English literature, and remained an avid reader of the latest novel until her death. Hedwig prided herself on her modern emancipated behaviour in sharp contrast with Karl's orthodox Jewish mother. However they were also very similar, Karl's mother was devoted to her husband and respectful of him, just as Hedwig was devoted to Karl, respectful of his profession and of his achievements.[592]

The second theme of Abraham's "Amenhotep" is the relationship between son and father. Is the essay really about his relationship with his father, as Hilda Abraham wrote? Like all Abraham's longer articles, "Amenhotep" is extremely complex.

There is an important similarity between Abraham and Akhenaten. Both dismissed their father's religion. Akhenaten foreswore the Amen cult and replaced it with his mother's Aten cult, of which he created a version entirely his own. Abraham became secular, having been an orthodox Jew, although he was not influenced in this by his mother, who remained orthodox. Abraham's wife was secular, but he took his first step in that direction before he met her, asking his father for permission to abandon the Jewish rituals because he would not be able to comply with them in the clinic at Dalldorf. This does not necessarily mean that he rejected the Jewish religion, but there are no indications in his later life that he or his family were practising Jews. His son even had himself baptised in England and became a member of the Anglican Church.[593]

There is another aspect of Abraham's interpretation that stands out. Abraham depicted Amenhotep IV as a man with a weak father and a strong mother from whom he could not detach himself. In Abraham's interpretation, the relationship between Akhenaten and his mother was quite remarkable. According to Abraham, Amenhotep III became more concerned with hunting than with ruling and in due course his wife, Queen Tiye, carried out his royal duties. Amenhotep III died when his son was ten years old, which meant that Abraham's Amenhotep IV had a father who was largely absent and did not carry out his duties as king, and a mother who was in power and governed the empire. After the death of Amenhotep III, Tiye became regent and remained so until her son took over from her at the age of fifteen. Until that time, Amenhotep IV mainly experienced a mother who held power. So he had a strong mother and a weak, absent father. He phantasied that he had a strong father, whose name he then erased.

Abraham wrote that something could be observed in Akhenaten that was a common phenomenon in neurotics. They reject their father in a religious or political sense only to replace him with another authority, thereby showing that their need for a paternal authority remains undiminished. Abraham foreswore the orthodox Jewish faith of his childhood and put Freud and psychoanalysis in its place. It would be very unfair to Abraham to say that psychoanalysis was a religion to him. He was far too scientific for that, a thorough professional, extremely well versed in diagnostics, and his contributions to psychoanalysis were fundamental. But there was something religious about the way he converted to psychoanalysis.

Compare his teacher Bleuler, who was hugely enthusiastic about psychoanalysis and saw in it a theory that at last made it possible to understand patients. Bleuler thought some aspects of psychoanalysis truly phenomenal, but there were other aspects he found more dubious.

Occasionally, he felt that assertions were insufficiently substantiated and wanted to see more thoroughgoing proof. Bleuler's attitude to psychoanalysis was extremely sympathetic, but it was also critical and scientific. Freud found this hard to tolerate and accused him of ambivalence.

Abraham's transition to psychoanalysis was radical and unconditional. It was as if he were adopting a new religion, with Freud as its authority. His critical, scientific stance developed only later.

The last of the three themes of "Amenhotep" was aggression, an extremely important subject in all of Abraham's work. He believed Akhenaten was neurotic because he repressed reality. The pharaoh was blind to hatred and animosity, absorbed in his dreams of love and beauty, and meanwhile his empire declined because he did not ensure it was properly defended. Abraham says the cause of this was Akhenaten's undue repression of sexuality, which disturbed his emotional contact with other people and made him lose all sense of reality. Abraham saw it as an auto-erotic curtailment, such that only his own wishful fantasies were of interest. The link Abraham makes with Christianity is striking. He stresses the preaching of love and peace, accompanied by a refusal to acknowledge the existence of aggression. Akhenaten disavowed aggression and was himself at the same time extremely aggressive, erasing the names of all gods except his own god Aten from inscriptions, even erasing the name of his father. The most aggressive act by Akhenaten was not named as such by Abraham: Akhenaten allowed the great Egyptian Empire of his forefathers to collapse.

Freud's criticism

Abraham's great teacher was critical, writing on 3 June 1912,

> Dear Friend,
>
> I have read your Egyptian study with the pleasure that I always derive both from your way of writing and your way of thinking, and should like to make only two objections, or, rather, suggestions for alteration. Firstly, you claim that when the mother is particularly important, the conflict with the father takes milder forms. I for my part have no evidence of this and must assume that you have had special experiences in this respect. As the matter is not clear to me, I ask you to revise this passage. Secondly, I have doubts about presenting the king as so distinctly a neurotic, which is in sharp contrast with his exceptional energy and achievements, as we associate neuroticism, a term that has become scientifically inexact, precisely with the idea of being inhibited. After all, we all have these complexes, and we must beware of not being called neurotic. If we have successfully stood up against them, we should be spared the name.[594]

Abraham changed his article on both points, so he complied with Freud to that extent. Freud was then full of praise and called it "an adornment of" the psychoanalytic journal *Imago*.[595] The fact that Abraham immediately complied with Freud's request to adjust the article nevertheless raises a number of questions. One major difference between articles by Freud and those by Abraham is that Freud sees everything as revolving around the father, Abraham the mother. In Freud's Oedipus complex, the father played the main role. Abraham's articles were all about constricting ties to the mother, problems in breaking free from the mother, the mother's dominance, and aggression towards the mother. When Abraham wrote that the conflict with the father took milder forms if the mother was particularly important, he was writing about himself. In his parental home, everything revolved around his mother. Abraham had a good, mild, friendly relationship with his father, without too much in the way of conflict. Freud was more likely to object in cases where articles were about the relationship with the mother. It would be a mistake, however, to think that, unlike Abraham, Freud had a dominant father, or a mother who was less of a prominent presence.

Louis Breger has written a biography of Freud in which he gives a central place to Freud's family circumstances in childhood. Freud's mother was so dominant that even as an older man he would get stomach ache when he had to visit her on a Sunday. Freud's father was far weaker than his mother.[596] Abraham's father, by contrast, was not weak at all; he occupied a special place in the household. He was respected and tolerant and more detached from family life. Freud developed a theory according to which the son fights a strong and powerful father to win the mother from him—a strong and powerful father such as Freud had never had and would have liked to have.[597] Freud never chose as a subject the direct relationship between mother and son.

Freud's second objection was fundamental and he advanced it on several occasions. Abraham divided the world into healthy and sick, normal and neurotic. It seems he was firmly resistant to Freud's idea that we all carry neurosis within us. Freud believed that when we have conquered neurosis to a reasonable extent—the victory is never absolute—we have no reason to continue calling ourselves neurotic. If we did, everyone would be neurotic. Freud thought Akhenaten was far too creative and energetic to be called neurotic, whereas Abraham had described him as neurotic above all things.

Moses and Monotheism

Years later, Freud himself wrote about Akhenaten. In *Moses and Monotheism*, Freud looked in detail at the figure of Amenhotep IV and his transition to monotheism.[598] Commentaries on Abraham's "Amenhotep" and on Freud's *Moses and Monotheism* often draw attention to the fact that Freud does not mention Abraham in his book. Leonard Shengold even devoted a whole article to the subject in 1972 called "A parapraxis of Freud in relation to Karl Abraham".[599] It was a striking omission, all the more so given that Freud began his *Moses* with a detailed review of Rank's *Der Mythos von der Geburt des Helden* (The Myth of the Birth of the Hero) of 1909. Bernard Lemaigre called it an astonishing omission, even if Abraham's "Amenhotep" is more modest in its aims than Freud's *Moses*.[600] "Amenhotep" was an investigation of the relationship between Akhenaten and both his father and his mother. In his *Moses*, Freud was not interested in the least in the influence that women, especially Akhenaten's mother, Tiye, had on the pharaoh. He was interested above all in monotheism.

Shengold assumed that Freud had forgotten about Abraham's article and tried to understand why. In 1911, Abraham had written a short article entitled "On the determining power of names".[601] In it, he pointed out that names have an influence on those who bear them, as if a name contains an obligation and prescribes certain behaviour. In Freud's *Moses*, Karl Abraham is not mentioned, but the patriarch Abraham is. In Genesis 17, we read how God made a covenant with Abraham, saying that all men and boys must have themselves circumcised. In his *Moses*, Freud took the origin of Judaism away from Abraham and ascribed it to Moses.

Shengold concludes, "In attempting to write a family romance of the Jews, Freud dismissed Father Abraham and his namesake Karl Abraham".[602] Shengold believed this had to do with the close contact between Abraham and Fließ at the end of Abraham's life, which caused Freud to identify Abraham with Fließ and to transfer to Abraham his perpetual love–hate feelings for Fließ.[603]

However, Shengold's explanation is contestable for three reasons. First, Abraham remained important to Freud even after his death. This is not generally known, because Freud hardly spoke about his friend ever again, except to Abraham's wife and children. But every time Freud saw them, they discussed Karl Abraham at length and they always ended up talking about the great loss they had suffered, all of them, Freud as well as Abraham's immediate family.[604]

Second, Freud and Abraham discussed the history of ancient Egypt during their very first meeting in 1907. Freud told Abraham about it and gave him two antique statuettes. They shared an interest in the subject and, during the journey to the Harz Mountains in 1921, Abraham went to the trouble of organising a visit to the Egyptian museum, mainly for himself and Freud.[605] It seems improbable, therefore, that Freud would forget about Abraham in connection with Akhenaten.

Third, Shengold compares the forgetting of Abraham's "Amenhotep" by Freud to the way Freud forgot that the original idea about bisexuality had come from Fließ. He sees Abraham as comparable with Fließ in this connection. He pays no attention to the political situation in which Freud wrote *Moses*. It was 1934 when Freud began to write that book, at the age of seventy-eight. The first version was finished during the summer, but he did not dare to publish it, partly for fear of the negative consequences for psychoanalysis and partly because he had doubts about the imperviousness of his arguments.[606] In 1933, the Nazis had come to power in Germany. The Berlin Psychoanalytic Society, bulwark of psychoanalysis, had been all but swept away. Jews were no longer allowed to practise their professions and were in great danger. Of the younger generation of psychoanalysts in whom Freud had placed his hopes, Abraham and Ferenczi had died, Rank had left after a conflict, Eitingon had emigrated to Palestine, and Sachs had left for the USA. Only Jones was still in Europe. Freud's three sons had fled Germany with their families, Martin to Vienna, Oliver to Paris, and Ernst to London. Freud's books had been thrown on the pyres at book-burnings in Germany and his health was poor. He had suffered heart trouble and pneumonia in the autumn of 1933.[607]

Freud had been fascinated by the figure of Moses for many years and when he stayed in Rome in 1912, not long after the exchange of letters with Abraham about Akhenaten, he went every day to look at the sculpture of Moses by Michelangelo, about which he later wrote *The Moses of Michelangelo*.[608]

In that difficult period, which began in 1933 when unprecedented persecution of the Jews arose that affected Freud's family, his friends, and his psychoanalytic following, Freud focused on the origins of the Jewish religion and set out to show that it lay with Moses. Freud was not, at that point, interested in a psychoanalysis of Akhenaten, as Abraham had been. He dismissed the stress Abraham had laid on the position of the woman and on Akhenaten's relationship with his mother. Freud had always avoided the subject of "the relationship with the mother". By not naming Abraham, he avoided having to look at Abraham's important theme: the love–hate relationship with the mother and the love–hate relationship with the wife that went with it. In this period, Freud was focused entirely on the origins of Judaism. He does not mention that Abraham had sought those origins long before him in the brief period of monotheism in Egypt during Akhenaten's reign.[609] It remains unclear whether the idea came from Abraham or from Freud.

In fact, Freud did refer to Abraham, only not by name:

> The kernel of my hypothesis – the dependence of Jewish monotheism on the monotheist episode in Egyptian history – has been suspected and mentioned by various writers. I spare myself the trouble of quoting these opinions here, since none of them is able to indicate how this influence can have come into operation.[610]

Moses and Monotheism was not published until 1939, in Amsterdam. By then, Freud was living in London.

Emergency talks in Munich in 1912

On 24 November 1912, a remarkable incident took place in connection with Abraham's "Amenhotep".[611] Jung had called together the presidents of the psychoanalytic societies that belonged to the IPA for emergency talks in Munich about the *Zentralblatt*. Stekel had cancelled his membership and was now threatening, as its editor-in-chief, to take the journal with him.[612] Present were Freud, Jung, Abraham, Jones, van Ophuijsen (representing Maeder), Riklin, and Seif.[613]

All this happened in a period when Jung was taking a distinctly different course from Freud, with his own libido theory. During the lunch, in a separate room of the Park Hotel from that in which the meeting had taken place, the conversation turned to Akhenaten. Jung's biographer mentions a man who spoke on the subject, although he is not named.[614] This must have been Abraham, who insisted that it was the pharaoh's wish for his father's death that led him to have his father's name erased wherever it appeared on inscriptions. Jung did not agree. He did not see this as resistance to the father. Instead, he claimed the pharaoh acted in this way because he was a creative man. Freud then reproached Jung and Riklin for having published psychoanalytic articles in Swiss journals without mentioning his name. When Jung defended himself by saying that Freud's name was known anyhow, Freud fainted, to everyone's consternation. Jung, who was a strong man, picked him up and carried him to a couch. Were the murderous impulses towards the father, as expressed by the erasure of his name from inscriptions, ultimately the same for Freud as the way Jung and Riklin had ceased to mention his name? It seems Freud was terrified in this period of being dethroned by Jung.[615]

CHAPTER ELEVEN

The secret committee

The years 1911–1913 were marked by major differences of opinion within the young psychoanalytic movement. Adler had left the Vienna Psychoanalytic Society in 1911, along with quite a number of other members. His theory that human beings are driven by power was ultimately incompatible with Freud's theory that they are driven by libido.[616] Freud did not regret Adler's departure; in fact, he had played a fairly active role in it. In early 1911, partly on Freud's initiative, Adler was asked to set out his position to the Vienna Society. A number of evenings were devoted to it and Adler was fiercely attacked by Freud and his allies. After that, he resigned his membership.[617]

Following Adler's departure, Wilhelm Stekel remained, even though he had been on Adler's side. Stekel was the managing editor of the *Zentralblatt für Psychoanalyse* at the time, and he increasingly came into conflict with Freud, all the more so because he was acting as if the journal was his own property, whereas it was a general journal with Freud as editor-in-chief.[618] The problems escalated when Stekel, after a quarrel, refused to work with Viktor Tausk any longer.[619] The intention had been for Tausk to take upon himself the review section of the journal. In November 1912, Stekel left the Society and Freud withdrew as editor-in-chief of the *Zentralblatt*. Stekel refused to give up his position as managing editor. Freud wrote to Abraham that he was extremely relieved by Stekel's departure from the Vienna Psychoanalytic Society, since he had lost all confidence in him.[620] He had thought of a way to displace Stekel from the editorship, since it looked as though the publisher of the *Zentralblatt* might take Stekel's side and opt to keep him. On 24 November 1912, a meeting was convened in Munich at which the chairs of the various psychoanalytic societies, including Abraham, were present.[621] There it was decided that a new journal would be established, the *Internationale Zeitschrift für ärztliche Psychoanalyse*. In 1920, the name was shortened to *Internationale Zeitschrift für Psychoanalyse*. The members of the various societies then cancelled their subscriptions to the *Zentralblatt* en masse.

Stekel remained its managing editor until the journal quietly died a death in 1914. Abraham offered his support to the new journal and said he was prepared to become editor if Ferenczi did not wish to do so. In the end, Ferenczi took on the editorship along with Rank.

The problems with Adler and Stekel troubled those involved a great deal, but they were as nothing to the problems with Jung, who was becoming an open threat to Freud.

From favourite son to enemy

The relationship between Jung and Freud worsened rapidly in 1912. Their difference of opinion about the libido theory, far from being resolved, intensified. Jung distanced himself openly from Freud and propagated a libido theory of his own that was diametrically opposed to Freud's. Jung believed the Oedipus drama should not be taken literally in the way that Freud believed it should. Children did not desire the parent of the opposite sex; girls did not want to go to bed with their fathers, or boys with their mothers. According to Jung, these presumed incestuous desires were symbols and phantasies.[622] Jung admitted that boys have a close bond with their mothers, but he said this had nothing to do with sexual desire; instead, it was connected with the dependence of children on their parents. The Oedipus saga was intended symbolically to prevent psychological incest, so that children were able to separate themselves from their parents.[623]

Jung wanted to expand the concept of libido to include psychic energy and to remove the emphasis on sexuality so that the theory would become more socially acceptable.[624] It was a hazardous situation. Jung was president of the IPA. He was very well known and had many followers. There was a real possibility that Jung's version of psychoanalysis might become the accepted version within the IPA and push Freud's theory into the background.

That risk became all the greater when Jung travelled to the USA in September 1912 to spend two months on a lecture tour there. He won a decisive victory with his new version of the libido theory. There was no longer any talk of sexuality in children or of the sexual origin of neuroses.[625] Neurosis was caused by the patient's current circumstances.

Shortly after Jung left for America, his wife, Emma, sent Freud volume two of his book *Psychology of the Unconscious*. Freud did not read it to the end. He knew for certain now that Jung had abandoned Freudian psychoanalysis.[626]

Immediately after his return, on 11 November 1912, Jung wrote a letter to Freud. It summed up all the successes he had achieved. He had given many lectures and held many seminars and in that short time he had even analysed several patients. His tone was full of bravura, almost coarse. He no longer wished to take account of Freud and he wrote, "Naturally I also made room for those of my views which deviate in places from the hitherto existing conceptions, particularly in regard to the libido theory. I found that my version of ΨA won over many people who until now had been put off by the problem of sexuality in neurosis".[627]

Freud replied, on 14 November, "You have reduced a good deal of resistance with your modifications, but I shouldn't advise you to enter this in the credit column because, as you know, the farther you remove yourself from what is new in ΨA, the more certain you will be of applause and the less resistance you will meet".[628]

These were the death spasms of a close friendship and collaboration. On 3 January 1913, a month and a half later, Freud proposed to Jung that they break off their personal contact. After that, the end of their business relationship was not long in coming. A secret committee was established and began to arm itself against the risk posed by the apostates, of whom Jung was seen as the most dangerous by far. The committee was set up mainly as a way of holding the line against Jung.

The secret committee

The idea of forming a secret committee arose when Jones, Ferenczi, and Rank met in Vienna in early July 1912.[629] They consulted about the difficult situation psychoanalysis now found itself in.[630] Ferenczi expressed a wish for a small group of men to be analysed by Freud, so that they could represent the pure theory, stripped of personal complexes. They would form a small unofficial group that would be at the centre of all the psychoanalytic societies, to which others could come to learn psychoanalysis.[631] Jones proposed this to Freud on 30 July 1912 and Freud addressed the matter in detail straight away, on 1 August:

> What took hold of my imagination immediately is your idea of a secret council composed of the best and most trustworthy among our men to take care of the further development of ΨA and defend the cause against personalities and accidents when I am no more. You say it was Ferenczi who expressed this idea, yet it may be mine own shaped in better times, when I hoped Jung would collect such a circle around himself composed of the official headmen of the local associations.[632] Now I am sorry to say such a union had to be formed independently of Jung and of the elected presidents. I dare say it would make living and dying easier for me if I knew of such an association existing to watch over my creation. I know there is a boyish, perhaps romantic element too in this conception, but perhaps it could be adapted to meet the necessities of reality. I will give my fancy free play and may leave to you the part of the Censor.
>
> First of all: This committee had to be strictly secret in its existence and its actions. It could be composed of you, Ferenczi and Rank, among whom the idea was generated. Sachs—in whom my confidence is illimited in spite of the shortness of our acquaintance—and Abraham could be called next, but only under condition of all of you consenting.[633]

In fact, Freud took charge of the initiative from the start. He made its aim the further development of psychoanalysis and the defence of the cause of psychoanalysis against "personalities and accidents" after his death. Freud proposed that both the existence of the committee and its activities should be strictly secret and he named the potential members. It was some time before the committee began to function, but the outlines of it were there and everyone Freud named did indeed become a member.

It is not entirely clear when Abraham first became involved. Jones mentions in his description of the origins of the committee that Ferenczi and Rank had made contact with Abraham when they were in Berlin.[634] In the same context, Jones refers to a letter from Abraham to Freud of 24 July 1912, in which Abraham mentions the visit and writes that he has obtained further information from Rank.[635] Jones assumed the secret committee must have been spoken about at that time. On 26 December 1912, Freud wrote to Jones that Abraham had recently visited him for three days and that he did not know whether Rank had persuaded Abraham to join the group.[636] This might mean that Abraham had his doubts about the enterprise at first and had to be talked round. Its secret character, outside the official IPA and the local psychoanalytic societies, might not have been to Abraham's liking initially, but in that case he must have reconsidered. On 25 May 1913, during the first official meeting of the committee, Freud gave each of the members a small piece of treasure from his collection of ancient Greek precious stones, set into gold rings.[637]

Smoking out Jung

On 29 July 1912, Freud wrote to Abraham, "I am preoccupied with what is going on in Zurich, which seems to prove the truth of an old prediction of yours, which I willingly ignored. I shall certainly contribute nothing to the break, and I hope that the scientific companionship can be sustained".[638] It was a recognition by Freud that Abraham had been right when he warned that Jung and the Zurich circle were distancing themselves from Freudian psychoanalysis. Contact between Abraham and Freud in this period was extremely warm-hearted.

The entire situation with Jung and then with Stekel hit Freud's self-confidence hard. On 21 October 1912, he wrote to Abraham, "Now to what preys on my mind. I find it embarrassing to think that we should get on so well because we meet so rarely. (With Ferenczi it goes just as well, incidentally, despite our frequently being together.)"[639]

The main goal of the secret committee was to ensure that Jung, with his divergent ideas, did not gain the upper hand in the psychoanalytic movement. The members decided to review Jung's work in detail in the journals and Freud would then follow up with an article about the history of psychoanalysis.[640] Jung was subjected to a bombardment of criticism. Ferenczi got the ball rolling with criticism of Jung's *Psychology of the Unconscious*.[641] He presented his review at the first meeting of the committee on 24 and 25 May 1913 in Vienna. At that same meeting, the members discussed how they should behave at the forthcoming psychoanalytic congress in Munich, which was to be chaired by Jung.[642]

Confrontation at the Munich congress

The congress took place on 7 and 8 September 1913. The secret committee met the day before at a different venue and shortly before that Abraham and Ferenczi visited Freud together for several days at San Martino di Castrozza in the South Tyrol, where he was staying on holiday. Abraham had spent the summer with Hedwig and the children in Noordwijk on the Dutch coast.[643]

The congress was the last time Freud and Jung met. There were eighty-seven participants, both members and guests. The IPA had a membership of 160 by this point. The report of the congress is the shortest ever to appear in the *Korrespondenzblatt*.[644] The tension must have been extraordinary. The committee had agreed beforehand that an open break must be avoided.

There was a risk that Jung and the Swiss might publicly withdraw from the IPA, which would cause the entire organisation to split.

Lou Andreas-Salomé was present at the congress and she described the situation in her diary as follows:

> The people from Zurich sat at their own table, across from the Freud table. There is one phrase that sums up what characterised their behaviour towards Freud: not that Freud was deviating from him (Jung) but that it was precisely by this deviation that he (Jung) must save Freud and his cause. When Freud resisted, the weapon was turned as if he could bear no scientific toleration, was dogmatic and so on. Who it is that's dogmatic and power-loving you could see at a glance. Whereas two years ago Jung had a kind of robust joviality and bursting vitality that revealed itself in his thundering laugh, he is now, in his solemnity, aggressive, ambitious, with a mental brutality. Freud was never so close to me as at that moment, not just because of the break with his "son" Jung, whom he loved, for whom he had as it were transferred his cause to Zurich, but because of the nature of the break—as if it was Freud who had approach him with ambitious rigidity. Freud was the same as ever, but he was finding it hard to quieten the profound emotion within him.[645]

According to Jones, with the exception of lectures by Freud, Abraham, and Ferenczi, the quality of the presentations in Munich was mediocre.[646] Abraham gave a talk about the neurotic curtailment of sight. His article on the subject was published in 1914 and became a classic of the psychoanalytic canon.[647] In the vote for the presidency of the IPA, Jung was re-elected, with thirty votes in favour and twenty-two abstentions.[648] The members of the committee abstained. Jung accepted the renewal of his presidency.

Further smoking out of Jung

In October 1913, in a letter to Maeder, Freud wrote that he wondered whether Jung was acting in good faith. At this point Maeder was president of the Zurich Psychoanalytic Society. The message reached Jung, deeply offended him and led him to decide that further collaboration with Freud was impossible. He withdrew as editor-in-chief of the *Jahrbuch*.[649] Abraham succeeded him, with the support of Eduard Hitschmann.[650] In late 1913 and early 1914, there was a great deal of contact between Abraham and Freud. Freud was happy with the criticism of Jung that Abraham was writing and in their letters the expression "Coraggio Casimiro" occurs a number of times. It was their way of giving each other courage.[651] "Coraggio Casimiro" was a reference to a mountain climb Abraham had undertaken with two guides, who had taken raw meat with them to eat. On arrival at the hut where they were to stay the night they discovered that the meat had started to smell bad. One guide encouraged the other to eat it with the words "Coraggio, Casimiro".[652]

Freud suggested the IPA should be wound up and a new association formed, in order to be rid of Jung as president.[653] The plan was dropped after objections by Abraham and Jones. In March 1914, Abraham proposed to the committee that the four groups they represented—Berlin, Budapest, Vienna, and London—should sign a petition asking Jung to step down. Jones responded by protesting fiercely against this in a letter to Abraham. His London group was barely holding together and Jung's supporters were too strongly represented.[654]

Then, in the first issue of the *Zeitschrift* for 1914, several extremely critical reviews of Jung's work were published. Abraham's article was a long review of Jung's American lectures. Abraham's criticism was imbued with a fierce indignation unusual for him, not just because Jung was being disloyal to Freud but because he kept contradicting himself.[655] That same issue included a critique by Jones of Jung's "Psycho-Analysis".[656] Next came criticism by Ferenczi of Jung's lecture in Munich.[657] Eitingon made a contribution, too, criticising Jung in an article called "Über das UBW bei Jung und seine Wendung ins Ethische" (On the UBW in Jung and his turn to the ethical) (UBW is the abbreviation for "Unbewusste", meaning "unconscious").[658]

Rank and Sachs were also planning to write an article critical of Jung called "What is psychoanalysis?", but Hitschmann thought the *Jahrbuch* was becoming too full, so they withdrew their piece.[659]

All this criticism was devastating. Jung took the honourable way out and wrote to all chairmen of the Societies on 20 April 1914 that he was withdrawing as president of the IPA.[660] This had been precisely the intention. On 22 April, Abraham and Eitingon sent Freud a telegram: "HEARTFELT CONGRATULATIONS ON THE ZURICH NEWS".[661]

Freud answered Abraham: "Dear Friend, You were certainly just as surprised as I was at how meticulously Jung carries out our own intentions. Our reserve has now indeed borne fruit; somehow we will get rid of him, and perhaps of the Swiss altogether".[662]

This was all before the publication of Freud's own contribution. His article "On the history of the psycho-analytic movement" was an attack on Jung.[663] In the committee, it was known as his "*Bombe*", his "bomb". Bleuler thought it extremely unpleasant that he was placed in the same category as Jung in the article and he wrote to Freud that he was far closer to Freudian psychoanalysis than to the Jungian version.[664] Abraham was pleased by Bleuler's reaction and wrote to Jones that he hoped that now Jung had resigned, Bleuler would rejoin their ranks.[665]

The committee members

The group that Freud had gathered around him was highly talented. The members of the committee were without exception extremely erudite and, aside from Eitingon, they had all published a great deal.

Ferenczi, a Hungarian, was the most spontaneous and exuberant of the committee's members, full of warmth and enthusiasm for his friends and no less unrestrained in demanding attention and love from Freud. A gifted speaker and analyst, who talked a great deal during his analyses, he was important in the development of psychoanalytic theory.[666]

Rank looked young, with large spectacles. He was shy and, despite his intelligence, sometimes felt awkward. His simple background sometimes got in his way. He was widely read and essential to Freud as a secretary. He was also an original thinker.[667]

Sachs was above all a man of literature, with a huge repertoire of Jewish jokes. He was witty, courteous, and great company, and always surrounded by women. He was particularly loyal to Freud.[668]

Abraham was calm, measured, firm, not quick to judge. He had a great sense of humour and he, too, was a gifted speaker. Jones thought him the most normal of the group. He was important in the development of psychoanalytic theory and in propagating psychoanalysis.

Eitingon, who joined the committee in 1919, was a small, inconspicuous man with a rather anxious look. He followed Freud in everything.[669] At the same time he lived in great wealth and luxury. He came into his own when able to help. The polyclinic he set up was of great importance to the development of psychoanalysis.

Jones was the only non-Jewish member of the committee and the only one for whom German was not his mother tongue. Both these things made his position less than easy. He was a small, resolute man with huge enthusiasm for work and great charm. He was extremely important to the development of psychoanalysis in the English-speaking countries.

Abraham's position on the committee

In the early years of the committee, Abraham occupied a special position. He had a good marriage with two children he doted on, as well as a psychoanalytic practice that carried out ten analyses per day. Berlin was one day's journey from Vienna. Abraham was extremely attached to Freud but not directly financially or emotionally dependent on him.

The same could not be said of the others, with the exception of Sachs. Ferenczi and Jones were involved in psychoanalytic relationships with Freud that could be described as extraordinarily complicated, almost incestuous. Both had partners who entered into analysis with Freud and both corresponded about this in detail with him. In both cases, those romantic relationships failed. Ferenczi's girlfriend, Elma Palos, and Jones' girlfriend, Loe Kann, married other men.[670] Loe Kann married a man who was also called Jones, whom Jones consistently referred to as Jones the Second, and Freud, who had become very fond of Loe Kann, was present at her wedding in Budapest in June 1913.[671]

Freud believed Jones needed analysis and tried to persuade him of this. In June 1913, Jones travelled to Budapest to undergo analysis for two hours a day with Ferenczi. Freud and Ferenczi discuss this at length in their letters. With all these analyses and a lack of discretion as to what they wrote in their letters, a complex emotional tangle developed. Freud seems to have become rather more cautious when both Ferenczi's relationship with Elma Palos and Jones' relationship with Loe Kann broke down after the women entered into analysis with him. He did not want to accept Ferenczi for analysis at that point.

The two non-doctors on the committee, Rank and Sachs, both started to practise analysis only after the First World War. Rank had a doctorate in philosophy and Sachs in law. Otto Rank was completely dependent on Freud.[672] When he met Freud in 1905 at the age of twenty-one, having been introduced by Adler, who was his family doctor, he was a turner and fitter who had read *The Interpretation of Dreams*. In 1906, he wrote the book *Der Künstler*, which was greatly valued by Freud.[673] Freud took care that he received a scholarship to enable him to attend grammar school and then university. In 1912, Rank gained his doctorate in philosophy with a book about the Lohengrin saga. Ever since 1906 he had been secretary to the Wednesday Society and later he performed the same function for the Vienna Psychoanalytic Society.[674] He was also Freud's personal secretary and right-hand man.

The co-ordinated move against Jung was the first act of the secret committee. After the First World War, it grew into a cabal that determined the shape of psychoanalysis from behind the scenes for many years and shared out all the leadership positions between its members.

CHAPTER TWELVE

An unhappy writer, scopophilia, and other peculiarities

An observation by Abraham, and the writer concerned

"Should patients write down their dreams?" was a short article that Abraham published in 1913.[675] It concerned the question of whether it was useful to ask patients to write down their dreams immediately upon waking. In a brief paper about the use of dream interpretation in psychoanalysis, Freud had said this was unnecessary.[676] It had turned out that if the narrative of a dream, which would otherwise have been forgotten, was laboriously saved in this way, no significant thoughts would come to the patient in the session of psychoanalysis that followed. The dream text might as well not have been saved at all. Abraham developed this theme further and described one of his patients, whom he had told that there was no point in writing down his dreams. The patient nevertheless put a notebook next to his bed. He had an elaborate, emotionally laden dream and when he woke he filled two pages with notes, which he brought to his analysis with Abraham the next morning. It soon turned out that what he had written down was completely unreadable. His desire to preserve the dream was thwarted by repression, and the resulting compromise took the form of two unreadable pages. The patient was not content to let the matter rest and decided to put dictation equipment next to his bed. It was interesting that in doing so he forgot that the equipment did not work very well. The recording turned out to be very indistinct and in his session of analysis the patient had to fill many gaps. Ideas came to him without any difficulty, but it could all have happened equally well without any recording. In this case there was little resistance, so the patient could easily fill gaps and associate.

Abraham wrote that taking a dream with you to analysis was rather like presenting a gift to the analyst. "I'm bringing you the most special thing I have." Particularly narcissistic patients might fall in love with the beauty of their dreams and preserve them against forgetting like treasures. The article gained additional significance later when it became clear that the patient described was the writer Oskar A. H. Schmitz, who, in his third volume of journals, wrote a detailed account of his analysis with Abraham.[677]

In early twentieth-century Germany, Oskar A. H. Schmitz (1873–1931) was a well-known writer.[678] He fell into obscurity for a while, but, since the publication of his diaries in 2007, interest in him has grown again.[679] He was the elder son of a railway director in Bad Homburg, and he grew up in a wealthy and protected environment in which music and general personal development were regarded as important.[680] He occupied a special position in the family, where he had a younger brother and two younger sisters. All the hopes of his parents, especially his father, were invested in him: he must study hard, he must be a success, he must have a brilliant career.

By the time he went to secondary school, Schmitz felt a powerful resistance to all this. He passed his school leaving exams only with great difficulty and went to Heidelberg to study law. In subsequent semesters, he attended the universities of Leipzig, Berlin, and Munich. As well as law, he went to lectures on economics, philosophy, and art history, but he felt attracted above all by artistic circles in Munich.[681] It was in this period that he started writing poetry. In 1894, he met Karl Wolfskehl in Rome, who introduced him to the poetry of Stefan George. Wolfskehl offered to give Schmitz's poems to George and to have them published in *Blätter für die Kunst*.[682] After that, Schmitz made several attempts to finish his university degree and to write a dissertation, encouraged by his father and by Wolfskehl. He switched from law to economics, then to art history and German.

All this time, until his sudden death in 1895, his father continued to hope that eventually a doctoral thesis would emerge. Schmitz said that he had always felt rather distant from his mother but had a profound relationship with his father and felt obliged to live up to his expectations. As a small child, he adored his father. So, for a while, he continued his attempts to graduate and to gain a doctorate, but, in 1896, he decided to become a writer and poet. He was enabled to do so by his inheritance from his father. The fact that in 1896 his first poems appeared in *Blätter für die Kunst* had a major influence on his decision. Schmitz tried to connect with the Schwabinger Bohème, a *fin-de-siècle* group made up of loners, eccentrics, and geniuses who wanted to live wild lives and be different.[683] (Schwabing was Munich's bohemian quarter.) Schmitz was never really accepted into this group, with its relentless insistence on nonconformism. He was regarded as too bourgeois. Franziska zu Reventlow describes him rather unflatteringly in her *roman à clef Herrn Dames Aufzeichnungen* through the character of Adriaan, a writer on the make whose origins were obvious from a long way off.[684] It was a period marked by an intensely apolitical attitude to life. Stefan George, Hugo von Hoffmannsthal, and Rainer Maria Rilke all wrote about their feelings and recorded fleeting impressions and moods. Wedekind, who was extremely critical of the zeitgeist, wrote the following poem largely as a reaction against the Bohème.[685]

> Greife wacker nach der Sünde,
> Aus der Sünde wächst Genuß.
> Ach du gleichest einem Kinde,
> Dem man alles zeigen muß.

Meide nicht die ird'schen Schätze:
Wo sie liegen, nimm sie mit.
Hat die Welt doch nur Gesetze,
Daß man sie mit Füßen tritt.

Glücklich, wer geschickt und heiter
Über frische Gräber hopst.
Tanzend auf der Galgenleiter
Hat sich keiner noch gemopst.

Reach out bravely for sin.
From sin enjoyment grows.
Ah, you are like a child
That has to be shown everything.

Don't eschew the worldly treasures.
Wherever they may lie, take them with you.
The world only has laws
So that people may trample on them.

Happy is he who, artfully and gaily,
Hops over fresh graves.
Dancing on the steps to the gallows
Has never yet bored anyone.[686]

Schmitz left for Paris, where he felt more at home.[687] He stayed there for almost a year and got to know Stefan George personally. In the years that followed, Schmitz became a productive and eventually rather successful writer. He travelled a great deal, to Italy, France, Britain, Spain, Algeria, and Egypt, and spent long periods in the major capital cities of Europe. He was a popular guest at literary salons and he was a compulsive visitor of brothels and prostitutes. A restless man, he led a hectic and nervous life, continually on the go, driven by loneliness.

Schmitz hoped to find peace in marriage and in 1901 he married the singer Nina Burk. After a year they separated, and in 1905 he married again. This time the marriage lasted six months. In lonely hours he would walk through the city to pick up a woman. As early as 1897, he wrote in his diary about his puzzling fear of demons in the small hours of the night and how they sent him into a panic. On 5 May 1907, this fear overcame him during a walk through a sunny English garden. After that the panic attacks increased, often in connection with his sexual escapades. When Schmitz was in Vienna in 1907, he met the publisher and bookseller Hugo Heller, who invited him to attend a lecture by Freud called "Creative writers and day-dreaming". Schmitz went with a friend, the writer Stefan Zweig.[688] After the lecture, Schmitz made an appointment with Freud for 13 December and then went to the whores with Zweig. Freud advised Schmitz to have his physical ailments treated before he began psychoanalysis, in particular the trouble with his bladder that he was experiencing. Afterwards, Schmitz had second thoughts about this advice, since he felt his bladder problems were connected with his mental state. In the years that followed, his difficulties continued unabated. Years later, in 1912, he was again in Vienna and he probably sought contact with Freud again, who referred him to Abraham in Berlin.

On 16 November 1912, Schmitz wrote in his diary, "On Wednesday 13 Nov. started sessions of psychoanalysis with Dr. Abraham".[689] From the notes in his diary it is not possible to form a precise impression of his psychoanalysis by Abraham; they are too fragmentary and it is unclear what was said. They do, however, give a general impression. Analysis began quickly. Abraham's way of working might have been to begin his interpretation while the patient was still, so to speak, on the threshold. We cannot exclude the possibility that Schmitz, who had read books about psychoanalysis, began that way himself. In any case, by the second day, based on a dream, they were already talking about Schmitz's erotic feelings for his father as a substitute for his mother.

He had been woken in the night from a dream that someone was in the room. In analysis, it emerged that this had to do with his father. The next day, the light world his father represented and the dark world connected with his mother were discussed. Shortly after that, a session was spent analysing the little book *Herr von Pepinster und seine Popanz* (1912), which Schmitz had written in collaboration with his brother-in-law and friend Alfred Kubin.[690] Kubin had created fourteen illustrations for the book. The story concerned a certain Lynx, a miserable ghost who could live only by sucking the strength out of living people like a vampire. People who did not have a powerful ego, who lacked a pronounced will to survive, became his victims. In the character of Pepinster, Schmitz seemed to be describing himself and his own lack of identity that made him wander astray. Pepinster leads a double life, like Schmitz, moving from the world of the intellect to the world of the passions and back again.

Wolfgang Martynkewicz, the editor of Schmitz's diaries, described what the pages of the journals that related to his psychoanalysis looked like. They were full of heavy crossings out in different kinds of ink and in highly inconsistent handwriting, which sometimes became illegible. Often pieces had been torn out afterwards, or cut away with a knife, and descriptions would abruptly stop.[691] Clearly a great deal of emotion and aggression was involved. Martynkewicz also pointed out that, in particular, many of the passages that related to Abraham's diagnosis had been destroyed. On 19 March 1913 we read "Analysis: At least a clear diagnosis now: 1) Narcissism, outwardly sublimated to striving for perfection in everything. . . ."[692] There the text breaks off; Schmitz has cut out the remainder with a razor blade. The word narcissism occurred regularly in the diaries and Martynkewicz seems to have taken that diagnosis at face value. Was it really narcissism in a man who sometimes had great difficulty keeping himself together mentally and later became psychotic? Schmitz certainly had an extremely narcissistic father, who regarded his son as a project: a boy who must study and go on to build a brilliant career; a boy who must make his father's dream come true. Schmitz Senior does not seem to have taken into consideration whether or not Schmitz Junior was suited to fulfilling his father's dream.

In "On narcissism", Freud wrote, "Parental love, which is so moving and at bottom so childish, is nothing but the parents' narcissism born again, which, transformed into object-love, unmistakably reveals its former nature".[693]

Schmitz began his analysis convinced that he adored his father and hated and despised his mother. Both parents were discussed at length during the sessions and the reverse side of adoration was addressed, that is, anger and fear in relation to the father.[694] Other subjects that arose were Schmitz's anal tendencies and problems with authority, his refusal to conform to the wishes of others, his enjoyment of being late, of travelling out of season, and of sleeping in the top bunk of a train compartment, with no one above him. By contrast, there was his fear of abandonment and wanting to be different from the way he was because he could not completely join in. Schmitz found it very hard to be alone.

After the analysis was broken off, Schmitz wrote an autobiographical book called *Der Vertriebene* (The Exile), in which he describes the moment when, as he sees it, he started to exhibit deviant behaviour. One day, when Schmitz was still a toddler, his father saw him jumping about the room naked. From that moment on, his upbringing changed. His father took control and taught him about shame and hygiene. Habits that until then had been entirely natural became problematic, such as the privilege, the daily morning ritual, of crawling into bed with his mother. This was no longer allowed, and neither was dancing naked in front of his sisters. Why not? the boy wanted to know. Because it is shameful, his father said. Schmitz says it split his soul in two, with one half in the light world and the other in the dark world. It was a theme to which he returned time and again. On 11 January 1916, after the session, he wrote in his diary,

> The ambivalence arose because of that: that what was experienced as a declaration of love should suddenly be evil and forbidden.
>
> Assumption: the parents "no longer love" their son. Now he no longer loves them either and refrains from any expression of love. That is however precisely what is desired. As a result a stubborn obedience to the mother arises, which at the same time is no longer love. There is a forced obedience to the father, which at the same time is lovelessness towards others.[695]

Schmitz's father regularly allowed his contempt for his wife to show through. The mother was belittled both by the father and by the paternal grandmother. Schmitz hated that, but nevertheless he began to see his mother as undeserving of his father. He, too, began to despise her. It must have been a case of identification with the aggressor, although that concept did not yet exist.[696] Fear caused Schmitz to identify with his father and to start imitating him. That fear was expressed in his dreams of those years. He had nightmares about a creature he called "Lieflam", a huge mud-brown beast. Later he described it as an animal with black beards all over it. He told of how as a child he once walked into the bathroom when his father was having a bath and noticed that his father "had black beards all over him". Freud had recently published *Totem and Taboo*, a collection of essays that discuss just such frightening animals in dreams. In the case of boys, they usually represented the father.[697] The birth of his younger brother, Richard, made Schmitz feel ousted. At that point, his father took over his upbringing completely from his mother, putting him to bed in the evenings, checking he had washed, and caring for him when he was ill. His little brother, whose appearance was marred by a birthmark that covered two thirds of his face, received all the attention.[698] Schmitz felt permanently discriminated against, purely because he had not come into the world with an abnormality. When he found out at secondary school that his mother was partly of Jewish extraction, it came as an enormous shock. After that, he connected the dark world inside him with his Jewish roots, yet took on a Jewish psychoanalyst.

Martynkewicz (2007c) wrote in the summary of his article about Schmitz's psychoanalysis by Abraham, "The case demonstrates the early treatment of a narcissistic neurosis, which ultimately fails because of the resistance and defensive mechanism of the patient" (translated for this edition). He wrote this with conviction, as if it were a foregone conclusion that the analysis would fail because of Schmitz's resistance, as if he had impenetrable narcissistic armour. Yet, the passion with which Schmitz's diary entries for the period of the analysis are written, so different from other parts of his journals, tends to suggest that there was too little armour, rather than too much. Those things that were discussed in analysis clearly went very deep. It seems that at first an unexpected amount was achieved with the desperately unhappy Schmitz. Fairly soon there was a positive transference, and Abraham in particular, as a trustworthy presence, seems to have been important in bringing it about. Schmitz was so bound up with himself that he seems barely to have registered Abraham as a person. His diary entries are quite unlike those of Horney in 1910, in which Abraham is far more clearly present in person. Schmitz stopped his constant travelling, which had been a way of fleeing his depression and fears. This was far from easy for him. On 7 June 1913, he wrote the following about his psychoanalysis:

> The effect is generally such that I have become calmer inside and no longer chase illusions. Those illusions were however a kind of self-defence against my inborn tendency to criticise. Now, without illusions, I am at the mercy of that criticism and for the time being that does not exactly strengthen the activities of life, especially with regard to women.[699]

When he undertook another trip to Russia in May 1914, he noticed that travelling alone was no longer easy for him.

In the analysis of Schmitz, who had become more or less stuck in an anal, childhood world, there was a great deal that could be talked about, such as Schmitz's adoration for his father, which enabled him to put that adoration into perspective. It became possible to talk about Schmitz's odd childhood dreams in which he was forced to eat faeces. The subject of his extreme rages arose as well. The relationship with his mother and his jealousy of his little brother remained largely shrouded in mystery, but his mother was discussed often and a little of the desire, rather than the aversion, was brought out.

We cannot say how the analysis might have ended had it continued. Schmitz had major problems that were difficult to treat. It is clear, however, that the sudden breaking off of his psychoanalysis was the worst thing that could have happened to him. In *Ergo Sum*, Schmitz recalls it as a huge crisis:

> The wife of the doctor mentioned to me on the phone that her husband was now being called up and my feelings at that moment were like those of a child that suddenly loses the loved one that is raising it . . .; with great difficulty I got through a "parting session", as if I could not live any longer without receiving some guidance, and whenever in the days that followed I passed the house of this very likeable man, I had the childish feeling that I had been deprived of my last refuge in this tough time, which apparently had no further use for me.[700]

It was 1915. There was a war on. Abraham had been called up and had no choice but to break off Schmitz's psychoanalysis. Schmitz became depressed. In 1916, his condition worsened and he became almost psychotic. In early 1916, he was called in for a medical examination prior to being drafted and he lived in a total panic with regard to the war. When he was actually called up, Abraham saved him at the last moment by writing a doctor's certificate for him, as a result of which he did not have to join the army.[701] Abraham had clearly become fond of Schmitz and even gave him permission to make use of his library in Berlin in his absence.[702] In 1916, it seems that Schmitz, along with his friend Alfred Kubin, became subject to megalomania and lost all contact with reality.

Why did Schmitz not return to Abraham after the war? His severe problems persisted. It was only when he happened to meet Abraham at a health resort in 1921 that they had a few more conversations. Aside from Schmitz's many rationalisations, including arguments that Freud's teachings were wrong after all, he probably simply did not have the courage to continue. The sudden end to his treatment had been devastating.

Several more psychoanalytic observations

In 1912–1913, Abraham published a series of short, concise articles about agoraphobia, fetishism, and rituals. They are best understood as psychoanalytic observations. They varied in length from two to eleven pages.

A short piece titled "On the psychogenesis of agoraphobia in childhood" was about a little boy of five who became anxious whenever his mother left, even if his nanny stayed with him.[703] The children Abraham describes always had nannies, as was usual in his circles. The little boy did not dare to go outside unless his mother was with him, even to go to the neighbour's house. When his mother instructed him to take a walk with the nanny, the little boy said firmly, "I do not want to be a walking-child, I want to be a mother's child."[704] Suddenly it was no longer a question of what he was afraid of, but rather of what he wanted. But the objection will be, Abraham writes, that if the boy so clearly knows what he wants, which is to be a mummy's boy, then what is the anxiety about, which indicates that something must be repressed? According to Abraham, what had to be repressed was the incestuous, forbidden desire to possess the mother sexually and have her all to himself.

This desire was expressed in things the little boy said. When his father was away for a few days, he was allowed to sleep next to his mother in the parental bed. On the morning that his mother told him his father would return that day, the little boy responded by saying, "How much nicer it would be if daddy never came back at all!"[705] By saying that, Abraham writes, he expressed both his wish that his father was dead and his desire to sleep with his mother.

In this brief case history, the little boy's wish regarding his mother is indeed striking, but Abraham seems to pay little attention to fearful situations in the real world. The boy was very anxious and wanted to have his mother to himself. Was he simply afraid, though, of his own forbidden incestuous desires?

According to Jones, Abraham suffered from agoraphobia himself in his early years. Perhaps Abraham was actually the little boy he was writing about. But in Abraham's case there was another fear as well. He was afraid that his mother would suddenly disappear in the sense that she had when he was two. He worried about this so much that he did not want to let her out of his sight.

Abraham wrote two articles on the subject. The second, in 1914, was about agoraphobia in combination with a powerful desire for movement.[706] In his view, enjoyment of walking or dancing that was obstructed by the fact that the child dared to go out only when accompanied by the mother or father was a sign that the child was too strongly attached to the parents and forbade itself to move in their absence. He called it a sign of an incestuous fixation. Jones wrote to Abraham on 29 December 1913 that he had read the article with great interest and went on to describe a symptom of his own that had to do with movement. He would always be put into a bad mood instantly if the person he was with on a walk insisted on deciding the route rather than leaving it to Jones. (Jones was generally speaking extremely coercive. He wanted everything to go the way it went in his head.) He connected the symptom with a rebellion against his father. Jones had once greatly enjoyed taking walks with his father. He felt it was a rebellion against unconscious homosexual desires, as well as resistance at a very early age to being told what to do, such as resistance to being taken to the toilet when you did not want to go, whether by a mother or by a nurse. Jones must have been immensely stubborn.[707]

Abraham's article "Remarks on the psycho-analysis of a case of foot and corset fetishism" was about a twenty-two-year-old student who, in puberty, felt attracted neither to men nor to women. He believed himself to be impotent. At the age of fourteen, he started to tie himself up and before long was doing so regularly, as soon as he was home alone. He liked reading books in which people were tied up and tortured, such as stories about "Red Indians". He never tried it on others. Later, he noticed that he was aroused by elegant ladies' shoes with high heels, especially when he imagined how uncomfortable they must be.[708] His interest then shifted to corsets, and the tighter they were laced the more arousing he found them. As a sixteen-year-old boy he even wore one of his mother's corsets outdoors on several occasions, under his clothes.

This psychoanalytic case history is very different from the way it would be written now. The interaction with the analyst and the countertransference are not mentioned. As was usual in those days, the patient was described along with his symptoms, and then a psychoanalytic explanation was sought based on associations made by the patient.

What struck Abraham in the case of this boy was the drastic curtailment of sexual activity. It consisted mainly of phantasy and of pleasure in looking, and it was entirely auto-erotic. Abraham's conclusion was that this had to do with extremely powerful congenital anal-sadistic urges and scopophilia, which had to be so strongly repressed that the boy perceived merely a part of other people, always the exterior.[709] He saw only a pinching shoe; the rest of the person was invisible to him. Because of repression, only one small aspect of sight remained.

In "A complicated ceremonial found in neurotic women", Abraham describes two women who did not know each other but who performed a very similar ritual before going to sleep at night.[710] They both laid out their clothes with meticulous neatness and paid particular attention to grooming their hair. At first, they explained this by saying that they might die suddenly in the night. One of the women would carefully tie her long hair with a white ribbon, just as she had when she was a young girl. As the analysis went on, it turned out that it was not death she expected but her father, who had died when she was an adolescent.

Transformations of scopophilia

In 1910, Freud wrote a short treatise entitled "The psycho-analytic view of psychogenic distur-bance of vision".[711] This was the first article in which he wrote about ego-drives. These are drives that serve the purposes of the individual's self-preservation and it is important to distin-guish between them and sexual drives. The subject of the article was hysterical blindness, or becoming unable to see as a reaction to looking as a stimulating sexual act. Freud wrote that a reproving voice was heard, telling the individual that because they had tried to use their sight for purposes of evil sensual desire, they would now get their just deserts and be unable to see any longer.[712] Freud wrote the following:

> The sexual and ego-instincts alike have in general the same organs and systems of organs at their disposal. Sexual pleasure is not attached merely to the function of the genitals. The mouth serves for kissing as well as for eating and communication by speech; the eyes perceive not only alter-ations in the external world which are important for the preservation of life, but also characteris-tics of objects which lead to their being chosen as objects of love—their charms.[713]

It is hard to serve two masters, and so it may happen that one of the partial urges that makes use of the eyesight, scopophilia, is extremely powerful. The ego-drive responds with repres-sion, so that ordinary sight becomes disturbed. Freud wondered in the article whether the repression of sexual component drives in itself would be enough to cause a functional disor-der of an organ, or whether there would have to be specific constitutional conditions that forced organs to exaggerate their erogenous role and, as a result, caused the repression of drives.[714] This would then be the bodily component of the disposition to psychogenic and neurotic dis-orders.

This fragment is of importance in connection with Abraham, who repeatedly pointed to constitutionally determined, strengthened drive organisation as among the causes of neurotic disorders, yet approached the subject in a different way from Freud.[715] Where Freud saw mainly a point of discussion and stressed the questions that should be asked, Abraham tended to assert that neuroses had to do with overactive drives, and they were, therefore, suddenly seen as an abnormality, something that in Freud's work, with its cautious formulations, does not emerge at all. It is noticeable time and again that Abraham, as a doctor of his time, divided the world into healthy and sick.

On 3 March 1913, Abraham wrote to Freud about sight in a quite different connection.[716] He had noticed a number of times that patients were unable to describe their parents. The patient would be incapable of calling to mind his or her parents' facial features, despite being able to recall those of other family members and acquaintances in detail. So there was a form of repres-sion of scopophilia specific to the relationship with the parents. This observation by Abraham later became important as a psychoanalytic diagnostic instrument. The inability to describe one or both parents came to be seen as a sign of a problematic relationship with the parent or parents concerned. It indicated that the patient did not dare to look at the parent. Freud responded by asking Abraham to develop his valuable observation into an item for the *Jahrbuch*.[717] Abraham eventually wrote a lengthy article on the subject, "Restrictions and transformations of scopophilia in psycho-neurotics; with remarks on analogous phenomena in folk-psychology".[718] He also gave a talk on the subject at the congress in Munich.

Freud was hugely enthusiastic about the article:

Dear Friend,

I read your paper for the *Jahrbuch* yesterday and cannot refrain from congratulating you on it. I think it the best clinical contribution that has appeared in any of the five volumes, unequalled in assurance, correctness, many-sidedness, and interest. Vivant sequentes![719]

CHAPTER THIRTEEN

The First World War

A t the start of 1914, none of the psychoanalysts of the time seems to have had the slightest suspicion of what was awaiting them. In their letters there is no trace of unease about the political situation.

This was one of the high points of Abraham's psychoanalytic career and of his contact with Freud. All his attention was focused there. As already mentioned, after Jung withdrew as editor-in-chief of the *Jahrbuch für Psychoanalyse* in late 1913, Freud asked Abraham to take over that task.[720] Abraham was happy to oblige.[721] Freud visited him in Berlin on 25 December 1913 and spent the afternoon at his house. In early 1914, Abraham sent Freud a photograph of himself. Freud had it framed and put it in the place of Jung's portrait.[722] In their correspondence, they frequently discussed the *Jahrbuch*. Freud sent Abraham his "On narcissism: an introduction". He was rather uncertain about it and clearly relieved by Abraham's enthusiastic reaction.[723] He wrote that he was moved by the fact that Abraham was willing to include the piece in the *Jahrbuch* and that they were now bound together yet more intimately.[724] It was as if, in his new role as editor, Abraham had suddenly become for Freud a person whose opinion was anxiously awaited, and if it turned out to be favourable he would accept the verdict with relief. That Freud had been so wrong about Jung and so right about Abraham seems also to have brought about a change in their relationship, as if Freud was now putting himself in Abraham's hands. Two days after Freud heard that Jung had withdrawn as president of the IPA, he asked Abraham to comply with his request to take over the leadership of the upcoming congress in Dresden. He also urged Abraham to arrange to spend the summer vacation, with his family, not far from the holiday home where Freud would be staying.[725] Because of the outbreak of the First World War, the congress in Dresden did not take place.

On 7 May, Freud wrote to Abraham, "You are now our President. We have the Association in our own hands and shall not soon let go of it".[726] In just a few months, Freud had transferred to Abraham all the functions Jung had fulfilled in the International Psychoanalytic Association. When making Abraham president, he had asked permission from the chairmen of all the Societies attached to the IPA. They all assented. Nevertheless, Abraham's reaction to the offer was cautious. He accepted the presidency *ad interim*, but he needed to think long and hard about taking the position permanently and he consulted with Sachs on the subject. He would have preferred Freud to take over the function himself, although without being burdened with the day-to-day concerns involved. It would become an honorary presidency, while the actual presidential duties would be carried out by Abraham or by whoever was, in due course, chosen. Freud answered that it was his personal wish that Abraham, with his "energy, correctness and devotion to duty" should become the definitive president, but he wanted to leave the decision to the committee, which planned to meet before the Dresden congress.[727]

Theodor Reik in analysis with Abraham

The Abrahams were very hospitable. Among their visitors were many fellow analysts. Hilda Abraham was particularly fond of Theodor Reik, who was devoted to her father. It was Freud who had advised Reik to turn to Abraham.[728]

Theodor Reik (1888–1969) was born in Vienna, the son of a Jewish bank inspector. He studied philosophy and gained his doctorate in 1912 with a thesis on the psychogenesis of Flaubert's *The Temptation of Saint Anthony*. It was the first ever psychoanalytic PhD. In 1911, Reik became a member of the Vienna Psychoanalytic Society.[729] He wanted to study medicine as soon as he had finished his studies in philosophy, but Freud advised him to focus instead on psychoanalysis.

Reik was extremely talented. He was a creative thinker and writer, well versed in literature. Freud had great respect for him. He was also extremely neurotic, however, continually standing in his own way. It was no accident that he later chose *Masochism in Modern Man* as the title of his *magnum opus*.[730] In February 1914, he went to Berlin and Freud wrote to Abraham that it would be good if he could do something for Reik, who was getting nowhere in Vienna.[731] Reik lacked a steady income in Vienna and was very hard up.

In this early period there was great solidarity and much co-operation between psychoanalysts. Freud could be extremely generous and caring.[732] He not only supported a large number of relatives but gave financial help to colleagues where necessary.[733] Abraham helped, too, where he could. He tried to find Reik a job in Berlin. Although he did not succeed, he was able to get Reik some work for two publishers of newspapers and magazines. Reik managed to obtain further commissions from others and threw himself into writing articles.[734]

On 6 July 1914, Reik entered into analysis with Abraham (free of charge) because he was severely depressed.[735] In their letters, Abraham and Freud discussed how he was doing. Reik was so poor that he was, at times, actually starving, yet he had such a strong tendency to make himself suffer that he refused to accept money. On 31 July 1914, he was due to marry a woman who had virtually nothing, which would mean poverty for the two of them. Abraham had finally persuaded Reik to accept a small contribution, but he asked Freud for help because Reik's relationship with him was so sensitive now that he was his analyst. Freud immediately sent two hundred marks. Reik remained in analysis with Abraham until he was called up for military service in 1915. He found Abraham to be a sharp observer with a rare gift of empathy and would later describe his analyst as follows:

> As a doctor, too, Abraham showed astonishing composure. He was not one of those doctors who conceal the inadequacy of their knowledge behind an overly self-assured performance. He recognised all too clearly that medicine was still a long way from an ideal therapy. But the sense of calm certainty he displayed gradually transferred itself to his patients. As removed from the overestimation as he was from the underestimation of the efficacy of psychoanalytic therapy, he could inspire in them the conviction that they were in good hands and that they could rely on his unconditional honesty. He spoke little, but his silence was justified and in an extraordinary way urgent and encouraging; his voice, with its dark timbre, was calm and calming. Cool and detached, but when necessary humanely intimate, he was certain of the trust of his students and patients. . . . Both in analysis and in his private conversations, an original, dry sense of humour would break through now and then, which was not present in his published work.[736]

The First World War

The debate about who caused the First World War is still going on a hundred years later. One thing historians do agree upon is that in mid-1914 Germany was not under threat of invasion by other great powers.[737]

On 28 June 1914, the heir to the throne of the Austro-Hungarian Dual Monarchy, Franz Ferdinand, was murdered in Sarajevo by Serbian nationalists.[738] The Serbian government was not behind the assassination but did know it was going to happen.

Austria decided on drastic measures against Serbia, whose ambitions were a threat to the Dual Monarchy, but a punitive expedition against Serbia would inevitably lead to a conflict with its ally and defender, Russia. The decision on what to do ultimately lay with Berlin, since Austria was allied with Germany and unable to act against Serbia without the support of the German Empire.

In Berlin there were doubts at first, but, on 6 July, the decision was made to give Austria full support in dealing with Serbia, whatever the consequences might be. This so-called "blank cheque" intensified the crisis. Austria still had doubts about military intervention but did not, in turn, want to disappoint its ally, Germany.[739]

Given its origins, the war ought to have been an Eastern European conflict with Germany and Austro-Hungary on one side and Serbia and Russia on the other. That was the concept on which the blank cheque was based.[740] The German general staff, however, had developed a war plan that, irrespective of where a crisis erupted, provided for a lightning war against France (Russia's ally), beginning with an advance through neutral Belgium.

It was known as the Schlieffen Plan. The aim was to bring about a rapid victory against France before Russia had time to mobilise. The plan inevitably placed Britain in the enemy camp. On 23 July 1914, Austria sent Serbia a forty-eight-hour ultimatum. Although Serbia complied with most of its demands, Austria broke off diplomatic relations on 25 July, the deadline named in the ultimatum, and started to mobilise. Despite feverish diplomatic activity, in which Britain played a mediating role, Austria-Hungary declared war on Serbia on 28 July 1914.[741]

Russia began to mobilise immediately and the Germans responded by putting the Schlieffen Plan into effect. German troops moved westwards rather than eastwards and, on 1 August, a telegram arrived from the German ambassador in London stating that Britain would guarantee French neutrality if German deployment in the west was purely defensive.[742] At an emergency conference, the kaiser declared that German troops would advance not westwards but eastwards; for all his bellicose rhetoric, Kaiser Wilhelm was not an advocate of war. He came up against desperate resistance from Moltke, chief of the general staff, who could no longer change troop movements in the west. Had he done so, a hopelessly disorganised force would have advanced in the east and defeat there would have been a foregone conclusion. Over the previous few years, the general staff had neglected to put together a plan of attack for the Eastern Front—a cardinal error.

The Schlieffen Plan failed miserably. The kaiser had promised the men that they would be home before the first autumn leaves fell. In early August, the German army marched through Belgium and three weeks later it was threatening Paris. The French government fled to Bordeaux. The Russians, however, attacked far sooner than expected, so part of the German army was forced to move east. Then German troops on the Western Front became bogged down at the Marne, their advance checked by the French and the British. The front line froze, from Flanders to Switzerland. The years of horror in the trenches that followed were chillingly described by Erich Maria Remarque in his novel *All Quiet on the Western Front*. Countless books have been written about the war in the west but remarkably little about the Eastern Front. In 1931, Winston Churchill published a book called *The Unknown War: The Eastern Front*, in which he wrote that in scholarly studies of the Great War the Eastern Front was left largely out of account. With a few exceptions, this has changed little. Abraham's involvement concerned the Eastern Front. He was stationed in the east as a doctor.

The Schlieffen Plan was predicated upon a swift victory over France, after which attention could turn to the east. This was based on the idea that the Russian armies would be incapable of rapid mobilisation. Reality proved otherwise. The Russians advanced in a disorganised fashion but extremely quickly. They notched up successes in Prussia, which was defended with limited forces because so much manpower had been sent west. The Cossacks implemented a scorched earth policy, plundering Prussia, burning its villages, and taking their prisoners of war back east. At that point, the decision was made to replace the army leadership. Von Hindenburg was brought out of retirement and he took charge along with Ludendorff. Using a clever tactic of maximum mobility, German forces achieved major victories.[743]

Hindenberg was the only one of the eight German army commanders to achieve this kind of success. After the Battle of Tannenburg in late August 1914, in which the Russians suffered a crushing defeat and 95,000 Russian troops were taken prisoner, he became the most famous man in Germany overnight.

Tensions between the great powers in Europe had been increasing for years before 1914, as had their weaponry. Yet, in Germany, few people seemed to realise that a war might break out. Schmitz calmly undertook a journey through Russia, suddenly finding himself amid troop movements on his way back.

Abraham was so absorbed in his work and his new central position in the world of psycho-analysis that the possibility of war does not seem to have occurred to him. Not until July 1914 is there any note of disquiet about the political situation in the correspondence between Freud and Abraham.

Just weeks before the war started, Abraham was making detailed plans for the summer.[744] On 5 July, Hedwig was to go to Arendsee in Mecklenburg with the children. Abraham would join them on 26 July and on 2 August (later changed to 3 August) the whole family would travel to Bremen to stay with his parents. They planned to be there for four days, then take the children to a childminder in Berlin, after which he and Hedwig would travel to the Tyrol and remain there until the end of August. They would walk in the Dolomites and stay in a hotel near Freud's holiday home. What actually happened was described by Hilda in a letter to Jones in the 1950s.[745]

In July, Hedwig was on the Baltic coast with the children, who were having a great time on the beach. Abraham had stayed in Berlin. He sent the children a long epistle full of drawings, rhymes, and riddles about how their toys and schoolbags were longing to be reunited with them.[746] At the end of July, Abraham joined them as planned. Then war broke out.

Hilda wrote to Jones that at first Abraham refused to believe that the war had started, so they stayed on the Baltic coast and had an uncomfortable night. She makes no further comment on the matter. In reality, it is clear from the letters from Abraham to Freud of 29 and 31 July 1914 that Abraham knew perfectly well war was coming. On 29 July, he wondered whether the journey to the Dolomites and the congress in Dresden in September would be able to go ahead. He was still assuming, however, that hostilities would be on a limited scale. At that point, only Austria had declared war. Sadly, Abraham could not have been more wrong in that respect, as he realised by the time he wrote his letter of 31 July. He had wanted to leave Ostseebad Brunshaupten within two days, but it was too late. Mobilisation had already begun. By 29 July, most of the tourists had gone. He had waited too long. It was almost impossible to travel during mobilisation.

Hilda wrote to Jones that generally Abraham's optimism did not affect his judgement, the implication being that she felt in this case it did. Abraham's reaction is understandable. He had only recently started to play an important role in the world of psychoanalysis. He was president of the IPA and organiser of the upcoming congress in Dresden. He had become editor of the *Jahrbuch*. His contact with Freud had never been so good and would never be so good again. Freud had written to him, "All my life I have been searching for friends who would not exploit and then betray me, and now, not far from its natural end, I hope I have found them".[747] Abraham was about to spend part of his holiday close to Freud for the first time, as Ferenczi had done so often. All of that was swept away at a stroke.

CHAPTER FOURTEEN

A great turnaround

Many lives were disrupted within just a few days

Germany was at war on two fronts. In early August 1914, in the middle of what was supposed to be a holiday, Abraham found himself back in Berlin, along with Hedwig and the children. Many of the city's younger men had already left. As a reservist, he had to make himself available for service in the military hospital. To give himself a little more financial security, he started receiving patients again. He lived from newspaper to newspaper and followed the war reports "in a state of utmost tension".[748] Eitingon had joined the Austrian army as a volunteer and departed.[749]

Correspondence was frequently interrupted. Mobilisation had delayed the post and letters did not always arrive. On 14 August 1914, Abraham wrote to Freud that he had received no news from anyone. What had happened to Rank, Sachs, and Ferenczi? He was feeling rather more positive now after the early successes of the war.[750] On 25 August, Freud wrote expressing his relief at having received a sign of life from Abraham at last. He, too, had been forced to leave his holiday home and was back in Vienna. His three sons were in the army. Anna was stuck in England, where she had been visiting friends including Jones.[751] Rank and Sachs were both in Vienna. Rank was cataloguing Freud's library and Ferenczi had been called up and was waiting to hear where he would be sent as a doctor.[752] Abraham expressed his own relief in response. He was in touch with his confidants again. A number of letters had been lost.[753]

A temporary military hospital was set up in the restaurant of the Grünewald Rennbahn near Berlin. Abraham was initially stationed there. Hilda and Gerd thought his uniform fabulous and the fact that soldiers saluted him on the street absolutely fantastic. In his letter to Freud of 28 August, Abraham was almost jubilant about German war successes after all the uncertainty caused by news reports of the previous month.[754] The German advance on the Western Front

141

went well in the early weeks, but it was not long before the troops were completely bogged down.[755]

Work at the military hospital was often extremely demanding. Abraham described a day on which a transport of wounded men arrived. He had to get up at half past four, travel to Grünewald, and work there without a break until two in the afternoon, then see patients in his own practice at home for several hours. This kind of thing went on day after day.[756]

The letters Abraham wrote to Freud leave no room for doubt that he did surgical work, but it is not clear precisely what. He probably had to apply bandages and perhaps assist with operations.[757] Hospitals far from the front line, like Abraham's in Berlin, were responsible for nursing soldiers who had already undergone treatment elsewhere.[758]

Early in the war, the border between Austria and Germany was still open and in September 1914 Freud visited his daughter, son-in-law, and grandson Ernst in Hamburg, calling in to see Abraham in Berlin both on his way there and on his way back.[759] They did not realise that this was the last time they would see each other for several years. Freud later wrote that he always thought back with "unclouded satisfaction" to those days with Abraham and his family.[760] Freud was still showing great interest in and enthusiasm for the war at this stage. In his introduction to the correspondence between Freud and Ferenczi, Falzeder writes at length about Freud's ambivalent attitude towards the First World War and the great admiration he intermittently felt for Germany.[761]

The Berlin Psychoanalytic Society had shrunk markedly and was barely functioning any longer. Abraham had only one category of patients in his practice: unmarried men with inherited wealth. He was busy with the fifty patients he cared for at the military hospital and he felt some satisfaction at being able to help them.[762] In December, he contracted severe influenza and had a cough for a long time afterwards, but the letters remain cheerful.

Freud was in a very different situation from Abraham. His practice, too, had declined significantly, but he was too old to be obliged to serve as an army doctor and in the extra time suddenly at his disposal he became astonishingly productive. During the First World War he wrote an impressive series of articles. His mood grew increasingly sombre, however. He was deeply worried about his three sons in the army and in need of Abraham's support, of his ability to buoy him up. On 21 December 1914, he wrote to Abraham,

> Dear Friend,
>
> I should like to hazard the paradox that your letters are always pleasing, even if they have uncheering things to report, as your last one. I hope you have now fully recovered, as have the patients in my house.
>
> You are right. I need someone to give me courage. I have little left. In your letter I cherish all the qualities our allies impress us with, and in addition your own personal qualities, your Coraggio Casimiro! Sometimes I dread the meal. If you can really manage to come and see me, you will be doing a great service to my morale, and we shall be able to discuss everything easily.[763]

In the end Abraham was unable to go. First Hedwig fell ill and contracted angina. She developed symptoms similar to those of scarlet fever. Then Abraham had to go to Bremen to help his parents. His seventy-six-year-old aunt, his father's sister, who lived with them, had had a stroke in the summer that meant she was now totally dependent as well as mentally disturbed.[764] There was a family conference to discuss what to do with her. Abraham's older brother still lived with his parents, but it seems they needed Abraham to come and be part of the discussion.

In late 1914, Freud wrote that he had always hated "helplessness and penury" most of all and both seemed to be approaching.[765] He was to prove correct about that.

Their correspondence faltered in early 1915. Letters sometimes took weeks to arrive or were lost altogether.[766] Both Abraham and Freud immediately started to worry whenever that happened. Freud's mood improved in January. He now told himself that the war situation was a long polar night in which it was a matter of waiting until the sun rose again.[767] In March 1915, Abraham was transferred to the military hospital in Allenstein, which, until the end of the Second World War, was in East Prussia, not far from the then German–Russian border. In 1945, it became part of Poland.[768] Hilda wrote positively about the town in her biography, saying it was in beautiful surroundings with lakes and forests, ideal for a walker and nature-lover like her father. Moreover, food was less scarce than in Berlin because Allenstein was set amid rich agricultural land.[769] It had a tough climate, however, with bitterly cold winters, and Hedwig and the children remained behind in Berlin.

In early 1915, the Germans went on the offensive in the east and by mid-March the front was entirely in enemy territory. The great advance across the whole of the Eastern Front began on 27 April 1915. Its immediate goal was to prevent any further attacks on Prussia like those of 1914. While German and Austrian troops moved eastwards, the Russians implemented a scorched earth policy, destroying everything in the territories they lost and stripping them of their population.[770]

In the autumn of 1915 the German advance was halted. German troops had captured 160,000 square kilometres of territory.[771] In the process, the Germans had suffered great losses, fewer than in the west but considerable all the same.[772] They now had to deal with an immense stretch of land that was unknown to them and seemed to consist mainly of endless plains, desolate after the Russian devastation.[773] It was named Ober Ost.[774] In 1914, Germany stretched far further to the east along the Baltic than it does now, directly bordering Russia. All of present-day Poland, Estonia, Latvia, and Lithuania belonged to Russia at the time. The victories of 1915 added mainly lands in what are now Poland, Lithuania, and Latvia.

When Abraham arrived in Allenstein in March 1915, the town was relatively close to the Eastern Front. Within a few months, the front had shifted so far to the east that it was 350 kilometres away. The early part of his time in Allenstein was a short respite in the long, overburdened years of war. He even had time to respond in detail to Freud's theory concerning melancholia and to work on his own article about the oral phase.[775]

In the first week of May, Hedwig came for a visit. They had a great week together, even though Abraham was now a good deal busier at the clinic. Hedwig had only just got back to Berlin when five-year-old Gerd became seriously ill. He had diphtheria and Abraham was filled with anxiety, phoning Berlin daily if at all possible.[776] In the early twentieth century, diphtheria was extremely dangerous and could kill. Years later, Hilda still vividly remembered her brother shivering when he accompanied her to school along with their mother. They did not yet realise how sick he was. Her mother's sister, Aunt Else, came to fetch her from school that day. Hilda remembered staying with Gerd and nursing him after the diagnosis. The long quarantine period that followed was terrible and nine-year-old Hilda felt desperately lonely.

Both Gerd and Hedwig were in quarantine and Hilda could only wave at her mother from a distance. She wrote about how difficult that was: "The four weeks of quarantine were very trying, although I was taken for an occasional walk by a self-sacrificing relative or by our housekeeper. I remember being allowed to see my mother only to wave to, and even looking back now it seems a time of terrifying loneliness and isolation".[777]

When the period of quarantine ended, Gerd was still suffering from quite serious after-effects, including renal trouble and paralysis of some of the muscles of the pharynx.[778]

In May 1915, with Gerd dangerously ill, Abraham wrote not a word to Freud. This can be explained in part by the fact that as well as worrying about Gerd he had to work extremely hard. The offensive in the east had been under way since 27 April, casualties were high and Abraham was at it almost non-stop night and day. Perhaps it was also typical of Abraham. When, in late 1914, Freud lost heart, he needed Abraham to buoy him up, but when Abraham went through a particularly difficult period he wrote to Freud only after the danger had passed, and his letter was full of amusing and odd anecdotes about Gerd. He made no mention of the serious crisis his son had been through. Was he cautious about burdening Freud, just as he could be immensely careful not to burden his mother? The contrast with Ferenczi is quite staggering. Ferenczi repeatedly poured out his heart to Freud, shared all his romantic adventures with him, and went into detail in his letters about every symptom of illness he detected in himself.[779]

Abraham wrote to Freud about Gerd, mentioning only the events of the day after Hedwig came back from Allenstein:

> On the day after her arrival, my wife's siblings came to dinner.[780] During the meal, the little chap asked to speak: "Mummy, while you were in Allenstein I kept having a dream" ("dream" is what both children call their daydreams). My wife unsuspectingly asked him what he had dreamt. The answer: "I kept on thinking when mama comes back from papa whether there would soon be a baby growing inside her."[781]

Abraham thought Gerd a "pillar of psychoanalysis" with such comments. They had told the children about pregnancy and birth but not about conception; Abraham thought that Gerd must have put two and two together. He had written to Freud on an earlier occasion about Gerd's jealousy and desire to have his mother all to himself. Gerd was beside himself with joy when he was allowed to sleep next to his mother in the parental bed for two nights because his room had to be disinfected after the quarantine. He asked questions like "Does papa allow this?" and "Does he allow me to put my hanky under his pillow, too?" He found the chamberpot in the bedside cabinet most intriguing of all and woke frequently during those two nights in order to use it.[782]

In his letters to Freud, Abraham says not a word about all the horrors he must have seen. Soldiers arrived not just wounded but often maimed. Many had become sick because of poor hygiene in Ober Ost.[783] The Germans regarded the eastern territories they conquered as above all dirty. Large-scale initiatives took place in which they forced the inhabitants to clean up.[784]

The Germans attributed all the parasites and lice that tormented them to the local population, although in those days every army suffered from infestations of lice and other vermin. The people of Ober Ost learnt to turn this to their advantage. Often their only opportunity to avoid arbitrary and cruel treatment by German soldiers was to shout "sick, sick". They were then promptly left in peace.[785]

Freud's answer to the long letter Abraham wrote after Gerd's illness gives food for thought. Only after a full month did he respond as follows:

Dear Friend,

My having failed to answer you for so long is due not to one single motivation, but to a very multiple one, which I shall now try to break down into its component parts.[786] First of all there was probably an intention to imitate you in your long silence, which had already caused me concern. This was, indeed, not groundless, as your child's severe illness fell into that interval. Then there was the impact of our splendid victories, which expressed itself in increased working ability, with the result that today I am already working on the 11th of the intended 12 papers.[787]

How should we understand what Freud writes here? He states that he may have deliberately waited before writing back to Abraham until an equivalent length of time had passed. Freud had been right to worry, as the letter from Abraham showed. Yet, deliberately waiting precisely because Abraham had written that his child was dangerously ill seems strange. Freud goes on:

As a result of the interval I got into a muddle and do not know what I have already sent to you. Some of what has already passed the manuscript stage is indeed transportable. I am in a similar situation with Ferenczi, who is so much nearer and turns up in Vienna occasionally. Our correspondence undergoes the strangest interruptions, and I cannot remember what I have told him and what I have not. I think I regard the situation as a repetition of the initial one, when I was productive and—isolated. All my friends and helpers have now really become soldiers, and it is as if they were removed from me. Even Rank, who has remained in Vienna, has not appeared since his call-up. He is serving with the heavy artillery. Sachs will be going into the army service corps in Linz.

Freud felt abandoned by everyone, as he had before 1907 when he had yet to gather a group of confidants around him. He generally found it hard to tolerate being made to wait for an answer to his letters. Breger wrote about this in his book *Freud. Darkness in the Midst of Vision*.[788] Freud's reaction to the delay in receiving a letter from Abraham might be described as rather egocentric given that Abraham had such worries to contend with. There is a possible explanation, however. Freud might have found it hard to tolerate being excluded like this, without even a short note from Abraham when something serious was wrong—and in wartime, when concern quickly arose if someone did not stay in touch. So possibly it was a reaction to the fact that Abraham did not confide in Freud when he found himself in a crisis.

In addition to the war, 1915 and 1916 were difficult years for Abraham with regard to his family. First there was Gerd's illness, then the deaths of his two aunts in Bremen and the death of his father.[789] Then Hedwig had health problems that lasted for several months.

In June 1915, Abraham received alarming news about his father and travelled with all speed to Bremen. Nathan Abraham had grown very weak that spring, with severe neuralgia in his left arm, which had to do with his heart, as well as bad bronchitis. When Abraham arrived in Bremen his father was recovering a little. In 1924 Abraham wrote the following in his "A short study of the development of the libido":

> I had seen my father for the last time a few months before his death, when I was home from the war on a short leave. I had found him very much aged and not at all strong, and I had especially noticed that his hair and his beard were almost white and were longer than usual on account of his having been confined to his bed. My recollection of my last visit to him was closely associated with this impression.[790]

On his way back, Abraham passed through Berlin, where little Gerd was still far from fully recovered.[791] The first thing his son said to him was "Daddy, where is your sword?" Abraham had left it in the train and Hedwig had to go to the station to fetch it. Regulations said that Abraham was not allowed out without it.[792]

Back in Allenstein, Abraham had to work unbelievably hard, at least ten hours a day. He was often called out at night as well. For a psychiatrist to work as a surgeon was far from easy. Surgical specialists usually stayed in the east for only three or four weeks and then moved to the more honourable Western Front, so there were continual changes in personnel.[793]

A holiday in August, which he was able to spend with his family in Fürstenberg in the lake-land area north of Berlin with its many forests, allowed Abraham to get his breath back to some extent. His efforts to meet up with Freud again that summer came to nothing. Freud did manage to visit Hedwig later in the year in Berlin, along with van Emden.[794] He was on his way to visit his daughter in Hamburg.[795]

In November 1915, Abraham began preparing to set up an observation ward for soldiers with mental problems. The intention was that from then on he would be doing only psychiatric and psychotherapeutic work and he hoped to be able to work on some new psychoanalytic theorising.[796] He was optimistic about the war at this point:

> I have good news from home. My wife is putting up bravely with the long separation; the restrictions imposed by the war are also not easy to bear. But that does not matter. In principle, the war has already been won. The other side just does not want to admit it yet. This is similar to what we see in some difficult cases. But we are used to the fact that these resistances, too, yield in the end.[797]

It is no wonder Abraham thought this way. On the Eastern Front, huge territories had been conquered. The advance had been extremely successful. It does, however, raise the question of exactly what news was available about the war, since on the Western Front things were not going at all well for Germany and it seems as if Abraham had no knowledge of that.

Abraham's father had recovered only briefly. In the autumn of 1915, the same symptoms returned, followed by some improvement. On 16 November he was so lucid and vivacious that Abraham's mother was hopeful. The turnaround came a day later. He complained that he could no longer read a word, then lost the power of speech, fell unconscious, and died on 20 November.[798] Abraham's reaction to his death was remarkable:

> Towards the end of the previous year my father had died. During the period of mourning which I went through certain things occurred which I was not at the time able to recognize as the

consequence of a process of introjection. The most striking event was that my hair rapidly turned very grey and then "later reverted to its normal color" in a few months' time.[799]

He also described his first reaction to Freud's "Mourning and melancholia" in 1916:

When Freud published his "Mourning and Melancholia", so often quoted in these pages, I noticed that I felt a quite unaccustomed difficulty in following his train of thought. I was aware of an inclination to reject the idea of an introjection of the loved object. I combated this feeling in myself, thinking that the fact that the genius of Freud had made a discovery in a field of interest so much my own had called forth in me an affective "no". It was not till later that I realized that this obvious motive was only of secondary importance compared with another.[800]

Abraham thought that he could not accept Freud's ideas about introjection because this process took place in him after the death of his father.[801]

In the exchange of letters with Freud there is no mention of the death of Abraham's father. This does not mean Freud was unaware of it. Telephone conversations took place in those days, although Freud rarely engaged in them. Abraham had informed Freud on 24 October that his father had recovered from his severe attack of pleurisy.[802] But in the entire period that followed, the subject of the death of Abraham's father is not addressed at all in the letters. This is a clear example of Abraham's way of corresponding. He wrote about facts and about psychoanalysis, but not about his inner emotional life. He did not write about his loss.

In her biography, Hilda does mention that her grandfather became ill, but not that he died. This is puzzling, since she knew him well and had visited Bremen often. She was nine years old at the time of his death, so she will have been well aware of what had happened.[803] Abraham was very fond of his father and the loss was a great blow. His blond hair turned grey overnight. However remote psychoanalysis may have been from him, Nathan Abraham had always been interested in what his son did and read all his articles.[804]

Abraham did write about his bereavement in two letters to Fließ of March 1916. From the few letters of Abraham's to Fließ that have survived, it is clear that at times when he badly needed help, Abraham sought contact with Fließ. When Hedwig was ill in early 1916 he wrote to Fließ, and when he was seriously ill himself in 1925 he called on Fließ for help.[805] We should be a little cautious here. So few of Abraham's letters remain that it is quite possible he confided in others with whom his correspondence has been lost.

In late 1915 and early 1916, Hedwig developed a number of unpleasant symptoms. Months of nursing Gerd and worrying about him, as well as the poor food situation in Berlin, must have considerably depleted her resistance. Treatment by the family doctor helped only in part, which is why Abraham turned to Fließ. Hedwig was suffering from persistent stomatitis aphthosa, or sores in the mouth, and was able to consume liquids only for several weeks. She also had lumps and swellings on her fingers. Abraham thought all this had to do with the poor quality of the food in wartime. The bread in particular had caused Hedwig intestinal problems from the start. He advised her to stop eating it.

In late December 1915, Abraham, to his surprise, was allowed to spend a brief period of leave in Berlin with his family. He also visited his mother in Bremen, but he told Freud nothing of her reaction to the death of her husband, and neither did he mention what it was like for him to visit, to be in his parental home without his father for the first time.

CHAPTER FIFTEEN

Creation of a theory about early childhood and ejaculatio praecox

A huge burden of surgical responsibilities and the exhaustion of wartime made it extremely difficult for Abraham to carry out his scientific work. He tried to do so, and it frustrated him that he was merely refining material that he had collected before the war. All the same, he wrote a number of important articles in this period. On 30 January 1915 he wrote to Freud that he was working on a short piece about the relationship between hunger and libido. This was probably in preparation for the writing of his "The first pregenital stage of the libido", which was published in 1916. It described the earliest signs of childhood sexuality.[806]

Freud was wildly enthusiastic about this paper and it would later win its author a prize:

> The paper with which you presented me is as excellent as—everything that you have been doing in recent years, distinguished by its many-sidedness, depth, correctness, and, incidentally, it is in full agreement with the truth as it is known to me. It is so crystal clear that it seems to cry out for a graphic representation of the intersecting and merging mental forces.[807]

Freud rewrote and adapted two of his main works, *The Interpretation of Dreams* and *Three Essays on the Theory of Sexuality*, several times.[808] Abraham's latest article tied in with the 1915 edition of the *Three Essays*, which Freud had extended with a piece about early childhood sexuality. In the 1920 edition, Freud returned to Abraham's 1916 article, and in the 1925 edition he made mention of Abraham's follow-up article on the same subject of 1924.[809]

Abraham began his article with a brief discussion of Freud's additional material in the 1915 edition of *Three Essays*. In it, Freud quoted Lindner, who, in 1879, had written about sexual activity in young children.[810] Lindner had studied the way babies suck and it had struck him that their sucking, even when it did not serve the function of relieving hunger, had an intensity that absorbed all their attention. He also observed that excitement during sucking increased to reach a kind of orgasm and he saw falling asleep afterwards as a consequence of the gratification the child had achieved. Lindner also drew attention to the grasping that was connected with this sucking and he recognised the smooth transition from sucking to masturbation, an activity that is unambiguously sexual. Freud took up Lindner's observations and described a number of important characteristics of this early sexuality. Abraham summarised them in three points:

1.   Very early sexuality is not directed on to another object, but is manifested auto-erotically.
2.   This most primitive form of sexual expression is not an independent phenomenon, but is dependent upon a function important for the preservation of life, namely sucking for nourishment; it is the reproduction of a pleasurable stimulus which the child has experienced during feeding.
3.   The attainment of the pleasure is attached to an "erotogenic zone"—the mucous membrane of the lips.[811]

As a consequence, in this early stage, there is no way of distinguishing between the satisfaction of hunger and the gratification of the erogenous zone.

According to Freud, the exit of the intestinal tract had a similar dual function. It served not only for excretion but as an erogenous zone in the service of childhood sexuality. Erogeneity differed from person to person both at the lips and at the anus. Freud distinguished between two pregenital stages of development, the oral–cannibalistic stage and the anal–sadistic stage.

In the oral–cannibalistic phase, sexuality and food intake are not yet separate. The goal is to incorporate the object. Sucking can be seen as a leftover of this phase, in which the function of absorbing food has been separated from sexual activity and one's own body has become an object.

In the anal–sadistic phase, the antitheses begins to take shape. There is a contrast between active and passive. The active aspect is the urge to conquer, arising from the body's musculature, while the passive is expressed mainly in the mucus membrane of the intestines, as erogenous zone and sexual target.

Abraham's article was about these manifestations of early childhood sexuality, but in adults and using case histories to illustrate his points. It is a good example of Abraham's general way of working. He was a craftsman who, by listening carefully and observing meticulously, tried to stay as close as possible to the material the patient brought him. He built upon psychoanalytic theory, based on a series of observations from his daily practice. If his work is read superficially, he seems mainly to be refining Freud's own theories. A more careful reading, however, makes it clear that he carved out his own paths. His work seems accessible but it is not; it demands detailed attention. The essence of his work is often completely lost in the poor English translations. This may be one of the reasons why he is so much better appreciated in Germany and France.[812]

In a letter to Jones dated 4 January 1920, Abraham wrote that he had received a letter from one Dr Bryan, who told him that he was going to publish a collection of Abraham's articles in English translation. Abraham told Jones:

I am of course very grateful that someone took the trouble, and I am glad that my texts will have a greater distribution in this way. But it seems to me it would be more proper in such cases for the author to be consulted *beforehand*, so that he could check the selection, test the completeness of the pieces and if necessary make additions and corrections. (Original emphasis)[813]

Abraham was, of course, right. Jones was quick to write back that it was a misunderstanding, probably arising because Bryan had expressed himself carelessly (as he did in the translations).[814] Bryan had told Jones that he had translated an article by Abraham for himself. Jones had then proposed translating all the articles and having them published by the British arm of the psychoanalytic publishing house. Jones wrote that Abraham would be able to make any corrections he liked. The English edition would not be published until later in the year. It seems as if Jones did not check whether Bryan was actually capable of translating. It is not clear from the letters what happened after that. How did it come about that so many translation errors remained in the text? Was Abraham not given the time to correct it or did he not spot the errors? Did he have Hedwig correct the articles? Hedwig occasionally translated from German to English herself. From a letter of 13 March 1914 from Jones to Abraham, it turns out that at that point Bryan could not even read German.[815] In the years that followed, therefore, he first had to master German and then psychoanalysis, which in those days was mostly written about in German articles and books.

In the current English edition of *Selected Papers on Psychoanalysis* by Karl Abraham, both Douglas Bryan and Alix Strachey are named as translators.[816] It is not clear who translated which passages and it does not seem that Strachey, who was a good translator, corrected Bryan's work.

Still, to return to Abraham's article, he reports on a patient who became psychotic while a university student. It was a mild form of psychosis, so psychoanalytic treatment was an option. The patient had some awareness of the mouth as an erogenous zone and spoke about ejaculation in his mouth as if it were the most normal thing in the world. When asked about this it emerged that he was talking about waking from an arousing dream after which he noticed that saliva was running out of his mouth. His other associations also concerned the erogenous significance of his mouth.

As a child, the patient had been unable to wean himself off his love of drinking milk.[817] He could never get enough milk and he drank it in a special way. He would press his tongue to the roof of his mouth, behind his front teeth, and suck the milk in. The milk must be neither hot nor cold but at body temperature. As a result he obtained an extremely pleasant sensation. He called it "sucking at the breast". When he was fifteen, he gave up this way of drinking milk and started to drink cold beverages. The desire for milk remained, however. Sometimes he lay awake at night with great sexual desires. He would get up and drink milk. If he could not find any, he would masturbate.

The patient also said that as a small boy loving someone meant the same as eating something tasty. As a four-year-old he had a nanny of whom he was extremely fond and he liked to phantasy about biting her breast or swallowing her whole. The patient had become stuck at the oral–cannibalistic phase.

In his *Three Essays* of 1915, Freud described the differences in erogeneity of specific zones in different people:

Just as we saw previously that it was possible to derive a multiplicity of innate sexual constitutions from variety in the development of the erotogenic zones, so we can now make a similar
attempt by including the indirect sources of sexual excitation. It may be assumed that, although
contributions are made from these sources in the case of everyone, they are not in all cases of equal
strength, and that further help towards the differentiation of sexual constitutions may be found in
the varying development of the individual sources of sexual excitation.[818]

Abraham concurred, but he seemed to attribute a far more prominent role to this congenital
sensitivity than Freud. He was interested in the differences between children when they were
weaned and especially the differences that originated in the child itself. There were children
who, of their own accord, not because of circumstances, did not want to leave the breast.[819]
Abraham seems to see this above all as a neurotic predisposition and writes of it as follows:

Now we have learned from observation that persons who cling to infantile pleasure-sucking are
invariably seriously hampered in the development of their sexuality. Their instincts of nutrition
and of sexuality remain to a certain extent intermingled. Their libido does not find the way to a
living, human object in a normal manner, but seeks its gratification in the first instance in sucking
up a material into the mouth.[820]

Abraham had found a strongly repressed libido and a passionate desire for sweetness,
which was slowly sucked at, in a patient whose normal male sexuality was completely
repressed. When he went to work in the morning, he pretended he was still a child, saying to
his wife in parting, "Sonny is going to school now." On the way he bought sweets, as children
do, which he slowly sucked. He spoke keenly and animatedly of this childish amusement,
while normal male sexuality interested him hardly at all. Abraham regarded him, with his
strongly libidinous emphasis on having sweet substances in his mouth, as a typical example of
a failure to separate the function of taking nourishment from that of sex: "There is no doubt
that in the normal person the gratification of his sexual needs exercises a marked influence on
his disposition. Yet the healthy person is capable of tolerating a temporary lack of his accustomed gratification within certain limits."[821]

In medical training in those days, there was a clear division between normal and abnormal
and between healthy and sick. Abraham also thought very much in black and white. This is
sometimes a pity, because a hint of disapproval quickly comes to hang over what he writes,
distracting from what he has to say. Abraham did not depart very far from Freud in these
matters, but he does not seem to have adopted Freud's view that we all contain pathology
within us to a greater or lesser extent.

This last quote comes from the start of part VI of Abraham's 1916 paper "The first pregenital stage of the libido". What followed was a discussion of neurotics who had got stuck in the
earliest phase of childhood sexuality, when there is not yet any distinction between sexuality
and food intake. Such patients had mood problems, or, to put it more precisely, they had problems regulating their moods.

Abraham discussed two kinds of problem. First, there was decreasing tolerance for any
delay to gratification, and the earlier the stage at which the their sexual development had
become stuck, the more pronounced this was. Such patients resembled spoilt children in this

sense. Their libido continually demanded the gratification to which they were accustomed. They reacted with great displeasure if they did not get it, and that displeasure would then turn into a bad mood. The second point, which Abraham argued was connected with the first, concerns the origin of depressive feelings that Abraham believed were insufficiently recognised. The accustomed gratification was needed to stave off bad moods. It served to prevent depression when it threatened. This explained the fact that the source of gratification was the first thing the patient turned to early in the morning, and, indeed, the patient's insistence on getting hold of it.[822]

Taking medicine for depression or nervousness therefore had a beneficial effect, however transitory, even if the substance concerned contained no tranquilliser of any kind. Abraham wrote,

> In the life of every person there was a time when he was freed from all excitement by taking a fluid. The "suggestive" effect of a bottle of medicine does not lie only in the physician's treatment by any means, but at least as much in its function of supplying something to the patient's mouth which arouses echoes in him of his earliest pleasurable memories.[823]

This brought Abraham back to his most important theme: depression. In fact Abraham spent all his psychoanalytic working life expanding and refining his theory on depression, at first alone and later to a great degree in consultation with Freud.

"Mourning and melancholia" and Abraham's concept of depression

The exchange of ideas with Freud on the subject of depression came to an end on 2 May 1912, when Freud quoted in his letter some critical remarks by Paul Federn about Abraham's article on manic–depressive disorder, without entering into discussion with Abraham about them.[824]

After that, the correspondence between Freud and Abraham was silent on the subject until February 1915. Then Freud sent Ferenczi a first version of "Mourning and melancholia", requesting him to send it on to Abraham.[825] In 1914, Freud had already taken an extremely important step with "On narcissism".[826] He had been using the word "narcissism" for several years. In 1909, during a meeting of the Vienna Psychoanalytic Society, he reacted to a case history by Sadger with a discussion of the subject. On that occasion, he described narcissism as something that did not occur in isolation but was a necessary step in the development of the transition from auto-eroticism to object-love. He regarded loving one's self as a necessary stage in development. From there, the step is taken to loving similar objects. Freud explained that the human being generally has two original sexual objects, the mother or carer and himself, and his later life was determined by which of the two he remained fixated upon. The challenge lay in losing both and not clinging to either one for too long.[827] In 1913, Freud had given narcissism a place between auto-eroticism and the pregenital stages.[828]

In "On narcissism", Freud distinguishes between two kinds of narcissism, primary and secondary. Primary, original narcissism is a normal phase of development between auto-eroticism and object-libido. Secondary narcissism is found in people who regressively take themselves as a love-object.[829] Narcissism was described by Freud as a magnification of the ego.

Libido is withdrawn from the outside world into the ego. Melancholia was more likely to be traced back to the narcissistic phase than to the auto-erotic phase.

Abraham reacted at length to Freud's first version of "Mourning and melancholia", which can be seen as a further development of his train of thought in "On narcissism".

Freud's explanation was complicated. His starting point was the similarity between mourning and melancholia. They produce phenomena that are almost identical. Both are a reaction to loss and characterised by despondency, loss of interest in the outside world, inhibition of activity, and so on. But melancholia is characterised by a loss of the sense of self-worth, which does not occur in grief. Freud explained this as follows. With mourning, the loved object is no longer there and the work of grieving that needs to be done consists of withdrawing all libido from its connection with the object. This is a painful and lengthy process in which, step by step, the memories and expectations connected with the object are first hypercathected and then ended. After completion of the work of grieving, the ego regains its freedom and lack of inhibition.

It is true that melancholia has the same characteristics, but there is no apparent way of finding out what has been lost. In mourning, the loss is conscious. Melancholia seems to be a matter of unconscious loss of an object, after which a comparable process of assimilation takes place in which all interest in the outside world disappears and energy is depleted. The loss of a sense of self-worth that occurs with melancholia seems, however, to suggest that the loss the melancholic has suffered is located not in the outside world, but in the ego. With mourning, the outside world becomes bare and empty; with melancholia, the ego becomes so. The melancholic expresses endless self-reproaches that, in many cases, when listened to carefully, seem barely to fit the person at all, but, rather, another person. There was once a loved object, an other; an attachment of the libido to a particular person had existed at one time. But as the result of a real affront by this loved person, the object-relationship was shattered. What follows is not the withdrawal of the libido as in mourning, which makes it available for another object. Instead, the freed libido is withdrawn into the ego. There it is used to bring about an identification of the ego with the relinquished object. The loss of the object now means a loss of ego.

There is also a rift between the ego and the ego changed by identification. The loss of ego causes the loss of a sense of self-esteem. The endless self-reproaches relate to the ego changed by identification; the ego expresses criticism of the ego changed by identification. These self-reproaches are, therefore, ultimately directed at the original object.

Freud goes on to write that the precondition for this whole process must be that there is a strong fixation on the loved object but, at the same time, the object cathexis must have had little power of resistance. This is a contradiction that implies the object choice has been made on a narcissistic basis, so that the object cathexis can regress to narcissism as soon as it meets with difficulties.[830] The narcissistic identification with the object then becomes a substitute for the erotic cathexis, so that despite the conflict with the object, the love relation need not be given up.[831] The replacement of object-love with identification is an important mechanism in the narcissistic disorder.

Abraham began his reaction by observing that there was one aspect he would like to emphasise more than Freud did:

I should like to remind you—not in order to stress any priority but merely to underline the points of agreement—that I also started from a comparison between melancholic depression and mourning. I found support in your paper on obsessional neurosis (the Rat Man), which had just been published, and stressed that sadism was important because its intensity does not allow the capacity for love to arise; and I deduced depression from a perception of one's inability to love. I had to leave completely unanswered the question of why melancholia develops in one case and obsession in another.[832]

In his article "Notes on the psycho-analytical treatment of manic depressive insanity and allied conditions" of 1912, Abraham was already assuming a correspondence between mourning and melancholia, having taken the first step towards a psychoanalytic theory about depression in his article on Segantini.[833] Freud mentioned Abraham in a note on the first page of "Mourning and melancholia", but he did not do him justice, as Abraham remarks in his letter. Freud's note is as follows: "Abraham, to whom we owe the most important of the few analytic studies on this subject, also took this comparison as his starting point".[834]

Freud's "Mourning and melancholia" was, as the title suggests, entirely based on the comparison between mourning and melancholia. The draft that he sent to Ferenczi and Abraham has been lost. Was the note already included in that version? Probably not, since Freud wrote in his letter responding to Abraham, dated 4 May 1915, "Your comments on melancholia were very valuable to me. . . . I also mention [your] link with mourning".[835]

Moreover, in this note, Freud refers to Abraham as someone who "also" started out from the comparison between mourning and melancholia. The word "also" is striking. It makes it seem as if they were both working on the same subject at the same time, but Abraham had thought of the comparison and Freud adopted it from him. Freud had once made a connection between the two, in 1897, but that had to do with self-reproaches in mourning the death of a parent that were identified as melancholia.[836] He had not, at that point, discussed any similarities in the ways the two manifested themselves.

Abraham does not seem to have regarded this as a problem. The recognition of his work was sufficient. He did not need to be in the foreground and he regarded his 1912 essay on depression as very much incomplete as yet. Freud had taken a major theoretical leap forward with "Mourning and melancholia".

In his response to Freud's article, Abraham stressed the part played by sadism. In the analyses of his depressive patients, many violent and criminal fantasies kept coming to light. The self-reproaches pointed to repressed hostility. The motor inhibition led to a suspicion that serious motor impulses needed to be kept in check. The tendency of depressive patients to torment those around them pointed in the same direction. The direct emergence of sadism in the manic phase was another indication. Sadism also played a prominent role in obsessional neuroses, but Abraham saw a distinction in that obsessional neurosis was clearly coupled with anal eroticism, whereas he had not come upon that link in depression. Depression seemed linked instead to the oral phase. The entire process could be traced back to a phase in early childhood in which the child identifies with his object and wants to incorporate it, to eat it up, to devour it. Abraham wrote about the patient's relationship with the object,

What harm has the melancholic in fact done to the object with whom he identifies?

The answer to this is suggested to me in one of your recent papers—I think it is the one on narcissism (?). There you discuss identification and you point to the infantile basis of this process: the child wants to *incorporate* its love-object: to put it briefly, it wants to *devour* it. I have strong reason to suspect that such cannibalistic tendencies exist in the melancholic's identification. It may be safely assumed that this identification has an ambivalent meaning—a manifestation of love as well as destruction.

The first argument I would advance is the melancholic's fear of *starvation*. Food has taken the place of love here. I would assume that the role played by the anal zone in obsessional neurosis is assigned to the mouth in melancholia.[837]

Abraham's explanation for the endless self-reproaches of the melancholic had a totally different cast from Freud's explanation. What Abraham thought he could see in his depressive patients was that they were unable to love and frantically tried to obtain a love-object. They identified with the loved object, could not bear its loss and were oversensitive to the slightest unfriendliness. Quite often, melancholics allowed themselves to be tormented by those they loved in masochistic self-punishment. The reproaches that they ought to make to the loved object they instead made to themselves because they wished far worse upon the loved object. Abraham regarded depression as a regression of the libido to the oral stage and he saw the self-reproaches as a reaction to the melancholic's own cannibalistic desires. In Abraham, the stress is very much on the person's aggression and feelings of guilt about it.

Freud reacted, as he always did in such theoretical debates, with great courtesy.[838] He had found Abraham's comments very valuable and had incorporated those parts he could use in his own paper. Most useful of all were the remarks about the oral phase of the libido.

He did have two objections, however. First, Freud found that Abraham took insufficient account of one essential feature of his hypothesis, the topographical aspect.[839] The regression of the libido and the abandonment of the unconscious object cathexis were central to it. The topographical aspect was different in mourning and in melancholia. In mourning, it was a matter of a conscious object relation, in melancholia, an unconscious one. Second, Freud argued that Abraham, instead of looking at the mechanism, had pushed sadism and anal eroticism to the fore as explanatory motifs. The mechanism, as described above, concerned the identification with the loved and abandoned object and the division in the ego between the ego and the ego changed by identification.

Freud followed up his elucidation with a third hypothesis, in which he incorporated Abraham's idea that the entire process linked up with the oral phase, the early childhood phase in which the child identifies with the object and wants to eat it up, to consume it.

Identification is the phase that precedes object choice. It is the first form of expression with which the ego distinguishes an object. It would like to incorporate this object according to the oral or cannibalistic phase of the development of the libido, by eating it.

Freud added that Abraham was probably right to trace back the refusal of food, which is seen in severe forms of melancholia, to this connection.

Bernard Lemaigre, who published a brief overview of Abraham's work, wrote that here Freud was returning to Abraham's hypothesis about the importance of the oral phase in depression.[840] That is undeniably the case, but in his account Lemaigre ignores one important question: Freud arrived at Abraham's ideas, but did Abraham arrive at Freud's?

In this period, in June 1915, Abraham could not go along with the direction of Freud's theory. On 3 June 1915, he wrote,

> As regards the question of melancholia, I am now fully in agreement with you on *one* point—that I had not sufficiently appreciated the mechanism, that is to say the topographical aspect. One other point remains: the postulation in your short manuscript that reproaches that are actually directed against another person are transposed to one's own ego. I am not yet convinced of this. I do not remember your bringing detailed proof in your paper. If it does not involve too much trouble, I should like to have a letter from you explaining more exactly what you mean and how you account for it.[841]

What Abraham could not follow at that point and what, in fact, until the 1920s hardly any of Freud's disciples really took in, was that from "On narcissism" onwards, Freud was developing two different theories in parallel. Perhaps it is not quite correct to say that Abraham could not follow Freud. Abraham asked Freud for proof of that which he had thought up. Freud was working on the vicissitudes of the ego: identification with the object and the withdrawal into the ego. It all has a high level of abstraction. Abraham wanted proof. He seems to have found it all very theoretical. It is as if, in 1915, Freud did not see this as two theories, but as a certain important mechanism that he had worked out within the existing theory.

Until 1914, there was only the libido theory. According to that theory, neurotic symptoms were a manifestation of a conflict between ego drives and sexual drives. Ego drives are the forces that cause repression. Sexual drives are everything that has to be repressed for reasons of self-preservation and adaptation.[842] The psychoanalytic technique applied here relied above all on the breaking of resistance. The patient had to be convinced that he or she was repressing infantile libidinous desires and must be persuaded to admit to these desires. Transference interpretations were hardly ever used as explanations. That started only in about 1922.

The detailed charting of the libido theory and the recognition of the libidinous organisation came into play only from 1913 onwards. First, the anal phase was described by Freud and Jones, then the oral phase by Freud and Abraham, and the phallic phase by Freud. Abraham rounded off this development in 1924 with his theory about the development of the libido and in doing so laid out a framework that has remained largely intact to this day. It was also Abraham who described the final goal, which, in many cases, was not reached. According to Abraham, these were steps towards a more mature object-love in which account could be taken of the object; a loving, non-egotistical relationship.

On the one hand, Freud, together with his pupils, developed the theory of the existence and the order of pregenital development and, on the other, initially almost entirely without his pupils, he concerned himself with the theory of the development of the ego.[843] This theory was about the ego, the ego drives and narcissism, and it was the precursor to Freud's later structural theory. Freud was convinced that the discovery of the structure and genesis of the ego would be of great importance for the understanding of neuroses and psychoses. This development was never summed up in a framework such as Abraham laid out for the development of the libido.

The confusing thing about the two theories was that the central points of the theory of the development of the ego, namely narcissism and narcissistic identification, were part of libido theory. The progress of the libido in libido theory was from auto-eroticism to identification with the object in the narcissistic phase and then to object-relations.

The identifying characteristic of the narcissistic phase was that a person fell in love with his or her own body and ego or objects that resembled it. Narcissism relates to love of self in contrast to more mature object-love. In object-love, narcissism is overcome, so a non-egotistic relationship with the object becomes possible. May-Tolzmann (1990) wrote that the simultaneous revision of the libido theory and the ego–narcissism theory may have produced the unclear relationship between the two. In the period between 1913 and 1920, Freud asserted that the narcissistic phase extended from the start of psychic development to the anal–sadistic phase, but elsewhere he said that narcissism—in the sense of the omnipotence of thoughts and the animistic worldview—was part of obsessional neurosis, which was a regression to the anal–sadistic stage.[844] "Mourning and melancholia" was again about the oral phase, however, to which narcissism was said to belong.[845] In this period, Freud regularly changed his ideas about the place where narcissism belonged.

Abraham was not working on the development of the ego but was instead expanding the libido theory. In that theory, narcissism was the phase that came after auto-eroticism and there the incorporation of the object was central. Abraham followed Freud's theory until 1915. With his "The first pregenital stage of the libido" he set off on a path of his own, which was fundamentally distinct from Freud's. To Abraham, repressed sadism was decisive. According to Abraham, a person's sense of guilt about their own sadism lay at the root of depression.[846]

For Freud, depression distinguished itself from other disorders by its narcissistic identification, which he saw as coming about through the dissolution of the unconscious libido cathexis of the object.[847]

Abraham's idea would eventually be greatly influential in psychoanalysis because it was taken up by the Kleinians, who regard depression as caused by the guilt reaction to one's own hostility. Segal wrote in her introduction to the work of Melanie Klein, "In the depressive position, anxieties spring from ambivalence, and the child's main anxiety is that his own destructive impulses have destroyed, or will destroy the object that he loves and totally depends on".[848]

Ejaculatio praecox

Another important article by Abraham that appeared in these war years was "Ejaculatio praecox".[849] Abraham had been planning to give a lecture on the subject at the congress in Dresden. When the congress was cancelled because of the outbreak of war, Abraham turned it into a published article, which appeared in 1917.

In his introduction, Abraham wrote that of all the disturbances to male potency seen by the neurologist in his consulting room, this was the most common. In psychoanalysis only limited attention had been paid to it up to that point. Ferenczi had written an article about disturbances to potency in 1908, but he did not treat ejaculation praecox as a subject in its own right.[850] After Abraham's article, it remained a little discussed subject in psychoanalysis, even though the disorder is common to this day.

Abraham regarded premature ejaculation as a phenomenon whose cause was mental, the male counterpart to female frigidity. He described in detail the striking characteristics of ejaculatio praecox:

> Emission does not take place as a rhythmical expulsion but as a simple outflow of the semen. If the emission is not accompanied by active bodily movements or a maximum erection or even rhythmical contractions of the perineum, and if it actually takes place *ante portas*, then the presence of the semen as a substance is all that is left to remind us of a normal emission of the sex products. On the other hand, the similarity of ejaculatio praecox to another physiological process, namely, micturition, becomes very striking. This latter process takes place with the body at rest and the penis flaccid, and to the accompaniment of constant (not rhythmical) muscular contractions. Ejaculation praecox can thus be looked upon as a combination of two processes: it is an ejaculation with regard to the *substance* of the emission, and a micturition with regard to the *manner* of it.[851]

Abraham wrote that a striking characteristic of patients who suffered from ejaculation praecox was that the emptying of the bladder had always been particularly pleasurable. He was also struck, mainly because of associations made by his patients, by the difference between the emptying of the bladder and ejaculatio praecox. The former took place from infancy prompted by a stimulus, true, but above all under the influence of the will of the patient, and, to a certain degree, this also applied to normal ejaculation. Premature ejaculation, by contrast, happened independently of the will of the patient, who consciously wanted a normal course of events during sexual intercourse; the premature discharge of semen surprised him every time. Many patients mentioned feelings of shame that were accompanied by anxiety and heart palpitations.

The comparison with the emptying of the bladder held true only in part, therefore. Ejaculation praecox mainly resembled the emptying of the bladder in early childhood, before potty training.

From the associations made by patients, it also became clear that they had often had great trouble being potty trained, they often passed urine involuntarily, and sometimes they continued to wet the bed into adulthood. Patients even mentioned that the bodily experience of involuntarily passing urine and of ejaculatio praecox were, to them, identical. Abraham argued that these were patients who had become stuck at a certain point in the development of their libido. They derived infantile pleasure from the outflow of their body products. So, ejaculatio praecox was at one and the same time a pleasure and a displeasure. The displeasure lay in the fact that they were unable to perform the sex act normally. The pleasure lay in the outflow.

Abraham wanted to place particular emphasis on the ambiguity of the whole situation and on the experience of pleasure, because the latter was often entirely missed in looking at premature ejaculation.

It was also striking that ejaculatio praecox occurred only during sexual intercourse and not during masturbation, which made it seem likely that the object-relationship was of relevance.

From the associations made by Abraham's patients, it emerged that they had a cruel and aggressive attitude to women. The phantasy of being able to kill a woman by coitus was prominent. The male genital organ was robbed of its dangerousness so that it could not get into a position in which it would serve sadism. There was also a fear of the female genitals—a fear of losing the penis.

The contribution of narcissism was considerable; there was an overvaluing of the penis. It concerned the phase in which the child felt itself to be the centre of its still small world and in which it accepted demonstrations of love from others without giving anything in return.

In normal sexual intercourse, both the man and the woman achieve gratification. With ejaculatio praecox, the woman is a substitute for the mother that can be both used and wetted. The man does not want to give love but to receive love and be touched. Some patients are even proud of the ejaculation that does not take place inside the woman but before her eyes, so to speak. It is a matter of both wanting to be admired by the woman and rejecting her in a way that is expressed as contempt for her.

Abraham regarded premature ejaculation above all as a narcissistic symptom, such that the man gave nothing and wanted only to get something from the woman, primarily admiration. He saw it as follows: in ejaculatio praecox the man saves his physical energy. He does not give his partner gratification; he spills his seed but does not give it to her, and neither does he give her a child. He creates expectation that he does not fulfil. He is unconsciously very much dependent on his mother/wife and avenges himself on her.[852]

CHAPTER SIXTEEN

The final war years in Allenstein

Reunited at last

In Allenstein, Abraham had found a furnished five-room apartment on the ground floor of an old house, in the midst of nature with woodland only few minutes' walk away.[853] Abraham moved in there on 1 May 1916 and Hedwig and the children followed two weeks later. The original plan was simply for them to spend the summer there, but they stayed until the end of the war.

The children loved it in Allenstein. They could go wherever they liked and they had a garden to play in. It was an old-fashioned house where they could play games without having to worry about the furniture. They preferred to climb through the window than to ring the bell.[854] The harsh East-Prussian climate did mean long winters with hard frosts and continual snow.[855] At first, Hilda did not go to school but was given private lessons at home. Once it had been decided that they would stay and give up the apartment in Berlin, both children started attending school in Allenstein. Gerd remembered later how at first he could not fully understand the dialect spoken at school. He also recalled how much he enjoyed putting on his father's uniform and parading in it after his father came home from his work at the military hospital.[856] Hilda wrote in her biography that her parents missed the cultural life of Berlin.[857] Especially for Hedwig, who could barely exist without her beloved Berlin, it must have been a monotonous existence and the friendship she developed with the wife of Abraham's colleague Hans Liebermann was extremely welcome. The beautiful summer made up for the long harsh winter to some extent. They spent almost every Sunday outdoors and had some memorable adventures. Abraham did not like asking the way, so they regularly got lost or were forced to take long unplanned detours.[858]

From June 1916 onwards, Abraham had his own psychiatric department in the military hospital and he was now head of psychiatry in the Twentieth Army Corps. He had worked tremendously hard to create such a position and collected piles of documentary evidence to show it was needed. The bureaucracy was formidable and this was the only way to get anything done.[859] He succeeded in organising things so that his colleague and pupil, Liebermann, came to assist him. Hans Liebermann (1883–1931) was from Hamburg. He had studied medicine and philosophy and gained his doctorate in Freiburg in 1910. He entered into analysis with Abraham in 1911 because of hay fever and, in 1913, he moved to Berlin. On 1 January 1914 he became a member of the Berlin Psychoanalytic Society. After the First World War, Liebermann succeeded Karen Horney as the Society's secretary.[860]

A psychiatric department of his own

Not a great deal is known about what actually went on in Abraham's psychiatric department, since so much documentation concerning military activities in the First World War was lost during the Second World War.[861] A short eye-witness account by Gershom Scholem has survived.

Gershom Scholem (1897–1982), later a famous German–Jewish historian and philosopher, was admitted to Abraham's psychiatric department in Allenstein in 1917. He was twenty years old and had been found fit for military service in March 1917. In May 1917, he was called up, with orders to join a military unit on 20 June.[862] This was right in the middle of the war. Scholem tried to get out of the army as quickly as possible. He pretended to be suffering delusions.[863] On 7 July 1917, he was examined by Stabsarzt Abraham.[864] As soon as a place became available, Scholem was to be sent to the overcrowded psychiatric department run by Abraham in Allenstein.[865] Meanwhile, he stayed in the barracks and had only to distribute the mail.[866] From the moment he was relieved of his duties, Scholem was tormented by the others in his barracks. He thought it was partly anti-Semitism. On 25 July, he found himself in Abraham's department. It had been ordered that he would stay there for six weeks, under observation. He wrote about the department to a friend:

> It is much better here than I expected. True, one is watched all the time, but within those tight boundaries you have freedom of movement. All day long you have peace and you can do whatever you like, even, if the nerves allow it, contemplate. All the doctors here are said to be Jews. The military hospital is small, with some seventy men. We are alone in this large house and the food is a bit better than in the recruits' depot.[867]

To his great relief, Gershom Scholem heard from the doctors after only two weeks that he would be discharged as soon as possible and everything would be done to prevent him having to enter military service again. Whether Abraham realised the delusions were feigned is not clear. They were probably the basis for Scholem's discharge. It was not the case that there was nothing wrong with him. He was in an extremely poor mental state.

Lack of contact with Freud

Abraham missed Freud and made all kinds of attempts to see him again. He was very much hoping for a meeting in late September 1916, in combination with a congress in Munich. He tried to arrange things so that he would meet up with Freud not far from the Austrian border. Freud spent part of the summer in Salzburg. Abraham was not allowed over the border at that time, since he was a serving soldier. When his attempts to arrange a meeting failed, Abraham was greatly discouraged and after the congress he wrote from Regensburg: "Dear Professor, So it was not to be! I am very put out to be staying here alone on the return journey. The town is splendid, and the Museum of Antiquities would certainly have satisfied you. So when are we going to see each other?"[868] Abraham had wanted to go to the congress in order to have the chance to see Freud, but Freud had already returned to Vienna, where Ferenczi had announced that he wanted to be in analysis with Freud for two weeks during his leave, beginning in mid-September. That was very early for Freud to be back in Vienna. He wrote that he had ended his travelling season for the moment and his early return no doubt had to do with Ferenczi's analysis. Ferenczi actually delayed his visit. On 26 September, when Freud received Abraham's letter, Ferenczi had yet to arrive.[869]

Abraham had to accept the fact that another pupil had taken precedence. Two months passed before Abraham wrote to Freud again and it was a gloomy letter. He felt under severe strain. Liebermann, who had been sent to assist him, had soon fallen ill and Abraham was having to do everything by himself.[870] He also regretted the fact that he had been unable to send Freud any scientific work. It had all been so different when he was able to write to Freud about new scientific insights and wait in suspense to see how Freud would react.[871] Abraham felt rejected and thought the one thing that might capture Freud's attention, a fresh series of scientific discoveries, was precisely what he was unable to deliver. Part of the picture must surely have been that he was now in mourning for his father and had a particular need to see Freud, his substitute father. The cancellation of the plan to meet up in September was almost unbearable for Abraham.

Freud was rather nonchalant about it. His focus was not on Abraham at the time. There were too many other urgent and dispiriting affairs in Freud's life: efforts to get hold of food and particularly cigars every day; having three sons in the army—miracle of miracles, all three survived the war. The things Freud said about Ferenczi had another significance, as Abraham probably realised perfectly well. After the difficult early years and the trouble with Jung, in 1914 Abraham had come to occupy the most important position within the psychoanalytic movement, and for Freud. He had now lost that position to Ferenczi.

This is illustrated by the frequency of the letters. In May 1914, Freud and Ferenczi wrote five letters to each other and Freud and Abraham eight. In May 1917, Ferenczi and Freud wrote thirteen letters to each other, Freud and Abraham only three. The tight bond that had always existed between Freud and Ferenczi reached its zenith in the war years, during which Ferenczi underwent a short analysis with Freud on three occasions.[872]

So, as well as the fact that the correspondence between the two of them regularly had the character of an analysis of Ferenczi, Ferenczi was actually in analysis with Freud, first of all during the three and a half weeks that passed in October 1914 before Ferenczi was called up as a doctor in the Hungarian cavalry and his analysis had to be broken off. Ferenczi had great difficulty with this abrupt termination and he tried to pursue a kind of self-analysis, which Freud advised him against. The remarkable thing, of course, was the fact that Ferenczi had entered into analysis with Freud when he knew it might be broken off at any moment, as soon as he was called up. But in those days no one worried greatly about a sudden end to analysis, not realising the damaging effects it could have. Ferenczi resumed his analysis from Wednesday 14 June 1916 to Wednesday 5 July 1916, while he was on leave. His third period of analysis, for which Freud returned early to Vienna, was from 29 September 1916 to 13 October 1916.

Abraham remained gloomy and exhausted. His letter of mid-December 1916 once again spoke volumes.[873] The winter in East Prussia was mercilessly cold and Abraham's health began to suffer.[874] Hedwig later said that Abraham had suffered from asthma as a child, which disappeared completely as he grew up, but in the tough climate of Allenstein, with its fierce cold and fog, the asthma returned, so badly that Abraham considered having himself transferred to another German city.[875] He developed further health problems. Towards the end of the war, he contracted severe dysentery and he was very slow to recover. He had relapses for years afterwards in which symptoms of dysentery recurred, the last time in the spring of 1924.[876] Jones later wrote that the war affected Abraham's health to such an extent that he suspected it had ultimately led to his death.[877] A group photograph taken at the congress in The Hague in 1920 shows clearly that at that point, two years after the end of the war, Abraham was still severely emaciated.

Holland as a bright spot

The psychoanalytic societies languished during the war years. Practically everyone with the exception of Freud was called up. The neutral Netherlands represented a bright spot, which greatly pleased both Freud and Abraham. On 28 April 1917, the Dutch Society for Psychoanalysis was founded.[878] Van Emden had objected for a long time to the setting up of a psychoanalytic society because a number of the Dutch analysts at that time were more Jungian than Freudian. Recently, however, van Ophuijsen had allied himself with Freud, at which point van Emden decided the time was ripe for a society.[879]

Interest in psychoanalysis had begun fairly early in the Netherlands. In 1905, August Stärcke, psychiatrist at a psychiatric clinic in Den Dolder called the Willem Arnsthoeve, read Freud's article "On dreams" and found it fascinating.[880] Along with his brother, Johan, he absorbed himself in the study of psychoanalysis and, from 1911 onwards, he published regularly on the subject. His work was very much appreciated by Freud and, in 1921, he received the Freud Prize for one of his psychoanalytic articles.[881] In March 1921 Ferenczi even advocated asking Stärcke to join the secret committee.[882] That did not happen.

Of great importance was Gerbrandus Jelgersma's interest in psychoanalysis. A Leiden university rector and professor of psychiatry, Jelgersma focused intensively on psychoanalysis in the years 1912–1914.[883] The outcome was a speech with the title "Ongeweten Geestesleven" (Unknown mental life), which Jelgersma delivered on 9 February 1914 on the occasion of the 339th anniversary of Leiden University. In it, he spoke frankly about his acceptance of psychoanalysis.[884] At that point, Jelgersma was fifty-five. He had a successful career behind him and enjoyed great prestige.

Abraham wrote an enthusiastic article in the annual overview in the *Internationale Zeitschrift für ärtzliche Psychoanalyse*:

Prof. Jelgersma on the unconscious. From a competent quarter and at an excellent institution, psychoanalysis has recently been given an evaluation that we must record as an exceptionally pleasing event. At the anniversary celebrations of the University of Leiden its rector, psychiatrist Prof. Jelgersma, gave the commemorative speech. As his subject he chose the unconscious.

After discussing a lengthy newspaper article of 9 February, Jelgersma discussed mainly Freud's teaching on dreams, in a way that demonstrated his total command of the material. He accepted the doctrine as a whole, seeing it as an extraordinarily important achievement for psychology. He also spoke without any reservations about Freud's theory of neuroses. He regards the stress on sexuality in the aetiology of neurosis as completely justified. He recognises that repressed sexual desires are at the centre of neurosis and finally he emphasised what a tremendous impression the rediscovery of the oedipus motif in the inner life of the individual has made on him.[885]

Freud, too, was both surprised and pleased by this unexpected support.[886]

Jelgersma's speech was extraordinarily important for psychoanalysis in the Netherlands. Many of the later Dutch psychoanalysts became interested because of it.

Van Ophuijsen, who had given the decisive push to van Emden to set up the Dutch Society for Psychoanalysis, had worked at the Burghölzli Clinic in Zurich and had been in analysis with Jung there. Later, he turned away from Jung to ally himself with Freud. In the 1920s, he became a good friend of Abraham's.

Depression

In May 1917, Abraham reached the age of forty. All was not well. He was unhealthy, over-strained, and perpetually tired. There seemed to be no end to the war in sight. His letters became more scarce. In the summer, he wrote to Freud that he had still not fully recovered from the asthma and bronchitis of the previous winter.[887] For Freud, wartime circumstances were hard, too, but from various sides he was kept supplied with food and cigars. Eitingon was important in that respect, but so were Ferenczi, Sachs, and several patients. That summer, Freud enjoyed a holiday in Csorbato in Hungary, with plenty of bread, butter, sausage, eggs, and cigars. Sachs spent three weeks with him there, Ferenczi two, and Rank and Eitingon also visited.[888]

During the war, Abraham continued to read every word Freud wrote, but, in the autumn of 1917, he was too tired and overworked to write a review of Freud's *Lectures* as he had promised.[889] On top of his heavy workload, he had started up a small practice of his own because his financial situation had become so bad. His letter of 23 September 1917 sounded gloomy and he had difficulty with the fact that the others were able to visit Freud and he could not.

The other faithful members of our small circle had the opportunity of meeting you this summer. Unfortunately *I* have had to forego this pleasure for exactly three years, as three years have passed since you and your brother were in Berlin in 1914! I constantly plan to make up for lost time, as far as possible, immediately once the war is over. But as long as "impotence of thoughts" is reigning, I shall be confined to wishing.[890]

Freud responded quickly to that letter, slightly alarmed at Abraham's sombre tone.[891] The frequency of their letters had declined sharply of late. To Ferenczi, Freud wrote, "I recently received a touching letter from Abraham with a muted complaint about the change in the times and relations".[892]

Abraham's gloomy mood continued. He wrote that he had turned grey and lost weight, even though there was enough to eat, and in November 1917, he added, "What, for instance, might have happened to Casimiro's courage during the last few days?"[893]

Looking back, it is clear that although he continually wrote about how the tough conditions of war and being overworked had made him depressed, Abraham's symptoms dated back to the year in which his father and two aunts died. That was same year in which first Gerd and then Hedwig became so ill. Abraham's depression began after a series of deaths and illnesses in the family, just like his mother's depression forty-seven years earlier. In her biography of her father Hilda wrote, "My father was obviously showing signs of prolonged stress".[894]

In late 1917 and early 1918, Abraham wrote more optimistic letters, but they are not completely convincing.[895] He was making all kinds of plans for after the war, had started on his *Habilitation* again, had spoken to Bonhoeffer in Berlin, and persuaded Freud to write a letter, although not to Bonhoeffer but to Kraus. The way in which he thanks Freud is strangely lacking in empathy:

Dear Professor,

Many thanks for your two letters and for complying with my wish concerning Kraus! I did gather from your first letter that you found it difficult to come to a decision, but I did not doubt for a moment that you would in fact write to K., and it was therefore unnecessary to set my mind at rest with the second letter! I am very sorry that my request made you feel so uncomfortable. Perhaps we shall both be rewarded by a favourable result![896]

Entanglements on the Eastern Front

For Germany, the course of the war was so bizarre that it is understandable that it took a while for many Germans to believe that Germany really had lost. The general staff, Hindenburg, and Ludendorff all continued to insist until well into 1918 that Germany was winning. From 1916 onwards, Ludendorff was, to all intents and purposes, the country's leader.[897]

Abraham was later reproached for the fact that he with "imperturbably naive optimism (and German nationalism), believed in the victory of the Austrians and Germans until the final year of the war".[898] Given the course of the war, this was not particularly strange at all.

Germany had been reasonably successful on the Eastern Front throughout the war. The Tsarist armies carried on fighting but kept losing. Because little has been written about the war on the Eastern Front, not many people realise this. In Russia, the February Revolution broke out in 1917. The tsar was deposed. As a consequence, Russia more or less withdrew from the war. The Germans helped by sending Lenin (who had been living in exile in Zurich) to Russia in a sealed train.[899]

The second Russian Revolution of October 1917 was a coup by the Bolsheviks, led by Lenin. After that, Russia was completely caught up in the revolution and the fighting within the country. Germany was able to force it to sign the Treaty of Brest-Litovsk on 3 March 1918, according to which Germany took control of so much territory that cracks appeared almost immediately. The area concerned was so vast that the Germans were not even able to deploy sufficient troops to stabilise the region and implement the treaty. Great swathes of the tsarist empire were brought into the German sphere of influence: Estonia, Latvia, Lithuania, Russian Poland, most of White Russia, and parts of southern Turkey. Finland and Ukraine became independent. Part of Poland had become independent at an earlier stage. Russia lost more than a million square kilometres of land, fifty million inhabitants, 90% of its coal mines, 54% of its industry, 35% of its railways, 32% of its urban territory, and almost all its oil and cotton production. Germany suddenly had a huge empire in the centre of Europe and many Germans concluded that the war had now been won.[900] All of this was to last just six months.

The final offensive

In March 1918, the Germans began a series of offensives in the west. They were in a hurry. The Americans had now sided with the Allies and were in a position to send troops. At first the Germans were successful, but, from September 1918 onwards, they were driven further and further back.

The commander of the German armies, General Ludendorff, omnipotent up to that point, had staked everything on victory in the spring of 1918 with a huge offensive in the west. In early October 1918, he wanted an immediate armistice because of the danger of the collapse of the Western Front. He was keen to avoid the blame falling on himself and his high command, however, and he immediately established a parliamentary democracy, so that the newly formed government would have to ask for a truce and take responsibility for it.[901] Historian Detlev Peukert described the manoeuvre as follows:

> The eventual effect of this cynical manoeuvre, which absolved the ruling conservative and military leadership from responsibility for the consequences of its own failed war policy, was to inflict on the democratic parties the odium of the nortorious *Dolchstoß*, directed by stay-at-home politicians against the fighting soldiers in the trenches.[902]

For a long time, hardly anyone in Germany knew that it was Ludendorff who had demanded an immediate truce. He did so at a highly disadvantageous moment, when most German troops found themselves on enemy territory. He seems to have been prompted by panic.[903] A stubborn rumour emerged that it was the government that had stabbed the army in the back by asking for a truce. Ludendorff's efforts to deflect blame from the army leadership on to the recently installed government succeeded. In the end this did not help Ludendorff himself, since the American president, Woodrow Wilson, demanded the resignation of all those responsible for the course taken by Germany up to that time, and Ludendorff disappeared from the stage.[904] General Ludendorff was not the only one to leave high office. The German emperor abdicated and fled to the Netherlands. In Austria, Emperor Charles I also abdicated.

Germany lost not only all the territories it had gained but an eighth of its home territory as well, along with ten per cent of its population, most of its iron ore deposits, and a significant proportion of its coal mines.[905]

On 11 November 1918, the war officially ended with the signing of the armistice at Compiègne. Europe was left in a state of total upheaval. Eight million Europeans had been killed and fifteen million seriously wounded, practically all of them frontline soldiers. There were five million widows, nine million orphans, and ten million refugees. Then Spanish influenza broke out, claiming more victims than the entire war. The Spanish 'flu killed twenty million.[906]

CHAPTER SEVENTEEN

The congress in Budapest of 1918

The war was not yet over, but a psychoanalytic congress was successfully organised in September 1918.[907] Initially, the congress was planned for 21 and 22 September in Breslau.[908] The Austro-Hungarian doctors, however, who were in the army, could not obtain visas to travel to Germany. Abraham wrote to Lou Andreas-Salomé that this meant fourteen registrations to attend the congress would have to be annulled, and with them a majority of the lectures. The congress was transferred to Budapest, in the hope that the two German psychoanalysts who were serving soldiers would be allowed a visa because there were so few of them.[909] It would be held a week later than planned, on 28 and 29 September.[910] Sachs was suddenly found to be seriously ill. He had already arrived in Budapest when, on the morning before the congress began, he suffered a severe pulmonary haemorrhage. He was urgently admitted to hospital, where tuberculosis was diagnosed. Sachs had to spend a long period at a sanatorium in Davos.[911]

The congress was a great success. True, the number of psychoanalysts taking part was relatively small because of the war. In total, there were just thirty-two members of the IPA, but the number of guests was unusually high.[912] Many of the members were in uniform. Four analysts came from Germany, two from the Netherlands, thirteen from Vienna, twelve from Budapest, and one from Warsaw. There were fifty-five guests, including Freud's wife and his children, Ernst and Anna.[913] Then there were eight high functionaries, which was extremely unusual for a psychoanalytic congress: two representatives of the city of Budapest, including the mayor, two senior military representatives of Hungarian government, two representing the German government, and two from the Austrian government.[914] They will have been interested above all in the first part of the scientific programme, which was about war neuroses.

The participants in the congress were royally received. The city of Budapest had made the recently opened Gellërt fürdõ thermal baths and hotel available, and, on the eve of the congress, a reception took place in the marble hall. On the first evening, 28 September, a banquet was held by the municipality of Budapest in the Bristol Hotel for all the congress participants. A steamboat was provided to ferry guests across the Danube from the hotel to the academy of sciences where the scientific programme took place.[915] After all those years of wartime deprivation, it must have been overwhelming. The congress was organised by Ferenczi, Von Freund, and Rank.[916]

The two Dutch participants, van Emden and van Ophuijsen, were given a special welcome by Abraham as chairman. They were the only participants from a neutral country. Both gave a lecture, van Emden on "Analyse einer Sensation am Kopfe im Traum" (Analysis of a sensation in the head in a dream) and van Ophuijsen on "Die Frigidität des Weibes" (The frigidity of the female).[917]

The surprise of the spring of 1918 was Dr Ernst Simmel (1882–1947), senior doctor and head of military hospital number XIX for war neuroses in Posen. Freud had written to Abraham about him for the first time on 17 February 1918, after Simmel published a book called *Kriegsneurosen und psychisches Trauma. Ihre gegenseitigen Beziehungen dargestellt auf Grund psychoanalytischer, hypnotischer Studien* (War Neuroses and Mental Trauma. Their mutual relationship described based on psychoanalytic, hypnotic studies). Freud was extremely enthusiastic about the book, as was Abraham.[918] Simmel had made a study of psychoanalysis on his own initiative, and, in his book, he expressed confidence in its usefulness and gave examples. Freud was of the opinion that Simmel had taken proper account of the sexual aetiology.[919] The book was written based on Simmel's work at the military hospital, and it led to an invitation to him to speak at the congress in Budapest. He would later enter into analysis with Abraham.[920]

The scientific part of the Budapest congress began with a lecture about war neuroses by Ferenczi, with Abraham and Simmel as fellow speakers. It was followed by a discussion. These three lectures later appeared in book form, first in German and, in 1921, in English with a fourth contribution by Jones, who, at the time of the 1918 congress, had belonged to an enemy power and was therefore unable to attend.[921]

The amount of attention devoted to the subject was so great because the war, as well as resulting in an unprecedented number of dead and wounded, had produced a huge number of soldiers with war neuroses. The symptoms were psychogenic paralysis, deafness, and blindness, as well as trembling, attacks of rage, sleeping disorders, anxiety, oversensitivity, headaches, delirium, depression, and so on.

At the congress, Ferenczi began with an overview of the literature on war neuroses. He touched upon a large number of writers of scientific articles, from Oppenheim and his view that such neuroses were caused by brain damage to Nonne, who found in Freud's research into the unconscious important support for their treatment.[922] Oppenheim's view was fairly generally abandoned during the First World War.[923] In its place interest arose in a psychodynamic theory that blamed both an original susceptibility and traumatic events. Ferenczi said that progress could be seen in the attitude of prominent neurologists towards psychoanalytic theory. But at the same time Nonne, for instance, was of the opinion that the war had shown beyond doubt that the idea of an almost exclusively sexual origin of hysteria was incorrect. According to Ferenczi, there was confusion about the concept of sexuality here. Sexuality was seen exclusively as genital sexuality, whereas psychoanalysis was about a far broader concept:

The war neuroses, according to psycho-analysis, belong to a group of neuroses in which not only is the genital sexuality affected, as in ordinary hysteria, but also its precursor, the so-called narcissism, self-love, just as in dementia praecox and paranoia. I grant that the sexual foundation of these so-called narcissistic neuroses is less easily apparent, particularly to those who equate sexuality and genitality and have neglected to use the word "sexual" in the sense of the old platonic Eros. Psycho-analysis, however, returns to this extremely ancient standpoint when it treats all tender and sensual relations of the man to his own or to the opposite sex, emotional feelings towards friends, relatives and fellow-creatures generally, even the affective behaviour towards one's own ego and body, partly under the rubric "erotism", otherwise "sexuality".[924]

Abraham spoke next and his story was a shocking low point in his oeuvre. It displayed a total lack of empathy for the soldiers' experiences of the horrors of war. In short, it amounted to a claim that people who started out with healthy minds could cope with the horrors, whereas degenerates developed neuroses. It was based on the sexual origin of war neuroses.

Abraham had written his lecture at a time when he was depressed, ill, and severely overstrained. Those circumstances seem to have seriously damaged his capacity for empathy. In addition, fear was a blind spot for Abraham. If there was anything the soldiers fell prey to, then it was enormous fear, under artillery bombardment, for example. Rainer Tölle remarked in his 2005 article about war neuroses that fear as experienced during such artillery attacks during the First World War, with shells falling all around, has been described by remarkably few writers. There are hardly any written references to actual situations and the fear that arose from them. Tölle wondered whether that was because the fear was taken for granted and, therefore, seen as not worth mentioning, or whether it was not written about because such fear was regarded as improper in a soldier.[925]

Abraham described the soldiers with war neuroses as failures from an early age:

It is found with great regularity that war neurotics were even before the trauma—to call it for the time being by the common name—emotionally unstable, especially with regard to their sexuality. Some of them were unable to fulfil their duties in everyday life; others were able to do so, although they showed little initiative or driving power. In all cases sexual activity was restricted, and libido inhibited by fixations. Many of them had already before the war shown poor or limited potency. Their relationship to the female sex was disturbed by partial fixation of the libido in the developmental phase of narcissism to a greater or lesser extent. Their social and sexual functioning was dependent on certain concessions to their narcissism.

In wartime these men are placed under entirely different conditions and are faced with extraordinary demands. They must at all times be prepared to sacrifice themselves unconditionally for the general good. This involves the renunciation of all narcissistic privileges. Healthy individuals are able to suppress their narcissism entirely. Just as they are able to transfer their love, so they are able to sacrifice their ego for the community. In this respect those predisposed to neurosis fall behind those who are healthy.

At the front they are obliged not only to endure perilous situations—a purely passive performance—but also to undertake something which is given far less attention. This is the aggressive action for which the soldier must be ready at all times; besides the readiness to die, a readiness to kill is demanded of him.[926]

It is as if the actual events were irrelevant to Abraham and only the development of the psyche mattered, whether complete or incomplete. In theory, that is, because in practice Abraham did the following:

> When in 1916 I opened a ward for neuroses and psychoses, I dispensed with all active interference, as well as hypnosis and other means of suggestion. I let the patients abreact in a waking state, and attempted by means of a simplified psycho-analysis to make them understand the origin and nature of their illness. I succeeded in giving them the feeling of being understood and of considerable relaxation and improvement.[927]

It sounds calm and caring. It is hard to understand how Abraham could be so judgemental in theory while behaving in practice as if he had quite the opposite attitude.

A letter he wrote to Lou Andreas-Salomé makes clear how depressed Abraham was in the period leading up to the congress. He wrote that he had completely lost contact with the others and added, "The congress will be a ray of hope in this endless isolation".[928] It sounded despairing.

Simmel's lecture contrasts starkly with what Tölle concluded about the literature. He did describe what the soldiers actually went through.

> One must have experienced the war occurrences themselves or their recapitulation under analytical–cathartic hypnosis in order to understand to what attacks the mental life of a man is exposed in time of war. For instance, a man after being wounded several times has to return to the front, or is separated from important events in his family for an indefinite time, or finds himself exposed irretrievably to that murderous monster, the tank, or to an enemy gas attack which is rolling towards him; again, shot and wounded by shrapnel he has often to lie for hours or days among the gory and mutilated bodies of his comrades, and, not least of all, his self-respect is sorely tried by unjust and cruel superiors who are themselves dominated by complexes, yet he has to remain calm and mutely allow himself to be overwhelmed by the fact that he has no individual value, but is merely one unimportant unit of the whole.[929]

In a letter to Ferenczi, Freud had earlier written that although Simmel's approach had a basis in psychoanalysis, aside from that it was mainly cathartic in nature.[930] In his lecture and in his book, Simmel described, based on a series of case histories, how he tried to draw the trauma to the surface by means of hypnosis and to bring about a kind of catharsis. He also mentioned that the unconscious significance of the symptoms of the war neurotics was largely non-sexual.[931] Abraham did not agree with that at all.[932] Oddly, the fact that the analysts embraced him to such an extent caused much resistance in Simmel for a long time. A considerable amount of time passed before he sent his review of the congress, causing the publication of works from the congress to be significantly delayed.[933] Freud awarded him the Freud Prize. Simmel wrote not a word in response, at which Freud was extremely piqued.[934] In the end, they agreed that he would enter into analysis with Abraham, but, at the time of their first appointment, Abraham sat down and wrote a letter to Freud, telling him Simmel had failed to appear.[935]

At the congress, Abraham proposed making Ferenczi the new president of the IPA. His proposal was accepted and Ferenczi chose Anton von Freund as secretary.

Abraham had never been able to make much of his presidency. He had only just become president of the IPA in 1914 when war broke out and now, towards the end of the war, Ferenczi took over the position. Abraham had said right at the start that he saw himself as an interim president.

Anton von Freund (1880–1920) was from Budapest. He was a rich and successful brewer as well as a doctor in philosophy. Both Von Freund and his wife had been analysed by Freud, Von Freund in 1916, 1918, and 1919. In 1917, he became active in the psychoanalytic societies in Vienna and Budapest. He supported psychoanalysis financially and enabled Freud to set up a publishing company in 1919, the Internationale Psychoanalytische Verlag, with Freud, Ferenczi, and Von Freund in charge and Rank as director.[936] Von Freund was due to become a member of the committee, but after he became ill—he developed cancer and died in 1920—Eitingon joined in his stead. Von Freund had also made a large sum of money available for the founding of a psychoanalytic institute in Budapest. There, psychoanalysis would be made available to all, and in addition a large number of doctors would be trained in psychoanalysis. Ferenczi would be given scientific leadership of the institute and Von Freund would be responsible for organisational matters. These plans came to nothing because the political situation in Budapest changed and those in power held on to the money.

The first publication to come from the new psychoanalytic publishing house was the collection about war neuroses, including the lectures delivered at the Budapest congress. That Freud did not think much of these lectures is clear from his remark about the Verlag's first book: "I do not regard it as an outstanding achievement, but perhaps for that very reason it will make an impression on our honoured contemporaries".[937]

After the congress in Budapest, three noteworthy things happened. First, the war neuroses vanished into thin air as soon as the war was over.[938] The special interest shown in psychoanalysis on that score therefore disappeared, although interest in psychoanalysis did remain greater than it had been before the war.

Second, although Freud was not particularly taken with the lectures at the Budapest congress, he did use them when he was engaged as an expert witness in the case against Wagner von Jauregg.[939] There, he formulated the psychodynamic factors in war neurosis as follows:

> It was therefore easy to infer that the immediate cause of all war neuroses was an unconscious inclination in the soldier to withdraw from the demands, dangerous or outrageous to his feelings, made upon him by active service. Fear of losing his own life, opposition to the command to kill other people, rebellion against the ruthless suppression of his own personality by his superiors—these were the most important affective sources on which the inclination to escape from war was nourished.[940]

What Freud described here as the cause was, in fact, the actual situation the soldiers had to deal with, as described by Simmel, rather than the sexual and constitutional causes on which Ferenczi and Abraham based their ideas.

Third, Freud's dissatisfied remark about the lectures at the Budapest congress could also be interpreted in another way: that he found his own libido theory insufficient when it came to war neuroses. What he wrote could be seen as relating to his change of course in his essay

"On narcissism", after which not only the development of the libido but the development of the ego became a major focus of attention.

For the unimaginable violence of the First World War that had turned men into a bunch of murderers, the libido theory—so fervently defended by Ferenczi and Abraham at the congress—no longer seemed enough. An important counter-argument was provided by the dreams of soldiers with shell shock. Simmel had observed that these were not dreams of wish-fulfilment but dreams of panic and fear, nightmares in which the traumas were experienced anew.

At the congress in The Hague in September 1920, Freud gave a lecture with the fairly inno-cent-sounding title "Ergänzungen zur Traumlehre" (Supplement to the teaching on dreams).[941] It was a short lecture that at first sight was not particularly remarkable, but, on further exami-nation, it meant nothing less than a total change of direction in Freud's thinking about dreams. It concerned the fact that besides dreams that represent the fulfilment of wishes, people can also have traumatic dreams.[942] Freud would work out these ideas further in *Beyond the Pleasure Principle*. Death suddenly began to play a major role in his work.

Germany in chaos, yet the creation of a psychoanalytic polyclinic in Berlin goes ahead

The war was over, but that did not mean that peace came to Germany. For a short time it had seemed as if the country would succeed in making the transition from an empire to a democracy. The forced resignation of General Ludendorff and the departure of the kaiser gave the new government, led by Prince Max von Baden, a chance to put through much needed reforms. The top army leadership, however, threw a spanner in the works. The supreme command of naval forces decided to carry out an attack even though a ceasefire had been requested and negotiations were under way. This was done on their own initiative, not on the orders of the new government, and it led to a strike by sailors on two ships on 28 October 1918 and a revolt by sailors in Kiel on 3 and 4 November. The consequence was a revolution, which spread with great speed. One German city after another was taken over by workers' and soldiers' councils without any blood being spilled. By 9 November, the revolution in Berlin was victorious.[943]

On 24 November 1918, Abraham wrote to Freud that in Allenstein the revolution had been rapid and bloodless. If everything continued so smoothly there would be no reason to complain. But what would happen next was highly unpredictable, and he had no idea what his personal fate would be. He did not know when he would be able to return to Berlin and whether it would be sensible to take his family back with him, given the drastic food shortages there.[944] In reality, however, their situation was far from safe. The Abrahams were in the far east of Germany. German troops were in total disarray and racing to get home as quickly as possible. The armistice had been signed on 11 November and the Russians had reacted by immediately breaking the treaty of Brest-Litovsk with Germany. They were assembling their troops.

Abraham was discharged from military service on 14 December 1918 and he hoped to return to Berlin on 30 December. Liebermann would have to stay in Allenstein a little longer. Abraham had already rented a flat in Berlin on a temporary basis, in Grünewald, at 6 Schleinitzstrasse:

We have the lower floor of a two-family villa with veranda and garden, seven rooms and entrance hall, respectably furnished. The practice promises well: two analyses certain, two probable, one still uncertain. When I have announced my return in B. there will probably be more to come. I hope that living outside town will be good for my health, which suffered from the eastern climate. It is glorious for the children, especially as there are excellent schools in the garden city.[945]

In Allenstein, where the possibilities for social contact were limited, the family had become friendly with one of Abraham's patients, Mrs Haas, who had been referred to him by Freud and had earlier been in treatment with van Ophuijsen. Her twelve-year-old nephew was also in analysis with Abraham because of educational problems. Hilda and this unnamed nephew were the same age and became good friends. Hilda was extremely impressed when he boasted of his poor marks at school, of which conscientious Hilda would have been deeply ashamed. They became childhood sweethearts. Mrs Haas initially went with them to Berlin, along with her nephew, but they left again in late January 1919. After that, Hilda heard nothing more from her friend. She was deeply hurt. Not until the 1950s did she learn what had actually happened. The nephew, who had made a successful career for himself by then, found her address through the psychoanalytic institute in Frankfurt and rang her in London. At one point Hilda asked why he had broken off contact so abruptly. He told her, "That is what your 'old man' demanded." Hilda, who generally wrote about her father with admiration in her biography, was staggered by this: "I think nowadays we would have been warned of the necessity of such a separation, which left me with a distinct feeling of insecurity and inferiority".[946]

Did Abraham chase off his daughter's first boyfriend like an old-fashioned jealous father? Just a year earlier, Abraham had published "Some illustrations on the emotional relationship of little girls towards their parents".[947] This short article is about Hilda, a four-year-old Hilda whose life revolves around her father rather than the twelve-year-old Hilda who was captivated by the nephew of Mrs Haas. What makes this event so unpleasant is that Abraham chased away not only Hilda's first boyfriend but practically her only male friend. Other than one brief affair, the adult Hilda never had a partner.

Abraham's health was far from good in this period. He had chronic bronchitis, was sleeping badly, and struggled to keep his practice going. Once back in Berlin he put himself in treatment with Fließ, which led to some improvement. Abraham even felt too ill to adapt his lecture at the Budapest congress into an article and to resume his editorship of the journal.

About Berlin, he wrote to Freud that he had the idea that the "worst of the riots" were over. Food supplies were a good deal more problematic than in East Prussia, however.[948]

Political tensions

The "worst of the riots" was a reference to the ongoing revolution in Germany. At that point the chaos was total. The Abraham family was fortunate not to be in the centre of Berlin but in a suburb, where there was less outright conflict. Within a period of three months the kaiser had fled, the general staff had lost its position of power, and democratic reforms had been quashed by a revolution in which workers' and soldiers' councils took power without a political programme or clear leadership, not knowing what they should do. Prince Max had abdicated when the revolution broke out and his position had passed to SPD leader Friedrich Ebert. After the armistice on 11 November, undisciplined, disillusioned soldiers stalked the land. In Berlin demonstrations, strikes, and attacks by armed gangs were an everyday occurrence in December 1918 and January 1919.[949] The only people with a clear programme were the communist Spartacists. In January 1919, they renamed themselves the Communist Party of Germany, the KPD. They had two extremely striking leaders, Karl Liebknecht and Rosa Luxemburg, but their following was limited.[950] Eventually the government, led by the SPD and put in power with the support of the workers' and soldiers' councils, crushed the councils with much bloodshed and with the help of the army. SPD leader Ebert was horrified by the situation in Russia, not so much by the Bolshevik coup as by the total collapse of the Russian empire that followed.[951] Such an outcome had to be avoided in Germany at all costs.

The weather was appalling as well. The winters of both 1918–1919 and 1919–1920 were extremely cold and fuel was scarce. Freud began a letter to Abraham from Vienna on 9 February 1919 with the words, "First, let me state that it is bitterly cold here in this room".[952]

In his biography of Freud, Jones described the situation in Vienna immediately after the war:

> The years succeeding the World War were extremely hard. Everything had come to a standstill in Vienna and life there was scarcely bearable. The monotonous diet of thin vegetable soup was far from being adequately nourishing and the pangs of hunger were continuous. The winters of 1918–19 and 1919–20 were the worst of all, with their completely unheated rooms and feeble illumination. It needed a tough spirit to endure sitting still and treating patients for hour after hour in that deadly cold, even if equipped with an overcoat and thick gloves.[953]

Conditions in Berlin were hardly any better.

The avoidance of free association

Despite the great unrest in Berlin, life went on. In February 1919, Abraham reported that the Berlin Psychoanalytic Society, to the extent that its members could be traced at that point, was meeting three times a month. Abraham had not yet succeeded in discovering the whereabouts of some of the former members, namely those who had come from abroad. He asked Rank whether the non-doctors could receive *Imago* instead of the psychoanalytic journal, which was aimed at members of the medical profession. There were a number of non-doctors who would soon be admitted to the Berlin society as associate members.[954]

On 23 January 1919, the Berlin group had its first post-war meeting. At the following meeting, on 6 February, Abraham became the first since the war to give a lecture: "Über ein besondere Form des neurotischen Widerstandes" (On a special form of neurotic resistance).[955] He always presented everything he wrote to his own group.[956] He gave many lectures.

This particular lecture was about patients who did not freely associate. One of his examples was a female patient he had treated in Allenstein.[957] The point of Abraham's lecture was as follows. The basic principle of analysis is free association, but patients' attitudes to it are enormously diverse.[958] All patients occasionally come out with well-considered thoughts or say that nothing occurs to them. The patients he is talking about here, however, rarely say nothing occurs to them. They speak continually and some do not even want to be interrupted by the doctor. These patients do not associate freely, but, rather, under the continual critical supervision of the ego. Moreover, they show a tireless willingness to throw the doctor off the scent. It was a form of resistance that should not be underestimated, and it could make a therapeutic result impossible.

Abraham thought that in the case of such patients there was a great deal of pride at play and that every remark made by the analyst was experienced by them as humiliating. These patients were extremely receptive to everything that could damage their sense of ego; they had a powerful narcissism. In analysis, there tended to be identification rather than transference, and, just as children like to pull adults' legs about defecation, saying that they cannot produce any excrement only to do so suddenly at a time of their own choosing, these patients wanted to make their own decision about how much to unburden themselves and when. Their apparent willingness and the stream of words meant that only an experienced doctor would succeed in getting to the bottom of what was going on, and even then such treatments were extremely difficult. Abraham had noticed that a result, often partial, could be achieved only if he discussed what was happening right from the start. Then there was sometimes an opportunity to break through the narcissism and a transference developed. That could be seen by the fact that the patient suddenly started freely associating after all.[959]

This brief lecture was typical of Abraham. He came upon a problem or odd behaviour in several patients, or among his family or friends, even perhaps in himself, something he had not seen described before. He observed it carefully, tried to investigate what was going on and how it could be interpreted psychoanalytically, and then wrote an article of great clarity on the subject. His professional craftsmanship remained close to his observations. Freud thought it was an excellent piece and very up-to-date; he would merely have liked to see more stress laid on the origins of this entire attitude in the father complex.

The setting up of a psychoanalytic polyclinic

In July 1919, the Berlin Psychoanalytic Society took an important decision. The members agreed with Eitingon's proposal to open a psychoanalytic polyclinic in Berlin that coming winter (Eitingon, 1922). It was inspired by an idea of Freud's, which he had expressed in his lecture at the Budapest congress in 1918. Freud's lecture at that time had been called "Lines of advance in psycho-analytic therapy" and he had written it during the summer before the congress, when he was staying with Anton von Freund. It must have been written in consultation with von Freund, who afterwards developed plans to finance a psychoanalytic polyclinic in Budapest. In his lecture, Freud referred to the huge amount of neurotic misery in the world. The psychoanalysts could deal with very little of it, and even then only in the well-off upper strata of society. They could do nothing whatsoever for all those in large swathes of society who were suffering terribly with their neuroses.

Freud foresaw—and correctly so—that the conscience of society would one day awaken and poor people would be given a right to psychiatric help. Institutes would be set up where they could be treated without payment. Freud thought it might be a long time before the state took upon itself this obligation, but meanwhile private charities could make a start. What von Freund had not been able to do because of his death at the age of forty, Eitingon was now taking upon himself.

On 21 July 1919, Eitingon wrote to Freud:

Dear Professor,

In the hope that you are well and enjoying being away from Vienna with all its agitations, I would like to tell you briefly about a small yet perhaps not unimportant psychoanalytic occurrence. Last Saturday our Society, as proposed by me, took the decision to open a psychoanalytic polyclinic in Berlin this coming winter. We will therefore make a start on "psychotherapy for the people" without waiting until our State, which is still under construction, or until the generous anthropophilic calling of a new private person à la Dr. v. F(reund) puts major resources at our proposal for such a purpose.[960] . . . The relatively modest resources required for a none too small polyclinic—approximately three doctors will be able to work there simultaneously—are already more or less guaranteed to us. The total amount of treatment time by doctors each day will in the short term be mostly free of charge, carried out by a number of the experienced colleagues of our Society, according to the time they have available. I have asked the Society to authorise leadership of the polyclinic for myself and Simmel.[961]

Eitingon was in an unusual position. His knowledge of psychoanalysis was extensive and profound.[962] Before he left for Palestine in 1933, however, he published hardly any scientific articles and treated hardly any patients.[963] He travelled a great deal and mainly acted as patron and organiser. His contact with Freud intensified during the First World War, when he supported Freud enormously, providing him with food and cigars. He carried on in that supportive role after the war. The extract from the letter quoted above is remarkable for a number of reasons. Eitingon wanted to implement Freud's idea of an institute where ordinary people would be treated. He did not want to wait for the state, which was being reconstituted at that point. This was sensible, since the state was more or less bankrupt after the war and its financial position soon worsened further as a result of the reparations imposed on Germany. Eitingon goes on to write, oddly, that he does not want to wait for someone like von Freund to stand up and offer large sums of money. What was odd about this was that Eitingon was now donating large sums of money himself. He paid for the polyclinic out of his own funds for many years. This raises the suspicion that he did not want to fall short of von Freund's grand gesture and, therefore, set up a polyclinic at his own expense. As a reward, he was offered von Freund's place on the secret committee.[964] Initially, it was agreed that Eitingon would be given von Freund's ring after his death, but in the end that did not happen.[965]

The opening of the polyclinic

The polyclinic was opened on 14 February 1920 with a wonderful celebratory party.[966] The clinic was a great success from the start and it gave a huge boost to psychoanalysis in Berlin. Freud was unable to attend the opening, but two of his children were there, Mathilde and Ernst.

Abraham's brother-in-law and friend, Hans Bürgner, came, too. He became the new polyclinic's lawyer and notary as well as personal adviser to many members of the Berlin Psychoanalytic Society. Hans Bürgner later vividly recalled the opening of the polyclinic, at which Abraham gave the opening speech and Simmel contributed a cheerful note with a toast.[967]

Eitingon wrote in the *Korrespondenzblatt* that it had been difficult to find a suitable location for the polyclinic, given the current housing crisis in Berlin.[968] In the end, a place was found with the help of the minister of culture. In January 1920, the Psychiatric Society was allocated a six-room apartment in the centre, at 29 Potsdamerstraße. Ernst Freud took responsibility for the decor and furnishings.[969] The polyclinic had five consulting rooms, in which five doctors could carry out analysis simultaneously. The largest of them also served as a conference room, where meetings of the Society could be held and courses and talks given. The leadership of the polyclinic was made up of Eitingon and Simmel, supported by Abraham as president of the Berlin Psychoanalytic Society. Eitingon and Simmel held a daily consultation. Patients began arriving as soon as the polyclinic opened its doors. Abraham was the first to give a course there, in March 1920: "Über ausgewählte Kapitel der Psychoanalyse" (On selected chapters of psychoanalysis).

There were also plans to set up a special department for children some time in the future. Abraham wanted to train a woman doctor for it.[970]

Continuing unrest in Berlin

On 13 March 1920, the Kapp Putsch took place in Berlin, another attempt by the army to take power. It was a critical moment and the government, seizing the only means available to it, called for a general strike. A huge number of people responded and from 14 to 21 March 1920, Germany came to a standstill. The strike made clear that the last thing the population wanted was another military dictatorship.[971] Abraham told Freud on 13 March that it was a good thing the polyclinic had been established, since it was totally unclear what awaited them after the radical change of that day.[972] In the period that followed, Abraham had plenty of time because of the strike, which he used to write: "I have done a great deal of writing during recent weeks. While it lasted, the general strike cut my practice down to half, and so I had sufficient free time."[973]

One thing he wrote was an article for *Die Neue Rundschau* titled "The cultural significance of psycho-analysis".[974] It was a valuable introduction to psychoanalysis and it also offered an overview of psychoanalytic literature up to that point, but it contained nothing new. It is interesting, nevertheless, because it reflects the way Abraham thought about psychoanalysis at the time. His firmness of tone is striking. When he writes of the revolutionary changes brought about by psychoanalysis, the first point he mentions is that it vindicates, or perhaps even establishes, the dominance of causality in the field of psychic life. That is not exactly untrue: psychoanalysis is a causal theory, but the stress on that point, its primacy in his account, is surprising. A very different starting point is equally possible, which is that psychoanalysis presumes and claims to have shown that people have an unconscious about which it is possible to learn something through free association but that cannot be known in itself. The unconscious is a force in psychic life that is hard to fathom, one that can be channelled only to a very limited degree. Think of the eight million dead of the First World War. In the period from 1914 to 1918, there was no sign of composure and nothing was any longer under control. It is notable that the war did not bring about any change in Abraham's way of thinking. It did not sow any doubts as it did in Freud and Simmel.

On the one hand, this seems astonishing. The war was an explosion of violence of a kind no one had ever thought possible. It presented a wholly new view of the human psyche. This was clearly recognised by Freud. On the other hand, Abraham had always stressed aggression far more than Freud did. Freud initially regarded aggression as an additional symptom that emerged when the experience of pleasure was interrupted. Abraham had always assumed the existence of an extremely strong, inborn urge towards aggression, different in each individual, a constitutionally determined sadism. It included an urge to destroy and annihilate.

A dangerous time

The years 1920–1923 were the most turbulent and, at times, downright dangerous years of the Weimar Republic. It was a thoroughly chaotic period, incomprehensible in its totality for the ordinary German citizen. The Treaty of Versailles came into force on 10 January 1920 and peace did not bring calm but, instead, a series of major conflicts. The Allies at first delayed the decision about the level of reparations and the means of payment. They then decided that Germany should pay not just for the direct war damage it had inflicted but for the entire cost of the war. The calculations, therefore, involved such huge sums of money that they were simply unimaginable. The debt was estimated at 269 billion gold marks, an impossible sum in those days. In London in the spring, this was reduced to 132 billion, which was still beyond anything it was possible to comprehend, let alone to pay.[975]

There was also the threat from Russia. In the summer of 1920, an apparently unstoppable Russian army marched through Poland with the undisguised aim of bringing the revolution to Germany. The idea was to use Germany as the springboard to other nations in Europe where the Bolsheviks wanted to impose a communist regime.[976]

The Russian advance was eventually stopped by the Poles, who fought with extraordinary courage because they were not prepared to fall under Russian rule again, having just gained their independence at the end of the war.[977]

Sunday neuroses

In these turbulent times. Abraham wrote a reaction to an article by Ferenczi in which he addressed a problem that is still of relevance today. Ferenczi had written about Sunday neuroses.[978] The patients concerned had symptoms specifically on Sundays, usually headaches or intestinal disorders. The cause was often unclear and it meant that for these mostly young people their only day off was spoilt. Ferenczi had heard about the problem from patients who had been troubled by it primarily in their youth. He proposed that when on Sundays and other holidays the external pressure of duties and obligations was removed, the internal pressure which kept the passions in check was reduced, so that people felt an urge to discharge themselves sexually. At parties and on outings, people could be seen giving such drives free rein.

In neurotics, an opposite reaction could be observed. This might be because the drives they curbed were all too dangerous, so that they had to be very much on their guard, or it might be that they had a particularly strong conscience that forbade even minor transgressions. Their passions had to be fiercely restrained. Along with the self-punishment phantasies aroused, this could lead to the physical symptoms mentioned above.

Abraham wrote in his reaction that he was not in any sense intending to contradict Ferenczi, but that he wanted to supplement the article. In essence, he wrote the following: a considerable number of people can ward off the outbreak of severe neurotic symptoms only by working hard. By labouring strenuously at their profession, studies, or other tasks, they tear themselves away forcibly from the demands of their libido. They impose tasks upon themselves that go far beyond what is truly necessary. Work becomes essential to them, increasingly so, as if they are addicted. When the neurosis does eventually break through, a sham diagnosis is attached to it, namely "overwork". Abraham went on to say that in some cases they did not succeed in preventing the libido from obtruding. It broke through by means of conversion.[979]

In other cases, and this is where Sunday neuroses come in, the neurotic symptoms showed themselves as soon as work was interrupted by external circumstances. The laboriously achieved balance disappeared on Sundays or during holidays. When work began again, patients immediately felt much better. Sunday was, moreover, particularly difficult because on that day neurotics were more clearly confronted with the consequences of their neurosis. They might see loving couples out walking, for example, when they had not succeeded in entering into such a relationship themselves. This gave them a profound sense of having failed.[980]

The point that Abraham addressed in his reaction to Ferenczi is of great relevance today. Overwork is seen as a result of working too hard. The possibility that there might be an earlier step, so that working too hard can in itself be a consequence of underlying problems, is not taken into account.

The Freud family

Abraham's health still left much to be desired. In his letters to Freud, he wrote a number of times that his health was reasonably good.[981] That was an ominous sign. In periods when he was healthy, Abraham never mentioned it.

The bronchitis that persisted until the summer of 1919 meant that Abraham was not able to do anything besides run his practice. He remarked that he did not any longer have the freshness of mind that used to enable him to fit in scientific work as well. The practice itself was going well. The patients were not troubled by having to travel all the way to Grünewald.

Meanwhile, the family was still living in a temporary apartment. All their belongings and most of their clothes were in storage. This had been the case for several years now and they longed for a home of their own.

Freud and his wife came to visit them in the apartment. Abraham and Eitingon had organised everything minutely:

Berlin-Grünewald, Schleinitzstrasse 6

14 September 1919

Dear Professor,

After consulting Eitingon, I can give you the following programme:

Your train, unfortunately, does not reach Lehrter Station until 1:40 in the afternoon, not at 12 o'clock, as my wish wanted to improve the timetable. I shall be at the station with Eitingon. He will look after your luggage and take it to Anhalter Station and bring the luggage ticket to you in the afternoon at our house. I myself will take you and your wife to Grünewald immediately by the quickest way. For lunch and supper you are our guests. If Eitingon has obtained sleeping-coach tickets, you can stay with us until about 8 o'clock in the evening. My wife and I are vastly looking forward to receiving you both in our house again, but we must ask you in advance to excuse the fact that our temporary lodging cannot offer you as comfortable a stay as we would wish.

In the evening I shall see to it that you catch your train at the right time. Meanwhile have some really lovely days in Hamburg with your children and grandchildren!

I would be grateful for a short confirmation that you agree with the programme. In any case, I will point out that my telephone number is post Pfalzburg number 1684.

With the most cordial greetings to all of you from my wife and me,

Yours,

Karl Abraham.[982]

Freud's reaction after the visit was beautifully worded: "Dear Friend, There is already something dream-like about the times behind us, when friendly solicitude kept the seriousness of life away from us".[983]

The members of the committee seem to have become a kind of family to Freud as time went on. Not only did Freud, and sometimes his wife, visit Abraham and Eitingon in Berlin, some of Freud's children came regularly. On 23 November 1919, Abraham wrote to Freud: "Gradually all your family are turning up here, and we hope to have sight of one or two more of them soon".[984]

Mathilde (1887–1978), Freud's eldest daughter, had recently visited the Abrahams along with Freud's sister-in-law, Minna Bernays.[985] Freud's youngest son, Ernst (1892–1970), who lived in Berlin, visited the Abrahams for the first time in December 1919. He became a regular visitor.[986] Ernst was an interior architect and, as mentioned earlier, he designed the interior of the new polyclinic and later that of Abraham's consulting room.[987] Oliver (Oli) Freud (1891–1961) came to Berlin in 1920. He was in a bad way after the war. Eitingon found a temporary job for him.[988] Oli was depressed and he turned to Eitingon for help. Anna Freud later wrote the following about Oli to Lou Andreas-Salomé:

He was then, in Berlin, in a very poor state and suffered greatly because of it. He asked Eitingon for help and advice. Eitingon felt—with reason—that he was himself too close to take him into analysis, but instead of drawing the correct conclusion from that and helping him to find another analyst, he delayed the matter for months without being able to make a decision and in the end left Berlin without having done anything. In the end Lampl intervened when he arrived and sorted things out.[989]

Eitingon's behaviour greatly disappointed Freud. Lampl saw to it that Oli entered into analysis with the young and promising Franz Alexander.[990]

Hans Lampl (1889–1958) had been good friends with Martin, Freud's eldest son, since their schooldays together. As a child, he often visited the Freuds' house and he went on holidays with them. After the First World War, he moved to Berlin to become a psychoanalyst there. In 1925, he married Jeanne De Groot (1895–1987), who came to occupy a central place in Dutch psychoanalysis.

Oliver visited the Abrahams regularly and got along very well with Gerd. His analysis with Alexander started in December 1921 and, in October 1922, Abraham wrote to Freud that he found Oliver definitely changed for the better. He had just been on an outing with the Abraham family.[991] Anna Freud also visited the Abrahams. She wrote to her parents on 21 November 1920, "Recently I spent the afternoon at the Abrahams; it was really nice and I was very charming".[992]

Finally, a home of their own

At last, in October 1919, the Abraham family was able to move into the new house at 14 Bismarckallee, a beautiful avenue. The house still stands. The part in which the Abraham family lived was bombed during the Second World War and rebuilt afterwards.[993]

Abraham's son, Gerd, talked about the house in 1988.[994] His face lit up during the interview when he spoke about Berlin and his father. Gerd (Grant) was seventy-eight by then. He lived in the Bismarckallee between the ages of nine and sixteen (1919–1926). He said they had a spacious apartment on the first floor of a large villa. The consulting room was at the centre of the apartment and everyone, children and servants, knew they had to be absolutely silent in the corridor outside, so that his father and the patients would not be disturbed. The children never saw most of the patients. The first of them arrived at eight in the morning and the bell kept ringing all day. The patients either found their own way to the waiting room or were taken there by the maid, Grant could not remember which.

Abraham worked without a break between patients until 1 o'clock in the afternoon. The family then had lunch together and his parents chatted a little, perhaps with the children as well although Grant no longer knew for certain. After lunch, Abraham slept for ten minutes and then worked on until six or seven in the evening. He often went to meetings after that. Sunday was reserved for the children from early morning until tea time. Their father played games with them, took them for walks or read to them. Good friends of his parents would visit for tea, usually the early founders of psychoanalysis in Berlin. Grant remembered, for example, visits by Eitingon and his wife.[995]

These were still difficult times. It was hard to get enough to eat. The food situation in Vienna was particularly dire. On 6 January 1920, Freud wrote to Abraham that Rank had brought supplies with him from Holland but that food sent from Britain and America had, of course, failed to arrive.[996]

The epidemic of Spanish 'flu was still raging. On 25 January, five days after Anton von Freund, Sophie died, Freud's second youngest daughter. She was living in Hamburg with her husband, Max Halberstadt, and their two sons. Sophie was pregnant with her third child. For the Freuds, the blow was too much. In late February, Freud wrote to Katá Lévy that he did not know whether they could ever be cheerful again, his poor wife had been hit so hard.[997]

Hedwig later said that Freud had visited them shortly after Sophie's death and that it was unimaginably awful. Freud was filled with sorrow.[998]

On 10 July 1920, Abraham gave a lecture to doctors in the clinic in Halle about neurotic complaints of the digestive organs. It was a success. Those attending were mainly from the Clinic for Internal Medicine; the psychiatrists stayed well away, making all kinds of excuses, apart from a doctor from the mental hospital in Halle. Abraham wrote to Freud that his listeners were at first sceptical and negative but their "supercilious smiles" gave way during the lecture to full attention and the discussion yielded far more agreement than disagreement. One of the doctors from the clinic said afterwards that he had previously completely rejected psychoanalysis, but that as a result of the paper he had come to see that there was something in it after all. Others enquired about training possibilities. Abraham had started to receive such invitations far more frequently.[999]

The marriage of Max Abraham

In the summer of 1920, the Abrahams stayed close to home because they were so content in their new house with its large garden. At the start of the holidays, the four of them visited Abraham's mother in Bremen and, on the way back, they took a look at a few of the little towns along the Weser.[1000] They then travelled to Nordhausen in the Harz to celebrate the engagement of Abraham's older brother Max.[1001]

Max's fiancée was Else Goldstein from Nordhausen, fifteen years his junior. Max was forty-seven years old and still living with his mother in the parental home where he had taken over the family business after his father's death in 1915. In 1897, Nathan, father to Max and Karl, had switched from a wholesale business in tobacco to a wholesale business in textiles. After grammar school, Max had trained as a textile merchant in Hannover.[1002] Unlike Karl, he had remained true to the orthodox Jewish faith of his parents. In her book about Max's daughter, Bettina Decke writes that with his adherence to the orthodox faith, Max was more or less swimming against the tide. Most German Jews had abandoned daily adherence to the Torah because it was in conflict with modern ideas that laid great stress on integration into German society. Orthodox believers were, however, highly respected within the Jewish community.[1003]

Max struggled to carry on his father's wholesale business. After his marriage to Else Goldstein in 1921, the couple moved with his mother to a house that was less "sought after" but more conveniently located for the company. Max increasingly regretted not having become a rabbi. He could sit "studying" for hours. His only daughter, Lottie, later spoke about how he would rock gently back and forth while reading. Max taught his daughter a little Hebrew and read poems and stories to her. Wilhelm Busch was their favourite. For birthdays and other celebrations, Max would write verse. He had a great sense of humour. Lottie was extremely fond of her father but she also rebelled against him because he was so terribly prim and proper.[1004] The age difference was so great that he could easily have been her grandfather. Mark Markreich wrote the following about Max Abraham:

> He had at his disposal an unfailing memory, sharpened by continual study of the Talmud, which had been left to him as a legacy by his forefathers in a large number of huge tomes. . . . Having grown up in an atmosphere of ancient Jewish tradition and provided with the resource of a good general knowledge, Max Abraham devoted himself all his life to the service of Judaism, modestly withdrawing behind the greatness of his father and the calling of his brother.[1005]

CHAPTER NINETEEN

The congress in The Hague from 8 to 11 September 1920

A rie van der Chijs (1874–1926) was a Dutch neurologist and one of the pioneers of psychoanalysis in the Netherlands. In 1920, he attended a psychoanalytic congress for the first time, in The Hague. He wrote that on such an occasion one wishes to meet the great personalities but imagines them as simply too awe-inspiring. He was referring to Abraham, among others. Van der Chijs envisaged Abraham as a biblical patriarch, a big and heavy man, with, at the very least, a full, greying beard. On the first evening of the congress, Chijs suddenly found himself standing with his colleagues in a tight huddle in front of someone who introduced himself as Abraham. Their disappointment could be read from their faces, it seems, because Abraham asked for an explanation. Van der Chijs wrote of that moment: "With his slim build and young, clean-shaven face he laughed heartily when we gave the answer. Far from awe-inspiring, Abraham was simplicity itself. It was impossible to tell from his looks that he played such a major leading role in the world of psychoanalysis".[1006]

Preparations for the congress

Abraham and Eitingon would have liked the sixth psychoanalytic congress to take place in Berlin. Jones was firmly opposed to that.[1007] On 4 January 1920, Abraham wrote to Jones that it would be impossible to hold a congress in The Hague. The Germans, Hungarians, and Austrians had hardly any currency. The train journey was impossible for them to afford, let alone the cost of a stay in Holland with the guilder valued at such a high rate. Even if the Dutch provided accommodation, it would still be unaffordable.[1008] Abraham wrote to Jones about this, rather than to Ferenczi, because Jones had been forced to replace Ferenczi as president. The political situation in Hungary made it impossible for Ferenczi to continue to act as president.[1009]

He did chair the congress in The Hague, however, at which Jones was unanimously chosen as the next president of the IPA.

Jones answered Abraham at length. He claimed first of all that the decision had already been made, first in Budapest and then during a meeting of the committee in October, which Abraham had been unable to attend because there was no train service at the time. Then he gave a friendly and detailed explanation, remarking in passing that he did have some knowledge of the situation in Austria, Hungary, and Germany, since that autumn he had married a woman who was originally from Moravia.[1010] The most important argument for choosing The Hague was that so soon after the war it was more sensible to hold a congress on neutral soil.

The position of Jones

Jones had some far from easy years behind him. In 1913, he had set up the London Psychoanalytic Society, where major difficulties arose because the Jungians were in a majority. They defended the view that Jung's method was a variation on a legitimate development in psychoanalysis. At that point, Jones had no allies other than Bryan, who had little grounding in psychoanalysis.[1011] Jones did have a highly successful psychoanalytic practice and during the war he had been able to stay in touch with Freud through van Emden in the Netherlands.

Psychoanalysis in Britain became properly organised only with the setting up of the British Psychoanalytical Society in 1919, also by Jones. To put an end to the problems, he dissolved the London psychoanalytic group that year. The new British Psychoanalytical Society was immediately recognised as coming under the umbrella of the IPA.

In February 1917, Jones married Morfydd Owen, Welsh by birth, who was a singer and composer.[1012] She died on 7 September 1918 during an operation for appendicitis.[1013] Just over a year later, on 9 October 1919, Jones married Katherine Jokl, whom he had met only a few weeks before in Zurich, when Sachs recommended her as a translator. Katherine, or Kitty, Jokl was of Jewish extraction and had grown up in Vienna, where she attended the same school as Anna Freud. The marriage was a great success from the start. Jones had, in effect, married into Freud's circle.[1014]

Dutch hospitality

The Dutch psychoanalysts made huge efforts to make it possible for their colleagues to attend the congress in The Hague. On 14 July 1920, van Ophuijsen wrote to Rank that all members of the Association who had applied to attend the congress would be able to stay with Dutch colleagues for the duration of the congress week, from 8 to 13 September. In Britain, money was collected to subsidise the travel expenses for IPA members from Germany, Austria, and Hungary.[1015]

The congress was very well attended. There were fifty-seven members of the IPA, of whom fourteen were from the Netherlands and nine from Britain. There were five associate members, all from Britain, and fifty-seven guests, thirty-seven of them from the Netherlands, seven from

Britain, and one from the USA.[1016] The number of those present was all the more surprising given that the participants from Central Europe not only had no money but had to apply for, and be granted, a complex visa.[1017]

The course of the congress in The Hague

On the eve of the congress, a reception was held for participants. Jones wrote that same evening to his wife, Kitty, "We have just come from meeting the Professor, who came from Hamburg, with Anna and Eitingon and Abraham. It was a rousing reception, about 30 people. . . . Everyone looks extremely well".[1018]

Abraham saw relatively little of Freud for most of the year and it had become a tradition that they would reserve some time before a congress to talk to each other. After Sophie's death, Freud regularly visited his widower son-in-law and two grandsons in Hamburg. Before the congress in The Hague, he first went to Hamburg with Anna and then travelled from there to The Hague with Eitingon. Abraham joined them in Bremen.[1019]

The van Ophuijsens lived in a small house in The Hague, yet they had many people to stay. Ans van Ophuijsen's baby son slept in the nanny's room. The Ferenczis slept in the van Ophuijsens' bedroom, Abraham in the guest room, Reik in the baby's room, and at the last moment Lampl joined them as well. Sachs and Rank stayed with the van Emdes. A room had been booked for Freud in the Hotel Paris, since he preferred not to stay with people, liking his freedom. Jones also stayed in Hotel Paris, which he was able to afford.[1020]

One of the Dutch participants, who made a good impression at the congress with his original ideas and witty performance, was August Stärcke.[1021] He wrote to his father-in-law about how things had gone in The Hague and described the atmosphere beautifully:

Dear father,

I returned enthusiastic from The Hague, and with the feeling that I had been part of a cultural event. There was no *discord*. British, Americans, Central Europeans, and neutrals, all were part of a universal brotherhood. It was like a stay in the Ur-Sippe, with the generally recognised tribal chief at the head. After my first lecture I was drunk and dizzy, like an officer given a chance to distinguish himself under the watchful eye of his commander-in-chief. Just before I started, Abraham, who spoke before me, overran his time by a long way and was urged to cut his lecture short by Ferenczi, the president.[1022] I too was in a stew, since the General Secretary had written that we would have forty minutes in which to speak, and I had carefully tailored my lecture to that, but at the meeting we were told we had thirty minutes. Moreover we were requested to speak freely and not read, because that was less tiring for the audience. So I began my lecture (on the castration complex, about which the previous speaker had also lectured, only about the female) as follows: "Ladies and Gentlemen, I intend to make a further contribution on the theory dealt with by Dr. Karl Abraham.[1023] Now two demands have been made of us by the president, 1. . . . that the lecture must be short, thirty minutes[1024] and 2. that we must speak freely. Freedom is an illusion, however, and one that we have learnt from Freud to do without. The other requirement, to reduce speaking time from forty minutes to thirty, has naturally awoken my own castration complex, since we have just seen how reluctant a man, too, is to see his privileges curtailed.

Fortunately I have remembered at just the right moment that the American poet Edgar Allan Poe set a maximum speaking time of five minutes, because no one can tolerate paying attention any longer than that, and so a compromise has been reached, a repeat of that culture-historical event whose aim is the removal of the trivial with retention of the essential, a kind of circumcision, in the hope that the Lord-God-Father-President will be satisfied with that."

Then I had my audience's attention and they hung on my every word. Ferenczi came up to me afterwards to say that it had been "exceptional". It went well the second time too. I spoke more freely than I ever could in Dutch, because of the realisation that all my paradoxes in crass sayings went in here like honey. The second time I was greeted with applause even as I took my place on the podium. The previous speaker, the young Binswanger, had spoken for an hour and a quarter, and it was a rather tough lecture, at the end of which Abraham brushed past and whispered in my ear: "You'll make up for that." So the unbelievable happened, that I was honoured as a witty cockroach. For the illustration of a point I had sought out a good case, but when I got to it I thought, wait, I'll take something else, and I took the example of applause as a pointless act, mindful of the fact that audiences like to be insulted. When I then compared applause with an epileptic attack, it burst out on all sides and a few moments passed before I could continue. But the main thing of all was: Freud was extremely content, my pieces must be published right away, including in English translation in London and New York.—I took my leave of him very warmly.—I heard wonderful things. Lofty thoughts with something of the future wafting through them. The debate was dropped. Freud believed I had brought so many new ideas that it must first be printed, so we had Friday afternoon free.[1025] I was invited to lunch with a few Viennese in the Pavilion, but I needed to be alone because I was completely overwhelmed by the unexpected success, so I ate a delicious bit of bread + butter + cheese with a cup of coffee sitting on the beach, and collected shells for the boys, and had my picture taken, a telegraph post blown askew just like in the wedding photo.

Afterwards Freud walked up to me with Sachs, and his daughter with Abraham. They had been on a long walk. And Rank and a couple of others had been bathing, and Róheim, a very pale ethereal Hungarian, an excellent ethnologist, who had spoken about totemism among the Central-Australians, got lost in the sea and didn't listen for the horn and had to be fetched out, and everyone said he was on his way to Central Australia.[1026]

I have the pleasant feeling that I made a number of friends, and enviers too of course. There was a general spirit of something rebellious in many of the lectures, something of necessary change in society instead of putting the patient in the foreground.[1027]

The congress must have been thrilling. The Treaty of Versailles had come into force a few months earlier, on 10 January 1920, and now a group of people had come together who until recently belonged to enemy powers: American and British people meeting with Germans, Austrians, and Hungarians. It was the first post-war scientific congress at which nationals of former enemy powers came together. There were no French among them. Pfister had invited the influential French psychiatrist Professor Dupré, but his name does not appear on the list of participants.[1028] Those present must have had the feeling they were walking on eggshells and the irrepressible bursts of laughter met with by Stärcke's lecture undoubtedly had to do with that. The neutral Dutchman broke the tension by larding his serious lecture with jokes.

Abraham had a great feeling for languages. As well as German he spoke English, Spanish, Italian, and Romansh, and he could read Danish, Dutch, and French. He was also at home in the classical languages and took the opportunity to refresh them when his children had Greek and Latin lessons at school. At the congress, he amazed all those present by giving a speech in Latin. It was a more neutral language than German.[1029]

Grosskurth (1991) wrote in her book about the secret committee titled *The Secret Ring*, "Abraham, a gifted linguist, gave the opening address in Latin in order to avoid offending any national sensibilities".[1030] Yet, neither in Jones' account nor in the *Korrespondenzblatt* is there any reference to Abraham opening the conference. It was not Abraham who was first to speak, but Ferenczi. As president, he gave a lengthy account of the state of affairs in psychoanalysis and spoke about the recently founded English-language journal *The International Journal of Psychoanalysis*. Abraham must have spoken at some other point during the banquet.

The female castration complex

On the Wednesday afternoon in The Hague, Abraham gave a lecture entitled "Manifestations of the female castration complex". It was a subject he had been working on for quite some time and, on 3 May 1919, he had given a lecture on it to the Berlin Psychoanalytic Society.[1031] A version that he had developed further was published some years later, in December 1921, in the *Zeitschrift*.[1032] Abraham based his lecture on two essays by Freud, *Three Essays on the Theory of Sexuality* and "The taboo of virginity (Contributions to the Psychology of Love III)".[1033] In his lecture, Abraham highlighted the fact that many women suffer either temporarily or continually from the fact that they are women. From dreams and other products of their unconscious, there emerged a repressed desire in many women to be male. Because that desire was so often present, Abraham concluded that it was a general desire on the part of women. Every woman, deep in her heart, wanted to be a man.

Abraham chose to call this not the genital complex but, instead, the female castration complex for the following reason: initially, the little girl, as befits her narcissism, does not have any sense of inferiority in regard to her own body. Neither is she capable of recognising that it is at a disadvantage compared to the body of a boy. She cannot accept her primary defect, so she phantasies that the member was there but has been taken from her by castration. It is, therefore, correct to speak of a castration complex in the girl. According to Abraham, this belief was closely connected with another idea, in which the female genitals are seen as a wound. That wound represents the effect of castration.

Abraham was of the opinion that being disadvantaged in comparison to men prompted the desire in many women to avenge themselves on men, who had the advantage. The aim of these impulses was an active castration of the man.

Abraham was following Freud with this explanation, but whereas, for Abraham, it was as clear as day that all women suffered from the castration complex, what Freud said on this point was more circumspect. He formulated it as follows:

> We have learnt from the analysis of many neurotic women that they go through an early age in which they envy their brothers their sign of masculinity and feel at a disadvantage and humiliated

because of the lack of it (actually because of its diminished size) in themselves. We include this "envy for the penis" in the "castration complex". . . . During this phase, little girls often make no secret of their envy, nor of the hostility towards their favoured brothers which arises from it. They even try to urinate standing upright like their brothers in order to prove the equality which they lay claim to. In the case already described in which the woman used to show uncontrolled aggression after intercourse towards her husband, whom otherwise she loved, I was able to establish that this phase had existed before that of object-choice. Only later was the little girl's libido directed towards her father, and then, instead of wanting to have a penis, she wanted—a child. . . . But the masculine phase in the girl in which she envies the boy for his penis is in any case developmentally the earlier, and it is closer to the original narcissism than it is to object-love.[1034]

Freud did not say that all women suffer from a castration complex but, rather, that all women go through a phase in which they feel disadvantaged by the lack of a penis, which he categorised under the castration complex.

Abraham followed up Freud's argument that the discovery of the male genitals was an affront to the girl's narcissism. In the narcissistic stage of development, the child carefully guards its possessions and looks at others' belongings with jealousy. It wants to keep what it has and also to get what it sees. If someone else has what it does not have, then two closely connected reactions are prompted in the child: hostility towards the privileged person and an impulse to take from him what he has.

The combination of these two reactions manifests itself in envy or, indeed, malice, a typical reaction that belongs to the sadistic–anal phase of libidinous development. As a result, the female castration complex expresses itself as penis envy. In many cases when the child regards something with envy, it can be reassured by being told: later, when you're big. A girl cannot be promised that a male organ will grow, although this does not alter the fact that the little girl is convinced for a long time that she will get one. When that does not happen, an adjustment is expected of the girl that is not expected of a little boy. She has to come to terms with being disadvantaged.

Abraham referred to Freud's observation that, for a child, the concept of a proof of love is closely connected with the concept of a gift. The proof of love that makes the biggest impression on the child is its repeated suckling by the mother. This act satisfies the child, increases, as it were, its material property, and stimulates its erotogenic zones at the same time.[1035]

The child responds to this gift from its mother to some degree by giving something back, by regulating its bodily evacuations in the way that she wants. Defecation is a material gift in return for all the proofs of love it has received. In this early period, the child sees its faeces as part of its body. The process of identification makes a link between the penis and defecation. So, the boy is afraid that he might lose his penis in the way that he loses his faeces. In the girl, a phantasy develops that by means of defecation she might gain a penis, or be given one, usually as a gift from her father. It is a matter of parallels: defecation = gift = penis.

But the girl has to reconcile herself to the reality that no penis is going to grow, and neither will she receive one as a gift. Following Freud's lead, Abraham claimed that the girl makes another comparison, however, namely the parallel with a child. She now hopes that instead of a penis, which has not come, she will have a child that will be a gift from the father, a compensation for her defect. By identifying her own ego with the mother, in the place of the original

Karl Abraham in his youth

Karl Abraham's parents
(Sue Brandon collection)

Max Abraham, the older brother
(Sue Brandon collection)

The house at the Bismarckstrasse, where Karl Abraham grew up
(Bettina Decke collection)

Else, Hans, and Hedwig Bürgner, about 1895
(Anja Amsel collection)

Eugen Bleuler, 1885
(Bleuler family archive,
by courtesy of Mr Mösli and Mrs Joos-Bleuler)

Eugen Bleuler with his eldest son,
Manfred, 1903
(Bleuler family archive,
by courtesy of Mrs Joos-Bleuler)

Sigmund Freud, 1906

Carl Gustav Jung on Baily Island, 1936
(by courtesy of the Kristine Mann Library, New York, and Deirdre Bair)

Karl Abraham with Hilda and Gerd, Noordwijk, 1913
(Estate of Grant Allan)

Karl Abraham with Hedwig, Hilda, and Gerd, Allenstein, around 1917
(Estate of Grant Allan)

Congress in The Hague, 1920. Seated, from the left: Flügel, Ferenczi, Freud, Jones, and van Emden Standing: van Ophuijsen, Stern, Meijer, an emaciated Abraham, Rank, and Sachs

The comité in 1922

Sandor Rado

Helene Deutsch

Nelly Wolffheim

Melanie Klein around 1912
(Wellcome Library London)

Melanie Klein around 1927
(Wellcome Library London)

The Abraham family in 1924 in Sils Maria
(Estate of Grant Allan)

Karl, Hedwig, Hilda,
and Gerd Abraham,
and James Glover's wife in 1924

Grant/Gerd as a British soldier in the Second World War

Hedwig and Hilda in England

penis envy a jealousy now arises of the mother's possession of children. According to Abraham, the girl has to sublimate these feelings of hostility towards the mother if she is to go through a normal female development, just as she has to sublimate the libidinal tendencies towards her father.

At puberty, the desire for a child must be detached from the father and the freed libido must find a new object. If this all goes according to plan, then the female libido has, from that point on, a wait-and-see attitude towards the man. Her self-expression is regulated by certain inhibitions (feelings of shame). Abraham: "The normal adult woman becomes reconciled to her own sexual rôle and to that of the man, and in particular to the facts of male and female genitality; she desires passive gratification and longs for a child. Her castration complex thus gives rise to no disturbing effects".[1036]

In comparison to the Abraham who, in 1910 and 1912, struggled with mothers and women in *Segantini* and "Amenhotep", here he seems to emerge as a man who has neatly divided women into normal and abnormal. He went on to specify abnormal or pathological developments, remarking that the aim described above often remained out of reach. An inhibiting factor were the many moments in a woman's life in which the castration complex was fostered, such as menstruation, loss of virginity, and childbirth, so in every woman traces of the castration complex could be found. Normal women, according to Abraham, regularly had dreams with masculine features, but he was mainly interested in the more serious expressions of the castration complex that had clear pathological sides to them and he mentions several.

There are women who take revenge for the injury done to their physical integrity. Abraham was here drawing upon Freud's "The taboo of virginity", where he writes of a woman's aggression towards the man who has deflowered her.[1037] Among some primitive peoples, the husband is forbidden to deflower his wife, because of the danger in which it places him. Abraham wrote that he knew of several cases in which women had attacks of rage after their first night with a husband and hit him or tried to strangle him. In his view, such rages could be seen as revenge for the violation of physical integrity. Moreover, the event deprived the woman of any possibility of denying the difference between male and female sexuality. It went even further back than that, however. It was revenge for the injustice done by the father—the father who did not give the child a member. The daughter does not ultimately take revenge on the father in person, but on the man who, as a result of libido transference, has taken over the role of the father. By preference, she takes revenge for her castration by castration. The woman, therefore, tends to have a sadistic–hostile attitude instead of an attitude of love.

Another pathological development is adoption of the male role, Abraham wrote. The bisexual disposition common to all humanity enables women to transform their desire to be male into homosexuality. They have a tendency to take the male role in relationships with other women. They like masculine clothing and hairstyles. There is also a sublimated form, in which latent homosexuality does not penetrate the consciousness but remains as a repressed desire to be a man. Male interests are then preferred. Such women are of the opinion that when it comes to intellectual performance, it does not matter whether you are male or female. Abraham added that this type of woman was strongly represented in the woman's movement.

In two groups of women, Abraham saw above all a neurotic transformation of the castration complex and he claimed that the two types could supplement each other or occur in the same individual. There was the wish-fulfilment type that arose from an unconscious desire to take the male role and was based on the phantasy of possessing a male sexual organ. Abraham gives the example of a patient who wanted to become a famous man and as a girl phantasied that she was a female Napoleon who defeated everyone. The second group consisted of women Abraham described as the vengeful type. Their vengefulness expressed itself in a rejection of the female role and the repressed desire to rob the privileged man of the longed-for organ. According to Abraham, this desire often expressed itself in dreams in which family members or others were run over. One patient dreamed that her father had been run over and lost a leg and his wealth (*Vermogen*). The repressed desire for revenge could also express itself in a perpetual fear that someone was going to be run over. Another patient, for example, was continually tormented by the fear that one of her male family members would be run over and lose an arm or a leg. The repeated disappointing of the man was another means of taking revenge, he wrote.

Another category Abraham distinguished was that of women who belittled men. Their desire to undermine the significance of the male organ expressed itself in a general belittling of the man. According to Abraham, such a woman would avoid men with a particularly active male character and would focus on passive, feminine men when looking for a partner. As well as having a desire to belittle, she was extremely sensitive to situations that might arouse a sense of inferiority in a woman. One of Abraham's patients refused to walk along the street in her husband's footsteps in deep snow.

The final section of Abraham's essay about the castration complex is about the influence that mothers with a castration complex have on their children. Abraham was well ahead of his time here. Hardly anything had yet been written about the effect of mothers on their children. Abraham was of the opinion that some mothers transfer the castration complex to their children by speaking disparagingly about female sexuality or by unconsciously allowing their daughters to become aware of their rejection of men. Their influence on their sons could be considerable as well, since their repudiation of the male sex damages the narcissism of the boy, who is proud of his penis.

Remarkably, feminists responded with enthusiasm to Abraham's article.[1038] This arose from the fact that he was the first analyst to develop serious, detailed ideas about the consequences of sexual difference for the mental development of girls. Until then, psychoanalysis had looked only at the male castration complex and female development was addressed only in contrast to male development.

Karen Horney's reaction

Abraham's lecture aroused the ire of Karen Horney. In 1910, she had been one of his first patients and she was now an established psychoanalyst. She had been an active member of the Berlin Psychoanalytic Society for years, several of them as its secretary. She reacted with an article called "Zur Genese des weiblichen Kastrationskomplexes" (On the genesis of the female castration complex).[1039] Horney wrote that Abraham assumed women felt inferior based on their genitals because he simply found this self-evident, looked at with a male, narcissistic eye.

According to Horney, Abraham's belief that a girl had a primary defect because her genitals were inferior to those of the man would mean that half of humanity was dissatisfied with the sex allotted to it. This view was absolutely unsatisfactory, according to Horney, not only as concerned female narcissism, but for biological science. Horney had no wish to deny the existence of penis envy, but she did not see it as the cause of the castration complex.

Horney developed a theory of her own. Her view was that women who want to be men have been through a phase in which they were extremely fixated on their fathers. The father was their love-object and they wanted to have his child. Such women phantasied a complete sexual recognition by the father, as a defence against the reality that the father did not return their love. This led to an even more bitter disappointment, since they then came to feel that their father, who had once been in love with them, had now deceived them or let them down. Disappointment led to the girl giving up the father as a love-object and, instead, identifying with him. The girl incorporated the lost love-object and identified herself with it. She identified herself with her father and acted as if she were herself a man. When the girl gives up the father as a love-object, she also abandons her desire to have his child. That is the point at which the pregenital desire for a penis is experienced again in an intensified form. The penis envy that occurs in the castration complex is not the pregenital penis envy, but a far stronger form that arises from disappointment of the oedipal desire in the girl and her subsequent distancing from, and identifying with, the father.[1040]

Melanie Klein's entrance into the psychoanalytic world

Melanie Klein had once attended a psychoanalytic congress as a guest, in Budapest in 1918.[1041] At the congress in The Hague, she attended for the first time as a member of a psychoanalytic society. Her meeting with Abraham at that congress was to have far-reaching consequences.

Melanie Klein was born in Vienna in 1882, the fourth child of a doctor. Her parents neither planned nor wanted this youngest daughter. The family lived in poverty. Melanie Klein's father had a strong preference for her older sister, who died when Melanie was four. Klein married at the age of twenty-one. Her husband was a chemist and they had three children. The marriage was not happy. Melanie Klein was often depressed and her mother involved herself far too intensely with the household.[1042] After her mother's death in 1914—the family had been living in Budapest since 1911—Klein's depression worsened and she entered into analysis with Ferenczi, who encouraged her to take up the analysis of children.[1043] In 1919, she gave a lecture about the psychoanalysis of children for the Hungarian Psychoanalytic Society and she was immediately accepted as a member.[1044] This was remarkable, since she had no university education, having only attended grammar school. The analysis later turned out to be of her younger son, Erik, and it was carried out without any supervision, as she later said herself.[1045] The next chapter of this book examines at greater length the issue of lay analysis.

Anton von Freund, secretary to the Hungarian Psychoanalytic Society, was not impressed by Klein's lecture and told her that she had not reached the unconscious of the child in any way at all. He suggested she should set aside a specific time each day for the boy's psychoanalysis.

The membership list of the Hungarian Psychoanalytic Society in late 1919 shows that at this point there were eighteen male members and two female members. They were Melanie Klein and the wife of Radó, Dr Erzsébet Radó-Révész, a qualified neurologist. Of the twenty members, seventeen, most of them medical doctors, had doctorates. They also included a bookseller and an editor.[1046] Melanie Klein must have been the odd one out, strongly protected by Ferenczi.

Ferenczi first wrote to Freud about Melanie Klein on 29 June 1919. He wrote that he was getting Anton von Freund to set up a course on child analysis for the Association and that Klein would assist with it. Ferenczi introduced her as "Frau Dr. Klein (not a physician)", who had recently made some good observations of children after being trained for some years by Ferenczi.[1047]

The letter gives the impression that Ferenczi was making Melanie Klein seem rather more important than she was. The title "Dr." was her husband's not hers, although this was not clear from the letter, and she had been in analysis with Ferenczi for years, whereas the letter describes this as training. It is possible to regard analysis as training, but why did he obfuscate here? Ferenczi had a special bond with Melanie Klein and, in 1919, he gave her a photograph of himself with the caption, "For Mela, my beloved student".

It was also Ferenczi who drew Klein's attention to the fact that members of the Hungarian Society could attend the congress in The Hague, at which point she wrote a long letter to Rank, requesting him to help her arrange for a visa and travel documents.[1048]

Abraham was impressed by Melanie Klein when he met her at the conference and he invited her to come and work in Berlin.[1049] He wasted no time and wrote in the first circular letter from Berlin on 6 October 1920, less than four weeks after the congress, that more staff were needed for the polyclinic and perhaps Ferenczi would like to persuade Melanie Klein to move to Berlin as soon as possible so that she could carry out child analyses there.

The secret committee and the circular letters

The relationship between members of the committee was very good in The Hague. Until 1920, contact had been maintained by means of personal letters.[1050] In The Hague, the circular letters were inaugurated. The decision was taken that every week, on a set day, from each of the four cities in which the committee members lived, a letter would be sent to the other three cities. That way, the members could stay in touch with developments in psychoanalysis and steer the IPA. The cities were Vienna with Freud and Rank, Berlin with Abraham, Eitingon and Sachs, Budapest with Ferenczi, and London with Jones.

Ferenczi started the ball rolling with the first circular letter on 20 September 1920:

Dear Professor

Dear colleagues and friends!

Please allow me, to mark the start of our formal exchange of letters, to send you my warmest greetings. Being together with you at the congress has refreshed my spirits, which were in urgent need of such stimulation. I hope that our exchange of ideas—over the year—will continue to sustain the sense of solidarity and not permit any feeling of tiredness to arise.[1051]

Ferenczi then asked the chairman (Jones) whether he would be able to collect together the statutes of all the psychoanalytic societies so that they could be unified, a subject that, in the case of Berlin, is touched upon further in the next chapter.

The bicycles

Freud always showed a great deal of interest in Abraham's children. When he returned from the congress in The Hague, he happened to hear that Hilda and Gerd would love to have bicycles. At that point, it was impossible for the Abrahams to give them such an expensive gift. There was high inflation and Abraham was trying to rebuild his practice. Freud had received extra money to enable him to enjoy his stay in The Hague. There was some left and he gave it to Abraham to buy bicycles for the children. It was an unexpectedly wonderful Christmas present.[1052] Abraham wrote to Freud, "It is virtually impossible to separate the children from their bicycles; if you have ever made anyone happy, dear Professor, you definitely have succeeded here!"[1053]

CHAPTER TWENTY

The issue of lay analysis and Abraham in a tight corner

fter becoming so ill during the congress in Budapest, Hanns Sachs had gone to Davos for a tuberculosis cure. He corresponded regularly with Freud.[1054] From Davos, he travelled on to Zurich in late 1919. His healing process lasted two years in total and he made a complete recovery. In this period, he decided to give up his legal practice and become a full-time psychoanalyst.[1055] In Zurich, Sachs gave a course in psychoanalysis for beginners as well as an advanced course. He also practised psychoanalysis. By late December 1919, he was able to make a living, since he was carrying out four analyses.[1056] He did not want to stay in Zurich, however, because all sorts of limitations were placed on foreigners there. They were not allowed to rent furnished rooms, could stay only in expensive lodgings, had to report to the immigration police regularly, and so on.[1057] Moreover, Sachs found himself unable to connect with the recently established Zurich Psychoanalytic Society.[1058]

Sachs wanted to move to Berlin.[1059] On 27 May 1920, Eitingon wrote to Freud that they had discussed this *"en petit comité"*, in other words with Abraham, Horney, and Liebermann, and considered how Sachs would be able to earn a living there. It might be possible to find work for him outside of analysis that would at least enable him to get by.[1060] Freud answered that he was greatly worried about Sachs, who must not be abandoned, but he did not know what to do.[1061] Work was indeed arranged for Sachs in Berlin and, on 21 June 1920, Freud wrote to Abraham that he was very pleased that Abraham, too, had started to see that psychoanalysis could no longer be restricted to doctors and that Sachs would be a great asset to Berlin.[1062] Abraham promptly answered that he had not in the least changed his view with regard to the practice of psychoanalysis by laymen. Sachs would be dealing with non-medical matters and he had always agreed that this part of psychoanalytic science should be extended to lay circles.[1063]

Abraham made a firm distinction between psychoanalysis, which was practised by doctors, and the involvement of laymen in psychoanalysis, a distinction that was certainly not made by

Freud. What Abraham had to say on the subject seems strange, because Sachs did, in fact, start to carry out many training analyses, up to nine a day. Did Abraham see these analyses more as teaching assignments than as treatments? Was he of the view that trainee psychoanalysts could be treated by laymen because it was a matter of teacher and pupil, whereas patients, who came because of problems, should be treated only by doctors?

Nowadays, it is usual for psychoanalysis to be carried out by both doctors and non-doctors, by psychologists, teachers, philosophers, and others. This is the outcome of a major struggle in which doctors defended their monopoly on psychoanalysis tooth and nail. It is regarded as one of the bigger conflicts within the world of psychoanalysis and it took place mainly in the latter half of the 1920s.[1064]

In early 1926, Reik was accused of quackery for performing analysis when he was not a doctor but a philosopher. The case was set in train by a patient who believed he had been damaged by Reik. It prompted Freud to write "The question of lay analysis", in which he sets out his own view on collaboration between doctors and non-doctors within psychoanalysis.[1065] The case against Reik was dropped, probably because of Freud's brochure as well as a lack of evidence, but it did bring to light a sharp difference of opinion within the psychoanalytic societies, so it was seen as advisable to have a broad discussion on the point. In 1927, twenty-eight responses on the subject by psychoanalysts from different countries were published, followed by an afterword by Freud.[1066]

In the USA the controversy broke out again in full force in 1980.[1067] In 1996, Schröter wrote an extensive article about lay analysis in which he showed that the entire question had been under discussion since the First World War and that Abraham had played an important role in it.

The problem of lay analysis was urgent because the psychoanalysts who did not have a medical background (Rank, Sachs, Reik, and Andreas-Salomé, for example) could barely manage to keep their heads above water. It was not easy for the doctors, but within a neurology practice it was not impossible to work as a psychoanalyst some of the time, or even continually.[1068] After Freud, Abraham had been the first to risk it, starting in 1908, and he had made a success of his practice. The position of the analysts who were not doctors was far more difficult. The lay psychoanalysts experienced constant financial difficulties. Rank and Reik earned a little extra with the psychoanalytic publishing house. Freud regularly gave Andreas-Salomé financial support. He was terribly worried about Sachs's future after his stay in Switzerland. The Berlin psychoanalysts eventually offered a solution, but Abraham, like Eitingon, was of the opinion that psychoanalysis should remain the preserve of doctors. He thought Sachs should not analyse patients but do other work.[1069]

The Berlin Psychoanalytic Society had decided in 1911 that only doctors who were involved with psychoanalysis practically or scientifically could be members.[1070] That excluded laymen. In 1912, a category was added: associate membership for non-doctors with an academic education who were involved with scientific work on Freudian psychology.[1071] In Vienna, there had always been a more tolerant attitude to non-doctors. The Wednesday Society was set up in 1902 by doctors, but non-doctors were allowed to participate that same year. In 1908, when it officially changed its name to the Vienna Psychoanalytic Society, it distinguished between two kinds of members: doctors, who carried out analysis, and non-doctors, who paid only half the membership fee.[1072]

Sachs began work on 8 October 1920 in Berlin.[1073] On 13 October, five days after Sachs's arrival, Abraham wrote in a circular letter that Sachs had come to live close to him, that they saw each other a great deal, and that they had already had two committee meetings with Eitingon. Sachs had organised two courses in the meantime. The first was an introduction to psychoanalytic theory with an emphasis on *The Interpretation of Dreams* and the second was about the application of psychoanalysis in the humanities. It had also been arranged that Sachs would do three or four training analyses and one therapeutic analysis.[1074] This meant that Abraham had immediately abandoned his view that Sachs, as a layman, ought not to treat patients. They had a good, friendly relationship. Hedwig later said that Sachs had become a good friend.[1075] The fact that Sachs almost immediately became a full member of the Berlin Psychoanalytic Society, even though, according to its statutes, full membership was reserved for doctors, might have had something to do with this friendship. The *Korrespondenzblatt* states that he was added to the membership list on 1 February 1921 as the only non-doctor.[1076] Liebermann, who at that point was secretary to the Berlin Psychoanalytic Society, wrote an extremely agitated letter to Eitingon a day earlier, on 31 January 1921. Eitingon, as usual, was travelling. Liebermann wrote that the general meeting of the Society had got no further than halfway through the agenda and would resume on 3 March.[1077] He added that Eitingon was expected to attend. They had spoken about inadequate statutes, which might have to be changed in the long run if the statutes of all the societies that came under the umbrella of the IPA were to be made compatible, including the rules concerning the admission of non-doctors. Sachs was, at that point, accepted as a member. This led to fierce protests by Müller-Braunschweig, because, Liebermann writes, Abraham and Sachs wanted to force through the acceptance of Sachs before fundamental aspects of the issue of lay analysis had been resolved or even discussed.[1078]

The conflict between Müller-Braunschweig and Abraham had been going on for some time. Schröter was of the opinion that Müller probably wanted to be admitted to the Berlin Psychoanalytic Society as a layman himself, whereas Abraham wanted to restrict membership to doctors only. Müller had also given unauthorised lectures about psychoanalysis and he may have carried out what were known as "wild analyses". These were analyses by an analyst who was not a member of a psychoanalytic society.[1079] In early 1921, Müller-Braunschweig seems to have been highly indignant that Sachs had been admitted as a member straight away whereas he had not. Along with Sachs and Melanie Klein, he would eventually become the third lay member accepted into the Berlin Psychoanalytic Society during Abraham's lifetime.

Liebermann explained that there had been such a lengthy debate about organisational matters that no time was left. According to Liebermann, when Müller's case was forced to a vote there was, of course, no unanimity in his favour. Liebermann claimed that Abraham, in the chair, had completely refused to show leadership in the matter. Liebermann decided that Eitingon had been missing like grease on a wagon wheel and that he absolutely must attend on 2 March.[1080] The almost shrieking emotional tone of the letter, directed mainly against Abraham, makes clear that Müller-Braunschweig was not the only one to have difficulty with Abraham.

Among other things, Abraham very much wanted Sachs to come to Berlin because he could take over the training analyses from him. Abraham believed that as president of the Society he would be in an impossible position if all its members had been in analysis with him.[1081] The bond between former analyst and former analysand remained strong and all kinds of negative and positive transference feelings could easily continue to play a role. This is clearly the case here. Müller and Liebermann were both former analysands of Abraham and emotions ran extremely high.

The conflict with Liebermann

The conflict with Liebermann had much more far-reaching consequences for Abraham than the conflict with Müller-Braunschweig, since suddenly it was taking place within his home. In Allenstein, Hedwig had become good friends with Liebermann's wife and she sided with them rather than with her husband, which must have been extremely painful for Abraham. Sachs wrote to Freud that the fact that Abraham was so strongly influenced by his wife only made things more difficult. It is the only situation in which Hedwig is known to have taken a position in direct opposition to him.[1082]

After the First World War, during which he had worked with Abraham in Allenstein, Liebermann took over the job of secretary to the Berlin Psychoanalytic Society from Horney. On the membership list for the Berlin Psychoanalytic Society, he is first named as secretary on 1 October 1919.[1083] Because Liebermann neglected his tasks as secretary, however, conflict arose between committee members in Vienna and Berlin. In the first circular letter from Vienna, dated 5 October 1920, there was already talk of negligence on the part of Berlin, specifically by the secretary, since there was no treasurer. Subscriptions had not yet been paid, and the year was almost over.

In March 1920, Liebermann had lost both his parents in a single week and his mental state deteriorated badly.[1084] He was barely functioning as secretary. It then transpired in a circular letter from Jones of 2 November 1920 and a letter accompanying it from Pfister to Jones, dated 23 October 1920, that two applications for membership of the Berlin Psychoanalytic Society had run into the sand, the first because the person in question was not a doctor and no one knew him, and the second, from a professor in Bonn, because he had received no reply for months. Both problems could be laid at Liebermann's door and Rank, who wrote a letter on 11 November 1920 partly on behalf of Freud, revealed that he, too, had many complaints to make about Liebermann's negligence as secretary and had regularly mentioned this to Abraham.[1085] Rank wrote that if Liebermann had too much work and was too taken up with personal matters, a colleague must perform his duties instead. Abraham answered on 17 November 1920: "In general you can hardly think me capable of allowing negligent leadership. Today I will limit myself to affirming that special relationships exist, that I feel the deficiencies myself more than anyone does and carry out the tasks of the Association myself as far as possible".[1086]

Abraham wanted to return to the subject the following week, after consulting Eitingon and Sachs. He defended Liebermann and he seems also to have done his best to fill the gaps left by him. Liebermann's wife was in analysis with Eitingon at that stage and Liebermann himself with Sachs. Moreover, Eitingon was supporting Liebermann financially.[1087] This meant that the people Abraham was consulting were far from impartial.

The outcome of the consultation was, therefore, determined by the two analysts of Liebermann and of his wife. Abraham wrote on 24 November 1920 that a change of personnel would be the simplest solution but that Sachs thought as follows about that:

> L. is deep in his neurosis, especially in a profound transference resistance in relation to Abraham, who has treated him in the past. Any reproach, even a hint in that direction will call up the strongest affect, without serving any purpose. All of L's circumstances in life have been seriously disrupted. In addition to the neurosis, the prognosis for which appears very unfavourable, there has recently been added a serious suspicion of a rectal carcinoma. L looks miserable. In such a condition a person cannot be rushed, any more than he can be deprived of his position.[1088]

Abraham added that Eitingon shared this opinion. In retrospect, it is a fascinating spectacle, and it makes clear that in those days there was no comprehension of the intensity of transference and acting out, and no ability at all to deal with them. Liebermann divided the world into good and bad. His former analyst was a scoundrel, his new analyst was good. He himself was, above all, extremely vulnerable and need to be treated with great care and circumspection, which the bullying Abraham, in Liebermann's view, was not doing. He was so convincing that he won Hedwig, Sachs, and Eitingon to his side. The above letter of 31 January 1921 shows how he could set people against Abraham.[1089]

Abraham returned to the two failed applications for membership in his circular letter of 1 December 1920.[1090] The professor from Bonn, Walter Frost, had actually been sent a response but had not replied himself. The other application had indeed fallen through because of Liebermann. Professor Pietsch of Breslau, not a medical doctor, who had applied to join, had sent a letter to Abraham back in August but it had failed to reach him. His second letter had been answered after a considerable delay. This must certainly have got on Abraham's nerves, given how dutiful and precise he was. He went on to write that he hoped Old Prussian order could be restored. Rank answered, partly on behalf of Freud, with great vehemence, saying that the case of Pietsch demonstrated there was a danger that the Berliners, with their intolerance regarding membership policy, would bring down on their own heads the reputation of being a closed sect, and would thereby frighten off serious and valuable candidates. It was still unclear what had happened with the two medical doctors in Frankfurt, and the subscriptions, which he had asked about so many times, had still not been paid.[1091] The fierce tone of his comment about Pietsch must have had to do with Rank's own lay status and frustration about it. He had to work extremely hard, yet he was not really seen as a full member by the doctors on the committee. In the circular letters up to that point, the problems with Pietsch had emerged primarily as a matter of negligence by Liebermann, and rather less as an example of the membership policy of the Berlin group. In his criticism, Rank appears to point to Abraham as the culprit rather than to Liebermann.

In mid-December, Abraham became very ill. It was a recurrence of his dysentery attack of the previous summer and it was accompanied by a high fever. He recovered, but it left him extremely tired. The problems with Liebermann continued unabated.

On 22 December, Abraham wrote in a circular letter that Rank had judged too harshly yet again. In the case of Pietsch, it was a matter of oversight by Liebermann. There was no reason at all to accuse the Berlin Psychoanalytic Society of intolerance.[1092] Abraham followed this up with a cry from the heart that was probably in part an outcome of his illness and state of exhaustion:

> The business with the subscription money is very painful for me. Right up to the last letter all three of us were unaware of it. Eitingon has now investigated the facts of the case. L(iebermann) long ago collected all the contributions. Several had yet to be paid. Meanwhile he has lost the list of sums received and does not know to whom he needs to send reminders. Instead of at least submitting the money received he kept putting it off.—So, again a very bad sign of an utterly disorganised system of administration.[1093] And I knew nothing of it! Things really cannot go on like this here. Our annual general meeting is a few weeks away. L. has said that he wants to relinquish his post. Until then let us leave the matter be. But something has to be done at once about the issue of subscription money. Because the telephone line is down I cannot speak with L. today but I promise to supply exhaustive details next time, including about the two doctors in Frankfurt.[1094]—I cannot resist commenting here that the management of our Society, which used to be faultless, is now in a truly grave situation. For reasons it would take too much time to go into here, I have had so little contact with L. over the past few months that our business was bound to suffer. When I proposed a change three months ago, E(itingon) and S(achs) declared themselves resolutely opposed; I have mentioned in the circular letter the reasons for that. I myself regard it as impossible to allow this situation to continue any further.

Abraham found himself in a kind of snake pit. He could see no way out and considered stepping down as president of the Berlin Psychoanalytic Society. Liebermann had lost his parents in March. Abraham wrote the above letter in late December 1920, a good nine months later. After his parents' deaths (it is not clear from the letters exactly how they died) Liebermann seems to have developed an extremely malicious sadistic transference with regard to Abraham, in which he exposed Abraham, who was, after all, rather coercive, to a great deal of inaction, mislaying of things, and chasing away of potential members when they were of crucial importance for the still small Berlin Psychoanalytic Society. Abraham showed understanding for a long time, continuing to defend him and doing the things Liebermann had neglected to do. This seems merely to have made matters worse.

That autumn, Liebermann and Abraham had hardly any contact, apparently at the suggestion of Sachs. It is difficult to imagine: a society in which so much happens yet in which the president is barely able to communicate with the secretary and cannot take on a replacement, while the secretary continues to mismanage everything completely. It appears as if Eitingon and Sachs became caught up in Liebermann's transference. That is precisely what makes Abraham's situation Kafkaesque. Were Sachs and Eitingon taking revenge as well?

In late January 1921, Sachs wrote Freud a letter about the situation as a whole. In it, he describes the relationship between Eitingon and Abraham as friendly, but says there were differences between them. Eitingon was completely the ever-helpful mother Russia, while Abraham was the orderly and consultation-seeking Prussian father. Fortunately, according to Sachs, they had intelligence and professionalism in common. The most dangerous reef seemed at that point to be Liebermann. The completely helpless and unbalanced state that Liebermann was in appealed strongly to Eitingon's compassion, and he wanted at all costs to protect

Liebermann against Abraham. Abraham, for his part, reacted fiercely to the sadistic attacks by Liebermann, which was understandable to a degree, since Liebermann had obeyed him for years. In addition, Abraham's wife had sided with Liebermann. Sachs requested Rank not to criticise him so fiercely, since it only made Abraham even more irritated and he might demand that Liebermann step down.[1095] There is every indication that both Eitingon and Sachs found themselves in a situation in which the main concern was that Liebermann, despite his impossible behaviour (three potential members lost in six months and a membership of just eighteen), should stay.

Remarkably, it was still being said that Rank should moderate his tone, as if the problems were caused by the way he expressed himself. But Rank was calling Berlin to account for negligence. He had not received the money for the journal subscriptions and potential members referred to Berlin disappeared into the morass. Even if he did not make such accusations particularly mildly, the problem certainly did not lie with him.

In the circular letter of 12 December 1920, Abraham had made it known that Liebermann was going to withdraw, but he would remain in place until the general meeting of late January 1921. It is quite bizarre that Eitingon and Sachs reversed that decision and insisted Liebermann must stay, even though his behaviour had not improved in the least. Eitingon was travelling at the time. All this was communicated by letter.[1096] In a circular letter of 31 January 1921, after the general meeting, Abraham announced that if Liebermann was found to have been negligent one more time he would step down himself. He was of the opinion that Liebermann must cease to be secretary, but Sachs and Eitingon did not agree and Abraham decided that if two of the three had the same standpoint then the third must concede.

Once more the reaction, this time from Ferenczi in a letter to Freud of 7 February 1921, was that Rank must moderate his tone and not that Sachs and Eitingon must curb their rescue fantasies:

In the Rundbriefen, Rank ought to be somewhat more considerate of Abraham's sensitivity, perhaps rather in the tone than in the content of his admonitions. Abraham's intent to resign shows that it is hard for him to bear recriminations. His bona fides and his diligence certainly remain elevated over all doubt.[1097]

Eitingon made his stance clear in a letter to Freud of 4 February 1921: Liebermann was falling overboard, barely able to cling to a plank of the ship. He had to be saved and remain secretary. That little bit of damage to the Society was not worth worrying about and could be dealt with.[1098] Eitingon the saviour was starting to go too far. A great deal of damage had already been done.

Jones adopted an unambiguous position. In a circular letter of 11 February 1921, he wrote the following, aimed specifically at Abraham,

You know we shall all fully understand your position as regards the business of the Berlin society, but remember that you are not allowed to resign without permission from the Committee, which will be rather hard to obtain! You have been President of a Ps-A society uninterruptedly for longer than anyone in the world, and you know what enormous importance we all attach to your remaining in control.[1099]

A reaction from Freud put an end to the whole affair. He answered Eitingon by return, saying he greatly regretted that the Liebermann affair, into which he had no further insight, had caused a rift between Eitingon and Abraham and that—although they would have to take account of the individual—the interests of the Society, which had suffered from mismanagement under Liebermann, must be put first.[1100] In the circular letter of 11 February 1921, Rank wrote that he and Freud had every sympathy for Liebermann in this business and were in favour of the mildest treatment, yet they hoped that a way could be found to avoid the damage to the general interest that was bound up with it.[1101] Freud's will was law to Eitingon. Finally, he was able to agree to have Liebermann step down as secretary. He took over the secretarial tasks himself.

CHAPTER TWENTY-ONE

Psychoanalysis flourishes in Berlin

F amous and still relevant are Abraham's "Psycho-analytic studies on character-formation".[1102] The complete work was to be published in 1925, but several years before, on 20
January 1921, Abraham gave a lecture to the Berlin Psychoanalytic Society about part
one, "Contributions to the theory of the anal character".[1103] The title was a reference to the fact
that several important works on the subject had already appeared and Abraham wanted to add
to them. He intended both to describe in more detail the complex manifestations of the anal
character and to investigate further the relationship between sadism and anal eroticism.[1104]

The lecture concerned the former, the description of the anal character. Abraham first
quoted Freud, who had specified the following anal characteristics: a predilection for ordering
things, which often degenerated into pettiness, a frugality that could easily become miserliness,
and a stubbornness that could tip over into severe obduracy.

Sadger had added to this that people with a pronounced anal character cherished a conviction that they could do everything better than anyone else. Their characters were marked by
stark contradictions: great determination along with a tendency to delay every accomplishment
to the last moment. Being able to do everything better than anyone else leads to the notion of
having to do everything oneself because no one else can do it so well. Abraham's opinion was
that this quite often developed into a feeling of being unique. Such people became pretentious
and haughty and tended to have a low opinion of all others. One of Abraham's patients
expressed himself on this point as follows: "Everything that is not me is dirt."

One well-known phenomenon is the inability to comply with the orderliness of an other,
but nevertheless expecting this of the other, as soon as one has devised a particular system.
Jones referred to it as holding fast obstinately to one's own system of doing things.[1105] Abraham
gave the example of a mother who made a written programme for her daughter, arranging
every minute detail of the little girl's day: 1. Get up. 2. Use the chamber. 3. Wash, etc. She would

knock on the door to her daughter's room in the morning to ask how far she had got and the daughter would have to answer that she had reached number 9 or number 15, so that the mother had absolute control over what was going on.

According to Abraham, the anal character had its origins in premature potty training. For a child, relieving itself produces feelings of lust, yet it is forced to regulate and restrain that act. Abraham's opinion was that toilet training would go well only if the child was mentally ready for it. This meant that the moment must have arrived at which the initial narcissistic feelings—the child focused mainly on itself—could be transferred to objects (to the mother or other carers). When the child is able to do that, it becomes potty trained for its mother's sake. The German word *zuliebe* (for the sake of) is actually more appropriate here, since it contains the word *Liebe*, love. If the demand is made too soon, the child becomes potty trained out of fear. The inner resistance remains, the libido stubbornly persists in a narcissistic fixation and the result is a permanent disturbance of the ability to love.

Abraham quoted Jones, who had pointed out the increased self-esteem a child acquires through its excretory acts. If this sense of greatness was disrupted prematurely, lasting feelings of inadequacy were frequently produced.

Toilet training that is demanded too soon and the inner resistance to it lead to the obstinacy displayed by anal neurotics whenever a demand or request is made of them. It is reminiscent of children who pretend to be constipated when they are required to defecate, so as to relieve themselves at a moment of their own choosing. They resist being forced to do it. Typical of the adult form is the frequent rejection of a request or demand, even though the person concerned is generous when giving of his or her own free will. Abraham regularly heard during his analyses about husbands who refused every request for money from their wives only to give more than the amount requested later, of their own volition. Such men enjoyed making their wives permanently dependent on them financially. They derived pleasure from giving money in portions the size of which they determined themselves.

Another striking characteristic is the doling out of food in portions as the anal neurotic sees fit. This could be taken to grotesque extremes. Abraham recounts the case of an old man who fed his goats by giving them each blade of grass separately. This demonstrates the accompanying sadism. Such a person liked to arouse desire and expectation and then afford gratification in small, often insufficient amounts.

Abraham described how neurotics who always wanted to introduce their own system into everything were inclined to criticise others exaggeratedly. In social life, they made up a large proportion of those who were continually discontented. Anal obstinacy could develop in one of two directions. It might lead to inaccessibility and stubbornness, if the asocial and unproductive characteristics predominated. Or it might lead to perseverance and thoroughness, characteristics that were socially valuable as long as they were not taken to extremes.

Abraham also pointed to a group to which not much attention had been paid until then. He wrote that there were patients with anal neurosis who avoided taking any kind of initiative. In daily life, they were in continual need of a kind father or attentive mother who would remove all obstacles from their path. In psychoanalysis, they resented having to engage in free association. They wanted only to lie still and have the analyst do all the work, or to be asked questions by the analyst. Free association was to them a mental evacuation that, like bodily evacuation, must not be demanded of them. They always expected someone else to do the work for them, as if an enema were being performed.

In February 1921 the collection *Klinische Beiträge zur Psychoanalyse aus den Jahren 1907–1920* (Clinical Contributions to Psychoanalysis, 1907–1920) was published, which included the majority of the articles published by Abraham between 1907 and 1920.[1106] Freud congratulated him warmly: "My hearty congratulations on the appearance of your book, which is generally appreciated by the analysts as a collection of classical, model papers".[1107]

The book was a great success and met with glowing reviews. W. Mayer-Groß, for example, wrote in the *Zentralblatt für die gesamte Neurologie und Psychiatrie*:

An extraordinarily careful and determined effort to build upon Freud's ideas. The way he thoroughly and lastingly researches, explains and reveals where Freud has shown him the way is heart-warming. One also gains the impression that here, in a way that rarely happens, great experience has been drawn upon.[1108]

The Glover brothers

Suddenly, there is a gap of several months in the correspondence between Freud and Abraham. It was caused by the circular letters. On 31 October 1920, Freud wrote to Abraham that he had never thought the circular letters would put an end to their private correspondence, but three and a half months had passed since the last letter written to him by Abraham. In 1921, too, they exchanged only a few letters. Freud was happy with the huge leap forwards made by psychoanalysis in Berlin and wrote, "We are all proud of the upswing in Berlin".[1109]

The Berlin Psychoanalytic Society was flourishing. The polyclinic gave it a tremendous boost and psychoanalysis was regarded far more favourably after the First World War than before. In 1920, a meeting was held every two weeks, with a lecture, and in 1921 the meetings became weekly. Many courses were given as well. It was not only within the city that psychoanalysis was doing so well. Aspiring analysts came from far and wide to be trained in Berlin.

Abraham was a great draw and people often came specially to be analysed by him. In December 1920, the Glover brothers arrived from England to enter into analysis with him. On 11 January 1921, Abraham reported that both brothers had started their analysis the previous week.[1110] They later became important figures in the British Psychoanalytical Society. Abraham was pleasantly surprised by them. He had expected them to know little about psychoanalysis and to have no idea at all of the essential issues, but that was not the case by any means. The brothers were very well informed, it was just that they were not yet familiar with all the literature.

James Glover (1882–1926) had been a guest at the congress in The Hague a few months earlier. He was a doctor who, since 1918, had been working in the Brunswick Square Clinic in London, a psychotherapeutic clinic founded in 1913. In 1920, the clinic was harshly criticised by Jones because the directors, Miss Turner and Miss Sharpe, were not doctors.[1111] In fact, none of the staff was a doctor, apart from Glover and a young assistant.[1112] The students at the clinic were all lay people, too, and they carried out almost all the treatments. According to Jones, the treatments they performed were more or less analytical in nature. The students would arrive as students or as patients and within a few weeks they were analysing others. A patient was first seen by a doctor, but after that the directors decided who would carry out the treatment and patients would have one analyst after another, sometimes four or five within a period of a few months. The procedures of the clinic produced a stream of so-called analysts, who were bringing psychoanalysis into disrepute.[1113] It was, therefore, of great importance to Jones and the British Psychoanalytical Society that James Glover was properly introduced to psychoanalysis.

James Glover returned to Britain in April 1921. Abraham was very pleased with him. He was convinced that Glover had improved greatly and that he was an extremely conscientious doctor with a considerable knowledge of psychoanalysis. On his return to London, James Glover made contact with Jones to consult with him about the Brunswick Square Clinic. He accepted Jones' criticism.[1114] They decided to try to reshape the clinic into a psychoanalytic polyclinic in co-operation with the British Psychoanalytical Society and on the model of the polyclinic in Berlin.[1115] One remarkable effect of these efforts was that a large number of the clinic's staff travelled to various parts of Europe to enter into analysis with Ferenczi, Rank, and Sachs.[1116] Jones also ensured that James Glover was accepted as a member of the British Psychoanalytical Society at its next meeting.[1117] The attempt to turn the Brunswick Square Clinic into a psychoanalytic polyclinic came to nothing, however.

James' younger brother, Edward (1888–1972), seems to have had a closer friendship with Abraham. He remained in analysis for several months longer than James. Also a doctor, he had been a successful lung specialist in Britain. After the death of his wife in childbirth, after a marriage of just eighteen months, he decided on a change of course in his career and followed his brother to Berlin for a training analysis. To Edward Glover, Abraham was not just an inspiring teacher with great powers of imagination but a kindred spirit whom he admired for his erudition and great scientific and personal integrity.[1118]

Abraham started the analysis of both the Glover brothers on 5 January 1921, in a period when his health was in a miserable state. He was in urgent need of convalescence, so he went to Merano for five weeks with Hedwig, staying in the same hotel as the Eitingons. The Glovers simply went with them.

Freud wrote to Abraham, witty as ever, "I hope your "hand luggage" [the two Glovers] will not disturb you too much".[1119] The trip did Abraham a great deal of good. On his return, he made a far more cheerful and energetic impression. His children had been away with him and an incident had occurred during that holiday that Gerd would never forget. There was an avalanche in the Austrian Alps. A mountain climber was brought in who had broken a leg in the avalanche. Edward Glover and Abraham immediately set about amputating the climber's leg. Abraham had been obliged to work as a surgeon in the war years in Allenstein and had carried out many operations, and Glover was a surgeon. Abraham allowed his son to watch, but warned him that he would have to pick himself up if he fainted.[1120] What is most striking is that Abraham did not realise how frightening it would be for his son to witness the operation. Gerd was eleven years old. It is reminiscent of his daughter Hilda's tonsillectomy, after which Abraham showed so little sense of how frightening it had been for her. Fear remained a blind spot for Abraham.

The tic debate and van Ophuijsen

Abraham had met van Ophuijsen in November 1912 in Munich, when the chairmen of all the psychoanalytic societies came together to discuss the problems surrounding Stekel and the *Zeitschrift*. Van Ophuijsen was there as a stand-in for Maeder.[1121] In the 1920s, after the congress in The Hague, they became friends.

In June 1921, van Ophuijsen came to Berlin. On 9 June, he attended a meeting of the Berlin Psychoanalytic Society and he stayed with Abraham for eight days. Together, they analysed urgent inner problems in that time.[1122] It seems van Ophuijsen used those eight days to undergo a short analysis by Abraham. A year later, he entered into analysis with Sachs.[1123] The meeting of the Berlin Psychoanalytic Society that van Ophuijsen attended was devoted to an article by Ferenczi called "Psychoanalytische Betrachtungen über den Tic" (Psychoanalytic considerations regarding the tic).[1124] What became known as the tic debate was published in the *Korrespondenzblatt*.[1125] Ferenczi had written a long article in which he closely investigated the tic, a phenomenon that had until then received little attention in psychoanalysis. Ferenczi compared the tic with a conversion-hysteria symptom.[1126] He said that both could be traced back to a traumatic event in which the resulting affect was insufficiently worked through. In hysteria, however, the physical symptom was merely a symbol of the mental shock; the affect was suppressed and the memory repressed. A tic, by contrast, was about a purely organic traumatic wound. It might be the pressing of the cheek in the case of an abscess in a molar, which continues even after the tooth has healed. There is a reminder of the situation in which the tic arose. Hysteria was about the relationship with the object, whereas, in the case of a tic, no object relation was at play but, rather, a repetition of the staving off of the trauma. Ferenczi was thinking of a continual repetition of the movements, which, in the time when the trauma took place, had the function of fending off the suffering or reducing it. Ferenczi also compared tics to compulsive acts. He believed that compulsive acts were more complicated. They were acts intended to achieve something in the outside world, whereas the tic was no more than a brief stereotypical act. Ferenczi also talked about Gilles de la Tourette syndrome, for which, like other tics, he tried to give a psychoanalytic explanation.[1127] Today, that syndrome is seen as primarily genetically determined.

On 2 June 1921, Jenö Harnik had given a lecture about Ferenczi's article to the Budapest Psychoanalytic Society, of which he had been a member since 1914. In 1920, he had moved to Berlin and started work in the polyclinic, and, in 1921, he became a member of the Berlin Psychoanalytic Society.[1128] Harnik reaffirmed above all Ferenczi's stress on the similarity between a traumatic neurosis and a tic. A week later, on 9 June 1921, when van Ophuijsen attended, another meeting of the Berlin Psychological Society was devoted to the subject of the tic. A debate was held about the article and the review of it by Harnik. On the panel were Abraham and van Ophuijsen.

Abraham opened the discussion. He examined in detail Ferenczi's article and stressed how difficult it was to distinguish between a tic and a compulsive act. He also saw a connection between the symptoms and the originating event, as is the case with hysteria. Patients attributed no significance to the tic in their mental lives, however, whereas those who suffered from compulsions attributed significance to their compulsive acts, fearing consequences if they failed to carry out those acts. Abraham, in contrast to Ferenczi, was convinced that the tic, like the compulsive act, was directed towards an object. In his analyses he came upon instances of tics that had to do with anal and sadistic relations with the object. Abraham had even drawn up a table to illustrate all this. Such things were his speciality.

In his table (Table 1), the tic was at the same level as compulsive neurosis, in which there was an anal–sadistic relationship with the object.

Next to speak was van Ophuijsen and something remarkable happened. Van Ophuijsen immediately began to criticise Ferenczi.[1129]

In his view, Ferenczi's treatment of the subject lacked a clear definition of the tic. Van Ophuijsen did not seem to realise that it was usual to intersperse criticism with a few words of praise. This was only the start of a torrent of criticism, at the end of which he also discussed Abraham's contribution briefly. His behaviour was all the more remarkable because he was more or less making his entrance into the Berlin Psychoanalytic Society. As far as the content was concerned, van Ophuijsen differed from Abraham hardly at all, but the form of his contribution diverged markedly from the norm.

Abraham gave Ferenczi an opportunity to react to the debate in writing. Ferenczi was furious. He wrote that all readers of his article would have to admit that their colleague van Ophuijsen was kicking at open doors. It was surely obvious that his article was an initial foray. It was a discussion paper and, in Ferenczi's own mind, a completely successful one, given the interesting contribution it had prompted from Abraham.

In December 1921, van Ophuijsen wrote a long letter to Ferenczi in which he showed himself to be deeply insulted by Ferenczi's reaction. Ferenczi made mention of the letter in his circular letter of 21 December 1921.[1130]

Abraham tried to reconcile the parties and wrote to Ferenczi, "But O[phuijsen] is extremely sensitive and easily feels hurt, in other words disparaged".[1131] Oddly, it seems Abraham did not think that van Ophuijsen had behaved at all rudely. Moreover, in the autumn of 1922, he sent his daughter Hilda to van Ophuijsen to undergo analysis with him.

Sequel to the issue of lay analysis

Meanwhile the issue of lay analysis continued to lurk in the background for the committee and from time to time it caused brief expressions of irritation. In June 1921, Jones had asked for advice in his circular letter from London. A group had formed in Porth, South Wales, made up

Table 1. Abraham's tabular illustration.

Object–love	Genital organisation	Normal state	Normal state
		Control of organ innervation	Capacity to deal with psychical stimuli
Object–love	Genital organisation	Conversion	Anxiety
		Hysteria	Hysteria
Object–love	Sadistic–anal organisation	Tic	Obsessional neurosis
Narcissism to autoerotism		Catatonia	Paranoic states

largely of teachers who had set themselves the goal of studying psychoanalysis. Their secretary had asked whether they could become members of the British Psychoanalytical Society.[1132] Freud and Rank answered from Vienna that a positive response should be given to the approach. They were of the opinion that the acceptance of this group into "our circle" was the only way for those involved to learn psychoanalysis.[1133] They observed that most doctors, after all, were laymen in the field of psychoanalysis. By saying this, Freud and Rank were making a different distinction. Lay people were those who had little or no knowledge or experience in the field of psychoanalysis. They might, therefore, also be doctors. Abraham responded to the lay issue in the circular letter from Berlin, and, oddly enough, he wrote as if the reaction from Vienna had come from Rank alone.[1134] Rank did write the letters, but he always did so on Freud's behalf as well as his own.

Here we see hints of what would later cause huge irritation: the unclear status of the letters from Vienna. Did those letters express Rank's opinion? Rank was lowest in the hierarchy. He was the youngest on the committee, he had the least experience with psychoanalysis, and he was not a doctor, but had a doctorate in philosophy. Or did the circular letters from Vienna express the opinions of Freud, who was at the top of the hierarchy?

The letters frequently gave the impression that they represented the opinion of Rank, with additions by Freud here and there. In any case, in his circular letter of 1 July 1921, Abraham wrote as if he had a difference of opinion with Rank about the status of lay people, not with Freud. Rank must have found this very unpleasant. Abraham wrote that Rank was right to claim that there was a need for analysts who were not doctors. He believed this was obvious as far as the scientific side was concerned, but the same did not apply to the practice of psycho-analytic therapy. He wrote that Rank and several others who had been schooled directly by Freud in Vienna could not compare themselves with those who had experienced only an analysis with Pfister lasting three weeks.[1135] By writing this, Abraham was, in fact, saying that lay people could not run a psychoanalytic practice, aside from a few who had been trained directly by Freud. Sachs was unable to agree with this point of view. He wrote in the margins next to the remark about Pfister that all this was no less true of doctors. Eitingon was travelling, so he did not sign his name to the letter. The implication here is surely that Abraham simply divided the world into doctors and non-doctors and, in his opinion, only the former (a few exceptions aside) could carry out psychoanalysis.[1136]

The trip to the Harz

This was the heyday of the committee. In 1921, no congress took place and the decision was made to hold a committee meeting in the autumn, from 21 to 29 September. The three Berlin members put forward a proposal to combine their scientific meeting with a visit to the old towns of Hildesheim (where Abraham's grandparents came from), Braunschweig, and perhaps Goslar. They also wanted to take a trip to the Harz Mountains.[1137] The entire journey was financed out of the Psychoanalytic Fund.

Abraham knew the area and organised the trip. Hedwig later said that he chose Hildesheim as the town to start from for Freud's sake, since there was a wonderful museum of Egyptian artefacts there. Freud and Abraham both enjoyed the visit to the museum enormously.[1138] From Hildesheim, they travelled on to the beautiful historic town of Goslar.[1139]

In a letter to the members of the committee dated 8 September, Abraham writes about the train times. It demonstrates how much effort was required in those days to get together in this way. The connections were very bad and most members had to travel for several days.[1140] Jones had the longest journey, all the way from London.

It was a huge success. Freud had written two articles specially for the event, which he read out to the committee members and which they then discussed. The articles were "Psycho-analysis and telepathy" (1941d), which was not published until after his death, and "Certain neurotic mechanisms in jealousy, paranoia, and homosexuality" (1922b), an article based on the treatment of a psychotic patient, Dr Bieber of New York.[1141] In her 2008 article about Freud's patients, May showed that the idea, current until then, that Freud had no psychotic patients was incorrect. Freud treated several psychotic patients, who greatly interested him. He did not succeed in adapting his piece on psychosis for use in analysis, but he did find the treatment therapeutically useful none the less, and scientifically necessary.[1142]

Freud had also asked the others to bring some scientific baggage with them. As well as scientific discussion, there was time for shared pleasure. They took long walks and went sight-seeing. They climbed the Brocken. Freud tested the vertigo of his fellow committee members by asking them to lean on the iron rail that surrounded a viewing point with their hands at their backs and then to imagine the rail was no longer there. Jones was of the opinion that they withstood the test well. All were profoundly impressed by Freud's stamina. He seemed inex-haustible.[1143] At that point Freud was sixty-five, twenty years older than the others on average. Both Abraham and Ferenczi later wrote about how much they had enjoyed the trip.[1144] The only one who did not think much of it was Jones, although he tried not to let that show.[1145] On 23 September, he wrote from Hildesheim to his wife, Kitty, that he had caught 'flu from Rank, who, of course, said that Jones had left a window open somewhere. Jones felt unwell and his German was bad. He found the trip itself very tiring: long walks with the group followed by endless meetings in stuffy cellars. He had heard some interesting new ideas from Freud, however, and from Abraham, too. Jones thought Ferenczi was less good than he had been.[1146]

It cannot have been easy for him. Jones spoke German well, but he was the only one for whom it was not his native language and the long discussions must therefore have been hard for him. Moreover, he had contracted 'flu for the second time that year. All the same, another factor must undoubtedly have been that Freud set a pace for the intensive daily programme with which hardly any of those present could keep up.

Freud's eldest son, Martin, wrote in his book *Glory Reflected* about Freud's working days, which started at eight in the morning and often continued until three at night.[1147] He stopped only for a midday meal with the whole family and a walk along the Ringstraße, at an unimag-inable pace. In the period 1910–1914, Freud received nine to eleven patients a day, at fifty minutes per patient. After the First World War, he received nine or ten patients a day, six days a week. This was not unusual; Jones and Abraham had similar working days.[1148] The difference was that Freud continued working long into the evening. He would write and read and corres-pond with others. He must have had astonishing energy.

CHAPTER TWENTY-TWO

Unrest in Germany and a successful congress in Berlin

The early 1920s must have been an extremely difficult time for Abraham and his family, as it was for an entire generation. After defeat in the war, with millions dead and wounded, the Spanish 'flu claimed even more lives. There was terrible inflation as well as severe political unrest, with strikes and shooting in the streets. The Freikorps made their presence felt. The name Freikorps had been in existence for many years, but, after 1918, it was used for paramilitary groups in Germany that often led a peripatetic existence. They were composed of former soldiers who would not or could not return to a normal existence, along with jobless young people and other malcontents. They were sometimes deployed by the government, against the communists, for instance.[1149]

The early years of the Weimar Republic were marked by a permanent state of crisis. The republic took its name from the decision to make Weimar, rather than turbulent Berlin, the seat of the parliament elected in January 1919. Weimar was quiet and easy to make secure, and it had historic significance as Goethe's home town.

One important factor in the permanent crisis was the rampant inflation that started straight after the First World War and increased rapidly, getting completely out of hand in 1923. In Germany, the war had been financed by printing money and by the time it ended five times as much was in circulation as at the start. The government was unwilling or unable to intervene, since a complete deadlock had been reached as a result of the astonishingly high reparation payments demanded by the Allies.[1150] The inflation of the time becomes starkly visible if the value of the mark is compared to that of the dollar. In January 1919, one dollar was worth 8.90 marks, in January 1922, a dollar was worth 191.80 marks, and in January 1923, a dollar was worth 17,972.00 marks.[1151] Germans with savings were particularly hard hit. They lost everything.

The position of German Jews

The emancipation of the German Jews became a reality only after the First World War. Equal rights were granted in the edict of 1812 and the constitution of 1871, but they became a reality only up to a point. Enthusiasm for the First World War was at least as great among German Jews as it was among their fellow Germans. One in six Jews joined the German army, 100,000 in total. Of those, 80,000 served at the front, 35,000 were decorated for valour and 12,000 died. A relatively large number of Jewish soldiers were killed. The Jewish population in Germany was 1.5 per cent. The proportion of troops killed who were Jewish was three per cent.[1152]

After the war, the German Jews were hugely influential, especially in Berlin, where five per cent of the population was Jewish. The Berlin Jews managed to occupy important positions. They were extremely influential in trade and dominated German banking, and they owned large department stores such as Wertheim, Tietz, and Kaufhaus Israel. The most important newspaper conglomerates, such as Ullstein and Mosse, were owned by Jews and much of cultural life between the wars was dominated by Jews, such as Max Reinhardt, Bruno Walter, and Albert Einstein.[1153] A remarkable number of German Jews won Nobel Prizes.[1154]

At the same time, anti-Semitism was ferocious. The Freikorps had a marching song, for instance, that went "Knallt ab den Walther Rathenau, die Gottverfluchte Judensau" (Knock down Walther Rathenau / The God-forsaken Jewish sow!).[1155] Rathenau was minister of foreign affairs and hugely influential.

In May 1922, a Catholic priest came to warn Chancellor Joseph Wirth that these words were threatening to become more than a marching song. There was a conspiracy to kill Rathenau. Wirth warned Walther Rathenau in person, who was terribly shocked but then became extremely calm, went to the chancellor, laid both hands on Wirth's shoulders and said: "My friend, it's nothing, who would want to do me any harm?"[1156]

Walther Rathenau (1867–1922) barely regarded himself as Jewish at all; he was a German with Jewish roots. He believed it was of great importance for the Jews to assimilate into German society. He was one of the most prominent German politicians of the 1920s and some even saw him as one of the greatest personalities of the twentieth century. His books about economics and politics had high print-runs. In mid-1922, he had been foreign minister for only six months, but he already seemed to be succeeding in restoring Germany's position as one of the great powers of Europe after years of vilification. He was also extremely rich. He was the son of Emil Rathenau, who had sold his iron foundry in about 1880, gone in search of a new business, visited the international Electrical Exhibition in Paris in 1881, where he became interested in an invention by the thirty-four-year-old Thomas Alva Edison, and decided to buy from Edison the patent on electric light bulbs and other patents for Germany. With borrowed money, he set up a company that later became AEG. By 1890, it employed several thousand workers; by 1910, there were 70,000.[1157]

Despite the warnings, Rathenau had himself driven to work in the centre of Berlin in an open-topped car. He lived in the Königsallee in Grünewald, which takes a rather winding course parallel to the Bismarckallee where Abraham lived with his family. The corner with the Erdener Strasse and the Wallotstrasse, where the attack took place on 24 June 1922, is not far from the Abrahams' house. They might even have heard the shots. Rathenau was assassinated by three members of the Freikorps.[1158]

In Abraham's surviving letters, no mention is made of the attack, but it must have been a huge shock to the Abraham family, as it was for most of the residents of Berlin. The impression the assassination made was comparable to the shock caused by the murder of John Kennedy in the early 1960s. Everyone remembered where they were at the moment when they heard that Rathenau had been murdered. When news of his death became known, hundreds of thousands of workers streamed out of the factories and walked through the streets in a sombre parade. The unions declared a day of mourning to coincide with Rathenau's funeral. In Berlin alone, the number of demonstrators was estimated at a million (there were millions more in other cities) and after the funeral they continued their angry march through the city for hours. The attack on Rathenau was the most shocking event of all, but it was not an isolated incident. Since the declaration of the Republic, several hundred attacks on politicians had taken place, some of them successful.

Rathenau's belief that he was a German first of all, although with a Jewish background, was shared by many Jews of his generation, including Abraham and his wife. Hilda Abraham wrote in her biography that it was very important to her father that his family had lived in Germany for centuries.[1159]

Lecture in Vienna

In early 1922, there were railway strikes. Abraham had been intending to travel to Vienna to give a short series of lectures along with Ferenczi and Róheim for a small number of Americans and for the Stracheys.[1160] They were analysands of Freud's who were to take a three-month course.[1161] Abraham was due to speak on 4 and 5 January, Ferenczi on 6 and 7 January, and Róheim on Sunday 8 January. Freud had one guest bedroom, where first Abraham could stay and then Ferenczi.[1162] In the end, Abraham was unable to travel because of the strike and he eventually arrived at the end of January.

He travelled back just in time before the next railway strike started. In early February, 700,000 German railway workers and officials stopped work.[1163]

On 23 and 24 January, Abraham gave his lectures to the Americans. The first was about the spider as a dream symbol and the second about the apostates Adler and Jung and the movements they led.[1164] He also delivered his lecture about the spider at a meeting of the Vienna Psychoanalytic Society on 25 January. Abraham later added to his article the discussion there, with contributions from Nunberg and Freud.[1165] The time he spent in Vienna with Rank and Freud was also used to make preparations for the next congress, which was to take place in Berlin in the autumn.[1166] In the circular letter of 11 February, he thanked Freud and Rank for the hospitality with which they and their families had received him.[1167]

On 10 January 1922, at a gathering of the Berlin Psychoanalytic Society held to discuss internal matters, Liebermann was at last formally replaced as secretary by Eitingon. The explanation given in the *Korrespondenzblatt* was "for health reasons".[1168] Whether this cleared the air of the entire Liebermann affair is questionable, given the way events subsequently developed.

Friction between Berlin and Vienna and a division into two camps

Preparations for the congress by the committee can be followed closely because they were very widely discussed in the circular letters of those months. The preparations themselves went well, the congress that eventuated was a great success, but there were clearly internal tensions.

On 11 February 1922, Abraham and Eitingon sent a circular letter from Berlin with a number of proposals for the congress. The first was to have a stenographer record everything, the second was that, given the appalling financial situation in Berlin, a small entrance fee should be charged and the third was that since the congress was private in nature, a number of lectures should be held afterwards for those interested.[1169] The answer from Vienna on 21 February 1922 was dismissive in tone. All three proposals were rejected outright.[1170]

> Point 1. We are absolutely opposed to stenographic recording . . . mainly because we are not planning to print *entire* lectures or to relieve someone of the trouble of writing.
>
> Point 2. We are decidedly opposed to charging for admission, let alone graded by currency.
>
> Point 3. Unfortunately we have to oppose this point as well. The idea of holding lectures after a tiring congress is simply overzealous.

As the French say, it is the tone that makes the music. Again, the problem arises that this letter was written in the third person plural. Was it really from both Rank and Freud? In the correspondence between Abraham and Freud, a number of letters can be found in which the latter was unfriendly, unpleasant, or unreasonable, but no letter from Freud is so dismissive, to the point of rudeness. This suggests that the tone of the letter from Vienna of 21 February should be ascribed to Rank. What was going on? Was Rank overtired and, therefore, abrupt and aggressive in tone? Rank mentions fairly often in the circular letters that he was under too much pressure. Or did his position of power directly beside Freud go to his head?

One remarkable coincidence was that on the same day as the rather shameful letter was written, the still oblivious Abraham invited Ferenczi to stay with him and his wife for the duration of the congress. If Ferenczi, as he had indicated earlier, preferred to stay with his brother, then Rank and his wife would be more than welcome.[1171] Rank replied on 15 March that he was happy to accept the invitation.[1172]

Abraham reacted quite calmly, but the rejection of all his proposals had an unpleasant impact, as is clear from the letter of 1 March 1922, "Unfortunately in all letters, especially the one from Vienna, there is only advice against our proposals, without a single positive proposal being made on any of the points raised".[1173]

The next few letters from Vienna are much the same, however. Many of Abraham's proposals were rejected. Rank's letters were strangely peremptory and often thoroughly dismissive. In the end, it clearly became too much for Abraham and he wrote back in a very irritated tone, specifying in detail all the points on which Rank had misunderstood him.[1174]

Rank responded by writing that Eitingon had told him, and Sachs had confirmed, that Abraham really lived too far away for him to stay there. He was going to look for lodgings elsewhere for the period of the congress. He also responded to Abraham's objections, admitting a few mistakes, and his tone was a good deal more friendly.[1175]

What Eitingon had done was actually rather pathetic and bad for Rank, Abraham, and the committee. Abraham lived in a suburb, quite some distance from the centre, but in Berlin that was not much of a problem. The transport links were good. Still, as in the Liebermann affair, Eitingon could not resist interfering in Abraham's business and again he brought Sachs in his wake. Given the rather tense relationships between them, it would have been far better if Rank had stayed with Abraham and they had been able to continue the friendly relations they had enjoyed in Vienna that January.

Matters came to a head when Jones put in his two pennies' worth in the circular letter from London of 3 July 1922:

> May I be allowed to say a word about Abraham's warmth about Rank? It is certain that Rank's comments could not have been personally intended in the sense Abraham thinks. We must by now all know that it is a quality of Rank's to express his thoughts in a forcible, and not always discriminating manner. It is an idiosyncrasy of his that we should willingly allow him if it gives him pleasure. Sometimes the blows fall on Ferenczi's head, often on mine, and at times in Berlin. I have always admired the sunny urbanity with which Ferenczi receives them and have striven to imitate such an excellent ideal. So let me counsel you, my dear Abraham, to smile back and Rank will at once be as amiable as ever.[1176]

There was a good deal of concealed aggression in this letter from Jones, which was supposedly intended to support Abraham but was mainly about Jones himself. At that point, there were serious problems between Freud and Rank on the one side and Jones on the other, because Jones had not done a good job of arranging the publication of the *International Journal* or of the English translations of works by Freud. On top of that, Freud had Joan Riviere in analysis with him. She had been in analysis with Jones and Freud was of the opinion that Jones had made major errors.[1177]

Both Freud and Rank reacted fiercely to Jones' letter on 1 August 1922 and the result was that, although the business between Abraham and Rank had actually been brought to a conclusion, Jones and Abraham were suddenly both labelled *"Angreifer"*, attackers.

Freud wrote that the *Angreifer* were not correct in his view and Rank wrote, clearly insulted,

> On which I would merely like to observe that I (Rank) am perfectly good at tolerating criticism, when it is in its place. As for the rest, I regard our personal friendship and professional bond as far above such little differences and outbursts of emotion, and I am certain that I am of the same opinion as the others in that respect. (Translated for this edition)[1178]

Jones had manufactured a Jones–Abraham camp.[1179]

Summer 1922

In the summer holidays, Abraham and his family first spent a few days with his mother in Bremen to celebrate her seventy-fifth birthday.[1180] They then travelled to St Anton am Arlberg in the Tyrol. To keep the costs down—because of the low exchange rate of the mark everything abroad was extremely expensive—Abraham took a patient with him.

Abraham went for walks in the mountains with Gerd, who was now twelve.[1181] Gerd talked about those walks later in an interview. Abraham was a fearless mountain climber. He always walked on ahead, taking the steepest mountain paths without any nervousness at all, sometimes holding his son dangling from the end of a rope and pulling him back to a safe place. Sometimes, Gerd had to withstand mortal terror.[1182] In contrast to his father, he was able to feel fear.

Hilda described how it was their habit to rent an apartment in the mountains for three months in the summer, so that her father could indulge his great passion. She also mentioned that Abraham took patients along to help pay the costs of the stay. The patients stayed nearby and Abraham worked for three or four hours every day. After that, he spent time with his family. Hilda recalled that, as children, they stayed in a hotel and there were always lots of people around, of whom two would disappear from the sitting room to reappear an hour later, at which point another pair disappeared. As children, they were mystified as to what was going on.[1183]

During the summer of 1922, Abraham, Rank, and Ferenczi met up in Seefeld, where they made further preparations for the congress in September.[1184]

The congress in Berlin

The congress in Berlin of 25 to 27 September 1922 was the last psychoanalytic congress that Freud attended.[1185] He made a deep impression with his lecture "Something of the unconscious". In it, he discussed the first two chapters of *The Ego and the Id*, which was to be published in the spring of 1923. *The Ego and the Id* was to mark a major upheaval in psychoanalysis.

Freud's was far from the only revelatory and innovative lecture. Ferenczi spoke about his genital theory, Horney about the female castration complex, Klein about early analysis of children, Piaget about symbolic thinking, Spielrein about time, Eitingon about the Berlin polyclinic, and Abraham about the development of the libido, a discourse that is fairly generally regarded as his main work.[1186] There were a good number of other contributions as well, thirty-one in total.

Freud had been staying in Hamburg since 12 September 1922 with his widowed son-in-law, Max Halberstadt, and his grandsons, Ernst and Heinerle, and from there he travelled on to Berlin, arriving on about the 20th.[1187] On Saturday 23 September, there was a meeting of the committee at Abraham's home. Hilda later told Eissler about that meeting. She was not sure whether it was a meeting of the presidents of the different psychoanalytic societies or of the committee.[1188] Hilda was allowed to meet the visitors briefly before dinner, and Freud took her arm and said he would accompany her to the table. Hilda, who was then almost sixteen, felt tremendously shy, not knowing how to deal with Freud's courtly humour. She found it simply very unpleasant, since they were all men and only her mother was supposed to eat with them. She went with Freud to the doorway and then made off. The professor, Hilda said to Eissler later, told her via her mother that he would insist that the children ate with them the next time.[1189] The Abrahams were a hospitable household. Jones wrote to his wife that he had had a hugely enjoyable evening with them. It must have been on the 21st, the Thursday before the congress. There were three ladies, Mrs Abraham, Mrs Ferenczi, and Anna Freud, who looked very attractive, according to Jones.[1190] During the congress Reik stayed with Abraham, as did van Ophuijsen and his wife.

The seventh psychoanalytic congress was the best attended psychoanalytic congress prior to the Second World War. There were 256 participants, of whom 112 were members of one of the psychoanalytic societies. The others were guests who had been given special permission to come. They were from all points of the compass: the USA, eleven, Belgium, three, Germany, 120 (ninety-one of them from Berlin), Britain, thirty-one, Hungary, twenty-two, India, two, Italy, four, *Journal of the American Psychoanalytic Association*, one, the Netherlands, nine, France, one, Riga, two, Czechoslovakia, one, Ukraine, one, Austria, twenty-eight (all from Vienna), and Switzerland, twenty. Most remarkable, of course, were the two participants from India and one from the *Journal of the American Psychoanalytic Association*. As the list shows, the connection with France was still minimal. An extensive account of the congress appeared in the *Korrespondenz-blatt*.[1191] Since, at the congress, Abraham was elected secretary of the IPA, the congress report must have been compiled by him.

On Sunday 24 September 1922, the evening before the congress began, a reception was held for the participants by the Berlin Psychoanalytic Society.

Abraham's lecture

In 1924 Abraham's magnum opus would be published: *A Short Study of the Development of the Libido, Viewed in the Light of Mental Disorders*. The book is in two parts. Part one is about manic–depressive states and the pregenital stages of the development of the libido. Part two is about the beginning and development of object-love.

At the congress in Berlin, Abraham read out a piece from the first part of his study, which he called "Neue Untersuchungen zur Psychologie der manisch-depressieven Zustände" (New investigations in the psychology of manic–depressive states). This work is examined in more detail in Chapter Twenty-five.

Eitingon's talk about the Berlin polyclinic[1192]

Before his departure for Palestine in 1933, Eitingon published hardly anything and gave few lectures. His contribution to the Berlin congress about the polyclinic was an exception. It was published in full in the *Korrespondenzblatt*.

The pathos of the first few pages makes them hard to read. The description of the practice, however, offers a clear picture of procedures at the polyclinic, which had now been in existence for two and a half years. Eitingon said the following in his introduction about psychoanalysis and the Great War:

It (psychoanalysis) had no part in the illusions that have now been lost. It has always been aware of the latent powers of the mind and the hidden mechanisms of individuals and groups, which are now becoming plainly evident after the falling and the tearing of so many masks. From the mood of the time people called more than before for psychotherapy, but that which named itself so could answer only with phrases and platitudes and did not know the way ahead. Psychoanalysis has, however, developed further without allowing itself to be swayed by war and misery. Firmly founded, properly secured, and far-reaching, it was present at that moment. Now there is a need to make it more practical and accessible.[1193]

This is far removed from the reality. Psychoanalysis had certainly always been aware of the aggressive forces in man, but not one analyst had predicted the unstoppable destructive aggression of the First World War. What Eitingon described here was a fantasy world, with himself as the implicit saviour of humanity by means of psychoanalysis in his polyclinic.

There was another striking point about Eitingon's lecture. Abraham was no longer mentioned in it. He was named only in relation to the training. Whereas in the description of the polyclinic in 1920 he was presented as the person who stood beside Eitingon and Simmel in the leadership, this was no longer the case in 1922. Eitingon had written to Freud about him at the time: "For reasons of prestige and to demonstrate in particular the close relationship between the polyclinic and the Berlin Psychoanalytic Society, we have included Abraham in the showcase of the leadership of the polyclinic".[1194] The first person Eitingon named as one of those who had made his time available to the polyclinic was his protégé Liebermann.

The polyclinic was free to those patients unable to pay for treatment. It was left to patients to make a contribution if they could afford to do so. The analysts who worked there received only a small fee. They provided mainly their time. Eitingon financed the entire infrastructure: the rent, furnishings, and other expenses.

Eitingon and Simmel were in charge of the polyclinic and were assisted by Anna Smeliansky, who lived in the clinic. Psychoanalyst Boehm, the Müller-Braunschweigs, Horney, Klein, Alexander, Harnik, Schott, and Lampl worked in the clinic, where training in psychoanalysis also took place.[1195]

In the first two and a half years of the polyclinic, six hundred applications were received. In the year prior to the congress, some fifty to sixty analyses had taken place at any one time. At the start, there were many chronic patients, who went from clinic to clinic for years, but later there were fewer of those. The clinic had only five consulting rooms, which were used intensively. An attempt to reduce the sessions to half an hour failed, so they continued to last between forty-five minutes and an hour. The patients came three or four times a week, only in extremely serious cases more often than that. So, even in the early years of psychoanalysis, three or four sessions a week was usual. In this first period, not including the many short trial analyses, 130 analyses were concluded. Many of the patients were declared improved, substantially improved, or cured. By present-day standards, the analyses were short. Of the 130, thirty-five lasted less than three months, forty-nine lasted three to six months, thirty lasted six to nine months, thirteen lasted nine to twelve months, six lasted twelve to eighteen months and eight lasted longer than eighteen months. Of the very short analyses in particular, the conclusion was often reached that the problems remained unchanged or that the analysis had failed (Fenichel, 1930).

In his lecture, Eitingon paid no attention to the frequency of analysis per week and he does not mention that point in his progress reports. It is, therefore, impossible to see how many patients came three, four, or more times per week. He clearly did not regard a high frequency as necessary to analysis and it does not seem to have been a subject of discussion in those days, which it certainly is today.[1196]

So, how many times a week did analysis take place at that time? The general impression is that six times a week was usual, Monday to Saturday. Freud saw patients less often, but sometimes for many more hours a week. Roszi von Freund, for example, came for twelve hours a week in the first period of her analysis with Freud, from 1 November 1915 to 15 July 1916. Patients who had travelled a long way sometimes came far more often.[1197] In the autumn of 1921, Freud had more patients than he could treat. He first tried to refer them to Rank and when that did not succeed he reduced the frequency from six to five times a week. He had six full working days, so he was able to give his patients all their sessions.[1198]

As far as we know, Abraham, who did not work at the polyclinic, analysed his patients six times a week.

The relationship between Abraham and Eitingon

During the congress, Joan Riviere, Freud's British analysand, was invited to lunch with Eitingon and she was clearly much impressed by the luxury in which the Eitingons lived. In a letter to her mother and sister that has since become famous, she wrote,

> I had been invited by Dr Eitingon to lunch at his house the next day, Wednesday. He is a rich man, a doctor, has practically founded the Clinic with his own money, is an old friend of Freud's and a very sound analyst. Dr Abraham is the scientific leader of P.A. in Berlin but Eitingon is the material and social leader. Freud & daughter were staying at his house. No doubt I owed the invitation to F. It was quite interesting. His wife was a well-known Russian actress—a very piquant & notable little apparition with piled-up masses of black hair & exquisite clothes—very Parisian in effect. Evidently there was unlimited money. The house was rather like this one in Vienna—a private house, so unusual, looking into a garden at the back—with glazed-in balcony—but all very new & grand, in beautiful modern taste—wonderful paint, panelling, Chinese wall-papers & influence on furniture, beautiful bookshelves, pictures, rugs, objets d'art—& marvellous food. We were 8 at lunch, a ceremonious affair, the two Freuds, father and daughter, self & 3 Viennese members, one a woman doctor, & Eitingon & wife—O I forgot there was also a certain Frau Lou Salomé.[1199]

What Riviere writes, that Abraham was the scientific leader and Eitingon the material and social leader, is not correct. But, perhaps intuitively, she had touched upon a problem within the Berlin Psychoanalytic Society. Eitingon was the material leader of the polyclinic, but not the social leader of psychoanalysis in Berlin. His wife did not want to receive any analysts. Only the Freud family and Lou Andreas-Salomé, who was of Russian extraction like Eitingon and his wife, were welcome. This alone made social leadership impossible for Eitingon, and, in any case, he was away far too often. After the congress, he travelled to Paris with his wife on 13 October, then on to London and Palermo, returning only in late January 1923. Lou Salomé stayed on in his house while he was away.[1200] Eitingon frequently took long trips like this. When Abraham wrote to Freud in early 1923 about the circular letters from Berlin, which were mainly written by him, he mentioned that he was finding it hard to get together with the other two Berlin committee members to write a letter. Abraham referred to the fact that Freud knew how careless Sachs had become about this kind of thing and that Eitingon's "domestic fixation" was impossible to break through. Eitingon's wife, Mirra, demanded a great deal of attention.[1201] Eitingon's tendency to want to save others was very strongly expressed in their relationship. Mirra Eitingon was often poorly and wanted extended stays at fashionable health resorts, hence their travels in winter.[1202]

Abraham was the undisputed leader of the Berlin Psychoanalytic Society, both in a social and in a scientific sense, from its founding until his death.

There was only one moment when his leadership wavered and that was during the Liebermann affair, when Eitingon played an active role in the attempt to dethrone him, which almost succeeded. We might wonder whether Eitingon could have tolerated Abraham's permanent leadership. At no point did he emerge from his letters and his meetings with Freud and Anna Freud as so cheerful and enterprising as he did immediately after Abraham's death, when he took all the leadership tasks upon himself.[1203]

The letters between Lou Salomé and Anna Freud also bring out Abraham's social function. On a number of occasions there were visits to the Abrahams' house in the period when Lou Salomé was staying in Berlin.[1204]

Riviere also wrote in her letter that after the congress ended on Friday 29 September, she ran into Jones, who had wanted to leave already but had missed his train.[1205] He proposed to her that they should both go to Abraham's house that evening. Riviere wrote the following:

> So about 9 we drove out there. They live still further out, in a sort of Hampstead Heath, with lovely trees & country round. However it was pouring with rain & pitch dark. A Dutch member & his wife were staying with the Abrahams & unfortunately the wife was an incessant talker, & as in Germany all the chairs in the drawing room are arranged round one small table, with coffee & liqueurs & sweets on it, everybody is crammed together & you can get no conversation if one person persists on talking. This lady talked about her own dogs precisely an hour & poor Jones' face got blacker and blacker—*he* likes to do the talking. The result was that I did not get to know the Abrahams in the least and we drove away again rather bored.[1206]

It must have been Ans van Maastrigt, van Ophuijsen's wife, who talked so incessantly.

CHAPTER TWENTY-THREE

Young talent pours in

The rapid growth of the polyclinic demanded more and more staff. How were all the new psychoanalysts to be trained?

Ever since 1910, the Berlin Psychoanalytic Society had been giving many courses. After the opening of the polyclinic in 1920, they took place in the clinic or, if there was insufficient room as with Abraham's courses from 1923 onwards, in a larger room elsewhere. Abraham gave a great many of the polyclinic's courses. In the spring and autumn of 1920, he taught an introduction to psychoanalysis, with twenty participants.[1207] In 1921, he held a psychoanalytic seminar for advanced students and a course in which new psychoanalytic works were studied, as well as two more introductory courses. The number of participants increased. In the spring of 1921 there were thirty, and in the autumn thirty to forty. In 1922, Abraham again held a psychoanalytic seminar, for twenty participants this time. He also gave an introductory course about experiences from psychoanalytic practice, for thirty participants.

The introduction to psychoanalysis in the autumn of 1922 was attended by eighty to ninety people. The numbers were rising spectacularly. Sachs, Horney, Simmel, and Eitingon were also involved with education.[1208] The number of doctors who wanted to train as analysts continued to grow.[1209] Gradually, a need emerged to offer a general training course rather than all kinds of separate courses. A commission was set up consisting of Abraham, Eitingon, and Simmel, supported by Horney and Liebermann. This group would organise a full training course that was to last a year to a year and a half. Ultimately, it became the Berlin model for training in psychoanalysis that would be emulated all over the world. The trainee's own training analysis played a decisive part in the course.[1210] From Eitingon's letters, it is clear that Freud was actively involved in all this.

In the new commission there was a debate about the timing of the training analysis. At what stage in the training should it take place? Eitingon favoured the second phase of training. That meant the candidate would first be given lessons in theory and read the most important psychoanalytic works. He would, therefore, have some idea what his options were.[1211] Then the training analysis would take place. Eitingon estimated that the resistances created by the candidate's prior knowledge would not be much greater than the resistances that would exist in any case.

Freud did not agree.[1212] He had discussed the timing of the training analysis with Rank and they had considered the following points: if the course began with theoretical teaching lasting five to six months, the candidate would conclude that the stress lay on the intellectual content of the course. This meant there would be less attention paid to the training analysis and the candidate would think that he had learnt enough about psychoanalysis no matter how the training analysis went. This would deprive the course of an opportunity to weed out candidates. It would be far harder to dismiss some of the participants. Freud was in favour of having the candidate start with their own analysis, and then follow the course and read the books only if that went well.

In his report about the Berlin polyclinic, Eitingon mentions that an important part of the training consisted of practical work in the polyclinic. Candidates would be allocated cases that were suitable for them and their analyses would be carefully guided by an experienced analyst. This was the precursor to the control analysis later applied everywhere, with one important difference: in Berlin, there was initially a possibility that the experienced analyst would take over the analysis if the candidate was not performing well. This was to protect the patients.

Berlin as a magnet

In this period, many great talents came to Berlin. From Hungary, and especially Budapest, there was an influx of young analysts who had fled their country after the overthrow of the Republic of Councils. Among them were Franz Alexander, Sándor Radó, Alice and Michael Balint, Barbara Lantos, and Jenö Harnik.[1213] Melanie Klein is often included in this list of Hungarians, but she had moved to Berlin earlier, and not specifically because of the political situation.

Analysts from Vienna also settled in Berlin, not just Sachs, but Hans Lampl, Walter Schmideberg, Siegfried Bernfeld, Helene Deutsch, Theodor Reik, and Marianne Rie (Kris).[1214]

Franz Alexander

One extremely talented newcomer was the Hungarian Franz Alexander (1891–1964) from Budapest, the son of a philosophy professor.[1215] He studied medicine and moved to Berlin after the war, where, in 1921, he became the first student of the Berlin Institute for Psychoanalysis and entered into analysis with Sachs. Abraham wrote about him in the circular letter of 11 February 1922: "At our last meeting Alexander gave a talk about 'Castration Complex and Character Formation'. The lecture demonstrated once again his superb talent". For that essay, Freud awarded him the prize for best clinical essay of the year. In 1923, he became a member of the Berlin Psychoanalytic Society.

Alexander then wanted to give courses, but Eitingon was worried by Alexander's rapid progress and stood in the way for two years. Only after much urging by Radó did Eitingon relent. Fenichel would later face the same obstruction.[1216] Alexander had a good relationship with Freud, whom he visited regularly when he was in Vienna. Freud always made time for him. They had got to know each other when Freud's middle son, Oliver, was in analysis with Alexander because of depression. Oli, as he was called, gained a great deal from the analysis.[1217] Freud often referred patients to Alexander after that.[1218] Alexander later said that he was surprised by his discussions with Freud. He had the impression that Freud's way of treating patients was extremely flexible and that he rarely followed any general rules. Freud could stimulate a patient to undertake certain activities if, for example, he thought they would be beneficial, and he took far more account of the patient's daily life than Alexander had thought possible based on his theoretical articles. Freud was very well informed about his patients' everyday lives.[1219]

In 1930, Alexander travelled to Chicago, where he set up the Chicago Psychoanalytic Institute on the Berlin model. He was its director for twenty-five years.

Sándor Radó

Sándor Radó (1890–1972) also came from Budapest. He was to develop into one of the most important analysts in Berlin. He had studied political science and medicine in Budapest and, in 1913, he became secretary to the recently established Hungarian Psychoanalytic Society.[1220] Radó was politically active in the Hungarian Republic of Councils. After the 1922 congress, he remained in Berlin and in December he entered into analysis with Abraham.

Fenichel, who also settled in Berlin after the congress, had entered into analysis with Radó a little over a month earlier, on 27 October 1922. Two years later, they both stopped their analysis at around the same time. Fenichel wrote in his diary on 19 December 1924 that he had been sitting that evening with Radó in the Romanische Café, where Löwenstein, Lampl, and Alexander later joined them, and that he had ended his analysis that day.[1221]

Because Fenichel was in analysis with Radó at the same time as Radó was in analysis with Abraham, the influence of Abraham must have been noticeable in Fenichel's analysis. It was a psychoanalytic grandfather–father–child relationship.

Sándor Radó became a member of the Berlin Psychoanalytic Society in 1924 and held many important functions. He was a teacher at the institute, a member of the education committee, secretary of the DPG, and eventually secretary to the education committee of the IPA. He succeeded Rank as editor of the *Internationale Zeitschrift für Psychoanalyse* and became one of the publishers of *Imago*. Radó was known as a brilliant teacher with a photographic memory, but he was also considered extremely imperious during his time in Berlin.[1222] According to Alexander, he was a phenomenal debater who usually succeeded in discovering weak points in his opponents.[1223] In 1931, he emigrated to New York and there he introduced the Berlin training model. In the 1930s, Radó broke with Freud after a critical review by Lampl-de Groot of his article "Fear of castration in women" (1933). Radó assumed that Freud shared the opinion of his pupil.[1224]

In the 1960s, Radó was interviewed by Bluma Swerdloff and he mentioned Abraham surprisingly frequently.[1225] Radó said that he was with Freud working on the *Zeitschrift* when Freud received the news of Abraham's death. Freud spoke to him about the death of Abraham, wrote an obituary, and then asked him what was going to happen now to the Berlin Psychoanalytic Society. Radó concluded, wrongly, that Freud's grief lasted five minutes.[1226]

Freud was, in fact, deeply affected by Abraham's death, but he would not have wanted to dwell on that in a business meeting. Something Freud probably failed to notice was what the news meant for Radó. Radó had only just started his analysis with Abraham when his wife and unborn child in Budapest died suddenly. His analysis lasted a long time by the standards of those days and he tried to come to terms with the death of his wife and child. Abraham had great faith in Radó. He immediately allowed him to teach, encouraged him to write articles, and worked closely with him until his death. It must have been almost impossible for Radó to cope with the fact that now his analyst, too, had died.

The large place occupied by the death of Abraham in the interview with Swerdloff forty years later seems to indicate stagnated grief. Radó said that at the time he thought that Abraham, who was already seriously ill, had committed suicide to escape the conflict with Freud.[1227] Radó was not entirely wrong, as will become clear.

Therese Benedek said in 1953 that she thought the later break between Radó and Freud had more to do with Abraham's death than with Freud himself. Benedek described in that interview the very close co-operation between Abraham and Radó up to Abraham's death. She also saw a connection between the work of Radó and Abraham on orality and grief and the working through of Radó's mourning for his wife.[1228] She thought that Radó had laid at Freud's door, years later, all his anger at Abraham, who had abandoned him by dying. The article by Radó about women's fear of castration that was so heavily criticised by Lampl-de Groot was an extension of Abraham's article about the castration complex in women (Lampl-de Groot, 1934).

Another notable point comes to the fore in the correspondence between Freud and Radó in the period immediately after Abraham's death. Freud absolutely wanted an entire issue of the journal to be devoted to Abraham after his death and before the issue planned to mark his own seventieth birthday.[1229] Radó at first prevented this and Eitingon supported him in doing so. After much insistence by Freud that they must honour the dead before they could celebrate, Radó finally gave way.[1230]

In his interview, Radó made a number of interesting remarks about the clinical aspects of psychoanalysis in that period. In Budapest, he had been a very close friend of Ferenczi. For that reason alone he could not enter into analysis with Ferenczi, but Radó also objected to Ferenczi's tendency to speculate, for example about evolution and what happened several million years ago. Months might pass in the Budapest Psychoanalytic Society without anyone discussing a case or a therapeutic approach, let alone talking about techniques.

Radó wanted a clinically orientated analyst and, to his mind, only Abraham fitted the bill. That was why Radó went to Berlin. He was extremely enthusiastic about the very different attitude in Berlin. At their first meeting, Abraham came in and started talking about the patients he had analysed. He described what he had discovered, how he had explained it, what was correct or incorrect, and which treatment was appropriate. The others followed his example. It was all very practical and clinical and it made everyone enthusiastic. Abraham feared that speculation would harm psychoanalysis, a young science in the making. It would become a speculative system rather than an empirical science based on observation.

Radó also talked about his analysis by Abraham. He said that in those days there was still no knowledge about how to approach a patient, what was important and what not, or what a therapist should work on and what should be left alone. This meant attention was paid to phenomena Freud had described. According to Radó, it was not the case that the analyst and the analysand together put the analysand's life under the microscope, investigated what the central problems were, and tried to do something about them. It was a more a matter of searching for possible ways of applying Freudian principles.

Radó remained in Berlin and never went back to Budapest. The death of his wife and child must have played a part in this, something Radó does not mention at all in his long interview.[1231]

Otto Fenichel

Otto Fenichel (1898–1946) also remained in Berlin after the congress. He was already a member of the Vienna Psychoanalytic Society, but now he wanted to follow a modern training course in Berlin. Alongside his teaching analysis and his theoretical education he treated patients at the institute.[1232] Fenichel was a great admirer of Abraham. In 1925, he took a course taught by Abraham, studied his work, and wrote an extremely positive review.[1233] In 1926, he gave a course on Abraham's work. It was not repeated. Fenichel fled Berlin in 1933 and, in 1938, after various peregrinations, emigrated to Los Angeles, where, among other things, he wrote his astonishingly erudite magnum opus *The Psychoanalytic Theory of Neuroses*, which became a standard work in the field of psychoanalysis.[1234]

There is every indication that Fenichel ultimately became a victim of the rigid anti-lay policy of the Americans. The American Psychoanalytic Society admitted only people with an American medical degree as full members. Fenichel was a doctor, but, like all émigré doctors, he was not recognised as such in the USA. Although he had been a full member of a psychoanalytic society in Europe, the American Psychoanalytic Society regarded him as a layman.

Fenichel had a flourishing practice in Los Angeles and was an important member and teacher at the Los Angeles Psychoanalytic Society, but he feared that his lay status would make it impossible for him to be influential on a larger scale in the American umbrella organisation. So, in his late forties, he began studying medicine again. This involved working in a clinic for a year as a resident doctor, with a demanding work schedule including night shifts. Fenichel's health had always been less than good and he had heart problems. He found his work as a resident doctor far harder than he had expected and he died rather suddenly before it was over.[1235] Like Abraham, Fenichel was forty-eight when he died.

Anna Freud

Several months before the congress in Berlin in September 1922, Anna Freud wanted to join a psychoanalytic society so that she could attend the congress as a member of the IPA, and she considered Berlin. If she wanted to become a member in Vienna, she would have to give a lecture, but the problem was that she was not yet analysing patients. Anna Freud asked Eitingon on 22 April 1922 whether she could not become a member of the Berlin Psychoanalytic Society on the basis of her translation of Varendonck.[1236] Eitingon's answer is not known, but it was probably negative.

Anna Freud finally did give a lecture to the Vienna Psychoanalytic Society on 31 May 1922. There is a strong suspicion that she solved the problem of the fact that she was not yet performing analyses by discussing her own analysis by her father, in an anonymised form.[1237]

The Berlin Psychoanalytic Society benefited from the unfavourable political situation in Hungary, but its flourishing is mainly attributable to Eitingon's polyclinic, where people could learn analysis, and to sound psychological training and inspiring leadership by Abraham.

CHAPTER TWENTY-FOUR

Psychoanalytic techniques and Helene Deutsch

Inflation

In 1923, inflation in German got completely out of hand. This is well illustrated by the value of the mark in relation to the dollar. In July 1914, one dollar was worth 4.20 marks. In July 1922, one dollar was worth 493.60 marks. Six months later, in January 1923, this had increased to 17,972.00 marks. In July 1923, the number of marks needed to buy one dollar had become inconceivable, at 353,412. It continued to rise rapidly, reaching 4,620,455 by August 1923, 98,860,000 in September 1923, 25,260,208,000 in October and 4,200,000,000,000 marks on 15 November 1923.[1238]

The devaluation of the currency was so rapid that every German who received a salary had to buy as much as possible as quickly as possible because the money would be worth almost nothing a couple of days later. Goods bought on that first day had to last the month. Savings had melted away long before. A kohlrabi suddenly cost fifty million and for the price of a postage stamp you could once have bought a villa in Dahlem.

In Remarque's novel, *Three Comrades*, the protagonist and narrator works in the advertising department of a rubber factory and earns 200 trillion marks a month.[1239] The money was paid out twice daily, followed by a half-hour pause in which employees could run to the shops to spend it before the latest devaluation of the mark was announced, since at that point it would halve in value.

As a result of the unstable currency, there were fortunes to be made on the stock exchange. Young speculators—some still in school—could react with lightning speed, dared to gamble, and became suddenly rich. Wholesale buyers took advantage. Fast money was spent on extreme luxury and noisy entertainment. It contributed to the decline of moral norms, to cynicism, contempt, and a rise in crime.

Remarkably enough, the fall of the mark was accompanied by a hectic cheerfulness, which expressed itself in, for example, a craze for dancing. There was dancing everywhere and all levels of society joined in, at lunch, at teatime, in ballrooms, garden restaurants and nightclubs, on the beach and in the street. The noise drowned out the fear. The middle classes in particular were forced to acknowledge that their frugality and concern for the future had counted for nothing. There was hunger, there were far more diseases, and the number of suicides increased dramatically.

In the summer of 1923, many strikes took place and they were increasingly violent. By June, the Cuno government had practically lost control of the country. On 11 August 1923, Chancellor Cuno stepped down and was succeeded by Stresemann.

In the autumn of 1923, the situation became extremely dangerous. In Saxony, in collaboration with Moscow, preparations were made for a communist revolution. In Hamburg, there was actually an attempted revolution, which was put down on 23 October within twenty-four hours. In Bavaria, the threat arose of an anti-republican coup by the right, which was eventually called off by the right itself, impressed by moves against the communists in Saxony. In its wake, Adolf Hitler decided, once the tension in Bavaria had eased, to carry out the now famous Bierkeller Putsch in Munich on 8 November 1923. The young Führer tried, with the moral support of General Ludendorff, to bring about an anti-republican coup with his National Socialists. Hitler was arrested and imprisoned.

A little Abraham is born

On 9 February 1923, Charlotte Abraham was born, the daughter of Abraham's brother Max and his wife, Else. Max had wanted a son, whom he planned to name after his brother Karl. Charlotte was a female version of the name Karl.

Charlotte was able to spend only a very little time with her uncle Karl Abraham, but she always remembered a present he gave her when she was two years old. Abraham had brought liquid for blowing bubbles. Charlotte was delighted by it. Her mother thought she was really too young for it, but eventually she permitted the blowing of bubbles. Else Abraham had a big soft spot for her brother-in-law.

Developments within the Berlin Psychoanalytic Society

Despite the adverse circumstances, the Berlin Psychoanalytic Society flourished. There was great affection for Abraham within the Society and he played a crucial role. In an interview with Michael Balint by Swerdloff in 1965, Balint described his time in Berlin and his experience of Abraham.[1240] He said, "When I started analysis, it was a revolution. We were all revolutionaries. We were excluded from universities, hardly admitted to scientific societies, just tolerated".[1241] He talked about the lively atmosphere in Berlin and all the people who were there: Radó, Melanie Klein, Helene Deutsch, van Ophuijsen, Alexander, and many others. Then he spoke about Abraham: "Abraham was—I really must emphasize it—the very best president I ever met in my life. He was simply magnificent, the things he could do".

Swerdloff then said "Fair?" Balint answered,

Fair and absolutely firm. No nonsense. He kept the place very well in hand. Again, he had his limitations. He did not like fantasy very much. He did not have much fantasy himself, but he was very much down to earth, excellent clinician, perfect clinician, and a really fair man. He was fair, I mean you should consult his correspondence; he was an absolutely reliable, firm, fair man. I could tell many anecdotes about him.

Swerdloff said "Go ahead", and Balint continued,

For instance one day Simmel—whom we all liked and at the same time were angry with, he was a most unruly man with excellent ideas—gave a god-awful paper. It was really terrible. There was a long table, the seniors sat in the first row, we youngsters sat in the second row behind them, and oh my, we were prepared for a slaughter. Then the paper was finished, and there was a pause. Abraham pulls Simmel into the window niche and has a word with him. Then he opened the meeting. Oh, now we have a slaughter! But Abraham said that during the pause Dr. Simmel informed him that he did not want his paper discussed. In consequence Abraham closes the meeting. That was the only way it could be done.[1242]

The psychoanalytic technique

Radó had already indicated when he was interviewed by Swerdloff that at the time of his own analysis, which ran from late 1922 to late 1924, it was, in his view, not yet clear how a patient should be approached.[1243] It was not obvious to him what an analyst in a treatment situation actually should and should not do. He was referring to the technique of psychoanalysis. On the one side, there was psychoanalytic theory, which had been developing further and further for almost thirty years, and, on the other, there was the practice of analysis. Radó was exaggerating when he said that around 1924 nothing was yet known, but he was certainly right that the technique was relatively neglected as a subject compared to the theory.

In 2001, Marina Leitner published *Ein gut gehütetes Geheimnis* (A Well-kept Secret), which looks at the technique of psychoanalysis. It examines the issue of what exactly a psychoanalyst does in the consulting room. Leitner writes that, in 1908, Abraham was the first person after Freud to open a psychoanalytic practice and make a living by it.[1244]

The number of people who were running a financially viable psychoanalytic practice before the First World War was indeed very small. Jung followed Abraham's example in March 1909, Ferenczi in 1910, Drosnès in 1910–1911, as did Stekel, then van Emden and Jones in 1912, Andreas-Salomé and Hattingberg in 1913.[1245] Of those who combined psychoanalysis with a neurological practice, such as Sadger and Hitschmann, it is not clear how many analyses they carried out. The lawyer Viktor Tausk started studying medicine in 1908 specifically in order to become an analyst.[1246]

The first group had to analyse based on Freud's theory without having anything more than summary indications from Freud regarding the technique. Therefore, they had to invent the wheel themselves. Freud's case histories were not particularly helpful. He expanded on the theory, something that was later advised against. Streams of associations were broken off, whereas the whole idea of free association was to leave the associations undisturbed. Freud stated that the explanation of the transference was the most important thing, but nowhere does he write exactly how this was to be done.[1247] Not for nothing did Freud procrastinate when it came to writing about technique. He thought the psychological factors that presented themselves in the psychoanalytic method (including the person of the analyst) were too complex and too variable to be subjected to strict rules.[1248] Moreover, the field was still under development.

From 1910 onwards, Freud did start to publish some indications as to technique, writing, for example, that association experiments were useful for research but not as treatment. Jung always had his patients start by associating from words he gave them.[1249]

In 1910, Freud wrote the following in his article about wild psychoanalysis:

> It is not enough, therefore, for a physician to know a few of the findings of psycho-analysis; he must also have familiarized himself with its technique if he wishes his medical procedure to be guided by a psycho-analytic point of view. This technique cannot yet be learnt from books, and it certainly cannot be discovered independently without great sacrifices of time, labour and success. Like other medical techniques, it is to be learnt from those who are already proficient in it.[1250]

Freud wrote of "wild psychoanalysis" in a time when there were very few analysts, when there were still no instructions for the practical side of analysis, and when everyone simply set to work in his or her own way. Suddenly, there was a risk of being labelled a "wild analyst" if you did not exercise the technique properly. One consequence of this seems to have been that everyone anxiously concealed their precise method of analysis and hardly any open discussions of the subject took place. At all those evening meetings of psychoanalytic societies, there was rarely any talk of techniques until the 1920s.[1251] Only in the training on offer in Berlin was technique taught as a separate subject.

Another important technical point was countertransference, the conscious and unconscious feelings evoked in the analyst by the patient. The concept was first named by Freud in a letter to Jung of 7 June 1909.[1252] Hardly any attention at all was paid to countertransference in the early years of psychoanalysis and it was mainly seen as interference that had to be cleared away so that it would not cause trouble.

In his essay "The future chances of psychoanalytic therapy" Freud wrote about countertransference and the influence it had on the unconscious feelings of the doctor. Freud was of the opinion that the demand should be made of the doctor that he must recognise and overcome countertransference. To do so, he must analyse himself, his own complexes and resistances.[1253] Only much later would countertransference be seen as an important instrument in analysis.

As was usual at the time, Abraham barely mentioned countertransference in his articles and letters. He did watch out for it, as demonstrated by that letter to Freud in which he wrote that he had noticed how he kept looking at a photograph of his parents when he investigated early childhood transference in a patient.[1254] In connection with Helene Deutsch, he said explicitly that he had not been troubled by it.

Technical complications in the relationship between Freud, Deutsch, and Tausk

Helene Deutsch (1884–1982) was one of the first women to study medicine in Vienna. That was in 1907. She gained her doctorate in 1912 and that same year married the Viennese doctor of internal medicine, Felix Deutsch. During the war, she worked as head of the psychiatric department at the clinic run by Wagner–Jauregg. She was forced to give up that position in 1918 because women had no official right to jobs in leadership roles.

In 1918, she entered into analysis with Freud.[1255] The outcome of her analysis was traumatic. When Eissler interviewed the Deutsch couple in 1954, the first thing Helene Deutsch mentioned was the suicide of Viktor Tausk, which took place thirty-five years before the interview.[1256]

In early 1919, Tausk entered into analysis with Helene Deutsch. It was not an obvious choice. Helene Deutsch was a complete beginner at the time. Tausk had been a member of the Vienna Psychoanalytic Society for ten years, had worked since 1914 as a neurologist in Vienna, regularly gave courses in psychoanalysis, and had published a great deal. His psychoanalytic career had been interrupted for a time by the war and was resumed in 1918. Tausk had wanted to be analysed by Freud, but Freud declined and referred the experienced Tausk to the beginner Helene Deutsch. Roazen has written about the entire affair in his biography of Helene Deutsch, based on her notes and hundreds of hours of interviews.[1257]

According to Helene Deutsch, Freud had explained to her why he did not want to analyse Tausk. He was afraid that Tausk would pick up his ideas and then think they were his own. Freud therefore referred Tausk on, insulting him deeply by sending him to Deutsch. Why did Tausk accept this, nevertheless?

The possibility cannot be excluded that, in his despair, he phantasied about a via-via analysis. The consequence was that Helene Deutsch's analysis with Freud was largely about Tausk. Much of what Tausk discussed with her was then discussed in her analysis with Freud. In his analysis, Tausk talked mainly about Freud.

Not much was left of Deutsch's own analysis. After three months, Freud put an end to the whole situation. He was of the opinion that Tausk had caused a disturbance to Deutsch's analysis. Freud, therefore, clearly blamed Tausk for causing the problem. According to Freud, Tausk had agreed to enter into analysis with Helene Deutsch because, through her, he could communicate with Freud.

Freud gave Helene Deutsch the choice between stopping with Tausk and continuing her analysis with Freud or stopping with Freud. Helene Deutsch opted for the former and stopped the analysis of Tausk in late March 1919. On 3 July 1919, Tausk killed himself.[1258]

In the autumn of 1919, Freud ended the analysis of Helene Deutsch, so that he could analyse the Wolf Man instead.[1259] Freud fairly often did this, stopping an analysis suddenly after a year, but, in this case, it was extremely unfortunate. Helene Deutsch was hugely disappointed and felt rejected.[1260]

Roazen wrote that Helene Deutsch felt strikingly little responsibility for the whole situation with Tausk. She blamed Freud, although, at the time when it happened, Deutsch was thirty-four years old. When she said to Freud in retrospect that Tausk might still be alive if she had not sent him away, Freud insisted she had made the right choice, in that she had chosen for herself. Perhaps Freud was trying to prevent her from feeling guilty, thought Roazen. Her reaction to Eissler's interview, however, suggests that Tausk's death continued to haunt her.

There was something else, too. Helene Deutsch always continued to describe herself as a pupil, a follower and admirer of Freud. If she did feel any anger at the misery Freud caused her, then she never discussed it any further. Her analysis with Abraham, which seems to have gone better than her analysis with Freud, was marginalised. This indicates that the negative transference in the analysis with Freud did not come to the fore and her idealisation of him continued. Freud ended her analysis before she could become angry with him.[1261]

The question is whether Freud might have avoided the negative transference on other occasions as well. It was a complaint also made by Ferenczi.

Helene Deutsch's analysis with Abraham

In early 1923, Helene Deutsch went to Berlin for a second analysis, this time with Abraham. A fair amount is known about the analysis because the letters Helene Deutsch wrote to her husband, Felix, in Vienna at the time have survived.[1262] One difficulty is that she did not date her letters but wrote merely, for example, "Tuesday at four thirty", or "Sunday afternoon".

Helene Deutsch was troubled by depression.[1263] Eduard Hitschmann said later that she was manic–depressive, and that was why she entered into analysis.[1264] This is far from unlikely, given the strong mood swings evident in the letters. In the autumn of 1923, they were gloomy and cheerful by turns, and she wrote of herself, "I am experiencing distinctly circular states of mind—perhaps in order to appear more interesting to Papa-Abraham".

Helene Deutsch travelled to Berlin with her six-year-old son, Martin. The little boy was devoted to his father and the separation was very hard for him. After the summer holidays of 1923, Martin was, therefore, due to stay with his father, Felix. Helene Deutsch took a couple of patients with her for analysis, to cover her living expenses. Berlin's psychoanalytic community took care of her. Schmideberg met her at the station and wore himself out in ensuring everything was to her liking. Melanie Klein visited. Happel and Smeliansky did what they could for her.[1265] The van Ophuijsens lived nearby and had a little boy of about the same age as Martin.[1266]

Deutsch started her analysis with Abraham almost immediately, six times a week. At first, she would travel from her home near the Tiergarten in central Berlin to Grünewald, the suburb where Abraham lived. It took three hours every morning, including the travelling time. Her chambermaid looked after Martin. Later, she rented a home close to Abraham.

Right from the start, Deutsch wrote about her analysis:

> Abraham is very intelligent and understands well what is going on, we are already involved in the most intensive work in the analysis. I am in a strange state of seclusion á deux with the analyst, so don't be surprised, my love, if my letters become short, lacking in content and impersonal—every little bit of psychic energy must go into this—...[1267]

In one of the next letters she wrote, "It's tremendous with Abraham!! Entirely objective, no transference befuddlement".[1268]

In that same letter, Deutsch also wrote that she was in urgent need of money and had already borrowed 100,000 marks from Abraham. All through the correspondence Helene Deutsch mentioned the rapid devaluation of the currency. She gave a good impression of how this affected the daily life of the analysts in Berlin. Naturally, it is impossible to reconstruct the course of her analysis accurately from the letters, but it is possible to draw certain conclusions. There was very soon a powerful positive transference, such that Deutsch thought Abraham wonderful and became completely engrossed in her analysis with him (state of seclusion *à deux*).[1269]

What can we deduce from her letters about Abraham's technique? The fact that she set to work intensively right from the beginning and that Abraham approached the case in that way must mean that he did not begin by watching and waiting but started quite energetically.

The remark that Abraham was entirely objective, without any trouble with transference, is almost certain to have come from Abraham himself. This may indicate that Abraham believed he did not have any problem with countertransference and was entirely objective when carrying out analysis. He probably saw himself as a doctor who made an objective diagnosis and then treated the patient based on that diagnosis.

This is a very different approach from, for example, Eitingon, who wrote to Freud as early as 1912 that with one patient he felt he was skimming the surface, could not get through, and was getting nowhere. He wondered whether something else was wrong with this patient. Here, Eitingon was using his own countertransference in his attempts to clarify what was going on.[1270]

Several letters later, Deutsch wrote, "Such classic technique and tremendous superiority you cannot begin to imagine. It is enough to make one want to retrain, and gives one a keen sense of only now coming to understand Ψ". [1271] This again says something about Abraham's technique, which is that he explained psychoanalysis, as was far from unusual in this period in Berlin. Balint said of his analysis with Sachs, which took place at around the same time, that he gained nothing from it because it was not an analysis at all. The sessions consisted mainly of theoretical explanation.[1272]

In her first period in Berlin, Helene Deutsch went out a lot, because she felt restless. She later called it her coffee house period. She also spent a great deal of time at the Abrahams' house.

Her letters frequently mention evenings with the Abrahams and walks with the Abrahams. In the months that followed her coffee house period, in which she spent much time at home and felt chronically sleepy, she was again with the Abrahams quite regularly.

She wrote about spending an entire Monday afternoon at Abraham's house with Martin, staying for dinner and then going with Abraham to a meeting of the Berlin Psychoanalytic Society. Of a supper she went to with the Abrahams she noted, "Abraham doesn't let any obstacles such situations might throw up get in his way".[1273]

As far as psychoanalytic technique is concerned, this is remarkable. Even in the 1920s, it was known that it was better to avoid personal contact between analyst and analysand, in the patient's own interest. But Helene Deutsch was a regular guest in the Abraham household and Abraham said this caused no disturbance because he did not allow himself to be disturbed by it. It seems as if Abraham did three things at once: analyse, maintain friendly contact, and educate. He apparently saw no problem at all in combining the three. Then a remarkable moment was reached in the analysis, which had been described by Helene Deutsch for some time prior to this as difficult and demanding. All she could do was cry:

> Following an admittedly unpleasant but not harrowing experience, I found myself in a state of continuous, compulsory crying for eight consecutive days. I cried my eyes out every night, so much that the linen was soaked; I cried when I was eating, on the streets, during analysis. The situation became so serious that A. clearly saw it as his duty to look after me, often inviting me and acting as a kindly, understanding father. During today's session this whole to-do dissolved into a final frenetic sob when I recalled father heartlessly throwing me out of the room for the first time. At the time I had braved the situation without crying, and by adopting a "I don't care a jot" pose. It conjured up a chain-reaction of similar experiences which rose to the surface, culminating in this last one that, having been brought to the fore in the analysis, led to a liberating release from all those dreadful feelings.

> Today, I feel as if I'd been given a gift: happy, calm, well.[1274]

To judge by this letter, it was a reaction to what in the analysis was experienced as a rejection. Roazen wrote in his biography that the analysis of Deutsch by Abraham failed because she was insufficiently detached from Freud and because Freud had told Abraham that Helene Deutsch's marriage must not be put at risk.[1275]

The question is whether this analysis, despite circumstances that seem odd by today's standards, did actually fail. First, Helene Deutsch revived, threw off her work disorder, and became extremely productive, writing articles, giving lectures, and holding courses (Deutsch, 1925). After her return to Vienna in 1924, she laid the foundations for a training institution based on the Berlin model. In 1925, she became the first president of the psychoanalytic institute and she remained in that position until she left for the USA in 1934. Second, Abraham generally operated quite independently of Freud. The fit of weeping suggests, however, that some other difficulty was involved in the analysis.

It was after a rejection that Helene Deutsch could not stop crying. In her own family she had been a latecomer, the fourth child of a famous lawyer. She adored her father and hated her mother, who would have preferred to have a son.[1276] This was a far-reaching division into good and bad. Deutsch adored both Freud and Abraham. It seems possible that the suicide of Tausk and the rejection by Freud that followed it became a handicap. She and Abraham connected that great fit of weeping after a rejection with a rejection by her father. What came to the surface in Helene Deutsch was that she had been thrown out of the room by her father in a loveless way—by the father she so adored—just as she was "thrown" out of analysis by Freud. But neither Helene Deutsch nor Abraham made the link with the situation with Freud. Helene Deutsch adored her teacher Freud and does not seem to have allowed in any other feelings. Yet, she was in analysis with an analyst who also adored Freud and who was also barely able to let any other feelings in. Did they discuss the Tausk affair during her analysis? Could it have been brought up in this constellation? The fact that the name Tausk does not occur once in her letters to Felix is an ominous sign. The entire problem seems to have been smothered by Abraham's motherly, rather than fatherly, solicitude.

Roazen's description of Helene Deutsch's stay in Berlin raises certain questions.[1277] He writes that Abraham said to Helene Deutsch that he had written to Freud and to Felix to say that he could not analyse her because he found her too nice.[1278] Nothing of the kind can be found in the letters. But if Abraham did indeed say such a thing, that would mean he recognised and thought about his own countertransference. This would be remarkable, and entirely at odds with his frequent friendly association with Helene Deutsch, which, in Abraham's view, could do no harm because he would not be troubled by transference. Roazen also wrote, "Her original transference to Freud was such that she could never seem to develop enough of an emotional attachment to Abraham to succeed in changing herself as she might have wished".

The letters give a different impression altogether. They tend to evoke surprise that there was such strong transference right from day one. Deutsch wrote about Abraham continually, about how wonderful he was and how difficult the analysis was. There is so much about Abraham in them that, for Felix Deutsch, the letters cannot have been easy to take. When Abraham starts using the analysis partly to guide Helene Deutsch in the writing of articles and the giving of lectures, the powerful transference and the intensity of the analysis remain.

Then Abraham made a cardinal error, one that occurred frequently in those days. In the summer of 1923, the analysis of Helene Deutsch had not yet been completed. It was scheduled to resume after the summer. Abraham told her they would not start again until 1 October, because in September he needed her place for another patient.

So, she was pushed aside once more. Helene Deutsch's reaction was profound. She had a crisis in the summer and became depressed. There is a heartrending letter from her to Felix in which she writes that she had been planning to see Abraham, somewhere abroad, but did not succeed in meeting up with him. She was totally at sea.[1279]

The analysis with Abraham continued in October 1923, but the letters show no sign of the powerful transference of earlier in the year. In those years no one knew that in psychoanalysis there was such a thing as separation anxiety.[1280]

The Ego and the Id

In late April 1923, Freud's *The Ego and the Id* was published. It caused a revolution in psychoanalytic theory.[1281] In it, Freud wrote that the basic starting point of psychoanalysis was the distinction in the psyche between conscious and unconscious. There was also another distinction to be made, which was between id, ego, and superego, the so-called structural model. The id is unconscious, the ego is partly conscious, the superego is largely unconscious.

In writing this book, Freud was powerfully inspired by Groddeck, who continually stressed that we are steered by unknown and uncontrollable forces.[1282] Freud located them in the id, towards which the ego, in effect, behaves passively. The individual, Freud wrote, consists of a psychic, unconscious id, which we cannot fathom, with, on its surface, the ego, developed from the system of perception. The ego, he claims, is largely pre-conscious and, to a very small degree, conscious, whereas what is repressed is found in the id. The ego is part of the id, but it is changed by the influence of the outside world, by perception. It has a mediating role between the id and the outside world.

Freud compared the ego to a rider who has to control the superior strength of a horse, with the difference that the rider tries to do this using his own strength, whereas the ego has to work with strength borrowed from the id, of which it is part. Just as the rider often has to resort to guiding the horse to where the horse wants to go, so the ego does the bidding of the id, pretending that the will of the ego is in charge, whereas in fact the will of the id is being followed.

It was, above all, the description of the superego that changed the course of psychoanalytic theory. The idea of the introjection of the lost love-object, as described by Freud in "Mourning and melancholia", is given a far more general interpretation in *The Ego and the Id* and far greater importance is attributed to it. Freud now argued that it played a role in every loss of a love-object and was of great importance in the formation of the ego. Through the abandonment of the parents as the love-object in the oedipal phase and through the identification with, and introjection of, the parents as love-object, the superego is created. The superego contains the conscience and ideals of the ego and continually expresses the influence of the parents. The tension between the demands of the conscience and the performances of the ego are experienced by the individual as feelings of guilt.

The fourth part of *The Ego and the Id* is the most controversial. It concerns the two kinds of drives, the sex drive and the death drive. Sadism is seen as a representation of the latter.

In the fifth and final part of the book, Freud describes how the ego is largely formed by identifications and how the earliest identifications behave as a separate authority in the ego and come to stand in opposition to the ego as a superego. The superego retains throughout life the ability to oppose the ego and to restrain it. Because the superego originates in the unconscious Oedipus complex, it is itself unconscious.

Freud distinguished between conscious and unconscious guilt feelings. In compulsive neurosis and in melancholy, the sense of guilt is conscious, but in compulsive neurosis the source of the sense of guilt is unconscious. In hysteria, the sense of guilt is unconscious.

Flügel described the immense importance of the unconscious character of the super-ego.[1283] It gives an important basis to the change in the practical approach of psychoanalysis from the treatment of symptoms to the analysis of the resistances. This also explains the unconscious need for punishment that is one of the most powerful resistances to improvement during analysis. Flügel thought that the great cruelty that can be displayed by the superego, for example in extreme moral behaviour, ought to find a certain satisfaction in the id.

Freud regarded it as remarkable that the more someone restricts his aggression towards the outside world, the more restrictive and, therefore, aggressive becomes his superego.

What were the reactions to Freud's new work at the time? A series of reviews appeared in medical journals, in a journal about sexology, and in the newspapers. Some were positive and some negative.[1284] There were no reviews of it in the *Zeitschrift für Psychoanalyse* or in *Imago*, however, and the review in the *International Journal* was four years in coming, appearing in 1927, shortly after the translation was published.[1285] So, at first, there was no response in journals within psychoanalytic circles. This was remarkable, since both books by Abraham, in 1924 and 1925, were reviewed promptly, as were *The Trauma of Birth* by Rank and *The Development of Psychoanalysis*, co-authored by Ferenczi and Rank.[1286]

There are a number of possible reasons why the response of the profession itself was so long delayed. They have to do both with the book and with all the things that distracted attention from it.

First, this was Freud's most difficult work so far. Some parts were unfathomable and extremely abstract. It is more than possible that it took quite a long time for the contemporary generation of psychoanalysts to comprehend it sufficiently to be able to write about it. Ferenczi had been sent parts I and II before publication and made a few remarks about it in a letter, about the unconscious sense of guilt, among other things, and about the effort required to read the book attentively.[1287] In the autumn of 1923, he was asked to write a review for the *Zeitschrift*. Ferenczi accepted the commission but no review by him was published.

Freud had told the publisher to send copies to all the members of the committee. Jones received the book on 1 May and he wrote to Freud on 2 July 1923 that he was reading it with enormous interest but that he would have to read it a second time and think about it before being able to comment.[1288]

That it was hard for Jones to fathom was confirmed by a short article he wrote in 1926, three years later, which demonstrates that the concept of the superego, which had such a prominent place in *The Ego and the Id*, raised a series of questions in his mind.[1289]

We know of no reaction from Eitingon, but the book was published in the period when he did no work.

Second, several weeks after the book came out, Freud became seriously ill and, in the course of the year, it became clear that he had cancer.

Third, the committee encountered huge internal problems and fell apart.

Fourth, Rank departed, first temporarily and then for good.

What Abraham thought of *The Ego and the Id* is not clear. He thanked Freud as follows, "I am just reading your book. I still have to thank you for sending it to me. I think it shows evidence of such an unchanged sprightliness that can only delight all of us who are attached to you".[1290] Abraham clearly felt it showed Freud had lost none of his vigour. He responded merely to the fact that Freud was still able to write such a book. On 31 October 1923, Radó and Sachs gave a lecture to the Berlin Psychoanalytic Society with the title "Die Probleme in Freuds *Das Ich und das Es*" (The problems in Freud's *The Ego and the Id*). Radó was in analysis with Abraham at the time and there is a chance that not only Radó, but Abraham, recognised certain problems. Unfortunately, it seems the lecture was never published.

The lack of a reaction by Abraham to the content of the book is not particularly strange given the fact that most of those around Freud responded only long afterwards. Abraham did not really live long enough to integrate the work into his own. His articles barely refer to it at all, but articles by him that were published after April 1923 were all compiled long before. That spring Abraham was entirely caught up in putting the finishing touches to his libido theory.

Still, given that Abraham thought of "Mourning and melancholia" that a theory had been put forward in it that was not yet sufficiently supported by evidence from clinical practice, there can be no doubt that he must have thought this was even more true of *The Ego and the Id*.

Aside from Sachs, it was mainly the young talents in Berlin who busied themselves with *The Ego and the Id* in 1923 and 1924. In Vienna in October 1923, Reik gave a lecture on unconscious feelings of guilt.[1291]

Over time, *The Ego and the Id* became one of the central paradigms of psychoanalytic theory.[1292] The development it went through in the psychology of the ego is interesting, also from a historical perspective. Ego psychology, with Heinz Hartmann as its most important representative, is based on *The Ego and the Id*, claiming to develop Freud's theory further, although, in fact, it developed a new theory that departs considerably from Freud's.

Ego psychology set the tone for psychoanalytic theory in the USA in the period from around 1945 to the 1980s.[1293] The most important representatives of ego psychology all fled continental Europe in the Nazi period: Ernst Kris, Rudolf Loewenstein, Edith Jacobson, Margaret Mahler, Annie Reich, Kurt Eissler, Max Schur, and David Rapaport. Anna Freud was in London.

Although they all had to flee house and home, the Second World War and Hitler are not mentioned in their writings. Bergmann wrote that this seems to have been a necessary defence for them. If they were to adapt to life in the USA, then it was essential that they did not occupy themselves with what was happening in Europe.

Another thing that is all but absent in the work of the ego psychologists—and this is entirely in line with the above—was the id. There was no talk of a horse, an id so strong that the ego had little choice but to pretend to be leading the horse when in reality it could only follow.

The ego psychologists wrote about neutralising drives, about the ego as an authority that above all regulated adaptation. It was certainly not an ego that was fairly passively wedged between an id and a strict superego, but instead an autonomous ego. They concerned themselves with the analysis of resistance. Theirs was an ego that is not at the mercy of an id. The ego psychologists actually created a theory that was diametrically opposed to Freud. As part of their resistance to the Second World War, they constructed a theory that claimed the ego, if sufficiently reinforced, could be the master of the id.

Abraham's way of thinking seems instead to have been carried on by Melanie Klein, who was opposed tooth and nail by the ego psychologists.

A congress in Oxford and a visit from Jones

In early 1923, Jones had arranged for Abraham to speak at the international congress for psychology that was to take place in Oxford on 27 July.

A couple of days before it began, on 25 July, Abraham attended a special meeting arranged for him at the British Psychoanalytical Society, where Jones gave a speech in his honour. On 2 July 1923, Abraham became an honorary member of the British Psychoanalytical Society.

The title of Abraham's lecture in Oxford was "Psychoanalytic views on some characteristics of early infantile thinking".[1294] He delivered it from memory. Hedwig attended the congress with him and afterwards they stayed with Jones. They greatly enjoyed their time as his guests. On 7 August 1923, Abraham wrote an extremely enthusiastic letter of thanks.[1295] It was the start of a close friendship. Together they took trips through England, including the South Downs, the area of chalk hills south of London. They went to Elsted, to the country home of the Joneses in West Sussex, where Abraham met his children, Gwenith and Mervyn. They toured Sussex and visited London and Jones' house at 42 York Terrace.

The Abrahams had an exhausting journey home. Hedwig suffered from seasickness and then grew very uncomfortable on the train because of the heat and the endless delays at the border. They stayed in Berlin for two days and then travelled on to Munich, where they found their children extremely content. The whole family made a twelve-hour journey to their holiday destination of St Christina and told each other their travel experiences. St Christina was a village in the South Tyrol, where they had a wonderful time. They stayed in a good hotel in beautiful surroundings and the weather was excellent.

The committee was due to meet in late August near Lavarone, where Freud was staying. Abraham proposed they should gather at San Cristoforo on Lake Caldonazzo.

Freud seriously ill and in mourning

In the summer of 1923, there was trouble within the committee. A number of factors were involved, but the most important was undoubtedly the fact that Freud was unwell. The indomitable Freud, who in Hildesheim in 1921 had shown he had more energy than any of them, had become seriously ill and soon turned out to have cancer.

Freud had spent the second half of 1922 working on *The Ego and the Id*. In April 1923, the book was published and that same month Freud underwent an operation on a swelling in his mouth.[1296] Freud had asked Felix Deutsch to look at the swelling. Deutsch suspected it was cancer but kept that to himself. Freud did not have the swelling investigated any further, although it is clear from his letters that he was certainly aware that something serious might be diagnosed. On top of that, Freud's favourite grandchild, Heinerle, the youngest son of his late daughter Sophie, died of tuberculosis on 19 June 1923. A few days before Heinerle's death, on 11 June 1923, when it was clear that the little boy could not be saved, Freud wrote to his Hungarian friends Katá and Lajos Lévy: "I find this loss very hard to bear. I don't think I have ever experienced such grief; perhaps my own sickness contributes to the shock. I work out of sheer necessity; fundamentally everything has lost its meaning for me".[1297]

The response of the members of the committee to Freud's illness was intense. Eitingon, who had been in close contact with Freud since the First World War, had visited him a great deal and continually supported him, suddenly failed to appear. From 3 to 7 May, shortly after the operation, he had stayed with Freud and after that nothing was heard from him for months and even in the months after that very little.[1298] There is every indication that Eitingon could not bear Freud's illness. Anna Freud, who was very fond of Eitingon and had been corresponding with him for some years, took great offence at this. She had the impression that he had been avoiding her since her father became ill.[1299] She wrote to Lou Salomé on 23 April 1924, a year after Freud's first operation:

Eitingon was in Vienna for two days. I barely saw him, however, and did not speak to him at all. He is obviously avoiding me, not only now but in the summer in Lavrone as well and during his previous visit in May. He probably doesn't want to talk about papa's illness. I don't know. But it's not very friendly and I'm angry with him. Justifiably so, don't you think?[1300]

The second to react strongly was Rank. His break with Freud, examined in Chapter Twenty-six, is often associated with Freud's illness, but the pressure on Rank over the years must also have had an effect.

CHAPTER TWENTY-FIVE

Innovative work

A Short Study of the Development of the Libido
and Psycho-analytical Studies on Character-formation

I n 1924 and 1925, Abraham published two books that are generally regarded as his main
work.[1301] Both were the fruits of years of preparation. Prior to their publication, Abraham
gave lectures based on them. He spoke about *A Short Study of the Development of the Libido*
both at the congress in Berlin in 1922 and to the Berlin Psychoanalytic Society on 27 March
1923.[1302]

On 1 April 1923, Abraham wrote to Freud that his lecture to the Berlin Psychoanalytic
Society had been very well received.[1303] His *A Short Study of the Development of the Libido*
completed the charting of the libidinous organisations. It concerned a theory originating with
Freud, who had worked on it along with several members of the committee. Efforts to chart the
libidinous organisations took place only after 1913. First the anal phase was described by Freud
and Jones and then the oral phase by Freud and Abraham. In 1923, Freud presented the phallic phase. Abraham then concluded the series in 1924 with a fully worked out theory of the
development of the libido.[1304]

A Short Study of the Development of the Libido is in two parts. Part one describes manic–
depressive conditions and the pregenital developmental stages of the libido. Part two focuses
on the development of object-love in the various phases. The book was a further extrapolation
from earlier articles by Abraham on depression, starting with *Segantini* (1911). Next came
Abraham's essay on manic depression of 1912, with a strong emphasis on a disposition to
hatred that paralyses the ability to love.[1305] Then he published "The first pregenital stage of
the libido" in 1916, in which depression is understood as a regression to the cannibalistic stage
with the desire to incorporate, devour, and destroy. In 1917, Freud published "Mourning and

melancholia", in which he made some use of Abraham's findings. In it, Freud describes how patients who lose their love-object absorb it into themselves by introjection, so that their self-reproaches are, in truth, aimed at the lost object.

The earliest developmental phases of childhood and how they relate to depression

Freud's *Three Essays on the Theory of Sexuality* was first published in 1905. The book was expanded several times and Abraham elaborated upon additional material found in the 1915 edition, in which Freud described early childhood development. Freud called the earliest phase of childhood development the cannibalistic phase, the phase in which the consumption of food has not yet been separated from sexual activity and both have as their aim the incorporation of the object.[1306]

Abraham now divided this into an earlier and a later oral phase.

The earlier oral phase is that of the suckling infant. According to Abraham, this phase is preambivalent and objectless. It is the stage of auto-eroticism. The libido of the child is bound up with the act of suckling. This is an incorporation that does not cancel out the existence of the other. In this phase, the child knows no object outside itself. There is no distinction between self and object.

The later oral phase, also called the oral–sadistic phase, would then, according to Abraham, be the cannibalistic phase. It starts at the time when the child grows teeth and can bite. Biting is the primal form of our sadistic impulses. In this phase, the child is aware of an object outside itself, but its sole aim is to incorporate it. This phase is all about the total incorporation of the object. It is a phase in which ambivalence occurs. Being attracted by the object immediately presents the danger of incorporation, of the destruction of the object.

Abraham connected this phase with the melancholy seen in depression. It is the stage towards which the melancholic regresses. Melancholy conceals within it ambivalence in its worst and most primitive form.

Abraham's book took as its starting point the idea that neurotic problems in adults are connected with the phase of early childhood in which patients have become stuck or to which they have regressed. To regress is to revert to an earlier stage of libido development and it can have all kinds of causes, such as defence against a psychic conflict, illness, exhaustion, and so on.

Abraham's ideas about the relationship between melancholy and the oral phase had a great deal of influence. From the time his study about the melancholic who unconsciously wants to devour and destroy his object was published in 1916, the relationship between oral desires and depression occupied an important place in the psychoanalytic literature of depression.[1307]

In both the cannibalistic phase and the early anal phase, the real relationship with the object is nullified, in the cannibalistic phase by the devouring of the object and in the early anal phase by its expulsion.

The anal phase and the relationship with the object

Abraham did not find it easy to distinguish between the manic depression that he associated with the cannibalistic phase and the compulsive neurosis that belonged to the next phase. They have a great deal in common. Manic–depressive patients fairly often exhibit compulsive behaviour in the relatively calm intermediate periods. Moreover, both phases are characterised by a marked ambivalence towards the object.

There is an important difference between the anal phase and the oral phase. In the oral phase, the object is eaten and, thereby, given up; in the later anal phase, it is clung to. In each phase a specific erogenous zone dominates: in the oral phase, the mouth, in the anal phase, the anus. This latter phase is strongly connected with sadism, although sadism also has a prominent place in the second oral phase. Abraham wrote that, in his analyses, it was confirmed time and again that in the anal phase the desired person is regarded as property. This meant that the person was equated with the most primitive form of property known to man: a certain body product, excreta. Because, in this phase, the ambivalence of the emotions was still unbridled, the positive attitude of the individual towards the object is expressed through the holding on to that property, while a negative attitude towards the object is expressed as a rejection of that property. So, the loss of the object means that, in compulsive neurosis, there is a danger of the expulsion of the object in the sense of excreta.

In Abraham's experience, there were quite a few neurotic patients who reacted anally to every loss, whether a bereavement or a material loss. Depending on their unconscious disposition, they suffered either from diarrhoea or from constipation. A message saying that someone had died quite often led to an urgent need to defecate, as if all of the intestines needed to be emptied at once.

He also described the example of a woman with a very strong anal disposition who was unable to throw away things that had become unusable. From time to time, however, she had the urge to rid herself of such things. She had now found a way of doing so. She would go from her house to a nearby wood. On leaving the house, she stuck the point of the item concerned under the strings of her apron, at the back. While walking through the wood, she would then lose the item from behind. So, to be rid of something, she had to drop it from the back of her body.

In Abraham's view, the keeping and controlling that were so characteristic of the anal phase made clear the degree to which the anal and sadistic urges reinforced each other within it. The extreme orderliness that accompanied this particular phase revealed an extreme lust for power. Things are subjected to violence; they are squeezed into a certain system that is adhered to meticulously. Fairly often, other people are forced to adjust to this system.

One good example is the cleaning compulsion of a neurotic housewife. She often behaves as if not a single item can be left alone. The entire house is turned upside down and other people are forced to adjust to the system. In markedly compulsive characters of the kind seen in housewife neurosis and in neurotically applied bureaucracy, both a lust for power and sadism become plainly visible.

The anal–sadistic phase is about both expulsion (of excreta) and holding on. Abraham divided the anal phase into two. There was the phase in which object-hostile destruction and loss dominated, which he saw as the earlier phase, and the phase in which holding on and controlling dominated, which came later.

Regression to the later of the two anal phases makes it possible for the compulsive neurotic to stay in contact with the object. Often, a sublimation of the sadistic and anal tendencies in quieter periods make it possible to relate to the object in such a way that, examined superficially, it seems normal. There is a boundary between the two anal phases. Above that boundary, it is possible to stay in contact with the object; something like a primitive stage of object-love is feasible. Below the boundary, contact with the object is lost. This breaking off of contact leads to a further regression in the direction of melancholia. According to Abraham, the boundary between neurotic and psychotic lies here, between the two anal phases.

Object-loss and introjection in normal mourning and in abnormal mental states

Abraham's field of study was manic depression, in which three phases can be distinguished: a depressive phase, a relatively quiet intermediate phase, and a manic phase. He wanted to discover what prompted melancholia, to enquire into the depressive phase or "that event which Freud has called the 'loss of object'—and into the process, so closely allied to it, of the introjection of the lost love-object".[1308]

Abraham's choice of words is striking because of the elements of Freud's argument that he omitted. Freud wrote about the ego, about the withdrawal of libido after an object-loss,

> But the free libido was not displaced on to another object; it was withdrawn into the ego. There, however, it was not employed in any unspecified way, but served to establish an *identification* of the ego with the abandoned object. Thus the shadow of the object fell upon the ego, and the latter could henceforth be judged by a special agency, as though it were an object, the forsaken object. In this way an object-loss was transformed into an ego-loss and the conflict between the ego and the loved person into a cleavage between the critical activity of the ego and the ego as altered by identification.[1309]

Abraham did mention the ego, but he said nothing about what happened in the ego. He said something else, however, which was that up to that point a thorough basis for Freud's theory, in the form of sufficient case histories, was lacking. This critical remark about "Mourning and melancholia", which Abraham made almost in passing, was entirely in line with the thinking of his old teacher, Bleuler.

Abraham and Freud had different ways of working when developing psychoanalytic theory. Abraham would expand upon a theory based on a series of cases analysed by him. Freud would extend his theory based on a further development that was often derived from just one case and was sometimes even a purely theoretical exercise. In his article "Rethinking dissidence and change in the history of pyschoanalysis", Bergmann quoted Ferenczi, who was critical of the fact that Freud's brilliant ideas were usually based on a single case.[1310] Bergmann agreed with what Ferenczi said but did not see it as criticism of Freud. He goes on, rather dogmatically, "In psychoanalysis major discoveries can be made on one particular case". It seems that there were doubts about this in the early phase of psychoanalysis, at any rate in the minds of Bleuler, Abraham, and Ferenczi.

In his chapter about object-loss, Abraham wrote that there was still little material available about normal mourning, because it was simply not a subject in psychoanalysis, but that he had now by chance experienced a process of normal mourning. This is interesting because he goes on to describe what is clearly the grief shown by Radó for his wife and child during his analysis with Abraham.[1311] The gist of what Abraham writes is this: one of my analysands was struck by the misfortune that during his treatment his wife became seriously ill. She was expecting their first child. Her serious illness eventually necessitated the interruption of the pregnancy by caesarean section. My analysand, who was called to his wife's side urgently, arrived after the operation had taken place. That operation did not, however, save the life of either his wife or the premature infant. After a while, the analysand returned to Berlin. The continuation of the analysis and one dream in particular left no room for doubt that the painful loss was followed by an introjection of an oral–cannibalistic nature.

One of the most striking phenomena in my analysand consisted of an aversion to eating that lasted for weeks. It was in striking contrast to his usual way of behaving and reminiscent of the refusal of food by melancholics. One day, the aversion to eating stopped and that evening my analysand enjoyed a copious meal. In the night that followed, he dreamed that he was attending the autopsy of his recently deceased wife. The dream had two contrasting scenes. In one scene, the dissected body parts grew back together, the dead woman began to show signs of life, and the dreamer caressed her, deliriously happy. In the other scene, a change took place during the autopsy and the corpse made the dreamer think of a slaughtered animal at a butcher's shop.

Abraham interpreted the dreams as follows. The autopsy in the dream linked up with the operation twice. In one part of the dream, it was connected with the re-experiencing of the deceased, whereas the other part of the dream involved cannibalistic associations. In the associations made by the dreamer, it was striking that his wife's corpse caused him to think of the meat dish he had consumed the evening before. Abraham saw this as a clear example of a dream in which "just like" was expressed. Twice the same dream, but with a different outcome. He saw it as a sign that part of the work of grieving had been carried out. The real, extremely painful loss had been given a sequel with the introjection of the loved person in an oral–cannibalistic manner. The first half of the dream was connected with the raising up of the loved object in the ego, the second half of the dream was linked with the way in which this happened: in an oral–cannibalistic manner. Mourning provides comfort; the love-object is not lost, because I now carry it within me and can never lose it again. This is in line with the course of depressive illness.

This chapter about object-loss and grieving contains quite a few autobiographical elements. The most obvious of them is the death of Abraham's father in 1915 and his reaction to it by means of an identification with, and introjection of, his father, such that Abraham's hair suddenly became as white as his father's hair.[1312]

It also contains a case history of a man who, as a small boy, was his parents' favourite but who, because of his mother's profound grief, suddenly lost his most important love-object. It happened to Abraham himself when he was two years old. In the case history, the little boy turns to his father as a love-object and after that feels the homosexual attraction towards him exhibited by older boys. Whether this was also an autobiographical element is not entered into by Abraham.

In 1968, Maria Torok wrote "Maladie du deuil et fantasme du cadavre exquis" (The fantasm of the exquisite cadaver).[1313] She began that article with a remarkable piece of correspondence between Abraham and Freud from 1922, which is reproduced below. This correspondence took place in a period in which Abraham was continually working on the similarities between mourning and manic depression. Abraham wrote the following to Freud on 13 March 1922:

> The taking in of the love-object is very striking in my cases. I can produce very nice material for this concept of yours, revealing the process in all its detail. In this connection I have a small request—for an offprint of "Mourning and Melancholia", which would be extremely helpful to me in my work. Many thanks in anticipation.
>
> One brief comment on this piece of work! You, dear Professor, state that you miss in the course of normal mourning a process that would correspond to the swing-over from melancholia to mania. I think, however, that I could identify such a process, without knowing whether this reaction is regularly found. My impression is that a fair number of people show an increase in libido some time after a bereavement. It shows itself in heightened sexual need and appears quite often to lead, e.g., to conception shortly after a bereavement. Sometime at your convenience I should like to know what you think about this and whether you can confirm this observation. The increase in libido some time after "object-loss" would seem to be a good addition to the parallel between mourning and melancholia.[1314]

Freud answered,

> Dear Friend,
>
> After more than a fortnight I decide to reread your kind private letter and discover your request for a reprint, which for some reason made no impact on me when I received it.
>
> I plunge with pleasure into the abundance of your scientific insights and intentions, only I wonder why you do not take into account at all my last suggestion about the nature of mania after melancholia (in the Mass Psychology). Might that be the motivation for my forgetting about the "Mourning and Melancholia"? For analysis, no absurdity is impossible. I would still have felt like discussing all these things—particularly with you—but no possibility of writing about them. In the evening I am lazy, and above all there is the urgent "business" correspondence, cancelling lectures, journeys, collaborations, and the like, which stands in the way of a decent exchange of ideas with one's friends.[1315]

To which Abraham wrote back,

> Berlin-Grünewald, 2 May 1922
>
> Dear Professor,
>
> ... Your letter of 30 March is still waiting for a reply, while I have already thanked you for the reprint of "Mourning and Melancholia". I fully understand your forgetting it. Your failure in

sending the paper I asked for was meant to indicate that I should first of all study the other source (Mass Psychology). Now, I am quite familiar with its contents concerning the subject of mania and melancholia, but, in spite of going through it once again, I cannot see where I went wrong. I can find no mention anywhere of a parallel in *normal* cases, i.e. the onset of a reaction state after mourning that can be compared to mania (after melancholia). I only know from you remark in "Mourning and M." that you *miss* something of that kind. And I referred to this in my comment. The increase in libido *after* mourning would be fully analogous to the "feast" of the manic. But I have not found this parallel from normal life in that section of "Mass Ψ" where the feast is discussed. Or have I been so struck by blindness that I am unable to see the actual reference?[1316]

and Freud answered,

Vienna

28 May 1922

Dear Friend,

Still with Eitingon's assistance, I have realised to my amusement that I completely misunderstood you through no fault of yours. You were looking for a normal example of the transition mel.[ancholia]/mania, and I was thinking of the explanation of the mechanism! Many apologies!

Cordially yours,

Freud[1317]

Why did Freud find this amusing?

Abraham had discovered something exceptional in his analyses, which was that in normal mourning a phenomenon occurred that might be comparable with the "swing-over" into mania in manic depression. Abraham had the impression that shortly after bereavement, many people felt an increased urge to have sex, which regularly led to the conceiving of children. This meant that mourning could swing over into mania in the form of increased sexual desire.

It was this specific point that interested Torok. In her patients, she regularly encountered this increase in sexual desire after bereavement. Her patients had great difficulty disclosing it because of their feelings of guilt and shame: how could you be filled with desire just after a death? Torok wondered why Freud did not go into the matter fully, asking herself what kind of resistance in the face of a clinical fact was going on here. She thought it illustrative of the aversion we experience when investigating mourning, as if such investigation is sacrilege.

Torok also thought that Abraham, because of the absence of any encouragement on the subject from the master, had decided not to work on it any further. In fact, if anything, he played down the scope of his findings. In *A Short Study of the Development of the Libido* it is mentioned, if only briefly.

It is naturally quite possible that the subject met with great resistance on Freud's part, but it seems that more was going on. Freud wrote to Abraham with some irritation, asking why he had not taken account of the mechanism as described in his *Group Psychology and the Analysis of the Ego*.[1318] It was not the first time that Freud had asked Abraham why he had failed to take account of this mechanism.

This point arose in Chapter Fifteen, in connection with Abraham's reaction to "Mourning and melancholia". The mechanisms concerned the identification with the loved and absent object and the splitting of the ego between the ego on the one hand and the ego altered by identification on the other. In "Mass psychology", Freud wrote about cyclical depression, which featured a regularly occurring depression followed by a rather more neutral period and then a manic period. Freud made use of the modern notion that saw such cases as non-psychogenic and also not as the outcome of external causes. This means that Freud presumed cyclical depression was inborn.

Freud also investigated the mechanism. In the manic, the ego and the ego-ideal had, he argued, flowed together so that the patient, in a mood of triumph and profound self-satisfaction, undisturbed by self-criticism, could delight in the falling away of restraints, scruples, and self-reproaches. The misery of the melancholic, according to Freud, was the expression of a severe discord between the two authorities in the ego, a discord in which the ego-ideal could express its condemnation of the ego mercilessly in micromania and self-abasement.[1319] In Freud, a central point is that the narcissistic identification comes about through the relinquishing of the unconscious object cathexis. The object, because in the unconscious it is no longer occupied, is no longer experienced as separate. The ego does not realise that it has ideas and feelings that originate in the object. There is a psychic process, a mechanism, by which the object becomes part of the ego.[1320]

Contribution to the psychogenesis of melancholia

Abraham tried to chart the factors that could lead to melancholia. In the transition from the early to the later oral phase, the child exchanges its conflict-free, pre-ambivalent disposition for an ambivalent and overwhelmingly object-hostile disposition. During the anal phase that follows, the transition from the early to the late anal phase means that the object from that moment on can be spared. Only in the genital phase is it possible to overcome the ambivalences and to take the object for what it is. The earliest object-relationship, which characterises melancholia, the second oral phase, is difficult and discordant. The reaction to object-loss is, in this phase, destruction and expulsion, so that the individual ends up in a depression.

Abraham summed up a number of peculiarities of melancholics. They are far from meek and subservient; rather, they are, to a great degree, a torment to those around them, behaving as if deeply hurt and as if a great injustice has been done to them. They usually have powerful feelings of superiority, which are turned against their family, acquaintances, colleagues, even against humanity as a whole. The doctor treating them feels this very clearly. Abraham described in this context a patient who entered the consulting room in an increasingly haughty pose each time, displaying great scepticism of psychoanalysis. According to Abraham, this disdain was aimed particularly at people who cast doubt on the reality content of the melancholic's ideas.

So, in the melancholic, ego-love and ego-hatred were opposites like overestimation and underestimation of oneself. Often, the melancholic saw himself as the biggest sinner ever and self-hatred, which was, in reality, hatred of the introjected love-object, was experienced as immense. This was the description of melancholia that Abraham gave, but he also wanted to try to offer an explanation for the development of melancholia. He specified a number of possible causes.

First, disenchantment in love. Abraham was convinced that disillusionment in love was the preparatory stage of melancholic depression. In psychoanalysis, he had observed that all fresh outbreaks of the sickness were connected to this disappointment in love. He did not mean unhappiness in love, but an object-loss in early childhood. Later events were experienced as a repeat of the early trauma.

Second, a constitutional factor was important. The inheritance of characteristics of earlier generations certainly played a role in manic depression.

Third, there was a special fixation of the libido on the oral stage of development. All things oral prompt strong desire and every denial in this area evokes a response of great unease. The desire to suck persists. Abnormal pleasure is derived from eating and especially from chewing.

Fourth, there was a profound injury to childhood narcissism through a convergence of disappointments in love. Abraham found in his patients a strikingly similar pattern in the early childhood years. A child that until then had felt itself to be its mother's favourite and imagined it could be confident of her love had experienced a disappointment at her hands that shook it to such a degree that it was barely able to recover. Further experiences of a similar kind convinced the child that the loss was irreparable. There was no alternative female person available. Even the attempt by the child to direct its love towards the father instead was unsuccessful. In the child, the impression therefore arose of complete abandonment. The first attacks of depression were the result of this impression. Abraham concluded that it was because of this course of events that the melancholic continually made fresh attempts to gain love.

Fifth, the great disappointment in love took place before the child had overcome the Oedipus complex. The consequence of this, Abraham argued, was that the oral–sadistic drives remained in force.

Sixth, repetition in later life of the early disappointments led to the onset of depression. The ambivalent emotional disposition with its hostile cannibalistic features was directed mainly against the mother.

The way he describes this process can best be quoted word for word, to give an impression of its intensity and character:

> If we want to realize the full strength of the melancholic's hostility towards his mother, and to understand the particular character of his castration complex, we must keep in mind Stärcke's theory that the withdrawal of the mother's breast is a "primal castration". As the analysis of many of his symptoms shows, the melancholiac wants to revenge himself on his mother for this by castrating her in his turn, either taking away her breasts or her imaginary penis. In his imagination he always chooses biting as the means of doing it, as I have already shown in some of the phantasies produced by such patients. I should like once more to lay stress on the ambivalent character of those phantasies. They involve on the one hand a total or partial incorporation of the mother, that is, an act of positive desire; and on the other, her castration or death, that is, a negative desire tending to her destruction.

> When melancholic persons suffer an unbearable disappointment from their love-object they tend to expel that object as though it were faeces and to destroy it. They thereupon accomplish the act

of introjecting and devouring it—an act which is a specifically melancholic form of narcissistic identification. Their sadistic thirst for vengeance now finds its satisfaction in tormenting the ego—an activity which is in part pleasurable. We have reason to suppose that that period of self-torment lasts until lapse of time and the gradual appeasement of sadistic desires have removed the love-object from the danger of being destroyed. When this has happened the object can, as it were, come out of its hiding-place in the ego. The melancholic can restore it to its place in the outer world.[1321]

These were ground-breaking ideas. Particularly new was the stress on the great importance of the mother–child relationship and the enormous aggression that played a major part in it, along with the influence of early abandonment that continued to be influential far into adult-hood. Here, another aspect came to the fore: not merely the development of the libido and not so much the development of the ego, but the development of the object-relations.

Differences between Abraham's and Freud's theory of depression

It is usual to describe the theories of Freud and Abraham about depression as the classic depression theory. This is to ignore the fact that they were totally different theories.[1322] In her article on Abraham's oral theory, May claimed that Freud's theory was originally the central one until, in 1924, in the period after Freud became ill, three of his pupils published theories of their own. They were Rank, Ferenczi, and Abraham.[1323] A start had been made on Abraham's theory long before, in 1910.

The differences in approach between Abraham and Freud were considerable. In Abraham's, there is a loss suffered in reality, the loss of a really existing object. Freud connects only mourning with a real object. Freud claimed that in depression something had been lost, but it was unclear what that was. So, for Freud, there was no stress at all on what had happened in reality; instead, all the emphasis was placed on what went on in the ego. Abraham referred to a loss of the most important object, the mother, in very early childhood. It was a loss in which at the same time nothing was available that could replace her. The consequence was a sense of total abandonment to which the depression became connected. If an object-loss took place in later life, then it became linked to the early loss. Freud, by contrast, made no mention at all of losses in early childhood.

Entirely new was Abraham's theory that, after teething, from the second oral phase onwards, there were feelings of both love and hatred towards the mother, and he strongly emphasised the hatred. The depressive patient regresses to the second oral stage, he wrote. In the depths of his unconscious, he wants to devour and destroy the object. Freud regarded the oral phase more as a preliminary phase without love or hatred, a time of auto-eroticism and narcissism.[1324] Abraham regarded a sense of guilt about one's own aggression as playing a central role in depression. In Freud's theory, there is no mention of the sense of guilt.[1325]

May stresses that, for Freud, love had a prominent place and aggression was an accompanying phenomenon.[1326] In her description, May comes to a negative value judgement. She concludes that Abraham prompted a development in psychoanalysis in which the entire doings of the patient are seen as object-orientated and as mainly aggressive—as if there were no phase in early childhood and, therefore, in analysis in which the patient is not object-orientated and where there is as yet no love and hate.

In Abraham's theory of depression, aggression certainly plays a far greater role than in Freud's theory of depression, but a further remark is called for here.

Freud published "Mourning and melancholia" in 1917, but he wrote it at the start of the First World War. Shortly after that war, influenced by the unprecedented outbursts of aggression that had taken place and that recurred in the dreams of front-line soldiers, Freud changed his theory. Love and lust were given a smaller place in it and aggression and the death-wish a far larger place.

Freud's depression theory is fairly abstract and he did not develop it any further. It seems that later psychoanalysts took Abraham's depression theory as their starting point, thinking that it had originated with Freud. In present-day psychoanalysis, it is common to identify a link between depression and aggression.[1327] This means that Abraham's theory tends to be followed rather than Freud's.

Development of object love

The second part of *A Short Study of the Development of the Libido* was about object relations. There are two ways to describe the route from early pregenital aims to the genital stage: by starting with the change to the leading erogenous zones or by starting with various kinds of object relations.[1328]

In the description from the perspective of object relations, Abraham's starting point was that neurotic object-relational problems in adults were connected with an early childhood phase in which they had become stuck or to which they had regressed. Object relations in adulthood are coloured by the early childhood physical relationship of the individual to his or her object.[1329] Abraham wrote that the normal development of psychosexuality led to an end result in which the individual was capable of object love. The development in the child is from objectless (auto-eroticism), via love of its own ego as the object to a turn towards the object in the stages that follow. This turn has an ambivalent character for a long time. Ultimately, if the development goes well, it results in a stable adult love relationship in which he or she takes account of the interests of the other and is capable of a genital–sexual relationship.

According to Abraham, the goal of psychoanalysis was to help the individual to reach the adult stage. Anyone who enters into analysis does so because he or she is not living as an adult in a some respect and has remained stuck at an earlier stage.

Abraham developed a table showing these developments (Table 2).

The table shows the psychosexual development of the libido in two directions, on one side with regard to the sexual goal and on the other with regard to the sexual object.

Another element that belongs here is what the inhibition of the drive looks like in the different phases, and the clinical picture that accompanies it. Regression to a certain phase produced a certain clinical picture. To each phase belongs a specific way in which the drive is inhibited. Only the earliest phase is without this inhibition.

The outline that emerges is as follows:

Table 2. Abraham's table illustrating the stages of development of the libido in two directions.

Stages of libidinal organisation		Stages of object love
VI Final genital stage	Object love	Post ambivalent
V Earlier genital phallic stage	Object love with exclusion of genitals	Ambivalent
IV Later anal–sadistic stage	Partial love	Ambivalent
II Earlier anal–sadistic stage	Partial love with incorporation	Ambivalent
II Later oral–sadistic or cannibalistic stage	Narcissism, total incorporation of objects	Ambivalent
I Earlier oral–sadistic or sucking stage	Autoerotism (without object)	Pre-ambivalent

Phase II—The inhibition consists of anxiety. The accompanying clinical presentation is melancholia. Melancholia may also be related to phase I.

Phase III—The inhibition consists of a sense of guilt and the accompanying clinical presentation is paranoia.

Phase IV—Empathy and disgust, and compulsive neurosis.

Phase V—Shame and hysteria.

Phase VI—Free of any clinical presentation.

Abraham saw the insights into the development of object love as given in his table as very much incomplete. They would require far more elaboration yet.

The melancholic regresses to Phase III, to the early anal–sadistic phase. He then continues back into Phase II, the oral–sadistic phase. The serious ambivalence conflicts of this phase give him a great desire for phase I, a longing for the breast, a longing to suckle. Phase I is the phase in which, in Abraham's opinion, the child cannot yet distinguish between itself and the other. It is also the phase in which there is no love–hate relationship.

Abraham also described the phases in between narcissism and object love.

With narcissism in the oral–cannibalistic phase, the individual is entirely focused on him- or herself and strives to incorporate the other, to devour and destroy the other.

In the phases that follow, the sexual goal is to incorporate not the object as a whole but a part of it only. The object can, therefore, largely be spared. The part consumed is often the breast, the penis, or the buttocks.

Abraham saw this phase as characteristic of paranoia. If the paranoid individual loses his or her love-object, there is a desire to incorporate it as a part-object. This does not have to be oral, it can also be imagined as anal. Abraham suspected that in paranoia there was regression to the first anal stage. This partial love with incorporation was again a preliminary stage of the next anal phase, in which the object was spared but seen as property. As indicated above, Abraham located the boundary between psychotic and neurotic between the two anal phases.

Abraham also discussed the phallic phase, in which there is object love with the exclusion of the genitals. He writes that this is characteristic of hysteria and plays a role in frigidity and impotence.

The genital phase, finally, is characterised by the fact that the object-love relates to the entire object. The individual can take account of the interests of the object. There is sympathy.

Fenichel wrote a glowing review of Abraham's *A Short Study of the Development of the Libido* in 1925. He said that Abraham had succeeded splendidly in his attempt to explain certain findings in manic–depressive patients by means of the libido theory. The book offered far more than that, however, since it described facts not hitherto understood and gave them a place in the libido theory.[1330] Later, in 1945, Fenichel wrote about the division into phases of development that it was important to realise that the phases are always relative. They are intended, above all, as a guide. In practice, the phases overlap, gradually merging into each other.[1331]

Abraham developed influential ideas in the field of depression in all the periods in which he worked on the subject. In this final period in 1924, he stressed the traumatic consequences of the loss of the mother as love-object. From 1910 onwards, Abraham emphasised the role of the mother, often to the displeasure of Freud, who laid the stress on the father. Perhaps it might even be better to say that this had been in play since 1908, when Abraham first attended a scientific meeting of the Vienna Psychoanalytic Society and pointed out the importance of the mother's tenderness.

"Psychoanalytic Studies on Personality Development"

Jones was full of praise when he discussed this essay in the *Zeitschrift für Psychoanalyse*.[1332] He actually called it a masterpiece.

Abraham wanted to supplement the generally accepted idea about the formation of character—that it is partly the product of innate dispositions and partly determined by the environment, in which upbringing occupies a special place—with a psychoanalytic view. He wrote that psychoanalytic research had added the following: aspects of childhood sexuality that can no longer occur in adult life lie at the root of certain traits of character. Anal eroticism, for example, partly continues to function in the adult sexual life, is partly sublimated, and is partly converted into character traits. These anal contributions to character development ensure, for example, that an individual is capable of adjusting to the demands of the environment concerning hygiene and cleanliness. Abraham kept the definition of character fairly broad: character encompasses the entirety of impulsive reactions by the individual to community life.

Abraham's study on the formation of character is in three sections. The first, which offers additions to the doctrine of the anal character, is discussed in Chapter Twenty-one. The second is about the contribution of oral eroticism to the formation of character. The third section concerns the formation of character in the genital stage of development.

In the infant stage, there is an intensive experience of desire bound up with suckling. The infant is not concerned purely with food; the mouth is experienced as an erogenous zone. The striking thing about the libidinous occupation of the mouth is that in later life it does not need to be given up nearly as much as, for example, the anal desires must be. Less needs to be sublimated; less needs to be converted into character. Much can remain.

Abraham thought that an oral phase that passed reasonably normally gave the best chance of normal social and sexual functioning later. However, a great deal could go wrong at this stage.

Both too much and too little satisfaction at the suckling stage could lead to an excessive fixation on the oral and the same was true of the next stage, in which the desire to bite came to the fore. The fixation expressed itself in hostile and envious traits and, above all, in powerful jealousy. This seems also to be able to connect with the previous, anal stage in which the urge to hold on to what one has is accompanied by a fear of losing even a small amount of it.

If the development of character is orally influenced, the individual has retained from this happy stage of life a deeply rooted conviction that things will always go well. Abraham wrote that, in his experience, these were people whose babyhood had been undisturbed and relished. Therefore, they faced life with unshakable optimism, an attitude that often helped them to achieve their goal. See Chapter One, in which Hilda attributes these characteristics to her father.

If the infant is too spoilt, the outcome can be far less favourable. Then the person in question expects to be handed everything on a plate, as if the mother's breast will flow for ever without any effort being required in return.

If there has been a major disappointment with regard to the oral desires, a very different scenario is created: not optimism, but worry. Everything requires effort. Even the most simple task is seen as excessively hard. In the social behaviour of such people, what continually comes to prominence is that they desire something. This sometimes expresses itself as a request, but it can be extremely demanding. The way in which the desires are expressed has an element of sucking about it. They are not held to facts or restrained by practical objections, but remain insistent. They will attach themselves to other people as if by suction and cannot stand to be alone even for a short time.

If the character showed more traits from the late oral stage, then biting was central and there was ambivalence, characterised by hostile and friendly tendencies.

The most important feature of character development in the genital stage is that the individual takes account of the interests of others. The destructive, object-hostile tendencies that have their source in sadism are reasonably under control. The miserliness and envy from the anal source are no longer dominant. This individual can feel sympathy for another person and have tender feelings. The victory is always relative and relapses are possible. The previous phases remain discernible. Energy can be derived from the early oral phase to enable a person to go for something directly. Energy can be derived from the anal phase to enable them to persist. Moreover, character changes can always take place by means of introjection.

Much of what Abraham wrote in his books and articles remains interesting today. On character formation and introjection, however, he wrote something that could only have been written ninety years ago: "It was Freud who first pointed out that important changes can take place at any time in the mental make-up of the individual through the process of introjection. Women in particular tend to assimilate their character to that of the man with whom they are living".[1333]

CHAPTER TWENTY-SIX

The conflict surrounding Rank and the disintegration of the committee

T he overture to the conflict was played in 1922, when Abraham criticised Rank in a circular letter for his dismissive attitude to proposals and for his gruff tone.[1334] Jones took the opportunity to side with Abraham, even though his conflict with Rank was far more substantial and of a different order.

As had happened before when Abraham criticised one of Freud's favourites, he was accused of jealousy. Abraham's irritability was said to be a product of his jealousy of Eitingon, who by this point had inevitably come to occupy the position of a member of the family, as Freud wrote to Rank.[1335] In that same letter, he wrote that Abraham was more important than Jones.

Freud's reaction to the squabble was rather anxious. He wrote a series of letters to Rank in July, August, and September 1922 that were to a large extent about publications and such matters, but that also addressed the difficulties in the committee. What stands out is that Freud took Rank's side completely, as if very afraid that Rank would feel hurt. In his biography of Rank, Lieberman writes in detail about the entire issue. One thing he mentions is that Freud realised only long afterwards how coarse Rank's behaviour was, but, interestingly, what he does not address is the fact that Rank's tone in the circular letters was unacceptably rude.[1336] He was so rude that the contemporary reader can only admire the patience with which the other committee members responded—until Abraham decided he had had enough, after every one of his proposals had been rejected in a staccato tone. Freud reacted like someone who was, on the one hand, fearful that something was up and, on the other hand, had absolutely no desire to know. If he had examined the other side even a little, specifically Rank's gruff tone, they could all have discussed what was going on with Rank. But Rank had become so important that it would have been disastrous for Freud if anything had been wrong with him. He tried to avert the danger by flattering Rank and telling him he was sorry that he had not encouraged him to study medicine. If Rank had a degree in medicine, he would have become his successor.[1337] This must have struck Rank as a strangely ambivalent comment. Like Reik, Rank had not studied medicine because Freud urged him not to.

Freud was greatly concerned about a successor and he kept pushing one person or another forward. Later, in the years after Abraham's death, he would name Abraham to Hedwig and Hilda as a successor.[1338] Hitschmann later described Rank and Reik as two paladins: the great Freud with his two young followers.[1339] It is a description that no longer applied by the 1920s.

Rank had become a central figure in the world of psychoanalysis. He was the editor of the *Internationale Zeitschrift für Psychoanalyse*. Since 1919, he had been director of the psychoanalytic publishing house. He was Freud's confidant and right-hand man. He also published a great deal and carried out analyses. He worked ceaselessly and got everything done, like a devil's disciple. But he paid a high price. Rank seems to have been driven by a sense that he had to do everything himself, megalomania that led to exhaustion.

In various circular letters it became clear that, since the setting up of the publishing house in 1919, he had found himself with too many responsibilities. On 23 December 1920 he wrote,

> . . . but in the last week before Christmas it was simply physically impossible for me to fulfil even the most urgent demands. Reik, who is leaving the publishing house in the new year to set up the bibliographical centre, has been on leave for the past few days, so that I also had to take over the distribution of the books, which he did up to now and had to be done particularly quickly just before Christmas, which was almost impossible because of the arrival of a whole series of new publications. On top of that, at precisely the same time Hiller arrived in Vienna and he needs to be made acquainted with his work. Furthermore, I had to balance the books and do all the other usual things that come up, which in any case I am never able to complete. So I do not have so much to report as I would have if there were not around thirty unopened letters to deal with and just as much printed matter and corrections to be done, among them probably plenty of important things to be communicated. The buying in of books and the bibliography will have to wait as well.[1340]

And, in the circular letter from Vienna of 1 August 1922,

> . . . since the supervision and editing of the *Zeitschrift* along with the editorial work of the publishing house—quite apart from my own work, which is also increasingly pressing—anyway gives me more to do than I can cope with. So I now find myself forced to engage a secretary in the autumn, in addition to the ten staff the publishing house now has at its disposal, who will have to take over part of my personal workload, since otherwise I will become irretrievably stuck.[1341]

These are two examples, but there are many more passages in which Rank mentions that he was tired or far too busy. Freud did see that Rank had too many responsibilities. On 23 January 1921, he wrote to Eitingon that Rank was sacrificing himself and could make a living only by performing three or four analyses a day alongside his editorial work. Freud considered paying Rank a little more, but Rank was keen to carry out analyses. This letter is the first indication that Rank had started his own psychoanalytic practice.[1342] Freud wrote about it as if it were entirely Rank's own business. But Rank was sacrificing his time to Freud's life's work, and therefore to Freud, for a minimal fee. Freud allowed that to happen. It was greatly to his advantage. Freud did suspect as early as 1920, however, that Rank was troubled by manic–depressive episodes. On 15 March 1920, he wrote the following to Ferenczi: "The Verlag is laboring on 10,000 external difficulties, and Rank, who is as well behaved as ever, does seem to me to be depressed and not properly capable of accomplishment. He is very probably a periodic [i.e. manic–depressive]".[1343]

Abraham as a wolf in sheep's clothing

Abraham emerges very badly from the secondary literature about the conflict surrounding Rank. When it was necessary to blame someone, thoughts remarkably often turn to him. Grosskurth goes furthest of all. In the introduction to her book about the secret committee she writes: ". . . how Abraham was intent on destroying Rank, and how Rank was almost destroyed".[1344] Grosskurth does not mention where she obtained that information from. It would not have been easy, since, in all the known literature by and about Abraham, nothing is to be found that gives any such indication. But the tone had been set. In his book *Das "Geheime Komitee" Sigmund Freuds* (The "Secret Committee" of Sigmund Freud), Wittenberger, too, is extremely critical of Abraham.[1345]

In 1922, two incidents took place involving Abraham and Rank. The first concerned Rank's rude tone and the second was about the division of tasks. In this period Jones was president of the IPA and, at the congress in Berlin in September 1922, Abraham was elected secretary of the IPA. In that capacity he was responsible for the *Korrespondenzblatt*, the journal in which reports from the various psychoanalytic societies under the umbrella of the IPA were published. But the *Korrespondenzblatt* was distributed as part of the *Zeitschrift*, of which Rank was the editor.

On 1 November 1922, Abraham sent a circular letter from Berlin saying that he was prepared to edit the *Korrespondenzblatt*. He described wanting to organise it so that he would receive all the reports from the psychoanalytic societies at the right time. The letter was addressed mainly to Jones, as president of the IPA.[1346]

On the same day, 1 November, Rank made a different proposal in his circular letter from Vienna. He wrote that the details of what the societies were doing should be sent to Abraham but at the same time to the editors, in other words to Rank and Rivière, for translation. The editing would be done by the editors, who would then compare their version with Abraham's version before publication.[1347] Rank was hereby in reality removing the editorship of the *Korrespondenzblatt* from Abraham. Although he had by then received Abraham's proposal, on 6 November he sent his own to all the secretaries of the psychoanalytic societies without consulting Abraham any further.

Abraham was indignant at the course of events. "This is no way to treat each other", he wrote on 12 November 1922.[1348] He found the procedure inefficient, too. Now Rank and Rivière, as translator, as well as he himself, would have to put together an entire *Korrespondenzblatt*, and Abraham, too, would need to get pieces translated. Abraham's version would then serve only for comparison, even though the *Korrespondenzblatt* would be published under Abraham's name.

The psychoanalytic societies had an umbrella organisation in the board of the IPA. Jones was its president and Abraham its secretary. Officially, they had ultimate responsibility and it was they who decided on the proceedings of the association, including the *Korrespondenzblatt*. What Rank made clear was that they had power only on paper. In reality, he made the decisions along with Freud. Abraham did not want to sow confusion among the psychoanalytic societies, so he went along with Rank's proposal.

On 15 November the next circular letter arrived from Vienna, in which was written: "Regarding Berlin: We hope that as of now the issue of the *Korrespondenzblatt* has been settled to everyone's satisfaction. Responsibility for it will naturally be taken by Abraham as central secretary". [1349]

Abraham was again confronted with the fact that his proposals had been ignored. Rank was going to edit, but Abraham would have to take ultimate responsibility.

The circular letter was otherwise largely devoted to a proposed move of the publishing house to Berlin in the hope that this would resolve its precarious financial position. On 16 November, a fierce protest was received from Jones. He was indignant that, as director of the British branch of the publishing house, he had not been consulted about the move to Berlin. About the *Korrespondenzblatt* he wrote the following:

> Abraham and I had to notify all the Group Secretaries of the future arrangements for regulating and coordinating the Society Reports and other work in connection with the *Korrespondenzblatt*, but before doing that we followed the usual Committee plan of first submitting our proposals to the rest of you for criticism. Judge of my astonishment when I learned that before our question could be answered and before we could take any action ourselves Rank and Hiller had taken it on themselves to make all the arrangements and issue orders to the Group Secretaries behind our back. It is now too late for us to do anything but accept fait accompli as usual; but I must express my opinion that the plan was deficient in some important technical respects, that the manner of carrying it out was decidedly disregardful of Abraham and myself, and that, since we hope to keep the Central Executive for some years in the hands of our Committee, it is detrimental to our own interest to impair its authority in the eyes of the Branch Societies. As it stands, the Societies expect orders from the Central Executive in a matter that is its direct function, while the latter is powerless to act.[1350]

Jones put it rather sharply here, but clearly and to the point. Then Freud responded, not on behalf of Rank as well, but alone, in a thundering letter of eight and a half pages.[1351]

Wittenberger wrote of this letter that while the members of the committee became lost in thousands of details when there was a problem that needed to be solved, Freud succeeded in bringing astonishing clarity and giving structure to the chaos of the group dynamic.[1352] Grosskurth, too, refers to Freud's letter as if it finally brought clarity.[1353] But Freud did not create clarity at all. On the contrary. Anger spatters from every page. Everything Rank did was good and what the others did was wrong. The letter is an extreme example of the improper use of his own ideas, a way of reasoning that means the substance of the difference of opinion is not discussed, instead it is interpreted psychoanalytically. Below are a few examples from the letter.

Abraham had been wondering whether the letters from Vienna, signed by Rank and Freud, were actually read by Freud, since the blunt tone of the letters was unusual for Freud. Freud answered that the outlines of all the letters were compiled together and the worked up version was shown to him later.[1354] He goes on, "I am sorry to see a sign of such sensitivity, surely from a remote source, in the so correct and fundamentally good friend Abraham".[1355] Here, Freud completely denies the cause of Abraham's suspicion, which was that the letters were so much coarser in tone than Freud's letters. He accuses Abraham of reacting in an overwrought manner, which must have deeper reasons. The actual argument is therefore pushed aside by an interpretation of Abraham's mental state.

With regard to Jones, Freud went even further. Rank was innocent and all Jones' criticism was actually intended for Freud. Rank served as a shield to catch the negative part of the expression of an ambivalence. Freud did not want to attend the next meeting of the committee and he said Jones must complete his short analysis with Ferenczi. Jones was wrong if he thought that he ought to have been consulted as director about the move to Berlin. There was just one director and that was Rank. Moreover, nothing had been decided and there was still plenty of time to raise objections. He concluded his letter with the following words: "This is how I see the situation and again I can see no grounds for reproaching Rank, who on this occasion as always before is giving of his utmost. In my opinion it would not have occurred to any of you if strange emotions had not strained the friendly attitude". Again Freud denies any real basis for the protests by Abraham and Jones. It is all caused by their own complexes.

What Freud did here was damaging. By denying there was any factual basis for the protests by Abraham and Jones, he made it impossible to talk matters through properly. There was, in truth, a factual basis. After all, Rank had refused to give Abraham ultimate responsibility for the *Korrespondenzblatt* as the statutes of the IPA required, while still demanding that Abraham put his name to it. By his denial, Freud also encouraged Rank's behaviour. It was all very well for him to write "seid einig-einnig-einig" (be united-united-united), but he was driving the parties away from each other.[1356] All this was played out in a period in which the psychoanalytic publishing house was in great danger because of financial problems. Freud seems to have been entirely focused on saving the publishing house, to which Rank was central, and all the rest was of secondary concern. The fact that the British publishing arm cost more than it brought in meant that Freud very much took sides against Jones.[1357]

Towards the end of 1922, emotions had calmed a little. At Freud's request, Rank wrote another reaction. It spoke volumes:

> . . . to direct an appeal to you to keep in mind, as firmly as I feel it myself every day and every hour, the complexity and responsibility of my position. This will ensure that you and I are prevented from tossing trivialities into my lap or making difficulties for me. For years I have done almost nothing but fight against a series of tremendous external difficulties. I would venture to say that I have done so with success up to now, although not without sometimes despairing at the magnitude of the task and the weakness of my powers, or a sense of paralysing exhaustion and tiredness.[1358]

Rank wrote of his exhaustion and his demanding duties, in which he must not be disturbed for trivial matters. But it is, of course, not a trivial matter if you do not wish to adhere to the statutes of the IPA. Rank was undoubtedly overtired, but he also placed himself pathetically in the role of the victim and made clear that he would tolerate no criticism at all.

San Cristoforo

It had become a tradition that the members of the committee would meet up for a few days in years when no international congress took place. In 1923, they planned to gather in San Cristoforo, close to Freud's holiday address in Lavarone, although without Freud. Because of his health and his deep grief over Heinerle, Freud preferred the committee members to consult between themselves and try to overcome their differences of opinion.[1359]

Doom hung heavy over it all. Felix Deutsch had offered to come to Lavarone to examine Freud, who accepted his offer on his daughter Anna's advice, since he wanted Deutsch to assess whether he would be able to go to Rome in September.[1360] Just before the committee meeting, Felix Deutsch had carried out an examination and concluded that the swelling in Freud's mouth was malignant and another operation would be needed. Again he said nothing to Freud. He feared Freud would refuse surgery and he was even afraid of suicide.[1361] The committee members were informed by Deutsch and they agreed with him that Freud should not be told until after Rome that he had cancer. They did not tell Anna either. The members were operating well beyond their authority in this matter. Freud never forgave Deutsch for it. Jones told Freud only in the last year of his life, in London, that the decision had been made by the committee. To which Freud answered: *"Mit welchem Recht?"* ("With what right?").[1362]

At a committee dinner that Anna Freud attended, Rank had an uncontrollable hysterical laughing fit when Freud's name was mentioned, which shocked Anna Freud.[1363]

In this tense atmosphere the committee members tried to talk through their internal difficulties. First of all there was a conflict between Rank and Jones about the publication of the *Zeitschrift* in German and the *International Journal* in English, and about the books that were published. The publishing house had financial problems and members blamed each other. Rank was being driven crazy by the way Jones wanted to check everything closely and Jones by the way Rank did everything behind his back.

In his book, *Freud and His Early Circle*, Brome wrote that it is good to keep in mind that in every conflict Jones had a habit of attributing mental illness to the other party.[1364] According to Brome, he usually did so unfairly, but perhaps in the case of Rank he was not entirely wrong. In Jones' opinion Rank was in the manic phase of manic depression.[1365] Rank regularly informed Freud about the problems and the two of them sided against Jones, so, in 1923, Freud was very critical of Jones:

> This last year brought a disappointment not easy to bear. I had to find out that you had less control of your moods and passions, were less consistent, sincere and reliable than I had a right to expect of you and than was required by your conspicuous position. And although you yourself had proposed the committee you did not refrain from endangering its intimacy by unjust susceptibilities.[1366]

Little account was taken of Jones' difficult situation. He was isolated, whereas the others lived close to each other. He was in England, where powerfully anti-German sentiments dominated after the First World War. This was the reason why he kept trying to remove Germanisms from the translations; they would immediately cause resistance in Britain—a consideration with which Rank had no patience. Moreover, in the British newspapers a smear campaign against psychoanalysis was under way. Jones was trying to strengthen ties with America and for that reason sometimes published articles he did not find particularly good, such as work by the president of the New York Psychoanalytic Society. Freud and Rank thought everything that came from America was "rubbish".[1367] In March 1923, the Psychoanalytic Press was separated from the parent company in Vienna and made independent, supported by the newly formed Institute of Psychoanalysis in London. Rank bore a powerful grudge towards Jones and is said to have told Ferenczi that Jones did not really belong among them and that he did nothing but send everyone instructions from London as if the others were all children. Rank wanted to have Jones removed from the committee, but Ferenczi prevented that.[1368]

Much has been written about the meeting of the committee in San Cristoforo. The biographers seem to be as much divided into hostile camps as the committee members were at the time.[1369] An entire day was devoted to the conflict between Rank and Jones, with Abraham playing a mediating role. Then Ferenczi picked up some words from Brill that Jones was said to have used and they came as a bombshell. Jones had supposedly called Rank a "swindling Jew". Ferenczi was furious, Rank livid. Jones offered Rank his apologies for the fact that he had unintentionally hurt him. Rank refused to accept the apology and demanded that Jones be thrown out of the committee. When that proposal was not accepted, Rank stormed out.

Illustrative of the extremely tense relations at the time, and probably also the tension that Freud's illness brought with it, is the fact that no one wondered whether what Brill had said was true, even though it was common knowledge that Brill's statements were not particularly reliable. Jones wrote that evening to his wife,

> The chief news is that Freud has a real cancer slowly growing and may last many years. He doesn't know it and it is a most deadly secret. Eitingon is here too. . . . We have spent the whole day thrashing out the Rank–Jones affair. Very painful but I hope our relations will now be better and believe so, but on the other hand expect Ferenczi will hardly speak to me for Brill has just been there and told him I had said Rank was a swindling Jew (stark übertrieben). Brill of course has gone to the US without seeing me.[1370]

What Jones had written to Brill was, in fact, something else entirely. Jones had complained to Brill that Rank was willing to send him hardly any figures and he had written, "Rank's general way of conducting business was distinctly Oriental".[1371] Months passed before Brill acknowledged that he had himself added the anti-Semitic sneer "swindling Jew" when he reported the remark to Ferenczi.[1372]

After their squabbles of 1922 and 1923, the relationship between Freud and Abraham had improved markedly. Abraham wrote to Freud quite regularly, giving him extensive reports from Berlin and trying to buoy him up.

Freud was very appreciative and he wrote an affectionate thank-you letter on 19 October 1923: "Dear Incurable Optimist, Tampon renewed today, got up, put what is left into clothes. Thanks for all news, letters, greetings, newspaper cuttings. If I can sleep without injection, I go home soon. Cordially yours, Freud".[1373]

The Trauma of Birth

The book that Rank published in 1924, however, *The Trauma of Birth*, brought about a greater estrangement between Freud and Abraham than ever before. In 1953, Hedwig talked in detail about this period that was so painful for Abraham.[1374] She described how difficult it was to deal with the fact that Abraham had a different opinion from Freud concerning Rank. Hedwig said that the professor believed to the last that Rank would never turn away from him. He had given Rank great trust and friendship and believed that in Rank he had a solidly reliable follower.

Abraham had doubts about *The Trauma of Birth*. Freud is said to have told Abraham he was too distrustful. Hedwig said that he might have thought her husband was jealous, which was not true at all. Freud had already blamed Abraham once before, said Hedwig, probably referring to the conflict with Jung. Abraham had seen then where the conflict would take them and the professor had not wanted to know or to believe it. Abraham was now convinced that Rank would eventually turn away from psychoanalysis and carve out his own path.

Because Abraham became so ill, he and Freud never discussed the matter again. Hedwig later heard from others how painful the whole matter was for Freud and that he had said, "Then Abraham was right again after all." Freud had done him an injustice.

Hedwig no longer knew who had told her about this remark by Freud. It must have been someone from Abraham's circle, probably Sachs, who was very close to him.

On 6 May 1923, Rank brought Freud the manuscript of *The Trauma of Birth* as a present for his sixty-seventh birthday. Shortly before, Freud had undergone his first operation on a swelling in his mouth. Hirschmann remembered how pale and tired Freud looked. They thought they were going to lose him.[1375] The book was published in 1924 and Rank dedicated it to Freud.

In retrospect, it is interesting to see what Freud later told Alexander about the book. Alexander had theoretical discussions with Freud fairly regularly when he visited him in Vienna:

> At another occasion Freud expressed his reservations about Rank's *Trauma of Birth* which had just been published. He showed a great deal of disappointment and even indignation. "Then all that we have discovered about the etiological importance of family influences is nonexistent!" he exclaimed. "Everything is decided by the event of birth itself." I recall that he added a strong expression such as: "Nonsense!" with a gesture of dismissal.[1376]

The Trauma of Birth was qualitatively substandard, which was a major problem.
The foreword begins as follows:

> The following arguments indicate a first attempt to apply the psychoanalytic way of thinking, as such, to the comprehension of the whole development of mankind, even of the actual fact of becoming human. It would be more correct not to use the word "apply", for it is not a question of one of the usual works on the "Application of Psychoanalysis to the Mental Sciences"; rather it is a matter of making psychoanalytic thought productive for our entire conception of mankind and history. This finally represents the history of mind, that is, the history of the development of the human mind and of the things created by it.[1377]

With this book, Rank wanted to make psychoanalysis fruitful for our overall image of humanity and the history of mankind, the human mind, and what the mind has brought forth. He used extremely inflated language. The first few lines make clear right away that what he had written down was a megalomaniac fantasy. In his book, Rank pushed aside the Oedipus complex, and with it Freud's theory, and put the birth trauma in its place as the source of all neuroses. The book is 200 pages long. Rank dictated it in just a few weeks, far too quickly for a book of its size.[1378]

It was not for nothing that Abraham kept insisting Rank should first have discussed the book in the committee, as Abraham had done in San Cristoforo with his new ideas about object relations. If Rank had spoken about his ideas, they could all have guided and protected him. He was, after all, by far the youngest and least experienced of the group.[1379] All the same, Abraham does not seem to have made a good assessment of Rank's condition. Megalomaniac fantasies do not admit of criticism or guidance. At best they burst apart.

The problem was most serious for Freud. Jones put it very clearly into words in a letter to Abraham of 8 April 1924:

> The Glovers gave a pitiless analysis of the Geburtstrauma at our last meeting, revealing the Vaterablehnung and flight from the oedipus complex as its essential motive. . . . The real tragedy is this. I fear that Prof. with his clear mind cannot be altogether blind to the unconscious tendency in Otto. Ten years ago he would surely have put his work before all else; but now, old, ill, and tied by the strongest claims of affection (which Otto has so fully justified in the past), he can hardly face the possibility of having once more to go through the Jung situation and this time nearer home, with someone who perhaps means more to him than his own sons.[1380]

In a time when Freud was writing a ground-breaking work about the development of the ego, titled *The Ego and the Id*, and Abraham was focusing on the early object relations in his *A Short Study of the Development of the Libido*, Rank had written a simplistic book in which all problems arose from the trauma of birth.[1381] This was certainly hard to take.

According to Rank, all fear could be traced back to the birth trauma. All patients identify the analyst with the mother, and they have themselves regressed to the position of the unborn child. Hysteria and conversion with symptoms of paralysis indicate a return to the womb. Migraine occurs because being born causes pain to the head. Asthma has to do with the struggle to breathe during birth. Castration anxiety is a repeat of the primal castration, the separation from the mother at birth. Discrimination against women has to do with the woman's relationship with birth trauma. And so on. How the mother treats her child is not mentioned once in the book, which is all about birth itself, described as a mechanical event.

It is also striking that whereas Freud attributes a greater role than ever to the unconscious in *The Ego and the Id*, an unconscious that can barely be known at all, Rank reduces the unconscious to the repressed birth trauma, which cannot be directly known because of repression but that can be understood in analysis. This point, too, is an astonishing simplification. The book was embarrassing, written in a manic phase, and it posed a threat to Rank's good reputation.

In the early months of 1924, Freud chose to defend Rank tooth and nail. He was warned about this by Eitingon in a letter from Ospedaletti on the Mediterranean coast dated 31 January 1924.[1382] Eitingon had manoeuvred himself into the position of outsider by disappearing almost completely from the stage ever since the start of Freud's illness in May 1923. He rarely even wrote letters to Freud any longer. He was present at San Cristoforo, though, and in late 1923 he became ill. In early 1924, he was briefly in Berlin but left almost immediately because he had still not recovered. In early January 1924, Abraham wrote to Jones about Eitingon: "No, I've heard nothing from Max since he left. You know, he is not very forthcoming. He has told me neither where he is travelling to nor for how long".[1383] Eitingon's disturbing letter to Freud was probably based on his brief visit to Berlin.

Eitingon wrote that in Berlin there was much agitation about two recently published books, *Development of Psychoanalysis* by Ferenczi and Rank, and *The Trauma of Birth* by Rank. Eitingon had good things to say about the first but thought very little of the second, which was too far removed from reality. Because it was by Rank and not Stekel, however, he was inclined to see what came of it without reacting himself. He then wrote about Abraham, saying he had climbed the hierarchy continually over recent years and had now gained a very prominent position in the international association. Eitingon regarded Abraham as, in a sense, the leader of the conservatives, who had been horrified by the leap made by Rank. Abraham was, there-fore, depicted by Eitingon as a conservative in contrast to the modern Rank and Ferenczi. This is an unjustified distortion. Abraham was still writing trail-blazingly innovative articles about the pre-oedipal phases and in Berlin he was very much open to new ideas. See, for example, later in this book, his attitude to Melanie Klein.

Alexander wrote a long, lucid review of *Development of Psychoanalysis*.[1384] The book advo-cated restricting the duration of analyses by placing a limit on them and at the same time intro-ducing a new phase in psychoanalysis in which, rather than recollection with elucidation by the analyst, repetition in the analytic situation would be at the forefront of psychoanalytic tech-nique. Alexander showed that Freud had put it exactly that way thirteen years earlier:

> In the process of seeking out the libido which has escaped from the patient's conscious, we have penetrated into the realm of the unconscious. The reactions which we bring about reveal at the same time some of the characteristics which we have come to know from the study of dreams. The unconscious impulses do not want to be remembered in the way the treatment desires them to be, but endeavour to reproduce themselves in accordance with the timelessness of the unconscious and its capacity for hallucination. Just as happens in dreams, the patient regards the products of the awakening of his unconscious impulses as contemporaneous and real; he seeks to put his passions into action without taking any account of the real situation. The doctor tries to compel him to fit these emotional impulses into the nexus of the treatment and of his life-history, to submit them to intellectual consideration and to understand them in the light of their psychical value. This struggle between the doctor and the patient, between intellect and instinctual life, between understanding and seeking to act, is played out almost exclusively in the phenomena of transference. It is on that field that the victory must be won—the victory whose expression is the permanent cure of the neurosis.[1385]

Furthermore, Alexander believed that the book was already outdated, now that *The Ego and the Id* had been published, since the necessary development of the ego as the goal of analysis was not mentioned in it.

Alarmed by Eitingon, Freud decided once again to write a long letter to the committee members, defending Rank. In his letter of 15 February 1924, he discussed both books,

Development of Psychoanalysis and *The Trauma of Birth*, and he treated both with great praise at first, followed by mild criticism.[1386]

Rank posted the letter and then wrote Freud a long response that same day.[1387] He found Freud's letter very well suited to its task, that is, keeping the peace in the committee, but Freud's stance with regard to his own book had disappointed him greatly. He writes that he does not want to be misunderstood by Freud, then continues with a sneer at his colleagues, saying he did not expect much understanding of his book from most of them. The overwrought tone of the letter and the rather angry summing up of all the points Freud had misunderstood makes clear immediately that the calming of Rank, at any rate, had not succeeded.

Abraham and Sachs reacted separately to Freud's long letter. They had clearly agreed to do so. Sachs wrote on 20 February that such a letter needed to be answered individually so that the individual differences would be brought out in full.

Sachs was extremely critical. He stressed the importance of the publication but wrote that a great deal was wrong with the way it had been executed. A theory like that of *The Trauma of Birth* cannot be proved on the basis of ethnological and religious–psychological material alone. Sachs found that, in the case of both books, too little was explained and too little evidence provided. Important points were not given a solid basis.[1388]

Abraham reacted to Freud's letter on 21 February by saying it had made a deep impression on him and that he had therefore thoroughly re-examined his own stance with regard to both books.[1389] He wrote that he was extremely uneasy about current developments, which had even robbed him of a good deal of his optimism about the progress psychoanalysis was making, and he urgently requested a meeting of the committee before the upcoming congress in Salzburg of 21–23 April 1924.

On 25 February, Freud wrote a second circular letter in which he responded to Abraham's request and declared himself in favour of a committee meeting before the start of the congress in Salzburg. These were months in which a great deal happened. There were the circular letters, but the committee members and Freud also wrote an unusual number of direct letters to each other. The correspondence between Freud and Ferenczi is of great importance to anyone wanting to follow developments in detail. On 21 January, Freud wrote to Ferenczi that he was not fully in agreement with *Development of Psychoanalysis*, the book Ferenczi had written with Rank.

Freud wrote that he had both admiration and criticism, and he had spoken at length with Rank about it. Ferenczi was utterly dismayed by this letter from Freud: "Your letter has shaken me considerably. For the first time since our acquaintance, which you soon elevated to friendship, I hear words of dissatisfaction from you. I didn't want to respond in the first affect, therefore I postponed this letter until today".[1390]

Freud had never criticised Ferenczi's work before and now that he was doing so, however mildly, Ferenczi could not bear it. He was deeply hurt. His letter was a full page of protest.

Freud's answer of 4 February was remarkable.[1391] Was he alarmed by Ferenczi's outburst?

Freud wrote back immediately the same day to say that he was sorry Ferenczi was suffering so much because of his letter and asking Ferenczi to tell him exactly what he had written, because he no longer knew, and he could not rightly say at this point what he disagreed with except that the theory in the book was still too sketchy. The book no longer appealed to him so much. Freud went on to say that he had received a letter from Eitingon telling him that

Abraham was extremely agitated by the form and content of Rank's publications, including the book written together with Ferenczi. What Freud was doing here was to criticise Ferenczi mildly and only in general terms. Then, when he received a fierce reaction from Ferenczi, he pushed Abraham to the fore as the critic.

Abraham, ignorant of all this, was extremely relieved that Freud, in his circular letter of 25 February, had supported his proposal for a meeting. He wrote to Freud on 28 February 1924 that now he had seen that Freud was prepared to listen to his criticism, even though it was stronger than Freud's and concerned a person to whom Freud was very close, he now wanted to write to Freud about the dangers he saw in it.[1392] Perhaps Freud would shake his head and not want to hear any more of his criticisms. He went on, "But it is no longer possible for me to keep them back, and I shall therefore state briefly what I intend to put before our meeting, giving full and detailed *reasons* for my opinion".

After careful study, Abraham wrote, he had come to the conclusion about both books that they were manifestations of a scientific regression that corresponded down to the smallest detail with the symptoms of Jung's renunciation of psychoanalysis. Two of our best people, Abraham wrote, were in danger of straying from psychoanalysis and being lost to it. He saw two further dangers as well: the disintegration of the committee and the damaging effect on the psychoanalytic movement of the two new books. Abraham regarded an extensive discussion of both works at the meeting as the only possible way of averting this danger.

The letter makes clear that Abraham was extremely worried and wanted to tell Freud why. Freud reacted with a very long letter in which, on the one hand, he wrote that the concerns voiced by Abraham were not far from his own mind, but, on the other hand, that he was not worried because Rank and Ferenczi were so totally different from Jung: "What further damage would ensue? We could remain under the same roof with the greatest calmness, and after a few years' work it would become evident whether one side had exaggerated a valuable finding or the other had underrated it".[1393] Freud proposed limiting the committee's discussion to one day. Two days, as Abraham had proposed, would be too exhausting for him.

Then, however, Freud did something that would not just have disastrous consequences for the committee, but actually put an end to it at a stroke. He allowed Rank to read the letter from Abraham. Rank informed Ferenczi. Both exploded.

The only person to have clearly seen and described the damaging nature of this move is Brome: "The gathering storm really broke not because of Abraham's suspicions about Rank and Ferenczi, but because Freud, in an amazingly tactless moment, revealed to Rank the analogy which Abraham had drawn with the early history of Jung's defection".[1394]

What possessed Freud? Abraham's letter was clearly personal in character. He wrote that he wanted to discuss the content of the letter at the committee meeting. Abraham was cautious and did not want to bring up this sensitive issue in a circular letter but to address it verbally. Abraham differed with Freud about how to address the problem. The difference of opinion was not about the content of the books; as time went on, it became clear that both were very critical of that. Freud wanted to let the issue drop. He thought that the value of the books would emerge of its own accord. Freud seems to have been more sensitive to Rank's vulnerability. Rank was so easily hurt that he could not stand any criticism at all. Abraham saw, above all, a great danger to psychoanalysis and wanted to take the point up with Rank. He does not seem to have been aware that Rank would be unable to deal with such a debate, although Abraham clearly realised he would have to move cautiously. That Freud allowed Rank to read Abraham's letter and that Rank then informed Ferenczi was a serious matter. What Abraham had wanted to bring up cautiously during a meeting was now experienced as heavy-handed. Ferenczi was furious. On 18 March he wrote to Freud,

> Only for that reason did Abraham's step not have a more depressing effect on me, because, behind his cautious politeness I always also recognized the signs of boundless ambition and jealousy. For only these passions could blind him in such a way that he—against all reason—could slander the joint work and "The Trauma of Birth" as garbage publications. He did not summon the courage to appear openly in opposition to us—he also waited—again, extremely cautiously—until, from certain statements from your Rundbrief, he received the—in my opinion, erroneous—impression that you are not in complete agreement with these works, in fact, consider them dangerous. But with this step he has also evidently sealed the fate of the Committee. Already in S. Cristoforo he behaved rather ambiguously toward Jones and could only be convinced with difficulty that the latter's anti-Semitism is not compatible with membership in the Committee; he also used every opportunity to put Rank in the wrong.[1395] And now he has decided upon a mode of operation which makes it impossible for us to work intimately with him. But I think that with this the question of his presidency is also being reopened, for it is certainly not to be expected of us, precisely in these critical times, to recognize as a leader someone who could misunderstand us so badly and defame us so insidiously. Since only you and Eitingon can be considered "impartial," I am of the opinion that the latter should become president; as founder of the polyclinic, he would have earned this position long ago.[1396]

The passing on of the letter seriously damaged relations between Abraham and Ferenczi.[1397] Ferenczi's accusation that Abraham had failed to find the courage to act against them openly was incorrect. Abraham had wanted to express his objections openly, but in a meeting. Freud got there before him. That this would seal the fate of the committee was no empty threat. On 10 April 1924, Rank, with the agreement of Ferenczi, dissolved the committee in a circular letter.[1398] In San Cristoforo, it had been agreed that Abraham would be the next to chair the committee, with Rank as secretary. Ferenczi and Rank now prevented that.

Freud reacted immediately to Ferenczi's letter of 18 March and was now rather clearer himself in his criticism of *The Trauma of Birth*. He wrote of Ferenczi's reaction to Abraham, "I am sorry that on this occasion your inimical brother complex, which we believed to have been settled, has reawakened".[1399]

What makes the entire situation so bizarre is that it now turns out Freud had, at this point, read only half of *The Trauma of Birth* and relatively superficially at that. He had defended Rank without studying the book properly, which deeply offended Rank.[1400] In his reaction to Ferenczi, Freud also said clearly that he supported Abraham's chairmanship of the IPA. The correspondence between Freud and Abraham attests to very cordial relations between them in this period, even if they were not in complete agreement.

If Abraham resented Freud's indiscretion, then there is no sign of it in his letters to Freud. The mood changed totally in late March. Laying Freud's correspondence with Abraham next to his correspondence with Ferenczi makes clear that the change came about after the angry letter from Ferenczi of 18 March 1924. On 31 March, Freud wrote the following to Abraham, in which no trace remains of the previous friendly and warm tone:

> For to whatever extent your reaction to F.[erenczi] and R.[ank] may have been justified, quite apart from that, the way you set about things was certainly not friendly, and it has become completely clear on this occasion that the committee no longer exists, because the ethos that would make a committee of this handful of people is no longer there. I think that it is now up to you to prevent a further disintegration, and I hope that Eitingon, whom I expect here on the 13th, will help in this. It cannot be your intention by reason of this apprehension of yours to cause the tearing down of the *Internationale Vereinigung* and everything connected with it.[1401]

Freud also wrote that, because of his health, he would probably not be coming to Salzburg. Freud had caused this escalation by allowing Rank and Ferenczi to read Abraham's concerned letter and now he was shifting the blame entirely on to Abraham.

Congress in Salzburg

Under the circumstances, it might be described as a miracle that the congress in Salzburg took place in reasonable harmony, with everyone doing their best to avoid any sharp polemic about the books. Abraham spoke to Ferenczi at length on several occasions and managed to restore their previous friendly relations. Hedwig said that the relationship between Ferenczi and Abraham had always been very good, with the exception of the affair surrounding Rank. Then Ferenczi was angry with Abraham for turning against Rank. This was resolved completely later, however, according to Hedwig. Hilda told Eissler that she had always been extremely fond of Ferenczi.[1402]

Ferenczi wrote to Freud, "Abraham and I did everything possible to approach the mutual personal relations of the old friendship; this also succeeded—actually, much more than with Jones, who, together with his entire group, acted strikingly reserved".[1403]

Abraham also tried to speak with Rank a number of times, but there he hit a brick wall. The committee members did indeed decide not to breathe new life into the committee. Abraham was very satisfied with the high standard of the congress. He was elected president of the IPA, with Eitingon as secretary.

Rank left for New York before the congress was over. He planned to travel around the USA for six months, carrying out analyses and giving lectures. At first, he was highly successful. He was seen as a prominent colleague of, and direct collaborator with, Freud. Rank gave lectures and his new ideas were found refreshing. On 3 June 1923, he became an honorary member of the American Psychoanalytic Association and people queued up for the chance to be analysed by him. In the summer, however, his popularity began to fade somewhat and he had to write to Ferenczi to say he had better not come to America since he had barely enough patients himself. (Ferenczi was also planning to spend a few months in the USA. There was a great deal of money to be made there.) It is clear from the correspondence with Freud in this period that Rank was developing almost paranoid ideas about Abraham. Take the letter from Rank to Freud of 9 August 1924:

Nor do I know the extent to which your judgment of, or prejudice against, my conception was influenced by certain rabble-rousers who seem to have the irresistible need to cast themselves from time to time as saviors of psa, or of your own person—without seeing that in so doing they only give rein to their childish envy. The latest plans and conspiracies I hear of in Berlin strike me as so stupid, and are so unworthy of a scientific movement, that I hope you won't pay much attention to them either. I'd like to know what anyone hopes to achieve through them. If there's a desire to drive me from my official positions, to which until now I was bound not by ambition but by duty and concern and work, this can be done without recourse to back-room politics—if you should wish it. If there is a desire to refute my conception, there's really no need to foment intrigue. The more light there is, the more pleasant it will be for me, as the profound ignorance of people like Abraham, among others, will be all the more apparent. Do you really believe, Professor, that an argument from someone like Abraham will impress me when I've lost faith even in your judgment in this matter? I think people are more interested in intrigue for its own sake than in attaining any definite goals.[1404]

It was a clearly deranged Rank who wrote this, one who saw Abraham as the evil genius determined to drive him out. He seemed to be obsessed by Abraham. There are no indications at all that Abraham was trying to get rid of Rank. On the contrary, he made repeated efforts to enter into conversation with Rank and to restore relations between them, but Rank was incapable of entering into debate with him. In his reply to this letter, Freud reprimanded Rank for insulting Abraham.[1405]

Shortly before writing his letter to Freud, Rank had written to tell Ferenczi that he had saved psychoanalysis in the USA, where he found himself at that moment, and had perhaps also ensured the continued existence of the entire IPA. Rank claimed that a large number of the analysands had not been cured and were dissatisfied with the treatment they had received from Freud.

He had heard that attempts were being made in Berlin, led by Abraham and Radó, to push him and Ferenczi out. Rank wrote that he did not know to what extent Ferenczi was aware of these intrigues and was keeping them secret so as not to confuse him. Rank concluded by saying that all this left him cold.[1406]

These are megalomaniac ideas of Rank's, and they play tricks on him here. He claimed to have saved the psychoanalytic movement, but he did not realise the extent of the problems with which he had saddled the others by leaving so suddenly. He was editor-in-chief of the journal and director of the publishing house; both positions were crucial to the psychoanalytic moment at that point.[1407] Naturally, assiduous attempts were made to find replacements. Rank seems to have regarded that as intrigue, as part of an attempt to oust him.

In October 1924, a depressed Rank returned to Vienna.[1408] He had a three-hour conversation with Freud in which he blamed his behaviour mainly on Abraham's provocations and announced he would be returning to the USA for six months. Freud regarded an editor-in-chief and director of a publishing house who was continually abroad as an impossibility. Fortunately, Radó was found willing to take over the task from him. On 19 November, Rank visited Freud to say goodbye. It was a painful and embarrassing conversation. Freud felt sorry for Rank because he so clearly had something on his mind that he could not express and he thought he would never see Rank again.[1409]

Shortly after that, Freud received a letter from Brill that made a deep impression on him. Brill described how Rank had pushed Freud's teachings aside in America and, in interpreting dreams, no longer gave a sexual origin any place, allowing only interpretations that pointed to the birth trauma.[1410]

Rank was planning to travel to America again and his wife, Beate, accompanied him to the station, but to her astonishment he was at the door again little later. He had changed his mind. In November, Rank left once more, but this time he got no further than Paris before turning round. Beate Rank said later that he was totally conflicted.[1411]

Meanwhile, Ferenczi wrote another circular letter on 16 November 1924, his first in six months. He wanted to support Freud's proposal to breathe new life into the committee. Jones agreed, as did the Berlin members. Several suggestions were made for a new committee member, among them the Dutchman August Stärcke. He enjoyed an excellent reputation. In the end, it was decided that Anna Freud would be made a member. She was delighted and asked Eitingon to convey her thanks to Sachs and Abraham.[1412]

Rank returned to Vienna from Paris and lay low there for two weeks, in a very bad state of mind. Then he wrote a note to Freud and asked to talk to him. In several long conversations he poured out his heart to Freud and discussed his situation. Anna Freud was amazed by the way he looked. His appearance had been totally different for a while, but now he resembled the old Rank again, only very shaken.[1413] Rank wrote a long letter to the members of the committee and expressed his apologies, especially to Abraham. The reaction of the Berlin members, Abraham, Eitingon, and Sachs, was reticent. They were glad of the turnabout, but regarded it as a first step. They asked Rank to enter into a debate about *The Trauma of Birth* after all.[1414] This was asking too much, however, from a depressed, exhausted Rank. Eitingon wrote another letter to stress that there was a readiness to restore old ties. Jones reacted with criticism but also goodwill to the idea of accepting Rank among them again if he would now follow the chosen course.

Jones wrote a long letter to Abraham in which he put the dilemma clearly into words. Because of the personal contact, it would be best to be generous and welcome Rank back. In a scientific sense, however, that would be too risky, since Rank's ideas were too much of a departure from psychoanalysis.[1415]

On 7 January 1925, Rank left again for the USA without any real reconciliation having taken place.

Jessie Taft

The question that remains is why Abraham was so negatively portrayed by several authors regarding the Rank affair. Jessie Taft undoubtedly played a role in this.

Jessie Taft (1882–1960) was an American psychologist who, on 3 June 1924, shortly after Rank arrived in the USA, attended a lecture by him at a meeting of the APsAa, the American Psychoanalytic Association in Atlantic City. The lecture was about the birth trauma. Later, Jessie Taft could no longer remember the content, but she recalled Rank all the better for that, since he had made a profound impression on her. With his slim appearance he perfectly fitted her notion of an erudite German student.[1416] At that point, Rank was forty years old.

Two years later, she entered into analysis with him, for eight or nine weeks. Rank's analyses were extremely short. After that, Taft returned home to Philadelphia and started treating patients based on the insights she had gained. In the spring of 1927, she joined a Rankian group in New York, taking part in a weekly seminar. She was mainly seeking technical and theoretical support. The group was made up largely of young psychiatrists who had been in analysis with Rank. When Rank launched another new theory in 1930, the will theory, and everyone turned away from him, Taft remained loyal. She worked closely with him for the next nine years, until his death in 1939. After he died, she was given his papers by Rank's wife and ex-wife.[1417]

Based on that legacy, which consisted mostly of letters, she wrote a biographical study of Rank.[1418] She emerges as a loyal and unshakable admirer and follower, who regarded her subject as a genius. Taft had read Rank's work. Apart from that, she had read little about psychoanalysis and, as secondary literature, only Jones' biography of Freud and Sachs' book about Freud.[1419]

When he fled the congress in Salzburg and rushed off to America, Rank was in a manic state. He described it as such in his letter to the committee of 7 January 1925.[1420] Taft deduced from this that Rank had always understood his manic–depressive mood swings and believed they were connected with periods of extreme creativity followed by extreme exhaustion. Taft played down Rank's manic depression by writing,

> It would be strange if Rank, who had travelled so little, now suddenly thrown into the midst of an unknown city, without personal friends, speaking the language with effort, had not experienced extreme swings of mood, from elation at finding himself able to help the analysts with whom Freud had been unsuccessful to revulsion against the nightmare of New York in summer, and fear of the lengths to which his own independence was taking him.[1421]

It is a romantic description of a heroic genius forced to break bonds to save his ideas. Taft knew nothing of the reality, which was that Rank had been in a manic state for some time, possibly fuelled by exhaustion, and in that state had dictated a muddled and ill-founded book that had brought him into conflict with his closest colleagues.

Abraham was depicted by Taft as blacker than black. Two things are relevant here.

First, from the moment that Freud allowed him to read Abraham's letter expressing the fear that Ferenczi and Rank would go the same way as Jung, Rank was obsessed with Abraham. That *faux-pas* by Freud might have been inspired by his need to deflect Rank's aggression from himself on to another. He succeeded only too well. From that moment on, Rank saw all evil as coming from Abraham. He scolded him in many of his letters. Taft wrote down all those remarks, without subjecting them to any critical thought.

Second, Taft often heightened the effect herself. For example, "Abraham soon became the particular enemy for Ferenczi and Rank, who had to deal with him in connection with his ambition for advancement in the psychoanalytic Congress".[1422] Taft seems to mean by this that Abraham was to become president of the IPA and Rank and Ferenczi were opposed. Regarding Abraham's objections to the fact that Rank decided what the *Korrespondenzblatt* would look like even though Abraham was ultimately responsible for it, Taft writes, "The mounting bitterness of the quarrels arising between the Press in London and the publishing house in Vienna combined with the constant complaints of Rank's mismanagement by Abraham".[1423]

Taft was throwing mud here out of loyalty to Rank. Abraham certainly did not complain "constantly". Taft also thought up a reason why Abraham and others had taken aim at Rank:

> It is hardly necessary even to point out that to the distant members, the privileges of a young, nonmedical, relatively inexperienced upstart like Rank, in almost daily contact with the Master and of necessity in his confidence, must have been a continuous source of unconscious envy and justifiable irritation, if not actual jealousy.[1424]

Why would that be so obvious? Rank's position was far from enviable. He earned little with work that was too much for him to handle. Moreover, there is no indication that Abraham was affected by jealousy. Hedwig and Hilda confirm this. What did Abraham have to be jealous about? He had a flourishing practice in Berlin and was making a good income. He had a strong position in the Berlin Psychoanalytic Society, and he was loved and valued. He was extremely content with his contact with Freud and became upset if it faltered in any way. Those times when it did falter, however, were caused not by jealousy, but by differences of insight.

Taft cannot really be blamed for the book. She frankly states that she was a faithful follower, who idolised Rank. She wrote a hagiography. She has regularly been quoted uncritically by other authors, however, so that Abraham has been systematically placed in an unfavourable light.[1425]

CHAPTER TWENTY-SEVEN

Melanie Klein and fellow analysands

Relations with Freud restored

On 28 March 1924, Freud congratulated Abraham on being elected president of the IPA and added:

> I have heard with pleasure that the Congress passed off without any disturbing clashes, and I am very glad to acknowledge your services in this matter. As for the affair itself, I am, as you know, in an uncomfortable position. As regards the scientific aspect, I am in fact very close to your standpoint, or rather I am growing closer and closer to it, but in the personal aspect I still cannot take your side. Though I am fully convinced of the correctness of your behaviour, I still think you might have done things differently.[1426]

Freud had retracted his sharp tone with regard to Abraham's behaviour towards Rank and merely wrote that Abraham ought to have dealt with the matter differently. Freud does not seem to have been aware of his own contribution.

Abraham responded with immense relief:

> I feel infinitely relieved since I know that there is no factual discrepancy. For the last six months I have been very seriously worried. I cannot, naturally, in principle refute the possibility of having made an error in *form*. If I were to try to give a fuller explanation of my behaviour, I would have to go into many things that I have so far intentionally left untouched in our correspondence. I believe it is better to leave them unsaid; instead, I promise in future to show every consideration necessary in this far from simple situation.[1427]

Good relations with Freud had been restored, not least because of all the efforts Abraham had made at the congress in Salzburg to repair relations between the committee members. With Ferenczi he had succeeded. Rank had remained unapproachable.

The summer of 1924

For the summer, Abraham rented a little house in Sils-Maria. The family travelled there at the end of June. Abraham had not been in the Engadin for eighteen years and he was as enchanted by the landscape as ever. The profusion of Alpine flowers in early summer was unparalleled. The small dwelling was completely self-contained. The living room was furnished in the local style with a three-cornered bay window, wooden panelling and ceiling, and built-in furniture. The bedrooms were light and spacious and beautifully furnished. Abraham had taken a patient with him. He was working on a new edition of *Segantini* and on the lecture he had delivered at Salzburg.[1428] At first, there had been no certainty that the trip would go ahead, since the government was demanding huge sums for permission to travel abroad, prompting the remark from Abraham that apart from the fact that dogs had to be kept permanently on a leash, human beings now had to be tied up as well.[1429] Abraham had a dog of which he was extremely fond.[1430] It clearly annoyed him that he was not allowed to let it off the leash.

At the end of his holiday Abraham visited Freud for a few days. On 31 July 1924, Freud had written to Abraham; ". . . and I am looking forward greatly to seeing you again".[1431] On 23 August, Abraham wrote to Freud that he was incomparably pleased to have found him, despite all he had been through, so well, sympathetic, and capable, and he thanked him for all the kindnesses shown to him. He had no idea that it was the last time he and Freud would see each other.[1432]

Helene and Felix Deutsch

Helene Deutsch had called on Abraham for help in connection with the difficulties she and her husband were experiencing with Freud. Felix Deutsch had already informed Abraham about those problems one evening during the Salzburg congress. Helene Deutsch suggested she should come to Sils Maria in the summer of 1924 to discuss the matter, but Abraham wrote to her that he was going to visit Freud on the Semmering and would therefore be in Vienna on the way there or on the way back. So she did not need to make the long journey and they could meet up in Vienna. Abraham agreed to talk to Freud about the things that concerned the Deutschs.[1433] He did so, but meanwhile the damage had been done. Freud wrote to Ferenczi on 6 August that he had dispensed with Felix Deutsch as his doctor.

Freud did not mince words. Felix Deutsch must be counted among the constitutionally stupid. Freud resented him most of all for not being discreet but instead telling other people everything. He had also lied to Freud about his true condition.[1434] Felix Deutsch had seen in 1923 that Freud had cancer, but did not tell him so.[1435] This was, of course, unforgiveable, but at the same time there was a shocking repetition at work regarding that other reproach, for indiscretion. During the period when his wife was in analysis, Felix Deutsch wanted to be analysed himself. Abraham and Ferenczi were the most obvious analysts for him, but they lived too far away and Abraham did not qualify since he was analysing Helene Deutsch. Freud recommended Bernfeld and Felix Deutsch took his advice.[1436] But Bernfeld was a beginner at analysis and younger than Deutsch. It was a repeat of the situation with Tausk and Helene

Deutsch. Felix Deutsch had felt humiliated by Freud's referral of him to Bernfeld and by the fact that he had agreed. The indiscretions that Freud was angry about concerned the fact that Felix Deutsch mentioned Freud and his illness in his analysis by Bernfeld. He was, after all, Freud's doctor. But these were not indiscretions, since in analysis it needs to be possible to talk about anything. The one who was indiscreet was Bernfeld. He was unable to keep his mouth shut.[1437]

After his visit to Freud, Abraham talked at length with Felix Deutsch in Vienna. He tried to persuade Freud to judge Deutsch less harshly.[1438] Helene Deutsch seemed, on the face of it, to be doing well in this period. Her lectures were praised and she was busy setting up the Vienna Psychoanalytic Institute. Her mental state in the years 1924–1925 was not at all good, however, and she agreed with Abraham that she would enter into analysis with him again in the summer of 1925.[1439] That never happened, because Abraham became ill.

Among Abraham's patients at this time were Alix Strachey, Nelly Wolffheim, and Melanie Klein. The first two were of great importance to the third.

Alix Strachey

James and Alix Strachey are famous above all for taking upon themselves the publication of the complete works of Freud in English, translating most of his books and articles themselves. Freud was published by Leonard Woolf's Hogarth Press from 1924 onwards mainly because the Stracheys were part of the Bloomsbury group.[1440]

Shortly after their wedding in 1920, James and Alix Strachey travelled to Vienna to enter into analysis with Freud. Etiquette in analysis was far more relaxed in those days than it is now and Freud asked after just a few weeks whether they would translate for him. The work in question was "'A child is being beaten'", which was soon followed by a request to translate the far more substantial *Group Psychology and the Analysis of the Ego*.[1441] Freud was an admirer of James' older brother Lytton.[1442] The Stracheys stayed in Vienna for two years. Alix's analysis was interrupted a number of times when she contracted severe pneumonia. In retrospect, she decided she had not benefited at all from Freud's analysis of her. Freud recommended she should continue her analysis with Abraham and, in the course of 1924, she took up his advice.[1443]

For her analysis, Alix moved to Berlin while James remained in London. They wrote to each other almost daily and much of their correspondence was published in 1985.[1444]

The letters of Alix Strachey paint an excellent picture of analytic Berlin in those days. One striking aspect of the correspondence is that Alix says almost nothing about the analysis itself, unlike Helene Deutsch, for instance, who wrote about almost nothing else in her letters to her husband. This might have to do with the fact that James Strachey also wanted to enter into analysis again, preferably in Berlin and ideally with Abraham. Alix Strachey did not want that at all. In the end, James was analysed by James Glover, himself an analysand of Abraham. James Glover died fairly shortly after Abraham, so both Stracheys lost their analysts in the middle of their analysis.

The motive for Alix's analysis is not clearly described anywhere, but Meisel and Kendrick write in their introduction to the letters that it was very probably melancholia.[1445] Virginia

Woolf's depiction of Alix Strachey seems to point in that direction. She described her as some-one with a good brain but not enough vitality to persist in using it.[1446] "Mired in sepulchral despair", Woolf wrote of her. Alix Strachey began her analysis with Abraham on 10 September 1924. James came with her but was due to return to England after a short time.[1447] On 20 October, Abraham wrote the following to Freud about her:

Perhaps, dear Professor, you may be interested in hearing something about Ψα from Mrs Str.[achey] from London. It struck me from the very beginning that the long period of work with you has been, as it were, obliterated. We have to discover everything afresh, as all the facts elicited by the first analysis have disappeared, while the general knowledge of Ψα is intact. You will remember that the patient lost her father in the first weeks of her life and has no memories of her own of him. Apart from other motives for the amnesia, there is a complete identification of your person with the father—she has no memories of either. On the other hand she has directed towards you the same rescue phantasies as towards her father.[1448]

Abraham thinks transference was the reason that Alix Strachey could recall almost nothing of her analysis with Freud, but it does seem odd. Possibly she was depersonalised. Freud does not seem to have had much success in making contact with her.

The analysis of Alix Strachey by Abraham is rather more informal than it would be today, as was the case with Helene Deutsch as well. Alix read German literature during the period she was in Berlin, Fontane and Heinrich Mann, for instance. Abraham gave her *Die kleine Stadt* by Heinrich Mann to read. She saw her analyst at a "tea party" and during her sessions of analy-sis the phone at Abraham's elbow would often ring and a short conversation would follow. She wrote to James: "... the telephone at Höhere Mächten's elbow frequently rings and a short conversation ensues, while my ideas whirl hopelessly round in my head". The nickname she gave Abraham, "Höhere Mächten" (Higher Powers), points to a great distance between them.[1449] Alix was extremely satisfied with her analysis and wrote on 9 February 1925,

Dearest James,

I had a non-analytical conversation with Dr. Abraham today about the length of my analysis. He wanted to know how long I should be able to go on with it. I said, indefinitely, i.e. till I was well. This is, I'm sure, the only line for me to take. Because until my symptoms and general state is cured, I shall remain practically useless in any capacity (that I knew before I came here); and also there is no doubt in my mind that Abraham is the best analyst I could be working with, and I really believe that it may be effective – anyhow, I am certain that more psychological work (not to mention an actual improvement, which may be only due to transference) has been done in these 5 months than was accomplished in 15 with Freud. (Curious isn't it? But I have heard of other people who also think that Abraham is a sounder person as an actual analyst. Frau Klein told me this.) So that, "kurzum", it is a question of now or never.[1450]

What the letters clearly demonstrate is how astonishingly active the Berlin Psychoanalytic Society was in those days. In 1924, it had twenty-seven to twenty-eight members, as well as trainee psychoanalysts who were not specifically named. The number of activities it held is remarkable in relation to the number of members.

The first event encountered by Alix Strachey was a two-day meeting in Würzburg on 11 and 12 October 1924, specially for German psychoanalysts. It had been Abraham's idea to bring together interested people living in central and southern Germany and possibly to set up a second German psychoanalytic society. Up to that point, practically all German psychoanalytic activity was concentrated in Berlin and analysts who lived elsewhere in the country were rather out on a limb. It was mainly through Karl Landauer that Abraham became aware of the problem. Landauer lived in Frankfurt and because of the war and the crisis of 1923 he had become very isolated from his colleagues. In January 1924, he travelled to Berlin for the first time and from then on Abraham looked after him by meeting up with him fairly regularly and above all by sending him supportive letters.[1451] Abraham was always ready to give Landauer advice, enabling him to throw off his sense of isolation completely.[1452] Abraham organised the two-day meeting in Würzburg with Landauer's help and the plan was to have such a meeting every year. When it was over, Abraham and Hedwig spent a day with Landauer and his wife on the Königssee in southern Germany.[1453]

The description by Alix Strachey of the meeting in Würzburg was hilarious. It started with an endless train journey on wooden seats. Just before departure, a swarm of analysts filled the entire compartment. The bed in the hotel room was far too short, but all this was made up for by the immense conviviality, with hardly any sleep, lots of good wine, and lectures of a high standard in beautiful old Würzburg. The van Emdens were guests of honour at the festive dinner.[1454]

Abraham was good at creating a bond with people. At the "Tagung", analysts from central and southern Germany spoke, but so did a number of Abraham's confidants such as Felix Deutsch, Helene Deutsch, Boehm, Landauer, Sachs, and Simmel.[1455]

In a letter to James of 31 October 1924, Alix gave a good impression of the vast range of activities of the Berlin Psychoanalytic Society.[1456] The courses were to start on Monday 3 November. She was planning to take three of the six courses. On Monday evenings she wanted to go to Sachs, who was giving a course about normal sexual development, on Wednesday evenings to Simmel about anxiety, and on Thursday to Abraham about the ontogenesis of personality.

In addition, there were courses given by Radó and Alexander and a technical seminar by Eitingon, Simmel, and Radó. Alix had heard that only advanced students were eligible for these two courses and the technical seminar.[1457]

Then there were the meetings of the Berlin Psychoanalytic Society on the first and third Thursday of the month and the last Saturday of the month.

The large number of courses had to do in part with the flourishing polyclinic. Eitingon reported on that during the congress in Salzburg.[1458] Of the twenty-seven members of the Berlin Psychoanalytic Society, fifteen performed work of some sort for the polyclinic. Eighty analyses were carried out at a time, twenty-eight of them by permanent staff. Then there were sixteen analyses by members who made their services available voluntarily, or by members of other psychoanalytic societies who were staying in Berlin for a period. Another thirty-eight analyses were carried out by aspiring psychoanalysts, under the supervision of Eitingon, Simmel, Harnik, and Radó. The patients continued to pay what they said they could afford. Most of the treatments lasted for several months to a year. Around twenty per cent lasted between one and two years. It is striking that they included quite a few child analyses.

An extensive training programme was put together on the initiative of Simmel under the chairmanship of Eitingon and with the collaboration of Abraham, Müller, Sachs, Simmel, and Horney.[1459] That programme has since been extremely influential. Broadly speaking, most of today's psychoanalytic societies still follow it, with one important difference. In 1924, anyone who was interested could take a course. There was much more openness.[1460] Only the courses on technique were reserved for aspiring psychoanalysts, since patients were discussed in them.

Alix Strachey began to feel at home in Berlin. At the end of the afternoon she often sat in Café Konditorei Schilling reading and writing letters.[1461] Schilling was a famous coffee house on the Kurfürstendamm. Alix was extremely keen on dancing and she danced as often as possible, although the Berliners had the bad habit of dancing on carpets, which made it difficult to move across the floor. Alix had an additional problem in that she was very tall, often far taller than her dancing partners. On 4 December 1924, she went to the Union Palace with Sachs to dance. Sachs was bulky and must have come to about Alix's shoulder. Radó had gone with them. He did not dance, but he said that he wrote his articles only to dance music. So there he sat, staring into the distance and making notes in a notebook. Alix was greatly charmed by him.[1462]

The most important contact Alix made in Berlin was Melanie Klein, with whom she often went out at night in Berlin from 1925 onwards to paint the town red. On 2 February 1925, she wrote to James:

I'm now sufficiently recovered from the great Dance to compose a letter about it. It really was much nicer and more gay than the other one. . . . Frau Klein took me off with her. She was most elaborately got up as a kind of Cleopatra—terrifically décolleté—and covered in bangles and rouge—exactly as I imagine C. did look in the late Anthonies. She was frightfully excited and determined to have a thousand adventures, and soon infected me with some of her spirits. . . . She's really a very good sort and makes no secret of her hopes, fears and pleasures, which are of the simplest sort. Only she's got a damned sharp eye for neurotics, and I was afraid she nosed something in my anticipatory looks of horror and despondency.—But this time I had luck. In the first place I somehow got the art of roving from partner to partner, instead of clinging feverishly, and with utmost boredom for both, to the first person I happened to meet. In the second place, I found a Dancer, a real dancer. . . . Now and then I met Cleo again, perfectly happy and grinning. Then appeared Simmel, most brilliantly got up as a Berlin nightwatchman. He really has got a talent for acting. . . . I spied Dr. Sachs in the distance, but he kept away from all his acquaintances, intent on his own business.[1463]

Melanie Klein and Alix Strachey became friends and many dance evenings were to follow. Alix wrote to James that Melanie Klein was unpopular with some of the Berlin Psychoanalytic Society, who claimed she was good at the practice but weak in the theory. Her opponents were led by Lampl, whom Alix described as follows: "Lampl, who, to tell you the truth is rather too silly. A regular Viennese—good-natured as long as he's not bored and extremely provincial out of laziness and self-content. But he is easy and nice and amusing (as that goes here) to get on with. I think Radó is probably the cleverest of the lot".[1464]

Lou Andreas-Salomé was regularly in Berlin. When in town, she would come to meetings of the Berlin Psychoanalytic Society. She also visited Abraham. He was a person she liked to talk to about all kinds of things.[1465] They corresponded quite regularly. On 28 October, Lou Andreas-Salomé wrote Abraham a letter several pages long because she was unable to come to Würzburg. Her letter dealt mainly with *A Short Study of the Development of the Libido*, about which she was extremely enthusiastic.[1466]

The same thing struck Lou Andreas-Salomé about the Berlin Psychoanalytic Society as had struck Alix Strachey, which was the enormous hostility towards Melanie Klein. Lou Andreas-Salomé wrote to Anna Freud on 18 October 1924 about how curious it was that the Berlin analysts, with the exception of Abraham, rejected Melanie Klein with great abhorrence.[1467]

Ferenczi had been concerned about this even before Melanie Klein moved to Berlin. On 22 April 1921, he wrote to Eitingon that he was afraid the anti-women and anti-layperson mood that he believed he had detected among the Berliners at the congress in The Hague would cause Melanie Klein to creep back into her shell.[1468] Around that time, Hermine Hug-Hellmuth had started sending out messages about Melanie Klein's lack of higher education.[1469]

Nelly Wolffheim

In the summer of 1921, kindergarten teacher Nelly Wolffheim contacted Abraham because of a number of serious symptoms she was suffering. She later described in her autobiography how she had found that first visit extremely encouraging. Abraham listened to her in a friendly way and gained her trust. He advised her to undergo analysis because otherwise she would not be in a condition to resume her work in the short term. He could take her on for six weeks, since another patient was away travelling. Abraham explained to Nelly Wolffheim that normally someone of her age—she was forty-two—would not be accepted for analysis (Abraham, 1920a). He had only once treated a patient so old. Nelly Wolffheim thought that her case interested Abraham and that this explained why he agreed to analyse her despite her age and continued when the six weeks were over. Nelly Wolffheim remained in analysis with Abraham for more than four years, until his death. It was an unusually long time for those days.[1470] She missed him hugely when he was no longer there.[1471]

The series of symptoms that had brought Nelly Wolffheim to Abraham was impressive. She was from the well-off Jewish middle class. She had a very anxious neurotic mother and the family lived a relatively isolated existence. Nelly Wolffheim had a brother two years older who not only looked very handsome but was extremely capable and gifted. Nelly Wolffheim had a squint for a long time, was troubled by a rash, was often in poor health, and thought herself terribly ugly. Her childhood had been marked by feelings of inferiority, envy, and jealousy with regard to her brother. She had all kinds of anxieties and was depressed. For a while, as a child, she had cried every time her parents said goodnight to her because she thought she was going to die in the night. Depression ran in the family. Two of her mother's brothers committed suicide.

Despite all this, Nelly Wolffheim became a kindergarten teacher and she had a day nursery of her own. But she was often unable to work because of all kinds of illnesses and depression. When she approached Abraham she was in a very poor state. She had serious stomach complaints, which later turned out to have to do with her gall bladder, and she was deeply depressed. She found Abraham's proposal that she enter into analysis with him extremely problematic. If she became ill again, as she so often had, then how was she to pay for analysis six times a week? Nevertheless, she started and the analysis gave her the strength to work more. As well as the day nursery, she had to take on all kinds of other work to pay Abraham's fee. In the mornings, she sometimes taught German for an hour before the day nursery opened. After it closed, she went to Abraham for her analysis. In the late afternoon, she taught. On free afternoons and on evenings when she was not following a course in psychoanalysis, she took dictation. Eventually, Nelly Wolffheim's condition improved immensely as a result of analysis. She was no longer too ill to work and she published many books and journal articles about pedagogy and especially psychoanalytic pedagogy. Because of Abraham, she started taking courses in psychoanalysis and even attending congresses, so that she became very well grounded in psychoanalysis.

Nelly Wolffheim and Melanie Klein

It was through Abraham that Nelly Wolffheim came into contact with Melanie Klein. Abraham advised Melanie Klein to observe children in Nelly Wolffheim's day nursery. She later vividly remembered Klein's first visit.[1472] Klein looked pretty and intelligent. She sat bolt upright on a bench. Talking continually, without asking questions, she laid out her vision of child psycho-analysis as the only correct one. Wolffheim was deeply impressed. After all, Klein was a psychoanalyst. But when Klein said that if a child made two toy cars crash into each other in a game it symbolically represented the parents' coitus, she was unable to believe it. After consultation with Abraham, a five-year-old girl from Wolffheim's day nursery entered into analysis with Klein. This was Erna, whom Klein later described at length. Several of Melanie Klein's young patients came from the day nursery and Nelly Wolffheim referred a number of young patients to her. There were regular telephone conversations between them about the children. Wolffheim later thought it typical of Klein's attitude to the pedagogic efforts of her day nursery that she never wrote a word about them. It was the daily environment of the children and they no doubt talked about it in their analysis, but, for Klein, only the inner world counted.

Nelly Wolffheim earned an important extra income by taking dictation from Melanie Klein. For two and a half years, Klein came three evenings a week, straight after work, to dictate articles and personal letters.

The articles were dictated from memory without any notes. Melanie Klein hopped from one thought to the next. Nelly Wolffheim, who became fond of Klein, did not find the articles scientific; they were more like art. In this period, Melanie Klein was finally able to visit Freud, as she had wished to do for so long. She was particularly eager to talk to him about her child analyses. Afterwards, she said not a word about the experience to Nelly Wolffheim, who concluded that the visit had not gone well. Freud is believed to have said afterwards, "Is that what's become of my analysis?"

At that time, Melanie Klein was insisting that all children should undergo analysis as part of their upbringing, just as they should all go to school. Nelly Wolffheim disagreed totally. She found the proposal worrying and discussed it in her analysis with Abraham. Abraham, who was generally positive about Melanie Klein's ideas, said that she had no need to worry. There would never be enough child analysts to fulfil that requirement.

The position of Melanie Klein

Melanie Klein's success in gaining such a central position in the world of analysis is, to an important degree, attributable to Karl Abraham and to Alix Strachey. Abraham gave her the opportunity to settle in Berlin and to develop her ideas further there, and she was initially very much guided by Abraham's theory, of which she adopted a great deal. Alix Strachey gave her lessons in English and saw to it that Klein was able to deliver a series of lectures in London in 1925. Alix Strachey translated the lectures into English and even partially rewrote them. Klein's lectures were extremely chaotic and Alix Strachey made each of them into a comprehensible whole. This enabled Klein to flee Berlin, the city so hostile to her, after Abraham's death and to settle in England.

Melanie Klein succeeded in winning important patrons to her side. First there was Ferenczi in Budapest, who allowed her to join the Budapest Psychoanalytic Society even though she had no academic training at all. He put her in touch with psychoanalysis and pointed out her gift for child analysis.[1473] Then there was Abraham, the central person in Berlin, the city where she settled at the age of thirty-eight and where she laid the foundations of her theory, which was closely related to Abraham's. Finally, there was Ernest Jones in London, who even allowed her to analyse his own children.

In her 1932 book, *The Psycho-Analysis of Children*, Melanie Klein wrote the following about Abraham:

> In Dr. Karl Abraham I had the great good fortune to find a second teacher with the faculty of inspiring his pupils to put out their best energies in the service of psycho-analysis. In Abraham's opinion the progress of psycho-analysis depended upon each individual analyst—upon the value of his work, the quality of his character and the level of his scientific attainments. These high standards have been before my mind, when, in this book on psycho-analysis, I have tried to repay some part of the great debt I owe to that science. Abraham clearly understood the great practical and theoretical potentialities of child analysis. At the First Conference of German Psycho-Analysts at Würzburg in 1924, in connection with a paper I had read upon an obsessional neurosis in a child, he said, in words that I shall never forget: "The future of psycho-analysis lies in play technique." The study of the mind of the small child taught me certain facts which seemed strange at first sight. But Abraham's confidence in my work encouraged me at that time to follow the path on which I had started. My theoretical conclusions are a natural development of his own discoveries, as I hope this book will show.[1474]

In 1920, Abraham had already been making plans for the development of child analysis in the polyclinic in Berlin and he had expressly invited Melanie Klein to take it on. In the circular letter of 11 January 1921, he wrote that she had arrived. A few weeks later, on 3 February,

Klein gave her first lecture to the Berlin Psychoanalytic Society, about child analysis. The week after that there was a discussion on the subject. On 19 May, she again delivered a lecture, this time about orientation disorders in children. As well as giving lectures, she spoke at the congresses. She lectured at the congress in Berlin in 1922 and she spoke at the congress in Salzburg in 1924 and at the congress in Würzburg later that year. She became a member of the Berlin Psychoanalytic Society in 1923 and that same year she taught a course on child sexuality for kindergarten teachers.

In 1923, Abraham supervised a child analysis by Melanie Klein and he wrote to Freud,

> I have something pleasant to report in the scientific field. In my work on melancholia etc., of which Rank has the manuscript, I have assumed the presence of a basic [mood disorder] in infancy as a prototype for later melancholia. In the last few months Frau Dr Klein has skilfully conducted the $\Psi\alpha$ of a three-year-old boy with good therapeutic results. This child faithfully presented the basic melancholia that I had assumed and in close combination with oral erotism. The case offers in general amazing insight into the infantile instinctual life.[1475]

It was a crucial moment, because Abraham saw the theory that he published shortly afterwards confirmed in practice in a three-year-old patient that Melanie Klein was treating. It was also crucial because Klein later used the ideas Abraham was then developing as the building blocks of her own work.

This was a difficult period for Melanie Klein. She had been living apart from her husband for some time, but in 1923 they decided to attempt a reconciliation and moved into a house in Berlin's wealthy Dahlem district along with their children. It was not a success and Melanie Klein left her husband for good in April 1923.[1476] She had earlier asked Abraham whether she could enter into analysis with him. She regarded her analysis with Ferenczi as deficient because the negative transference had not arisen. At first, Abraham did not want to analyse her. After the problems with Liebermann, he had decided not to psychoanalyse colleagues any longer, but he must have allowed Melanie Klein to persuade him. In early 1924, she began her analysis with Abraham. Grosskurth, Klein's biographer, wondered whether she might have started before then. Melanie Klein said in her interview with Eissler that she had been in analysis with Abraham for fourteen months when he died.[1477]

Abraham's family was not charmed by her. His son Grant, still Gerd in those days, later said that, as children, they generally never met Abraham's patients, with the exception of Melanie Klein, whom they were apparently allowed to see more than the others. Grant remembered her as haughty and condescending. His mother and sister spoke with considerable anger about Klein. Grant thought they disliked her because she was so pushy.[1478] Hedwig developed such animosity towards Melanie Klein that after Abraham's death she asked Jones to remove her name from his obituary. Jones did not comply with her request.[1479]

In 1987, Pines mentioned an interesting aspect of Melanie Klein's analysis: Abraham sometimes kept interpretations to himself, for fear that Melanie Klein would make use of them before he had published his findings.[1480] It seems Abraham was a little apprehensive about Klein's use of his theoretical insights.

Melanie Klein's early years in psychoanalysis

Primarily because of the research done by Claudia Frank, a clear picture has emerged of how crucial the Berlin years were to the theory developed by Melanie Klein.[1481]

In her now classic book, *Introduction to the Work of Melanie Klein*, Hannah Segal omitted the Berlin years altogether.[1482]

Grosskurth, Melanie Klein's biographer, continued to assume that many of Klein's case histories could be traced back to her own children. Frank showed that this was true only of the lecture with which she became a member of the Budapest Psychoanalytic Society and the two articles based on that lecture.[1483] Melanie Klein carried out at least twenty-two child analyses in Berlin and much of her later work was based on those analyses and the case histories belonging to them. Immediately after she arrived in Berlin, she began her first child analysis at the polyclinic, on 1 February 1921.

Of the twenty-two analyses she carried out in Berlin, only five were of children of colleagues. At first, she analysed the children three times a week, from 1923 onwards perhaps daily. In the Wellcome Library in London, an overwhelming amount of material can be found about her Berlin analyses.[1484]

Abraham not only supported Melanie Klein in her research in the field of child analysis, he protected her against the far from mild attacks by her colleagues. They thought it was outrageous that she was transferring the psychoanalytic technique, complete with all its interpretations, to child analysis lock stock and barrel. Could the tender mind of a child cope with it? Melanie Klein's eccentric performance also contributed to the opposition she evoked. Alix Strachey described her as a chaotic waterfall of words, but also as very original. Klein's articles and lectures from that time consisted of long case histories with little theory. It is important to remember that listening to and observing children in such detail was something very new. The application to children of psychoanalytic interpretations—and they were often sexual interpretations—without any restraint was a revolution in technique.

Klein had carried out one analysis in Budapest before she moved to Berlin, that of her own son Erik. The lecture she gave about it on the occasion of her admission to the Budapest Psychoanalytic Society was published in 1920.[1485] Klein described what Erik said and did and the questions she put to him, and she added hardly any theory or interpretations. The criticism of von Freund, that she had not touched the unconscious of the child in any way, seems correct, as does his advice that she should analyse the boy at a fixed time each day. In early 1921, Klein moved to Berlin. In that same year, a sixty-page article by her was published in *Imago*.[1486] This article was an expanded version of the above-mentioned article in the *Zeitschrift*. To protect his privacy, she had changed the name of the boy from Erik to Fritz. The article in *Imago* was, above all, a case history with a tiny bit of theory from Freud, Abraham, Ferenczi, and Róheim. No technique is mentioned at all, really, only the idea that by allowing children to talk about where they come from, for example, and whether they have always been a boy and whether their sister was always a girl and so on, it is possible to work prophylactically, to prevent shame and inhibitions later.

In 1922, the year that Klein became an associate member of the Berlin Psychoanalytic Society, a short report appeared in the *Korrespondenzblatt* of her lecture at the Berlin congress, called "Zur Frühanalyse" (On early analysis).[1487] In 1923, she published an extended version in *Imago*. It was a fairly chaotic article, again on the subject of preventing inhibitions by analysing children at a very young age.[1488] In 1922, another article by her about inhibitions appeared, this time about inhibitions in puberty, in the journal *Die neue Erziehung*.[1489] In 1923, Klein became a member of the Berlin Psychoanalytic Society and in that year Abraham began to supervise her. From the article, it becomes clear that Melanie Klein began to develop theories of her own only when she came under the supervision of Abraham and later entered into analysis with him.

The work of Abraham and Klein

An in-depth comparison of the theories of Abraham and Klein would require a book of its own and it falls outside the remit of this biography. There are, however, several remarks to be made on the subject.

Melanie Klein and the later Kleinians continually referred to Freud and never to Abraham, even though Klein's theory is far more closely related to Abraham's ideas than to Freud's. It was not the case that Melanie Klein renounced Abraham; in fact, she specifically mentioned him. Her famous book of 1932, *The Psycho-Analysis of Children*, was dedicated to him: "To the memory of Karl Abraham in gratitude and admiration".[1490] Oddly, however, it stopped there. Melanie Klein and the later Kleinians did not discuss Abraham's work. If they used his ideas, then they did not do so explicitly. They did not develop his ideas further, and neither did they criticise him. Instead, they always quoted Freud.

It is possible to point to two reasons for this.

First, status. After his death, Abraham rapidly lost status, whereas Freud's status only increased. Quoting Freud lent much more weight than quoting Abraham. Second, it was a survival strategy, and an extremely successful one. Continually referring to Freud was a strategic emergency measure taken by Melanie Klein that was adopted by her followers as well. By always writing that she was basing her ideas on Freud and by never taking a stance in opposition to him, even if her theory did not resemble Freud's theory, she managed to hold her own within the psychoanalytic world and could not be described as a dissident and excluded. Melanie Klein took this approach right from her very first articles, but it came to the fore most strongly during what became known as the controversial discussions.

In 1942, Anna Freud and Melanie Klein found themselves up against each other in London.[1491] During the controversial discussions, their battle was fought out within the British Psychoanalytical Society. Both regarded their own theory as the true psychoanalytic theory and comparison between them was difficult. In the end, there remained only one basis for comparison in the debate and that was to look at whether their ideas were "based on Freud". This degenerated into basing their arguments on literal quotations from Freud. The result: Melanie Klein was not excluded, which was what Anna Freud wanted, but instead gained an official place in the world of psychoanalysis. The British Psychoanalytical Society developed a Freudian branch, a Kleinian branch, and an independent branch.

Two technical innovations formed the foundations of Melanie Klein's work. The first was to allow children to talk and to listen very closely, and the second was the playing technique, which she applied from 1923 onwards. In the consulting room, the child was given simple toys and allowed to do with them whatever it liked. The game was watched in the same way as free association in adults was observed, and it, too, was interpreted. Hannah Segal has described Klein's fundamental principles, which were formulated much later, as follows:

—Transference based on the projection of the inner parent figures onto the analyst.

—A psychoanalytic situation that must not be disturbed by any moral, educational or reassuring stance.

—A playing technique in which the analyst tries to understand and to interpret, playing with the child as little as possible, only as much as is necessary to allow the child to express itself.[1492]

The influence of Abraham on Klein's theory

"Klein's theory in tandem with Abraham's theory" was how Taylor described it in relation to the years around 1924.[1493] Perhaps this can best be clarified by defining the points on which Klein obviously took her inspiration from Abraham

First, in the period when Klein was being supervised by him and was in analysis with him, Abraham developed a theory about the first year of life. He distinguished between a first and a second oral phase, such that the first oral phase was auto-erotic and the second oral–cannibalistic. Depressions could be traced back to the second oral phase. The first year of life was a phase that Freud hardly concerned himself with at all. Melanie Klein made that first year a spearhead of her theory and saw the oedipal phase as beginning earlier. Whereas Abraham saw no ambivalence or object relations in the first oral phase, Klein regarded both as present from birth.

Second, both Abraham and Klein identified a powerful aggression in the first year of life: Abraham from the moment the teeth started to come through, Klein far earlier even than that.

Third, the drives play a major part in both theories. Abraham's theory is entirely an outcome of the libido theory, as was Klein's theory at the beginning.

Fourth, both point to a pattern in object relations whereby a development takes place from the destruction of possessions to valuing them.

Fifth, in Abraham, guilt about one's own aggression is of great importance and leads to depression. According to Klein, from a very early age the strict superego that condemns one's own aggression is of great importance. They both write of the same processes, but using different terminology.

Sixth, both theories are a combination of drive theory and object-relations theory and both strongly emphasise component objects. Klein indicates that above all the penis and the breast are the earliest objects of unconscious infantile preoccupation. Abraham also strongly emphasises the component objects, but he claims that the vengefulness of the melancholic, in regression to the second half of the first year of life, desires a castration of the mother, whether of her breast or of the penis she is credited with having.

Seventh, the interpretation of negative transference was of importance to both Klein and Abraham. Klein's objection to her analysis with Ferenczi was that the negative transference was never discussed and both Klein and Abraham were of the opinion that in humans there is inborn aggression that can burst out with problematic force.

Finally, anxiety is important in the work of both Abraham and Klein. They strongly associated anxiety with a person's own cannibalistic desires.[1494]

There was also a fundamental difference between them. For Abraham, real interactions with the outside world and traumas experienced in it were central, for Klein, the inner world.

CHAPTER TWENTY-EIGHT

Abraham's death

The year 1925 began promisingly

On 14 February, the fifth anniversary of the founding of the polyclinic was celebrated. The clinic had turned out to be a great success. Ninety analyses were now taking place there at any one time.[1495]

Moreover, for the first time a prominent Berlin medical group, the association for gynaecology and obstetrics, had asked for a lecture about gynaecology and psychoanalysis.

Abraham gave that lecture on 13 March 1925, and it was broadly in line with his article "Manifestations of the female castration complex" of 1921.[1496] There, he wrote that the normal reaction of women to the difference in sex is jealousy. The girl feels castrated and regards her sexual organs as a wound. She wants to be a man. In the course of her development, she abandons that desire, identifies herself with her mother, focuses on the father as a love-object, and wants to have his child. Abraham saw this as the first manifestation of the mothering instinct. From his speech, it turns out that he saw very many physical things as mental. He saw the start of menstruation outside of the normal cycle as resistance to having sexual intercourse with the husband. Vomiting during pregnancy was, in his view, partly caused by unconscious resistance to the pregnancy and to bearing a child, while an inability to produce breast milk could often be traced back to an unconscious hostility in the mother towards the child. That last point was particularly striking, because it had happened to his wife, Hedwig, when she tried to breast-feed their daughter, Hilda.

The response of the gynaecologists to Abraham's lecture was extremely critical, but that did not bother Abraham in the least. In his closing speech, he calmly addressed their criticism point by point. Afterwards, he was extremely satisfied with how the evening had gone. The lecture hall at the university clinic had been filled to the rafters. The gynaecologists knew little about psychoanalysis and at first they listened with the familiar sceptical smiles on their faces, but those smiles disappeared in the course of the evening and they became interested, especially during the discussion. Abraham heard from various sides afterwards that the evening had been a success for psychoanalysis.

A final meeting falls through

Abraham wanted to visit Freud at Easter, but Freud prevented that. Freud's health was not good.[1497] On 20 March 1925 he wrote that he was terribly sorry not to be able to receive Abraham but that he was still not completely "ready for use". Freud felt conscience-stricken because Eitingon, by contrast, was able to come. He used the excuse of consultation about the publishing house, because otherwise Abraham might feel offended.[1498] A letter from Freud to Ferenczi makes clear what was going on:

> Abraham has announced himself with his wife for Easter. But I will probably ask him not to visit me. I am too tired from the more than six months' work and the incessant treatment with its torments, so that I would like to take a rest over Easter in Vienna, or elsewhere, free from respon-sibilities. Abraham is an optimist, rather presumptuous in his relations with people, and he evidently cannot see eye to eye with the demands of my condition.[1499]

Abraham, however caring he may have been, had difficulty attuning himself to others. In his enthusiasm, he would want to discuss things at length with Freud and Freud did not feel up to it. He was afraid Abraham would demand too much of him. Neither Freud nor Abraham had the slightest idea that this was a crucial moment. They would never see each other again.

Receiving Eitingon was easier for Freud, because Eitingon always went along with what-ever he said. Rank, who had just returned from America, will have played a role here as well. Freud was now in agreement with Abraham's criticism of Rank, but his priority was to get Rank to rejoin the rest of them. He entered into a debate with Rank about *The Trauma of Birth* and tried to persuade him to debate with others about it as well, but Rank was far too depressed. He went to meetings of the Vienna Psychoanalytic Society without showing any sign of engagement at all. Anna Freud was annoyed by him, writing to Eitingon that he was behaving like a proud and very badly brought up child.[1500] Mildness was not Anna Freud's strong point. Rank complained to Freud that he was totally incapable of work and felt extremely unhappy.[1501]

Things were going well with Abraham, with his family, with the Berlin Psychoanalytic Society, and with psychoanalysis in Berlin. As ever, he was giving a lot of courses, which were well attended.

Abraham's children were at the Grünewald Grammar School, not far from their house.[1502] Hilda, now eighteen, was in her last year at school. Gerd at fifteen was as tall as his mother and sister, and his parents' pride and joy. Abraham was planning to go on a major moun-taineering trip with him in the summer.[1503] At school, Hilda had been asked to write an essay about dream psychology and her teacher specifically requested that she describe Freud's theory uninhibitedly. She had been interested in psychoanalysis from a young age. Abraham gave her books to read and she went to lectures.[1504]

A cry for help from Reik

On 11 April 1925, Abraham received an eight-page letter from Reik. It was a cry for help concerning the ban on lay analysis.[1505] Freud had advised Rank, Reik, and his daughter Anna, among others, against studying medicine because he thought it must be possible for psychoanalysis to be carried out by non-doctors. In other words, he approved of lay analysis. Freud had a clear view on the matter, but he got his pupils into great difficulties because practically everyone, including psychoanalysts, thought that medical studies were an essential requirement, which made it hard for lay practitioners to acquire patients.

Reik wrote in his letter that unfortunately he had carried out only four analyses, that there were no foreigners among them, and that he and his wife could only just manage on the income this produced.[1506] Now something terrible had happened. Stekel had wanted to set up a psychoanalytic polyclinic. The municipal authorities refused him permission, however, and in his fury he had pointed out, in a medical journal, that Rank, Reik, and Bernfeld were carrying out psychoanalysis although they were not doctors. As a direct result, Reik had received a writ for running a medical practice without being a qualified doctor. He was threatened with a ban, which would mean the loss of his entire income.[1507] In 1926, a second indictment was lodged against Reik, this time by a patient. Freud supported Reik during legal proceedings and wrote "The question of lay analysis" to defend him.[1508] In the end, Reik was not prosecuted.

Abraham's lectures in the Netherlands and financial misappropriation by van Ophuijsen

Abraham was asked, through van Ophuijsen, to give three lectures in The Hague and Leiden in late May 1925. On 27 and 29 May, he lectured to a group of neurologists and students at the Leiden Society for Psychoanalysis and Psychopathology.[1509] There were around thirty people in the audience. The lecture was about the psychoanalysis of schizophrenic conditions. Abraham spoke about a hebephrenic patient and a more paranoid patient. He described the course of their psychoanalysis and its difficulties. The results had been astonishingly good.

The annual reports of the Leiden Society are preserved in a small hand-written book that is still in the possession of G. W. Muller, son of F. P. Muller.[1510] The latter became a member of the Dutch Psychoanalytic Society in 1920 and was president of the Leiden Society for Psychoanalysis and Psychopathology when Abraham gave his lecture there. In the annual report of 1924–1925, the minutes record that Abraham delivered two lectures about the psychology of, and therapy for, schizophrenia, which were very interesting. Only it was a shame that attendance was disappointing. Signed by the president, F. P. Muller, and the secretary, H. C. Jelgersma.[1511]

On 28 May, Abraham gave a lecture to The Hague branch of the Dutch Medical Association in front of a large audience, most of them doctors who had not been trained in psychoanalysis. The lecture, about hysterical symptoms, was a great success.[1512]

From a postcard from Abraham to Freud dated 29 May, we can conclude that the Abrahams very probably stayed with the van Ophuijsens. Abraham wrote that they were enjoying a splendid afternoon in the Wassenaar Park. The card was signed by him, by Hedwig, and by the van Ophuijsens.[1513]

After Abraham's death, there was an extremely unpleasant aftermath to their friendship of many years. On 5 March 1926, just over two months after Abraham died, van Ophuijsen wrote a long letter to Eitingon in which, at the end, he described his problematic financial situation.[1514] He had lost his savings in 1920. Van Ophuijsen does not mention whether it was through speculation or in some other way. In 1922–1923 van Ophuijsen and his family spent a considerable time in Berlin, where they lived rather comfortably. The mark was worth little in those days compared to the guilder. When he returned to The Hague in April 1923 with his family, he was expecting his practice to flourish again from the start. That was not the case at all, and he had no financial reserves. Van Ophuijsen found himself in financial difficulties. Freud, Abraham, and van Ophuijsen's mother helped him to keep his head above water.[1515]

A few months after that first letter, on 30 September 1926, van Ophuijsen sent Eitingon what he himself described as a cry for help. He needed a great deal of money to pay his debts. It seems Eitingon was immediately willing to help, because a few days later, on 3 October, van Ophuijsen wrote to Eitingon that he surely had no idea how relieved he had been after receiving the telegram. Van Ophuijsen, however, did not want Eitingon to assist him without knowing exactly what was going on.

During the problematic financial period in Germany with rampant inflation, Abraham had put money aside in the Netherlands by buying bonds. He had given van Ophuijsen permission to use these bonds, which van Ophuijsen was managing for him, as security for a loan to help him deal with his severe financial difficulties in 1923. Van Ophuijsen had made all too generous use of that permission. In his letter to Eitingon, he wrote that, in late 1925, Hans Bürgner had let him know that his sister, Hedwig, did not want to sell the bonds straight away. In September 1926, however, Hedwig had written to him asking him to sell all the bonds and to send her the money immediately. Hedwig was in urgent need of money, but van Ophuijsen had pledged it all.

Worse, in early 1926, van Ophuijsen had speculated with what was left and lost everything. Like a true gambler, he must have thought he could clear his debts by taking one more risk. He needed 7,500 guilders, a huge sum in those days, when a working man earned twenty-six guilders a week. Eitingon eventually lent him 3,500 guilders at an annual interest rate of 7%.[1516]

In September 1925, van Ophuijsen became a member of the board of the IPA. It is interesting that van Ophuijsen, despite his financial misappropriation, was proposed by Eitingon at the congress in 1927 as treasurer of the IPA, and, indeed, was elected as such.

Abraham's illness

On 7 June, Abraham wrote to Freud from his bed that he had brought an acute feverish bronchial catarrh back with him from Holland, which appeared persistent.[1517] This letter gives the impression that he contracted bronchitis in the Netherlands, but information from

Hedwig makes clear that before he travelled to The Hague and Leiden, Abraham got a fish-bone stuck in his throat.[1518] The clearest description of what happened comes from a letter from Abraham to Fließ of 1 July 1925, in which he reports to Fließ on the course of his own illness and connects it with Fließ's theory of vital periodicity.[1519] Between the lines, the letter is a cry for help.

Abraham wrote that he was recovering from a fairly serious illness. On Saturday 23 May, shortly before his departure for the Netherlands, he went on a trip with his wife and a group of acquaintances during which they stayed the night in Fürstenberg.[1520] That evening an unfortunate incident occurred. Someone spoke to Abraham and when he tried to reply, a small piece of fishbone, no larger than half a grain of pepper, got stuck in his throat. The considerable pain in his throat eased later and the following day he had the impression that perhaps he had coughed up the bone after all. He decided to go on the day's outing as planned. In the afternoon, however, he had more and more trouble with his throat. He wanted to go home, but the next train was not until eight in the evening. He arrived in Berlin at ten. In a sudden coughing fit that evening, he coughed up a tiny piece of bone, without being able to tell if all of it was out. But the sense of having something stuck in his throat had gone.

On Tuesday 26 May, Abraham left for Holland with Hedwig to deliver his lectures. He had various symptoms during his time in the Netherlands, and they now seemed more indicative of bronchitis. When he returned to Berlin, he developed a fever. From 5 June onwards, he had such a high temperature that he was confined to bed. He had severe pneumonia. On 15 June, there was a slight improvement for a while, but then he experienced severe attacks of fever again, which fluctuated markedly in the course of the day. In the morning his temperature was 36.8 and in the evening 39.5. On 19 June he was in a very bad way, but on 20 June his condition suddenly improved.[1521] In his next letter to Fließ there is something that seems odd given the seriousness of Abraham's illness. He applied Fließ's theory of vital periodicity to the dates of his illness and arrived at twenty-three days for one lung and twenty-eight days for the other.

There were no antibiotics at the time. Abraham's illness was life-threatening and he had never been good at feeling fear. Abraham seems to have wanted to gain control of his fear of a life-threatening illness by means of numbers. He sought sanctuary in Fließ, his substitute father, a substitute both for his own father and for Freud: Fließ as a transference figure. In times of need, he always turned to Fließ. Abraham asked whether Fließ could come during the next week to examine his bronchial tubes.

For Abraham's patients this was a difficult situation of great uncertainty. Their appointments were cancelled. Alix Strachey rang Abraham's house on Thursday 11 June to ask how he was doing. She was told to call again on Sunday 14 June. It was possible that Abraham would be able to resume work on the Monday. Alix wrote to James that it had not sounded very convincing. Her letter makes a sombre impression. Being let down by Abraham was hard for her to bear. On Sunday she rang again and spoke to Hedwig, who told her that Abraham had suffered a relapse and would definitely be unable to work for another week. Alix's reaction was to want to leave for England immediately. On 16 June she wrote, "Well, here I sit, struggling against the impending gloom. Die Klein says she thinks Abraham will not be able to start work again as soon as he gets well—whenever that is . . ."[1522] Alix became more and more despondent and started writing even more than one letter a day. On 18 June she wrote, "My only hope now is in this same Prussian character, tho'—that is, that Dr. Abraham will be analysing before he is well enough to leave the house or even walk".[1523] Then, two days later, on 20 June,

> At present I hardly know what to do. It seems impossible to get authentic news about Abraham. I either hear from a servant, or via the Ballys through Abraham mère, fils or fille. They say it's alright, that the lungs are freer, etc., but he continues to have temperatures at night, is very weak, & so on. . . . for I simply *must* get on with it & be cured. It's hell to be in my present state, and that's the truth. Ridiculous and hellish.[1524]

Later that same day, Alix sent a telegram to James: "COULD YOU COME IMMEDIATELY—ALIX."[1525] James came to fetch her and took her back to England.

Alix's extreme reaction to Abraham's sickness was by no means strange. She was in the middle of an analysis that was going well. There was a powerful transference. At that moment everything depended on the analysis and on Abraham. His sudden unavailability caused complete panic.

Alix Strachey was one of nine patients who were in analysis with Abraham at that time. She cannot have been the only one who reacted so strongly to his illness, but it was she who wrote down that reaction in detail.

On 25 June, Abraham wrote to Freud that the illness itself had run its course but that his lungs were still sensitive in part, so he had to stay in bed for the time being. He was planning to go to the mountains in about a fortnight to recuperate. He felt weakened by the illness but hoped everything would clear up.[1526] Freud replied that he was glad to hear he was getting better and hoped Abraham would be conscientious about his convalescence, "for your own sake as well as ours".[1527] Abraham had arranged to go with his family to Wengen in the Berner Oberland, a place he had chosen because there were mountain railways, so they could get high into the mountains even if Abraham was not fit enough to climb.

Meanwhile, preparations for a congress in Bad Homburg were well under way. Abraham would lead the congress as president of the IPA and Eitingon, as secretary, had already been doing much of the work during Abraham's illness along with Sachs. Preparations on the spot were taken in hand by Landauer and his wife, and by Clara Happel.[1528]

Abraham wrote in his letter to Freud of 6 July that they would not see each other for the time being if Freud did not come to the congress in Homburg. It was only now that he realised how much of his strength his illness had cost him. He would not be able to visit Freud that year.[1529]

Many letters were exchanged in this period. Freud was clearly worried. Abraham wrote from his deck chair in Werner that he was now conscientiously resting, the cure Freud had prescribed.[1530] He had not yet lost his sense of humour, but he was extremely weak. He had never realised that a person could walk so slowly or that a lift could become one of the necessities of life. Hedwig was also totally exhausted from nursing him.

Abraham was not doing any scientific work. That was highly unusual, but he simply did not have the energy for it. He read his favourite writer, Aristophanes, in Greek. He also read Heine. Sachs came to visit him in Werner.[1531]

By mid-August Abraham was a bit better, but he was still far from healthy. They had travelled on from Werner to Sils-Maria, which was his favourite place, "unequalled by anything else in the Alps".

Eitingon had written to Abraham about a patient he wanted to refer to him and on 12 August Abraham answered that he would like very much in theory to do the analysis but doubted whether he would be up to it. He was slightly better but only recently even a short conversation had proven too much for him. Abraham had a patient with him at his holiday address. Until recently this analysis was still interrupted frequently by coughing fits.

For the first few hours after getting up he also had trouble breathing. His wife was to stay with him until Friday 14 August and then return to Berlin. He wanted to start making preparations for the congress as soon as he was alone: the opening speech, which he had to give as president, the daily programme, and so on.[1532] In August 1925, Abraham was still not at all well.

The film by Pabst

On 30 November 2010, a documentary was broadcast on Dutch television titled "Van Hitchcock tot David Lynch, film en onderbewuste" (From Hitchcock to David Lynch, film and the unconscious).[1533] It addressed the fact that, in 1925, psychoanalysis and film were both thirty years old. The first film was shown in Paris in 1895 and in that same year Freud published *Studies on Hysteria*.[1534]

In 1925, the two came together for the first time. It was not new for psychoanalysis to feature in a film, but never before had filmmakers and psychoanalysts really worked together. Abraham and Sachs collaborated on the production of *Secrets of a Soul*. Among analysts, a storm of protest arose about this first psychoanalytic film. It was intolerable that a thing as complicated as psychoanalysis should be shown on the silver screen. In the Rank affair, Eitingon had wrongly accused Abraham of conservatism.[1535] In reality, Abraham was, if anything, the opposite of conservative. He did not close himself off from new developments, whether it was a matter of Melanie Klein or the portrayal of psychoanalysis in a film, even though he did have his reservations about the latter. Jones wrote of Abraham that he was always open to new ideas.[1536] The film caused such a disturbance in psychoanalytic circles that it cost Sachs his position. Because Abraham died shortly before the film came out, all the anger was directed at Sachs. It became a fierce campaign that lasted almost until the end of the twentieth century. Until then, watching the film was taboo among psychoanalysts. The remarkable result was that a campaign of denigration was carried on among psychoanalysts against a film that hardly any of them had seen. The film itself was a huge success with a broad public, a real box-office hit. As a silent film about psychoanalysis, it remains interesting to watch.

It all started harmoniously enough. Abraham wrote to Freud from his sick bed that just before he became ill he had received a request in person:

> The owner of an important film company came to see me and told me of his decision to produce a popular scientific Ψα film with your authorisation and with the collaboration and supervision of your recognized scholars. With regard to the latter, I am to have the right to make suggestions.
>
> I need hardly mention that this kind of thing is really *not* up my street; nor that this type of product is typical of our times and that it is *sure* to be carried out, if not *with us* then with people who know nothing about it. We have so many "wild" analysts in Berlin—if only to mention Kronfeld,

Schultz and Hattingberg, who would be only too keen to grasp at such an offer should we decline. In that event, they would have the financial gain and our cause would be damaged.[1537]

At this point, it was to be an informative film of the kind that had existed since the First World War, the kind of film that, for example, taught soldiers who had lost limbs in the war how to care for their wounds. As a result of the war, there were very many amputees in Germany. Such a film was usually accompanied by a book.[1538] For this film, made with Abraham's collaboration, a popular science book about psychoanalysis was to be published, which Sachs would write. In the end, however, it became an ordinary feature film rather than an informative film. It was directed by the famous G. W. Pabst.[1539] Abraham and Sachs were not involved in the decision to turn it into a piece of pure entertainment.

Shortly before this, Freud had been offered $100,000 by the American film producer Samuel Goldwyn to collaborate on a film about famous love stories. He wanted nothing to do with it. In America in 1909, he had seen a film for the first time and he thought it was terrible. Ferenczi, who was with him on that occasion, thought film a wonderful medium.[1540]

Neumann immediately sent a contract to gain the authorisation of Abraham and Freud. Abraham forwarded it to Freud.[1541] Freud answered Neumann that he had no objection to a contract between Abraham and Neumann, but did not want to be involved in the making of such a film. To Abraham he wrote on 9 June 1925, "My chief objection is still that I do not believe that satisfactory plastic representation of our abstractions is at all possible. We do not want to give our consent to anything insipid".[1542]

On 14 June 1925, Sachs wrote a long letter to Freud in which he said he was convinced that film would, in the long run, play the same role in cultural development as the printing of books in its time. Printing had pushed out the handwritten, aesthetically perfect book, but it had also made a universal culture possible.[1543]

The tone of the letters written by Freud, Abraham, and Sachs in June 1925 was cordial. Grosskurth wrote in her book about the secret committee that Freud was implacably opposed to the film.[1544] That is a gross over-simplification. Freud did not want to be involved with the film himself, but at first he had no objection to the involvement of Abraham and Sachs. He did not even exclude the possibility that if both he and Abraham approved of the script, he might authorise the film later.[1545] On 21 June, he wrote another affectionate, joking letter to Abraham after he had heard from Sachs that Abraham was still unwell:

> Dear Friend,
>
> I hear from Sachs, to my surprise and also to my dismay, that your illness is still not a thing of the past. That does not fit in with my picture of you. I like to think of you only as a man continually and unfailingly at work. I feel your illness to be a kind of unfair competition and appeal to you to stop it as quickly as possible. I expect news about your condition from someone very close to you and meanwhile send you my cordial good wishes.
>
> Yours,
>
> Freud[1546]

On 24 June, Sachs wrote to Freud that because of Abraham's illness, he had taken over the film negotiations. Freud did not need to authorise anything. Abraham and Sachs would be named as scientific compilers and be given a veto.[1547] Freud would be named only as the founder of psychoanalysis.

In his article of 1995, Ries shows in detail how carefully Abraham and Sachs went to work, on the assumption that here was an opportunity that psychoanalysis must not let slip, and how they were later blamed by the world of psychoanalysis. The film seriously damaged relations between Freud and Abraham, just before Abraham's death. There were two reasons for this. First, the following advertisement was published by the film company in June 1925:[1548]

> The treatment of nervous diseases by Psycho-Analysis according to Professor Freud is one of the most topical problems of our day: Although the Freudian teaching is mentioned and discussed by thousands of people only very few have a real idea about its nature. In Ufa's Neumann film *Secrets of a Soul* . . . everything worth knowing about Psycho-Analysis will be disclosed by means of an interesting story. The director is Hans Neumann.[1549]

Abraham and Sachs had always said that no film could possibly portray psychoanalysis in all its complexity, but in the advertising for a film there was, of course, no room for such nuances. Neumann stuck to the agreement that Freud would be named only as founder of psychoanalysis, but this agreement was now being stretched to its limits by giving such a prominent place to his name. Freud only became truly incensed, however, when he received from Ferenczi a cutting from *The New York Times* of 23 July 1925 in which he was depicted as the supervisor of the entire project. He wrote to Abraham: "One should not, after all, get mixed up with such people".[1550]

The second reason had much more far-reaching consequences and it originated within their own ranks.

Bitter rivalry between Vienna and Berlin

After the press in Vienna had reported in June 1925 about the Berlin plans for a film, on 21 August 1925 a press release appeared from the central psychoanalytic publishing house.

> Recently in film industry circles various projects concerning "psychoanalytic films" have surfaced. One of the largest American film industrialists is known to have tried in vain to persuade Prof. Freud himself to give his authorisation for such a film. Since the project of creating such a film has now been picked up in Germany as well, the International Psychoanalytic Publishing House in Vienna, which is the publishing centre for the entire psychoanalytic movement and the publisher of Prof. Freud, has decided to take upon itself the making of a psychoanalytic film, so that the danger of a misleading depiction or of an offensive or nonsensical parody can be averted.[1551]

The message was from Storfer, the brand new director of the publishing house, Rank's successor, who, after the message about the Berlin film in June, had decided to make a film himself. He asked Bernfeld to write a script.[1552] On 4 July 1925, Bernfeld wrote to his mistress, the actress Liesl Neumann, that he had accepted Storfer's offer to make a competing film. He wrote to her again on 16 August to say that the script was almost finished but he had not yet decided which of the two leading roles she would be given.[1553]

Abraham and Sachs were understandably outraged. After all their careful work on the Berlin film, they were suddenly being portrayed as some kind of charlatans and now they had to deal with a competing film that was intended to represent the true stance of the psychoanalytic world. The always so phlegmatic Sachs wrote a furious letter to Freud on 25 August.[1554]

Some of the reporting of this episode places Abraham and Sachs in a very bad light. Eppsteiner and colleagues wrote in 1986, "For both Berlin psychoanalysts reasons of power and prestige above all, and the fear that other 'wild analysts' might have the 'material profits', were decisive reasons for their cooperation with the UFA project". Reichmayer (Bernfeld's biographer), who was also involved in composing the above article, wrote in 1990 that they competed with every psychoanalytic project in Vienna for the sake of prestige.[1555] Ries contradicted that with great firmness in 1995. Abraham and Sachs had been the first to take on a film project and it was Storfer and Bernfeld in Vienna who decided to make a competing film. Moreover, Abraham and Sachs did not have financial gain in mind. They expected only to make a profit on Sachs' book and had agreed that no matter how much money was made, it would all go into the coffers of the publishing house. They received only a meagre fee for their own contributions to the film.

The congress in Bad Homburg

Why did Abraham insist on attending the congress, which took place from 3 to 5 September? Was he so dutiful that he preferred to work himself to death than fail to do what he had agreed to do?

Perhaps the decisive factor was the honour of leading the congress as president of the IPA. Abraham was re-elected at the congress by a large majority.

The portents were not good. Abraham had been planning to return to Berlin in mid-August but he delayed his departure and remained in the mountains to recuperate further. Hedwig left in mid-August, alone. On 16 August, Abraham asked in a letter to Eitingon whether in planning the committee meetings they could take him into account, since according to his current plans he would have to leave a day earlier, whereas he needed every possible hour for his recovery.[1556] This message makes it clear that Abraham was far from fully restored to health. At the congress, a large group photograph was taken in which Abraham does not look well at all. Furthermore, he suffered a piece of great bad luck. During the congress the weather was freezing cold, even though it was only early September. In the hall where they gathered, the participants wore fur coats, and at night they laid their coats on the beds.[1557] Nowadays, the heating would be turned on if such a thing happened at a congress, even if it was summer, but not in 1925. Abraham later thought it was because of the cold that he became ill again.

The congress went well. There were many interesting lectures. Abraham was enormously busy chairing it. Everyone was eager to speak to him and all those occasions when people wanted just a moment of his time were a great strain.[1558] During the banquet he managed to have a proper talk with Rank, which was reasonably harmonious. He had the impression that Rank was manic again. Rank read his lecture so quickly that practically no one could follow it. Abraham wrote to Freud afterwards that Rank's paper was full of unfounded claims and it lacked any attempt at proof, just as had been the case before.[1559]

Storfer and Bernfeld were the biggest problem at the congress. It seems that they told anyone who would listen about their film, and accusations of disloyalty by Abraham and Sachs began there. The Viennese film about psychoanalysis fell through in the end; the script was never finished, Liesl Neumann was never assigned a role, Freud never gave permission, and a film contract was never signed. But at the congress in Bad Homburg, the rival film was continually at the centre of attention.[1560] Both Jones and Abraham, as far as he was able to speak, tried to keep the situation under control and spent many hours in consultation. Eventually, Eitingon organised a special meeting to discuss the matter. Abraham wrote to Freud that he had exerted himself in those hours-long discussions more than was good for him.[1561]

Jealousy of Berlin in Vienna

In this period, Berlin was the centre of the world of psychoanalysis, with Abraham as its undisputed leader and the most important analyst after Freud.

The film affair seems to have been a symptom of the jealousy and increasingly strong sense of rivalry among the Viennese, which was noticeable in other fields as well. On 30 September, shortly after the congress, some of the Viennese psychoanalysts held a protest meeting because the young Berliners, such as Alexander, had been given the chance to write in the Festschrift to be published to mark Freud's seventieth birthday in May 1926, whereas the young Viennese, such as Nunberg and Reich, had not. Furious, they wanted to make their own Festschrift that would be published at their own expense.[1562] At the same time, Helen Deutsch was mercilessly attacked. In a letter to Eitingon, Anna Freud wrote the following about that meeting:

Questions about the training institute were raised and such hostility and total distrust were thereby expressed that a fierce altercation resulted between her and the others. Remarkably, what she is reproached for is her attachment to Berlin and her efforts to shape the Vienna institute after the example of the Berlin institute. Apparently she has thereby damaged the interests of the Vienna institute and was directly intending to do so.[1563]

Crucial advice from Freud is brushed aside

On Thursday evening, 3 September 1925, at the congress in Bad Homburg, a meeting about training took place with the representatives of the various psychoanalytic societies. With almost forty people present, all the societies were represented. Eitingon proposed setting up an international training commission that would ensure that all the training by the societies looked the same. He wanted institutes to be established in all the countries involved where aspiring psychoanalysts could be trained according to the same guidelines. The rules would be compiled by the IPA, which would draw up the entire training programme. After that, only people who had completed the whole programme would be able to become members of the IPA.

Eitingon regarded training analysis as a central element of the training programme and referred to Nunberg's observation seven years before at the congress in Budapest that everyone ought to undergo a training analysis. At that time, in Budapest, most of those present saw such a requirement as unworkable. By 1925, the training analysis had become an undisputed part of training. Eitingon proposed the Berlin institute as a point of departure, along with the Vienna institute, which was developing along the same lines. Such institutes must now be set up by the other psychoanalytic societies. Budapest and London were already taking steps in that direction.

Eitingon's exposition stressed the exemplary function Berlin now had. That must have aroused jealousy. A great deal of emphasis would be placed on the analyses that were to be carried out as part of the training, under the supervision of an experienced analyst. Analysts outside those institutes would have to give up the right to train others.[1564]

The proposal was accepted at the general meeting. All the psychoanalytic societies would establish their own training commissions and these would then come under the umbrella of the IPA's training commission, of which Eitingon would be president.[1565]

Freud was not present at the congress. He had stayed away for health reasons and sent Anna Freud in his place—strikingly, since Freud did not agree with the proposals. In the circular letter of 20 October 1925 he wrote,

> From a distance I am trying to limit certain curtailments at the training institute that are now being established. I am known to be an advocate of lay analysis and I want to make psychoanalytic teachings available in a liberal manner to all those who have that aspiration, even if they are not able to fulfil the strict requirements of a complete course.[1566]

The point Freud touched on here was extremely important. He was in favour of welcoming anyone who wished to become seriously involved in psychoanalysis, even if they were not doctors, had little free time, or did not want to be full-time psychoanalysts.

Eitingon's proposals seemed in every way reasonable and necessary. Analysts would be given standard training, which meant it would be possible to offer a certain guarantee of quality. But there were huge disadvantages to them as well, especially the limited admission that would result and the need to manage the entire process. They seemed to set in motion a development that would make the world of psychoanalysis an increasingly closed bulwark to which only a small group, after a long and difficult period of training, would be admitted. There was little space for the equally large or even larger number of people who wanted to engage in psychoanalysis less intensively and perhaps not as a full-time profession.

Abraham's health

Only a few days after the congress, Abraham wrote to Freud that it had been a very great strain and he would now need several days to rest his breathing organs. He then added, "I will in any case have to undergo some treatment for my nose and throat from Fließ".[1567]

Why did Abraham have to undergo treatment to his nose and throat from Fließ when it was mainly his lungs that were continually giving him problems? Hedwig later said that throughout his illness Abraham had complete faith in Fließ, but that she did not entirely share it.[1568]

On Saturday 12 September, Abraham again had a high fever with cold shivers, and immediately afterwards a lower than normal temperature. This acute attack then seemed to come to an end, but, on the evening of Tuesday 15 September, he was feverish again.[1569] After the congress in Bad Homburg, van Emden had stayed in Berlin for a holiday and he concerned himself intensively with Abraham. Sachs wrote to Freud that a certain Dr May was now Abraham's Berlin doctor. Simmel, too, was involved in his treatment, but the doctors did not know precisely what was wrong with him.

Anna Freud wrote crabbily to Eitingon that Abraham again had a fever and therefore had again been proved right. His disagreeable behaviour at the congress might have had to do with not feeling well. One was not even allowed to be annoyed with him, she added childishly: it was awful that he was sick again, but she still found him far from pleasant.[1570] Anna Freud had become a friend of Bernfeld's, whom she greatly admired, and in the film affair she was clearly on Bernfeld's side.[1571]

On 23 September, Sachs wrote to Freud that Abraham's temperature had gradually gone down over the previous few days and that he was coughing less. He hoped there would be no further complications. Sachs was of the opinion that Abraham must now immediately go to the mountains—taking several analysands with him, otherwise it would be unaffordable—and not return until April. He made an urgent appeal to Freud to use his influence to persuade Abraham to take this course.[1572] Freud ignored Sachs' request.

Eitingon's role

In the autumn of 1924, Rank had set aside his tasks at the psychoanalytic publishing house, so a replacement was needed. Freud had feared all along that this would happen. To him, the publishing house was the most important thing of all and a good successor to Rank must now be found. In the correspondence between Eitingon and Freud there is a whole discussion between the two of them about who the successor should be.[1573]

Storfer, assistant to Rank since 1921, was made manager and officially appointed to that post on 6 May 1925.[1574] Freud wrote to Eitingon that the two rich men, he himself and Eitingon, would have to reach into their own pockets to pay him, but Eitingon answered that he would bear the entire cost. The publishing house had always been a financial worry and it seems it was unable to afford Storfer's salary.

Freud thought Ferenczi unsuitable for the function of desk editor because he was too slap-dash. He would be suitable as senior editor. The task of text editor was given to Radó. The post of editor-in-chief had yet to be filled, however, and, according to Eitingon, it would be rather indelicate to give the job to Abraham after the difficulties between him and Rank. He offered his own services. Freud, however, saw no reason to take account of Rank's sensitivities now and he objected to the appointment of Eitingon, who took on far too many tasks and was away far too often.

He wrote to Eitingon, "And the concern, that a time might come again in which the other front-line service asserts its claim and takes you away from your workplace for long months?"[1575] By the other front-line service, Freud meant Eitingon's wife.

Despite Freud's objections, Eitingon continued to edit. He saw himself as having a supervisory role. It was a departure from the previous norm. Until then, all the editors at the psychoanalytic publishing house had worked at building upon psychoanalytic theory and they all wrote scientific articles themselves. Eitingon did not do that. He published hardly anything, just a few reports about the polyclinic.

Eitingon was responsible for the fact that in August 1925, three months after his official appointment, Storfer, without consulting the editors, announced the making of a film on behalf of the publishing house. Eitingon was, after all, editor-in-chief and he was paying Storfer's salary. Eitingon wrote to Storfer on 27 August 1925, just before the congress in Bad Homburg, that he was absolutely opposed to the publishing house's film project.[1576]

Eitingon was secretary to the board of the IPA. Abraham was president of the IPA. Eitingon had done a huge amount of work of late. He had taken a great deal of the weight off Abraham during preparations for the congress in Bad Homburg. Why did he not continue to do so at the congress? Eitingon knew from Abraham's letters that he had still not recovered. Why did he not spare him the misery with Storfer and Bernfeld, who were bent on making money?[1577] Instead, he waited a long time, allowed the issue to escalate, and only then organised a meeting, which lasted for hours and was naturally far too taxing for Abraham. There are no records of the meeting, but it seems Eitingon eventually did the same as he had done several years before with Liebermann. He sided with the man who had caused the problem, in this case Storfer, who, with a great song and dance, threatened to resign, which he did not do.

From Eitingon's letter to Freud of 3 November, it turns out that Abraham and Sachs wanted Storfer to withdraw his press release about a film being made by the publishing house.[1578] Abraham had signed a contract with UFA which stated that for a period of three years no other psychoanalytic film would receive official support.[1579] Storfer's press release on behalf of the psychoanalytic publishing house therefore put a severe strain on Abraham's relations with UFA. The press release was not withdrawn, however, either then or later. Eitingon wanted Abraham to admit that Storfer had meant well, but Abraham had no intention of doing so. Eitingon attacked Abraham. Those present at the meeting were Abraham, Sachs, Jones, Eitingon, Ferenczi, Anna Freud, Bernfeld, and Storfer. The latter six turned against the first two en masse. Given Abraham's illness and difficulty speaking, which meant he could not defend himself properly, it must have been rather like a flock of chickens attacking the sick chicken in their midst. Because Abraham refused to say that Storfer had meant well, he was reproached for rudeness.

The others greatly resented the way Abraham behaved at that meeting. In his ill and exhausted state, just like at the end of the war, he will have been neither flexible nor humorous. He no doubt lacked empathy, but also, of course, he was simply correct. Why should he have to say of Storfer that he had done everything with the best of intentions, for the sake of the publishing house, if Storfer was not prepared to withdraw his press release? It had been a one-man operation about which Storfer had not conferred with the publishing house.

Eitingon's concealed and covert aggression against Abraham had been going on for some time. In those days Abraham was, after Freud, the undisputed leader of the psychoanalytic movement. Despite everything he had done, Eitingon's role was minor. He had mainly himself to thank for that, since he was often absent for half the year.

From mid-September 1925 onwards, Eitingon was in Italy. He did not come back when Abraham fell seriously ill. He did not come back when Alexander wrote to him that in the Berlin Psychoanalytic Society everyone was deeply concerned about Abraham's condition and that he was doubly missed.[1580] He did not come back to say a few final words to Abraham. He came back only after Abraham had died and he could take over the presidency of the IPA, only to leave for Italy again a few weeks later.

He did not let go of the presidency until 1932. Previously, the members of the committee had always passed the presidency on every few years. Never were Eitingon's letters to Freud so cheerful, energetic and zestful in tone as in the weeks after Abraham's death.[1581] He was rid of his rival.[1582]

Abraham and Freud

Until Bad Homburg, the relationship between Abraham and Freud had always been excellent. Not even the film had detracted from it. After Bad Homburg, their relationship was completely wrecked. Abraham wrote Freud a long letter on 8 September about how the congress had gone. On 11 September, Freud wrote an extremely sour letter in response, clearly angry about the entire film dispute. He defended Bernfeld and Storfer and laid the blame on Abraham and Sachs. He reproached Abraham for his harshness.[1583]

After the congress, Anna Freud and Eitingon travelled together to the Semmering, where Freud was staying. Eitingon remained there for a few days and also consulted with Storfer.[1584] Freud's anger with Abraham must have had to do with information he received from Eitingon and Anna. It seems Freud, too, failed to take account of the fact that in all his conscientiousness Abraham had exerted himself far too much. Freud allowed himself to be drawn into the anti-Abraham sentiment that had arisen.

Next there is a gap of five weeks in their correspondence. Abraham had pneumonia.[1585] Sachs kept Freud informed. On 28 September, Sachs was able to visit Abraham for the first time and he thought he looked better but was still plagued by a cough and asthma. Abraham's mood was good, Sachs wrote. He was calm and optimistic and was writing again. Sachs told Freud he had the impression that, as he had said before, Abraham needed a long period of recuperation.[1586] Sachs and Abraham had gradually become very good friends and Hedwig later called him her help and stay during this difficult period.[1587] On 17 October, after five weeks of illness, Abraham wrote in a circular letter that he had at last recovered. During his illness he had been helped a great deal by van Emden, who, as his doctor, had cared for him intensively throughout. He wrote that the treatment by Fließ had been of great importance:

> Secondly the intervention by Fließ in the treatment was of great importance for me. I have become conscious of his extremely unusual qualities as a doctor. He really is worth three Berlin professors of internal medicine, and even if you add a couple of extraordinary ones, it makes little difference. On top of that the entire course of my illness confirmed his theory of vital periodicity in a remarkable manner.[1588]

Abraham also wrote that in Germany the debate about psychoanalysis in newspapers and journals had really taken off. Everyone was talking about psychoanalysis. The film was coming along well. In three weeks, filming would be completed. He did not want to say much more about the Storfer–Bernfeld affair, but the Viennese initiative had turned out to be no more than a bluff.

The letter was signed by Abraham alone. Sachs was too busy with the film and Eitingon had been travelling since mid-September and was now in Florence. An angry response came immediately from Vienna, from Anna Freud on behalf of her father:

> Unfortunately I also have to admit that the matter of the film has left me with a bad taste in my mouth. I find that our Berlin friends have shown a degree of coarseness by continuing their hard judgments about the people involved, which I cannot see as in any way justified.[1589]

Seven days later, on 27 October 1925, there followed a response several pages long from Abraham to Freud. Abraham wrote that because of the accusation of harshness he had again been placed in a situation he had found himself in several times before:

> You know, dear Professor, that I am very unwilling to enter once again into a discussion of the Bernfeld and Storfer affair. But because of your reproach of harshness (in your circular letter), I find myself in the same position again as on several previous occasions. In almost 20 years, we have had no differences of opinion except where personalities were concerned whom I, very much to my regret, had to criticize. The same sequence of events repeated itself each time; you indulgently overlooked everything that could be challenged in the behaviour of the persons concerned, while all the blame—which you subsequently recognized as unjustified—was directed against me. In Jung's case your criticism was that of "jealousy"; in the case of Rank "unfriendly behaviour", and this time "harshness". Could the sequence of events not be the same once again? I advanced an opinion that is basically yours as well, but which you did not admit into consciousness. All the unpleasure linked to the relevant facts is then turned against the person who had drawn attention to them.

> What has actually happened—I mean on the part of Sachs and myself—that could leave you with so unpleasant an "after-taste"? Neither of us ever thought to plan a $\Psi\alpha$ film and to seek a company to make it. *We* were approached by "Neumann Productions" to work with them because they wanted competent analysts. If we had refused, all the "wild" analysts in Berlin would eagerly have rushed in. The "Ufa" already had "$\Psi\alpha$" film outlines of the most minor sort waiting to be tried. Besides, I told you about the situation immediately, even though I was already ill in bed. In addition, Sachs and I have not done the slightest thing that would have been open to ethical objections.

> I know that Sachs got very worked up about the notice issued by Storfer, but that is simply a matter of temperament. But I must say that in the last few months he has worked with more enthusiasm and spirit of self-sacrifice than anyone else would have done.

> On the other side there are the following facts: (1.) the nasty notice about the "bowdlerization" directed against Sachs and me. (2.) the offering of Bernfeld's draft to various firms, none of which had spontaneously approached St. and B. (3.) the underhandedness of the letter to Sachs and me, dripping with loyalty while *at the same* time they sent the notice to the press that I have mentioned. Thus an unfair competitive manoeuvre under the cloak of friendship. (4.) Storfer wrote to Eitingon

that he would comply with his instructions. When Eitingon gave him some, he did not follow them. (5.) The "resignation" was an empty gesture. Immediately after announcing his resignation in Homburg, Storfer took part in a meeting about matters of the Verlag (Fräulein Anna was present as well) and let nobody get a word in, but went on developing his plans for the future of the Verlag. The "resignation" was thus as untrue as everything else. I saw this at once but did not protest because I wanted to keep the peace. (Harshness?) (6.) Bernfeld tried to get me to break my word or my contract with regard to the Neumann Company, always juggling with promises of gigantic sums in dollars. After that, he spread it about in Homburg that I wanted to eliminate his film out of greed for money. He knew that Sachs and I had only had a moderate fixed amount for our work, and because of it had accused the Ufa of deceiving us, whereas *he* had assured us of enormous profits. He left the Congress prematurely because—according to his own statement— he could not bear to be there when I was elected President again. A strange repetition; Rank had said and done exactly the same in Salzburg. (7.) The news that you doubted, dear Professor, certainly did not come from the Ufa. It is as such that the head of the only company that could make such a film in Vienna (Pan-company), Dr Robert Wiene, gave Sachs the verbal explanation that St. and B. had approached "Pan" with the statement that they had an offer from the Ufa but were waiting in Homburg for an even higher one from the American side. Negotiations came to a swift and negative end.

These are a *few* main points that show that on that side an underhanded and untruthful game was being played from the very beginning.

And where is the harshness I am accused of? Sachs and I demanded that the notice in the press should be withdrawn; that did *not* happen. The "satisfaction" given to us was St.'s resignation, which—as I have said—was only a manner of speaking. We gave in and did everything to keep the "Ufa" out of all proceedings, and we did it successfully. As I have recently mentioned, I am corresponding with Storfer as though nothing had happened. Thus *we* gave in all along the line, and when some time ago you wrote about the "causa victrix of the Ufa", it was a great mistake. So what is there left that could be called harshness on our part? *Only* a few open statements in the circular letters (and in other correspondence), which is actually intended for free utterances. In addition, as far as my means of voice allowed, I mediated and smoothed things over in Homburg at every turn, and the whole of my behaviour within the Society makes it improbable that I would be so hard and harsh towards a few people.[1590]

The letter was a cry from the heart by Abraham, who felt unjustly treated.

Freud was cast into doubt by this letter from Abraham. He forwarded it to Eitingon to ask his opinion; he had not been there himself, after all, whereas Eitingon had been. Freud thought he might have done Abraham an injustice through sympathy for those who lived near him. He also wrote that he had never seen himself as a good judge of character and that given his experiences he had little reason to do so. Yet, objectively speaking, it was difficult to maintain that someone could always be right.[1591]

Eitingon wrote back almost immediately from Florence and his answer was astonishing. Was the always so restrained Eitingon showing his true nature here as a competitor of Abraham's? As if it would be unbearable for him if Freud embraced Abraham again, he wrote,

In its entirety Abraham's letter is "a real Abraham". Having a grain of truth, he of course did not notice how crooked, essentially off target and as a result wrong his attitude, his behaviour is. His reference to the two other great conflicts, which cannot be compared to the current one, is as superfluous as it is typical, since we know perfectly well that A. made mistakes regarding Rank too, if perhaps to a lesser degree in deed then certainly in manner.[1592]

He went on to say that Abraham had taken Bernfeld's fantasies far too seriously and that he had no sense of humour.[1593] The letter continues in the same vein all the way through: ". . . Since aside from his own typically heated self-love, it seems not much emotion clouds his view".[1594] And later:

> This intellectual self-righteousness results of course in practical moral self-satisfaction. When in the debate about the film in the Homburg committee meeting I wanted at least to have Storfer's selflessness acknowledged, pointing out that with his wheeling and dealing he did ultimately want to help the publishing house, Abraham replied that they had planned that the publishing house would publish the popular brochure to be written by Sachs for the UFA film, "so that we too would enable the publishing house to benefit". That certainly disarmed me completely.[1595]

Here, Eitingon was committing a form of character assassination. It resembled the situation with Liebermann. He defended Storfer tooth and nail, even though there is no indication that Storfer's intentions with regard to the publishing house were good. Had that been the case, he would have consulted the editors beforehand. Storfer wanted to make a competing film and play a nasty trick on Abraham and Sachs, and in the latter he succeeded mightily.

Eitingon managed to do here what he had failed to do in the case of Liebermann: he convinced Freud.

On 5 November, Freud wrote Abraham an extremely unfriendly letter saying that the entire matter would have gone far better if they had not taken it so very seriously in Berlin and that Abraham should not think he was always right.[1596] It was the last letter between the two of them.

Over the course of November, Abraham became ill again. He had gall attacks that caused him a great deal of pain. He had to interrupt his work, which he had resumed just a few weeks before.[1597] Around 20 November, he was admitted to a sanatorium and the doctors planned to operate. On 25 November, Sachs wrote to Freud that the evening before he had finally heard a little more from Abraham's brother-in-law.[1598] The doctors treating him—Borchardt, regarded as the best surgeon in Berlin, two specialists in internal medicine, and Fließ—were at a loss as to the diagnosis. Repeated X-rays, blood tests, and so forth provided no clues at all.[1599] Hedwig later said that Abraham was in such terrible pain that the doctors thought his gall bladder was infected, which was the reason they wanted to operate.[1600]

In late November, Felix Deutsch travelled from Vienna to Berlin to see what he could do.[1601] It was not until around this time that Freud realised Abraham might not survive his illness.[1602] Up to that point, Freud had been preoccupied with his own health problems and he regarded the much younger Abraham as far more robust by definition.[1603] From that moment on, Freud kept himself informed daily by telephone about Abraham's condition and everything in the Freud household was dominated by Abraham's illness: "Our situation is dominated by the news about Abraham's illness, news that sounds very unsatisfactory, incomprehensible and far from reassuring".[1604]

In early November, Freud had sent a short response to Eitingon's crushing letter about Abraham. After that, Freud did not write to him again until mid-December. Eitingon was now in Sicily and he wrote Freud one letter after another.[1605]

Storfer's financial management of the publishing house created a great many difficulties. In mid-December, Freud wrote to Eitingon about Storfer, about Abraham, and about the Berlin Psychoanalytic Society. He said that as far as Abraham was concerned, things looked bad and that he felt sorry for the Berlin society and the Berlin group, which were now without leadership.[1606] That was a direct reproach to Eitingon, who simply stayed in Sicily, even though there were fears for Abraham's life and the Berlin Psychoanalytic Society had been forced to manage without a president for months. Eitingon answered both Anna Freud and Freud to say that for a few days he had been about to leave for Berlin, but that things had then started to go a little better with Abraham.[1607]

On 10 December, Sachs wrote to Freud that he had spoken to Hedwig at length the previous day. The operation was over and it had revealed an inflamed gall bladder, without pus but with deformities and small gall stones. The gall bladder had been removed. The healing process was slow but normal. The patient had no fever but, in the first few days, a great deal of pain. Abraham felt extremely ill and was apathetic, probably both because of the pain he had been through and because of the morphine he had been given in the days before the operation. Abraham was still receiving a small dose of morphine in the evenings. The doctors were expressing optimism.[1608]

Jones wrote later that Abraham had a very swollen liver and had urged the doctors to perform the gall bladder operation on a day that fitted with Fließ's theory of vital periodicity.[1609] Jones was the only person to mention the numbers theory. He had the feeling that the operation had done Abraham more harm than good.

On 16 December, Freud wrote to Ferenczi that he had heard from Berlin that today Abraham was getting better as if by a miracle. He had been told that one should not despair too soon when it came to abscesses on the lung. Freud wrote that he still had a tendency to take Abraham's illness very seriously and that he had prepared himself for a fatal outcome. He asked Ferenczi to travel to Berlin. Freud wrote, "We may not, as long as he lives, portray what we have lost in him. But it is hard, especially for me".[1610]

Events then followed each other with great speed. For two days reports about Abraham were extremely bad. His death seemed to be approaching. On 21 December, however, he was marvellously recovered. In the last telephone conversation, the message came that his life was no longer in immediate danger. Deutsch was in Berlin and his presence meant so much to Abraham that he could not leave. There was a fear that the patient would relapse if he did. The previous report had said that there was now also an inflammation of the peritoneum. Abraham had seemed almost unconscious for several days, but that was now over. For Freud the situation was extremely hard.[1611]

Meanwhile, there were all kinds of difficulties with Storfer and Anna Freud wrote to Eitingon saying: might Abraham have been right after all?[1612]

Deutsch telephoned the Freuds on the afternoon of 21 December to say he had returned from Berlin and had left Abraham in a satisfactory condition. That same afternoon, however,

Radó rang to say that there had been a turn for the worse and Abraham had a high fever. He asked whether Deutsch could come at once.

In the summer of 1925, Abraham and Hedwig had bought a piece of land and made plans to build a house in Sils Maria. The building plans for the house reached them just before Christmas.

Felix Deutsch arrived back in Berlin on Christmas Eve. When he went to see Abraham the following morning with Hedwig and her brother Hans, they found him dead.[1613]

Abraham had breakfasted that morning at eight. An hour later he died suddenly, probably of an embolism.[1614]

On 25 December, Jones wrote to Freud,

Dear Professor,

What is to be said about today's frightful news? You know that I share your feelings to the full. It seems as if very little is to be spared to you in the way of suffering—and I too know what suffering means. There is no way of meeting this blow: it cannot be dealt with, for nothing can ever cure it—not even time. Karl was my best friend, and his wife one of my wife's best friends. We all understood each other completely. The loss is quite irreplaceable, both personally and to the movement.[1615]

Freud answered,

Dear Jones,

I can only repeat what you said: Abr.'s death is perhaps the greatest loss that could have hit us, and it has hit us. In letters I jokingly called him my "rocher de bronze"; I felt safe in the absolute confidence he inspired in me, as in everyone else. In the brief obituary I wrote for him for the *Zeitschrift* . . . I applied to him the line from Horace:[1616]

Integer vitae scelerisque purus[1617]

In his obituary in the *Zeitschrift*, Freud wrote the following,

On December 25, 1925, Dr. Karl Abraham, President and founder of the Berlin Psycho-Analytical Society and President for the time being of the International Psycho-Analytical Association, died in Berlin. He had not yet reached the age of fifty years when he succumbed to an illness against which his vigorous physique had been struggling ever since the early summer. At the Congress at Homburg his apparent recovery delighted us all; but to our grievous disappointment there followed a relapse.

We bury with him—integer vitoe scelerisque purus—one of the surest hopes we had for our science, young as it is and still so bitterly assailed, and a part of its future which will now, perhaps, never come to fruition. So high a place had he won for himself that, of all who have followed me through the dark pathways of psycho-analytic research, there is only one whose name could be put beside his. Colleagues and younger workers had an unbounded faith in him, so that it is likely that the leadership would have been his. And indeed, he would have been a model leader in the pursuit of truth, led astray neither by the praise and blame of the many nor by the tempting illusion of his own phantasies.

I am writing these lines for friends and fellow-workers who knew and valued him as I did. They will easily understand what the loss of this friend, who was so much younger than myself, means to me, and they will forgive me if I make no further attempt to express things for which it is hard to find words. An account of Abraham's scientific personality and an appreciation of his work will be written for our Journal by another hand.[1618]

CHAPTER TWENTY-NINE

Upheaval

On 26 December 1925, the day after Abraham died, Jones travelled to the continent by boat. There was such a thick fog that the ship had to drop anchor and he missed his train. He finally arrived in Berlin at ten in the evening and was met by Ernst Freud, Sachs, and van Ophuijsen.[1619] The next afternoon, on Monday 27 December, Abraham was buried in a new, wooded area of the Lichterfelde cemetery.[1620] Jones wrote to his wife, Kitty, that the funeral was terrible. Two hundred people attended and the scenes were heartrending. Ferenczi spoke rather formally on behalf of the IPA. In Jones' opinion he did so to keep himself under control. Sachs spoke on behalf of the Berlin Psychoanalytic Society. His was an extremely moving speech that made many of those present, including Jones himself, burst into sobs. Jones thought that aside from Abraham's family it was worst of all for Sachs, van Ophuijsen, and himself.[1621] Abraham's dog did not want to leave the graveside, but Hedwig had no desire to keep the dog and gave it to Abraham's brother, Max.[1622]

The day after the funeral, Jones visited Hedwig both in the morning and in the afternoon. On the Wednesday he visited her again. Hedwig was terribly sad but brave and very grateful to him for coming and for the letter from Kitty that he had brought with him. Gerd held up well. Hilda broke down completely, shattered. Hedwig's brother, Hans Bürgner, spoke at length with Jones and told him that he would take care of the three remaining family members and pay for the children's education.

In the Berlin Psychoanalytic Society, the reaction to Abraham's death was extreme. Everyone started arguing and they blamed each other, right from the evening of Abraham's funeral.[1623]

Ferenczi wrote to Freud that, on the morning after the funeral, Eitingon arrived energetic and enterprising.[1624] Ferenczi requested him to take over the leadership of the Berlin Psychoanalytic Society, to put a stop to the squabbling. Eitingon did so for a short time and then passed the task on to Simmel. Simmel formed an executive committee consisting of himself as president, Radó as secretary, and Horney as treasurer.[1625] Ferenczi cautiously enquired of Eitingon what he would think if he were to take over the presidency of the IPA. That was by far the most obvious solution. It was Ferenczi's turn. The members of the committee had always passed the presidency around between them. Since the congress in 1918, Ferenczi had been president for only a very short time, because he was forced to hand over leadership to Jones as a result of political developments in Hungary. It was quieter in Hungary now and he would be able to function as president, but Eitingon refused to listen. As he saw it, that would mean a loss of face for him. It would create the impression that he was not suitable as president.[1626]

It seems Eitingon managed to browbeat Ferenczi. There was no reason at all to think that Eitingon had more right to the position than Ferenczi. In fact, quite the opposite. Eitingon had been a member of the committee for the shortest time, and he had become so not for his services to psychoanalysis but because he provided money. Eitingon carried out hardly any analyses, made no contribution to the theory, did not publish, and was away travelling for much of the year. Ferenczi had been a committee member right from the start and he was an extremely experienced analyst. He had published a great deal and was of great importance to the development of psychoanalytic theory. Ferenczi said to Eitingon that in that case he would simply have to be the acting president until the next congress. He warned, however, that the function was incompatible with Eitingon's endless travelling. Eitingon answered that his wife had taken the heroic decision to subordinate her private wishes to her husband's working schedule.[1627] It was clear that Eitingon absolutely did not want to miss out on the post of president. He arrived back just in time for Abraham's funeral, but he had arranged in advance that on the Tuesday afternoon, the day after the funeral, there would be a meeting with a number of the presidents of the societies affiliated to the IPA, so that the decision to appoint him as acting president could be taken immediately. Those present, according to Ferenczi, were himself, Eitingon, van Emden, van Ophuijsen, Jones, and Sachs. Eitingon wrote a report in the *Korrespondenzblatt* about that meeting, which did indeed decide to make him acting president. He named Hitschmann as one of those present and, strikingly, did not mention Sachs.[1628] Sachs was slowly but surely being sidelined.

Eitingon had now got a grip on all the important functions in the psychoanalytic world: president of the IPA, editor-in-chief of the publishing house, director of the Berlin polyclinic, chair of the IPA's training commission. He had simply arrogated to himself both the presidency of the IPA and the editorship of the publishing house, despite protests from Freud and Ferenczi.

Abraham's family

Hedwig had been a dignified presence at the funeral, but afterwards she was seized by despair.

Jones had taken on the task of writing an obituary for a special issue of the *Zeitschrift* that would be dedicated to Abraham. He spent all his free time on it and reread Abraham's complete works.[1629] Freud and his daughter, Anna, translated the obituary into German.[1630] Hedwig was extremely grateful to Jones and did her best to help him with information about

Abraham's life. It was a heavy task. Looking through Abraham's papers in his desk was extremely upsetting. It was clear that, despite his long illness, Abraham had still been in high spirits. His love of study stayed with him right to the end and he did not predict the outcome of his illness at all. It overwhelmed Hedwig.[1631] In late March, she wrote to Jones that she was being driven completely crazy by her longing for Karl and her nostalgia for the happy past.[1632] Tom Burgner, son of Hedwig's brother Hans, said much later in an interview that Hedwig had completely collapsed after Abraham's death. She was deeply depressed and became menopausal overnight.[1633]

Kitty Jones visited Hedwig in September 1926. She was greatly shocked. Hedwig was pale and beautiful but her joviality had gone. She was a broken woman. She could not manage a smile for Kitty. Her face was as if carved in stone. Hans Bürgner took them out for a drive in his new car. Hedwig thawed a little then and was able to enjoy the trip, but she had not yet fully accepted Abraham's death. She kept wondering whether it had been avoidable and whether she had done the right things.[1634] When Freud saw Hedwig again for the first time in early 1927, he barely recognised her. He wrote to Ferenczi that fate had marked her deeply.[1635]

Hedwig found herself in financial difficulties because all their money had been spent in combating Abraham's illness. Therefore, she let out five of the eight rooms in their house. Hans Bürgner was a great support to her, as was Gerd. According to Hedwig, Gerd became far more mature and serious, although, appropriately at his age, he was also involved with school and sport.[1636] Hilda passed her school leaving exams and then went to her former analyst van Ophuijsen in the Netherlands. Her father's death hit her terribly hard.[1637]

Freud in mourning

Abraham's death was a huge blow to Freud, not only because he was extremely fond of Abraham but because he had placed all his hopes for the future in him.[1638]

He found it impossible to comprehend that Abraham, of all people, had been taken away from him like that, the man who seemed to be most alive of all, powerful and healthy. "Who would have thought, when we met that time in the Harz, that he would be the first to depart this irrational life?" Freud wrote to Jones.[1639]

On 3 January 1926, Freud reported to Pfister,

> The situation, not to say the mood, is dominated here by the death of Abraham, which—as you know—took place at Christmas. We have lost a great deal in him; he is almost impossible to replace. I write this laying aside all emotional reaction and valuing him purely for his objective worth.[1640]

It sounded deeply sad. Freud was sombre and in mourning. He became quite seriously ill in this period. It started with two days of 'flu in January, which kept him in bed with a fever for two days, and after that he was in poor health on and off for some time.[1641] In a committee letter of 20 January 1926, he wrote, "Furthermore the deplorable loss of our friend Karl Abraham is having a crippling effect on us and robbing us of any desire to turn our attention to minor events".[1642]

On 17 February, during his walk after lunch, Freud suffered chest pains on the street, which recurred twice.[1643] Doctors Braun and Lévy came to the conclusion that it was slight angina and prescribed rest.[1644] On 5 March 1926, Freud left to spend four weeks at the Cottage Sanatorium. His wife, his sister-in-law, and Anna took turns keeping him company.[1645]

It is clear from Freud's correspondence that he felt bad in the first few months of 1926. He wrote relatively few letters. The only thing he was intensively concerned with was the next issue of the *Zeitschrift*, which was to be dedicated to Abraham.[1646] Eitingon and Radó had suggested postponing it until December, but Freud was categorically opposed to that. First, they must honour the dead before they could think about his seventieth birthday, which, in itself, was something Freud was absolutely dreading.[1647]

The fate of the secret committee

The committee, which had been brought back to life after all the difficulties with Rank, became less and less active after Abraham's death. Some circular letters were still sent, but they were irregular and their tone was flat.[1648] Eitingon wrote only with long gaps in between and half the letters from Berlin were not signed by Sachs. Eitingon described his own opinion about the committee in a letter to Freud of 6 February 1926. He claimed that the committee served at best only to prevent conflicts between the members and by doing so to keep Jones in check somewhat: "Taugt es wenig gegen den Feind, so nutzt es vielleicht gegen den Freund." (roughly: "What doesn't work against the enemy may perhaps be of use against the friend.")[1649] It was clear that Eitingon had no fellow feeling at all for the committee. The lively and inspiring exchange that had made the committee what it was and the stimulating effect it produced that spurred the creation of new theories seem to have passed Eitingon by. He had never really acted as part of it.

Eitingon had played two nasty tricks on Ferenczi. Not only had he prevented Ferenczi from succeeding Abraham as president of the IPA, he had prevented him from becoming president of the Berlin Psychoanalytic Society, a role Alexander had asked Ferenczi to take on after Abraham's death. Ferenczi had liked the idea, since the presidency of the Berlin Psychoanalytic Society was one of the most prestigious positions at that point. Without consulting the committee, Eitingon transferred that function to Simmel in January 1926.

Freud wrote to Ferenczi that Eitingon had asked him to intervene in the Berlin group to secure its agreement with Eitingon's decision to step down as president. Freud did so.[1650] Eitingon then appointed Simmel his successor. Freud wrote to Ferenczi that Eitingon realised this was a provisional decision. According to Freud, Eitingon wanted Ferenczi to try to become president of the Berlin Psychoanalytic Society and Eitingon assumed that in due course Ferenczi would naturally be elected to that post if he came to Berlin.[1651] It was one of those typically complicated series of machinations by Eitingon, and he had even persuaded Freud to collaborate. Eitingon said that he assumed Ferenczi would become president in Berlin, but meanwhile he arranged things such that this could not happen. There was, of course, no chance at all that Ferenczi, with his record of service, was going to move to Berlin without the certainty that he would be elected president, especially in the knowledge that he would first have to compete with Simmel, who had just been given the post.

Ferenczi reconciled himself to the situation and wrote in his circular letter of 31 January 1926 that Eitingon's solution for Berlin was correct. In September 1926, he left for the USA for nine months. Prior to his departure, the committee met just once, shortly before Freud's birthday in May, and it was decided that at the next congress, in 1927, Ferenczi should become president of the IPA, as he wanted to be. Freud was not at all happy that Ferenczi was leaving for the USA for a long period. In early 1925, he had lost Rank, at the end of 1925, Abraham, and now Ferenczi was leaving as well. It seems Freud did not realise the extent to which Ferenczi had been passed over.

The correspondence between Freud and Eitingon was intense in this period. Freud leaned on Eitingon heavily in practical organisational matters. The things Eitingon said about his fellow committee members around this time were denigrating almost without exception.[1652] When Ferenczi returned in 1927, not he but Eitingon was elected the new president of the IPA. That had, meanwhile, become Freud's preference as well. Jones would have liked the presidency, and he was partly responsible for the fact that it did not go to Ferenczi.[1653] Eitingon, as usual, had said he did not want the post but got it all the same.

The committee was disbanded. Eitingon remained president of the IPA until 1932, after which Jones took over until 1949. Ferenczi died in 1933.

The family's change of course

Hedwig looked for a source of income that would allow her to stay in touch with the psychoanalytic world. In the end, in consultation with her brother, she started a guest house where, by preference, she would house psychoanalysts or psychoanalytic patients who were in Berlin for a while for training or for analysis. Abraham's former colleagues tried to help her. On the advice of Ernst Freud, she decided to buy a suitable house and adapt it. Hans Bürgner would pay part of the price, but she needed a mortgage of 80,000 marks. He asked Jones to borrow the sum in Britain because interest rates were far lower there. Jones had to use his own property as security, but he could do so for a maximum of 60,000 marks. He asked Eitingon to provide the remaining 20,000.[1654] It was also because of the guest house that Hedwig asked van Ophuijsen to return the money of Abraham's that he had been given for safe keeping.

Hilda started a degree in medicine. She had difficulty coming to terms with her father's death. In 1929, she wrote Jones a heartrending letter. Jones had remained extremely solicitous of the Abraham family and, in 1929, he sent a letter and a small present for Hilda's birthday.[1655] Hilda wrote him a thank-you note: "When I have not seen a person who is dear to me for a long time, I suddenly get overwhelmed by the fear that he is slowly gliding away from my outstretched fingers while I'm trying to get hold of him".[1656]

Hilda was afraid that those she loved, including Jones, might suddenly disappear. She was enjoying her medical studies but had recently been missing her father more than ever. She still had so much to tell him and there was so much she wanted to ask him. She added, "One can't expect to find the image of one's father in every man, can one?"[1657]

Freud did not cease to be concerned about the Abrahams. In 1930, Hilda studied in Vienna for a term and she was welcomed very warmly in the Freud household. The Abraham family was struggling financially at the time. Freud knew this, and he told Hilda that he had deposited a sum of money in the bank for her with his son in Berlin. He had arranged things in such a way that he would not know how much Hilda took from it, so that it would not be embarrassing for her. In the end, Hilda did not use the money at all, but she thought the gesture unbelievably generous, and the way Freud had arranged it, too.[1658]

Gerd studied law. The intention was that he would enter his uncle's practice, but the seizure of power by the Nazis prevented that.

The loss of the ring

Freud had given all members a ring when the secret committee was set up. Abraham's ring, which Hedwig said was very beautiful, was a small cameo.[1659] Two masks were cut into it, one in profile and the other full face. Abraham had often made prints with it, which Hedwig no longer had in later years. She gave the ring to Gerd when he became an adult. Gerd valued it extremely highly and he wore it, even when he was sent to India as a British officer in the Second World War. He took it off one night and an Indian crept in while he slept. The Indian stole all Gerd's possessions: his wallet, the ring, and various other things. Hedwig was appalled by the loss and said that unfortunately he had worn the ring too much.[1660]

Emigration after 1933

When the Nazis took power, Hedwig, Hilda, and Gerd fled to Britain, helped in doing so by Jones, van Ophuijsen, and Freud. Hilda was nearing the end of her medical studies and was given permission to spend the last four months of her degree course practising as a doctor in the Jewish hospital in Berlin. Jones thought the condition was that she would leave immediately afterwards. Hilda had entered into analysis with Dr Kemper and planned to become a psychoanalyst.[1661] In 1933, Hans Bürgner immediately lost all his work. Jones wrote that he was ruined, but that seems not, in fact, to have been the case. Bürgner managed to hold his own in Berlin until 1938, when he, too, fled to Britain. His wife, Dodo, had divorced him by then and had already left for Britain with their two children, Tom and Anja. In 1945, Hans and Dodo Bürgner remarried. After Kristallnacht in 1938, Gerd sent one letter after another to his uncle and aunt in Bremen, to persuade them at least to ensure that his cousin Lotte, fifteen at the time, would get out of the country.[1662] By doing so, he saved her life. Gerd arranged for a foster family for her in Manchester and she left in 1939, at the very last moment, with the kinder-transport. On 3 May 1939, she and fifty other children set out for Britain by train. Lotte did not really want to leave her parents at all. Abraham's brother Max and his wife were working on getting a visa for the USA but they did not make it. In 1941, they were murdered in Minsk.[1663]

Freud remained in touch with the Abraham family even after he was forced to flee the Nazis himself and found himself in London in 1938. The Abrahams visited him and Martha Freud there. In the 1950s, Hilda told Eissler that at that meeting Freud had spoken with great sorrow about Abraham. The last time Hilda saw him, Freud said that it was a loss from which psycho-analysis would never recover. Hilda also said that Freud had repeated his view that apart from Abraham there had been only one man who could have succeeded him.

Eissler asked her whether Freud had said whom he meant. Hilda answered that he had not. She assumed it was Ferenczi and that Freud, after Abraham and Ferenczi died, had no one left to succeed him. Hilda had the impression that it was a blow from which Freud never recovered.[1664]

Afterword

A number of facts and connections emerged during the research for this book. The role of Max Eitingon in the history of psychoanalysis, for example, turned out to be far greater than expected, and with it the importance of money. Both are deserving of further study. Abraham was already known to have been the first to develop a psychoanalytic theory on depression, but the question arose as to whether he might also have been the first to study the earliest pre-oedipal phases, even before they were mentioned by Freud. That point also merits further investigation.

Life story

Karl Abraham was a pioneer of psychoanalysis and among the first of the doctors who ventured to set up their own psychoanalytic practices. During his lifetime, he became the most important psychoanalyst after Freud. He had a profound influence on the development of psychoanalytic theory and his efforts to propagate it were of inestimable value.

Abraham's life was powerfully influenced by the turbulent times in which he lived. On the one hand, he was able to benefit from the rapid rise of a Jewish middle class in the Germany of Wilhelm II, which meant he was able to attend university. On the other hand, his options were limited by his Jewish background. The only careers open to him were those of a doctor or a lawyer. The First World War and, in its wake, revolution, inflation, and changing power structures left their mark on his life. They interrupted his psychoanalytic career but did not fundamentally obstruct it. His health, however, was permanently damaged by the war and the hardships of the post-war period.

Contact with Freud

The relationship between Abraham and Freud went through a number of major changes. Abraham became familiar with Freud's work while he was at the Burghölzli Clinic. He was enthusiastic about it and sent Freud an article he had written that was clearly influenced by psychoanalysis. Freud was pleasantly surprised and invited Abraham to visit him. It was the start of intensive contact between the two men that consisted mainly of written correspondence. At first, Abraham was the admiring pupil, although he soon noticed, during a conflict with Jung, that Freud was capable of suddenly turning against him. Far from damaging the bond between them, it deepened their relationship after Abraham, with his warnings about Jung, turned out to have been right. Freud always had his favourites and after Jung it was Abraham, although that position was lost when contact between them became impossible during the First World War. Research into Abraham makes clear that his importance to Freud was far greater than would be expected based on the literature published over the years. Freud knew that he could rely on Abraham under all circumstances and both seem to have greatly enjoyed their lively scientific exchange. Freud was sometimes fiercely critical of Abraham but he seems to have assumed that this "rocher de bronze" was more than able to take it. He held Abraham in high esteem. Perhaps it was partly because Freud had such firm confidence in Abraham that it took him so long to realise that his friend of twenty-one years younger was dying.

A letter from Freud to Eitingon of 14 December 1932 and the interviews with Hedwig and Hilda point to the fact that Freud continued to miss Abraham after his early death, but he spoke about him only with Ans van Maastrigt and Abraham's remaining family.[1665]

Theoretical and practical development as a psychoanalyst

When, in late 1907, Abraham settled in Berlin as an independent psychoanalyst, he could base what he was doing only on a few books by Freud in which the theory was articulated.[1666] At that point, there was no single practical work describing exactly how to set about working as a psychoanalyst, so Abraham had to teach himself his profession by trial and error. Freud tried to support him as far as possible in his letters. In these early years, Abraham worked hard at researching and dealing with his own problems. He wrote about them, without naming himself, in his essays on Segantini and Akhenaten. This was ground-breaking work. From *Segantini* (1911) onwards, the central theme that Abraham continually elaborated upon was depression and manic depression, which we now call bipolar disorder.

What drove Karl Abraham? Why did he become first a psychiatrist and then a psychoanalyst? The lives of Sigmund Freud, Karl Abraham, and the French psychoanalyst, André Green, took a similar course in one sense. Freud's mother lost her eight-month-old son Julius a month before Freud's second birthday. Abraham's mother, as described in Chapter One, had a stillborn daughter when Abraham was two, and André Green's mother lost her younger sister in a fire when he was two years old.[1667] The reaction of Freud's mother is not known, but the mothers of both Abraham and Green became deeply depressed in response to their loss. For both of them that event, which in Abraham's case took place in 1879 and in Green's case in 1929, grew to become a central theme of their work and interesting parallels can be drawn. Abraham was the first to develop, even before Freud, a psychoanalytic theory about depression. It was a theme he concentrated on all his working life, in later years also focusing on the consequences for the child and its further course in life.

In his patients, Abraham often found a striking pattern in the early childhood years. A child who had always felt itself to be its mother's favourite, imagining itself assured of her love, experienced through her a disappointment that shook it to such an extent that it was barely able to recover. Because of further experiences of a similar kind, the child became convinced the loss was irrevocable. No alternative female figure was available. Moreover, an attempt by the child to turn to its father instead was unsuccessful. This created in the child an impression of total abandonment. This impression brought with it early eruptions of depressive feelings. Later disappointments were then experienced as a repeat of the early trauma, so that the sense of total abandonment and emptiness recurred and once more gave rise to depression. Abraham thought that the original disillusionment in love must have taken place before the child had overcome the Oedipus complex. As a result, the oral–sadistic drives had not yet been eliminated. Unbearable disappointment prompted it to expel and destroy the love-object as bodily content. Then followed the introjection, the cannibalistic incorporation of the object in the special form of a narcissistic identification.

André Green covered the same subject. Where Abraham wrote about the "bad mother", André Green wrote of the "dead mother" (la mère morte). The dead mother is not physically dead but, because of sudden intense grief, she is no longer available for the child.[1668] André Green described the "dead mother complex" as follows: we are not talking about depression (in the child) after a real loss, but about depression that occurs in the presence of an object that has itself been absorbed by grief. Of prime importance is the sudden absence of any interest in the child. The most serious cases are those of a brother or sister who died very young, or a miscarriage kept secret from the child, who cannot understand what has happened. The motherly image is changed by this in a brutal manner. Until then, the child felt loved. The mother's grief is experienced by the child as a catastrophe. As well as the loss of love, it entails a loss of meaning, since the child has no explanation at all for what has happened and thinks it is itself to blame. Often, the father does not respond to the child's misery. At first, the child protests at the course of events. When that has no effect, the following happens: investment in the mother object ceases, the child identifies with the dead mother, and a loss of significance occurs. Identification with the dead mother creates a hole in the fabric of the child's object relations with the mother. At the centre is always the lifeless mother. The child feels responsible for the change in its mother but cannot bridge the discrepancy between that for which it reproaches itself and the intensity of its mother's reaction. As a result, it tends to make a connection with its way of being rather than with a forbidden drive. Consequently, it is forbidden to exist. This is all played out at an unconscious level. There is a triangulation between the child, the motherly object, and the lifeless mother. The child attempts to get over the trauma by means of a powerful precocious urge to creativity or to intellectual achievement. It has been through a cruel experience with its dependency on the changing moods of its mother. From this point on, it makes a determined effort to anticipate those changes of mood. The painting by Segantini portraying the bad mother that Abraham describes seems to fit Green's account remarkably well.

As a child and as an adult, Abraham was vigorous, intelligent, and high-spirited, with a great sense of humour. He also had enormous integrity. He was detached, however, with a reserve the depths of which even Abraham's best friends could not plumb, or even, probably, Abraham himself. This unconscious reserve must have had to do with the trauma Abraham suffered at the age of two when his mother, from one moment to the next, became unavailable.

Abraham had a number of characteristics that call to mind Green's dead mother complex. There were his immense intellectual feats at too young an age, to fill the gap left by the dead mother. The thoroughness of Abraham's linguistic research as a fifteen-year-old boy, for example, was extreme for his age. At university, he took far more subjects than other students. Early in life he was intellectually very active.

Abraham's decision to become a psychiatrist is also understandable based on Green's concept. He chose a profession concerned with the treatment of mental disorders. Psychoanalysis was a logical next step, since it revolves around early childhood sexuality. It was love of and by the mother, after all, that had been so disturbed. Abraham's ability to empathise and his focus on the other are signs of excessive attention to, and orientation towards, the wellbeing of other people. At play here, at an unconscious level, is the urge to prevent a repeat of the trauma by whatever means possible. This was undoubtedly of relevance in his relationship with Hedwig and their decision to return to Berlin, a city where she felt at home but he did not. The love-object had to be cherished and protected, even at a cost to Abraham himself. The role played by the mother was central to his work at that time.

Abraham took great risks with his personal safety. He felt no fear. He was a fanatical mountain climber even though his defective eyesight meant he could not judge depth. It is as if, at an unconscious level, he was uncertain of his right to exist and therefore found it easy to risk his life.

Abraham knew what a sense of total abandonment and the accompanying depression felt like. In his childhood, he sought refuge in the company of older boys and there will have been a homosexual component to that. In later life, he became depressed when his father died and when contact with Freud was broken off, as it was at the end of the First World War and when Freud turned away from him in the late summer of 1925. It is undeniable that Abraham more or less drove himself to death, if by a completely unconscious process. Just before the summer of 1925, he became seriously ill. That summer, in the mountains, he recovered bit by bit, but he ought to have spent months longer convalescing. Instead, he fulfilled his task of chairing the congress even though it was far too demanding. He allowed Freud's psychoanalysis to weigh more heavily than his own health. It is painful to read the letters in which Sachs asks Freud time after time to intervene. Sachs seems to have realised that Freud was the only person who could persuade Abraham to go to the mountains to rest. Freud, however, turned away from Abraham, under the influence of Eitingon, and became aware of the seriousness of the situation only when it was too late.

Abraham's theoretical development can be followed through his writing and his many case histories. (See Chapters Eight, Ten, Twelve, Fifteen, Nineteen, and Twenty-five.) Right from the start, his main themes were depression and manic depression. In that connection, he increasingly focused on the pre-oedipal phases and then on the oral phase in particular, with its powerful feelings of love and hatred. In one of his tabular diagrams, Abraham described the consequences for the object relations when the early pre-oedipal libido organisations become too dominant: no relationship is possible in which account is truly taken of the other. There is also too much aggression, which stands in the way of a permanent bond with a partner.

Abraham's early writings are very much focused on the relationship with the mother. Later, he became the first to take as his subject the sexual development of the woman. His ideas about early abandonment, as described above, were well ahead of his time.

How Abraham developed as an analyst in a practical sense and exactly what he did during treatments cannot be discovered in detail because, in his case histories, he describes his patients but not the interaction with them or the countertransference. This was usual in those days (see Chapter Twenty-four). He was initially fairly actively in search of the phenomena Freud had described; later, he became quieter, with more of a wait-and-see attitude. He continued to do a lot of explaining. He seems to have been caring towards his patients. They benefited from the treatment and apparently had a great deal of faith in him.

One of Abraham's great merits was that he did not evade negative transference. His own theory, which attributed considerable importance to aggression, will have been part of the reason for this.

Differences and similarities between Abraham and Freud

Abraham made a series of original contributions to psychoanalytic theory that were adopted after his death, often without any mention of his name. His theory about depression, early abandonment by the mother, and aggression in childhood and the feelings of guilt it aroused placed a lasting stamp on psychoanalytic theory. Abraham stuck closely to Freud's theory, but, as early as 1910, he began to carve out his own path. He seems to have wanted to avoid excessive abstraction as he developed new theories. He became entirely absorbed in the development of the libido theory, as time went on concentrating much of his effort on the very early pre-oedipal phases, right back into the first year of life. Abraham was by no means a clone of Freud. That misunderstanding can only have arisen based on a lack of familiarity with his work.

How exactly did Abraham differ from Freud?

First, for Abraham, the relationship with the mother was central from the start. Freud did not write about the relationship with the mother. For him, the father was central.

Second, Abraham assumed the existence of a powerful innate aggressive drive, which differed from person to person but was always a major influence. It was an inborn sadism and destructiveness that revealed itself as soon as the teeth came through. In fact, Abraham assumed both a sexual and an aggressive drive. Freud, by contrast, took as his starting point only the sexual drive. He saw aggression as derived from it, arising when the sexual drive was frustrated. After the First World War, Freud altered his theory, allocating a more important place to aggression and introducing the idea of a death drive (Freud, 1920g).

Third, Abraham focused intensively on the development of a psychoanalytic theory about the first year of life. The ambivalent feelings of love and hatred towards the mother are of great importance here: the powerful sadism that arises in the child; the desire to incorporate and to destroy. Abraham developed a theory about those first twelve months in which he distinguished between a first and a second oral phase, the first being auto-erotic and the second oral–cannibalistic. In 1915, Freud had added the pregenital phases to his *Three Essays on the Theory of Sexuality*, writing of an oral or cannibalistic phase in which the sexual goal is the incorporation of the object. He did not develop his theories on the first year of life any further, however. There is no mention of destruction, or of extreme aggression towards the mother. At that point, he was still basing all his work on the sexual drive as the motivating force.

Fourth, Abraham and Freud had completely different ideas about depression.[1669] For Abraham, there was a strong connection between depression and the oral phases; the melancholic unconsciously wants to devour and destroy the object. Depression is connected with strong feelings of guilt about aggression towards the object and Abraham focuses on the feelings of hatred that paralyse the ability to love. Depression, as Abraham discovered while treating patients, can arise because of a real and significant loss of love in the childhood years, as described above, so that the child finds itself in a situation of utter abandonment.

Freud's theory on depression had a quite different starting point.[1670] He, too, writes of loss, but it is not clear exactly what has been lost. Freud saw in depression the same symptoms as in grief: despondency, lack of interest in the outside world, and reduced activity. His theory seems to focus on unconscious object-loss, in which the loss of a sense of self-worth is a major element. The libido released after loss is drawn back into the ego, where it is used to bring about identification with the lost object. A split arises between the ego and the ego changed by identification, and self-reproaches are directed against the latter. Freud did not examine the consequences of, and reaction to, loss at a very young age.

One important difference between Abraham and Freud is that although both assume identification with, and incorporation of, the lost object, Abraham did not focus on vicissitudes within the ego. He did not write of a divided ego in which one part turns against the other. On the one hand, this might be because he did not live long enough truly to absorb the structural theory in full; on the other hand, Abraham seems to have thought this particular theory extremely abstract and insufficiently based on case histories.

Abraham saw the sense of guilt as arising less from the demands of a strong conscience that have not been complied with than from aggressive fantasies about what one would like to do to someone else.

Fifth, Abraham and Freud had different ways of working. Abraham took a series of case histories as the basis for his work, using them in his attempts to develop psychoanalytic theory further. Freud was content to base his work on a single case.

Sixth, Abraham, as a true doctor of his time, continued to make a clear distinction between normal and abnormal. Freud was of the opinion that everyone carries pathology within them. For Freud, it was a question of the degree of pathology. He did not regard as neurotic a person who could function well despite their pathology.

Seventh, Abraham did not seek to evade negative transference, whereas Freud does seem to have done so. For more on this, see Chapter Twenty-four, which looks at the treatment of Helene Deutsch. The evasion of negative transference probably contributed significantly to the fact that Helene Deutsch came to idealise Freud intensely.

Abraham's place in the world of psychoanalysis

In the last few years of his life, Abraham was the most important person in the world of psycho-analysis after Freud. His theoretical contributions were important for the development of psychoanalysis and were highly valued. He was popular for his way of giving leadership and the fact that, whenever possible, he helped and supported his colleagues. There were fierce conflicts within the committee, but he showed great dedication in trying to resolve them. Despite the fact that he tended to take the position of an all-knowing doctor, Abraham's psycho-analytic treatments seem to have been very successful. There are many positive testimonies. After his death, however, he quickly faded from view and the same applies to much of his work. The explanation usually given is that Abraham elaborated upon the libido theory, whereas the time of the structural theory had arrived. This explanation is valid only in part. The libido theory remained in existence alongside the structural theory, and, until shortly before his death, Abraham continued to deliver innovative work.

The fact that when feeling ill or depressed Abraham might have given the impression of being somewhat aggressive does not seem to have been a decisive factor. Appreciation of him was too great for that.

It may be the case that in the era of Eitingon and Anna Freud, who together gave leader-ship to the world of psychoanalysis after Abraham's death, there was no longer any place for Abraham. Eitingon seems to have wanted to see the back of Abraham even when he was alive. For a long time, Anna Freud was involved in a major battle with Melanie Klein, who had adopted many of Abraham's ideas. Furthermore, Anna Freud advocated a different kind of psychoanalysis, one that focused more on defence and control and was more directed towards the development of an ego that would be capable of bringing those uncontrolled drives, which had their roots in the unconscious, under control. Anna Freud, in any case, disliked Abraham.[1671] Eitingon became interim president of the IPA in 1926 and in 1927 was officially chosen as president. In 1927, Anna Freud became secretary to the IPA. Eitingon remained in his post until 1932, when Jones became president. Anna Freud was secretary until 1935, when Glover took over her function, and she stayed on after that as a member of the board of the IPA.

Since, for a long time, there was no place for Abraham, the influence of his theory on subse-quent generations of psychoanalysts seems to have been lost from view, although that influ-ence was considerable. His theory about depression and aggression has stood the test of time, but it has been presented as a theory of Freud's. The influence of early abandonment and its relationship with later depression and bipolar disorder, as identified by Abraham, has become widely known. It is presented in psychiatric textbooks as an established fact, confirmed by much research.[1672] An overview of recent studies can be found in an article by Nicolai about childhood trauma, which is so often discovered in people with depressive disorders.[1673]

Meticulous research into the early pre-oedipal phases has become central to psychoanalytic theory, as has the relationship with the mother. Abraham's influence on Melanie Klein is inter-esting. She was in analysis with him when he died. As a grief reaction, she seems to have incor-porated Abraham, or at least Abraham's theory, to such an extent that she could no longer tell the difference between his theory and her own. She absorbed it. Later, she departed from his theory to a considerable extent. Klein abandoned Freud's version of the Oedipus complex and moved it to the first year of life. She also changed the theory about the first oral phase fundamentally by claiming that both aggression and the ambivalence of object relations are present from birth. (See Chapter Twenty-seven.)

Was Eitingon a cuckoo in the nest?

This rather provocative question is an expression of the fact that one of the results of my research was the discovery that Eitingon's role in the history of psychoanalysis has been significantly underestimated. He was certainly constructive, but he had an undermining effect as well.

Eitingon was given a place on the committee because he was able to make a reality of Freud's dream of an institute where even those without the means to pay could receive psychoanalytic treatment. That was his great merit and that step was important to the development of psychoanalysis. Eitingon had a dark side, too, however. He became a member of the committee in 1919, and eight years later all the committee members had left with the exception of Jones, who was tolerated because he could keep the English-speaking world and himself under control. Ferenczi, like Jones, was vice-president of the IPA, but his position was marginal. The disintegration of the committee cannot be blamed on Eitingon alone, but he bears part of the responsibility.

Eitingon does not seem to have been interested in the other members of the committee. Having become a member, he took no part in the continual intellectual exchange that went on within it. He wrote no articles, he was often away, and when Freud became ill he disappeared from the stage altogether for a long time. It seems he was concerned purely about his relationship with Freud. A place on the committee brought him closer to Freud. This might explain why he was eager to receive only the Freud family and Lou Andreas-Salomé in his large, luxurious house in Berlin, not any of his other colleagues. In 1921, he almost caused Abraham to step down as president of the Berlin Psychoanalytic Society. He played only a marginal role in the conflict with Rank, but, against Freud's wishes, he stepped into the vacancy when Rank left the publishing house. Eitingon took over its leadership, with Radó as editor-in-chief. He also acquired the presidency of the umbrella training commission. Again contrary to Freud's wishes, he became interim president of the IPA on the day after Abraham's funeral. Shortly after that, both Ferenczi and Sachs were sidetracked. So, was Eitingon a cuckoo in the nest, who from 1926 onwards at last had the nest to himself, with Jones at a safe distance? The things he said about the secret committee make clear that he saw no value at all in continuing it.[1674]

Strikingly, Eitingon almost caused the disappearance of all the letters from Abraham.

On 14 December 1932, Eitingon wrote to Freud that he was making preparations to carry out an old plan, the writing of the history of psychoanalysis. Eitingon asked Freud whether he could see the correspondence between Freud and Abraham.[1675] Freud agreed. He sent Abraham's letters to Eitingon and gave him permission to see his own letters as well, which were in the possession of Hedwig. He wrote sadly, "In memory of those so much better past times, I send you a cordial greeting".[1676] Freud still missed Abraham terribly. The book Eitingon intended to produce was never written, but he took the letters with him to Palestine in 1933 and did not return them. After Eitingon's death, Arnold Zweig wrote to Eitingon's wife in 1944 that "Frau Dr. Abraham" would like to have Abraham's letters back. They must be part of the Eitingon estate.[1677] The letters were eventually found. Without those letters, this biography could not have been written.

Time for a different view

Why was Abraham so often negatively portrayed after his death?

It is possible to point to a range of factors, but Abraham's early death and the dismissive attitude of Eitingon and Anna Freud are certainly of relevance. Furthermore, in his three-volume biography of Freud, Jones exaggerated his own role and underplayed that of Abraham.

Abraham was good at tolerating criticism and he was himself sometimes critical. Several of Abraham's colleagues were very easily hurt. Rank, for example, never forgave Abraham for his criticism of *The Trauma of Birth*.

Abraham was involved in a number of major conflicts that to this day have been described in histories of psychoanalysis mainly from the point of view of his opponents of those years, such as Jung, Eitingon, and Rank. It is now time for a more balanced portrayal of Karl Abraham, so that his position can at last be explored and appreciated to the full.

SOURCES

Archives consulted

Amsterdam: Archive of F. Muller. Private collection of G. W. Muller.

Berlin: University Archive of the Humboldt University of Berlin

Berlin: Archives of the Karl-Abraham-Institut.

Boston, MA: Archives of the Boston Psychoanalytic Society and Institute.

Cambridge, MA: Schlesinger Library, Radcliffe Institute, Harvard University, Helene Deutsch Collection.

Freiburg im Breisgau: University Archive of the Albert-Ludwigs University.

Freiburg im Breisgau: Federal Archives.

Jerusalem: State Archives, Eitingon Archive.

London: Archives of the British Psychoanalytical Society.

London: Freud Museum.

Potsdam: Library of the Military History Research Office.

Tübingen: Institute of History of Medicine, G. Fichtner Databanks.

Würzburg: University Archive, Julius-Maximilians University.

New Haven, CT: Manuscripts and Archives, Yale University Library, Karen Horney Papers, Manuscript Group 1604.

Washington: Library of Congress, Manuscript Reading Room, Sigmund Freud collection, Karl Abraham correspondence (1877–1925), Anna Freud correspondence (1895–1982), Theodor Reik correspondence (1888–1969), Hanns Sachs correspondence (1881–1947), Ernst Simmel correspondence (1882–1947).

Zurich: State Archives of the Canton of Zurich, Burghölzli Archive.

Lotte Levy-Abraham, daughter of Abraham's brother Max. The interviews were recorded on 27 January 2006 and 16 October 2006.

Anja Amsel and Steven Burgner, daughter and grandson of Hans Bürgner, brother of Hedwig, 11 and 12 November 2006.

Jeremy Lewison, son of Dinorah Pines, 26 June 2009.

Interviews by K. R. Eissler with the following, consulted at the Library of Congress (Manuscript reading room, Sigmund Freud collection):

Alexander, Franz (1953–1954), box 112.

Allan-Abraham, Hedwig (1953), box 115.

Abraham, Hilda (1953), box 115.

Benedek, Therese (1953), box 115.

Deutsch, Helene en Felix (1954), box 115.

Hitschmann, Eduard (1952–1953), box 115.

Klein, Melanie (1953), box × 12.

Van Maastrigt (1954), box × 13.

Rank, Beate (1953–1954), box × 15.

NOTES

INTRODUCTION

1. Jones, 1926a, p. 179, 180.
2. Jones, 1955, p. 156.
3. Both Abraham's wife Hedwig and his patient Theodor Reik mention Abraham's extraordinary empathy. Interview with Hedwig by Eissler (Reik,1926, p. 211).
4. Sachs, 1926, p. 201.

CHAPTER ONE

5. Blackbourn, 2003, pp. 104–120.
6. Idem, p. 184.
7. Blackbourn, 2003, p. 157ff.
8. Craig, 1978, p. 78–85.
9. Haffner, 1973.
10. Abraham, 1909a, p. 21.
11. HA, p. 26. Hilda C. Abraham (1906–1971), daughter of Karl Abraham and a psychoanalyst in London, wrote a biography of her father towards the end of her life. She became ill and died before she could finish the book. Dinora Pines was a colleague and good friend of Hilda in London, and it was she who had encouraged Hilda to write the biography. After Hilda's death, she edited the book, along with Tom and Marion Burgner, and helped to ensure it was published. Tom and Marion Burgner were the son and daughter-in-law of Hans Burgner, Abraham's best friend as well as the brother of his wife Hedwig. Before fleeing Nazi Germany, Hans spelled his name with an umlaut: Bürgner.
12. In Germany, marriages between first cousins were allowed. They were most common in Jewish families. In Prussia between 1872 and 1875 there were fourteen such marriages per 1,000 among

Protestants, ten per 1,000 among Catholics and twenty-three per 1,000 among Jews. The Jewish tradition accepted first-cousin marriages and, in some cases, advocated them. Kaplan (1991, pp. 115–116).

13. HA, p. 18. Hilda Abraham writes that her father was interested in his forebears and their family tree, and he shared his discoveries with her. She also writes that those familiar with long-established Jewish families will know how important they found it to be able to refer back to earlier generations who had lived in Germany.

14. Decke, 1997, pp. 10–11). The combination of religious teacher and ritual slaughterer was not unusual, partly because of the great importance that was attached to that particular ritual (Gay, 1992, p. 39).

15. Decke, 1997, p. 10.

16. Decke, 1997, p. 11.

17. Decke, 1997, pp. 12–13.

18. Decke, 1997, p. 12.

19. Letter dated 14 July 1992 from Dr Schleier of the Bremen municipal archives to Mr Glocker of the University of Tübingen.

20. *Grote Winkler Prins, Encyclopedie* (1979–1984, 8th impression, Volume 5), Bremen.

21. Decke, 1997, p. 13. When Freud travelled to America in 1909 with Jung and Ferenczi, he left from Bremen.

22. In Bremen in 1871, just 0.39% of the population was Jewish, whereas in Hamburg in the same year the figure was 4.06%. Decke (1997, p. 50, n. 20).

23. Decke, 1997, p. 13.

24. Max Markreich, in his book about the history of the Jews in Bremen (1955), describes Jewish education there and mentions Karl Abraham's father, of whom he was himself a pupil (p. 82).

> Next came Nathan Abraham, from Nienburg on the Weser, a still young man who had been educated at the Jewish Teachers' Seminary in Hannover and was clearly capable of taking on the duties of a preacher alongside his normal duties. The classroom had been moved to Tiefer no. 9 in Bremen-Altstadt and furnished appropriately. The nature of the education was now essentially different. We learned to write Hebrew as well and to translate several commandments into the German language, but in those few lessons there was no time to gain an insight into Jewish life and Jewish history. Abraham was there until 1872 and then went into commerce.

25. Decke, 1997, p. 14.

26. In 1897, he shut down the business and set himself up as a wholesaler in haberdashery and men's fashions (Decke, 1997, pp. 14–15).

27. HA, pp. 19–21. In describing Nathan, Hilda uses terminology that exhibits some similarities with the way Kaplan describes the role of the father in Jewish families in the German Empire. At home, everything was focused on the father, who was treated with respect and could have peace and comfort without being disturbed. Personal contact with the children was not a priority. Everything was placed at the service of the career of the patriarch outside the home, in a world that could be extremely hostile. He needed to devote all his energies to that. The mother had an important and fairly independent position within the home (Kaplan, 1991, p. 53).

28. The Bremen municipal archives record that in 1898–1915 Nathan Abraham was the leader of the Jewish community in Bremen. See note 15.

29. Gay, 1992, p. 125ff.
30. Gay, 1992, p. 131.
31. Gay, 1992, p. 165.
32. Decke, 1997, p. 13.
33. Decke, 1997, p. 51, n. 22.
34. Gay, 1992, p. 165.
35. HA, p. 18.
36. HA, pp. 18–19.
37. Decke, 1997, p. 14.
38. Jeanette Abraham destroyed the furniture in her room and smeared herself with excrement.
39. HA, p. 19.
40. HA, p. 19.
41. See Chapter Twenty.
42. Decke, 1997, p. 17.
43. Parentification involves a child feeling responsible for the wellbeing of its parents, because of family circumstances.
44. Bettina Decke has written a book about Lotte Abraham, later Lottie Levy-Abraham, entitled *Du muß raus hier* (1998).
45. Interview with Lottie Levy-Abraham, 27 January 2006.
46. Draft and notes of a lecture by Dinora Pines on Karl Abraham, 1987, Dinora Pines Collection, ABPAS, Part of 39. All further references to Dinora Pines relate to this draft and notes.
47. HA, p. 21.
48. Decke, 1997, p. 29.
49. See Chapters Eight and Ten.
50. Interview with Lottie Levy-Abraham.
51. The theme of anxiety returns a number of times in his work.
52. Interview with Hedwig Abraham/Allan by Eissler. LoC, Sigmund Freud papers, set B, Box 115, Folder 1. (After her flight to England Hedwig adopted a new surname, Allan.) (Reik, 1926).
53. Decke, 1997, pp. 29–30.
54. HA, p. 21.
55. Balkanyi, 1975. The article from which information about the book is derived was handed to Jill Duncan of the Psychoanalytic Institute in London by Bettina Decke in July 1979.
56. Decke, 1997, p. 39.
57. Decke, 1997, pp. 40–42.
58. Information about the essay is from Decke (1997, pp. 40–42).
59. Decke, 1997, p. 61.
60. Decke, 1997, p. 62. Abraham's essay for his final school exam is from February 1896. Decke found the text in the municipal archives in Bremen, where it had been kept with other exam essays by pupils in his class. When she came to transcribe it, not everything was legible, so she placed question marks here and there. In this passage there is a question mark after *"Vorgange"* (precedent) and another after *"dann"* (then) in "then he must always".

CHAPTER TWO

61. Interview with Lotte Levy, 27 Jan 2006.

62. After the death of his father on 20 November 1915, Max had great difficulty keeping the business going. He had married by then and he and his family could keep their heads above water only because his very energetic wife let out rooms. Interview with Lotte Levy.

63. See also Chapter One. In 1896 the situation was far worse than in 1871 because of the growth of powerful anti-Semitic tendencies, especially among students. Kampe (1988) believed that professional jealousy played a role in this. In the late nineteenth century, the number of students increased spectacularly and there were too few graduate-level jobs for them. See Kampe, Chapter 1.3. "Status anxiety and change in mentality: The attack on Jewish students".

64. HA, p. 22.

65. Decke, 1997, p. 40.

66. The *"Inscriptionsliste"* are the lists giving the subjects a student has registered to take. They are held in the university archive of the Julius Maximilian University of Würzburg. UWue ARS 4139.

67. Decke, 1997, p. 43.

68. Paulsen, 1902, p. 409.

69. Heutger, N. (2004), *Die Mark: Geschichte und Kaufkracht einer Währung*. Accessed on 9 Aug 2012 via http://www.numismatikforum.de/ftopic6831.html.

70. HA, p. 22.

71. Iwan Bloch (1872–1922) later became a dermatologist in Berlin. An erudite man, in 1907 he proposed establishing a new science, sexology. He published much on the subject and was a great organiser. In 1913, along with Magnus Hirschfeld and Albert Eulenburger, he set up the Ärztliche Gesellschaft für Sexualwissenschaft und Eugenik. Bloch's magnum opus, *Das Sexualleben unserer Zeit in seinen Beziehungen zur modernen Kultur* was published in 1907 (Egger, 1988, p. 8).

72. From the *Inscriptionsliste* for the summer term at the University of Würzburg, university archive. Abraham registered for the following subjects: Heidenhain: bones and ligaments; Sobotta: microscope course on normal tissues; Röntgen: experimental physics II (optics, electricity); Von Sachs: natural history of the plant kingdom; Külpe: history of modern philosophy; Marbe: Schopenhauer.

73. Paulsen, 1902, p. 222ff.

74. See Chapter Nine.

75. Paulsen, p. 384.

76. In the Second World War, Freiburg was largely spared until 27 November 1944. Then, in twenty-five minutes, the old city centre was completely destroyed by bombers of the British Royal Air Force. The bombs fell so close together that in ten minutes everything was engulfed by a firestorm. Only the Freiburg Minster, built in the early thirteenth century remained, by chance, practically undamaged. All the buildings of the medical faculty were close to the old city and almost all were bombed. Photographs taken shortly after the bombing show a vast area of blackened rubble with the lonely steeple of the Minster towering above it all. "Ueberschär, G.R. In 25 minuten sank die Altstadt in Schutt und Asche" (In 25 minutes the old city was reduced to ash and rubble), *Freiburger Zeitung*, 26 Nov 1994. Acknowledgements to G. Fichtner.

77. Adolph and Kamp (1992). "Sie sol blühen, wachsen und gedeihen. Die Abert-Ludwigs-Universität und die Stadt Freiburg", in Haumann and Schadek, 1992, p. 473ff.

78. Seidler and Leven, 2007, p. 218ff.

79. Adolph and Kamp, in Haumann and Schadek, 1992, p. 474.

80. Quinn, 1988, p. 93.

81. "Immatrikulationen Wintersemester 1896/97." Freiburg, university archive.

82. Seidler and Leven, 2007, p. 288ff.

83. Idem, p. 374.
84. Quinn, 1988, p. 93.
85. Curriculum vitae, written by Abraham. Freiburg, university archive. B 54/1002 part 2075. In the CV that Abraham sent to the Burghölzli when he applied for a job there in 1904, he wrote the following:

> From the fifth semester I spent more than two years with Prof. Dr. Keibel in Freiburg compiling an embryological atlas. It was published in 1900 under the title: Keibel und Abraham, Normentafel zur Entwicklungsgeschichte des Huhnes (Verlag von G. Fischer in Jena, fol. 1200 u. Tafeln). My dissertation, too, was on an embryological theme.

86. Melopsittacus Undulatus. Freiburg, University Archive D 29/9/2911 and B 54/1002. Abraham, K. (1901). *Beträge zur Entwicklungsgeschichte des Wellensittichs*. Wiesbaden: von JF Bergmann.
87. Freiburg, University Archive. B 54 1002 part 5078. On that same day, 27 February 1901, Prof. Wiedersheim signed a form saying that Abraham's dissertation complied with all the conditions.
88. Freiburg, University Archive B 54 1002, part 3076. Freiburg in Brsg. D. 27/11 1901.

> Report on the work of Mr. Karl Abraham, trainee doctor from Bremen. Contributions to the developmental history of the budgerigar (Melopsittacus undulatus). The contributions to the developmental history of the budgerigar (Melopsittacus undulatus) are based on a meticulous study of thirty-six embryos. The findings for each embryo have been entered into diagrams and then compared with each other and with those for other birds. It was found that the development of the budgerigar is not essentially different from that of other birds, to the extent that these have been studied, the chicken for example. There were however a number of interesting divergences. I would draw attention to the development of the eye, the ductus endolymphaticus and the liver. The latter two in particular are of importance for further study. The ductus endolymphaticus develops in the budgerigar *before* the ear vesicle has closed. This makes it possible to determine the precise position of the closure of the ear vesicle in relation to the ductus endolymphaticus. It lies close to the base. The liver is constructed in pairs. This is the *first time* such a finding has been made in a vertebrate. The circumstances may be the same here as with the construction in pairs of the heart in amniotes. A number explain these most important observations. In a formal sense also the work is good, so that I have judged the work as a whole to be very good.

Wiedersheim
    The emphasis is by Wiedersheim, who clearly believed that Abraham had made a number of interesting new discoveries and had presented an excellent study.
89. HA, p. 23.
90. Dinora Pines collection. ABPAS, Part of 39.
91. HA, p. 26.
92. Information from W. Melching.
93. Wasserman, 1921, pp. 43–44.
94. Kampe, 1988, p. 15.
95. Important representatives were Bernard Förster, Max Liebermann von Sonnenberg, Ernst Henrici, and Professor Friedrich Zöllner. Idem, p. 23.
96. Kampe, 1988, p. 23.

97. Idem, p. 33

98. Idem, p. 11.

99. Idem, p. 127. This was a paragraph from the "Taschenbuch für die Mitglieder der Vereine Deutscher Studenten", which gave guidance to members who aspired to the "Kyfferhaus-gedanke".

100. Idem, p. 131.

101. Idem, p. 157.

102. Idem, p. 170.

CHAPTER THREE

103. Curriculum vitae of Karl Abraham. State Archive of the Canton of Zurich, Burghölzli archive.

104. Interview with Hedwig.

105. HA, pp. 22–23.

106. Interview with Anja Amsel and Steven Burgner.

107. HA, p. 29.

108. The facts about Dalldorf are from Damm and Emmerich, 1989, and Bratz, 1929.

109. The senior doctor or *Oberarzt* is the doctor with ultimate responsibility.

110. An extremely dark period in the history of the clinic began in 1933, nineteen years after Abraham left Dalldorf. In the view of the Nazis, "*war der rassenreine Volkskörper, seine Gesundheit und Aufartung durch die erbbiologische Minderwertigen bedroht*" (the racially pure body of the people, its health and the improvement of the species is threatened by hereditarily biological inferiors). Those *Minderwertigen* or "inferiors" were, among others, psychiatric patients and from 1933 they were compulsorily sterilised on a large scale. In Germany as a whole, 360,000 forced sterilisations took place after the Nazis came to power in January 1933. The Dalldorf clinic was no exception. By then, it had become part of the Wittenauer Heilstätten, whose doctors co-operated with the programme. After 1939, hardly any sterilisations took place: instead involuntary euthanasia was used. Between 1939 and 1945 in Berlin alone, 10,000 supposedly sick citizens, including children, were killed with the co-operation of the institutions in which they lived. In 1957, the Wittenauer Heilstätten changed its name again, becoming the Karl Bonhoeffer Nervenklinik (Hühn, 1989).

111. HA, p. 22.

112. Information about Liepmann is from Isserlin (1925).

113. While working at Dalldorf, Abraham published the following articles:

    (1902) "Beiträge zur Kenntnis des Delirium tremens der Morphinisten".

    (1904a) "Ueber Versuche mit 'Veronal' bei Erregungszuständen der Paralytiker." This article was about a department at Dalldorf that housed 209 sick and paralysed male patients, 150 of whom were in wards. An average of fifty to sixty at any one time were extremely restless, so it was unavoidable that they were prescribed sedatives. Abraham tried Veronal on four patients and found it less suitable than the Trional that was already in use.

    (1904b) "Über einige seltene Zustandsbilder bei progressiver Paralyse. Apraxie, transkortikale sensorische Aphasie, subkortikale sensorische Aphasie, sensorisch-motorische Asymbolie". In this article, four case histories are discussed that came under the heading of apraxia or were closely related to it. One patient died shortly after the study ended, so his brain was available for study as well.

    (1904c) Abraham and Ziegenhagen. "Cytodiagnostische Untersuchungen bei Dementia Paralytica." A short note on research into leucocytes in twenty-five men and women with Dementia Paralytica (dementia caused by the decay of the brain).

(1904d) "Vorstellung eines Kranken mit Hemianopsie und Rotgrünblindheit im erhaltenen Gesichtsfeld".

(1907a) "Beiträge zur Kenntnis der motorischen Apraxie auf Grund eines Falles von einseitger Apraxie".

114. Fechtboden: "Inszenierung von mannlichkeit in jüdischen Studentenverbindungen in Kaiserreich und Weimarer Republik." A talk given to the "Arbeitsgemeinschaft für geschichtliche Landeskunde am Oberrhein e.V".

115. Idem.

116. Schreiber, 1928. For the fiftieth birthday of S. P. Altmann. In: Braune, 2003.

117. Braune, 2003, p. 99:

> The seminar in the summerhouse was an entirely unpretentious scientific exchange. In this environment they were equals among equals. Many personalities famous in their day emerged from the seminar. Along with Alice Salomon, who gained a doctorate and became head of the Social School for Women in Berlin, Adele Schreiber studied there, as did the future psychoanalyst Dr. Karl Abraham, who died young, and Walter Kaesbach, future director of the Art Academy in Düsseldorf who, as Adele Schreiber reports, stood out even then with his artistic cravat and betrayed his real interest despite taking part in the political economy seminar. Other members of the seminar group were the blind student Ludwig Cohn, the future lawyers Hans Bürgner and Kurt Alexander, and Elisabeth Gottheiner and S. P. Altmann, who became a couple. Adele Schreiber wrote about the seminar's loving couple: "They found each other as in a fairy tale and because fortunately they have not died, they are still living. And now, watch out, here comes something fabulous that is nevertheless true. They put up with each other for a quarter of a century, they both became professors, and they are perhaps the only professorial married couple in Germany, which has meanwhile become a German Republic".

118. Wieler. "Alice Salomon (1872–1948)." Consulted on 11 Aug 2012 via http://www.jwa.org/encyclopedia/article/salomon-alice.

119. Bauer and Stark, 2008.

120. Interview with Anja Amsel and Steven Burgner.

121. May, 1999, p. 154. May was so astonished at the tone adopted by Abraham, who, in his later articles, demonstrated such poise, that he wondered whether he could really be the author. Yet, he undoubtedly was.

122. Idem, p. 155.

123. Hedwig Marie Bürgner (1878–1967).

124. HA, pp. 25–26.

125. Email from Anja Amsel, 8 Oct 2006.

126. "Helene Lange (1848–1930), German feminist and educationalist", http://www.absolutefacts.nl/vrouwen/data/langehelene1848.htm, accessed on 4 April 2015.

127. Georg Simmel (1858–1918) was an important philosopher and sociologist, teaching in the late nineteenth and early twentieth century. His lectures were famous and attended by many young intellectuals.

128. Dinora Pines collection. ABPAS, Part of 39. Dinora Pines was a good friend of Hilda Abraham in London. She was a dermatologist. Both Dinora's brother, Malcolm, and Hilda influenced her decision to become a psychoanalyst. Jeremy Lewinson donated his mother's psychoanalysis archive

to the ABPAS. (Interview with Jeremy Lewinson, 24 June 2009). Pines gave a talk in 1987 about Abraham at the Goethe Institute in Paris, in preparation for which she interviewed Abraham's son, then aged seventy-eight.

129. HA, p. 27.
130. Letter from Hedwig Abraham to Jones, 24 Feb. 1926. Ernest Jones collection, ABPAS, P04-C-B-01.
131. HA, p. 28.
132. HA, p. 29.
133. HA, p. 26. Abraham, 1909a, 1914d.
134. Abraham, 1914c, pp. 48–49.
135. Lotte Levy said, when interviewed, that she barely saw her nephew and niece, Gerd and Hilda, after Abraham's death. This was in the period 1926–1933, before Hedwig left for London with her two children.
136. See Chapter Thirty-one. It was mainly thanks to Gerd that Lotte, Max's daughter, was saved in 1939. She was on the last Kindertransport taking Jewish children to England. Lotte was sixteen, but it seems not to have occurred to Hedwig, who had been living in Britain for several years already, to invite the girl to live with her. She was taken in by foster families, where she helped with housework and looked after the children. Hedwig was condescending towards her. Interview with Lotte Levy.

CHAPTER FOUR

137. Letter from Bleuler of 25 November 1904 to the "hohe Sanitätsdirection" in Zurich. Burghölzli archive.
138. F/A, p. 10.
139. HA, p. 28.
140. Letter from Bleuler of 25 Nov. 1904 to the "hohe Sanitätsdirection" in Zurich. Burghölzli archive.
141. Ernest Jones (1879–1958) was a neurologist, born in Wales. He was eventually to become one of the most influential psychoanalysts of his day. Despite his many publications, his influence lay more in the organisational than the theoretical field. He set up both the American and the British psychoanalytic associations. Freud at first did not have a very high opinion of him, but he was glad to have a follower in the English-speaking countries. F/J, p. 145; Brome (1982); Maddox (2006).
142. Sándor Ferenczi (1873–1933) was a Hungarian neurologist who later became one of Freud's most important collaborators. He made important theoretical contributions to psychoanalysis.
143. Loewenberg, 1995, p. 46.
144. Idem.
145. Idem, p. 53.
146. Bair, 2003, p. 56.
147. Charcot (1825–1893) was one of the founders of neurology. He worked and taught at the famous Salpêtrière Hospital in Paris and attracted students from all over the world. His study of hypnosis and hysteria was influential. Both Bleuler and Freud studied under Charcot.
148. Loewenberg, 1995, p. 53.
149. Ellenberger, 1970, p. 286.
150. Loewenberg (1995), pp. 54–55.
151. Letter from Bleuler to Freud of 14 Oct. 1905. Schröter, 2012, p. 76.

152. Freud, 1914d, p. 26.

153. Clark, 1980, p. 237.

154. Haynal and Falzeder write in their introduction to the English edition of the collected letters of Freud and Abraham that not Jung but Bleuler introduced psychoanalysis at the Burghölzli (Haynal & Falzeder, 2002, p. xx).

155. Bair, 2003, p. 60. Schröter, 2012, p. 14, n. 15, indicates that what Jung read was not the great *The Interpretation of Dreams* (1900a) but a shorter version of it, entitled "On dreams" (Freud, 1901a).

156. Jones, 1953, 1955, 1957. In this biography, Jones attributed to himself a more important role than he in fact had.

157. Jones, 1955, p. 30.

158. Jones, 1955, p. 72.

159. Idem.

160. Bair, 2003, p. 55.

161. Idem, p. 53.

162. Idem, p. 13ff.

163. Idem, p. 13ff.

164. Gay, 1988, p. 198.

165. Idem.

166. Van Waning, 1992, p. 398.

167. Minder, 1994, p. 59.

168. Ellenberger, 1970, p. 666.

169. Ellenberger, 1970, pp. 666–667.

170. Idem.

171. Idem, p. 667. Alphonse Maeder (1882–1971) worked as an assistant in the Burghölzli clinic from 1906 to 1910.

172. Idem, p. 667.

173. Idem, p. 287.

174. In association experiments, patients were read a list of 100 words, one by one, and asked to respond each time with the first word that came to their minds (Bair, 2003, p. 65).

175. Minder, p. 55ff.

176. Franz Riklin (1878–1938). Riklin worked as a doctor's assistant at the Burghölzli along with Jung.

177. Graf-Nold, 2006, p. 110.

178. Van Waning, 1992, p. 399.

179. HA, p. 30.

180. HA, p. 29.

181. For example, the letter from Abraham to the health authorities in Zurich of 12 January 1906, in which he asks for permission for a holiday because he is getting married. Burghölzli archive.

182. HA, p. 28.

183. Letter from Abraham "An die h. Direktion des Gesundheitswesens des Kantons Zürich" of 29 August 1905.
    Letter from Bleuler "An die h. Direktion des Gesundheitswesens des Kantons Zürich" of 29 August 1905. Burghölzli archive.

184. HA, p. 31.

185. Graf-Nold, pp. 115–116.

186. Interview with Hedwig Abraham by Eissler.

187. HA, p. 20.
188. HA, p. 30.
189. HA, p. 31.
190. Idem.
191. For discussion of this incident, see Mächtlinger, 1997.
192. Hedwig's family disagrees. They have the impression that Hedwig would have liked a son. When Gerd was born ("the golden boy"), far more attention was paid to him than to Hilda. Interview with Anja Amsel and Steven Burgner.
193. Letter from Abraham to Fließ of 24 March 1916 (Hermanns & Schröter, 2010, pp. 96–97). Abraham wrote to Fließ that Hilda started having intestinal cramps after twenty-three days. In Fließ's theory of vital periodicity, twenty-three stood for female. Hilda was healthy at first, but could not tolerate milk from the bottle.
194. HA, p. 32.
195. F/A, p. 10
196. See Chapters Eight and Eleven.

CHAPTER FIVE

197. Bleuler had discovered Freud's work in the 1890s and followed him from that moment on. In 1896, for example, he wrote a review of *Studien über Hysterie* (Küchenhoff, 2001, p. 57).
198. Fichtner, 1992a, p. x.
199. Jung, 1906a; Minder, 1994, pp. 75, 76.
200. F/J, p 3.
201. F/J, 29 December 1906, pp. 13, 14; Jung, 1907a.
202. F/J, 1 January 1907, p. 17.
203. Graf-Nold, 2006, p. 139.
204. Minder, 1994, pp. 73, 74.
205. Schröter, 2004, pp. 2, 3.
206. National Archives, Zurich, Burghölzli Archives.
207. Jones, 1955, part II, pp. 31, 32.
208. Freud, 1914d.
209. This point will be examined in more detail later.
210. See the introduction by Fichtner to the correspondence between Freud and Binswanger (1992a).
211. Binswanger, 1956.
212. Bleuler, 1911.
213. Fichtner, 1992a, pp. xxxiv–xxxvii.
214. Jones, 1955, part II, p. 32.
215. F/J, 31 March 1907, pp. 25, 26.
216. F/J, p. 25.
217. F/J, p. 37.
218. Abraham, 1907b.
219. Minder, 1994, p. 71. Schröter (2004) writes in his introduction to the exchange of letters between Freud and Eitingon (p. 3), that Abraham and Eitingon soon started to do therapeutic analyses themselves at the Burghölzli Clinic. Given the strict way the Burghölzli was run, this cannot have been the case. Neither is there any evidence of it in Abraham's work. Moreover, Eitingon was not

working at the Burghölzli in 1906–1908. In 1906 he was a volunteer there for three weeks and in 1908 for a little over seven weeks, National Archives, Zurich; Burghölzli archive. In the remaining periods, he might possibly have helped with Jung's association experiments, but he will not have had any opportunity to carry out analyses (Wieser, 2001, p. 84).

220. Abraham, 1907c.
221. Idem, p. 125.
222. F/A, 25 June 1907, p. 1.
223. F/A, pp. 1–4.
224. This text, taken from May (2006), is not included in the collected works of Abraham published by Cremerius. In 1921, a book appeared with a great many of Abraham's articles to date: *Klinische Beiträge aus den Jahren 1907–1920*. It includes a short afterword by Abraham to his 1907 article.
225. May, 2006, p. 69.
226. Idem, pp. 74–76.
227. F/J, p. 78.
228. F/J, 8 November 1909, p. 257.
229. F/J, 15 November 1909, p. 262.
230. F/J, 14 December 1909, p. 274.
231. F/J, 15 November 1909, p. 262.
232. Fichtner, 1992b, p. 3, n. 2.
233. Idem and F/J, 25 Nov. 1910, p. 372.
234. Schröter, 2012
235. F/J, 25 November 1910, p. 372.
236. HA, 1976, pp. 29–30.
237. Letters from Jung to Abraham of 3 January 1908 and of 28 January 1908. Abraham papers. LoC.
238. F/J, 19 August 1907, p. 78.
239. They included Sabina Spielrein, who helped Jung with his association experiments (van Waning, 1992, p. 399).
240. Information from, and with acknowledgements to, Professor Hirschmüller.
241. Abraham (1907a): "Beiträge zur Kenntnis der motorischen Apraxie auf Grund eines Falles von einseitiger Apraxie." This is a detailed case study of apraxia following a stroke.
242. Letter dated 2 Aug 1905 from Bleuler to the *hohe Sanitätsdirektion*, in other words to the highest level of the bureaucracy under which the Burghölzli clinic fell. National Archives, Zurich; Burghölzli archive.
243. F/J, 5 October 1906, p. 4.
244. F/J, p. 5.
245. F/J, 27 August 1907, pp. 79, 80.
246. Letter from Hedwig Abraham to Jones dated 24 February 1926. Ernest Jones Collection, ABPAS, P04-C-B-01.
247. Bair (2003), p. 122.
248. From a letter written by Bleuler to the *hohe Sanitätsdirektion* dated 28 October 1907, it is clear that a complaint had been received that none of those responsible for the clinic had been present that summer. Bleuler responded with a long letter explaining the situation. Among other things, it was a result of the fact he had been ill. In the same letter, he also writes that Dr Abraham, the senior assistant, had been working as a psychiatrist just as long as Jung and was no less well versed in the procedures of the clinic. National Archives, Zurich; Burghölzli archive.

249.   Kampe, 1988, pp. 64, 65.

250.   F/A, p. 8.

251.   Idem, p. 9.

252.   Idem.

253.   Sadger, 2006, p. 29; also Epilogue by Huppke & Schröter (Eds.), p. 136.

254.   F/A, 13 October 1907, p. 10.

CHAPTER SIX

255.   F/A, p. 12. On 24 November 1907, Abraham wrote to Freud that he has now been in Berlin for a fortnight and had settled in to some extent. He was hoping to start his practice soon.

256.   HA, p. 36.

257.   Idem.

258.   Herzfeld, 1968, p. 82ff.

259.   Since 1902, Freud and his Viennese disciples had met on Wednesday evenings in Freud's waiting room. From 1908 onwards they used a different room and took to calling themselves the Vienna Psychoanalytic Society.

260.   Nunberg and Federn, 2008, part I, p. 254–256; Abraham, 1907c.

261.   Eitingon had met Freud during a summer holiday in Florence and had then travelled after him to Rome. He visited Freud on the evening of 19 September 1907, took a walk with him through Rome from 8.30 to 11.30 p.m. and then left again (Schröter, 2004, part I, p. 51). Schröter questions just how coincidental their meeting in Florence was.

262.   Freud (1907a). Friedrich Hebbels (1813–1863), a famous nineteenth-century German poet and playwright, kept a journal from 1822, when he was nine years old. His revealing journal entries were published posthumously in 1885–1887.

263.   The first international meeting of psychoanalysts was in 1908 in Salzburg. It will be looked at later in this chapter.

264.   Isidor Isaak Sadger (1867–1942), neurologist in Vienna. He became a member of the Wednesday Society in 1906. He cancelled his membership of the Vienna Psychoanalytic Society in 1933 after he was viciously attacked, especially by Jones, in relation to his book *Erinnerungen an Freud* (Sadger, 2006). He died in Theresienstadt in 1942 (Mühlleitner, 1992).

265.   Abraham's verdict on Freud's Wednesday Society corresponds with the verdict that Binswanger noted as originating with Freud (Fichtner, 1992a, p. xxxix). It seems plausible that Freud said something similar to Abraham at the time.

266.   Letter from Abraham to Eitingon of 1 January 1908 (HA, p. 38).

267.   Letter from Hedwig to Jones, 1 April 1952. Ernest Jones Collection, ABPAS, P04-C-B-01.

268.   Interview with Hedwig by Eissler. Summer 1953. LoC. Freud Archives. Interviews.

269.   Hedwig Abraham to Jones, 24 February 1926. Ernest Jones Collection, ABPAS, P04-C-B-01.

270.   Eitingon eventually gained his doctorate on 20 September 1909 with a treatise that fitted within a series of association studies written in Zurich: "Über die Wirkung des Anfalls auf die Associationen der Epileptischen". His study had taken ten years in all, an unusually long time for this period (Schröter, 2004, part I, p. 4).

271.   Hedwig Abraham to Eitingon (HA, p. 36).

272.   Hedwig Abraham to Eitingon, 2 January 1908. LoC, Karl Abraham correspondence, box 1, folder 1. Transcription by U. Heyl-Keese.

273.   F/J, p. 109.

274. Oppenheim was not an advocate of psychoanalysis.

275. In 1913, Abraham published an article about this patient: "A screen memory concerning a child-hood event of apparently aetiological significance" (*CP*, 1913b, pp. 36–41).

276. F/A, 8 January 1908, pp. 17, 18.

277. F/A, 9 January 1908, p. 21. NB. Freud and the analysts around him often used the symbols Ψ, Ψα, or ΨA when referring to psychoanalysis (see list of abbreviations).

278. F/A, p. 24.

279. HA, p. 38.

280. HA, pp. 23–24.

281. F/A, p. 32.

282. Freud, 1900a, p. 317ff.

283. HA, pp. 23–24.

284. F/A, p. 33.

285. In 1907, Jung received a series of visitors at the Burghölzli. They included Fülop Stein and Sándor Ferenczi from Budapest and Ernest Jones from London. Jones heard the men from Budapest talking about a meeting at which Freud's work could be discussed and he immediately adopted the idea, whereupon Jung made clear he wanted to retain the initiative (Bair, 2003, p. 129). In his biography of Freud, Jones makes no mention of the Hungarians, saying the idea was his own and Jung implemented it (Jones, 1955, part II, p. 39).

286. F/J, p. 106.

287. Letter from Jung to Abraham. Abraham papers, LoC.

288. F/J, p. 111.

289. Idem, p. 114.

290. Letter from Jung to Abraham of 30 January 1908. Abraham papers. LoC.

291. F/J, p. 127.

292. Idem, p. 130.

293. Idem, p. 134.

294. It was one of the few congresses, three in total, to which Hedwig accompanied Abraham. She was also present in Berlin in 1922 and Bad Homburg in 1925. Eissler, interview with Hedwig.

295. Gay writes the following:

> although during his three-year stay at the Burghölzli Abraham got along well with Jung, who was both interesting and surly, he also had obvious doubts about him. Once he had left the Burghölzli and started a practice in Berlin, he let no chance slip to irritate his former superior, especially when they met at psychoanalytic congresses. (Gay, 1988, p. 204)

296. Clark, too, concluded in his biography of Freud (1980, p. 252) that Abraham had done something wrong, which was failing to mention Bleuler and Jung in his talk in Salzburg. He writes that Freud mediated and Abraham soon saw the error of his ways and apologised to Jung.

297. Jones, E., 1955, part II, p. 40ff. It was not a professional meeting and the organisational side of psychoanalysis was not discussed.

298. Idem, p. 42:

> Most of the papers were subsequently published, but the only one that concerns us here is Freud's. Jung had begged him to relate a case history, so he described the analysis of an obsessional case, one which afterwards we used to refer to as that of "The man with the rats".

He sat at the end of a long table along the sides of which we were gathered and spoke in his usual low but distinct conversational tone. He began at the Continental hour of eight in the morning and we listened with rapt attention. At eleven he broke off, suggesting we had had enough. But we were so absorbed that we insisted on his continuation, which he did until nearly one o'clock.

Sadger (2006), p. 57, gives a different description:

And then the professor first spoke for a little under half an hour, which had been set as the time allotted to each speaker. At that point he broke off to ask the assembly whether it would permit him to continue saying what he had to say. And when he was granted that permission amid cheers, he continued speaking for another three quarters of an hour, making one and a quarter hours in total.

Jones writes that Freud spoke for five hours, whereas Sadger claims it was only one and a quarter hours.

299. Jones, 1955, part II, p. 47.
300. Brome, 1968, p. 87.
301. Cremerius, 1997, pp. 65–67.
302. Kuhn, 2000.
303. F/A, p. 53.
304. See, for example, the letter from Bleuler to Freud of 21 March 1907 (Schröter, 2012, pp. 102–103).
305. Kuhn, 2000, p. 714; Jung, 1908.
306. F/J, p. 111.
307. F/A, p. 26.
308. Kuhn, 2000, p. 711.
309. Abraham, 1908a.
310. F/J, p. 149.
311. Kuhn, 2000, p. 717.
312. Jones, 1955, p. 42.
313. Abraham, 1907b.
314. Kuhn, 2000, p. 716; Jung, 1910. This is Jung's own review of the speech he gave at the congress in Salzburg. Z., I, p. 128. The review cannot be found in Jung's collected works. It is remarkable in that he is the only one of the speakers to review their own work. The text is short and less than clear, barely giving any impression of what Jung actually said.
315. F/J, p. 144.
316. Idem.
317. F/J, pp. 145, 146.
318. F/A, pp. 38–39.
319. F/A, 9 May 1908, p. 39.
320. F/A, pp. 39–40.
321. Kuhn, 2000, p. 718.
322. F/J, p 134.
323. F/J, p. 144.
324. It is unclear to whom this refers. Once we exclude the Swiss and the Viennese, who felt themselves seriously disadvantaged by Freud with regard to Jung, not many candidates are left. It will

probably have been Jones, who, at that point, did not have much knowledge of psychoanalysis (F/J, 30 November 1907, p. 101) and was extremely impressed by Jung. This is supported by the fact that, despite his great friendship with Abraham in later years, Jones noted down the story in his biography of Freud, with Abraham as the culprit.

325. F/J, p. 149.

326. Jones, 1955, p. 40ff.

327. F/J, 10 May 1908, pp. 150, 151.

328. F/A, 27 October 1925, p. 564ff.

329. Otto Gross (1877–1919), son of a professor of criminology, studied medicine in Graz and worked as an assistant in Kraepelin's clinic in Munich. He was an advocate of psychoanalysis, as well as a champion of anarchist ideas and of free sex. He was admitted to mental hospitals many times for serious drug addiction, including stays in the Burghölzli Clinic in 1902, 1904, and 1908, on the last occasion with a special recommendation from Freud that he should be treated by Jung. The intention was that Jung would start the treatment and Freud would continue it in Vienna in October 1908. Gross was extremely handsome and a compelling, but also unmanageable, person, perpetually subject to megalomania and temper tantrums. Jung was completely gripped by him, devoted a great deal of time to him, and even started to engage in reciprocal analysis. None of this helped. Gross was forcibly detained but was allowed to walk in the garden unsupervised. He fled the clinic by climbing over the wall (Bair, 2003, p. 136ff).

330. F/J, 21 June 1908, pp. 157–160.

331. F/A, 9 July 1908, p. 48.

332. F/A, pp. 48, 49.

333. F/A, p. 38.

334. F/A, pp. 49–50.

335. F/A, p. 53.

336. Cremerius, J. (1997), "Karl Abraham, Freuds Sündenbock und 'Führer zur Wahrheitsforschung'." *Luzifer-Amor, 20*: 64–80.

CHAPTER SEVEN

337. Ellenberger, 1970, pp. 799–800. Hedwig wrote to Jones on 24 February 1926 that in that early period in Berlin, Abraham had tried to introduce others to psychoanalytic ideas and showed great courage in speaking to all kinds of associations of physicians. As a reaction he never received substantive criticism, however, but instead emotional rejection, so in the end he gave up the struggle. Ernest Jones Collection, ABPAS, P04-C-B-01.

338. F/A, p. 56.

339. Egger, 1988.

340. Idem.

341. Herzer, 2001, p. 107.

342. Idem, p. 108.

343. Idem, p. 109.

344. Herzer, 2001, pp. 183–184.

345. Idem, pp. 180–181; Freud, 1910c, p. 98ff.

346. F/A, 14 February 1909, p. 80.

347. F/A, p. 58.

348. Kloocke, 2002, p. 20.

349. Juliusburger, 1907. Juliusburger gave his talk on 14 December 1908 (Hermanns, 1994).

350. Later, Einstein would urge his friend to emigrate and in 1941 he paid Juliusburger's fare for the journey to the USA (Hermanns, 2008, pp. 27, 29).

351. The Monistenbund advocated a philosophy based on natural laws. Later the monists adopted a socialist and pacifist stance and campaigned against anti-Semitism and racism (Falzeder & Hermanns, 2009, p. 57, n. 2).

352. Jaffé, 1966, p. 200.

353. Eitingon wrote in his final circular letter of 25 December 1933:

> Now I would like to give you a message that some of you will already know and that is certainly pleasant. It is a request to make the newly founded Palestine Psychoanalytic Society (Chewra Psychoanalytith b'Erez Israel) a part of our umbrella organisation. On my first visit to Tel Aviv at around the end of September, where I found Dr. Wulff (Tel Aviv), Miss Smeliansky (Tel Aviv), Dr. Schalit (Haifa), and Dr. Kluge (Jerusalem) together at Wulff's home, I founded the Palestine Psychoanalytic Society from the five members of the German Psychoanalytic Society who were present there at that moment, of which I was chosen to be president and Dr. Schalit secretary.

354. Eitingon was working on his doctorate, which he would not gain until 1909 (Schröter, 2004, p. 4).

355. HA, p. 37. This series was called *Schriften zur angewandten Seelenkunde*, a series of monographs with Freud as editor-in-chief. Volume one was Freud's Gradiva study, volume two Riklin's study of fairytales, both published by Hugo Heller. Starting with volume three, Jung's *Der Inhalt der Psychose*, the books were published by Deuticke. Abraham's monograph appeared as volume four. Hugo Heller (1870–1923) was a Viennese bookseller and publisher. His bookshop, which was also an art dealership, was a meeting point for intellectuals and artists in Vienna. From 1902, he was a member of the Wednesday Society, which later became the Vienna Psychoanalytic Society (Mühlleitner, 1992). Frans Deuticke (1850–1919) was to become the publisher of the *Jahrbuch für Psychoanalyse*, which was founded later. Until the First World War, he was the main publisher of Freud's work.

356. Abraham, 1909b.

357. Sadger, 2006, p. 32.

358. Freud, 1908e.

359. F/A pp. 44–45.

360. F/J, p. 140.

361. Abraham, 1911a, p. 29ff.

362. Jones, 1955, p. 44.

363. Idem. These grievances would erupt two years later at the congress in Nuremburg.

364. Abraham, 1909c, d.

365. Abraham, 1908b.

366. Freud, 1905c.

367. Letter from Bleuler to Abraham of 29 August 1908, LoC, Abraham correspondence.

368. Freud, 1900a, 1905d.

369. F/A, p. 60.

370. Emil Kraepelin (1856–1926) was professor of psychiatry in Heidelberg and later in Munich. Gustav Aschaffenburg (1866–1944) was professor of neurology and psychiatry in Heidelberg, later in Cologne and finally in the United States.

371. F/A, p. 118.

372. F/Bleuler, p. 152.

373. F/Bleuler, p. 153.

374. Hilda Abraham's talk of 1970 has been preserved in the archives of the Karl Abraham Institute in Berlin: "Die Anfänge der Psychoanalytischen Vereinigung in Berlin (1908–1933)".

375. Abraham, 1909a. See also Chapter One.

376. F/A, p. 64–65.

377. Theodor Ziehen (1862–1950) was professor of psychiatry at the university in Berlin and at the Charité, the psychiatric clinic.

378. In the second half of his biography of Freud, Jones gave a rather distorted picture of the contact between Freud and Abraham at this time by reproducing only the letters that touch on the conflict with Jung and making no mention of all the warm letters between them (Jones, 1955, ii, p. 47ff).

379. F/A, p. 69.

380. F/A, p. 71.

381. Abraham's article "Die Stellung der Verwandtenehe in der Psychologie der Neurosen" [The significance of intermarriage between close relatives in the psychology of the neuroses] (1909a) was also published in the first *Jahrbuch*. Might Jung have found this too much Abraham in one number?

382. This relates to a visit to Berlin in September 1908, on the way from England to Jung in Zurich. Freud had visited family only and had not called on Abraham.

383. F/A, p. 74.

384. F/A, p. 75.

385. Jones, 1927, p. 43.

386. F/A, 16 May 1909, p. 90.

387. F/A, 9 March 1909, p. 86.

388. F/A, p. 94.

389. F/A, 13 July 1909, p. 95.

390. Letter from Hedwig Abraham to Jones of 1 April 1952. Ernest Jones Collection, ABPAS, P04-C-B-01.

391. F/A, p. 88.

392. Abraham, 1909c, p. 568.

393. Abraham, H., 1970b: "The start of Karl Abraham's scientific work in Berlin". Speech to mark the fiftieth anniversary of the founding of the Berlin Psychoanalytic Society.

394. See Chapter Ten.

395. F/A, 7 April 1909, p. 87.

396. F/A, 10 November 1909, p. 96.

397. Abraham, 1910a.

398. Löwenfeld, 1909, pp. 539–552, 587–598.

399. Abraham's explanation was as follows: a neurotic can be recognised by on the one hand powerful drives and on the other a strong tendency to repression. The neurosis emerges from the conflict between drive and repression. The power and variety of such instinctive drives and the overwhelming number of repressed desires turns the neurotic into a phantasist.

400. Abraham, H., 1970b.

401. See Chapter Three.
402. Schröter, 2004, p. 4.
403. Abraham, H., 1970b.
404. F/A, 14 March 1910, p. 108.
405. F/Fer, *1*, 1 January 1910, p. 119.
406. F/Fer, *1*, 2 January 1910, p. 121.
407. Letter from Bleuler to Freud of 26 March 1910 (Schröter, 2012, pp. 107–108).
408. The first clash between Jung and Abraham had taken place at the first congress in Salzburg, although most of the participants had failed to notice.
409. Ferenczi was less than tactful at this point. He said that it was simply the natural way for things to go because the Viennese, with the exception of Freud, were inferior to the people of Zurich (Clark, 1980, p. 297).
410. Clark, 1980, p. 195ff. See also Sadger, 2006, p. 58ff.
      Alfred Adler (1870–1937) was a member of the Wednesday Society from the beginning, in 1902. On the recommendation of Stekel he was invited to the first meeting by postcard. He remained an active participant until his departure in 1911. Adler developed his own theory, which would later come to be called individual psychology. As the result of a fundamental difference of opinion with Freud – for Adler aggressive urges were central – he left the Vienna Psychoanalytic Society, taking nine of the thirty-five members with him, and set up the Association for Free Psychoanalysis (Selesnick, 1966).
411. F/A, 28 April 1910, p. 109.
412. *Korrespondenzblatt, CB, 1*, 1910, 2. The *Korrespondenzblatt* was in existence from 1910 to 1941. It contained all the announcements and reports of the organisations under the umbrella of the IPA, as well as reports of congresses and was edited by the secretary of the IPA. The first issues, of 1910 and 1911, were published separately, then from late 1911 to early 1913 it appeared as a supplement to the *Zentralblatt für Psychoanalyse* and from 1913 it was part of the *Internationale Zeitschrift für ärztliche Psychoanalyse*. Abraham wrote in his overview of German and Austrian psychoanalytic literature up to 1909 that Warda was the first author to have taken a view based on his own observations that favoured the Breuer–Freud theory (Abraham, 1909c, p. 593).
413. Kloocke, 2002, p. 22.
414. This would mean that Paris did not use the correct dates of Karin Horney's analysis by Abraham in his biography of her (Paris 1994). On page 57 he writes, "The fifth diary records a very bad period for Karen, which began in April 1910, in the midst of her first analysis with Karl Abraham". Abraham himself refers to her in his letter to Freud of 28 April 1910 as one of the three patients that he has recently begun treating, so he cannot have been halfway through her treatment by then. Carl Müller-Braunschweig (1881–1958) had tried to get Freud to analyse her as early as 1908. He later became a member and trainer at the Berlin Psychoanalytic Society (later the German Psychoanalytic Association). In the 1930s, he played a controversial role by collaborating with the Nazis as an Aryan psychoanalyst while his Jewish colleagues had to leave the German Psychoanalytic Association and flee abroad.
415. In Berlin, women were not admitted to the university until 1908.
416. Paris, 1994, p. 55.
417. As stated earlier, Abraham wrote to Freud in May 1909 that he was treating six psychoanalytic cases. By the time Horney's analysis began he probably had more than a year's experience as a psychoanalyst.

418. Quinn, 1988, p. 143.
419. Idem, p. 145.
420. Horney papers, Yale University Library.
421. See Chapter Twenty-five.
422. See note 83. See also Paris, 1994, p. 57ff.
423. Freud, 1914g.
424. The above-mentioned archive also holds Horney's original diaries and a transcript. The transcript was bowdlerised, without this fact being mentioned in the text of the transcript itself. The explicitly sexual passages, such as a sentence about coitus and masturbation, were omitted from the transcript.
425. Bergmann (2004, p. 39–40), thought that Horney's analysis had failed because of a difference of opinion between her and Abraham about female sexuality. But Abraham published his article about female sexuality in 1921, eleven years after Horney's psychoanalysis. Horney was indeed indignant about that article and published a reaction in 1924 (see Chapter Twenty). This was so long after her analysis by Abraham, however, that it is hard to make a connection. The main reason for the failure was Abraham's lack of experience.
426. Horney papers.
427. Paris, 1994, p. 180ff.
428. Quinn, 1988, p. 160.
429. In those days the effect of separation anxiety had not yet been recognised by psychoanalysis.

CHAPTER EIGHT

430. Interview with Anja Amsel.
431. HA, p. 41. Care must have played its part here. Hilda was used to being an only child and suddenly all the attention was going to her brother. Abraham also wanted to observe, however. At four, Hilda was in the Oedipal phase and he wanted to study her relationship with him.
432. Idem.
433. Idem, p. 46.
434. Abraham, H., 1970a: Talk.
    At other meetings, too, attacks were made on psychoanalysis. In Hamburg on 29 March 1910, at the meeting of doctors, there were emphatic warnings against referring patients to a clinic where Freud's methods were applied. On 28 May 1910, Hoche spoke at a meeting of psychiatrists from southwest Germany about an epidemic of insanity among doctors and about psychoanalysts who were ripe for admission to mental hospital. F/A, p. 114, n. 2, pp. 116–117.
435. Abraham, 1911d, 1925.
436. May-Tolzmann, 1997, p. 98ff.
437. F/A, pp. 81, 126.
438. F/A, p. 129. The latter phrase is not included in the German edition of the correspondence.
439. F/A, p. 129; Freud, 1910c. Freud saw similarities between the personality traits of Segantini and Leonardo da Vinci. He had published an article on Leonardo in 1910. He saw both artists as anarchistic because of the absence of paternal authority, fixated on their mothers and influenced by events in their childhoods. Abraham first wrote to Freud about Segantini on 14 February 1909 and Freud mentioned writing about Leonardo da Vinci in the autumn of that year (Strachey, 1957). Both wrote about a painter in the same year.

440. Recently, fresh attention has been paid to Segantini to some extent. In 2011, in Riehen near Basel, a large retrospective exhibition was held by the Basler Fondation Beyeler, *Süddeutsche Zeitung*, 17 Feb. 2011. In 2009, a biography was published, written by A. Scheib. With thanks to W. Graf zu Castell-Castell.

441. Other authors, among them Frehner (1999), give 1865 as the year when his mother died. In that case, Giovanni Segantini would have been seven (Frehner, 1999, p. 11).

442. Von Petersdorf, 1997, p. 133.

443. Servaes, 1907; Segantini, 1909.

444. *Süddeutsche Zeitung*, 17 February 2011, p. 13.

445. F/A, p. 81.

446. Freud, 1909d.

447. Abraham, 1911d, pp. 218–219, 1922a.

448. Abraham, 1911d and 1925, pp. 258–261. This is the epilogue to Abraham, 1911d, added in 1925.

449. May-Tolzmann, 1997, p. 98; Freud, 1917e.

450. May-Tolzmann, 1997, p. 106. The article has been translated into English (see May-Tolzmann, 2001), but in an altered form that does not include this passage.

451. This point will be examined more closely later. It concerns a fundamental difference between Abraham and Freud. For Abraham, aggression plays a far greater role.

452. Abraham's speech to at the congress was called "Die psychosexuelle Grundlage der Depressions- und Exaltationszustände". *Korrespondenzblatt, C, II*, 1912, p. 232. It was published in a slightly more developed form in 1912 under the title "Ansätze zur psychoanalytischen Erforschung und Behandlung des manisch-depressiven Irreseins und verwandter Zustände" ("Notes on the psycho-analytical treatment of manic depressive insanity and allied conditions") (Abraham, 1912a; Cremerius, 1999).

    The congress in Weimar was a great success. There were fifty-five participants, including for the first time a number of women. Lou Andreas-Salomé (1861–1937) came with Poul Bjerre from Stockholm and from that moment on she would be a prominent presence in the psychoanalytic world. Freud gave a talk about Schreber: "Nachtrag zur Analyse Schrebers". Two Dutchmen attended the congress, Albert Willem van Renterghem (1848–1939) from Amsterdam, who then became a member of the Berlin Psychoanalytic Society, and Jan van Emden (1868–1950) from Leiden, who joined the Vienna Psychoanalytic Society after the congress was over. Van Emden had been in analysis with Freud and became friends with him. Dutchman August Stärcke was a member in Vienna at the same time as van Emden. There was also a note of discord at the congress; Jung insulted Hirschfeld to such an extent that he immediately cancelled his membership. (On 1 October 1911, ten days after the congress, Hirschfeld insisted on leaving the Berlin Psychoanalytic Society.) The cause was not just Jung's open aversion to homosexuality but an irresolvable theoretical difference. Hirschfeld regarded homosexuality as congenital and his goal was moral equality of status between homosexuals and heterosexuals. Psychoanalysts saw homosexuality as a stage in sexual development that should be overcome and if it was not then it became a perversion. See Herzer, 1992, p. 185 and Chapter Four.

453. Minutes of meetings of the Vienna Psychoanalytic Society were taken from 1906 onwards by Rank. In those days the meetings were still called the Wednesday Society. Brome (1968, pp. 34–35), describes it as follows:

    From 1906, he (Rank) duly recorded, on large sheets of paper in neat, crabbed handwriting, the protocols of the scientific meetings while the 'attendance lists and communications' were kept in a small black book. The quality of the discussions varies from the brilliant to the dull, from the logically exact to the emotionally confused, and Rank did not attempt to make a verbatim record which would have been impossible in longhand. Instead, he took extensive notes while the discussions were actually in progress and edited the notes afterwards. A certain amount of confusion was inevitable with this primitive technique. Some papers were condensed to notes which makes them unintelligible, and others are discussed without being named. Moreover it was possible for each member to read and correct his personal record, a process which could lead to important deletions. As the years advance, the minutes become less and less satisfactory, until it needs considerable imaginative powers to deduce precisely what is being said.

In 1976 these reports were published under the title *Protokolle der Wiener Psychoanalytischen Vereinigung*. Federn's criticism is noted in the report for 1 May 1912 (Nunberg & Federn, 2008[1976]).

454.   Idem. For further details see the report for 1 May 1912.
455.   Abraham wrote that in general little had been written about clinical depression and very little about alternating patterns of mania and depression. He had the idea that both concerned the same thing, excessively powerful drives, both love and hate. In depression, patients allow themselves to be weighed down by such drives and see no way out other than death. Mania occurs when repression is no longer effective. Patients are then propelled by their drives. Positive and negative libido, erotic desires, and aggressive hostility occur simultaneously.
456.   F/A, 2 May 1912, p. 151
457.   F/A, pp. 120–121
458.   F/A, p. 126.
459.   HA, p. 40.
460.   Interview with Hedwig by Eissler.
461.   See Chapter Seventeen. Anja Amsel said in her interview that Hedwig was cared for from marriage onwards, first by Abraham, and after his death by Hilda. It is, therefore, doubtful whether she would have agreed to let Abraham go off to Vienna or Budapest for analysis.
462.   Mächtlinger, 1997, p. 81.
463.   HA, p. 23.
464.   Interview with Lotte Levy.
465.   Idem.
466.   Interview with Anja Amsel and Steven Burgner.
467.   Mächtlinger, 1997, p. 84.
468.   Widlöcher, 1977, pp. 62–63. With thanks to D. Widlöcher.
469.   Idem, pp. 62–63.
470.   Interview with Lotte Levy.
471.   F/A, 14 February 1909, p. 81
472.   See Chapter Four. Mächtlinger, 1997, p. 91.
473.   HA, p. 22
474.   Abraham (1911d) wrote about this in a note (p. 248n):

The following observations may help to explain the strange fact that among those who love the Alps there exists a particular variety of Engadine enthusiasts. This enthusiasm appears to coincide with certain character-traits which in Segantini were developed to an unusually high degree. If love of the Alps in general often serves as an outlet for sublimated drives, this particular form of Alpine-worship seems to arise from the gratification of a specific complex.

Those "Hinweise" were related to the fact that Segantini felt a particular affinity for the inhabitants of the Engadin, who were characterised by hard work and indomitable energy.

475. HA, p. 22. When Abraham bought a Zeiss telescope, he had it made for his left eye only.
476. Abraham, 1925b.
477. Abraham, 1907c; Abraham et al., 1919.
478. What he described was both depersonalisation and derealisation. In the former, a person has a sense of being a stranger to themselves. In derealisation, the sense of contact with the environment is lost and everything seems strange. It is often associated with depression.
479. HA, p. 51.
480. Abraham, 1911d, p. 257.
481. May-Tolzmann, 1997, p. 123.
482. F/A, p. 127.
483. F/A, 13 February 1911, pp. 127–128.
484. Gay, 1988, p. 56.
485. Masson, 1985, Introduction, p. 1.
486. Idem, p. 15.
487. Hermann Swoboda (1873–1963) was a psychologist who was treated by Freud. Freud is said to have told him about Fließ's theory of bisexuality, which Swoboda then passed on to his friend Otto Weininger (1880–1903), who published it in his book *Sex and Character*.
488. F/A, p. 130.
489. F/A, p. 131.
490. Hermanns and Schröter, 2010, p. 89.
491. HA, p. 45.
492. Idem.
493. HA, pp. 45–46.
494. F/A, p. 2.
495. Pines, 1974; Freud, 1909b.
496. Abraham, 1917a.
497. Pines, 1974, ABPAS.
498. Abraham, 1917a, p. 53.
499. HA, p. 57.
500. Pines, 1974.
501. With Hilde Maas, Hilda had her third analysis. Her first analyst was van Ophuijsen, a friend of her father's (Pines, 1974). Her second analysis was shortly before she fled Germany in 1933, with Dr Kemper (see Chapter Twenty-nine).
502. Falzeder, 1994.
503. Idem, p. 185.
504. Idem, p. 184.
505. Pfeiffer, 1972b.
506. Hilda continued to have concentration problems for a long time afterwards.
507. HA, p. 57; Abraham, 1974, p. 6.

508. In Chapter Twenty, Abraham's theory about the castration complex in women is discussed.

509. HA, p. 57.

510. Interview with Anja Amsel and Steven Burgner.

511. Idem. Anja Amsel said that both Hedwig and Hilda were later focused mainly on men. Anja's brother Tom, for example, was seen as more important than she was.

512. HA, p. 58.

513. HA, p. 58.

514. HA, p. 58.

515. F/A, 5 December 1911, pp. 142–143.

516. Abraham's summary of the situation is not entirely clear, since the list of members of the Berlin Psychoanalytic Society for the autumn of 1911 is far longer. Here, he was probably counting only those members who lived in Berlin and could participate in meetings. Juliusburger gave a talk again in 1912 and seems to have stopped grumbling by then. The other Berlin-based members were Dutchmen Van Renterghem and van der Linde. Then there was Bjerre in Stockholm, Lenz in Berlin, Simon in Greifswald, Stegmann in Dresden, Vollrath in Jena, and Wanke in Thüringen. *Korrespondenzblatt*, C, 11, 1912, p. 239.

517. Mühlleitner, 1992). Margarethe Hilferding was one of the first women doctors in Vienna. She gained her doctorate in 1903. In April 1910, Federn proposed allowing her to join the Vienna Psychoanalytic Society. Sadger was generally opposed to the admission of women, but in a secret ballot the members voted to allow her in.

518. F/A, p. 145.

519. F/A, 29 October 1911, p. 140, 25 February 1912, pp. 147–148.

520. Idem, p. 148

521. Idem, p. 148.

522. Lou Andreas-Salomé (1861–1937) was born in St. Petersburg. She was the only daughter, with five older brothers, of the Russian general Von Salomé. Her mother, Louise Wilm, came from a Hamburg merchant family. The family belonged to the upper classes of St Petersburg. They were protestants. Lou Salomé attended the grammar school and in 1880 she went to Zurich to study philosophy, with an emphasis on theology. Because of a lung disease she broke off her studies and went to the Netherlands and Italy to recover her health. There she met Nietzsche and Paul Rée. In 1882, Lou Salomé went to live in Berlin and moved in philosophical circles around Paul Rée. In 1885, her first book was published, *Im Kampf um Gott*. In 1887, she married orientalist Carl Friedrich Andreas in Santpoort and moved with him to Berlin. In the years that followed she published several books, including *Friedrich Nietzsche in seinen Werken* (1894), one of the first analyses of Nietzsche's work. It brought her fame as a writer. In the early twentieth century, Lou Andreas-Salomé was known as one of the most important women in Europe in the field of philosophy. Her relationship with Rainer Maria Rilke became public knowledge only later. Through him she discovered psychoanalysis (Mühlleitner, 1992; Pfeiffer, 1972a; Winship, 1999).

523. Winship, 1999, p. 223.

524. F/A, p. 150.

525. Pfeiffer, 1972a.

526. This was in between two periods of analysis when Anna Freud was treated by her father.

527. Jones, 1955, pp. 176–177. In this period, Lou Andreas-Salomé also became good friends with Victor Tausk, eighteen years her junior, in Vienna. Various biographers of Freud wrote that they had a

sexual relationship, including Gay (1988, p. 390), and Clark (1980, p. 314). Her biographers refer only to a friendship (Welsch & Pfeiffer, 2006, p. 139).

528.   When Abraham was away for several years during the First World War, Lou Andreas-Salomé in Berlin missed him greatly. At the end of the war she wrote,

> My dear Doctor, thank you for being so friendly as to send the congress programme. Yes, it will be my pleasure to attend. Our separation has lasted far too long for all of us, as has the desire for an exchange of ideas. Every time I've been in Berlin, I've regretted intensely that there was no longer any road that led to you. I'll stay in Breslau, probably with people I know. Otherwise I'll write to you again. Is your wife coming with you? Kind regards to you both until we see each other again. Yours, Lou Andreas, 7 Sept. 1918.

529.   HA, p. 46.
530.   This may be a reference to Dr R. Gerstein, who became a member of the Berlin Psychoanalytic Society in 1912. *Korrespondenzblatt, C, 11*, 1912, p. 545.
531.   See Chapter Eleven.
532.   Interview with Anja Amsel and Steven Burgner.
533.   For a *Habilitation*, the candidate writes a second dissertation, having already written one to gain a doctorate. The standard required is considerably higher than for an ordinary dissertation and in Germany it is a necessary step for anyone intending to become a professor.
534.   Karl Bonhoeffer (1868–1948) was a famous neurologist and psychiatrist. In 1912, he succeeded Theodor Ziehen as professor of psychiatry and neurology at the Charité in Berlin, the university clinic attached to Humboldt University.
535.   F/A, 1 December 1912, p. 169.
536.   F/A, 3 December 1912, p. 169, 12 December 1912, p. 170.
537.   Abraham arrived in Vienna in the early morning of 21 December. F/A 18 December 1912, p. 171. He stayed until Christmas. F/Fer, *1*, 16 December 1912, p. 441.
538.   F/A, 17 December 1912, p. 171.
539.   F/Fer, *1*, 26 December 1912, pp. 449–455. Idem, 29 December 1912, pp. 456–457.
540.   Idem, 30 December 1912.
541.   F/A, 1 January 1913, p. 173.
542.   F/Fer, *1*, 7 February 1912, p. 343.
543.   F/A, 5 January 1913, p. 174.
544.   Idem, pp. 176, 178.
545.   Idem, p. 179.
546.   F/A, 3 March 1913, p. 178.
547.   F/A, 5 May 1912 and subsequently, p. 182ff. Abraham probably carried out his research in the Städtische Hospital- und Siechenanstalten, where his tutor Liepmann, his boss at Dalldorf, had carried out research before him.
548.   Falzeder and Burnham, 2007, p. 1222ff.
549.   F/A p. 178. No copies of the programme have survived.
550.   F/A, 27 March 1913, p. 181.
551.   Alfred Erich Hoche (1865–1943).
552.   Seidler and Leven, 2007, p. 328. In April 1933, after the takeover of power by the National Socialists, all Jewish staff at the University of Freiburg were dismissed. Hoche resigned. He

wanted nothing to do with the National Socialists. In the same month, Heidegger became rector of Freiburg University.

553. The letter from Hoche was published in the *Korrespondenzblatt*, *IZP*, *1*, 1913, 197 under the heading "Ein Gegner der Psychoanalyse". The letter went as follows:

> Freiburg i B, 1 February 1913
>
> Dear honoured colleague,
>
> For the annual general meeting of the German Psychiatric Association (in Breslau in May) I am undertaking, along with Bleuler, a review of the value of psychoanalysis. It is of great importance to me to have a reliable verdict on the nature and extent of the damage done to patients. If you do have such factual material, I request you to be so kind as to let me know of it in a manner you deem suitable. (I have in mind neither precise figures nor detailed personal case histories.) I will use it without naming names and in such a way that I will not anticipate any discussion points you may have. I know from my own experience that it is far from pleasant when someone asks around like this, but unfortunately I can see no other way to acquire this important material.
>
> With expressions of my most grateful thanks.
>
> Your humble servant, Hoche.

554. Falzeder and Burnham, 2007, p. 1230.

555. Idem.

556. Falzeder and Burnham, p. 1231; Bleuler (1910):

> Bleuler opened the congress. He stipulated that his paper was only a further development of his 1910 publication, but now with additional critical material. He tried to take up, point by point, the various fields covered by psychoanalytic theory and practice and then show which parts, in his view, withstood closer scrutiny, and which not. He saw Freud as "the discoverer" and himself as "the one who checks and examines his statements, not the one who wants to defend at all costs". On the one hand, he criticized the general structure and the premises of Freud's theory, which would suffer from a "lack of clarity, incompleteness and contradictions" and use "imprecise" terms. . . . On the other hand Bleuler listed an impressive number of such "details" that he regarded as "important contributions to our knowledge": the theory of affects, repression, the concept of the unconscious, projection and transference, infantile sexuality, the Oedipus complex, sexual aetiology, bisexuality, resistance, symbolism, displacement, condensation, overdetermination, Freud's theories of religion and obsessional neurosis, flight into and gain from illness etc. Regarding psychoses and, in particular, schizophrenia, he again stated that "I cannot agree with Freud's basic assumptions" but that many symptoms, the manifestation and the improvement of the illness could be explained by Freud's theory.

557. Falzeder and Burnham, 2007, p. 1233.

558. Abraham wrote to Freud on 5 May 1913 (F/A, p. 182), "The last bit of desire to attend the Congress left me when I read Bleuler's contradictory stuff". He was talking about a summary of Bleuler's talk that was sent out in advance of the congress.

559. Letter from Bleuler to Freud, 24 July 1913 (Schröter, 2012, p. 197).

560. Falzeder and Burnham, 2007, p. 1235.

561. Falzeder and Burnham, 2007, p. 1238. Smith Ely Jelliffe (1866–1945) was an American neurologist, psychiatrist, and psychoanalyst, and owner and editor in chief of the *Journal of Nervous and Mental Disease*. In 1913, he founded *The Psychoanalytic Review*. William John Sweasy Powers (1875–1938) was an American doctor who attended university in Germany. The letter was written when he was studying under Kraepelin.

562. Idem, p. 1237.

563. Letter from Oberholzer to Eitingon of 3 June 1913. Eitingon archive. Emil Oberholzer (1883–1958), psychiatrist and psychoanalyst, founded the Swiss Psychoanalytic Association after the dissolution of the Zurich Psychoanalytic Society in 1919 along with his wife Mira (*née* Ginzburg) (1887–1948).

564. See Chapter Eighteen.

565. Idem.

566. F/A 29 December 1919, pp. 412–413.

567. Idem.

568. See Chapter Nine.

569. Kaderas, 1998, p. 212.

570. Eitingon Archive.

CHAPTER TEN

571. Tietze, 2010, p. 37.

572. Dick, 2010, p. 130.

573. Else Lasker-Schüler was one of the few women in the German expressionist movement. She was highly regarded by Karl Kraus, among others.

574. Dick, 2010, p. 31.

575. Abraham, 1912c.

576. HA, p. 42.

577. Abraham had written to Freud on 5 December 1911 about the immense effort it had taken to win a place for psychoanalysis in Berlin. F/A, pp. 142–143. Freud had responded encouragingly on 2 January 1912, saying he admired Abraham's spirit and confidence. F/A, p. 146.

578. F/A, p. 146.

579. F/A, 14 January 1912, p. 147.

580. Abraham, 1912c, p. 263.

581. Abraham, 1912c, p. 267–268.

582. Abraham, 1912c, p. 268.

583. Abraham, 1911d, p. 221: "We find in Segantini an unusual limitation of choice of sexual objects. He was not able, as young people usually are, to form relationships and dissolve them again; his choice, once made, was final. This monogamous trait, which we also meet in neurotics, showed itself in a remarkable manner in Segantini".

584. See also Lemaigre, 2003, p. 88.

585. English spellings of the names of Akhenaten and his relatives vary. *CP* uses the older spelling, Ikhnaton; others' spellings include Echnaton, Akhenaton, and Khuenaten.

586. Abraham, 1912c, pp. 289–290.

587. Bryan, 2000.

588. Tutankhamen, pharaoh of the eighteenth dynasty, was a son of Akhenaten. He died young at the age of nineteen, and was famous mainly because in 1922 his grave was discovered untouched. He restored the old Amen religion, which had been abolished by Akhenaten. DNA research has recently shown that he was the child of Akhenaten and his sister, not the king's wife Nefertiti (Journal of the American Medical Association, 2010, 303(7): 638–647).

589. Abraham, 1912c. Two examples of the sources mentioned are Breasted (1905) and Weigall (1910).

590. Breasted (1905).

591. Weigall (1910). Breasted was the most important source for Freud in writing his book about Moses.

592. Dinora Pines collection. ABPAS, Part of 39.

593. Interview with Anja Amsel and Steven Burgner. It seems probable that Gerd, later Grant, did this in response to the horrors he experienced in 1933 when the Nazis came to power in Germany. Anti-Semitism in England must have played its part, too. Both Gerd and Hedwig changed their Jewish surname Abraham to Allan.

594. F/A, p. 154.

595. F/A, p. 154. F/A p. 164: "I like your Amenhotep in its revised form very much better, it is an adornment of our *Imago*, which continues to count on you". In 1912, young Otto Rank and Hanns Sachs established the journal *Imago* for applied psychoanalysis, with a particular focus on art and society. Otto Rank (1884–1939) is described at the end of Chapter Eleven. Hanns Sachs (1881–1947) was from Vienna, the son of a Jewish lawyer. In 1904, he gained his doctorate in law and he worked until 1918 as a lawyer. Sachs was extremely interested in literature. In the winter semesters of 1905–1906 and 1906–1907, he and his wife, Emmy Pisko, attended lectures by Freud at the university. In 1910, he introduced himself to Freud with a translation of Kipling's Barrack Room Ballads. That same year he became a member of the Vienna Psychoanalytic Society, giving his first talk in February 1911 on the subject of the application of psychoanalysis to prose and poetry. In March 1911 he became librarian of the Vienna Psychoanalytic Society and later its treasurer. Mühlleitner (1992), p. 279–280.

596. Breger, 2000, p. 27ff.

597. Idem.

598. Freud, 1939a.

599. Shengold, 1972.

600. Lemaigre, 2003, p. 82.

601. Abraham (1911b).

602. Shengold, 1972, p. 157.

603. Idem, p. 157ff.

604. Interview with Hilda Abraham by Eissler.

605. See Chapter Twenty-two.

606. *S. E.*, 23, p. 3.

607. Weissweiler, 2006, p. 364.

608. Freud, 1914b.

609. Van der Berg, 2012, pp. 11, 12.

610. Freud, 1939a, p. 31.

611. For a description of these events, see Bair, 2003, p. 236ff.

612. See also Chapter Eleven.

613. Franz Riklin (1878–1938) was a Swiss psychiatrist. He worked on Jung's association studies. At the congress in Nuremberg, he became secretary of the IPA and, along with Jung, editor of the *Korrespondenzblatt* that was set up there. After Jung's break with Freud he followed Jung. F/A p. 167–168, n. 1. Neurologist Leonhard Seif (1866–1949) was the founder (1911) and chair of the Munich Psychoanalytic Society. In 1913, he distanced himself from Freud and joined Adler. F/A, p. 168, n. 1. Seif wrote Jones a long letter about events in Munich (Seif to Jones, 26 December 1912, ABPAS), which shows that this was indeed all about Abraham's "Amenhotep IV". Seif also writes that Freud responded to Jung with such over-sensitivity that it was clear that Freud's own problems were involved. He reacted with great irritation, reproaching Jung for not enquiring sufficiently after Freud's mother, who was ill. Seif thought that Freud himself had great difficulties with the father–son relationship and wanted to impose a kind of forceful patriarchy. Alphonse Maeder (1882–1971) was a Swiss psychiatrist. In 1906, he had been taken on at the Burghölzli clinic as an assistant. He followed Jung after the break with Freud. F/A, p. 20, n. 12.

614. Bair, 2003, p. 236.

615. Freud had fainted once before in the presence of Jung and Ferenczi. In 1909, he travelled with them on the ship to America. They met up at the port in Bremen and had dinner together there. Jung kept talking about the "bog bodies", mummified corpses recently discovered in peat bogs in northern Germany, which he had been reading about. Freud found this very annoying and asked him a couple of times what it was that he found so interesting about those bodies. Then Freud fainted. Afterwards, he told Jung that all that talk about corpses meant Jung wanted him dead (Bruns, 2004, p. 105ff).

616. See note 410.

617. Clark, 1980, p. 305ff.

618. See the end of the previous chapter.

619. Viktor Tausk (1879–1919) originally graduated in law but began reading medicine in 1908. In 1909, he became a member of the Vienna Psychoanalytic Society. Freud and several other members helped to finance his university studies. He gained his doctorate in 1914 and established himself as a neurologist. Even while still at university he gave courses in psychoanalysis. Tausk committed suicide in 1919. See Chapter Twenty-four.

620. F/A, 21 November 1912, p. 167.

621. See previous chapter.

622. Schultz, 1990, p. 192ff.

623. Idem.

624. Gay, 1988, p. 226.

625. Idem, p. 231.

626. Schultz, 1990, p. 197.

627. F/J, 11 November 1912, p. 515.

628. F/J, 14 November 1912, p. 517.

629. The secret committee around Freud has been described in sufficient detail by others. Brome (1968), Grosskurth (1991), Schröter (1995), and Wittenberger (1995) are among those to have written about it. The latter, along with Tögel, published the circular that members of the committee sent each other.

630. Schröter (1995) gives 5–7 July as a possible date for this meeting, p. 515.

631. F/Jones, 30 July 1912, p. 146. Jones writes here that he thought it was Ferenczi.

632. The problems between Freud and Jung were not confined to the libido theory. Jung turned out to be unsuitable as editor-in-chief of the *Jahrbuch*. He was so involved in his own research that he had far too little time to devote to it.

633. F/Jones, 1 August 1912, pp. 147–148.

634. Jones, 1955, p. 153.

635. F/A, 24 July 1912, p. 158.

636. F/Jones, 26 December 1912, p. 186.

637. Jones, 1955, p. 154. Years later, a new member of the secret committee was added. At Freud's suggestion, Eitingon joined in 1919. He replaced Von Freund (1880–1920). Von Freund became a member but soon grew seriously ill, so he never fully joined. See Chapter Nineteen.

638. F/A, p. 159.

639. F/A, p. 164.

640. Freud, 1914d.

641. Ferenczi, 1913.

642. Schröter, 1995, p. 525.

643. Abraham initially planned to go to the South Tyrol with Hedwig. F/A, 5 May 1913, pp. 182–183.

644. *Korrespondenzblatt, IZP*, 2, 1914, 407.

645. Wittenberger, 1995, pp. 119–120.

646. Brome, 1968, p. 133.

647. "Restrictions and transformations of scopophilia in psycho-neurotics; with remarks on analogous phenomena in folk-psychology", *Korrespondenzblatt, IZP*, 2, 1914, 406. *SP*, pp. 169–234. See Chapter Twelve.

648. *Korrespondenzblatt, IZP*, 2, 1914, 407.

649. Brome, 1968, pp. 136–137.

650. F/A, 2 November 1913, pp. 203–204. Eduard Hitschmann (1871–1957) was a doctor in Vienna. He was introduced to Freud in 1905 by his friend Paul Federn, then became a member of the Wednesday Society and a psychoanalyst as well as continuing his work as a doctor. He was extremely erudite and wrote a series of psychoanalytic biographies (Mühlleitner, 1992, p. 149ff).

651. There are many examples, but to name two, F/A, 13 September 1913, p. 193 and 26 October 1913, p. 202.

652. Martin Freud, Freud's eldest son, wrote in his book about his father that this happened on a skiing trip in which he took part (M. Freud, 1957, p. 167).

653. Idem.

654. Wittenberger and Tögel, 1999, p. 35ff.

655. Abraham, 1914e, pp. 101–102.

656. Jones, 1914, *IZP*, 2: 83–86. Jung, "Psycho-Analysis", *Transactions of the Psycho-Medical Society*, *IV*(II): 19ff.

657. Ferenczi, 1914, pp. 86–87.

658. Eitingon, 1914, pp. 99–104.

659. F/A, p. 222.

660. F/A, pp. 232–233, n. 2.

661. Idem, 22 April 1914, p. 232.

662. Idem, 24 April 1914, p. 233.

663. Freud, 1914d.
664. Letter from Bleuler to Freud dated 4 July 1914 (Schröter, 2012, p. 206).
665. Letter from Abraham to Jones, 18 July 1914, Ernest Jones Collection, ABPAS, P04-C-B-01.
666. Brome, 1968, p. 155.
667. Idem, p. 156.
668. Idem, p. 156.
669. Idem, p. 157.
670. Ferenczi had a relationship with an older married woman, Gizella Palos. In 1911, he started to analyse her daughter, Elma, which led them to fall in love. Another of Gizella's daughters was married to one of Ferenczi's brothers. Ferenczi, who became unable to choose between the mother and the daughter, asked Freud to analyse Elma. Freud really had no time, but wanted to do it for Ferenczi's sake. Elma was in analysis with him for the first three months of 1912 and Ferenczi and Freud discussed her progress in their letters. Then Elma continued her analysis with Ferenczi, who remained in doubt, while Freud urged him to marry Gizella. It was an exceptionally murky situation in a time when the rules of behaviour surrounding psychoanalysis were not yet fully developed. Elma married someone else and eventually, in 1919, Ferenczi married her mother, Gizella.
671. These details are from Brome (1982) and Maddox (2006). In mid-1912, Jones came to Vienna with his Dutch partner Loe Kann. Loe was depressed, had a serious morphine addiction and entered into analysis with Freud, who was greatly charmed by her. Meanwhile Jones had become involved in a scandal in Toronto, where he was accused of making sexual advances to a former patient. According to Brome, the advances were mainly made by the patient. Freud asked Jones to leave Vienna in June 1912 in connection with his analysis of Loe Kann. At Christmas, Jones returned to Vienna and, for the second time, started a relationship with Loe's chambermaid, Lina. Loe Kann was distraught. For her this was the end. She became more self-reliant in analysis and left Jones not long afterwards. In May 1913, Jones left Toronto for good to set up a practice in England.
672. Otto Rank (1884–1934).
673. Rank, 1907.
674. Mühlleitner, 1992, pp. 250–251.

CHAPTER TWELVE

675. Abraham, 1913a.
676. Freud, 1911e, p. 96.
677. Martynkewicz, 2007b, 3.
678. Schmitz, 1916. From the correspondence between Freud and Ferenczi it is clear that Freud read and appreciated Schmitz's books. Ferenczi read one of the novels recommended to him by Freud, *The Growth of a Soul* by August Strindberg, and found it longwinded. F/Fer, 2, 25 January 1917, p. 177. Freud did not understand which book he was talking about and asked whether he meant *Der Vertriebene* (The Displaced) by Schmitz, saying he had found it original. F/Fer, 2, 28 January 1917, p. 180. Eighteen months later, Freud wrote to Ferenczi that he thought *Menschheitsdämmerung* (The Twilight of Humanity, Schmitz, 1918) an interesting book.
679. Martynkewicz, 2006, 2007a,b.
680. Martynkewicz, 2006, p. 343ff.
681. In his *History of Germany*, Blackbourn (2003) argued that the culture of Weimar had its precursors during the reign of Emperor Wilhelm II (p. 294ff.). Paris was the cultural capital of the nineteenth

century, and in the early twentieth century Berlin was developing into the cultural centre of the 1920s. Munich was also attractive, however, as an alternative to Berlin. Many writers and reviewers lived there, as did Germany's most important cartoonists and political cabaret artists. As a proportion of the population, three times as many artists lived there as in Berlin, and they included Kandinsky and the other members of the Blaue Reiter.

682. Stefan George (1868–1933) wrote exalted and detached poetry. He was from Bingen in the Rhineland. His father was a wine trader, while his mother was from a farming family. They had a close connection with France through French ancestors on the father's side (Groppe, 1997). George spent some time in Paris, where he attended Mallarmé's soirées. He published poetry from about 1890 onwards and became world famous. Stefan George made a cult of his life and surroundings, and his circle included important young writers of the time such as Friedrich Gundolf and Ludwig Klages. The circle of writers around George had an important influence on modernism.

683. Martynkewicz, 2006, p. 346ff.

684. Reventlow, 1913, 2004.

685. Benjamin Franklin Wedekind (1864–1918) was a German writer and actor. Among his works are "Frühlings Erwachen" (1891), and he collaborated on the Munich cabaret "Die elf Scharfrichter".

686. Wedekind, 1960. Both the original and the English translation are quoted in Craig, 1978, pp. 219–220, 768.

687. Martynkewicz, 2007c, p. 116ff. The details that follow are also taken from this article.

688. Freud, 1908e.

689. Martynkewicz, 2007b, p. 9.

690. Alfred Kubin (1877–1959) was a painter, illustrator, and writer. From 1912, he was part of the Blaue Reiter group. He was married to Schmitz's sister.

691. Martynkewicz, 2007b, 3, p. 127.

692. Idem, p. 129.

693. Freud, 1914c, p. 91.

694. Taken from Martynkewicz, 2007b, 3, p. 26ff.

695. Martynkewicz, 2007a, 2, p. 96 (translated for this edition).

696. Identification with the aggressor: the identification with and imitation of the person of whom one is afraid as a way of allaying that fear (Freud, A., 1992).

697. Freud, 1912–1913.

698. Martynkewicz (2007b, 3), Afterword to *Durch das Land der Dämonen*, p. 273. Schmitz, 1912, p. 206ff.

699. Martynkewicz, 2007b, 3, p. 39 (translated for this edition).

700. Martynkewicz, 2007b, 3, p. 301 (translated for this edition).

701. Abraham formulated his note about the state of Schmitz's health as follows:

For two years before the war and for nine months into the war (i.e. until I was called up) I, as doctor and specialist, examined and treated Mr. Oscar Schmitz in Berlin. Judging from my precise knowledge of his condition, which is based on a very penetrating, at first almost daily course of treatment, I declare the following: Mr. Schmitz is physically healthy aside from a groin hernia. His intellect is excellent, but from early childhood he has had symptoms of a psychopathic constitution. This poor mental disposition expresses itself in anxiety and depression, in sudden changes of mood, in pathological irritability, and sometimes in the failure of physical and mental capacities. These symptoms alone cast serious doubt on his suitability for military service. Decisive in this sense, however, is the fact that there is an extreme degree of irritability, which, as I can testify, can easily lead to aggressive utterances and acts. These impulsive utterances are usually denounced by the patient's conscious mind, but they nevertheless emerge with an irascible vehemence. He belongs in the category of psychopaths with explosive irritability, who according to the regulations of the war ministry's medical department must be excluded from medical service. As Mr. Schmitz has mentioned to me, he finds himself at this time once more in a depressive state and is therefore not in any condition to work and serve. Without being able to look further into this information now, it seems to me based on my experience certainly to be relied upon. Dr. Karl Abraham, currently army doctor in the psychiatric department, XX A.K. Reserve barracks II, Allenstein.

702.   Martynkewicz, 2007b, 3, p. 104ff.
703.   Abraham, 1913c.
704.   Idem, p. 42.
705.   Idem, p. 43.
706.   Abraham, 1914c.
707.   Letter from Jones to Abraham, 29 December 1913, Ernest Jones Collection, ABPAS, P04-C-B-01.
708.   Abraham, 1910b. At the second psychoanalytic congress in Nuremberg, Abraham gave a talk on the subject of foot and corset fetishism. He adapted it into an article that appeared in 1912 in the third *Jahrbuch*. It was also published as "The man who loved corsets", in Greenwald (1959), *Great Cases in Psychoanalysis*.
709.   The anal character and sadism are looked at in more detail in Chapter Twenty-four.
710.   Abraham, 1912b.
711.   Freud, 1910i.
712.   Idem, p. 317.
713.   Freud, 1910i, pp. 214–215.
714.   Freud is referring here to the idea that the sexual drive is composed of countless partial or component drives, connected to specific areas of the body. These separate drives have to go through a complicated development before they are fit for the goals of reproduction. Idem, p. 98.
715.   See, for example, Abraham, 1910a, p. 93.
716.   F/A, 3 March 1913, p. 179.
717.   F/A, p. 181.
718.   Abraham, 1914b.
719.   F/A, pp. 244–245. "Long live those that follow!"

CHAPTER THIRTEEN

720.   F/A, 2 November1913, pp. 203–204.
721.   F/A, 4 November 1913, p. 205. See also Chapter Eleven.
722.   F/A, 16 March 1914, p. 223. "Your picture will return tomorrow from the framer's and will then take the place of Jung's. It does not quite do you justice, but I thank you very much for it."
723.   F/A 16 March 1914, p. 222. "Tomorrow I am sending you the narcissism, which was a difficult birth and bears all the marks of it. Naturally, I do not like it particularly, but I cannot give anything else at the moment" Freud (1914c).

724. F/A 6 April 1914, p. 228.

725. F/A, 24 April 1914, p. 233. The next congress was planned for 20 and 21 September in Dresden. F/A, 2 April 1914, p. 226.

726. F/A, 7 May 1914, p. 234.

727. F/A, 13 May 1914, p. 239.

728. Interview with Hilda by Eissler.

729. Biographical details are taken from Mühlleitner, 1992 and Natterson, 1966.

730. Reik, 1941.

731. F/A, 15 February 1914, p. 218.

732. Freud also showed great concern for Abraham, regularly urging him to raise his fees so that he could generate a good income for himself. Abraham indeed did so, as is clear, for example, from his letter to Freud of 5 May 1913. F/A p. 182.

733. Among them was Lou Andreas-Salomé.

734. F/A, 9 March 1914, p. 220.

735. F/A, pp. 255–256.

736. Reik, 1926, p. 211ff. In 1918, Reik returned to Vienna, where he was elected second secretary and librarian of the Vienna Psychoanalytic Society. He started his own psychoanalytic practice. In 1934, he fled with his wife and family to the Netherlands to escape Nazi rule and lived for some years in The Hague. From there he emigrated to the USA in 1938, where he became famous through his books.

737. Retallack, 1996, p. 82.

738. Idem, p. 683.

739. Idem, p. 684.

740. Haffner, 1989, pp. 89–90.

741. F/Fer, 2, 27 July 1914, p. 9, n. 1.

742. The telegram was misunderstood. The British did not mean they would guarantee French neutrality but that they themselves would remain neutral if the Germans deployed defensively in the west.

743. Liulevicius, 2000, p. 14.

744. F/A, 10 May 1914 and 2 June 1914, pp. 237, 244.

745. Letter from Hilda Abraham to Jones, undated. Ernest Jones Collection, ABPAS, P04-C-B-01. The letter must be from the 1950s, since Jones was working on his biography of Freud.

746. HA, p. 62.

747. When Jung withdrew for good, Freud wrote the following to Abraham, F/A, 26 July 1914, pp. 264–265:

> Dear Friend,
>
> Simultaneously with the declaration of war, which transforms our peaceful spa, your letter arrives, at last bringing the liberating news. So we are at last rid of them, the brutal, sanctimonious Jung and his parrots! I feel impelled now to thank you for the vast amount of trouble, for the exceptional, goal-oriented activity, with which you supported me and with which you steered our common cause. All my life I have been searching for friends who would not exploit and then betray me, and now, not far from its natural end, I have found them.

CHAPTER FOURTEEN

748. F/A, 14 August 1914, p. 271.

749. F/A, 8 August 1914, p. 270.

750. F/A, 14 August 1914, p. 271.

751. Eighteen-year-old Anna Freud had qualified as a primary school teacher in June 1914 and left for England in mid-July. The Freuds were still assuming at that point that it would not come to war. Anna Freud visited her uncle Emanuel in Manchester and took a trip around southern England with Ernest Jones' former girlfriend Loe Kann, whom she much admired. Because of the outbreak of war she was unable to go home. They had quite a job getting her back to Vienna. Loe Kann and her husband, Herbert Jones, eventually managed to have Anna travel with the departing Austrian ambassador, first by ship to Gibraltar, from there to Malta, and then on to Genoa, from where she could take the train to Vienna (Young-Bruehl, 1988, pp. 64–69). Emanuel Freud (1833–1914), Freud's eldest half-brother from his father's first marriage, killed himself that same year, at the age of eighty-one. On 17 October 1914, he jumped from a moving train. Freud believed the outbreak of war had been too much for him to bear. F/Fer, 2, 11 November 1914, pp. 26–27 and n. 1.

752. F/A, 25 August and 3 Septtember 1914, pp. 271–272; 275–276.

753. F/A, 28 August 1914, p. 273.

754. Idem pp. 270, 271. At the start of the First World War, a patriotic mood prevailed among the Germans and Austrians. Abraham was no exception and even Freud did not escape it. He wrote to Abraham on 26 July 1914,

   Perhaps for the first time in 30 years I feel myself to be an Austrian and would like to try it once again with this not very hopeful Empire. Morale everywhere is excellent. The liberating effect of the courageous action and the secure prop of Germany contribute a great deal to this. – One observes the most genuine symptomatic actions in everyone. F/A, p. 265.

   Abraham's good friend and brother-in-law, Hans Bürgner, had a quite different response, seeing no reason at all for enthusiasm. Interview with Anja Amsel and Steven Burgner.

755. See Chapter Thirteen.

756. F/A, 9 September 1913, p. 276.

757. Later, in Allenstein, Abraham had to carry out surgery himself. From his correspondence with Freud it can be deduced that he had not been required to do so before then.

758. Lefebvre, 1987, p. 3–15.

759. Sophie, Max, and Ernst Halberstadt. HA, p. 62.

760. F/A, 18 October 1914, p. 280.

761. Falzeder, 1996.

762. F/A, 19 November 1914, p. 284. The date is erroneously given as 28 October in the correspondence.

763. F/A 21 December 1914, p. 291.

764. This must have been Jeanette Abraham (1838–1915), who lived with her brother Nathan all her life and was already mentally disturbed. See Chapter One. She died on 27 April 1915.

765. F/A, 30 December 1914, p. 294.

766. F/A, 30 January 1915, p. 296 and 18 February 1915, pp. 297–298.

767. F/A, 25 January 1915, p. 295.

768. Allenstein, founded in 1353, had 40,000 residents in 1915 (HA, p. 63). During the first division of Poland in 1772 it was allocated to the Kingdom of Prussia. At the Treaty of Versailles after the First World War, Germany lost large parts of its eastern territory, but Allenstein was not taken

from it at that stage because, in a plebiscite in 1920, the population voted almost unanimously to remain part of Germany. It is now a Polish town called Olsztyn with a population of 175,000.

769. HA, p. 63.
770. Liulevicius, 2000, p. 17.
771. Idem, p. 89.
772. Idem, p. 23.
773. Idem, pp. 152–153, 159. P. 153 reads,

> Letters from soldiers at the front expressed horror at the land. With spring thaws, lakes appeared out of nowhere, flooding bunkers and positions, and men on watch drowned at their posts or were swept away in icy currents. Hostile nature loomed large during lulls in the fighting as "days passed in monotony. Snow and fog, fog and snow—that was more or less the whole variation." In the trenches, "life took its usual course: standing watch, bad food, the torment of lice." On the Eastern Front, soldiers found themselves battling nature as much as human enemies, a decisive feature of this front-experience.

774. Liulevicius, 2000, p. 7.
775. Abraham, 1916. See Chapter Fifteen.
776. F/A, 3 June 1915, p. 310.
777. HA, p. 64.
778. Idem, p. 64.
779. See, for example, F/Fer, 2, 10 November 1914, p. 25.
780. Else and Hans Bürgner.
781. F/A 3 June 1915, pp. 310–311.
782. Idem.
783. Liulevicius, 2000, p. 23.
784. Idem, p. 154.
785. Idem, p. 81.
786. In the original text, the verb at the beginning of the sentence is missing.
787. F/A 3 July 1915, p. 312. Of the twelve papers on metapsychology mentioned here, five would eventually be published.
788. Breger, 2000, pp. 59–60. He writes of Freud's reaction to the lack of replies to his letters: "Throughout the engagement . . . he would become anxious if she did not respond to his letters immediately, a reaction that was present in his teenage correspondence with Silberstein and that continued throughout his life with his intimate male friends".
789. Aunt Jeanette and Aunt Johanna (1836–1916). See Chapter One.
790. Abraham, 1924, p. 438.
791. F/A, 6 July 1915, p. 314.
792. HA, p. 64.
793. Abraham, H., 1970b, p. 12.
794. Jan van Emden, Dutch psychiatrist and psychoanalyst (1868–1950). Freud met him in 1910 in Leiden. Van Emden entered into analysis with Freud and became a good friend of the family. They spent holidays together. During the First World War, van Emden made it possible for Freud to keep in touch with Jones in England. The exchange of letters went via him. In 1917, he was one of the founders of the Dutch Psychoanalytic Society, of which he became president in 1919 (Mühlleitner, 1992).

795. HA, p. 63.
796. F/A, 13 Nov. 1915, p. 319. The extensive correspondence Abraham engaged in at this time in connection with the setting up of an observation ward seems to have disappeared. Large parts of the archive of the First World War were lost at the end of the Second World War. Information from K. Erdmann, Bundesarchiv Freiburg im Breisgau.
797. F/A, 13 November 1915, p. 320.
798. Letter from Abraham to Fließ dated 2 March 1916. *Luzifer-Amor*, 46: 93–95.

The striking thing about this letter and Abraham's reply to Fließ of 12 March 1916 (idem, pp. 95–96) is that Abraham went along in all sincerity with Fließ's theory of vital periodicity. He described the three deaths in his family that had come in quick succession. His father was the sixth of six brothers and sisters. Three had died shortly after each other, on 27 April 1915 one of his father's sisters, on 20 November 1915 his father, and, on 3 March 1916, his father's oldest sister. Abraham did some calculations. The oldest sister was born on 20 August 1936 and died at the age of seventy-nine years and 196 days. That was 7×28 days (letter dated 12 March 1916).

Hans, Hedwig's brother, seems also to have been influenced by Fließ's numbers theory, since from the trenches of the eastern front he wrote about two brief bouts of 'flu. The first started on 12 January 1916 with cold shivers (twice twenty-eight days after his birthday on 17 November) and the second in the same way on 4 February, so twenty-three days after the first (letter from Abraham to Fließ dated 2 March 1916).

799. Abraham, 1924, p. 437. A mistake in the original English translation of the German text. The German text says: later reverted to its normal color. The English translation says: went black again. But Abraham's hair was blond.
800. Idem.
801. See Chapters Fifteen and Twenty-Five for a further discussion of the concept of introjection.
802. F/A, 24 October 1915, p. 318.
803. Pines stresses that the children were extremely fond of their grandmother, Abraham's mother. Dinora Pines collection. ABPAS, Part of 39.
804. Dinora Pines collection. ABPAS, Part of 39.
805. Letters from Abraham to Fließ of 2 March 1916 and 1 July 1925, *Luzifer-Amor*, 46: 93–94, 100–101.
806. Abraham, 1916.
807. F/A, 8 May 1916, p. 327.
808. *The Interpretation of Dreams* first appeared in 1900 and revised editions were published in 1909, 1911, 1914, 1919, 1925, and 1930. *Three Essays on the Theory of Sexuality* first appeared in 1905 and was revised in 1910, 1915, 1920, and 1924.
809. Abraham, 1924.
810. Lindner, 1879.
811. Abraham, 1916 p. 249. It is striking that in the English translation of this article the German "lustvoll" is translated as "pleasurable", losing all the sexual connotations of the original. Here the translation has been adjusted, in point 1. because "instinct" was used whereas it is clear that "very early sexuality" is meant and in point 2. because "so that" added after the semi-colon implied a cause and effect relationship not given in the original. *Selected Papers of Karl Abraham* was translated by Douglas Bryan and Alix Strachey and first published in 1927, with a reprint in 1988. These are not the only examples of maladroit translation in that publication and it must now surely be high time for a new translation to be produced.

812. Articles about Abraham have appeared regularly in both Germany and France in recent years. In English-speaking countries, they are rare.

813. Letter from Abraham to Jones, 4 January 1920, Ernest Jones collection, ABPAS, P04-C-B-01.

814. Letter from Jones to Abraham, 16 January 1920, Ernest Jones Collection, ABPAS, P04-G-B-02.

815. Jones to Abraham, 13 March 1914. Jones writes of Bryan: "He does not read German." LoC, Abraham papers.

816. London: Maresfield Library 1988. Reprint of the 1927 edition.

817. It would be going too far to name all the translation errors. Here are two examples: 1. Where Abraham wrote that as a schoolboy the patient had never been able to get sufficient milk to drink, we read that the patient had never been able to get sufficient milk to drink at school. (*PS, I*, p. 91; *SP*, p. 255). 2. Where Abraham wrote of "a not so small group of patients" in whom the pleasure in sucking was strongly accentuated from the beginning, the translation speaks of "a large group". (*SP*, p. 268).

818. Freud, 1905d, p. 106.

819. It does not seem to have occurred to Abraham that this distinction, between innate and determined by the environment, is one that is extremely difficult to make. He writes about it as if the difference is immediately obvious.

820. Abraham, 1916, p. 260.

821. Idem. p. 271.

822. In contemporary research, a link is quite often found between depression and eating disorders.

823. Abraham, 1916, p. 273.

824. Freud, 1917e; F/Fer, 2, 7 February 1915 and 18 February 1915.

825. Freud, 1917e; F/Fer, 2, 7 February 1915 and 18 February 1915.

826. Freud, 1914c.

827. Nunberg and Federn, 2008[1976], *II*, p. 282. This statement by Freud is recorded in the *Protokolle der Wiener Psychoanalytischen Vereinigung*. Bos (1996) has written an article about the *Protokolle*. As mentioned earlier, the Vienna Psychoanalytic Society appointed Rank as a paid secretary in 1906, and he was asked to compile records of its weekly meetings. Those records have survived and half a century later they were published by Nunberg and Federn. They provide a wealth of material: four volumes of 300 to 500 pages each, 250 records in total that cover the period 1906–1915. Bos points out that the *Protokolle* are *ad hoc* reconstructions by one person, Rank, who also took part in the discussions. They are not word for word reports, and neither are they transcripts from an account in shorthand or from a recording. So, how reliable is the material? The remarkable thing is that the *Protokolle* have been quoted by historians as if they are accurate transcriptions.

828. May-Tolzmann, 1990, p. 690.

829. Holmes, 2001 describes them as people who are pathologically focused on themselves and not able to enter into a relationship with another person. They approach others not as goals in themselves but as a means to their own egotistical ends.

830. Regression refers to a reversion to an earlier stage of psychosexual development (Stroeken, 2008, p. 163).

831. Freud, 1917e, p. 249.

832. F/A, 31 March 1915, p. 303.

833. Abraham, 1912a, pp. 137–156.

834. Freud, 1917e, p. 243, note.

835.   F/A, 4 May 1915, p. 308. This quote has been adjusted to match the original text. The published English edition of the correspondence has 'the link' rather than 'your link'.

836.   Correspondence Freud/Fließ, 31 May 1897, p. 267.

837.   F/A, 31 March 1915, pp. 304–305. A letter from Freud to Abraham has been lost in which he writes that Abraham takes insufficient account of hysterical anorexia. Abraham's answer to that is interesting in light of his own eating behaviour:

> You are quite right, dear Herr Professor, in remarking that I could have given more consideration in my paper to hysterical anorexia. I can explain why I only mentioned this condition in passing and did not investigate it in detail by the fact that I have not yet thoroughly analysed such a case. But there must be a deeper personal reason, just as you consider your passion for smoking to be a hindrance in your investigation of certain problems. I know from experience that my reaction to unpleasant events regularly makes itself felt by a loss of appetite. Therefore, inadvertently, I have avoided analysis of this symptom. However, I believe I have analysed it quite fully in myself and therefore could have taken myself as an example! Instead of this, I paid tribute to repression while working on the paper. Perhaps it will be possible to make a small addition to the text before the final printing. (F/A, 13 February 1916, p. 324)

838.   F/A, 4 May 1915, pp. 308–309.

839.   Consciously and unconsciously.

840.   Lemaigre, 2003, p. 41.

841.   F/A, 3 June 1915, p. 311.

842.   See also the article by May-Tolzmann (1990). The account of libido and narcissism theory that follows is based on that article.

843.   Idem, pp. 697, 707. Of the 130 articles published in the *Internationale Zeitschrift für Psychoanalyse* between 1914, when Freud's article on narcissism appeared, and 1922, only a handful extrapolated upon Freud's ideas about the ego and narcissism. An important contribution was made by Tausk in 1919 with his article "On the origin of the 'Influencing Machine' in schizophrenia". In it, Tausk laid out his idea that the spectrum of narcissistic problems, which run from feelings of alienation via hypochondriac anxieties to delusions of manipulation and persecution, is grounded in a pathological course of development of the ego and object finding, and connected with a loss of ego boundaries. This is a phenomenon very probably discovered and named by Tausk.
    1919 was also the year in which Tausk committed suicide. Freud wrote of him, "Despite his outstanding talents, he was of no use to us" (F/A, 6 July 1919, p. 400). A puzzling comment given Tausk's contributions.

844.   May-Tolzmann, 1990, p. 691.

845.   Freud (1917e).

846.   May, 2010, p. 73.

847.   Idem.

848.   Segal, 1973, p. 69.

849.   Abraham, 1917b.

850.   Ferenczi, 1908. In addition to Freud, Abraham named Sadger's 1910b article, "Über Urethralerotik", as a source of inspiration.

851.   Abraham, 1917b, p. 281.

852. Tausk wrote an extensive criticism of Abraham's article (Tausk, 1917). In it, he argues that ejaculatio praecox should instead be attributed to a surfeit of sexual phantasies and excessive masturbation. His argumentation is not convincing, since the case history he draws upon concerns a man who had no difficulty with premature ejaculation during sex with his wife but only in adulterous sex. He turned out to be afraid of sexually transmitted diseases and of unwanted pregnancy. With the ejaculation praecox that Abraham describes, premature discharge of semen takes place on every occasion,

CHAPTER SIXTEEN

853. F/A, 1 May 1916, p. 326.
854. HA, p. 65.
855. Dönhoff, 1990. In recalling her childhood in East Prussia, she describes how icy cold and long the winters were (pp. 75–76).
856. Interview with Grant Allan, Abraham's son, 1987, Dinora Pines collection. ABPAS, Part of 39. "He remembered his pleasure when his father came home from service in the military hospital and his fun in trying on his military clothes and strutting up and down with them."
857. HA, p. 65.
858. Idem.
859. HA, p. 65. No reference can any longer be found in the military archives in Potsdam to Allenstein and the clinic Abraham set up there. On 14 April 1945, the archive was destroyed and most of the papers burned. Information from Dr Gabriele Bosch, MBGA Bibliothek, Potsdam. See also Frank Unger (1999), "War neurosis—a form of male hysteria?"
860. In 1920, problems arose between Abraham and Liebermann because the latter had been neglecting his tasks as secretary (Kaderas, 2000, p. 113ff). For the events of 1920, see Chapter Twenty. Karen Horney and Liebermann were very good friends. According to two of Horney's biographers, they had a relationship in the 1920s (Paris, 1994, p. 141; Quinn, 1988, p. 199). Liebermann was in poor health. He became addicted to painkillers and died at the age of forty-eight (Kaderas, 2000, idem).
861. See Chapter Fourteen.
862. Skinner, 2007, p. 162.
863. Idem.
864. Medical corps captain.
865. With thanks to I. Shedletzky for information about Gershom Scholem.
866. Shedletzky, 1994, p. 70ff.
867. Idem, p. 83.
868. F/A, 23 September 1916, p. 336.
869. F/A, 26 September 1916, p. 336. The number of hours of analysis Ferenczi had per week in 1916 was between thirteen and 19.5 (May, 2007).
870. Liebermann developed a severe ear infection that lasted a long time. F/A, 12 November 1916 and 10 December 1916, pp. 337–338.
871. F/A, 12 November 1916, pp. 337–338.
872. Haynal, introduction to the correspondence between Freud and Ferenczi, II/I, p. 8.
873. F/A, 10 December 1916, pp. 338–339.
874. F/A 18 Mar. 1917, p. 345. "Here the winter was and is unusually stubborn, which also has not been beneficial to my health."

875. Interview with Hedwig by Eissler.

876. Jones, 1926a.

877. Idem.

878. F/A, 11 February 1917, pp. 343–344.

879. F/A, pp. 343–344. The founders included van Renterghem (who had been in analysis with Jung), van der Chijs (idem), Meyer (who had been in analysis with Jung), van Emden (who had been in analysis with both Jung and Freud and was a good friend of Freud's), Bouman, both the Stärckes, van Ophuijsen (who had been in analysis with Jung), and van der Hoop (idem) (Brinkgreve, 1984, pp. 78–82; Bulhof, 1983, p. 23).

880. Freud, 1901a.

881. Brinkgreve, 1984, p. 54; Stärcke, 1921.

882. F/Fer, 3, 28 March 1921, p. 53:

> An idea, which I would only like for the moment to express to you, is as follows: The lazy Dutch are mired in their good life and aren't participating properly. So I, for the moment personally, would like to get into closer contact with the only one among them who really amounts to anything: Stärcke. You see, I hope that in the foreseeable future he will be able to be accepted into our Committee.

883. Brinkgreve, 1984, p. 61.

884. Bulhof, 1983, pp. 135–138. Bulhof called Jelgersma the first professor in Europe who officially spoke in favour of psychoanalysis, but that position seems to have been taken by Bleuler at a much earlier stage. Brinkgreve (1984, p. 63) writes the same as Bulhof and both base what they say on Freud (1914d), who wrote, p. 33 n. 2, "The first *official* recognition of dream-interpretation and psychoanalysis in Europe was extended to them by the psychiatrist Jelgersma, Rector of the University of Leyden, in his rectorial address on February 9, 1914". This article by Freud was a settling of accounts, however, not just with Jung, but also with Bleuler, who is here written out of history by Freud.

885. Abraham, 1914, *IZP*, 2: 203.

886. Brinkgreve, 1984, p. 62.

887. F/A, 10 August 1917, p. 354.

888. F/A, 21 August 1917, p. 355.

889. The *Lectures* was a series of lectures given by Freud during the First World War at the University of Vienna, in the winter semester of 1915–1916 and in the winter semester of 1916–1917. They are an inventory of Freud's ideas in that period and they have an introductory character (James Strachey, Editor's Introduction to *Introductory Lectures on Psycho-Analysis*, SE, 15, p. 7).

890. F/A, p. 356.

891. F/A, pp. 357–358.

892. F/Fer, 2, 9 October 1917, p. 242.

893. F/A, 2 November 1917, p. 360.

894. HA, p. 68.

895. F/A, 16 December 1917, pp. 364–365.

896. F/A, 6 January 1918, p. 368.

897. Craig, 1978, p. 374.

898. It is surely far too simple, given the course of events, to accuse Abraham of great naivety and strange optimism. On the Eastern Front, where Abraham was posted, there was more reason for optimism than on the Western Front, but even in the west it was unclear until the latter part of 1918 who would emerge victorious (van Rossem, 2008).

899. Blackbourn, 2003, p. 365. According to Blackbourn, Lenin insisted on paying for his own train ticket, to stress the fact that he was not a German spy. But Lenin might, in fact, have been given a large amount of money by the Germans and used it for a large-scale propaganda offensive (Alnaes, 2007, 4, p. 260).

900. Liulevicius, 2000, pp. 206–207.

901. Peukert, 1991, p. 26.

902. Idem.

903. Idem.

904. Idem. Ludendorff would later be instrumental in the rise of Hitler.

905. Mann, 2008, p. 673.

906. Van Rossem, 2008, CD 4, 1.

CHAPTER SEVENTEEN

907. *Korrespondenzblatt. IZP*, 5, 1919, 52–55. According to the reports in the *Korrespondenzblatt*, Sachs, secretary to the Vienna Psychoanalytic Society, had proposed that Abraham, president of the IPA, should try to organise an international congress, because five years had passed since the previous such gathering.

908. Breslau was in Germany in 1918. After the Second World War, it became part of Poland.

909. Letter from Abraham to Lou Andreas-Salomé of 15 September 1918. LoC, Abraham correspondence. Transcription by U. Heyl-Keese.

910. At first, Freud was not in favour of the transfer to Budapest. It was difficult for the Germans to get permission to travel abroad, and Freud feared that Abraham, who had been unable to make anything of his presidency because of the war, would now miss his only chance to chair a congress. F/Fer, 2, 17 September 1918, p. 295. His worries proved unfounded. Abraham was able to attend and acted as chairman.

911. Ferenczi proposed giving Sachs 10,000 crowns from the "Literature Fund" for that year to cover the TB treatment. F/Fer, 2, 8 October 1918, p. 298. Freud agreed immediately. F/Fer, 2, 11 October 1918, p. 299. Later, he regretted it. On 16 October 1918, Freud wrote, "Perhaps I would only have exercised the beneficence less impulsively if I had been alone. Now that everything has been settled, I can say that. His family is quite well-to-do, you see, and they would hardly have begrudged him the means to recovery". F/Fer, 2, p. 300.

912. *Korrespondenzblatt. IZP*, 5, 1919: 52–55.

913. Idem.

914. Idem.

915. Idem.

916. F/Fer, 2, 10 September 1918, pp. 292–293.

917. See note 1.

918. Simmel, 1918. The book was discussed by Abraham and Harnik in *Bericht über die Fortschritte der Psychoanalyse 1914–1919*, p. 157 (1921).

919. F/A, 17 February 1918, p. 372.

920. Simmel was to play an important role in Berlin. In 1920, he set up the Berlin Psychoanalytic Institute's polyclinic along with Eitingon and, in 1922, he became a member of the Institute's new educational committee. In 1927, he opened the psychoanalytic clinic, Schloss Tegel, for which he had Ernst Freud design the interior. It was the first psychoanalytic clinic, but it had to close its doors in 1931 for lack of financial resources. Freud spent a good deal of time staying in the clinic when he came to Berlin for treatment to his jaw.
921. Ferenczi, Abraham, Simmel, and Jones, 1921.
922. Idem, p. 6. Max Nonne (1861–1959), professor of neurology in Hamburg, was a good example of the changed attitude to psychoanalysis in the First World War. Before the war, it had almost never happened that a professor expressed positive comments about psychoanalysis like this. Nonne (1922, pp. 112–113) wrote the following:

> Psychoanalysis is generally to be recommended for the treatment of military neurosis, both theoretically and practically. Mohr is correct in saying that as long as it is applied in a sensible form and without hazardous techniques of interpretation, it is basically nothing other than an attempt to give the sick man access to dictates in his mental life that have remained or become unconscious, thereby placing him in a position gradually to free himself from these influences, insofar as they have caused pathological symptoms. As in practice in civilian life, there is no way to resolve severe psychoneuroses such as depression, obsessions, and especially phobias of various kinds without psychoanalysis.

> We may well wonder exactly what Nonne understood psychoanalysis to be. He wrote that interpretations should not be too audacious and, earlier in his essay (p. 103), he wrote of psychoanalysis in the spirit of Freud but without the boundless exaggeration and one-sided focus on the sexual aspect. With thanks to A. Hirschfeld, Tübingen.

923. Tölle, 2005, p. 338.
924. Ferenczi et al., 1921, p. 17.
925. Tölle, 2005, p. 338.
926. Abraham, 1918, pp. 22–23.
927. *CP*, p. 66.
928. Abraham to Lou Andreas-Salomé, 2 September 1918, LoC, Abraham correspondence. Transcription by U. Heyl-Keese.
929. Ferenczi et al., 1921, p. 31.
930. F/Fer, 2, 17 February 1918, pp. 264–265.
931. Ferenczi et al., 1919, pp. 29–42.
932. F/A, 27 October 1918, p. 383.

> On the return journey from Budapest, and also more recently in Berlin, I have become more closely acquainted with Simmel. He has not yet in any way moved beyond the Breuer–Freud point of view, has strong resistances against sexuality, which he himself does not see clearly, and has unfortunately even stressed, at the Berlin meeting, that, according to his own experience, sexuality does not play an essential part in the war neuroses and the analyses. Perhaps he will develop further. But we must by no means overrate him.

933. F/A, 1 September 1919, p. 393.

934.   F/A, 13 September 1919, p. 395.

935.   F/A, 1 April 1919, p. 394. Simmel was to enter into analysis with Abraham for his work disorder. Abraham discussed the analysis, which eventually did go ahead, at length in his letters to Freud. He believed Simmel was above all narcissistic. As long as he was alone and could feel like a discoverer, everything was fine, but he could not stand being made part of an organisation. Abraham found his resistances to be enormous (5 May 1919, p. 396). Freud responded that it might be more economical to let him go; then he would not complete anything again anyhow (18 May 1919, p. 397). On 3 June 1919, p. 399, Abraham wrote that their colleague Simmel was now definitely making progress.

936.   Mühlleitner, 1992, pp. 107–108; F/A, 27 August 1918, pp. 381–382. Freud wrote,

> I ascribe a good share of my better spirits to the prospects that have opened up in Budapest for the development of our cause. Materially we shall be strong, we shall be able to maintain and expand our journals and exert an influence, and there will be an end to the begging we have had to do heretofore. The man whom we shall have to thank for this is not merely a wealthy man, but a man of sterling worth and high intellectual gifts, who is greatly interested in analysis; he is in fact the sort of person whom one would have to invent if he did not already exist. Faithlessness on his part is out of the question. He is a Ph.D. but a beer brewer.

> Von Freund had mentioned the prospect of a donation of a million crowns to support psychoanalysis.

937.   F/A, 18 May 1919, p. 398.

938.   Freud had a great sense of humour. In a letter to Ferenczi dated 9 November 1918, F/Fer, 2, p. 310, he wrote, "Is it true that all the war neurotics suddenly became healthy, except for one? What will Oppenheim say to that?" Oppenheim had, after all, been of the opinion that these neuroses were caused by changes in the brain due to brain damage. In his next letter, Freud went on: "Our analysis has actually also had trouble. No sooner does it begin to interest the world on account of the war neuroses than the war ends . . ." (F/Fer, 2, 17 November 1918, p. 311).

939.   Julius Wagner von Jauregg (1857–1940) won the Nobel Prize for medicine in 1927. He was an Austrian psychiatrist and head of the first psychiatric clinic in Vienna. In 1920, considerable criticism arose in Austria of the neurologists who had used electrical stimulation in treating war neurosis during the war. It was said to have led to suicides and deaths. A special investigatory commission was set up of which Wagner von Jauregg was initially part, until he was accused himself. Freud was an expert witness. He said that Wagner von Jauregg had been wrong to use such stimulation on the patient who had complained and that the patient could have been treated with psychoanalysis. It developed into a debate about psychoanalysis. Wagner von Jauregg was acquitted (Ellenberger, 1970, p. 839ff. See also Gunther and Trosman, 1974).

940.   Freud, 1919d, p. 213 (Memorandum on the electrical treatment of war neurotics).

941.   *Korrespondenzblatt, IZP, 6,* 1920: 379.

942.   See also Makari, 2008, p. 316ff, who looks at this point in detail.

CHAPTER EIGHTEEN

943.   Peukert, 1991, p. 27.

944.   F/A, 24 November 1918, pp. 384–385.

945. F/A, 15 December 1918, p. 388. Grünewald is both a forest in the southwest of Berlin and a suburb with beautiful large houses amid woods and meadows. In 1920, it became part of the city of Berlin. Since 1880, it had been a district popular with politicians, rich businessmen, famous artists, and academics.

946. HA, p. 66.

947. Abraham, 1917a. Hilda said in a talk in Berlin in 1970 that this was about her. Berlin, Karl-Abraham-Institut, Archive.

948. F/A, 20 January 1919, p. 390.

949. Craig, 1978, 406ff.

950. On 18 January 1919, Eitingon wrote to Freud,

> We are slowly starting to get used to the revolution, despite the fact that fighting with machine guns and artillery is making the city centre especially very disagreeable and the fact that the second phase of the revolution that has just ended, with the horrific end of the stage-couple Liebknecht–Luxemburg, was a particular emotional strain for my wife. Now it is calm here again, something like a mixture of the calm of the grave and the calm before the storm. (F/Eit, p. 146)

   On 4 January 1919, the Spartacist uprising broke out, which was put down by government troops. The leaders of the Spartacists, Karl Liebknecht and Rosa Luxemburg, were taken prisoner and murdered on 15 January.

951. Peukert, 1991, p. 29.

952. F/A, p. 391.

953. Jones, 1957, p. 3.

954. Letter from Abraham to Rank dated 2 February 1919. Eitingon Archive. Transcription by U. Heyl-Keese. The Berlin Psychoanalytic Society had twelve members at that point. *Korrespondenzblatt, IZP, 5*, 1919: 145. They were Dr Abraham, Dr Byerr, Dr Eitingon, Dr Gerstein, Dr Horney, Dr Koerber, Dr Liebermann, Dr Marcinowski, Dr Simmel, Dr Simonson, Dr Vollrath, and Dr Wanke.

955. *Korrespondenzblatt, IZP, 5*, 1919: 230.

956. In 1919, for example, Abraham gave six lectures to the Berlin Psychoanalytic Society. See note 14 and *Korrespondenzblatt, IZP, 6*, 1920: 100. On 6 November 1919, he delivered "Über die Prognose der psychoanalytischen Behandlung in vorgeschrittenem Alter" and on 18 December 1919, "Über narzißtische Bewertung der Exkretion in Traum und Neurose".

957. See the letters F/A of 11 August 1918 and 2 September 1918.

958. Free association is without any preconceived goal and without any censuring of what occurs to you at that moment.

959. Abraham, 1919a.

960. "Psychotherapie fürs Volk" (Psychotherapy for the people) was about the lecture Freud had delivered at the congress in Budapest, "Lines of advance in psycho-analytic therapy". The lecture was quoted by Eitingon in the *Korrespondenzblatt* in a piece devoted to the opening of the new poly-clinic in Berlin. *IZP, 6*, 1920: 97. Freud said the following (1919a, p. 167),

> It is possible to foresee that at some time or other the conscience of society will awake and remind it that the poor man should have just as much right to assistance for his mind as he now has to the life-saving help offered by surgery; and that the neuroses threaten public

health no less than tuberculosis, and can be left as little as the latter to the impotent care of individual members of the community. When this happens, institutions or out-patient clinics will be started, to which analytically-trained physicians will be appointed, so that men who would otherwise give way to drink, women who have nearly succumbed under their burden of privations, children for whom there is no choice but between running wild or neurosis, may be made capable, by analysis, of resistance and of efficient work.

961. F/Eit, 21 July 1919, pp. 158–159.

962. F/Fer, 2, 25 March 1918, p. 274: "On this occasion I have been together with Eitingon frequently, and I am astonished at the depth and clarity of his psychoanalytic knowledge". By "this occasion", Ferenczi is referring to the fact that Eitingon had at that point been staying with him for three days because his Russian wife was not allowed to travel any further until her papers were in order.

963. Rolnik, 2008, p. 88.

964. F/A, 3 October 1919, p. 404:

Another point on which your opinion will be decisive is the following. It is proposed on the occasion of the foundation of the Berlin polyclinic to admit Eitingon to full membership of the Committee. If you to agree with this, please mention it to him without further delay. In any other eventuality please let us know.

965. F/Eit, 21 January 1920, p. 187:

My dear Doctor, Toni Freund died yesterday, peacefully released from his incurable suffering. A great loss to our cause, a sharp pain for me, which I have however been able to assimilate over recent months. He bore his hopeless situation with heroic clarity, and brought no shame on analysis. When he received your letter in which you greeted him as a member of the committee, he wept and said: I know he will be my successor. As he said it, he indicated the committee ring, which he received from me. With his usual acumen he judged correctly. I had intended this ring for you. It has a particularly interesting stone and I did not take the trouble of finding another for you. A while later he actually took off the ring and gave word that it should be returned after his death. Yesterday, however, the young widow asked for the ring to be left to her because it is the only one he ever wore. I agreed of course, but am now pleased that Ernst has sent me your finger size and am now seeking a stone.

966. Brecht et al., 1985, p. 32.

967. Lecture by Hilda Abraham (1970a): "Die Anfänge der Psychoanalytischen Vereinigung in Berlin (1908–1933)", pp. 13, 14, Berlin, Karl-Abraham-Institut, Archive.

968. IZP, 6, 1920: 97.

969. On 1 December 1919, Freud wrote to Abraham that Ernst would leave for Berlin the day after Martin's wedding on 8 December and Abraham was certain to see him there. Ernst Ludwig Freud (1892–1970) was Freud's youngest son. He settled in Berlin as an architect and was given many commissions by analysts, including the interior of Abraham's consulting room. He worked in the Art Deco style. He married Lucie (Lux) Brasch and his youngest son, Lucian Freud (1922–2011) became a painter whose fame would rival that of his grandfather.

970. F/A, 13 March 1920, p. 418.

971. Haffner, 1973, p. 180ff.

972. F/A, p. 418.
973. F/A, 4 April 1920, p. 419.
974. Abraham, 1920b. *Die Neue Rundschau* is a well-known periodical for literature and essays, founded in 1890. In the period of Abraham's article, Alfred Döblin was writing for it under the pseudonym "Linke Poot", mostly sketches of Berlin in those years. Alfred Döblin (1878–1957) was one of the most important German writers of the early twentieth century. He was a doctor and well informed about psychoanalysis. His novel, *Berlin Alexanderplatz* (1929), made him world famous.
975. Peukert, 1991, p. 53ff.
976. Zamoyski, 2008, p. 2.
977. In 1795, Poland was divided between Russia, Prussia, and Austria. From that point on, Germany and Russia had a shared border. After the First World War, with the signing of the Treaty of Versailles on 28 June 1919, Poland became an independent nation again (Zamoyski, 2008, p. 1).
978. Ferenczi, 1921.
979. Conversion: the psychic conflict expresses itself in physical symptoms.
980. Abraham, 1919b, pp. 55–56.
981. F/A, pp. 390, 393, 396.
982. F/A, pp. 403, 404. On 9 September 1919, Freud and his wife, along with the Eitingons, travelled from the Badersee to Hamburg to visit the Halberstadts (Freud's daughter, Sophie, with her husband and children). On the way back, they visited Abraham in Berlin.
983. F/A, 3 October 1919, p. 404.
984. F/A, p. 407.
985. Mathilde Hollitscher-Freud (1887–1978) was Freud's eldest daughter. In 1909, she married Robert Hollitscher, a representative of large foreign silk factories. See Schröter, 2010, p. 25ff.
Minna Bernays (1865–1941) was Freud's wife's sister, four years younger. After her fiancé's death she remained unmarried. From 1896 onwards, she was part of the Freud household. Hedwig felt that she sometimes overshadowed Freud's wife, Martha, rather too much. Interview with Hedwig by Eissler, LoC.
986. Ernst Freud, 1892–1970.
987. F/A, 16 August 1921, p. 448.
988. Schröter, 2010, p. 225.
989. Rothe and Weber, 2003, p. 310.
990. Idem.
991. F/A, 22 October 1922, p. 459.
992. Meyer-Palmedo, 2006, p. 311. Anna Freud (1895–1982) was Freud's youngest daughter and the only one of his children to become a psychoanalyst.
993. Verbal account by the current resident.
994. Interview with Grant Allan by Pines. Dinora Pines collection. ABPAS, Part of 39.
995. Dinora Pines collection. ABPAS, Part of 39. Grant had probably become so English that he said tea, whereas in Germany "Kaffee und Kuchen" (coffee and cake) was usual in the afternoons.
996. F/A, p. 416.
997. Gay, 1988, pp. 391–392. Katá Lévy was the sister of Anton von Freund.
998. Interview with Hedwig by Eissler.
999. F/A, 16 July 1920, p. 431.
1000. The Weser is a river in northern Germany that flows into the North Sea at Bremen.

1001. F/A, 7 August 1920, p. 671 in the German edition (this letter is not included in the English edition of the correspondence).

1002. The description of Max and his family is from the book by Bettina Decke about Lottie Levy-Abraham, Decke (1998), and from interviews with Lotte Levy, as she called herself in adulthood.

1003. Decke, 1998, pp. 47–48.

1004. Idem., p. 52.

1005. Decke, 1998, p. 57. Max Markreich was a merchant in Bremen. From 1924 to 1938, he was president of the Jewish council in Bremen. In those years, he researched the history of the Jews in northern Germany. After the November pogrom of 1938, during which Jewish residents of Bremen were taken to the concentration camp, Sachsenhausen, Markreich managed to flee Germany before the year was out. His chronicle of the Bremen Jews was written in exile in San Francisco. He sent a copy of his manuscript, 500 pages in length, to Bremen in 1955, where it was kept in the municipal archive. It was published in 2003.

CHAPTER NINETEEN

1006. Van der Chijs, 1926.

1007. Freud wrote the following about this to Abraham: F/A 1 December 1919, p. 409: "I do not know whether it will really be possible to get the British and Americans to come to Berlin next autumn. Hostile prejudice is indeed stronger than you suppose".

1008. Abraham to Jones, 4 January 1920. Ernest Jones Collection, ABPAS, P04-C-B-01.

1009. On 21 March 1919, the Revolutionary Governing Council under Bela Kun (1866–1939) and Sándor Gabai (1879–1947) had taken power in Hungary and declared the Hungarian Republic of Councils. F/Fer, 2, pp. 346–347.

During the Republic of Councils, Ferenczi became a professor of psychoanalysis, through the mediation of Radó. Idem, 23 May 1919, p. 357. His appointment was short-lived. On 31 July 1919, the communists handed over power to the Social Democrats, who were overthrown by a counter-revolutionary movement that took power under Horthy. There followed a white terror, of which the Jews were the main victims. They were accused above all of collaborating with the communists. At the university, Jewish research assistants were dismissed and the Jewish students were thrown out and beaten up. Ferenczi lost his professorship. Idem, 28 August 1919. He was even excluded from the Budapest Medical Society because of his Bolshevik professorship. F/A, 21 June 1920, p. 428. At Freud's suggestion, Ferenczi handed over the presidency of the IPA to Jones. F/Fer, 2, p. 368, n. 3.

1010. Katharina Jokl was born in 1892 in Brünn, Moravia, which became Brno, Czechoslovakia. The family later moved to Vienna.

1011. F/Jones, 15 November 1914, p. 303. Dr C. A. Douglas Bryan had been involved in the setting up of the London Psychoanalytic Society in 1913 and became its vice-president. He was particularly interested in hypnosis and was an honorary member of the Psycho-Medical Association in London (Paskauskas, 1993). Bryan was the translator of works by Abraham who made so many mistakes. He wanted to publish a collection of Abraham's writings.

1012. In 1918, Morfydd Owen became associate professor at the Royal Academy of Music in London.

1013. Maddox, 2006, p. 135ff.

1014. Paskauskas, 1993, p. 357; Maddox, 2006, p. 153ff.

1015. Van Ophuijsen to Rank, 14 July 1920. Eitingon archive.

1016.   *Korrespondenzblatt, IZP, 6,* 1920: 377, 378. F/A, p. 432, n. 2. In contrast to the figures given in the *Korrespondenzblatt,* the note in the original version of the correspondence between Abraham and Freud speaks of two Americans and seven British.

1017.   One of those who did not attend the congress was Lou Andreas-Salomé. She would have liked to go, but had no money and was not a member of a psychoanalytic society, so she was not among those offered free accommodation. Freud did his best to enable her to attend. On 29 July 1920, Rank asked Abraham on Freud's behalf whether anything could be done for Frau Lou Salomé and whether she might be able to attend as a representative of the Berlin Psychoanalytic Society. (Letter from Rank to Abraham dated 29 July 1920, Eitingon archive.) Lou Andreas-Salomé had been practising analysis since late 1913, but she was not a doctor, so she could not become a full member of a psychoanalytic society (Welsch & Pfeiffer, 2006, p. 141). She was eventually allowed to join the Vienna Psychoanalytic Society along with Anna Freud in 1922. *Korrespondenzblatt. IZP, 8,* 1922: 245.

1018.   Ernest Jones to Katherine Jones, 7 September 1920. Ernest Jones collection, ABPAS, P02-C-02.

1019.   F/A, 7 August 1920, p. 671 in the German edition (this letter is not included in the English edition of the correspondence).

1020.   Interview with Ans van Maastrigt by Eissler. LoC.

1021.   Bulhof, 1983 p. 195.

1022.   One striking thing about what Stärcke says here is that, as he recalls it, Abraham spoke before him, whereas Deutsch is listed in the programme as speaking between Abraham and Stärcke. *Korrespondenzblatt, IZP, 6,* 1920: 379.

    Stärcke had been given a major role at the congress, more so than anyone else. On day one, Wednesday 8 September 1920, he gave a lecture entitled "Castration Complex". Then on the Friday there was a morning about psychoanalysis and psychiatry, with both Binswanger and Stärcke moderating. Stärcke's major role was not surprising. He stood head and shoulders above his Dutch colleagues and was greatly valued.

1023.   Bulhof had difficulty reading what Stärcke had written. He did not correct several apparent linguistic errors when editing the text of this letter. Bulhof (1983), p. 380.

1024.   Bulhof, idem, p. 380. The text is hard to read but it probably said that the lecture needed to be short.

1025.   For Friday, the programme does indeed feature only "Psychoanalysis and Psychiatry" with the two moderators. It seems the debate was cancelled.

1026.   Géza Róheim (1891–1953), Hungarian anthropologist. He was in analysis with Ferenczi in 1915 and 1916 and they became good friends. He became deeply involved with psychoanalysis and in 1921 Freud gave him a prize for the best article on the subject of applied psychoanalysis. His article was about totemism in Australia.

1027.   Bulhof, 1983, pp. 195–196.

1028.   Letter from Rank to Jones dated 28 July 1920. Eitingon archive. *Korrespondenzblatt, IZP, 6,* 1920: 337–338.

1029.   Jones, 1927, p. 14.

1030.   Grosskurth, 1991, p. 96.

1031.   Letter from Abraham to Rank dated 4 May 1919. Eitingon archive.

1032.   Abraham, 1921c.

1033.   Freud, 1905d and later versions; Freud, 1918a.

1034. Freud, 1918a, pp. 203–204.
1035. Freud, 1917c, p. 128.
1036. Abraham, 1921c, p. 344.
1037. Freud, 1918a.
1038. Kurzweil, 1995, p. 20.
1039. Horney, 1924.
1040. Paris, 1994, p. 66ff. In 1923, in response to Abraham, Horney wrote the article "On the genesis of the castration complex in women". Between 1923 and 1935, she published a total of nineteen articles about female psychology.
1041. *Korrespondenzblatt*, *IZP*, 5, 1919: 54.
1042. These facts about Melanie Klein are taken from Grosskurth, 1986.
1043. Ferenczi was stationed in Papa in Hungary in the early years of the war. From 1916 onwards, he was in Budapest again, so Melanie Klein's analysis probably started then, but they might have had occasional contact earlier. This is not made completely clear in Grosskurth's biography.
1044. In the reports of the Hungarian Psychoanalytic Society for 1919 in the *Korrespondenzblatt* the following is mentioned: "13 July: Frau M. Klein: 'Beobachtungen über die intellektuelle Entwickling eines Kindes" (Observations on the intellectual development of a child)". *IZP*, 6, 1920: 111.
1045. Grosskurth, 1991, p. 75.
1046. *Korrespondenzblatt*, *IZP*, 6, 1920: 111.
1047. F/Fer, 2, 29 June 1919, p. 361.
1048. Letter from Melanie Klein to Rank of 4 August 1920. Rank must have helped her, because, on 21 August 1920 she thanks him for his repeated efforts. Eitingon archive.
1049. Lindon, 1966, p. 361.
1050. Wittenberger & Tögel, 1999, p. 7.
1051. Idem, p. 47.
1052. Interview with Hedwig by Eissler. LoC.
1053. F/A, 9 February 1921, p. 438.

CHAPTER TWENTY

1054. The correspondence between Freud and Sachs is held at the LoC in Washington.
1055. Moellenhof, 1966, p. 181.
1056. Letters from Sachs to Freud, 16 November and 5 December 1919. LoC. Transcription by U. Heyl-Keese.
1057. Letter from Sachs to Freud, 21 November 1919. LoC. Transcription by U. Heyl-Keese.
1058. Schröter, 1996, p. 1150.
1059. Letter from Sachs to Freud, 23 November 1919. Transcription by U. Heyl-Keese.
1060. Schröter, 2004, pp. 103–104.
1061. Schröter, 2004, p. 105.
1062. F/A, 21 June 1920, p. 427.
1063. Idem, 27 June 1920, p. 429.
1064. Schröter (1996) describes the problems surrounding lay analysis in the period before about 1930 extensively.
1065. Freud, 1926e; Mühlleitner, 1992, p. 260ff.

1066.   Editor's introduction to "The question of lay analysis" (Freud, 1926e).

1067.   See also Eissler (1965), *Medical Orthodoxy and the Future of Psychoanalysis* and, on the battle in the USA, Wallerstein (1998), *Lay Analysis: Life Inside the Controversy*.

1068.   Schröter, 1996, p. 1134.

1069.   Schröter, 2004, p. 22.

1070.   Schröter, 1996, p. 1138.

1071.   Idem, p. 1142.

1072.   Idem, p. 1141.

1073.   Circular letter from Berlin dated 6 October 1920 (Wittenberger & Tögel, 1999, p. 65).

1074.   Idem, pp. 80–81.

1075.   Interview with Hedwig by Eissler.

1076.   *Korrespondenzblatt, IZP, 7,* 1921: 118, 119. On 21 December 1920, Müller became an associate member.

1077.   Letter from Liebermann to Eitingon of 31 January 1921. Eitingon archive.

1078.   Idem. Müller-Braunschweig had been in analysis with Abraham in 1910, at the same time as Karen Horney. He was a philosopher, so he was unable at first to become a member of the Berlin Psychoanalytic Society and had to be content with associate membership. On 1 February 1922, he was finally registered as a member for the first time. In 1933, Müller-Braunschweig published the memorandum "Psychoanalyse und Weltanschauung" (Psychoanalysis and worldview), in which the usefulness of psychoanalysis for National Socialism is described, and he remained active after all the Jewish members of the DPG, two thirds of the membership, were driven out of Germany. In 1926, the Berlin Psychoanalytic Society had been renamed the German Psychoanalytic Society (DPG). When, in 1936, the DPG became part of the German Institute for Psychological Research and Psychotherapy under Matthias Göring, he became president of its training committee.

1079.   See Schröter, 1996, p. 1158, 2004, p. 181.

1080.   Letter from Liebermann to Eitingon of 31 January 1921. Eitingon archive.

1081.   Wittenberger and Tögel, 1999, p. 173. Abraham wrote, "In our group enough difficulties have arisen from the fact that the majority of members were analysed by me".

1082.   Letter from Sachs to Freud, 23 January 1921. LoC. Transcription by U. Heyl-Keese.

1083.   *Korrespondenzblatt, IZP, 5,* 1919: 331.

1084.   For the problems with Liebermann, see also Kaderas, 2000.

1085.   Circular letter from Vienna, 11 November 1920 (Wittenberger & Tögel, 1999, p. 165).

1086.   Idem, p. 171.

1087.   In the Eitingon archive is a signed letter from Liebermann stating that, on 25 December 1920, he received the sum of 6,000 marks from Eitingon.

1088.   Circular letter from Berlin, 24 November 1920 (Wittenberger & Tögel, 1999, p. 182).

1089.   Letter from Liebermann to Eitingon of 31 January 1921. Eitingon archive.

1090.   Circular letter from Berlin, 1 December 1920 (Wittenberger & Tögel, 1999, p. 194).

1091.   Circular letter from Vienna, 11 December 1920 (Wittenberger & Tögel, 1999, p. 208).

1092.   Circular letter from Berlin, 22 December 1920 (Wittenberger & Tögel, 1999, p. 229).

1093.   This letter is dated 22 December 1920.

1094.   This concerns two doctors in Frankfurt, a professor and his pupil. They were K. Goldstein, head of the neurological department of the University of Frankfurt, and W. Rise. They had turned to Freud with a request for membership of the Vienna Psychoanalytic Society and the decision had been made to refer them to Berlin. The intention was that more information would be sought about the extent to which the two gentlemen were familiar with psychoanalysis. Depending on the outcome, they would be able to become either guests or members. Rank had informed them that they needed to contact Liebermann (Rank to Abraham 29 July 1920, Eitingon archive).

1095.   Letter from Sachs to Freud of 23 January 1921. LoC. Transcription by U. Heyl-Keese.

1096.   Circular letter from Berlin, 31 January 1921 (Wittenberger & Tögel, 2001, p. 45). Letter from Abraham to Eitingon dated 14 February 1921. Eitingon archive.

From this last letter, it appears that Sachs was tending towards Abraham's point of view, that Eitingon reproached Abraham for hostility towards Liebermann and that Abraham was extremely critical of Eitingon. Abraham wrote that Eitingon had a tendency to allow goodwill and indulgence to go too far and that too much lenience is a cardinal error in the treatment of neurotics.

1097.   F/Fer, 3, 7 February 1921, pp. 47–48.

1098.   Eitingon to Freud, F/Eit, 4 February 1921, pp. 236–238.

> I hasten to write to you again because I fear that the last few paragraphs of Abraham's latest committee letter—dealing with the Liebermann situation—were far more incomprehensible to you even than they were to me. Abraham's memory has played a trick on him when he speaks of a sudden change in my opinion. I have never said or desired anything other than that L. should not be dismissed. That would be to drop a person who finds himself in a desperate situation. Abraham is seizing upon the 'willingness' of L. to withdraw, without examining it any more closely, whereas I believe that it would be an enormous sacrifice for L.—it feels to him like fresh proof of his lack of capacity—and we must not accept this as long as there is any hope that this valuable and decent person will overcome the present crisis of his neurosis. For that reason I have always said one thing and never the other: as long as he is not better and it is viable from a business point of view, L. must remain at his post. And I am of the opinion that it can be managed. There is no possibility of serious damage to our cause. . . . Of course I understand that Abraham sees as extremely unpleasant the turning negative of years of intensive transference. . . . The great difference in attitude to L.'s acts and omissions between Abraham and myself can be explained first of all by the difference in the way in which we relate to a person who has fallen overboard from our ship and is still holding on to just one plank of that ship.

It is a breathtaking piece of prose in which Eitingon's greatness as guardian angel comes to the fore and Abraham is depicted as a scoundrel who is allowing Liebermann to drown. The division caused by Liebermann was, therefore, indeed infectious. The letter must have rung alarm bells in Freud, who knew all too well Eitingon's extreme tendency to want to save others.

1099.   Circular letter from London, 11 Februry 1921 (Wittenberger & Tögel, 2001, p. 71).

1100.   F/Eit, 4 February 1921, p. 240.

1101.   Circular letter from Vienna, 11 (13) February 1921 (Wittenberger & Tögel, 2001, pp. 59–60).

CHAPTER TWENTY-ONE

1102.   Abraham, 1925a.

1103.   Abraham, 1921, under 1925a, p. 370.

1104.   Abraham named the following sources: Freud (1908b), "Character and anal eroticism"; Sadger (1910a), "Analerotik und Analcharakter" (Anal eroticism and anal character); Ferenczi (1911), "Reizung der analen erogenen Zone als auslösende Ursache der Paranoia" (Stimulation of the anal erogenous zone as a trigger for paranoia); Jones (1919), "Über analerotische Characterzüge" (Anal-erotic character traits).

1105. Abraham, 1921, under 1925a, p. 376.
1106. Abraham, 1921c.
1107. F/A, 4 February 1921, p. 437.
1108. *Almanach* (1926), p. xxii and xxiii. Other reviews are interesting as well, such as one published in the *Archiv für Frauenkunde* (Archive of Gynaecology, translated for this edition): "Everyone who has been introduced to psychoanalytic thought will take this book in hand with thanks and benefit from it". Then there is the *IZP*: Ferenczi (1922, pp. 353–354, translated for this edition):

> Most of Abraham's ideas have proved themselves. Many have become common property among all psychoanalysts. Many of these works are frankly glowing achievements, the product of the author's great experience and sharp intellect. It is not possible, out of the wealth of new knowledge these essays offer, to create even a distant impression in a single paper.

1109. F/A, 31 October 1920, p. 433.
1110. Circular letter from Berlin, 11 January 1921 (Wittenberger & Tögel, 2001, p. 22).
1111. Ella Freeman Sharpe (1875–1947) was originally an English teacher and deputy headmistress. In 1917, she began studying psychoanalysis at the Brunswick Square Clinic, then continued her training in Berlin in 1920 and started analysis with Sachs. For several years, she continued her analysis in the summer months. In 1923, she became a member of the British Psychoanalytic Society and came to occupy a prominent place in it (Payne, 1947).
1112. Julia Turner, along with Jessie Murray, had set up the Brunswick Square Clinic in 1913. It remained in existence until 1922. Circular letter from London, 2 November 1920 (Wittenberger & Tögel, 1999, pp. 141–142).
1113. Idem.
1114. James Glover visited Jones on 21 May 1921. Circular letter from Berlin, 2 November 1920 (Wittenberger & Tögel, 1999, p. 138).
1115. Circular letter from London, 21 May 1921 (Wittenberger & Tögel, 2001, p. 170).
1116. Circular letter from Vienna, 1 July 1921 (Wittenberger & Tögel, 2001, p. 205).
1117. Circular letter from London, 21 May 1921 (Wittenberger & Tögel, 2001, p. 170).
1118. Bromley, 1973.
1119. F/A, 6 March 1921, p. 439.
1120. Dinora Pines collection. ABPAS, Part of 39.
1121. See Chapter Eleven.
1122. Circular letter from Berlin, 11 June 1921 (Wittenberger & Tögel, 2001, p. 189).
1123. Stroeken, 2009, p. 15.
1124. Ferenczi, 1921.
1125. *Korrespondenzblatt*, *IZP*, 7, 1921: 393–396.
1126. In conversion, a mental conflict expresses itself in physical symptoms.
1127. Gilles de la Tourette Syndrome involves both motor and vocal tics, of which the motor tics are more frequent, occurring many times a day.
1128. Jenö Harnik became an important training psychoanalyst in Berlin. In 1933, he fled to Copenhagen, where he became psychotic and died. See *Identity's Architect* by Friedman on Erikson, p. 106.

1129. *Korrespondenzblatt, IZP, 7,* 1921: 395.

1130. Circular letter from Budapest, 21 December 1921 (Wittenberger & Tögel, 2001, p. 317).

1131. Circular letter from Berlin, 11 January 1922 (Wittenberger & Tögel, 2002, p. 15).

1132. Circular letter from London, 11 June 1921 (Wittenberger & Tögel, 2001, p. 192).

1133. Circular letter from Vienna, 1 July 1921 (Wittenberger & Tögel, 2001, pp. 206 and 207).

1134. Circular letter from Berlin, 1 July 1921 (Wittenberger & Tögel, p. 209).

1135. Oskar Pfister (1873–1956), preacher and psychoanalyst in Zurich and one of the founders of the Swiss branch of the IPA.

1136. The view that psychoanalysis could be carried out only by doctors was not abandoned in the USA until around 1980.

1137. Abraham's maternal grandparents had lived in Hildesheim (Decke, 1998, p. 50).

1138. Interview with Hedwig by Eissler. LoC.

1139. Jones, 1957, p. 81. Goslar is on the northern side of the Harz. Its historic centre is on the World Heritage List.

1140. Circular letter from Berlin, 8 September 1921 (Wittenberger & Tögel, 2001, p. 239–240).

1141. Jones, 1957, p. 81.

1142. May, 2008, p. 94.

1143. Jones, 1957, p. 81.

1144. Circular letter from Berlin, 11 October 1921 (Wittenberger & Tögel, 2001, p. 244, 247).

1145. Circular letter from London, 11 October 1921 (Wittenberger & Tögel, 2001, p. 249).

1146. Letter from Jones to his wife, dated 23 September 1921. ABPAS.

1147. Freud, M., 1957.

1148. May, 2008, p. 45.

CHAPTER TWENTY-TWO

1149. The information about the Freikorps is taken from www.britannica.com/EBchecked/topic/218844/Freikorps, accessed on 13 October 2012.

1150. Craig, 1978, pp. 448–456.

1151. Idem, p. 450.

1152. Friedrich, 1995, p. 110ff.

1153. Max Reinhardt (1873–1943) was one of the most famous stage and film directors of his day, Bruno Walter (1876–1962) an equally famous conductor.

1154. Friedrich, 1995, p. 110ff.

1155. Friedrich, 1995, p. 98.

1156. Idem.

1157. Gall, 2009, p. 48ff. Walther Rathenau was highly intelligent. He went to work at his father's company but felt torn because he really wanted to be a writer and artist. He was in touch with all the great industrialists of the time and many important artists and writers as well. He was a good friend of Stefan Zweig and Frank Wedekind and with Graf Kessler, not to mention the German emperor.

1158. Schulze, 1982, p. 238ff.

1159. Hilda Abraham, 1974, p. 18.

1160. For more on the Stracheys, see Chapter Twenty-seven.

1161. Note on p. 696 of the German edition of the correspondence between Freud and Abraham. Guest lectures were to be given by Abraham, Ferenczi, Róheim and Sachs.

1162. Circular letter from Vienna, 21 December 1921 (Wittenberger & Tögel, 2001, p. 314).

1163. Circular letter from Berlin, 11 February 1922 (Wittenberger & Tögel, 2002, p. 43, n. 2).

1164. Abraham, 1922b.
   Circular letter from Berlin, 21 January 1922, p. 23, n. 2. The information given by Wittenberger and Tögel is contradictory here. On page 23 they say in note 2 that Abraham did not give his lecture about the breakaway movements, whereas, based on page 43, it seems he did give it. There were even requests to publish the lecture, although it seems it was not ultimately printed. They also give 22 January as the date of the lecture to the Vienna Psychoanalytic Society, whereas, according to the *Korrespondenzblatt*, it was delivered on 25 January. *IZP*, *8*, 1922: 117.

1165. Abraham, 1922b. Hermann Nunberg (1884–1970) had been a member of the Vienna Psycho-analytic Society since 1915 and he held an important position within it. In 1932, he fled to the USA, where he became a member and, later, president of the New York Psychoanalytic Society. Along with Ernst Federn, the son of Paul Federn, he published the protocols of the Vienna Psycho-analytic Society.

1166. Circular letter from Vienna, 3 February 1922 (Wittenberger & Tögel, 2002, p. 41).

1167. Circular letter from Berlin, 11 February 1922 (Wittenberger & Tögel, 2002, p. 43).

1168. *IZP*, *8*, 1922: 107.

1169. Circular letter from Berlin, 11 February 1922 (Wittenberger & Tögel, 2002, pp. 46–47). Schröter (2007) writes that it was extremely innovative in those days to use stenography.

1170. Circular letter from Vienna, 21 February 1922 (Wittenberger & Tögel, 2002, pp. 59–60).

1171. Circular letter from Berlin, 21 February 1922 (Wittenberger & Tögel, 2002, p. 64).

1172. Circular letter from Vienna 15 March 1922 (Wittenberger & Tögel, 2002, p. 87).

1173. Circular letter from Berlin, 1 March 1922 (Wittenberger & Tögel, 2002, p. 72).

1174. Circular letter from Berlin, 16 June 1922 (Wittenberger & Tögel, 2002, pp. 171–172).

1175. Circular letter from Vienna, 1 July 1922 (Wittenberger & Tögel, 2002, p. 175ff).

1176. Circular letter from London, 3 July 1922 (Wittenberger & Tögel, 2002, pp. 182–183).

1177. F/Eit, 12 June 1922, p. 289 (Maddox, 2006, p. 171).

1178. Circular letter from Vienna, signed by Ferenczi as well as Rank, 1 August 1922 (Wittenberger & Tögel, 2002, p. 187).

1179. See also the letter from Freud to Rank of 8 July 1922, in which Freud wrote the following to Rank, "I feel I should apologize for Abraham's and Jones's little unkindness, for they were actually reactions applying to me, deflected to you" (Liebermann & Kramer, 2012, F/Rank, p. 121).

1180. F/A, 2 May 1922, p. 458.

1181. F/A, 3 August 1922, pp. 458–459.

1182. Dinora Pines collection, ABPAS, Part of 39.

1183. Idem.

1184. Circular letter from Vienna, 16 August 1922 (Wittenberger & Tögel, 2002, p. 191).

1185. Freud developed cancer in 1923 and no longer appeared in public after that.

1186. See also Schröter (2007) on the seventh psychoanalytic congress in Berlin. Piaget (1896–1980) was a developmental psychologist. He had studied biology. After long observation, he developed a theory about the cognitive development of knowledge in children. He was in analysis with Spielrein.

1187. Tögel (2006) writes that Freud arrived in Berlin on 23 September. In the correspondence between Freud and Eitingon, there is a note on page 295 stating that Freud wanted to come two or three days earlier. That seems more likely, since, from Jones' letter of 22 September, it is clear that he had already met Freud. Jones wrote that the professor had caught a cold, the usual congress cold, and he wondered how long it would be before he had one himself. Jones was obsessed with the subject of catching colds. It is mentioned in many of his letters.

1188. Interview with Hilda by Eissler. Eitingon had proposed that the committee meeting should take place at his house.

1189. Interview with Hilda by Eissler.

1190. Letter from Jones to his wife, Katherine, 22 September 1922, Ernest Jones Collection, ABPAS, P04-G-B-02.

1191. *IZP*, *8*, 1922: 478ff.

1192. In the nineteenth century, polyclinics were set up in Germany in a good number of different medical fields. Such polyclinics often had a dual aim: to care for poorer segments of the population and to train students. Christoph Wilhelm Hufeland had started the first of them in the early eighteenth century. He organised a polyclinic in Jena and later, in 1810, at the university in Berlin (Winau, 1987, p. 132ff). The Berlin psychoanalytic polyclinic had the same dual aim. Patients who were unable to pay could enter into psychoanalysis there and, at the same time, it was a training institution.

1193. *IZP*, *8*, 1922: 506 (translated for this edition).

1194. Schröter, 2004, p. 192 (translated for this edition).

1195. Anna Smeliansky (1879–1961) was from Russia and studied medicine in Bern and Zurich. She had been a friend of Eitingon's since her student days. She was the polyclinic's resident doctor, lived there, and carried out many psychoanalyses. Smeliansky emigrated to Palestine in 1933, where she set up a new psychoanalytic polyclinic along with Eitingon and others. For a description of the Berlin polyclinic see also Dante (1999).

1196. In 1996, for instance, a panel discussion was organised by Arnold Rothstein that spent a full day discussing the relevance of the frequency of analysis for the creation of a psychoanalytic experience (Richards, 1997).

1197. May, 2008. Roszi von Freund was the wife of Anton von Freund.

1198. F/Fer, *3*, p. 71.

1199. Letter from Joan Riviere to her mother and sister, 3 October 1922. Joan Riviere collection, ABPAS, P02-C-02. Therese Benedek said in her interview with Eissler that during the congress she saw Freud coming in off the street with Lou Salomé. That sight made a great impression on her. Lou Salomé was a famous woman with her love for Nietzsche and Rainer Maria Rilke and for Freud. On Freud's other side was Erzsébet Révész-Radó. Therese Benedek thought Freud and Lou Salomé very old; she was herself thirty. Interview with Therese Benedek by Eissler, LoC. Therese Benedek (1892–1977) was a paediatrician and came originally from Hungary, where she was a member of the Budapest Psychoanalytic Society. She emigrated to Germany because of the political situation and there she became a member of the Berlin Psychoanalytic Society. She settled in Leipzig, where she set up another psychoanalytic society. Lou Andreas-Salomé became a member of the Vienna Psychoanalytic Society on 21 June 1922, shortly before the Berlin congress, but without having to give the usual lecture (Wittenberger & Tögel, 2003, pp. 134–135, n. 8). During her stay in Berlin in the Eitingons' house, she treated patients at the polyclinic (Rothe & Weber, 2003, *1*, pp. 79, 81.

1200. Rothe and Weber, 2003, p. 79.

1201. F/A, 7 January 1923, pp. 463–464.

1202. Schröter, 2004, p. 6.

1203.   Idem, p. 435ff. Anna Freud to Lou Andreas-Salomé on 21 January 1926: "Eitingon's visit was very nice. He is much refreshed by the journey, has taken on a number of new businesses, and is far more active and energetic, and also more cheerful than in recent years".

1204.   Lou Andreas-Salomé was Abraham's guest on the evening of 13 October along with Walter Schmiedeberg. Schmiedeberg was an analysand of Eitingon's and he, too, was staying in Eitingon's house. He later married Melanie Klein's daughter, Melitta (Rothe & Weber, 2003, pp. 81, 86).

1205.   Letter of 3 October 1922 from Riviere to her mother and sister Molly. Joan Riviere collection, ABPAS, P02-C-02. Joan Riviere-Hodgson (1883–1962) was one of the founders of the British Psychoanalytic Society in 1919. She had no academic training, as was usual in the upper-class circles in Britain from which she came. In 1916, she had entered into analysis with Jones. The analysis was complicated by the fact that Riviere openly fell in love with Jones, who lent her his house right at the start of the analysis. Jones was generally hugely attractive to women. In 1922 and 1924, Riviere entered into analysis with Freud and became an important translator of his work (see also Maddox, 2006, p. 125ff). Riviere would later ally herself with Melanie Klein.

1206.   Idem.

CHAPTER TWENTY-THREE

1207.   Circular letter from Berlin, 3 November 1920 (Wittenberger & Tögel, 1999, p. 149).

1208.   A/F, 16 October 1923, p. 727.

1209.   Circular letter from Berlin, 11 January 1922 (Wittenberger & Tögel, 2002, p. 14)..

1210.   A training analysis was compulsory for anyone who wanted to be trained in psychoanalysis.

1211.   F/Eit, 18 March 1923, p. 235.

1212.   F/Eit, 25 March 1923, p. 326.

1213.   Mühlleitner, 2008, p. 127.

1214.   Siegfried Bernfeld (1892–1953) was from Vienna. He studied physics, educational theory, and psychology. He was always extremely interested in social issues and upbringing. In 1919, he became a member of the Vienna Psychoanalytic Society and, that same year, he set up a children's home for Jewish war orphans. In the children's home, new methods of upbringing were applied that incorporated psychoanalytic ideas. The children's home had to close after a year because of financial problems. Encouraged by Freud, Bernfeld began to analyse patients in 1922. He was a gifted speaker and managed to win a great deal of support for psychoanalysis. In 1925, he moved to Berlin and became a member of the Berlin Psychoanalytic Society. Theodor Reik, who had already been to Berlin during his analysis with Abraham, returned in 1928 (Mühlleitner, 2008, p. 260). On Freud's advice, Marianne Kris (nee Rie) went to Berlin in 1925 to be trained. She entered into analysis with Alexander (Mühlleitner, 2008, p. 190).

1215.   Grotjahn, 1966, p. 384ff.

1216.   Mühlleitner, 2008, p. 161; Roazen and Swerdloff, 1995, p. 97.

1217.   Abraham wrote to Freud on 22 October 1922, "Last Sunday Oliver accompanied us on an excursion. I am glad to be able to say that I find him definitely changed for the better". F/A, p. 459. Oliver had entered into analysis with Alexander in December 1921.

1218.   Interview with Alexander by Eissler.

1219.   Idem.

1220.   Alexander et al., 1966, p. 241.

1221.   Mühlleitner, 2008, p. 130. The Romanische Café was famous in those days. Its clientele was a mixture of artists and journalists, along with people from Berlin's financial sector. You could sit as long as you liked with just one drink. Only in exceptional cases, if someone spent twelve hours over a cup of coffee, it might happen that the manager laid a card next to them saying "You are requested to leave this establishment after paying your bill and not to return" (Schebera, 2005, pp. 39–85).

1222.   Mühlleitner, 2008, p. 130.

1223.   Alexander, 1966, p. 241.

1224.   Roazen and Swerdloff, 1995, p. 9. This is a remarkable story. Lampl-de Groot's review of the article by Radó does indeed consist of a stream of fairly supercilious criticism, without a single positive note, comparable to van Ophuijsen's criticism of Ferenczi. Just as Ferenczi had been, Radó was furious. It remains unclear why Freud had anything to do with the review and why such criticism would cause a rift. Helene Deutsch wrote to her husband, Felix, in 1935, that Radó was totally obsessed with Lampl's review and filled with hatred towards everyone who had anything to do with it.

1225.   In the 1960s, the Psychoanalytic Movement Project was carried out by Bluma Swerdloff, within the framework of the Oral History Office at Columbia University in New York. As part of that project, psychoanalysts who were important from a historical point of view were interviewed extensively. One of the first to be interviewed was Sándor Radó. Paul Roazen wrote a book based on the interview with Radó. It was published under Roazen's name and the name of the interviewer, Bluma Swerdloff (Roazen & Swerdloff, 1995).

1226.   Idem, p. 90.

1227.   The conflict about Rank and about the film. See Chapter Twenty-eight.

1228.   Interview with Therese Benedek by Eissler.

1229.   See, for example, the letter from Freud to Radó of 28 November 1926. Freud Museum London.

1230.   F/Eit, 25 January 1926, p. 437.

1231.   Erzsébet Radó-Révész (1887–1923), doctor and psychiatrist, was from Nagyvarad in Hungary. In 1918, she went to Vienna to enter into analysis with Freud. From April 1918, she was a member of the Vienna Psychoanalytic Society. In late 1919, she married Sándor Radó and became a teacher of analysis at the Budapest Psychoanalytic Society. She died in early 1923. At that point she was in analysis with Ferenczi (Mühlleitner, 2008, p. 269).

1232.   Mühlleitner, 2008, p. 129ff.

1233.   Idem, p. 90. After Abraham's death, van Ophuijsen and his wife, Ans van Maastrigt, visited Freud at the Semmering. Ans van Maastrigt later told Eissler that Freud had been terribly sad about Abraham's death. She said that Freud spoke of how he had valued Abraham, who was impossible to replace, saying that Abraham was the only person suitable as president, that Eitingon did not have the authority for it, and how sad he was about that. He said: such a valuable man who dies so young and such an old man as I am who is sick and has to live. Interview with Ans van Maastrigt by Eissler.

1234.   Fenichel, 1945.

1235.   Mühlleitner, 2008, p. 384ff.

1236.   Letter from Anna Freud to Eitingon dated 15 April 1922, LoC.

1237.   Young-Bruehl, 1988, pp. 103–104.

CHAPTER TWENTY-FOUR

1238.   The description of the situation in Germany in 1923 is largely borrowed from Craig (1978, p. 448ff).

1239. Remarque, 1937.

1240. Swerdloff, 2002. Bluma Swerdloff interviewed Michael Balint on 6 and 7 August 1965 for the Columbia University Oral History Research Office. Later, she turned the interview into an article. Along with his wife, Alice, Michael Balint moved to Berlin in 1921. They both entered into analysis with Sachs. Balint later considered his analysis far too theoretical. A chemist and researcher by training, he became fascinated by psychoanalysis and, after a year, both Balints started working at the institute. They attended meetings of the Berlin Psychoanalytic Society. Balint also continued working as a chemist. After his return to Budapest, he entered into analysis with Ferenczi.

1241. Swerdloff, 2002, p. 401.

1242. Idem, pp. 388–389.

1243. See Chapter Twenty-three.

1244. See also Chapter Six of this book. In 1908, Abraham had read Freud's work, but he had no idea how to set about psychoanalysis in practice. He consulted Freud, who gave him general indications: take your time, don't try to force success. They were, in fact, indications as to what Abraham should avoid doing, rather than what he should do. F/A, 9 January 1908, p. 21.

1245. Leitner, 2001, p. 88.

1246. Mühlleitner, 1992, p. 82.

1247. Leitner, 2001, pp. 114–115.

1248. Strachey, 2006.

1249. Leitner, 2001, p. 173.

1250. Freud, 1910k.

1251. May, 1990, p. 697. May describes how, until well into the 1920s, the majority of psychoanalysts stuck to the theory of the conflict between the ego drives and sexual drives. In treatment, they sought unconscious libidinous wishes towards the object that were in conflict with the ego and, therefore, repressed, distorted into phantasies, and satisfied in symptoms and character traits. The technique seems to have consisted mainly of this search.

1252. F/J, p. 145.

1253. Freud, 1910d.

1254. See Chapter Seven.

1255. Mühlleitner, 1992, p. 75.

1256. Interview with the Deutsch couple by Eissler. LoC.

1257. Roazen, 1985, pp. xi, 190ff.

1258. Idem, p. 165ff.

1259. The Wolf Man is one of Freud's most famous case histories. He was a young Russian from a wealthy family. The treatment took place from 1910 onwards. The Wolf Man is referred to quite often in this period (Freud, 1918b).

1260. Briehl, 1966, p. 285.

1261. Email from N. L. Thompson of 18 April 2013:

> I always found it striking that Helene Deutsch emphasized that she had been Freud's analysand, while rarely referring to her second analysis with Karl Abraham. I think, however, that it gratified her narcissism to be identified with Freud rather than Abraham. Yet it was following Deutsch's analysis with Abraham that she began to publish her first papers on women. To me this suggests that her analysis with him had a meaningful influence on her capacity to make seminal, if sometimes controversial, contributions to psychoanalytic theory and clinical practice.

1262. Details about Helene Deutsche's stay in Berlin and analysis with Abraham are taken from the letters sent by Helene Deutsch to her husband, Felix Deutsch, in the period 1923–1924. Schlesinger Library, Helene Deutsch papers, 82-M143–85-M247, folder 16.

1263. Idem.

1264. Interview with Eduard Hitschmann by Eissler. LoC.

1265. Clara Happel (1889–1945) was a doctor who was trained at the Berlin institute. She became a member of the Berlin Psychoanalytic Society.

1266. Schlesinger Library. Helene Deutsch collection.

1267. See above note. The letters are undated.

1268. Idem.

1269. Idem.

1270. F/E, 9 February 1912, p. 69.

1271. See above note about the letters of Helene Deutsch.

1272. Interview with Helene and Felix Deutsch by Eissler.

1273. See above note about the letters of Helene Deutsch.

1274. Idem.

1275. Roazen, 1985, p. 193.

1276. Idem, p. 6ff.

1277. Idem, pp. 190–207.

1278. Idem, p. 193.

1279. Letter from Abraham to Felix Deutsch dated 2 December 1923 about the condition of Helene Deutsch. Abraham blamed the crisis over the summer on masochism. Schlesinger archive.

1280. Separation anxiety was not seen as an important factor in psychoanalytic treatment until the 1950s and 1960s.

1281. Freud, 1923b.

1282. Groddeck, 1923.

1283. Flügel, 1927.

1284. They include Arndt (1923–1924), *Zeitschrift für Sexualwissenschaft, 10*; Bleuler and Münch (1923), *Medizinische Wochenschrift, 70*: 989; Döblin (1926), *Vossische Zeitung in Almanach*. With thanks to G. Fichtner.

1285. Flügel, 1927.

1286. Ferenczi and Rank, 1924.

1287. F/Fer, 3, 18 March 1923 and 15 April 1923, pp. 96, 100.

1288. F/Jones, pp. 522, 524.

1289. Jones, 1926b.

1290. F/A, 3 May 1923, p. 469.

1291. Radó and Sachs lectured on 30 October 1923 about the problems in Freud's *The Ego and the Id*. *Korrespondenzblatt, IZP, 10*, 1924: 106. On 31 October, Reik spoke in Vienna about unconscious feelings of guilt. Idem, p. 119. Sachs spoke about *The Ego and the Id* in his lecture to the congress in Salzburg of 21–23 April 1924, and Alexander gave a lecture there called "Versuch einer metapsychologischen Darstellung des psychoanalytischen Heilungsvorganges. (Anwendung von Freuds topisch-dynamischer Theorie des Ich auf die Therapie)." Idem, p. 216.

1292. Modell, 1975, p. 57.

1293. Bergmann, who was trained in the ego-psychology tradition, described this period in his essay "The Hartmann era and its contribution to psychoanalytic technique" (Bergmann, 2000). Observations here about the Hartmann period are borrowed from that essay.

1294.   Abraham (1923) p. 86ff.

1295.   The trip through England is described in Abraham's letter to Jones of 7 August 1923. Ernest Jones Collection, ABPAS, P04-C-B-01.

1296.   The details of Freud's illness are from the biography by Schur (1972), who was Freud's personal physician from 1928 onwards.

1297.   Schur, 1972, p. 358.

1298.   F/Eit, p. 328ff.

1299.   In the letters written by Anna Freud to Eitingon that are held by the LoC there is a gap of sixteen months in 1923–1924. A letter dated 27 April 1923 is held there and one dated 1 August 1924, with nothing in between. In the August letter, Anna Freud complains that Eitingon has not given them his holiday address as he used to do. LoC, Anna Freud correspondence.

1300.   From the moment Freud became ill it was Anna Freud who cared for him and went with him everywhere (Rothe & Weber, 2003, p. 298).

CHAPTER TWENTY-FIVE

1301.   Abraham, 1924, 1925a.

1302.   *Korrespondenzblatt, IZP, 9*, 1923: 242.

1303.   F/A, p. 467.

1304.   May-Tolzmann, 1990, p. 690.

1305.   Nowadays, manic depression is known as bipolar disorder.

1306.   Freud, 1905d.

1307.   Fischer, 1976, p. 926.

1308.   Freud, 1917e. As described by Freud in "Mourning and melancholia". *SP*, p. 433. See also Chapter Fifteen.

1309.   Freud, 1917e, p. 248.

1310.   Bergmann, 2004, p. 32.

1311.   See Chapter Twenty-three.

1312.   See Chapter Fourteen.

1313.   Torok, 1968. Maria Torok (1925–1998) was Hungarian. After the Second World War, she fled to France and became a psychoanalyst there. She published a great deal, some of it about introjection and incorporation, in collaboration with Nicolas Abraham.

1314.   F/A, pp. 453–454.

1315.   F/A, p. 455.

1316.   F/A, pp. 457–458.

1317.   F/A, p. 458.

1318.   Freud, 1921c.

1319.   Idem, p. 148.

1320.   May, 2010, p. 74.

1321.   Abraham, 1924, pp. 463–464.

1322.   Fischer, 1976, p. 924ff.

1323.   May, 2010, p. 59; Ferenczi, 1924; Rank, 2007.

1324.   May, 2010, p. 68.

1325.   Fischer, 1976.

1326.   May, 2010, p. 69.

1327.   Van Tilburg, 1994. In this article, van Tilburg pointed out that contemporary research also shows real loss to be an important factor in depression, as Abraham claimed. At the same time, he warned against the unilateral linking of aggression with depression that has become usual among psychoanalysts.

1328.   Fenichel, 1945, p. 61.

1329.   See also Symington, 1986, pp. 155–169.

1330.   Fenichel, 1925.

1331.   Fenichel, 1945, p. 62.

1332.   Jones, 1925.

1333.   Abraham, 1925a, p. 412.

CHAPTER TWENTY-SIX

1334.   See Chapter Twenty-four.

1335.   F/Rank, 20 July 1922, p. 127.

1336.   Lieberman, 1985, p. 161ff. It was not until 1924 that Freud recognised that Rank had behaved far too rudely. On 20 March 1924, he wrote to Ferenczi, "Rank is terribly uncouth, pits people against him". F/Fer, 3, p. 128.

1337.   Letter from Freud to Rank dated 4 August 1922 (Lieberman, 1985, p. 181). Haynal and Falzeder (2002, p. 34), wrote that Freud even said to Rank that he preferred him to anyone else as leader of the psychoanalytic movement. The letter that they quote was dated 4 June 1922, from Freud to Rank. No such letter is known, however. (With thanks to Professor Fichtner.) They probably mean the letter of 4 August 1922. If so, then Haynal and Falzeder give far too positive an impression of it by omitting to mention that Freud would have given preference to Rank had Rank had a medical degree.

1338.   Interviews with Hedwig and Hilda Abraham by Eissler. LoC.

1339.   Interview with Hitschmann by Eissler. LoC.

1340.   Wittenberger and Tögel, 1999, p. 232.

1341.   Wittenberger and Tögel, 2003, p. 188.

1342.   F/Eit, p. 232 and note 8.

1343.   F/Fer, 3, p. 13.

1344.   Grosskurth, 1991, p. 16.

1345.   Wittenberger, 1995.

1346.   Wittenberger and Tögel, 2003, p. 217.

1347.   Idem, p. 215.

1348.   Idem, p. 219.

1349.   Idem, p. 221ff.

1350.   Idem, p. 228 (translated for this edition).

1351.   Idem, p. 231ff.

1352.   Wittenberger, 1995, p. 229.

1353.   Grosskurth, 1991, p. 121ff.

1354.   From the correspondence between Freud and Rank it is possible to deduce that the first assertion, that all the letters were compiled jointly, was not true and the second, that all the letters were shown to Freud, was true in most cases (Lieberman & Kramer, 2012).

1355.   Wittenberger and Tögel, 2003, pp. 231–232.

1356. Wittenberger and Tögel, 2003, p. 235.

1357. On 13 January 1923, Eitingon wrote to Freud that it was a shame Rank had only now (in a circular letter of 3 January 1923) produced the figures for the publishing house. They showed that the English branch of the company had debts of £700. At the congress in September, there was extensive discussion of the future of the publishing house, when these figures were not yet available.

1358. Wittenberger and Tögel, 2003, p. 260 (translated for this edition).

1359. Schur, 1972, pp. 358–361.

1360. Letter dated 17 August 1923 from Freud to Felix Deutsch. ABPAS.

1361. Lieberman, 1985, p. 189. Schur (1972, p. 351) goes into detail on the matter. He is convinced that Freud suspected from the start that he had cancer.

1362. Schur, 1972, p. 361.

1363. Gay, 1988, pp. 470–471.

1364. Brome, 1968, p. 167.

1365. Rank wrote to Freud during the First World War, when he was stationed in Kraków, that for as long as he could remember he had suffered from depressive episodes, which he usually kept to himself. F/Rank, 14 May 1918. In a letter to the committee of 7 January 1925, Rank wrote that he had been manic in response to Freud's illness. Circular letters, p. 219.

1366. F/Jones, letter dated 7 January 1923, p. 507.

1367. Brome, 1968, p. 170ff.

1368. Idem, p. 176.

1369. This includes Brome (1968, p. 177), Grosskurth (1991, p. 131ff.), Maddox (2006, p. 175ff.), Lieberman (1985, p. 189ff.), and Wittenberger (1995, p. 266ff.).

1370. Letter from Jones to his wife, Katherine, 26 August 1923, Ernest Jones Collection, ABPAS, P04-G-B-02. Grosskurth, 1991, p. 132.

1371. Jones wrote to Abraham on 17 March 1924 that he had been unable to go into detail on the issue in San Cristoforo because it would have meant sifting through the extremely unpleasant financial problems between the Press and the Verlag. That would only have led to even more rancour in Otto Rank, Jones thought, and it would have been impossible to come to a judgement without a great deal of documentation and several witnesses (ABPAS). Jones had not defended himself in San Cristoforo against the charge that he had called Rank a "swindling Jew".

1372. Maddox, 2006, p. 176.

1373. F/A, p. 475. Freud heard he had cancer and would need another operation only after his trip to Rome in September 1923. Professor Hans Pichler was his new doctor. Freud underwent a major operation on 12 October. Afterwards, he had a high fever for two days and was unable to return home until 28 October (Schur, 1972, p. 363).

1374. Interview with Hedwig by Eissler. LoC.

1375. Interview with Hitschmann by Eissler. LoC.

1376. Interview with Alexander by Eissler. LoC.

1377. Rank, 2007, p. 1 (translated for this edition).

1378. Janus, 2007, p. ii.

1379. Rank had been carrying out analyses only since 1920 and did three or four at a time. He was still relatively inexperienced when he wrote the book in 1922. Abraham and Jones had been analysing for many years and did nine or ten analyses per day. Sachs had also started late, but from the time he began working in Berlin (1920) he carried out nine analyses per day. Eitingon analysed very little.

1380. Lieberman, 1985, pp. 223–224.

1381. Freud, 1923b; Abraham, 1924.

1382. Schröter, 2004, p. 337ff.

1383. Card from Abraham to Jones dated 2 January 1924. Ernest Jones collection. ABPAS, P04-C-B-01.

1384. Alexander, 1925.

1385. Freud, 1912b, pp. 107–108.

1386. Circular letter from Vienna by Freud alone (Wittenberger & Tögel, 2006, pp. 169–172).

1387. F/Rank, 15 February 1924, p. 187ff.

1388. Letter from Sachs to Freud, 20 February 1924. LoC, Sachs correspondence. Sachs had always been very good friends with Rank. They had set up *Imago* together. In May 1924, Sachs took over the editorship of *Imago* from Rank.

1389. F/A, p. 483. Abraham's copy of *The Trauma of Birth* is still in the archive of the Karl Abraham Institute in Berlin. The book is full of notes, which shows that Abraham studied it extremely thoroughly. He had major objections to the lack of an empirical basis. In the margins are many comments such as "what does that mean?" and "not to be accepted without examples", or "how does he know that?", "careless", "one-sided explanation", "hasty conclusion". Zienert-Eilts has written an article about negative image-formation by Abraham in the Rank conflict that is not compatible with the sources (Zienert-Eilts, 2010, p. 24ff.).

1390. F/Fer, 3, p. 119.

1391. F/Fer, 3, pp. 122–124.

1392. F/A, p. 485. NB: The English edition of the correspondence gives the date of this letter as 26 February.

1393. F/A, p. 487.

1394. Brome, 1968, p. 184.

1395. It seems as if Ferenczi did not know why Jones had failed to defend himself in San Cristoforo. See the letter from Jones to Abraham of 12 November 1924. He also seems not to have been informed about the further discussions with Brill about Brill's "swindling Jew". Freud did know about it. On 5 November 1924, he apologised to Jones. F/Jones, p. 559.

1396. F/Fer, 3, pp. 127–128.

1397. All authors writing about the history of psychoanalysis, with the exception of Brome, have always pointed to Abraham as to blame for the disintegration of the committee. Even the editors of the German edition of the letters between Abraham and Freud, Falzeder and Hermanns, do not write that Freud committed a major indiscretion. Instead, they write that because of Abraham's "denunciation", Rank dissolved the committee and they place all the blame for that at Abraham's door (Falzeder & Hermanns, 2009, pp. 37–38).

1398. Wittenberger and Tögel, 2006, p. 194.

1399. F/Fer, 3, 20 March 1924, p. 130.

1400. Lieberman, 1985, p. 219

1401. F/A, p. 491.

1402. Interview with Hedwig and with Hilda by Eissler. LoC.

1403. F/Fer, 3, p. 142.

1404. The original German text is in a style characteristic of Rank. Cited from Lieberman, 1985, p. 242.

1405. Idem, p. 243.

1406. Idem, p. 245.

1407. On 16 September 1924, Anna Freud wrote to Eitingon, "I am also very well aware that for the publishing house and the journals it is virtually a matter of life and death whether Rank can still be held back". LoC.

1408. Brome, 1968, p. 191.

1409. Jones, 1957, p. 71.

1410. Brome, 1968, p. 191.

1411. Interview with Beate Rank by Eissler.

1412. Anna Freud to Eitingon, 4 December 1924. LoC.

1413. Idem, 24 December 1924.

1414. Wittenberger and Tögel, 2006, p. 213ff.

1415. Letter from Jones to Abraham dated 29 December 1924. LoC.

1416. Taft, 1958, p. ix.

1417. These details are taken from the introduction to Taft's book.

1418. Taft, 1958.

1419. Jones, 1953, 1955, 1957; Sachs, 1944.

1420. Wittenberger and Tögel, 2006, p. 219.

1421. Taft, 1958, p. 98.

1422. Idem, p. 86.

1423. Idem, p. 79.

1424. Idem, p. 82.

1425. To name but two: Lieberman (1985) quotes Taft frequently in his biography of Rank and Leitner (1998) also bases her work extensively on Taft.

CHAPTER TWENTY-SEVEN

1426. F/A, p. 500.

1427. F/A, p. 503.

1428. F/A, p. 508. The speech was called "The influence of oral erotism on character-formation".

1429. F/A, p. 506.

1430. Interview with Lotte Levy.

1431. F/A, p. 510.

1432. F/A, p. 511.

1433. Letter from Abraham to Helene Deutsch. Sils Maria 14 July 1924. LoC, Abraham correspondence. Transcription by U. Heyl-Keese.

1434. F/Fer, 3, p. 160.

1435. See Chapter Twenty-eight.

1436. When Freud recommended him to Felix Deutsch, Bernfeld was thirty-two years old. He had two years' experience at analysis.

1437. See Roazen, 1985, pp. 212–220.

1438. F/A, p. 512.

1439. Letter from Abraham to Helene Deutsch dated 15 February 1925. With thanks to S. Gifford and G. Fichtner for the transcription.

1440. Alix Strachey (1892–1973) was born in New Jersey but grew up in Britain. Her father died in a swimming accident six weeks after she was born. Her mother, from a well-to-do family, was a painter. Alix and her older brother, Philip, grew up in a very artistic milieu in London and travelled widely. In 1898, Alix's mother, Mary Sargent-Florence, bought land called Lord's Wood in Buckinghamshire and had a house built on it. She was a firm feminist and she wanted to rename the land Lady's Wood but gave up the idea under pressure from other residents of the area. After the death of Alix's mother in 1954, the Stracheys settled there. Alix studied modern languages at Cambridge, where she came into contact with Freud's work.

1441. Meisel and Kendrick, 1985, Introduction. Freud, 1919a, 1921c.

1442. Lytton Strachey (1880–1932). Famous British essayist and writer. Member of the Bloomsbury group and of the Apostles.

1443. Meisel and Kendrick, 1985, Introduction.

1444. Meisel and Kendrick, 1985.

1445. Idem, Introduction.

1446. Virginia and Leonard Woolf had got to know Alix Sargent-Florence when James Strachey brought her with him when he came to dine on 21 June 1916. They thought she was nice, saw her a number of times that summer, and arranged that she would come and work as an apprentice printer at the Hogarth Press in October. Alix stuck it for precisely two hours. Then she began to feel bored and stopped (Meisel & Kendrick, 1985, p. 7). *The Diary of Virginia Woolf*, Bell, 1981, pp. 41, 60–61.

1447. F/A, p. 514.

1448. F/A, p. 519.

1449. Meisel and Kendrick, 1985, p. 111. Idem, p. 191 in a note that this was about a message added to a pile of corrected proofs.

1450. Idem, p. 198.

1451. F/A, p. 497. Karl Landauer was originally from Munich. He studied medicine, entered into analysis with Freud in 1912 and in 1913, not yet twenty-six, he became a member of the Vienna Psychoanalytic Society. After the First World War, he settled in Frankfurt and, in 1923, he set up a psychoanalytic practice there. In 1929, he founded the Frankfurt Psychoanalytic Institute along with Erich Fromm and Frieda Fromm-Reichmann. In 1933, he fled with his family to Amsterdam where he became a training analyst. During the German occupation, Landauer was arrested in a raid and he died in Bergen-Belsen (Mühlleitner, 1992).

1452. Letter from Landauer to Eitingon, 29 December 1925, Eitingon archive.

1453. Idem. After Abraham's death, Landauer wrote in a letter to Eitingon how important Abraham had been for him. He felt orphaned now that Abraham was no longer there.

1454. Meisel and Kendrick, 1985, pp. 84–88.

1455. Felix Boehm (1881–1958) was a doctor, born in Riga. He became a member of the Munich Psychoanalytic Society in 1913. Boehm settled in Berlin in 1919 and entered into analysis with Abraham. His role in the Nazi era is extremely controversial. When Hitler came to power, Eitingon resigned as president of the German Psychoanalytic Society and fled to Palestine. Boehm succeeded him and, in 1935, he removed all Jewish members from the German Psychoanalytic Society.

1456. Meisel and Kendrick, 1985, pp. 104–105.

1457. *Korrespondenzblatt, IZP, 11*, 1925: 132:

In the fourth quarter of 1924 the Society is organising in its institute (Berlin W. 35, Potsdamerstraße 29) the following courses:

1. Dr. Sándor Radó: Introduction to Psychoanalysis, part 1 (The place of psychoanalysis in medicine, the basis of analytic psychology, dream theory, libido theory, the psychology of childhood). For medical students and educationalists. Six hours. (Listeners: 35)

2. Dr. Hanns Sachs: Normal sexual development. Six hours. (Listeners: 24)

3. Dr. Karl Abraham: Character development. For medical students and educationalists. Six hours. (Listeners: 30)

4. Dr. Ernst Simmel: Anxiety. Six hours. (Listeners: 13)

5. Dr. Franz Alexander: Neurosis and the entire personality. (New developments in psycho-analytic theory and its application in practice.) For advanced, already practising analysts. Six hours. (Listeners: 20)

6. Drs. Eitingon, Simmel, Radó: Technical seminar as an introduction to psychoanalytic therapy. For candidates only. (9 candidates).

Dr. Max Eitingon, secretary.

In the technical seminar or the "Practical Exercises", the candidates discussed their own patients.

1458.   The following details about the guidelines for the training come from the lecture given by Eitingon at the congress in Salzburg on 23 April 1924. *IZP*, *10*, 1924: 231, 232, 233:

Task, namely the training of the next generation of analysts. On the initiative of our colleague Simmel and as requested by the Berlin Psychoanalytic Society, a committee consisting of Messrs Abraham, Eitingon, Müller, Sachs, and Simmel, and Mrs. Horney, chaired by the reviewer, has set out the first firm rules for such training, which I will lay before you now.

Guidelines for education and training:

General

1. The purpose of the education and training offered by the institute is:

    a.   theoretical and practical training in psychoanalysis

    b.   the encouragement of psychoanalytic research

    c.   the expansion of psychoanalytic knowledge.

2. The leadership of education and training at the institute is entrusted to a six-member committee from the Berlin Psychoanalytic Society.

The guidelines

I   Preconditions for the training of psychoanalytic psychotherapists.

    a)   For training as a psychoanalytic therapist (analysis for adults) a medical degree is regarded as a necessary preparation and, in addition, psychiatric-neurological train-ing. Only in very rare cases can an exception be made.

Note: It is not necessary for medical studies to have been completed before admission to training can take place. The theoretical study of psychoanalysis can certainly be started during medical training. The training analysis in particular must start as soon as possible. Practical training, by contrast, is deferred until medical studies have been completed.

b) The same demands are made regarding training for child analysis as for therapeutic analysis, except that in place of medical studies an equally thorough theoretical and practical pedagogical study suffices, as long as it includes child pathology.

For a) and b): The training committee decides on the admission of candidates, after they have presented themselves personally to three of its members.

II The training of psychoanalytic therapists.

a) Training analysis

The training analysis takes place at the start of psychoanalytic training. Regarding the taking of courses and the reading of analytic works during the training analysis, the judgment of the training analyst is decisive. The training analysis must last at least six months.

The training committee decides on the allocation of each candidate to a training analyst.

Before the training analysis begins, the analysand undertakes not to engage in an independent psychoanalytic practice without the permission of the training committee and not to claim to be a practising analyst.

b) Courses

A.   Introductory course

Note: The first part of the introductory course can be followed by all faculties; the second part can if necessary be followed separately by doctors and non-doctors (educationalists in particular).

B.   Specialist courses

Groups of lectures and exercises:

1.   Drive theory (libido theory, perversions, repression, unconscious etc.)

2.   Dream

3.   Technique

4.   General and special teaching on neurosis

5.   Practical extra-therapeutic applications of psychoanalysis (Pedagogic etc.)

6.   Theoretical non-therapeutic applications of psychoanalysis (Aesthetics)

For therapists in training, the introductory courses and the first four groups of specialist courses are compulsory. The four groups need not all be taken in their entirety, only the parts that are delivered at a given moment, but in each group both a theoretical course and a practical course must be followed. The respective programme will be laid down and made public well in advance by the training committee. The theoretical courses must not last more than two or three semesters before practical training begins and they must continue alongside it.

c) Practical training in the polyclinic

1.   Practical training in the polyclinic begins when sufficient theoretical preparatory training has been received and the training analysis has ended or is sufficiently

advanced. Theoretical training can in exceptional cases be acquired by means of studies other than those included in the courses.

2.   Practical training in the polyclinic generally lasts at least two years in the case of work that takes up half the day. In the second year, with the permission of the training committee, the candidate can embark on independent psychoanalytic work.

d)   Transition to independent work as a psychoanalyst. The start of independent psychoanalytic work is dependent upon a decision by the training committee, which must consult with the training analyst and the teachers at the polyclinic.

III The training of non-therapeutic psychoanalysts.

1. Those who wish to study psychoanalysis without being trained as therapists can follow all courses and exercises to the extent that these are not about psychoanalytic technique and to the extent that individual course leaders do not make a particular selection.

2. For those courses for which insufficient teachers are available, external experts are engaged as far as possible.

IV A.   Aside from the courses under IIb, the following are given:

1.   A purely informative course of three to four hours on the subject: "What is psychoanalysis?" (for general educational purposes).

2.   The general psychoanalytic foundation course. This is intended to offer information about the subfields and the various theoretical and practical potentials of psychoanalysis to those who belong to the various scientific disciplines, so that afterwards they are in a position to make a decision concerning their training.

B.   Separately from the courses for those with scientific training, courses offering popular lectures about psychoanalysis will be held for the general public.

The demand that training must begin with a training analysis, the necessity of which was recognised by the old analytic circle only after many years, now seems clear and entirely self-evident not only to us but to those who, with the aim of learning psychoanalysis, have joined us more recently.

1459.   *Korrespondenzblatt, IZP, 10,* 1924: 229.
1460.   With a few exceptions, today's psychoanalytic societies allow only members and aspiring members to take courses.
1461.   Meisel and Kendrick, 1985, p. 137.
1462.   Idem, p. 137.
1463.   Idem, pp. 193–194.
1464.   Idem, p. 180.
1465.   Rothe and Weber, 2003, p. 411.
1466.   Letter from Lou Andreas-Salomé to Abraham, 28 October 1924. LoC, Karl Abraham correspondence. Transcription by G. Fichtner.
1467.   Idem.
1468.   Letter from Ferenczi to Eitingon, Eitingon archive.

1469. Hermine Hug-Hellmuth (1871–1924) was from Vienna. She initially worked as a teacher, then gained a doctorate in philosophy. In 1913, she became a member of the Vienna Psychoanalytic Society. She published a great deal and was regarded as an expert in child psychology and pedagogy. She started working as an analyst in 1919 and, in 1921, gave a course in Berlin. In 1924, she was murdered by her eighteen-year-old nephew (Mühlleitner, 1992, pp. 163–164).

1470. The autobiographical details are from Wolffheim, 1997a, p. 164ff.

1471. Letter from Nelly Wolffheim to Hedwig Abraham dated 23 September 1930. LoC, Abraham correspondence:

> I'm sending you my psychoanalytic book, just published, which I have dedicated in spirit— since outward declarations do not appeal to me—to the memory of your husband. When I wrote the book it was encouraging to me that he had described my task as not only to place my psychoanalytic studies at the service of my practice but the reverse as well, to place my observations and investigations at the service of psychoanalysis. I am filled with sadness by the fact that I cannot present my book to my analyst and teacher. So, my dear Mrs. Abraham, I want to share this with you and perhaps also your daughter.

1472. Details in this passage about Nelly Wolffheim and Melanie Klein are from Nelly Wolffheim (1997b).

1473. Klein, 1932, p. 9.

1474. Idem, p. xi.

1475. F/A, 7 October 1923, p. 471. The translated version of this quotation has been altered to read "mood disorder" in place of "irritation".

1476. Grosskurth, 1986, p. 114.

1477. Folder of the Melanie Klein Trust (2007). Melanie Klein in Berlin. Interview with Melanie Klein by Eissler.

1478. Dinora Pines collection. ABPAS, Part of 39.

1479. Jones, 1926a.

1480. Lecture given by Dinora Pines at the Goethe Institute in Paris in 1987. Dinora Pines collection. ABPAS, Part of 39.

1481. Frank, 1999.

1482. Segal, 1973. In Chapter One of the book, which looks at Melanie Klein's early work, all articles dating from before 1926 are omitted.

1483. Klein, 1920, 1923.

1484. Frank, 1999.

1485. Klein, 1920.

1486. Klein, 1921.

1487. *IZP*, 7, 1922: 493.

1488. Klein, 1923b.

1489. Klein, 1922.

1490. Klein, 1932.

1491. The description of the "controversial discussions" is from Brühmann, 1996.

1492. Frank, 1999, p. 55.

1493. Taylor, 1996, p. 114.

1494. Frank, 1999, p. 51.

CHAPTER TWENTY-EIGHT

1495. *Korrespondenzblatt, IZP,* 11, 1925: 525.

1496. Abraham, 1921c, 1925c.

1497. In 1923 Freud was diagnosed with cancer. The first operation took place on 20 April 1923, the second on 4 October, the third on 12 October, and the fourth on 7 November 1923. On that occasion, the malignant tissue was successfully removed, but the operation in Freud's mouth was such that a well-fitting prosthesis was impossible. From then on, Freud could eat, smoke, and talk only with great effort accompanied by pain. After the operations came X-ray treatments, and because the prosthesis never fitted properly it was continually being adjusted. On top of this, Freud could not give up smoking, which kept leading to new leucoplakias and after 1926 necessitated more than thirty further operations (Schur, 1972, p. 364).

1498. F/Eit, 1 April 1925, p. 394. Eitingon answered Freud's letter on 9 April 1925, saying that Abraham was not so quick to take offence. F/Eit, p. 395.

1499. F/Fer, 3, p. 209.

1500. Anna Freud to Eitingon, 1 April 1925. LoC, Anna Freud correspondence.

1501. Idem.

1502. In 1946, it was renamed the Walther Rathenau Grammar school. Note F/A, German edition, pp. 811–812.

1503. F/A, p. 542.

1504. Interview with Hilda by Eissler.

1505. Letter from Reik to Abraham, 11 April 1925. LoC, Abraham correspondence. The editors' introduction to "The question of lay analysis", S. E., pp. 179–181, states that an ex-patient had initiated proceedings against Reik. Mühlleitner (1992, p. 261) also mentions this. It was the second case against him. The case regarding the complaint by an American patient took place on 24 May 1927. After a few weeks of treatment, an American doctor had lodged a complaint because he was becoming worse rather than better. The patient had been referred to Reik by Freud by means of a message on a business card: "obsessive neurosis; full psychoanalytic treatment". Reik said that during treatment the patient developed the illusion that from across the rooftops men came into his room to castrate him. The complaint was judged to be unfounded (Sherman, 1988; Freud, 1926e, p. 177).

1506. A far higher fee could be asked of foreigners.

1507. These details are taken from a letter from Reik to Abraham dated 11 April 1925. LoC, Abraham correspondence.

1508. Freud, 1926e.

1509. A Dutch Psychoanalytic Society had been set up in the Netherlands in 1917. Jelgersma was one of the founders. In addition, a Leiden Society for Psychoanalysis and Psychopathology was set up around Jelgersma in Leiden.

1510. F. P. Muller (1883–1973), psychiatrist and psychoanalyst, was, for a time, Jelgersma's assistant. He occupied a prominent position in the Dutch Psychoanalytic Society, as its president among other things, taught at Leiden University, and published regularly (Bakker, 1975).

1511. With thanks to G. W. Muller.

1512. *Korrespondenzblatt. IZP,* 11, 1925: 505. Report by Dr. A. Endtz.

1513. F/A, 29 May 1925, p. 543.

1514. Van Ophuijsen to Eitingon, 5 March 1926. Eitingon archive.

1515. Idem, letters of 30 September 1926 and 3 October 1926.

1516. Idem.

1517. F/A, p. 543.

1518. Interview with Hedwig by Eissler. LoC.

1519. Hermanns and Schröter, 2010, pp. 100–101.

1520. Fürstenberg is a small town fifty kilometres north of Berlin, surrounded by lakes and woods.

1521. Hermanns and Schröter, 2010, pp. 100–101.

1522. Meisel and Kendrick, 1985, p. 283. Melanie Klein was also in analysis with Abraham.

1523. Idem, p. 287.

1524. Bally was a former pupil of Jung's who, at this point, was in analysis with Simmel. Meisel and Kendrick, note p. 282, pp. 289–290.

1525. Idem, p. 290.

1526. F/A, p. 548. "... the bronchial pneumonic foci have healed, but part of the pleura is still sensitive". NB: the English edition gives the date of this letter as 26 June.

1527. Idem, p. 549.

1528. *Korrespondenzblatt. IZP*, *11*, 1925: 507. Clara Happel (1889–1954) was a doctor who became a member of the Berlin Psychoanalytic Society and was in analysis with Sachs. In 1920, she and her family moved to Frankfurt, where she was involved in the setting up of the Frankfurt Psychoanalytic Institute.

1529. F/A, pp. 549–550.

1530. Idem, p. 551.

1531. Idem, pp. 551–552.

1532. Letter from Abraham to Eitingon of 12 August 1925. Eitingon archive. Transcription by U. Heyl-Keese.

1533. Directed by E. Kapnist (2005). Produced by Doc en Stock. Avro. With thanks to A. Gietelink.

1534. Freud (1895d).

1535. F/Eit, p. 340. The label conservative was far more appropriate to Eitingon himself than to Abraham. It was Eitingon who felt threatened by talented young people with new ideas and felt the need to place restrictions on them.

1536. Jones, 1927, p. 43.

1537. F/A, pp. 543–544.

1538. Ries, 1995. Details about the film affair are from Ries unless otherwise stated.

1539. Pabst (1885–1967) was one of the most important filmmakers in Germany.

1540. Jones, 1955, p. 62.

1541. F/A pp. 544–545.

1542. F/A, p. 547.

1543. Letter from Sachs to Freud, 14 June 1925. LoC, Sachs correspondence.

1544. Grosskurth, 1991, p. 174.

1545. F/A, p. 547.

1546. F/A, pp. 547–548.

1547. Letter from Sachs to Freud, 24 June 1926. LoC, Sachs correspondence.

1548. UFA, 1926a.

1549. Ries, 1995, p. 764. Translation by P. Ries.

1550. F/A, p. 554.

1551. Eppensteiner et al., 1985, pp. 132–133.

1552.   Adolf Storfer (1888–1944) was the son of a wealthy timber merchant from Bukovina. He studied law in Vienna and Zurich but never graduated. In Zurich he was in the Burghölzli clinic for a time after a suicide attempt, with a diagnosis of schizophrenia. He then worked in Zurich for the *Frankfurter Zeitung*. He was wounded in the First World War and became a journalist in Budapest. In 1919, he was accepted as a member of the Vienna Psychoanalytic Society, having been a member of the Budapest Psychoanalytic Society. In 1921, he replaced Reik as Rank's assistant, and in 1925 he replaced Rank as manager of the publishing house. He was in analysis with Freud. Storfer was intelligent, energetic, and unpredictable. He was a bohemian and his book-keeping methods caused many problems (Mühlleitner, 1992).

1553.   Ries, 1995, p. 773.

1554.   Letter from Sachs to Freud, 25 August 1925, LoC, Sachs correspondence.

1555.   Eppensteiner et al., 1985, p. 130.

1556.   Abraham to Eitingon, 16 August 1925, Eitingon archive.

1557.   Rothe and Weber, 2003, p. 471.

1558.   F/A, p. 558.

1559.   F/A, p. 557.

1560.   Ries, 1995, p. 774.

1561.   F/A, p. 559.

1562.   Anna Freud to Eitingon, 2 October 1925. LoC, Anna Freud correspondence.

1563.   Idem.

1564.   *Korrespondenzblatt. IZP, 11,* 1925: 676–680.

1565.   Idem, p. 688.

1566.   Wittenberger and Tögel, 2006, p. 280.

1567.   F/A, p. 558.

1568.   Interview with Hedwig by Eissler.

1569.   Letter from Sachs to Freud, 16 September 1925. LoC, Sachs correspondence.

1570.   Anna Freud to Eitingon, 20 September 1925. LoC, Anna Freud correspondence.

1571.   For Anna Freud and Bernfeld, see Young-Bruehl, 1988, pp. 99–102.

1572.   Sachs to Freud, 23 September 1925. LoC, Sachs correspondence.

1573.   F/Eit, p. 353ff.

1574.   F/Eit, p. 370, n. 4.

1575.   Idem, p. 367.

1576.   Idem, p. 408.

1577.   Bernfeld, one of the most talented of the young analysts of the Vienna Psychoanalytic Society, had become convinced that a great deal of money could be earned by the film. He wrote to his mistress (Bernfeld to Neumann, 16 August 1925) that she might have to go without a few days of sunshine at her health resort, which would not be a problem if there was a chance that within a few months she would be bathing in the sunshine of fame and riches. On 2 September, the day before the congress began, he wrote to her that he was staying in Hotel Metropol, which was very expensive, but he had to make sure he was close to the Abraham–Sachs rabble, otherwise they might run off with the spoils (Ries, 1995, pp. 775–776). Abraham wrote to Freud on 8 September 1925 that Bernfeld had admitted to him that he and Storfer were in the wrong. F/A, p. 559. Bernfeld tried to persuade Abraham to break his contract with the film company and offered him fantastic amounts of dollars for participation in his film project.

1578. F/Eit, p. 420ff.

1579. Jones, 1957, p. 115.

1580. Doubly missed in the sense that he was absent both from the polyclinic and from the Berlin Psychoanalytic Society. Alexander to Eitingon, 14 December 1925. Eitingon archive.

1581. F/Eit, including the letters of 22 January, 25 January, and 6 February 1926. Letter from Anna Freud to Lou Andreas-Salomé of 21 January 1926 (Rothe & Weber, 2003, p. 499).

1582. Eitingon was also involved in an attempt by Lampl to persuade the Berlin Psychoanalytic Society to distance itself officially from the film authorised by Abraham and Sachs. Lampl had written a protest against the film. He discussed it with Eitingon, who encouraged him to persist. Lampl read out his protest at a meeting of the Berlin Psychoanalytic Society and demanded it officially distance itself from the film. Sachs responded by saying that if that happened he would resign his membership. Eitingon said nothing at the meeting and left Lampl in the lurch. The proposal was not adopted. Many of those present were analysands or former analysands of Sachs. Sachs resented Lampl for years as a result. Letter from Lampl to Jones of 24 Nov. 1957. ABPAS.

1583. F/A, p. 561. Freud later revised his opinion on Storfer and Bernfeld totally. By his boasting and mismanagement, Storfer brought the publishing house to the edge of the abyss. Letter from Freud to Jeanne Lampl-de Groot of 17 January 1932. Freud later came to see Bernfeld as a fantasist. Idem, 10 February 1933 (Bögels, 2012).

1584. Rothe and Weber, 2003, p. 470.

1585. Interview with Hedwig by Eissler. LoC.

1586. Letter from Sachs to Freud, 23 September 1925. LoC, Sachs correspondence.

1587. Interview with Hedwig by Eissler. LoC. On 25 September 1925 Sachs wrote a heartrending letter to Freud about the downfall of the committee and the treatment meted out to him. He described how wonderful he had found it to be one of this group of men and to be able to be close to Freud. The friendship with Rank had been very important. He had given up on Rank after the congress in Homburg. Before that, when Rank was depressed, he had still had hope. In Homburg he noticed that Rank felt nothing but indifference towards him, but it had been easier for his purposes to be on speaking terms. Now Sachs had only Ferenczi and Abraham left, the latter as a true friend. Eitingon was not that. Sachs described Eitingon as follows: "Since Eitingon, so distinguished and profound by nature, is so surrounded by inhibitions that no one but you can get anywhere close to him." LoC, Sachs correspondence.

Eitingon's problem was that he could not associate with people on terms of equality. He surrounded himself with people he aided, such as Anna Freud, for example, whom he gave endless gifts and whose help and stay he was; Freud himself, whom he gave endless presents, money for Freud's projects and advice; van Ophuijsen etc. A whole list could be named. He could function only in the role of helper, to such an extent that when he lost much of his money in 1929 he never told his sickness-plagued wife.

1588. Wittenberger and Tögel, 2006, p. 276. For the relationship between Abraham and Flieβ, see also Shengold, 1972.

1589. Wittenberger and Tögel, 2006, p. 279.

1590. F/A, pp. 564–566.

1591. Storfer and Bernfeld. F/Eit, pp. 416–417. In this same period, Storfer turns out to have caused all kinds of financial problems. F/Eit, pp. 418–420.

1592. Idem, pp. 420–421.

1593. From descriptions of Abraham, it is clear that he certainly did have a sense of humour. In this situation, in which he was ill, he did not. From the correspondence of Bernfeld with his mistress it is clear that Bernfeld was, in fact, serious (Ries, 1995).
1594. F/Eit, p. 421.
1595. Schröter, 2004, p. 421, translated for this edition.
1596. F/A, pp. 566–567.
1597. Letter from Anna Freud to Eitingon, 19 November 1925. LoC, Anna Freud correspondence.
1598. Hans Bürgner.
1599. Letter from Sachs to Freud, 25 November 1925. LoC, Sachs correspondence.
1600. Interview with Hedwig by Eissler, 1953. LoC.
1601. Anna Freud to Eitingon, 26 November 1925. LoC, Anna Freud correspondence.
1602. On 4 December 1925, Freud wrote to Radó that he was extremely worried that things might not turn out well with Abraham.
1603. Freud had a great many physical problems from 1923 onwards, when he was discovered to have cancer. Around this time he had an infection in his jaw. A small operation was performed, after which he was in a great deal of pain, could only consume liquids and so on. F/Fer, 3, p. 238.
1604. F/Eit, p. 432.
1605. Idem, p. 425ff.
1606. Idem, pp. 432–433.
1607. Idem, 18 December 1925, p. 434.
1608. Letter from Sachs to Freud, 10 December 1925. LoC, Sachs correspondence.
1609. Jones, 1957, pp. 115–116.
1610. F/Fer, 3, p. 239.
1611. Anna Freud to Eitingon, 21 December 1925. LoC, Anna Freud correspondence.
1612. Idem.
1613. Pines, 1987.
1614. Jones to his wife, Katherine, 28 December 1925. Ernest Jones Collection, ABPAS, P04-G-B-02.
1615. F/Jones, p. 590.
1616. Idem, p. 115.
1617. He whose life is blameless and free of guilt.
1618. Freud, 1926, *International Journal of Psychoanalysis* 1926, 7: 1–1.

CHAPTER TWENTY-NINE

1619. Letter from Jones to his wife, Katherine, 27 December 1925, Ernest Jones Collection, ABPAS, P04-G-B-02.
1620. Groß-Lichterfelde became part of Berlin in 1920, making the graveyard there a cemetery for the whole of the city.
1621. Letter from Jones to his wife, Katherine, 28 December 1925. ABPAS.
1622. Things did not go well for Abraham's dog. In Bremen, it bit the postman and was put down. Interview with Lotte Levy.
1623. Letter from Jones to his wife, Katherine, 28 December 1925, Ernest Jones Collection, ABPAS, P04-G-B-02. Letter from Simmel to Freud, 2 February 1926, LoC.
1624. F/Fer, 3, p. 242.
1625. Letter from Simmel to Freud, 2 February 1926. LoC.

1626. F/Fer, *3*, p. 242.

1627. Idem.

1628. *Korrespondenzblatt, IZP, 12*, 1926: 119.

1629. Radó complimented Jones on his obituary and wrote that the appraisal of Abraham's personality had made a particularly deep impression on him. He wrote, "An honest and arresting image of his essence as we knew him and as we loved him". Letter from Radó to Jones, 18 April 1926, Ernest Jones Collection, ABPAS, P04-C-B-01.

1630. F/Eit, p. 450.

1631. Letter from Hedwig Abraham to Jones, 24 February 1926, Ernest Jones Collection, ABPAS, CAB/F01/01A.

1632. Idem, 23 March 1926.

1633. Dinora Pines collection. ABPAS. After emigrating to England, the Burgner family changed its name from Bürgner to Burgner.

1634. Letter from Katherine Jones to Jones, 13 September 1926, Ernest Jones Collection, ABPAS, P04-G-B-02.

1635. F/Fer, *3*, p. 292.

1636. Letter from Katherine Jones to Jones, 13 September 1926, Ernest Jones Collection, ABPAS, P04-GB-02.

1637. Rothe and Weber, 2003, pp. 503–504.

1638. Rothe and Weber, 2003, p. 495.

1639. F/Jones, p. 591.

1640. Freud and Meng, 1963, p. 106. Oskar Pfister (1875–1956) was a Swiss preacher who came upon the work of Freud in 1908 and studied it in depth. He used it in his work. He became a friend of Freud's and came to occupy an important place in the Swiss psychoanalytic world.

1641. Rothe and Weber, 2003, p. 499.

1642. Circular letters, p. 293.

1643. Anna Freud to Eitingon, 4 March 1926. LoC, Anna Freud correspondence. Anna Freud wrote to Eitingon that Freud's heart problems on the street had recurred twice. Anna Freud should be regarded as the most reliable source. She was closely involved with Freud's health condition. Other sources state that Freud had heart problems twice. See, for example, Jones, 1957, p. 120. See also Lajos Lévy to Eitingon, 7 March 1926. Eitingon archive.

1644. Idem.

1645. The Cottage Sanatorium for Nervous and Metabolic Illness had been set up in 1908 by Dr Rudolf Urbantschitsch. It was a sanatorium for the elite. See also Mühlleitner, 1992, p. 348ff.

1646. *IZP, 12*, 1926.

1647. Freud wrote to Radó on 28 January 1926 that Abraham must be given precedence. Circular letters, p. 294–295. Freud repeated this on 5 February 1926. Freud Museum. In the second letter Freud wrote that it would be no problem at all if the issue marking his seventieth birthday on 6 May 1926 did not appear until the summer.

1648. Wittenberger and Tögel, 2006.

1649. F/Eit, p. 440. The quote is from Wagner's *Die Walküre* (*The Valkyrie*) II.

1650. F/Fer, *3*, p. 245.

1651. Idem.

1652. F/Eit. On 3 August 1927, for instance, Eitingon wrote to Freud, "I received the enclosed letter from Ferenczi today in response to a very detailed letter; the impression I have of his way of describing things and situations, which is vaguer now than ever, has naturally not been ameli- orated by the letter". Earlier, on 12 July 1927, Eitingon had written that in Ferenczi he had encoun- tered unfriendly affect towards him for some time. Freud refused to believe it. F/Eit, 15 July 1927.

1653.   F/Fer, 3, p. 316.
1654.   Letter from Jones to Eitingon, 9 October 1926, Eitingon archive.
1655.   Letter from Jones to Hilda Abraham, 1 November 1929. Ernest Jones Collection, ABPAS, P04-C-B-01.
1656.   Letter from Hilda Abraham to Jones, 29 November 1929. Ernest Jones Collection, ABPAS, P04-C-B-01.
1657.   Idem.
1658.   Interview with Hilda by Eissler. LoC.
1659.   Idem.
1660.   Idem.
1661.   Letter from Jones to Anna Freud, 2 May 1933, Ernest Jones Collection, ABPAS, P04-C-C-06. Letter from Freud to Jeanne Lampl-de Groot, 8 April 1933 (Bögels, 2012).
1662.   Decke, 1998.
1663.   Idem.
1664.   Interview with Hilda by Eissler.

AFTERWORD

1665.   F/Eit, p. 846. Interviews with Hedwig and Hilda by Eissler. LoC.
1666.   These included *The Interpretation of Dreams* (1900a), the first edition of *Three Essays on the Theory of Sexuality* (1905d) and the case history of Dora (1905e).
1667.   Green, 2006, pp. 19, 49.
1668.   These remarks on Green's theory are derived from Green, 2005, pp. 142–173.
1669.   For a detailed discussion, see Chapter Twenty-five.
1670.   See Chapter Fifteen.
1671.   Anna Freud to Eitingon, 20 Sept. 1925. LoC, Anna Freud correspondence. See Chapter Twenty-eight. It is not clear why she disliked Abraham.
1672.   The Dutch *Leerboek Psychiatrie* (Psychiatry Textbook) of 2009 states on page 295, "The risk of depres- sion is therefore increased in people who were separated from parental figures in childhood, who lost a parent, or who were neglected or sexually abused" (Hengeveld & van Balkom, 2009) Similarly, in the *Textbook of Psychiatry* of 1999, Chapter Thirteen, entitled "Mood disorders": "In a majority of studies comparing depressed patients with normal controls, childhood loss—especially loss of a parent—has a positive association with adult depression and mania" (Dubovsky & Buzan).
1673.   Nicolai, 2012.
1674.   See, for example, his letter to Freud of 22 January 1926. Eitingon refers to Jones' proposal to provide the committee with new members: "His proposal for the expansion of the committee reminds me of that conversation we had, in which we so strongly doubted whether the commit- tee is still viable at all". F/Eit, p. 436.
1675.   F/Eit, p. 842.
1676.   F/Eit, p. 846
1677.   F/Eit, note, p. 845.

REFERENCES

Abraham, H. C. (1970a). Die Anfänge der Psychoanalytischen Vereinigung in Berlin (1908–1933). Manuskript eines Vortrags. Archiv des Karl-Abraham-Instituts, Berlin.

Abraham, H. C. (1970b). Die Anfänge von Karl Abrahams wissenschaftlicher Arbeit in Berlin. Manuskript eines Vortrags. Archiv des Karl-Abraham-Instituts, Berlin.

Abraham, H. C. (1974). Karl Abraham. An unfinished biography. *International Review of Psycho-Analysis, 1*: 17–72.

Abraham, H. C., & Freud, E. L. (Eds.) (1980). *Sigmund Freud—Karl Abraham, Briefe 1907–1926*. Frankfurt: Fischer.

Abraham, K. (1901). *Beiträge zur Entwicklungsgeschichte des Wellensittichs*. Wiesbaden: J. F. Bergmann.

Abraham, K. (1902). Beiträge zur Kenntnis des Delirium Tremens der Morphinisten. *Centralblatt für Nervenheilkunde und Psychiatrie, 25*: 369–380.

Abraham, K. (1904a). Ueber Versuche mit "Veronal" bei Erregungszuständen der Paralytiker. *Centralblatt für Nervenheilkunde und Psychiatrie, 170*: 176–180.

Abraham, K. (1904b). Über einige seltene Zustandsbilder bei progressiver Paralyse. *Allgemeine Zeitschrift für Psychiatrie und psychisch-gerichtliche Medizin, 61*: 502–523.

Abraham, K. (1904d). Vorstellung eines Kranken mit Hemianopsie und Rotgrünblindheit im erhaltenen Gesichtsfeld. Abriß. *Centralblatt für Nervenheilkunde und Psychiatrie, 27*: 578–579.

Abraham, K. (1907a). Beiträge zur Kenntnis der motorischen Apraxie auf Grund eines Falles von einseitiger Apraxie. *Centralblatt für Nervenheilkunde und Psychiatrie, 18*: 161–176.

Abraham, K. (1907b). On the significance of sexual trauma in childhood for the symptomatology of dementia praecox. *CP* (pp. 13–21).

Abraham, K. (1907c). The experiencing of sexual traumas as a form of sexual activity. *SP* (pp. 47–63).

Abraham, K. (1908a). The psycho-sexual differences between hysteria and dementia praecox. *SP* (pp. 64–79).

Abraham, K. (1908b). The psychological relations between sexuality and alcoholism. *SP* (pp. 80–89).

Abraham, K. (1909a). The significance of intermarriage between close relatives in the psychology of the neuroses. *CP* (pp. 21–28).

Abraham, K. (1909b). Dreams and myths: a study in folk-psychology. *CP* (pp. 153–209).

Abraham, K. (1909c). Freuds Schriften aus den Jahren 1893–1909 (Sammelreferat). *Jahrbuch der Psychoanalyse*, I, 546–574.

Abraham, K. (1909d). Bericht über die österreichische und deutsche psychoanalytische Literatur bis zum Jahr 1909 (Sammelreferat). *Jahrbuch*, I, 575–594.

Abraham, K. (1910a). Hysterical dream-states. *SP* (pp. 90–124).

Abraham, K. (1910b). Remarks on the psycho-analysis of a case of foot and corset fetishism. *SP* (pp. 125–136).

Abraham, K. (1911a). Observations on the cult of the mother and its symbolism in individual and folk psychology. *CP* (pp. 29–30).

Abraham, K. (1911b). On the determining power of names. *CP* (pp. 31–32).

Abraham, K. (1911c & 1925). Giovanni Segantini: a psycho-analytical study. *CP* (pp. 210–261).

Abraham, K. (1912a). Notes on the psycho-analytical treatment of manic depressive insanity and allied conditions. *SP* (137–156)

Abraham, K. (1912b). A complicated ceremonial found in neurotic women. *SP* (pp. 157–163).

Abraham, K. (1912c). Amenhotep IV—Psychoanalytic contributions to the understanding of his personality and of the monotheistic cult of Aton. *CP* (pp. 262–291).

Abraham, K. (1913a). Should patients write down their dreams? *CP* (pp. 33–35).

Abraham, K. (1913b). A screen memory concerning a childhood event of apparently aetiological significance. *CP* (pp. 36–41).

Abraham, K. (1913c). On the psychogenesis of agoraphobia in childhood. *CP* (pp. 42–43).

Abraham, K. (1914a). *De droom en de mythologie. Een bijdrage tot de psychologie van de menschheid*, J. Stärcke (Trans.). Leiden: S. C. van Doesburgh.

Abraham, K. (1914b). Restrictions and transformations of scopophilia in psycho-neurotics; with remarks on analogous phenomena in folk-psychology. *SP* (pp. 169–234).

Abraham, K. (1914c). A constitutional basis of locomotor anxiety. *SP* (pp. 235–243).

Abraham, K. (1914d). On neurotic exogamy: a contribution to the similarities in the psychic life of neurotics and of primitive man. *CP* (pp. 48–50).

Abraham, K. (1914e). Review of C. G. Jung's *Versuch einer Darstellung der psychoanalytischen Theorie* (Attempt at a representation of psychoanalytical theory). *CP* (pp. 101–115).

Abraham, K. (1916). The first pregenital stage of the libido. *SP* (pp. 248–279).

Abraham, K. (1917a). Some illustrations on the emotional relationship of little girls towards their parents. *CP* (pp. 52–54).

Abraham, K. (1917b). Ejaculatio praecox. *SP* (pp. 280–298).

Abraham, K. (1918). Dreikäsehoch. Zur Psychoanalyse des Wortwitzes. *Imago*, 4: 294–295.

Abraham, K. (1919a). A particular form of neurotic resistance against the psycho-analytic method. *SP* (pp. 303–311).

Abraham, K. (1919b). Observations on Ferenczi's paper on "Sunday neuroses". In: Robert Fließ (Ed.), *The Psychoanalytic Reader*, 1 (pp. 349–352). New York: International Universities Press, 1948.

Abraham, K. (1920a). The applicability of psycho-analytic treatment to patients at an advanced age. *SP* (312–317).

Abraham, K. (1920b). Die Psychoanalyse als Erkenntnisquelle für die Geisteswissenschaften. *Die neue Rundschau, 31*: 10.

Abraham, K. (1921a). Psychoanalysis and the war neuroses. In: S. Ferenczi, K, Abraham, E. Simmel & E. Jones, *Psychoanalysis and the War Neuroses*. London: International Psychoanalytic Press.

Abraham, K. (1921b). Contribution to a discussion on tic. *SP* (pp. 323–325).

Abraham, K. (1921c). *Klinische Beiträge zur Psychoanalyse aus den Jahren 1907–1920. Internationale Psychoanalytische Bibliothek, 10*. Leipzig, Vienna, Zurich: Internationaler Psychoanalytischer Verlag.

Abraham, K. (1921d). Manifestations of the female castration complex. *SP* (pp. 338–369).

Abraham, K. (1922a). The rescue and murder of the father in neurotic phantasy-formations. *CP* (pp. 68–75).

Abraham, K. (1922b). The spider as a dream symbol. *SP* (pp. 326–332).

Abraham, K. (1923). Psychoanalytic views of some characteristics of early infantile thinking. C. Baines (Trans.). 7th Congress of Psychology, Oxford, 31 July 1923. *British Journal of Medical Psychology* (1923), 283–287.

Abraham, K. (1924). A short study of the development of the libido, viewed in the light of mental disorders. *SP* (pp. 418–501).

Abraham, K. (1925a). Psycho-analytical studies on character-formation. *SP* (pp. 370–417): XXIII. Contributions to the theory of the anal character (1921). XXIV. The influence of oral erotism on character-formation (1924). XXV. Character-formation on the genital level of the libido (1925).

Abraham, K. (1925b). The history of an imposter in the light of psycho-analytical knowledge. *CP* (pp. 291–305).

Abraham, K. (1925c). Psycho-analysis and gynaecology. *CP* (pp. 91–97).

Abraham, K. (1927). *Selected Papers of Karl Abraham*. London: Karnac, 1988.

Abraham, K. (1955). *Clinical Papers and Essays on Psychoanalysis*. London: Karnac, 1979.

Abraham, K. (1974). Little Hilda: daydreams and a syptom in a seven-year-old girl. *International Review of Psycho-Analysis, 1*: 5–14.

Abraham, K. (1999). *Psychoanalytische Studien. Gesammelte Werken in zwei Bänden*, J. Cremerius (Ed.). Giessen: Psychosozial.

Abraham, K., & Ziegenhagen, A. (1904). Cytodiagnostische Untersuchungen bei Dementia Paralytica. Eigener Bericht. *Centralblatt für Nervenheilkunde und Psychiatrie, 27*, 15: 323–324.

Abraham, K., Freud, S., Ferenczi, S., Simmel, E., & Jones, E. (1919). *Zur Psychoanalyse der Kriegsneurosen*. Leipzig: Psychoanalytischer.

Alexander, F. (1925). Recensie K. Abraham, Versuch einer Entwicklungsgeschichte der Libido auf Grund der Psychoanalyse seelischer Störungen. *IZP, 11*: 113–122.

Alexander, F., Eisenstein, S., & Grotjahn, M. (Eds.) (1966). *Psychoanalytic Pioneers*. New York: Basic Books.

Alnaes, K. (2007). *De geschiedenis van Europa. 4. 1900-heden*, L. Pijttersen, K. Snoeijing, & C. Joustra (Trans.). Amsterdam: Ambo/Anthos.

Bair, D. (2003). *Jung, A Biography*. New York, Boston: Back Bay Books.

Bakker, J. E. M. (1975). F. P. Muller (1883–1973). *International Journal of Psychoanalysis, 56*, 481–482.

Balkanyi, C. (1975). The linguistic studies of Karl Abraham. Unpublished manuscript.

Bauer, C., & Stark, B. (Eds.) (2008). *Walter Kaesbach, Mentor der Moderne*. Lengwill: Libelle.

Bell, A. O. (Ed.). (1981). *The Diary of Virginia Woolf, 1*. Harmondsworth: Penguin.

Bell, Q. (1981). Introduction. In: Bell, A. O. (Ed.), *The Diary of Virginia Woolf, 1* (pp. vii–x). Harmondsworth: Penguin.

Bergmann, M. S. (Ed.) (2000). *The Hartmann Era*. New York: Other Press.

Bergmann, M. S. (2004). Rethinking dissidence and change in the history of psychoanalysis. In: M. S. Bergmann (Ed.), *Understanding Dissidence and Controversy in the History of Psychoanalysis* (pp. 1–109). New York: Other Press.

Binswanger, L. (1956). Der erste Besuch bei Freud in Wien (März 1907) (pp. xxxiv–xxxix). Reprinted in: G. Fichtner (Ed.). (1992), *Sigmund Freud, Ludwig Binswanger Briefwechsel 1908–1938*. Frankfurt: Fischer.

Blackbourn, D. (2003). *History of Germany. 1780–1918. The Long Nineteenth Century* (2nd edn). Malden, MA: Blackwell.

Bleuler, E. (1910). Die Psychoanalyse Freuds. Verteidigung und kritische Bemerkungen. *Jahrbuch, I,* 2, 623–730.

Bleuler, E. (1911). Dementia praecox, oder Gruppe der Schizophrenien. In: G. Aschaffenburg, *Handbuch der Psychiatrie, spezieller Teil*, 4. Abt. I. Vienna: F. Deuticke.

Bleuler, E. (1916). *Lehrbuch der Psychiatrie*. Berlin: Springer.

Bloch, I. (1907). *Das Sexualleben unserer Zeit in seinen Beziehungen zur modernen Kultur*. Berlin.

Bögels, G. (Ed.) (2012). *Sigmund Freud, brieven aan Jeanne Lampl-de Groot. 1921–1939*. Amsterdam: Sjibbolet.

Bratz, E. (1929). 50 Jahre Dalldorf. In: *Festschrift zum 50 jährigen Bestehen der Anstalt Dalldorf* (Hauptanstalt der Wittenauer Heilstätten).

Braune, A. (2003). *Konsequent den unbequemen Weg gegangen*. Adele Schreiber (1872–1957) Politikerin, Frauenrechtlerin, Journalistin. http://edoc.hu.berlin.de/dissertationen/braune-asja-2003-01-27/HTML/front.

Breasted, J. H. (1905). *A History of Egypt from the Earliest Times to the Persian Conquest*. New York: Charles Scribner's Sons.

Brecht, K., Friedrich, V., Hermanns, L. M., Kaminer, I. J., & Dierk, H. (Eds.). (1985). *Hier geht das Leben auf eine sehr merkwürdige Weise weiter. Zur Geschichte der Psychoanalyse in Deutschland*. Hamburg: Michael Kellner.

Breger, L. (2000). *Freud, Darkness in the Midst of Vision*. New York: Wiley.

Briehl, M. H. (1966). Helene Deutsch. The maturation of women. In: F. Alexander, S. Eisenstein, & M. Grotjahn (Eds.), *Psychoanalytic Pioneers* (pp. 282–298). New York: Basic Books.

Brinkgreve, C. (1984). *Psychoanalyse in Nederland*. Amsterdam: Synopsis.

Brome, V. (1968). *Freud and his Early Circle*. New York: William Morrow.

Brome, V. (1982). *Ernest Jones: Freud's Alter Ego*. Pittsburg, PA: Caliban Books.

Bromley, A. (1973). Edward Glover 1888–1972. *Psychoanalytic Quarterly, 42*: 173–177.

Brühmann, H. (1996). Metapsychologie und Standespolitik. Die Freud/Klein controverse. *Luzifer-Amor, 17*: 49–112.

Bruns, G. (2004). Zwei Ohnmachten Freuds in der Begegnung mit Jung. *Jahrbuch, 48*: 105–133.

Bryan, B. M. (2000). The 18th dynasty before the Amarna period. In: I. Shaw, (Ed.) *The Oxford History of Ancient Egypt* (pp. 207–264). Oxford: Oxford University Press.

Bulhof, I. N. (1983). *Freud en Nederland*. Baarn: Amboboeken.

Churchill, W. S. (1931). *The Unknown War: The Eastern Front*. New York: Scribner's Sons.

Clark, R. W. (1980). *Freud, the Man and the Cause*. New York: Random House.

Craig, G. A. (1978). *Germany 1866–1945*. Oxford: Oxford University Press.

Cremerius, J. (1997). Karl Abraham, Freuds Sündenbock und "Führer zur Wahrheitsforschung". *Luzifer-Amor, 20*: 64–80.

Cremerius, J. (1999). Einleitung zu Karl Abraham: Psychoanalytische Studien. *PS, I*: 11–33.

Damm, S., & Emmerich, N. (1989). Die Irrenanstalt Dalldorf-Wittenau bis 1933. *Publikation der Arbeitsgruppe zur Erforschung der Geschichte der Karl-Bonhoeffer-Nervenklink*. Berlin.

Dante, E. A. (1999). The Berlin poliklinik. Psychoanalytic innovation in Weimar Germany. *Journal of the American Psychoanalytic Association, 47*(4): 1269–1293.

Decke, B. (1997). Karl Abraham, Familie, Kindheit und Jugend in Bremen. *Luzifer-Amor, 20*: 7–60.

Decke, B. (1998). *"Du mußt raus hier." Lottie Abraham-Levy: Eine Jugend in Bremen*. Bremen: Donat.

Deutsch, H. (1925). The psychology of women in relation to the functions of reproduction. *International Journal of Psychoanalysis, 6*: 405–418.

Dick, R. (2010). *Else Lasker-Schuler. Die Bilder*. Berlin: Suhrkamp.

Dönhoff, M. (1990). *Before the Storm. Memories of My Youth in Old Prussia*, J. Steinberg (Trans.). New York: Knopf.

Dubovsky, S. L., & Buzan, P. (1999). Mood disorders. In: R. E. Hales, S. C. Yudofsky, & J. A. Talbott (Eds.), *American Psychiatric Press Textbook of Psychiatry* (pp. 479–566). Washington, DC: American Psychiatric Press.

Egger, B. (1988). Iwan Bloch und die Konstituierung der Sexualwissenschaft als eigene Disziplin. Dissertation medizinischen Fakultät Düsseldorf.

Eissler, K. R. (1965). *Medical Orthodoxy and the Future of Psychoanalysis*. New York: International Universities Press.

Eitingon, M. (1914). Über das Ubw. Bei Jung und seine Wendung ins Ethische. *IZP, 2*: 99–104.

Eitingon, M. (1922). Bericht über die Berliner Psychoanalytische Poliklinik (März 1920 bis Juni 1922). *Korrespondenzblatt, IZP, 8*: 506–520.

Ellenberger, H. F. (1970). *The Discovery of the Unconcious*. New York: Basic Books.

Eppensteiner, B., Fallend, K., & Reichmayr, J. (1986). Die Psychoanalyse im Film 1925/26 (Berlin/Wien). *Psyche, 41*: 129–139.

Falzeder, E. M. (1994). The threads of psychoanalytic filiations or psychoanalysis taking effect. *Cahiers Psychiatriques genevois, Special Issue: 100 years of psychoanalysis*: 169–194.

Falzeder, E. M. (1996). Introduction. In: E. Brabant, F. M. Falzeder, & P. Giampieri-Deutsch (Eds.), *Sigmund Freud–Sándor Ferenczi. Briefwechsel. Band I/2, 1908–1933* (pp. 7–25). Vienna: Bohlau.

Falzeder, E. M. (Ed.) (2002). *The Complete Correspondence of Sigmund Freud and Karl Abraham*, C. Schwarzacher (Trans.). London: Karnac.

Falzeder, E. M., & Brabant, E. (Eds.) (1993, 1996, 2000). *The Correspondence of Sigmund Freud and Sándor Ferenczi (Volumes 1–3)*. Cambridge, MA: Belknap Press of Harvard University Press.

Falzeder, E. M., & Burnham, J. C. (2007). A perfectly staged "concerted action" against psychoanalysis: the 1913 congress of German psychiatrists. *International Journal of Psychoanalysis, 88*(5): 1223–1244.

Falzeder, E. M., & Hermanns, L. M. (Eds.) (2009). *Sigmund Freud—Karl Abraham. Briefwechsel, vollständige Ausgabe*. Vienna: Turia + Kant.

Fenichel, O. (1925). Referat: Abraham, Karl: Versuch einer Entwicklungsgechichte der Libido auf Grund der Psychoanalyse seelischer Störungen. *IZP, 11*, 104–122.

Fenichel, O. (1930). Statistischer Bericht über die Therapeutische Tätigkeit 1920–1930. *In Zehn Jahre Berliner Psychoanalytisches Institut*. Vienna: Internationaler Psychoanalytischer Verlag.

Fenichel, O. (1945). *The Psychoanalytic Theory of Neurosis*. New York: W. W. Norton.

Ferenczi, S. (1908). Analytische Deutung und Behandlung der psychosexuellen Impotenz des Mannes. *Psychiatrisch-neurologische Wochenschrift, 10*, 298–301, 305–309.

Ferenczi, S. (1911). Reizung der analen erogenen Zone als auslösende Ursache der Paranoia. *IZP, 1:* 557–559.

Ferenczi, S. (1913). Rezension C. G. Jung (1911 & 1912). Wandlungen und Symbole der Libido. *IZP, 1:* 391–403.

Ferenczi, S. (1914). Kritik C. G. Jung. Contribution á l'étude des types psychologiques. Communication présentée au Congrès Psychoanalytique de Munich, 1913. *Archives de Psychologie, T.XIII(52),* Déc. 1913.

Ferenczi, S. (1921). Psychoanalytische Betrachtungen über den Tic. *Schriften zur Psychoanalyse, II* (2004) (pp. 92–93). Gießen: Psychosozial.

Ferenczi, S. (1922). Recensie: Abraham, K., Klinische Beiträge zur Psychoanalyse. *IZP, 8:* 352–353.

Ferenczi, S. (1924). Versuch einer Genitaltheorie. *Schriften zur Psychoanalyse, II* (2004) (pp. 317–400). Gießen: Psychosozial.

Ferenczi, S., & Rank, O. (1924). *Entwicklungsziele der Psychoanalyse.* Leipzig: Internationaler Psychoanalytischer.

Ferenczi, S., Abraham, K., Simmel, E., & Jones, E. (1921). *Psycho-Analysis and the War Neuroses.* London: International Psycho-Analytical Press.

Festschrift zum 50jährigen Bestehen der Anstalt Dalldorf. (1929). Berlin: Walter de Gruyter.

Fichtner, G. (1992a). Introdution. In: *Sigmund Freud–Ludwig Binswanger, Briefwechsel 1908–1938.* (pp. ix–xxxi).

Fichtner, G. (Ed.) (1992b). *Sigmund Freud–Ludwig Binswanger, Briefwechsel 1908–1938.* Frankfurt: Fischer.

Fischer, R. (1976). Die klassische und die ichpsychologische Theorie der Depression. *Psyche 30(10):* 924–946.

Flügel, J. C. (1927). Review. The Ego and the Id. *International Journal of Psychoanalysis, 8:* 407–416.

Frank, C. (1999). *Melanie Kleins erste Kinderanalysen.* Stuttgart: Fromann-Holzboog.

Frehner, M. (1999). The path to modernism. Giovanni Segantini—life and work, F. Elliot (Trans.). In: B. Stutzer & I. Chappius, (Eds.), *Giovanni Segantini* (pp. 8–33). Ostfildern: Hatje Kantz.

Freud, A. (1936). *The Ego and the Mechanisms of Defence.* London: Karnac, 1992.

Freud, E. L., & Meng, H. (Eds.) (1963). *Sigmund Freud—Oskar Pfister, Briefe 1909–1939.* Frankfurt: Fischer.

Freud, M. (1957). *Glory Reflected. Sigmund Freud. Man and Father.* London: Angus and Robertson.

Freud, S. (with Breuer, J.) (1895d). *Studies on Hysteria. S. E., 2.* London: Hogarth.

Freud, S. (1900a). *The Interpretation of Dreams. S. E., 4–5.* London: Hogarth.

Freud, S. (1901a). On dreams. *S. E., 5:* 633–686. London: Hogarth.

Freud, S. (1905c). *Jokes and their Relation to the Unconscious. S. E., 8:* 9–236. London: Hogarth.

Freud, S. (1905d). *Three Essays on the Theory of Sexuality. S. E., 7:* 123, 135–243. London: Hogarth.

Freud, S. (1905e). *Fragment of an Analysis of a Case of Hysteria. S. E., 7:* 1–122. London: Hogarth.

Freud, S. (1907a). Jensen's "Gradiva". *S. E., 9:* 1–95). London: Hogarth.

Freud, S. (1908b). Character and anal erotism. *S. E., 9:* 167–176. London: Hogarth.

Freud, S. (1908e). Creative writers and day-dreaming. *S. E, 9:* 143–153. London: Hogarth.

Freud, S. (1909b). *Analysis of a Phobia in a Five-year-old Boy. S. E., 10:* 1–147. London: Hogarth.

Freud, S. (1909d). *Notes upon a Case of Obsessional Neurosis. S. E., 10:* 151–249. London: Hogarth.

Freud, S. (1910c). *Leonardo da Vinci and a Memory of his Childhood. S. E., 11:* 62–138. London: Hogarth.

Freud, S. (1910d). The future prospects of psychoanalytic therapy. *S. E., 11:* 139–151. London: Hogarth.

Freud, S. (1910i). The psycho-analytic view of psychogenic disturbance of vision. *S. E.*, *11*: 209–218. London: Hogarth.

Freud, S. (1910k). "Wild" psychoanalysis. *S. E.*, *11*: 221–227. London: Hogarth.

Freud, S. (1911e). The handling of dream-interpretation in psycho-analysis. *S. E.*, *12*: 89–96. London: Hogarth.

Freud, S. (1912b). The dynamics of transference. *S. E.*, *12*: 97–108. London: Hogarth.

Freud, S. (1912–1913). *Totem and Taboo*. *S. E.*, *13*: vii-162. London: Hogarth.

Freud, S. (1914b). *The Moses of Michelangelo*. *S. E.*, *13*: 211–236. London: Hogarth.

Freud, S. (1914c). On narcissism: an introduction. *S. E.*, *14*: 67–102. London: Hogarth.

Freud, S. (1914d). On the history of the psycho-analytic movement. *S. E.*, *14*: 7–66. London: Hogarth.

Freud, S. (1914g). Remembering, repeating and working-through. *S. E.*, *12*: 145–156. London: Hogarth.

Freud, S. (1916–1917). *Introductory Lectures on Psycho-Analysis*. *S. E.*, *15*. London: Hogarth.

Freud, S. (1917c). On transformations of instinct as exemplified in anal erotism. *S. E.*, *17*: 125–133. London: Hogarth.

Freud, S. (1917e). Mourning and melancholia. *S. E.*, *14*: 237–258. London: Hogarth.

Freud, S. (1918a). The taboo of virginity. *S. E.*, *11*: 191–208. London: Hogarth.

Freud, S. (1918b). *From the History of an Infantile Neurosis*. *S. E.*, *17*: 1–122. London: Hogarth.

Freud, S. (1919a). Lines of advance in psycho-analytic therapy. *S. E.*, *17*: 157–168. London: Hogarth.

Freud, S. (1919d). Introduction to psycho-analysis and the war neuroses. *S. E.*, *17*: 211–250. London: Hogarth.

Freud, S. (1920g). *Beyond the Pleasure Principle*. *S. E.*, *18*: 1–64. London: Hogarth.

Freud, S. (1921c). *Group Psychology and the Analysis of the Ego*. *S. E.*, *18*: 65–143. London: Hogarth.

Freud, S. (1922b). Some neurotic mechanisms in jealousy, paranoia and homosexuality. *S. E.*, *18*: 223–232. London: Hogarth.

Freud, S. (1923b). *The Ego and the Id*. *S. E.*, *19*: 12–59. London: Hogarth.

Freud, S. (1926e). The question of lay analysis. *S. E.*, *20*: 177–250. London: Hogarth.

Freud, S. (1939a). *Moses and Monotheism*. *S. E.*, *23*: 1–137. London: Hogarth.

Freud, S. (1941d). Psycho-analysis and telepathy. *S. E.*, *18*: 177–193. London: Hogarth.

Friedrich, O. (1995). *Before the Deluge. A Portrait of Berlin in the 1920s*. New York: HarperCollins.

Gall, L. (2009). *Walther Rathenau, Portrait einer Epoche*. Munich: C. H. Beck

Gay, P. (1988). *Freud. A Life for Our Time*. New York: W. W. Norton.

Gay, R. (1992). *The Jews of Germany*. New Haven, CT: Yale University Press.

Giefer, M. (Ed.) (2007). *Korrespondenzblatt der Internationalen Psychoanalytische Vereinigung 1910–1940*. Bad Homburg (CD-ROM).

Graf-Nold, A. (2006). 100 Jahre Peinlichkeit—und kein Ende. *Jahrbuch*, *52*, 93–135.

Green, A. (1986). *On Private Madness*. London: Karnac, 2005.

Green, A. (2006). *Associations (presque libres) d'un psychanalyste. Entretiens avec Maurice Corcos*. Paris: Albin Michel.

Greenwald, H. (1959). *Great Cases in Psychoanalyis*. New York: Ballentine Books.

Groddeck, G. (1923). *Das Buch vom Es. Psychoanalytische Briefe an eine Freundin*. Leipzig: Internationaler Psychoanalytischer.

Groppe, C. (1997). *Die Macht der Bildung. Das Deutsche Bürgertum und der George-Kreis 1890–1933*. Cologne: Böhlau Verlag.

Grosskurth, P. (1986). *Melanie Klein, Her World and Her Work*. New York: Knopf.

Grosskurth, P. (1991). *The Secret Ring. Freud's Inner Circle and the Politics of Psychoanalysis*. New York: Addison Wesley.

Grotjahn, M. (1966). Franz Alexander. The Western mind in transition. In: F. Alexander, S. Eisenstein, & M. Grotjahn (Eds.), *Psychoanalytic Pioneers*. New York-London: Basic Books.

Gunther, M. S., & Trosman, H. (1974). Freud as expert witness: Wagner-Jauregg and the problem of war neuroses. *The Annual of Psychoanalysis*, 2: 3–23.

Haffner, S. (1973). *Failure of a Revolution: Germany 1918–1919*, G. Rapp (Trans.). London: André Deutsch.

Haffner, S. (1989). *The Ailing Empire. Germany from Bismarck to Hitler*, J. Steinberg (Trans.). New York: Fromm International.

Hales, R. E., Yudofsky, S. C., & Talbott, J. A. (Eds.) (1999). *Textbook of Psychiatry* (3rd edn). Washington, DC: American Psychiatric Press.

Haumann, H., & Schadek, H. (1992). *Geschichte der Stadt Freiburg im Breisgau*. Stuttgart: Konrad Theiss.

Haynal, A. (1993). Introduction, M. L. Ascher (Trans.). In: E. M. Falzeder & E. Brabant (Eds.), *The Correspondence of Sigmund Freud and Sándor Ferenczi (Volume 1)* (pp. xvii–xxxv). Cambridge, MA: Belknap Press of Harvard University Press.

Haynal, A., & Falzeder, E. M. (2002). Introduction. In: *The Complete Correspondence of Sigmund Freud and Karl Abraham* (pp. xix–xxx). London: Karnac.

Hengeveld, M. W., & van Balkom, A. J. L. M. (Eds.) (2009). *Leerboek Psychiatrie* (2nd edn). Utrecht: De Tijdstroom.

Hermanns, L. M. (1994). Karl Abraham und die Anfänge der Berliner psychoanalytischen Vereinigung. *Luzifer-Amor*, 7: 30–39.

Hermanns, L. M. (2008). Über die fünf Gründungsmitglieder der Berliner Psychoanalytischen Vereinigung im August 1908. In: *Berlin ist ein schwieriger aber bedeutungsvoller Boden. 100-Jahr Gedenkfeier der Gründung der Berliner Psychoanalytischen Vereinigung*.

Hermanns, L. M., & Schröter, M. (2010). Karl Abraham und Wilhelm Fließ. Briefwechsel 1911–1925. *Luzifer-Amor*, 46: 86–104.

Herzer, M. (2001). *Magnus Hirschfeld. Leben und Werk eines jüdischen, schwulen und sozialistischen Sexologen* (2nd edn). Hamburg: MännerschwarmSkript.

Herzfeld, H. (Ed.) (1968). *Berlin und die Provinz Brandenburg im 19. und 20. Jahrhundert*. Berlin: Walter de Gruyter.

Holmes, J. (2001). *Narcissism*. Cambridge: Totem Books.

Horney, K. (1924). On the genesis of the castration complex in women. *International Journal of Psychoanalysis*, 5: 50–65.

Hühn, M. (1989). *Rasseideologie wird Gesetz*. Berlin: Arbeitsgruppe zur Erforschung der Geschichte der Karl-Bonhoeffer-Nervenklink.

Huppke, A., & Schröter, M. (2006). Annäherung an einen ungeliebten Psychoanalytiker. In: I. Sadger (2006). *Sigmund Freud. Persönliche Erinnerungen*, H. Huppke & M. Schröter (Eds.), Tübingen: Edition Diskord.

Isserlin, M. (1925). Hugo Liepmann zum Gedächtnis. *Zeitschrift für die Gesamte Neurologie und Psychiatrie*, 99: 635–650.

Jaffé, R. (1966). Moshe Woolf, pioneering in Russia and Israel. In: F. Alexander, S. Eisenstein, & M. Grotjahn (Eds.), *Psychoanalytic Pioneers* (pp. 200–209). New York: Basic Books..

Janus, L. (2007). Introduction. In: O. Rank, *Das Trauma der Geburt* (pp. i–v). Giessen: Psychosozial.

Jones, E. (1914). Kritik: C. G. Jung: Psycho-analysis. *IZP*, 2: 83–86.

Jones, E. (1919). Über analerotische Characterzüge. *IZP*, 5: 69–92.

Jones, E. (1925). Referat Psychoanalytische Studien zur Charakterbildung. *IZP*, 11: 377–378.

Jones, E. (1926a). Karl Abraham 1877–1925. *International Journal of Psychoanalysis*, 7: 155–181.

Jones, E. (1926b). The origin and structure of the super-ego. *International Journal of Psychoanalysis*, 7: 303–311.

Jones, E. (1927). Introductory memoir. In: *Karl Abraham Selected Papers on Psychoanalysis*, D. Bryan & A. Strachey (Trans.) (pp. 13–45). London: Karnac, 1988.

Jones, E. (1953). *The Life and Work of Sigmund Freud (Volume 1)*. New York: Basic Books.

Jones, E. (1955). *The Life and Work of Sigmund Freud (Volume 2)*. New York: Basic Books.

Jones, E. (1957). *The Life and Work of Sigmund Freud (Volume 3)*. New York: Basic Books.

Juliusburger, O. (1907). Beitrag zur Lehre von der Psychoanalyse. *Allgemeine Zeitschrift für Psychiatrie und psychisch-gerichtliche Medizin*, 64: 1002–1010.

Jung, C. G. (Ed.) (1906a). *Diagnostische Assoziationsstudien: Beiträge zur experimentellen Psychopatholgie (Volume 1)*. Leipzig: Barth.

Jung, C. G. (1907a). Über die Psychologie der Dementia praecox: Ein Versuch. *GW*, 3: 1–170. Zurich: Rascher.

Jung, C. G. (1908). Der Inhalt der Psychose. *GW*, 3: 171–215.

Jung, C. G. (1910). Lecture at Salzburg Congress. Dementia praecox. Autoreferaat. *Jahrbuch*, I: 128.

Jung, C. G. (1916). Psychology of the unconscious. *Jahrbuch*, III & IV.

Jung, C. G. (1958–1970). *Die Gesammelte Werken*, M. Niehus-Jung, L. Hurwitz-Eisner, F. Riklin, & L. Zander (Eds.). Zurich: Rascher.

Kaderas, B. (1998). Karl Abrahams Bemühungen um einen Lehrauftrag für Psychoanalyse an der Friedrich-Wilhelms-Universität. In: *Jahrbuch für Universitätsgeschichte, 1*.

Kaderas, B. (2000). Hans Liebermanns Plädoyer für die Einführung der Psychoanalyse als Unterrichtsfach an der Universität. *Luzifer-Amor*, 26: 113–124.

Kampe, N. (1988). *Studenten und "Judenfrage" im Deutschen Kaiserreich*. Göttingen: Vandenhoeck & Ruprecht.

Kaplan, M. (1991). *The Making of the Jewish Middle Class. Women, Family and Identity in Imperial Germany*. New York: Oxford University Press.

Keibel, F., & Abraham, K. (1900). *Normentafel zur Entwicklungsgeschichte des Huhnes. Heft 2 der Normentafeln zur Entwicklungsgeschichte der Wirbeltiere*. Jena.

Klein, M. (1920). Der Familienroman in statu nascendi. *Gesammelte Schriften, 1* (pp. 1–9). Stuttgart: Fromann-Holzboog.

Klein, M. (1921). Eine Kinderentwicklung. *Imago*, 7, 251–310.

Klein, M. (1922). Hemmungen und Schwierigkeiten in Pubertätsalter. *Die Neue Erziehung, 4*.

Klein, M. (1923a). The development of a child. *International Journal of Psychoanalysis, 4*: 419–474.

Klein, M. (1923b). Zur früh Analyse. *Imago*, 9, 222–263.

Klein, M. (1932). *The Psycho-Analysis of Children*. London: The Hogarth Press.

Klein, M. (1995). *Gesammelte Schriften*, R. von Cycon with the collaboration of H. Erb (Eds.). Stuttgart-Bad Cannstatt: Fromann-Holzboog.

Kloocke, R. (2002). *Mosche Wulff*. Tübingen: Edition Diskord.

Küchenhoff, B. (2001). Die Auseinandersetzung Eugen Bleulers mit Sigmund Freud. In: D. Hell, C. Scharfetter, & A. Möller (Eds.), *Eugen Bleuler, Leben und Werk* (pp. 57–71). Bern: Hans Huber.

Kuhn, P. (2000). A scandal in Salzburg. Or Freud's surreptious role in the 1908 Abraham–Jung dispute. *International Journal of Psychoanalysis, 81,* 705–731.

Kurzweil, E. (1995). *Freudians and Feminists.* Boulder, CO: Westview Press.

Lampl-de Groot, J. (1934). Review of "Fear of castration in women" by Sándor Radó. In: J. Lampl-de Groot (1985). *Collected Papers* (pp. 32–39). Assen: van Gorcum.

Lefebvre, P. (Ed.) (1987). *Histoire de la médicine aux armées, Volume 3.* Paris: Edition Charles la Vauzette.

Leitner, M. (1998). *Freud, Rank und die Folgen.* Vienna: Turia + Kant.

Leitner, M. (2001). *Ein gut gehütetes Geheimnis.* Gießen: Psychosozial.

Lemaigre, B. (2003). *Karl Abraham.* Paris: Presses Universitaires de France.

Lieberman, E. J. (1985). *Acts of Will. The Life and Work of Otto Rank.* New York: Free Press.

Lieberman, E. J., & Kramer, R. (Eds.) (2012). *The Letters of Sigmund Freud & Otto Rank.* Baltimore, MD: Johns Hopkins University Press.

Lindner, S. (1879). Das saugen an den Fingern, Lippen etc. bei den Kindern (Ludeln). *Jahrbuch für Kinderheilkunde und psychische Erziehung, Neue Folge, 14:* 68–91.

Lindon, J. A. (1966). Melanie Klein, her view of the unconscious. In: F. Alexander, S. Eisenstein, & M. Grotjahn (Eds.), *Psychoanalytic Pioneers* (pp. 360–372). New York: Basic Books.

Liulevicius, V. G. (2000). *War Land on the Eastern Front. Culture, National Identity, and German Occupation in World War I.* Cambridge: Cambridge University Press.

Lowenberg, P. (1995). The creation of a scientific community: the Burghölzli, 1902–1914. In: *Fantasy and Reality in History* (pp. 46–89). Oxford: Oxford University Press.

Löwenfeld, L. (1909). Über traumartige und verwandte Zustände. *Centralblatt für Nervenheilkunde und Psychiatrie.*

Mächtlinger, V. (1997). Karl Abraham und Giovanni Segantini. *Luzifer-Amor, 20:* 81–97.

Maddox, B. (2006). *Freud's Wizard. The Enigma of Ernest Jones.* London: John Murray.

Makari, G. (2008). *Revolution in Mind.* New York: HarperCollins.

Mann, G. (2008). *Deutsche Geschichte des 19. und 20. Jahrhunderts.* Frankfurt: Fischer Taschenbuch.

Markreich, M. (2003). *Geschichte der Juden in Bremen und Umgegend.* Bremen: Edition Temmen.

Martynkewicz, W. (2006). *Tagebücher Oscar A. H. Schmitz, 1.* Berlin: Aufbau.

Martynkewicz, W. (2007a). *Tagebücher Oscar A. H. Schmitz, 2.* Berlin: Aufbau.

Martynkewicz, W. (2007b). *Tagebücher Oscar A. H. Schmitz, 3.* Berlin: Aufbau.

Martynkewicz, W. (2007c). Die dunklen Seiten eines Dandys. Der Schriftsteller Oskar A. H. Schmitz in der Analyse bei Karl Abraham. *Jahrbuch, 55:* 113–142.

Masson, J. M. (1985). Introduction. In: *The Complete Letters of Sigmund Freud and Wilhelm Fließ, 1887–1904.* Cambridge, MA: Belknap Press of Harvard University Press.

May, U. (1999). Ein Zeitungsartikel des jungen Karl Abraham (1902). *Luzifer-Amor, 24:* 154–157.

May, U. (2001). Abrahams discovery of the "bad mother". *International Journal of Psychoanalysis, 82:* 283–305.

May, U. (2006). Erbitterung und Nachdenklichkeit – Über Freuds Kommentar zu einem frühen Aufsatz von Karl Abraham. *Jahrbuch der Psychoanalyse, 52:* 63–92.

May, U. (2008). Nineteen patients in analysis with Freud (1910–1920). *American Imago, 65:* 41–106.

May, U. (2010). Karl Abrahams Revolution: Vom Wonnesaugen zum oral-agressiven Vernichtungswunch. *Luzifer-Amor, 46:* 58–85.

May-Tolzmann, U. (1990). Ich- und Narcismußtheorie zwischen 1914 und 1922 im Spiegel der Internationalen Zeitschrift für ärztliche Psychoanalyse. *Psyche, 44:* 689–723.

May-Tolzmann, U. (1997). Die Entdeckung der "bösen Mutter". *Luzifer-Amor, 20*: 98–131.

McGuire, W., & Sauerländer, W. (Eds.) (1974). *Sigmund Freud—C.G. Jung, Briefwechsel*. Frankfurt: Fischer.

Meisel, P. M., & Kendrick, W. (Eds.) (1985). *The Letters of James and Alix Strachey*. New York: Basic Books.

Meyer-Palmedo, I. (Ed.) (2014). *Sigmund Freud—Anna Freud: Correspondence 1904–1938*, N. Somers (Trans.). Cambridge: Polity Press.

Minder, B. (1994). Sabina Spielrein. Jungs Patientin am Burghölzli. *Luzifer-Amor, 14*: 55–127.

Modell, A. H. (1975). The ego and the id: fifty years later. *International Journal of Psychoanalysis, 56*: 57–68.

Mühlleitner, E. (1992). *Biographisches Lexikon der Psychoanalyse*. Tübingen: Edition Diskord.

Mühlleitner, E. (2008). *Ich-Fenichel*. Vienna: Paul Zsolnay.

Natterson, J. M. (1966). Theodor Reik. In: F. Alexander, S. Eisenstein, & M. Grotjahn (Eds.), *Psychoanalytic Pioneers* (pp. 249–264). New York: Basic Books.

Nicolai, N. (2012). De ontmanteling van het zelfgevoel—Schaamte en schuld na trauma's als voedings-bodem voor depressies. In: J. Dirks & N. Nicolai (Eds.), *Depressie & Psychodynamiek* (pp. 75–91). Amsterdam: Sjibbolet.

Nonne, M. (1922). Therapeutische Erfahrungen an den Kriegsneurosen in den Jahren 1914–1918. In: O. Schjerning (Ed.), *Handbuch der Ärztlichen Erfahrungen in Weltkriege 1914/1918. Band IV. Geistes- und Nervenkrankheiten* (pp. 102–121). Leipzig: Bonhoeffer.

Nunberg, H., & Federn, E. (Eds.) (1976). *Protokolle der Wiener Psychoanalytischen Vereinigung. Band I-IV*. Giessen: Psychosozial, 2008.

Paris, B. J. (1994). *Karen Horney*. New Haven, CT: Yale University Press.

Paskauskas, R. A. (Ed.) (1993). *The Complete Correspondence of Sigmund Freud and Ernest Jones*. Cambridge, MA: Belknap Press of Harvard University Press.

Paulsen, F. (1902). *Die Deutsche Universitäten und das Universitätsstudium*. Berlin: Asher.

Payne, S. M. (1947). Ella Freeman Sharpe: an appreciation. *International Journal of Psychoanalysis, 28*: 54–56.

Peukert, D. (1991). *The Weimar Republic: The Crisis of Classical Modernity*. London: Allen Lane.

Pfeiffer E. (1972a). Introduction. In: E. Pfeiffer (Ed.), *Sigmund Freud and Lou Andreas-Salomé. Letters*. London: The Hogarth Press and the Institute of Psychoanalysis.

Pfeiffer, E. (Ed.) (1972b). *Sigmund Freud and Lou Andreas-Salomé, Letters*, W. Robson-Scott & E. Robson-Scott (Trans.). London: Hogarth Press.

Pines, D. (1974). Introductory note to "Little Hilda". *International Review of Psychoanalysis, 1*, 4–5.

Pines, D. (1987). Written report of a lecture about Karl Abraham, held at the Goethe Institute in Paris. Part of 39 (Dinorah Pines collection). Archives of the British Psychoanalytical Society.

Quinn, S. (1988). *A Mind of her Own. The life of Karen Horney*. Reading, MA: Addison-Wesley.

Radó, S. (1933). Fear of castration in women. *Psychoanalytic Quarterly, 2*: 425–475.

Rank, O. (1907). *Der Künstler. Ansätze zu einer Sexualpsychologie*. Vienna: Hugo Heller.

Rank, O. (1909). *Der Mythos von der Geburt des Helden*. Leipzig und Wien.

Rank, O. (2007). *Das Trauma der Geburt und seine Bedeutung für die Psychoanalyse*. Gießen: Psychosozial.

Reik, T. (1926). Gedenkrede Karl Abraham. *IZP, 12*(2).

Reik, T. (1941). *Masochism in Modern Man*. New York: Toronto, Farrar & Rinehart.

Remarque, E. M. (1929). *All Quiet on the Western Front*, A.W. Wheen (Trans.). London: Little, Brown.

Remarque, E. M. (1937). *Three Comrades*, A. W. Wheen (Trans.). London: Hutchinson.

Retallack, J. (1996). *Germany in the Age of Kaiser Wilhelm II*. London: Macmillan.

Reventlow, F. zu (1913). *Herrn Dames Aufzeichnungen oder Begebenheiten zu einem merkwürdigen Stadtteil. Bd. 2. Romane 2. Sämtliche Werke in Fünf Bänden*, M. Schardt (Ed.). Oldenburg: Igel, 2004.

Richards, A. K. (1997). The relevance of frequency of sessions to the creation of an analytic experience. *Journal of the American Psychoanalytic Association, 45*: 1241–1251.

Ries, P. (1995). Popularise and/or be damned: psychoanalysis and film at the crossroads in 1925. *International Journal of Psychoanalysis, 76*: 759–791.

Roazen, P. (1985). *Helene Deutsch. A Psychoanalyst's Life*. New York: New American Library.

Roazen, P., & Swerdloff, B. (1995). *Heresy. Sándor Radó and the Psychoanalytic Movement*. London: Jason Aronson.

Rolnik, E. J. (2008). Wo sich die Intellektuellen gegenseitig im Wege stehen. Albert Einstein, Max Eitingon, Anna Freud und die Migration der deutschsprachigen Psychoanalyse nach Palästina. *Luzifer-Amor, 42*: 88–99.

Rothe, D. A., & Weber, I. (Eds.) (2003). *Lou Andreas-Salomé—Anna Freud Briefwechsel*. Göttingen: Wallstein.

Sachs, H. (1926). Gedenkrede Karl Abraham. *IZP, 12*(2): 198–202.

Sachs, H. (1944). *Freud, Master and Friend*. Cambridge, MA: Harvard University Press.

Sadger, I. (1910a). Analerotik und Analcharacter. *Die Heilkunde*, 43–46.

Sadger, I. (1910b). Über Urethralerotik. *Jahrbuch, II*, 409–450.

Sadger, I. (2006). *Sigmund Freud. Persönliche Erinnerungen*, H. Huppke & M. Schröter (Eds.). Tübingen: Edition Diskord.

Schebera, J. (2005). *Damals im Romanisches Café*. Berlin: Das neue Berlin.

Scheib, A. (2009). *Das Schönste was ich sah*. Hamburg: Hoffmann und Campe.

Schmitz, O. A. H. (1912). Herr von Pepinster und sein Popanz. Eine Gespenstergeschichte. *Die neue Rundschau, 23*: 1709–1723.

Schmitz, O. A. H. (1916). *Der Vertriebene. Ein Entwicklungsroman*. Munich: Georg Müller.

Schmitz, O. A. H. (1918). *Menschheitsdämmerung, Märchenhafte Geschichten*. Munich: Georg Müller.

Schmitz, O. A. H. (1927). *Ergo Sum, Jahre des Reifens*. Munich: Georg Müller.

Schröter, M. (1995). Freuds Komitee 1912–1914. Ein Beitrag zum Verständnis psychoanalytischer Gruppenbildung. *Psyche, 49*: 513–563.

Schröter, M. (1996). Zur Frühgeschichte der Laienanalyse. Strukturen eines Kernkonflikts der Freud-Schule. *Psyche, 50*: 1127–1175.

Schröter, M. (Ed.) (2004). *Sigmund Freud und Max Eitingon, Briefwechsel 1906–1936*. Tübingen: Edition Diskord.

Schröter, M. (2007). Volle Kraft voraus: Der 7. Internationale Psychoanalytische Kongress in Berlin (25–27 Sept. 1922). *Psyche, 61*(4): 412–437.

Schröter, M. (Ed.) (2010). *Sigmund Freud. Unterdess halten wir zusammen. Briefe an die Kinder*. Berlin: Aufbau.

Schröter, M. (Ed.) (2012). *Sigmund Freud—Eugen Bleuler. Ich bin zuversichtlich, wir erobern bald die Psychiatrie. Briefwechsel 1904–1937*. Basel: Schwabe.

Schultz, D. (1990). *Intimate Friends, Dangerous Rivals*. Los Angeles, CA: Jeremy P. Tarcher.

Schulze, H. (1982). *Weimar. Deutschland 1917–1933*. Berlin: Severin und Siedler.

Schur, M. (1972). *Freud: Living and Dying*, Madison, CT: International Universities Press.

Segal, H. (1973). *Introduction to the Work of Melanie Klein*. London: Karnac.

Segantini, B. (1909). *Giovanni Segantinis Schriften und Briefe*. Georg Bierman (Trans.). Leipzig: Klinkhardt & Bierman.

Seidler, E., & Leven, K. H. (2007). *Die medizinische Fakultät der Albert-Ludwigs-Universität Freiburg im Breisgau*. Freiburg: Karl Albert.

Selesnick, S. T. (1966). Alfred Adler. The psychology of the inferiority complex. In: F. Alexander, S. Eisenstein, & M. Grotjahn (Eds.), *Psychoanalytic Pioneers* (pp. 78–86). London: Basic Books.

Servaes, F. (1907). *Giovanni Segantini. Sein Leben und sein Werk*. Leipzig: Klinkhardt und Bierman.

Shedletzky, I. (Ed.) (1994). *Gershom Gerhard Scholem, Briefe 1, 1914–1947*. Munich: Beck.

Shengold, L. (1972). A parapraxis of Freud in relation to Karl Abraham. *American Imago, 29*(2): 123–164.

Sherman, M. H. (1988). Theodor Reik and lay analysis. *Psychoanalytic Review, 75*: 380–392.

Simmel, E. (1918). *Kriegsneurosen und psychisches Trauma. Ihre gegenseitigen Beziehungen dargestellt auf Grund psychoanalytischer, hypnotischer Studien*. Munich: O. Nemnich.

Skinner, A. D. (2007). *Lamentations of Youth. The Diaries of Gershom Scholem (1913–1919)*. Cambridge, MA: Harvard University Press.

Stärcke, A. (1921). Psychoanalysis and psychiatry. *International Journal of Psychoanalysis, 2*: 361–415.

Strachey, J. (1957). Editor's note to Leonardo da Vinci. *S. E., 11*: 58–59.

Strachey, J. (1958). Introduction to papers on technique. *S. E., 12*: 85–88. London: Hogarth.

Stroeken, H. (2008). *Psychoanalytisch woordenboek*. Amsterdam: Boom.

Stroeken, H. (2009). Johan van Ophuijsen, Padang/Indonesien 1882–New York 1950. *Luzifer-Amor, 22*: 7–44.

Swerdloff, B. (2002). An interview with Michael Balint. *American Journal of Psychoanalysis, 62*(4): 383–413.

Symington, A. (1986). *The Analytic Experience*. London: Free Association Books.

Taft, J. (1958). *Otto Rank. A Biographical Study based on Notebooks, Letters, Collected Writings, Therapeutic Achievements and Personal Associations*. New York: Julian Press.

Tausk, V. (1917). Bemerkungen zu Abrahams Aufsatz "Über Ejaculatio praecox". *IZP, 4*: 315–327.

Tausk, V. (1933). On the origin of the "influencing machine" in schizophrenia. *Psychoanalytic Quarterly, 2*: 519–556.

Taylor, D. (1996). Über einige Aspekte von Melanie Kleins Einfluß auf die British Psycho-Analytical Society. *Luzifer-Amor, 17*: 113–123.

Tietze, C. (Ed.). (2010). *Amarna*. Weimar: Arcus.

Tögel, C. (2006). *Freud und Berlin*. Berlin: Aufbau.

Tölle, R. (2005). Die "Kriegsneurose": Ein frühes Modell der pluridimensional verstandenen psychiatrischen Traumatologie. *Psychiatrische Praxis: Zeitschrift für Psychiatrie und Psychotherapie, 7*: 336–341.

Torok, M. (1968). Maladie du deuil et fantasme du cadavre exquis. *Revue Francaise de Psychoanalyse, 32*: 4.

Ufa (1926a). *Geheimnisse einer Seele*. Reklame-Ratschläge. Neumann-Film der Ufa. Berlin: Max Stadthagen.

Unger, F. (1999). Die Kriegsneurose—eine Form männlicher Hysterie. *Wehrmedizinische Monatschrift, 43*, 5–6.

Van der Berg, P. J. (2012). *Freud, Moses und die monotheistische Religion – Ein Essay*. Berlin: Frank & Timme.

Van der Chijs, A. (1926). In memoriam Dr. Karl Abraham 1877–1925. *Psychiatrische en neurologische bladen, 30*: 142–144.

Van Rossem, M. (2008). *Eerste wereldoorlog*. The Hague: Home Academy. CD-ROM.

Van Tilburg, W. (1994). De psychoanalyse, het sociologisch depressie-onderzoek en wat varia. In: J. J. Baneke & G. F. Koerselman (Eds.), *Psychoanalyse en depressive* (pp. 29–41). Amsterdam: Infobook.

Van Waning, A. (1992). The works of pioneering psychoanalyst Sabina Spielrein—Destruction as a cause of coming into being. *International Review of Psycho-Analysis, 19*, 399–414.

Von Petersdof, C. (1997). Der frühe Tod des Giovanni Segantini und des Karl Abraham. *Luzifer-Amor, 20*: 132–150.

Wallerstein, R. S. (1998). *Lay Analysis: Life Inside the Controversy*. Hillsdale, NJ: Analytic Press.

Wassermann, J. (1921). *Mein Weg als Deutscher und Jude*. Munich: Deutscher Taschenbuch, 1994.

Weigall, A. E. P. B. (1910). *The Life and Times of Akhnaton, Pharaoh of Egypt*. Edinburgh: Thornton Butterworth.

Weiniger, O. (1906). *Sex and Character*, L. Löb (Trans.). Bloomington, IN: Indiana University Press, 2005.

Weissweiler, E. (2006). *Die Freuds*. Cologne: Kiepenheuer & Witsch.

Welsch, U., & Pfeiffer, D. (2006). *Lou Andreas-Salomé*. Leipzig: Reclam.

Westermann Holsteijn, A. J. (1924). Professor G. Jelgersma und die Leidener psychiatrische Schule. *IZP, 10*, 253–257.

Widlöcher, D. (1977). Un peintre et son psychanalyste: Giovanni Segantini et Karl Abraham. *Psychanalyse à l'université, 3*(9): 55–68.

Wiedersheim, R. (1908). *Der Bau des Menschen als Zeugnis für seine Vergangenheit*. Tübingen: Laupp.

Wieser, A. (2001). Zur frühen Psychoanalyse in Zürich. In: D. Hell, C. Scharfetter, & A. Möller (Eds.), *Eugen Bleuler, Leben und Werk* (pp. 78–84). Bern: Hans Huber.

Wilson, J. A. (2008). Aknaton. www.brittannica.com. Accessed 9 August 2009.

Winau, R. (1987). *Medizin in Berlin*. Berlin: Walter de Gruijter.

Winship, G. (1999). Louise Andreas Salomé: at the high noon of culture in the shadows of psycho-analysis. *Psychoanalysis & History, 1*(2): 219–236.

Wittenberger, G. (1995). *Das "Geheime Komitee" Sigmund Freuds*. Tübingen: Edition Diskord,

Wittenberger, G., & Tögel, C. (1999). Introduction. In: G. Wittenberger & C. Tögel, (Eds.), *Die Rundbriefe des "Geheimen Komitees". Band 1: 1913–1920* (pp. 7–26). Tübingen: Edition Diskord.

Wittenberger, G., & Tögel, C. (Eds.) (2001). *Die Rundbriefe des "Geheimen Komitees". Band 2: 1921*. Tübingen: Edition Diskord.

Wittenberger, G., & Tögel, C. (Eds.) (2003). *Die Rundbriefe des "Geheimen Komitees". Band 3: 1922*. Tübingen: Edition Diskord.

Wittenberger, G., & Tögel, C. (Eds.) (2006). *Die Rundbriefe des "Geheimen Komitees". Band 4: 1923–1927*. Tübingen: Edition Diskord.

Wolffheim, N. (1997a). Die Rätselhaftigkeit menschlichen Lebens. In: G. Bierman (Ed.), *Nelly Wolffheim und die Psychoanalytische Pädagogik* (pp. 123–190). Gießen: Psychosozial.

Wolffheim, N. (1997b). Erinnerungen an Melanie Klein. In: G. Bierman (Ed.), *Nelly Wolffheim und die Psychoanalytische Pädagogik* (pp. 191–204). Gießen: Psychosozial.

Young-Bruehl, E. (1988). *Anna Freud. A Biography*. New York: Summit Books.

Zamoyski, A. (2008). *Warsaw 1920. Lenin's Failed Conquest of Europe*. London: HarperCollins.

Zienert-Eilts, K. (2010). Karl Abrahams Rolle im Rank-Konflikt. *Luzifer-Amor, 46*: 24–43.